HUMAN MEMORY

Second Edition

GABRIEL A. RADVANSKY

University of Notre Dame

Allyn & Bacon

Boston Columbus Indianapolis New York San Francisco Upper Saddle River
Amsterdam Cape Town Dubai London Madrid Milan Munich Paris Montreal Toronto
Delhi Mexico City São Paulo Sydney Hong Kong Seoul Singapore Taipei Tokyo

Executive Editor: *Susan Hartman*
Project Manager: *Kara Kikel*
Series Editorial Assistant: *Laura Barry*
Marketing Manager: *Nicole Kunzmann*
Production Manager: *Meghan DeMaio*
Creative Director: *Jayne Conte*
Cover Designer: *Jodi Notowitz*
Editorial Production and Composition Service: *Saraswathi Muralidhar/PreMediaGlobal*
Printer/Binder/Cover Printer: *Courier Companies*

10 9 8 7 6 5 4 3 2 1 14 13 12 11 10

Allyn & Bacon
is an imprint of

ISBN-10: 0-205-02452-1
ISBN-13: 978-0-205-02452-0

CONTENTS

CHAPTER TWO

Neuroscience of Memory 19

CHAPTER THREE

Methods and Principles 38

CHAPTER FIVE

Working Memory 83

CHAPTER SIX

Nondeclarative Memory 105

CHAPTER TEN
Formal Models of Memory 198

CHAPTER ELEVEN
Autobiographical Memory 219

CHAPTER FIFTEEN

Memory and Development 299

CHAPTER SIXTEEN

Amnesia 318

PREFACE

This book is a student's guide to human memory, its properties, theories about how memory works, and how an understanding of memory can give us a better idea of who we are and why we do what we do. Although I have tried to provide a reasonably comprehensive survey of many issues of the modern study of human memory, my main concern is the audience. Most college classes on human memory consist largely of psychology majors who are planning to go on to some field of psychology other than memory research, such as clinical or social psychology. Many others plan to go on to nonpsychology fields, such as medical or law school. Other students are not psychology majors, but they are taking the class because they think human memory would be something interesting to learn about (and they are right). Only a small minority of students will plan to do research on memory. As such, I have tried to write this book with the goals, interests, and backgrounds of the majority of the students in mind, while still providing enough information and detail to satisfy the "memory" student. I have taken a number of steps along these lines.

First, in addition to fundamental topics that are necessary for a basic understanding of how memory works, I have tried to focus on topics that will be helpful and useful whatever the student's ultimate goal. I have tried to avoid going into detail about the minutiae of various topics and have instead focused on the big picture. However, there may be cases where I do present a number of different experimental outcomes or theoretical positions. I have done this to provide the student with a sense of the difficulty and complexity of studying human memory, and the degree of careful and rigorous thinking and action that are needed to get at the truth of the human condition.

I mention several times that a particular study was conducted using students from this college or that university so that readers can associate with the information presented in this book. The participants in these studies are the same sort of people sitting in your classroom. I have tried to avoid language that would alienate a student—for example, using the word "subject," which can put up a barrier between the student and the material.

I have also tried to present the materials about memory from a number of different perspectives. Some of these come from experimental research on memory itself, such as perspectives from behavioral data, neurological data, and computational modeling. In addition, I present details about how various topics relate to work outside the realm of memory research, such as work in social, clinical, or developmental psychology, or even as fields as far-flung as law enforcement.

ACKNOWLEDGMENTS

I would also like to thank the following reviewers whose invaluable comments helped in the writing of this book: Harriet Amster, University of Texas at Arlington; Bryan C. Auday, Gordon College; Alan Brown, Southern Methodist University; Katinka Dijkstra,

Erasmus University; Warren Fass, University of Pittsburgh at Bradford; Ira Fischler, University of Florida; Dawn McBride, Illinois State University; Joanna Salapska-Gelleri, University of Nevada, Reno; J. Scott Saults, University of Missouri; Dominic Simon, New Mexico State University; Jeremy K. Miller, Willamette University and Annette Taylor, University of San Diego.

I would like to thank all those students at Notre Dame who helped me refine the text as I was writing it, including Janie Alderette, Katie Allberry, Valerie Baur, Sarah Benton, Lisa Brintnall, Chris Broughton, Gretchen Bryant, Jimmy Carrera, Carrie Coffield, Ashly Cumberworth, Kyla Davis, Kate DeCarlo, Catherine Eichers, Elizabeth Goodhue, Richard Herbst, Katie Hesmond, Lauren Hogel, Sally Hosey, Jeneka Joyce, Laura Kent, Beth Kessler, Jessica Kinder, Michael Kwiatt, Margaret Laracy, Chris Letkewicz, Celine McConville, Gerald Meskill, Tiffany Milligan, Kendra Morlock, Mary (Clare) O'Brien, Colleen O'Connor, Kevin O'Rourke, Leslie Pechkurow, Laurie Perez, Jon Pribaz, Maggie Priest, Meghan Rigney, Kristy Robinson, Ariana Salas, Austin Santesteban, Emily Schulte, Lindsay Slevinski, Brian Stouffer, Jon Streit, Scott Sutton, Justin Szalanski, J. R. Teddy, Katie Wade, John Wahoske, Lauren Walsh, and Lauren White.

Thanks to all the help from Allyn & Bacon: Paige Clunie, Meghan DeMaio, and Susan Hartman.

SUPPLEMENTS

Pearson Education is pleased to offer the following supplements to qualified adopters.

Instructor's Manual and Test Bank (0205827799)

Prepared by the author, the instructor's manual is a wonderful tool for classroom preparation and management. Corresponding to the chapters in the text, each of the manual's 17 chapters contains syllabus suggestions, instruction tips, discussion questions, in-class demonstrations, and a test bank, which includes over 1,100 multiple choice and short answer questions.

PowerPoint Presentation (0205827780)

Also prepared by Gabriel Radvansky, the PowerPoint Presentation is an exciting interactive tool for use in the classroom. Each chapter pairs key concepts with images from the textbook to reinforce student learning.
www.pearsonhighered.com

CHAPTER ONE

OVERVIEW AND HISTORY OF MEMORY RESEARCH

Memory is perhaps the most central aspect of human thought. Any question about human behavior, cognition, development, and nature requires an understanding of memory. Our memory makes us who we are, and it is one of the most intimate parts of ourselves. This may be why when we get close to someone, when we want them to know who we are and we want to know who they are, there is a sharing of memories. Many feel that the study of human memory is the closest one can get to a systematic study of the human soul. The aim of this book is to provide you, the student, with a survey and guide to what is known about human memory. As with most courses, there are a number of facts and ideas to learn. However, as any good professor will tell you, the slow accumulation of facts is not the main point of course work. The primary aim is to provide you with a deeper understanding and appreciation of some aspect of the world—and, hopefully, yourself. I trust that the ideas presented in this book will be useful in your life after this course is completed.

A SMATTERING OF DEFINITIONS

Before diving into the subject matter, we need to establish some points. Specifically, we need to define how the terms *memory* and *learning* are used. The primary subject of this book is, of course, memory. So what is *memory*? Well, the problem, and the beauty, of this term is that it has many meanings.

Memory

The word **memory** has three primary definitions (Spear & Riccio, 1994). First, memory is the location where information is kept, as in a storehouse, or memory store. Second, memory can refer to the thing that holds the contents of experience, as in a memory trace or **engram.** In this sense, each memory is a different mental representation. Finally, memory is the mental process used to acquire (learn), store, or retrieve (remember) information of all sorts. Memory processes are acts of using information in specific ways to make it available later or to bring back that information into the current stream of processing, the flow of one's thoughts.

Learning

The other term that needs to be defined is **learning,** which is any change in the potential of people to alter their behavior as a consequence of experience. Obviously, learning and memory are closely related: For something to be remembered, it must first be learned. Because of historical circumstances, however, these terms have become somewhat disconnected in the language of psychology. "Learning" has come to refer more to the acquisition of associations, often in the context of studies of conditioning. Moreover, these studies are often performed on animals, such as a rat learning a maze. This is not the learning people often refer to when they are in school. In this book I use the term the way it is conventionally used, although I may occasionally use the more restricted sense.

Synopsis

The terms *memory* and *learning* are used in specific ways in experimental psychology. In general, *memory* refers to the storage of information and the processes used to retrieve it. When referring to research, there is a greater likelihood that this will be work with humans. *Learning* is a term that has a greater association with studies of conditioning that are more likely to involve animals. However, both are clearly relevant to the topic of this book.

METAPHORS FOR MEMORY

There are several striking things about the human mind. One is that it is the part of ourselves of which we have the most intimate awareness. Our experiences are our thoughts. Another is that many, if not most, of the operations of the human mind are not open to direct inspection. You can't see thinking. In addition, there is the problem that every experience that the mind has changes it in some way. By reading this sentence, you are changed. These issues lead to a number of problems in trying to understand memory. One has to be clever and develop ways to assess how memory works. Many issues involved in the study of memory are covered in Chapter 3. More relevant here is the idea that there is no simple and direct way to talk about what memory is and how it works. Because of this, people often talk about it in indirect ways, using **metaphors.**

Roediger (1980) has compiled a list of metaphors that have been used over the centuries to capture various aspects of memory (see Table 1.1). Some of these metaphors express the idea that memory is a recorder of experience, such as a wax tablet, a record player, a writing pad, a tape recorder, or a video camera. Other metaphors imply that different types of memories, different types of knowledge, and different times in our lives are stored in different places. These include such metaphors as memory being like a house, a library, or a dictionary. In contrast to the idea that some memories are somehow distinguished from one another, another concept is that they can also become intertwined and interconnected, like a switchboard or network.

Memory is not passive. Some metaphors capture some of its more dynamic characteristics. For example, the process of retrieving a specific memory from the chaotic jumble we have accumulated during our lives has led to the idea of searching for memories as being something like trying to catch birds in an aviary or searching for something in a junk

TABLE 1.1 Metaphors Used to Describe Memory

METAPHOR	EXAMPLES
Recorder of Experience	Wax tablet, record player, writing pad, tape recorder, video camera
Storage Locations	House, library, dictionary
Interconnections	Switchboard, network
Jumbled Storage	Bird in an aviary, pocketbook, junk drawer, garbage can
Temporal Availability	Conveyor belt
Content Addressability	Lock and key, tuning fork
Forgetting of Details	Leaky bucket, cow's stomach, acid bath
Reconstruction	Building an entire dinosaur skeleton from fossils
Active Processing	Workbench, computer program

drawer, or even a garbage can. This also goes along with the idea that memories become harder to get at over time, as if they were being led away on a conveyor belt. Often a search is required to find the appropriate memories that match or meet the current need, like a lock and key. Memory retrieval is further complicated by the fact that much of what gets stored is forgotten, leaving only a portion of the original, like water in a leaky bucket. This loss of knowledge requires people to re-create the missing pieces of a memory, using a constructive process, perhaps like reconstructing a whole dinosaur from the fragments of bones left behind. Finally, metaphors capture the active nature of memory in manipulating information, as if it were a workbench or a computer program.

The large number of metaphors should give you the idea that memory is a complex thing that we have only begun to understand. Because of its ephemeral nature, we must rely on our knowledge of other more concrete and better understood concepts to help us make sense of it. Probably the most dominant metaphor for memory is the literacy metaphor (Danziger, 2008). The advent of written language led the ancients, and most people since, to view memories as something that are written down and put somewhere. This leads to the near-universal (though not necessarily completely accurate) conception of memory involving encoding, storage, and retrieval, much like writing books and storing them on a shelf. This metaphor treats memories as discrete packets, like books or papers, which may or may not correspond to how the brain parses up our experiences. The dominant modern version of literary metaphor is the computer metaphor which drove and dominated the cognitive revolution of the mid-twentieth century.

Before moving on, let's look at one more metaphor for memory that is very inaccurate: the idea that memory is a muscle. The idea is that the more you use your memory, the better it will be. In other words, simply memorizing information will make memory better in the future. There is no evidence to support this idea. Instead, it is not how much you use your memory but how much information you have in it that is important. So, memory is not like a muscle, but more like a key collection. The more keys you have, the more locks you can open.

Synopsis

Memory is not open to direct inspection. As such, we must use a variety of metaphors to capture its various aspects, such as its recording of experience, its organization, and its chaos. While each of these metaphors carries a degree of imprecision, each one effectively captures some characteristics of memory that makes it easier for us to understand.

HISTORY OF MEMORY RESEARCH

Questions about the nature of memory extend back millennia to the ancient philosophers. However, a true systematic, quantified, and rigorous assessment of the nature and limits of human memory did not begin until the end of the nineteenth century. In this section, we review some of the major players in the history of memory research starting from the ancients and leading up to about the mid-twentieth century.

From the Ancients to Modern Precursors

A great deal of scientific thought about memory has developed over time or has been influenced by people from the great philosophers of ancient Greece to more modern times. This began with Plato (428?–347? B.C.), a rationalist philosopher who emphasized rational thought as a means of understanding of the world. For him, memory serves as the bridge between the perceptual world and a rational world of idealized abstractions (Viney & King, 1998). Plato's ideas were further developed by other rationalists philosophers, including Rene Descartes (1596–1650) and Immanuel Kant (1724–1804). Plato's most prominent pupil was Aristotle (384–322 B.C.); he was an empiricist who believed reality itself was the basis of inquiry.

One of Aristotle's most powerful contributions is the idea that memories are primarily composed of associations among various stimuli or experiences. Aristotle's ideas later worked into grand form by the British empiricists, including George Berkeley (1685–1753), John Locke (1632–1704), John Stuart Mill (1806–1873), and David Hume (1711–1776). As you will see, there are many theories of memory that are associationistic, such as accounts of priming, interference, or even the creation of false memories that use Aristotle's ideas of how various elements are mentally linked to one another. These linking relationships often follow Aristotle's three laws of association: similarity, contrast, and contiguity such that memory associations link ideas that are similar in nature, are the opposite on some critical dimension (and thus a form of similarity in that the dimension is present and is important), or occurred near one another in time. In medieval times, St. Augustine (A.D. 354–430), in Book X of his *Confessions,* considers the topic of memory in a way that would be familiar in modern times. More recently Robert Hooke (1635–1703) developed a theory of memory with a surprising number of modern insights. However, his work was generally overshadowed by his rivalry with Sir Isaac Newton, which further hurried his ideas into obscurity (Hintzman, 2003).

Charles Darwin's (1809–1882) ideas also had an impact on scientific thinking about human memory (see the entire February–March 2009 issue of *American Psychologist*). Many memory theorists are guided by the idea that it has developed through the process of evolution to capture major characteristics of the environment and to perform specific tasks (Glenberg, 1997; Klein, Cosmides, Tooby, & Chance, 2002; Shepard, 1984). This evolutionary aspect of human memory has an influence on how people think about the mind, behavior, and genetic influences. It is important to note that in some sense all human behavior has a genetic component (Turkheimer, 1998). The existence of our brains requires that we have brain-building DNA and all of our thoughts depend on this brain. Thus, our memories have a genetic component. However, our DNA does not directly cause our brains to have the exact configuration that we happen to have at the moment, but this is due to our history of experiences.

Early Memory Researchers in Psychology

Psychology as an independent discipline arose in the latter half of the nineteenth century. Since then many people have influenced memory research. While we cover a few prominent ones here, it should be kept in mind that the study of memory did not always move at a steady pace. Sometimes in science people develop ideas that move the field forward but, for whatever reason, are not noticed at the time. These theories fall by the wayside, never to be heard again. However, a few may capture the attention of future generations, who discover in the earlier, neglected work parallels to modern ideas. For example, in memory research, Richard Semon (1859–1918) developed a theory of memory in the first decade of the twentieth century that incorporated many ideas about the process of retrieval. However, his contemporaries largely ignored these ideas, and his insights were not appreciated until 70 years later (Schacter, Eich, & Tulving, 1978). Now let's look at some people whose work had a more immediate impact.

Ebbinghaus. One of the first true students of memory in a scientific form was Hermann Ebbinghaus (1850–1909). He is best known for his 1885 publication *Memory: A Contribution to Experimental Psychology* (*Über das Gedächtnis* in the original German). This work conveyed his detailed studies of memory, using himself as both experimenter and subject, because formal methods of obtaining research participants were not available at that time. Also, this was a time of psychological research when the study of one's self was more acceptable. Currently, it is viewed as more objective if the experimenter tests another person who knows little to nothing about the experimental hypothesis. There are still a few people who do test their own memories, but these efforts are quite rare. Soon after Ebbinghaus's work, researchers at the University of Göttingen developed Ebbinghaus's methods into the experimenter-participant model we know today (Danziger, 2008).

Ebbinghaus tried to study memory in as pure a form as possible, in the absence of an influence of prior knowledge. To do this, he devised a form of test stimulus called the **nonsense syllable,** which is a consonant-vowel-consonant trigram that has no clear meaning in the language. Nonsense syllables for English would be PAB, SER, and NID. Ebbinghaus created and used about 2,300 of these. These nonsense syllables had a tremendous effect on the study of human memory for many decades. Researchers not only used nonsense syllables but also spent a great deal of effort studying them, even to the point where nonsense syllables were rated for meaningfulness (Glaze, 1928). People recognized that some nonsense syllables were more word-like than others. For example, "BAL" is rated high in meaningfulness (because of "ball"), whereas "XAD" is rated very low.

Ebbinghaus spent a lot of time memorizing lists of nonsense syllables of various lengths, under various learning conditions, and for various retention intervals before he tested himself. (In some of his later studies he did allow some real words to enter his lists on the premise that it would have little effect.) For memory retrieval he would give himself the first nonsense syllable, and he would then try to recall the rest in the series. Using this simple approach, he was able to discover a wide range of basic principles of human memory that have withstood the test of time. Some of the more important ones are the concepts of the learning curve, the forgetting curve, overlearning, and savings. It should be noted that although Ebbinghaus discovered these using nonsense syllables, these same patterns are observed with all types of information.

The **learning curve** reflects the idea that there is a period of time needed for information to be memorized, such as the number of times a person needs to practice information, and it can be affected by a number of things, such as the amount of information to be learned. The learning curve is a negatively accelerated function in which most of the action occurs early on, with smaller and smaller benefits gained later on. So, the largest amount of information is learned in the first segment. In the second, although more is learned, the gain is not as much as during the first. A similar description applies to the third segment, and so on. Thus, through this process, information is gradually committed to memory. Furthermore, Ebbinghaus showed that how a person went about learning, in terms of the distribution of practice, influenced how well information was learned. Specifically, memory is better when practice is spread out over time, rather than lumped together—a distinction that is currently known as **distributed practice** and **massed practice.**

The **forgetting curve** is the opposite of the learning curve, and yet it is strongly similar to it. It conveys the loss of old information rather than the acquisition of new information. However, the forgetting curve is like the learning curve in that it is also a negatively accelerating function. As we'll see in Chapter 3, most of what is forgotten is lost during the initial period. As time goes on, the process of forgetting continues but at a slower pace. The more time that passes, the slower the rate of forgetting.

Forgetting is clearly the most problematic aspect of memory, and the forgetting curve suggests that we are doomed, sooner or later, to lose just about every memory we acquire. However, it should be apparent that this is not strictly the case. There are some pieces of knowledge that you've had for years and are unlikely to ever forget. One way to do this is by a process called **overlearning,** in which a person continues to study information after perfect recall has been achieved. This continued learning insulates a person against forgetting. If there is substantial overlearning, forgetting may be delayed for quite some time, perhaps indefinitely.

When information has been forgotten to the point that no pieces can be recalled with accuracy or reliability, it might seem that a person must start at square one and repeat all of the previous effort. However, this is not the case. Ebbinghaus found that after seemingly complete forgetting, subsequent attempts to relearn the information required less effort than the first time. This difference between the amount of effort required on a subsequent and prior learning attempt is called **savings.** The existence of savings is very important. For one thing, it demonstrates that knowledge that appears to be lost may be residing somewhere in the darkened corners of our mind. It is no longer consciously available, but it can still exert an unconscious influence on behavior—in this case, serving as a platform on which to build a new set of consciously available memories.

Bartlett. Another major figure in the study of human memory is Sir Fredrick Bartlett (1886–1969). Bartlett was, in some ways, the opposite of Ebbinghaus. Whereas Ebbinghaus was interested in the operations of memory independent of prior knowledge, Bartlett was directly interested in how prior knowledge influenced memory. He found that prior knowledge has a profound influence on memory. Specifically, he suggested that what is stored in memory is often fragmentary and incomplete. When people are remembering, in some sense, they are reconstructing the information from the bits that are stored and from other prior knowledge that they have about such circumstances. This reconstruction is guided by what Bartlett called "schemas" (a theoretical construct also used by Gestalt psychologists, such as Kurt Koffka). Schemas are general world knowledge structures about commonly experienced aspects of life. (There will be more about schemas in Chapter 9.) To illustrate the effects of schemas, Bartlett had people read a story and then later try to recall it anywhere from immediately after they read it to several months or years later. What he found was that as memories for the story became more fragmented, the story content was altered to make it more consistent with a stereotypical story.

James. One of the most prominent of the early psychologists was William James (1842–1910). James is so highly regarded that, even among current researchers, it is not usual to find a quote by James leading off a research or review article, particularly by Americans. Much of this influence comes through his famous textbook, *The Principles of Psychology* (1890/1950). In general, James was a primary mover in the functionalist movement in early psychology. In terms of memory, James was able to provide descriptions that are remarkably similar to theories in use today. For example, his distinction between primary and secondary memory closely parallels the distinction between short-term and long-term memory. Similarly, he was one of the first academics to describe memory retrieval problems, such as the tip-of-the-tongue phenomenon (see Chapter 14) in which a person is not able to remember something, such as someone's name, but there is this strong feeling that retrieval is imminent.

Gestalt Psychology

Modern views of memory were influenced by a number of movements in psychology. Two important ones were the Gestalt and behaviorist movements. The **Gestalt** movement, mostly advanced by German researchers such as Wolfgang Kohler (1887–1967), Max Wertheimer (1880–1943), and Kurt Koffka (1886–1941), suggested that strictly reductionistic approaches to mental life were incomplete. Instead, one needed the idea that complex mental representations and processes have a quality that is different from the component parts that make them up. This is not to say that the Gestalt psychologists completely rejected reductionistism. They most certainly did not. Instead, they argued that an understanding of more complex phenomena was important in its own right because it could be qualitatively different. For example, a melody is something that is qualitatively different from the individual notes that make it up, although it is certainly very dependent on them.

One of the ideas of the Gestalt movement that has influenced thinking about memory was that the whole is different from the sum of its parts. This idea can be seen in modern views that memories are built up of a configuration of simpler elements to take on a new quality. For example, the finding that people remember the causally important elements of a story better than others (Trabasso & van den Broek, 1985) is directly in line with this idea. Gestalt psychologists also stated that the observed behavior of a person depends on both the context in which people find themselves as well as a frame of reference. This is reflected in the context effects that are observed in memory and perspective effects, such as the hindsight bias. Moreover, because our context and goals can change, the way we use and organize our memories were thought to change according to these demands as well (Danziger, 2008).

A final concept to come out of the Gestalt movement is the idea that mental representations are isomorphic. That is, their mental structure and operation are analogous to the structure and function of information in the world. The influence of this idea is clearly seen when spatial memory is discussed (see Chapter 8). The idea is that the structure of a memory trace reflects the structure of the event, as it would be experienced, although in not as complete a form. It should be noted that for the Gestalt psychologists this isomorphism was a functional one. The memory trace functioned "as if" it has the same structure as external events, not that it actually did.

Behaviorism

As we will see in Chapter 6, there are many aspects of memory that operate on a basic and unconscious level. Some of these involve the encoding, storage, and retrieval of relatively simple contingencies that fall under the heading of "conditioning." This was the domain of the behaviorists. **Behaviorism** is a school of thought that originally sought to bring greater credibility to psychology as a science. It was a line of thinking that had a strong grip on psychology for much of the early- to mid-twentieth century. Part of this effort was to avoid mentalistic constructs because they could not be objectively observed and to focus entirely on observables. Although the workings of the mind could not be observed, behavior could be. So, much of the experimental work that was done during the behaviorist era did not directly address issues of memory. However, there were some important insights and discoveries that are relevant here.

Two of the more salient forms of conditioning are classical and operant conditioning. Classical conditioning is a form of memory that allows one to prepare for contingencies that are present in the environment, whereas operant conditioning allows one to remember the consequences of one's own actions. Both of these concepts came into the vocabulary of psychology early on in the twentieth century. Classical conditioning was first described by the Russian physiologist Ivan Pavlov (1849–1936), who had won the Nobel Prize for his work on digestion. Operant conditioning was first described by an until then little-known American named Edward Thorndike (1874–1949), who discovered these principles because, in part, he wasn't able to do what he really wanted to do as a graduate student: study hypnosis.

The discovery and study of these forms of conditioning are important because for decades they shaped much of the research in learning and memory. There was great interest in studying the principles that guided these forms of learning and the implications they had on behavior. One of the salient qualities of classical and operant conditioning studies is that one can take these principles pretty far without having to posit much about what is going on mentally. One can just observe the stimulus conditions and the responses produced by an organism.

Despite this generally antimentalistic view during the behaviorist era, there were some behaviorists who had important insights into issues of memory. Perhaps the most prominent of these was Edward Tolman (1886–1959), who did a number of studies with rats running through mazes. According to strict behaviorist analyses of maze running, what the rat is learning is to make specific turns at specific junctures. Each turn that the rat makes in the maze would either be reinforced or not. If this is true, then any change in the maze should result in the rat needing to learn the route all over again. However, Tolman observed that rats often did not need to undergo a relearning but adapted to changes very quickly. This observation led him to suggest that rats had a mental representation in memory for that spatial location. Tolman called this the "mental map." The rats presumably could consult this mental map in memory to adapt to the changes in the maze. Thus, working within the behaviorist context, people such as Tolman were able to bring a discussion of memory and mental activity back into mainstream psychology.

Tolman was a molar behaviorist, although the term he preferred was *purposive behaviorism*. That is, he was interested in larger behaviors as opposed to the more microscopic behaviors that interested many of his behaviorist colleagues. An example of a molar behavior might be something like getting to the end box of a maze or going to a movie, whereas a microscopic behavior might be an action like "turn left." This interest in molar behavior can be seen in an approach to memory that takes into account the goals and context of a person in the memory situation.

Verbal Learning

The **verbal learning** tradition existed in the context of a behaviorist psychology and stemmed from Ebbinghaus's work with nonsense syllables. The term *verbal learning* itself reflects the behaviorism of many of its practitioners, although what was being studied was a form of memory. Because the verbal learners were behaviorists of a sort, the studies they did often had clearly defined stimulus and response components. Memorization was referred to as "attachment of responses to stimuli," and forgetting was "loss of response availability." (For a nice summary of verbal learning and its relationship to memory, see Tulving & Madigan, 1970.) The verbal learning tradition gave psychologists a way to study memory during the antimentalistic era of behaviorism.

One of the dominant methods in the verbal learning tradition is the **paired associate** learning paradigm. In this approach, people memorize pairs of items, often words, letters, or nonsense syllables. An example of a pair would be something like "BIRD-FANCY." During testing, people would be presented with the first item of the pair and would be asked to produce the second (e.g., "BIRD-?"). The first item served as the stimulus and the second as the response.

There were many variations on this theme. The simple A-B paradigm would present people with a list of paired associates and have them recall the B items in the presence of the A cues. This is clearly memory in a behaviorist guise. Other paradigms are more complicated, where people must learn a second list of items. If this second list was unrelated to the first, this was called an A-B C-D paradigm (easy). An example of this would be learning the pair "BIRD-FANCY" in the first list, and "TABLE-ARROW" on the second. If the second list retained the initial cues with the first list, it was called an A-B A-D paradigm (hard). An example of this would be learning the pair "BIRD-FANCY" in the first list, and "BIRD-ARROW" on the second. Alternatively, one could have the second list be combinations of the A items with synonyms of the B items, called an A-B A-B' paradigm (very hard). An example of this would be learning the pair "BIRD-FANCY" in the first list, and "BIRD-DRESSY" on the second. Finally, there could be a recombination of the A and B items from the first list, an A-B A-Br paradigm (very, very hard). An example of this would be learning the pairs "BIRD-FANCY" and "TABLE-ARROW" on the first list and "BIRD-ARROW" and "TABLE-FANCY" on the second. Often what researchers were doing was looking at the effects of interference of prior learning on new learning. Issues of interference continue to be of interest to memory researchers, and some still use paired associate learning paradigms. We'll see that some of the ideas developed by the verbal learners explored in the sections on interference in Chapter 7.

Early Efforts in Neuroscience

Memories are stored in the brain, but the brain is a complex and busy place. So where exactly is each memory stored? Is it possible to locate individual memories in the brain? This is the basic question asked by neuropsychologists such as Carl Lashley (1890–1958). Lashley (1950) did a series of studies in search of what he referred to as the "engram"—the neural representation of a memory trace. Lashley first trained rats to run through a maze and then surgically removed part of their brains. After the rats recovered from the surgery, they would be placed back into the maze. If memories for the maze were localized in one part of the brain, then destroying that part would destroy the memory, and the rats would then run the maze just as if they were entering it for the first time. The major outcome of these studies was that no matter what part of the brain was removed, the lesioned rats were still able to perform better than control rats that were placed in the maze for the first time. The critical factor was how much tissue had been removed, not where (see Figure 1.1). (A similar study was done by J. P. Flourens, with pigeons, in the nineteenth century, as reported by Danziger, 2008.) This led Lashley to conclude that engrams were not localized in one part of the brain but were distributed throughout the cortex. While more recent studies have shown that some forms of memory may be localized in different parts of the brain, the general conclusion that many different and distributed parts of the brain are used during memory processing is well supported.

In addition to understanding what different parts of the brain do, it is important to understand how the brain works. That is, how do the interconnections among neurons influence the processing of information? One of the pioneers along this line of research was Donald Hebb. Hebb's classic contribution was his book *The Organization of Behavior* (1949). Hebb is one of the forerunners of computational neuroscience—mathematical modeling of brain activity. According to Hebb, memories were encoded in the nervous system in a two-stage process. In the first stage, neural excitation would reverberate around in cell assemblies. A collection of cells that corresponds to a new pattern or idea would be stimulated, and this stimulation would continue for some time. In the second stage, the interconnections among the neurons would physically change, with some connections actually growing stronger. This is similar to the idea of long-term potentiation, discussed in Chapter 2. According to Hebb, it takes some time for memories to move from stage 1 to stage 2. This is why if people suffer some sort of trauma to the brain, such as a blow to the head, they may lose recent memories. (We will discuss this in Chapter 16

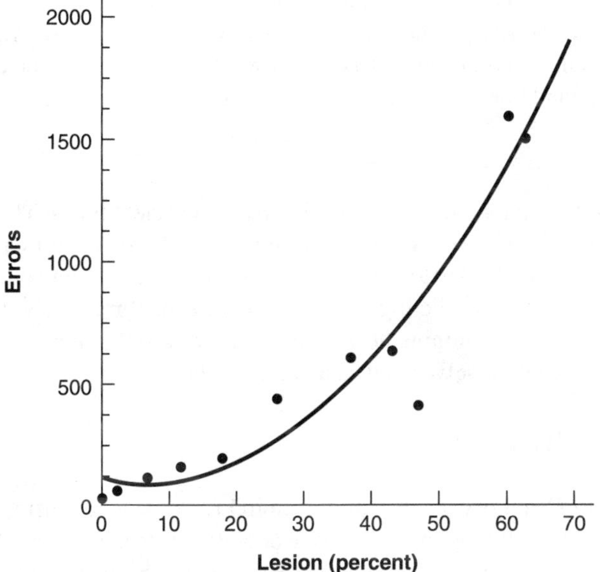

FIGURE 1.1 Results of Lashley's Experiment

Source: Lashley, K. S. (1950). In search of the engram. Symposia of the Society for Experimental Biology: Physiological Mechanisms of Animal Behavior (Vol. 4). New York: Academic Press.

when we examine amnesia.) In addition, these ideas of neural organization and change help lead to the development of computational models of the nervous system, such as the parallel distributed processing (PDP) models, discussed in Chapter 10.

The Cognitive Revolution

Over time, psychologists became frustrated with the constraints imposed by behaviorism. There was a desire to study mental activity as mental activity, not simply as a black box between the input of the stimulus and the output of the response behavior. The so-called **cognitive revolution** of the 1950s and 1960s marked a return of mental states to legitimate study. It made the study of memory a palatable topic once again.

Many people contributed to the cognitive revolution. We focus here on one whose efforts serve as an example of the work and ideas that brought about this change. George Miller provided a number of important findings for memory research, such as his work on the capacity of short-term memory in his paper "The Magical Number Seven: Plus or Minus Two" (Miller, 1956). This work took the idea of mental processing seriously and demonstrated how it was a limited system, much a like a computer's processing is limited by the amount of memory it has. These studies were some of the first to show that memory could be studied with the methodological rigor that the behaviorists were so fond of.

Miller also showed that how people mentally organized information has an influence on memory. Specifically, the more highly organized a set of information was, the better the memory. In other words, how information is actively thought about can affect later memory. In addition, the knowledge that a person has stored in long-term memory can influence current memory performance in profound ways. Thus, work by Miller, and people like him, showed that in order to understand how memory works in the current situation, one must understand how it is structured over the long term.

Synopsis

The study of memory has a long history stretching back to ancient times. There have been a long line of thinkers who have revealed important characteristics of memory that we continue to uphold. While this history is long, it has not always been smooth. Even in recent times, there have been conflicting opinions about the importance and nature of various aspects of memory. By examining how we have progressed through time, we can better understand why we find ourselves in the state that we do.

THE MODAL MODEL OF MEMORY

The standard model of memory, or the **modal model** (Atkinson & Shiffrin, 1968), is a heuristic guide for understanding how memory works. It has been successful enough that it has limped along for years as one the guiding frameworks for discussing issues about how information is stored over time, so it is worth discussing. This model has four primary components: (1) the sensory registers, (2) short-term store, (3) long-term store, and (4) control processes. An outline of the model is shown in Figure 1.2.

The first component of the model, the **sensory registers,** is best thought of as a collection of memory stores. Each of these stores corresponds to a different sensory modality. For example, there is one sensory register for vision, one for audition, one for touch, and so forth. The world is full of information that is in a constant state of flux. Our sensory registers allow us to hold on to this information for brief periods of time to determine if it is worthy of further attention. If we did not possess such memory stores, our minds would be constantly locked into only the very current state of affairs. In such a situation, we would not be able to detect patterns that involve very brief memories, such as determining that two frames of a film can be interpreted as continuous movement or that a sequence of sounds forms a word.

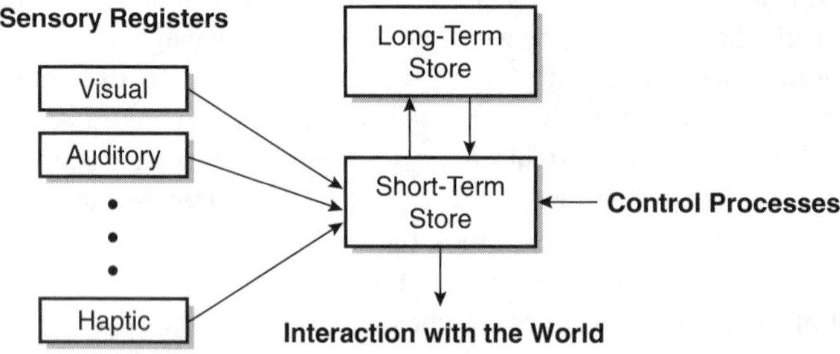

FIGURE 1.2 The Modal Model of Memory

Source: Reprinted from *The Psychology of Learning and Motivation,* 2, Atkinson, R.C., & Shiffrin, R.M., Human memory: A proposed system and its control processes, pp. 89–195, 1968, with permission from Elsevier.

Once information has been attended to, it needs to be kept in the current stream of thought. Because what we are currently thinking about can change and drift relatively quickly, this information needs to be kept available for a short period of time. This part of the standard model is a **short-term memory** that generally retains information for less than a minute if nothing is actively done with it. If consciousness is associated with any part of memory, it would be the information in short-term memory. This is knowledge that is either currently in conscious awareness or just beyond it. Another characteristic of short-term memory is its capacity—the amount of information that can be held in an active state. This amount is humblingly small—somewhere on the order of seven items. Issues dealing with the sensory registers and short-term memory are considered in more detail in Chapter 4.

The third component of the modal model is the idea that there are also control processes that actively manipulate information in short-term memory. This can include processes from rehearsing information to transferring knowledge to or from long-term memory, or perhaps even reasoning. This component of memory makes it an active participant in reality rather than just a passive absorption and retrieval mechanism. The idea that control processes in short-term memory work with knowledge in the service of some goal has led to the idea that short-term memory should be considered more of a working memory system. Issues of working memory are considered in detail in Chapter 5.

The fourth component of memory—the one that interests most people and that much of this text is devoted to—is long-term memory. **Long-term memory** encompasses a wide variety of different types of long-term knowledge and different ways of using that knowledge. Issues of long-term memory are covered extensively in Chapters 6 through 17.

Again, it should be noted that this model is a heuristic for thinking about the broad memory system, but no one uses this as an accurate theory of memory. For example, incoming information does not need to pass through short-term memory to actually reach long-term memory. Instead, the information appears to activate knowledge in long-term memory, and this activated knowledge is actively manipulated in short-term memory (van der Meulen, Logie, & Della Sala, 2009).

Synopsis

The modal model of memory is the standard heuristic that is used to guide discussions of memory. One component of this model is the sensory registers, which are brief memory systems that hold sensory information. Short-term memory holds small amounts of information for short periods of time, usually under a minute. The control processes are used to actively manipulate information. Finally, long-term memory is responsible for storing information for very long periods of time.

MULTIPLE MEMORY SYSTEMS

As is illustrated by the modal model, memory is not a unitary thing. Instead, it has several different subcomponents. Each subcomponent has evolved, as a result of selection pressures, to handle a different job (Klein et al., 2002; Sherry & Schacter, 1987). Some of our long-term memories are implicit and act on us outside of consciousness. In contrast, others are explicit and can enter conscious awareness. Long-term memories can also differ in whether they refer to specific events or to general knowledge.

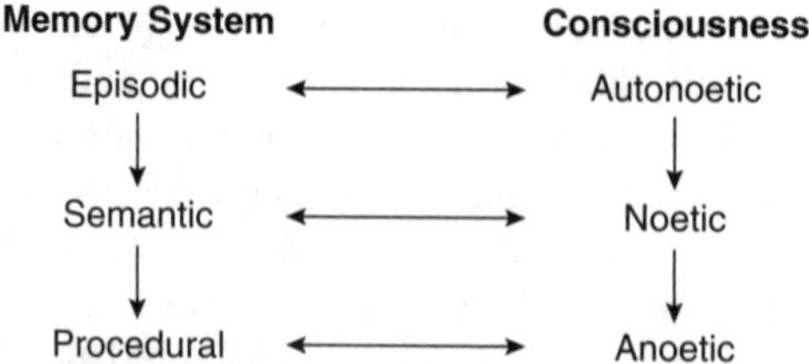

FIGURE 1.3 Tulving's Triarchic Theory of Memory

Source: Tulving, E. (1985a). How many memory systems are there? *American Psychologist*, 40, 385–398.

A number of different classifications of long-term memory can be identified. One organizational guide is Tulving's (1985) *Triarchic Theory of Memory,* shown in Figure 1.3. This view divides long-term memory into three classes: procedural, semantic, and episodic. These divisions reflect the different tasks required of memory, as well as different levels of control and conscious awareness.

Procedural memory is an evolutionarily old memory system. Even relatively primitive organisms have some kind of procedural memory. More recently, people have referred to this as the nondeclarative memory and have grouped semantic and episodic memory in a declarative memory. This more elaborate view of the organization of long-term memory is illustrated in Figure 1.4, which first reflects the **declarative-nondeclarative distinction.** Declarative memory refers to memories that are easy for a person to articulate and talk about. In contrast, nondeclarative memory refers to information in long-term memory that is difficult to articulate but that still has profound influences on our lives. As can be seen in Figure 1.4, nondeclarative memories can be divided into various types, and in Chapter 6 we discuss many of these. One type of nondeclarative memory is the procedural memory of Tulving's classification. This is memory for how to do things, like ride a bicycle or speak your native language. However, other types of memories are included in this category, including condition responses and priming effects. This memory system is described as "anoetic" in Tulving's system because it does not require conscious awareness.

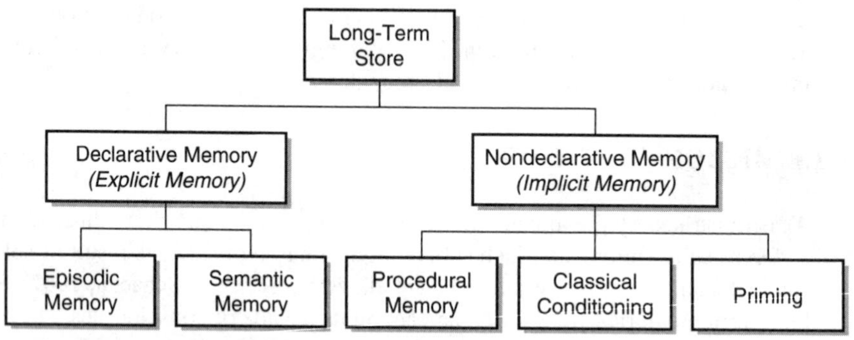

FIGURE 1.4 The Division of Long-Term Memory Systems

Source: Squire, L. R. (1988). Mechanisms of memory. *Science*, 232, 1612–1619.

As shown in Figure 1.4, declarative memory can be divided into two categories as defined by the **episodic-semantic distinction** (Tulving, 1972). Semantic memories are generalized and encyclopedic and are not tied to a specific time or place. This is stable knowledge that you share with your community. For example, knowing what a bird is, what a stop sign means, and what you do in a restaurant are all semantic memories. Semantic memories are highly interrelated and are forgotten rather slowly once established. In **Tulving's Triarchic Theory,** semantic memory is noetic because it requires conscious awareness. You have to be consciously aware to know that an object is a bird or a tree and that it is similar to other members of that category.

In contrast, episodic memories refer to specific episodes or events in our lives. They are tied to the time and place in which the information was learned. For example, where did you go on your first date? Who told you that funny joke? Did you just see the word *apple* in a list of words. Also, unlike semantic memories, episodic memories for each event are compartmentalized and forgotten very rapidly. Episodic memory uses autonoetic knowledge in Tulving's Triarchic Theory because it requires knowledge of the self. For example, in order to know whether you've recently seen an action film, you need to have some memory of yourself as a separate identity to which past events can be referenced. In fact neurological measures, such as ERP recordings (see Chapter 2), show different types of brain activity for memories that refer to the self in some way compared to more semantic memories (Magno & Allen, 2007).

In addition to the different types of memory systems, we can also point out differences in how people use their memories. One of the more prominent of these is the **explicit-implicit distinction** (Schacter, 1987), which roughly corresponds to the distinction between declarative and nondeclarative memories. The important point here is how information is retrieved from memory, not the content of the information.

Explicit memory refers to when a person is actively and consciously trying to remember something. When you are trying to recall someone's name or when you recognize a suspect in a police lineup, this is explicit memory. Implicit memory refers to when a person is unaware that memory is being used. Even though most of this book is dedicated to issues of explicit memory, much of our lives, both thinking and action, are governed by implicit memory. Familiar things that are recognized more quickly, are preferred in choices, and guide our thinking are all examples of the influence of implicit memory operating.

Synopsis

Human memory is not a unitary thing. Instead, there are multiple memory systems that perform different tasks and are responsible for different types of information. Often these capture various levels of involvement of conscious awareness, such as the Triarchic Theory of memory, the declarative-nondeclarative, and implicit-explicit distinctions. Other divisions capture the type of knowledge that the memory systems are processing, such as the episodic-semantic distinction.

RECURRING ISSUES

Before we move on to the specific topics, there are some issues that bear clarification. These issues reoccur throughout the chapters, so it would be helpful if you are alerted to them. In general, these issues have been lurking in the background of most memory research but are now coming to the forefront.

Neurological Bases

It is important to understand the neurological bases because memory exists as a property of the nervous system. The better one understands how the nervous system operates, the better one's insight into human memory. Early in the "cognitive age," much of the study of human thought, including memory, was dominated by the computer metaphor. Part of this metaphor was the distinction between the hardware and the software. The idea was that a person could have an understanding of how software operates with little knowledge of the underlying hardware. For example, some programming languages, such as C and JAVA, are designed to be hardware-independent. To an extent, human memory and thought, the software, can be studied without a detailed understanding of the neural hardware (sometimes called "wetware") on which it is instantiated.

However, some aspects of memory can be understood only if one is familiar with the underlying neurophysiology, and there are many aspects of memory that are better understood or defined when the neurological underpinnings are made clear. Finally, if nothing else, knowing that a theoretical mental process can be associated with a real neural process lends confidence to one's findings and ideas. As we advance into the future, cognitive neuroscience becomes more and more important.

Emotion

A growing trend in cognitive psychology is to look at issues of emotion, which is a critical component of our everyday experiences. More and more memory researchers are incorporating emotion into their theories (see Kensinger, 2009). The importance of emotions has been shown in both behavioral and neurological data. We will discuss the use of emotion to study human memory from time to time throughout the book to better capture its intertwined involvement with memory. Certain sections will present findings that are critically dependent on the emotional state of a person. In this way you will be able to see how these issues of memory, in general, that are often described apart from emotional experience are an important part of a larger psychological system.

Multiple Memory Sources

Another idea is that memory often uses multiple sources rather than a single source on nearly any memory task. Some of the clearest examples of this idea are what are known as **fuzzy trace theories** (e.g., Brainerd, Reyna, & Mojardin, 1999). According to this view, there are at least two memory traces involved in any act of remembering. One is a memory trace that contains detailed information about a specific instance. The other is a more general, categorical trace that captures general information. What is remembered reflects a combination of these. Information in the detailed memory trace dominates when a person has a good memory of a specific event and is trying to remember what happened during that one event. In contrast, information in the general memory trace dominates when a person's memory for a specific event is poor or if knowledge is used in a general way, such as trying to remember what a flywheel is.

Embodied Cognition

Recently, there has been increased interest in **embodied cognition.** While this phrase can mean many different things (Wilson, 2002), there are clear ways that this perspective can have particular influences on the study of human memory. Although the term *grounded cognition* (Barsalou, 2008) may be more descriptive and inclusive, we use the phrase embodied cognition to be consistent with the majority of the literature on this topic. The basic idea is that mental activity does not occur in a vacuum but is grounded in the type of worlds our bodies inhabit and the ways we can use our bodies in this world. Thought is affected by how we interact with the world. This can be seen when memory is affected by the situations people find themselves in. That is, people use context to help guide the encoding and retrieval of information. Second, memory often operates in real time as events are unfolding. As anyone taking a college exam knows, memories often need to be adequately retrieved in a set time limit. Finally, memory is influenced by both the structure of the perceptual information it receives as well as the types of activities a person will likely need to perform in the future—for example, remembering how to navigate around town. All of these ideas are consistent with an embodied cognition perspective.

Scientific Rigor and Converging Evidence

Memory is a tricky thing to study. Each person's memories are different in important ways from everyone else's. There are also different aspects of memory that are qualitatively distinct. However, to have the clearest picture of what our memories are like, and who we are, we need to take as objective a view as possible. We need to avoid being led astray by our biases, momentary intentions, and other prejudices. Taking a rigorous, scientific approach can do this. Psychology, after all, is a science. To emphasize this, various approaches or methods of looking at the data from memory experiments are presented throughout the book to illustrate how the data from memory studies can be analyzed and interpreted to gain a more refined insight into the depths of our mental storehouses. Also, we will see that opinions and theories formed as a science are better supported when evidence comes from different methods of collecting and analyzing data. If these multiple sources of information are all consistent with the same explanation, this gives us greater confidence that the theory is closer to the truth. This is something known as *converging operations.*

Synopsis

While the focus of this book is on the various aspects of memory, there are a number of recurring threads that will reappear across the various topics that represent emerging ways of thinking about memory. These include an increased desire to understand the neurological underpinnings of memory, the involvement of experienced emotions, the division of information across multiple memories, and a need to understand how memory operates in the real world. All of these, as well as every other topic in memory, are approached from a scientific perspective that seeks to derive answers about memory that help us have an accurate and durable understanding of ourselves.

SUMMARY

Understanding human memory is one of the most introspective tasks we can undertake as a species. By looking at how our own memories are created, structured, stored, and retrieved, we can gain a great deal of insight into who we are collectively and as individuals. The study of memory, however, is difficult. Memory is a very complex thing, incorporating issues of representation, storage, and process. People have been trying since ancient times to uncover the mysteries of human memory. Throughout history, particularly since the advent of psychology proper and especially since the advent of the cognitive revolution, we've gained a clearer and more consistent picture of what memory is all about, but much of the canvas is still obscured. Although there are many different theories about the nature of memory, many people at least implicitly follow the idea that short-term and long-term memory have different characteristics and that the operation of memory can be intimately influenced by the mental processes applied to the contents of memories. Moreover, different types of knowledge are handled by different memory systems. From this background, we will survey various aspects of memory, often touching on common themes of neuropsychological issues, emotions, multitrace influences, and issues of scientific rigor.

STUDY QUESTIONS

1. What do the terms *learning* and *memory* mean in the context of this chapter? How are they referring to similar things? How do they diverge?
2. Why do we need metaphors for memory? What are some metaphors? What do they tell us about the nature of memory?
3. What were some of the major figures and some of the major schools of thought that dominated thinking about human memory? What were the contributions of each?
4. What are some of the major divisions of human memory? What sort of processing is done by each of those divisions?
5. What are some of the emerging themes that will be recurring at various points in our discussion of memory?

KEY TERMS

behaviorism, cognitive revolution, declarative-nondeclarative distinction, distributed practice, embodied cognition, engram, episodic-semantic distinction, explicit-implicit distinction, forgetting curve, fuzzy trace theories, Gestalt psychology, learning, learning curve, long-term memory, massed practice, memory, metaphors for memory, modal model, nonsense syllable, overlearning, paired associates, savings, sensory registers, short-term memory, Tulving's Triarchic Theory, verbal learning

CHAPTER TWO

NEUROSCIENCE OF MEMORY

How are memories encoded? Where are they stored? How are they retrieved? Using the computer analogy, thoughts and memories are the software and data, and the nervous system is the hardware. A person can understand many aspects of the software without knowing much about the hardware. Many computer users don't really understand how the machine works, but they can still use the software. Still, to gain a truer insight into the software, how it represents and processes information, why some processes are fast and others are slow, one needs an understanding of the hardware. The same is true for memory and the nervous system.

Memory, like any mental process, is an **emergent property** of the nervous system, not a property of the individual neurons, that emerges when the neurons work together. To more clearly illustrate this, think of six square boards. None of those boards by themselves have the property of containment. However, when the boards are arranged to make a box, then it is possible to place something inside it. The property of containment emerges out of the arrangement of the elements that lack that property individually (see Minsky, 1986).

Without a working understanding of the nervous system, your knowledge of memory will be limited and incomplete. The operation of the nervous system is intertwined with an understanding of how memory works and operates in our interactive world (e.g., Marshall, 2009). The aim of this chapter is to provide an understanding of the major components of the nervous system and how they are involved in memory. We first consider the simplest component, the neuron, then how neural communication occurs and how this changes as a result of experience (the first step in encoding a memory). After that, we'll skip to higher levels of processing, such as the cortex, and how they are involved in memory. Finally, we examine ways to study how the underlying neurobiology is related to the observed psychology.

NEURONS

To understand how neurophysiology relates to mental experience, it is good to have a working understanding of the nervous system. Let's look at the components of individual neurons, followed by a presentation of neural communication.

Neural Structure

The most basic parts of the nervous system are neurons. A **neuron** is a specialized cell in the body that plays a role in the transmission and retention of information. The structure of a neuron is shown in Figure 2.1. Some of these components are shared with other cells. For example, the neuron has a cell body, or **soma,** that contains all of the general cell processing components, such as mitochondria, RNA, and so forth.

Other structures are for the specialized jobs of neurons. Extending out of each neuron are dendrites. **Dendrites** are largely used for receiving signals either from sensory cells or from other neurons. Generally, dendrites are responsible for collecting information. Neurons have another protruding structure called an axon. **Axons** are used for transmitting information either to other neurons or to other structures, such as muscles and glands. At the end of each axon are the **terminal buttons** that contain the neurotransmitters. **Neurotransmitters** are the chemicals that are used to send signals to other neurons. Because axons can sometimes be quite lengthy, to avoid the loss or confusion of signals, some neurons have axons that are encased in a fatty substance called a **myelin sheath** that acts as a neural insulator. The myelin sheath has gaps along its length that are called the **nodes of Ranvier.** They facilitate the transmission of information within a neuron by allowing the neural signal to jump from one point to the next without having to continuously traverse the entire length of the axon. Thus, the distance that the neural signal travels is functionally shortened.

Neural Communication

Let's now look at the transmission of information. Neural communication can be broken down into two components, one electrical and the other chemical.

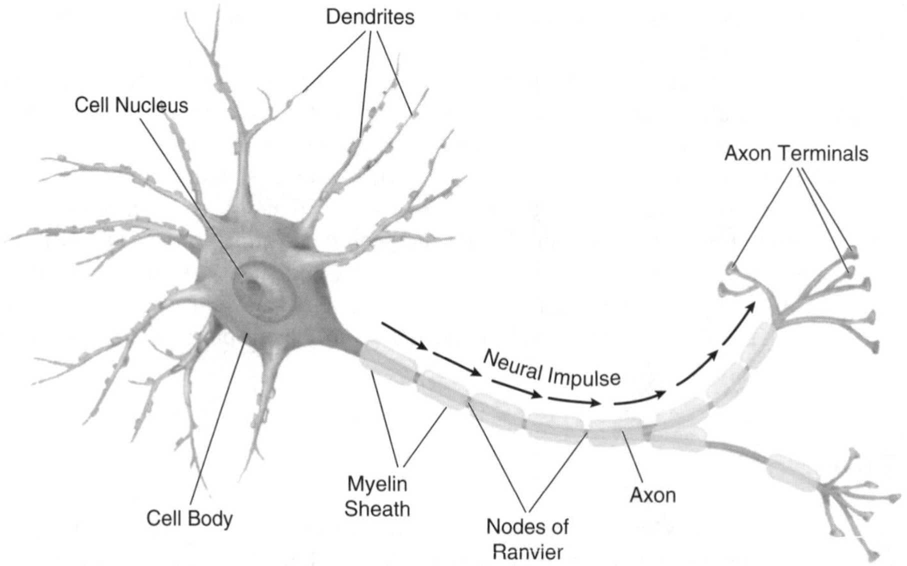

FIGURE 2.1 A Neuron

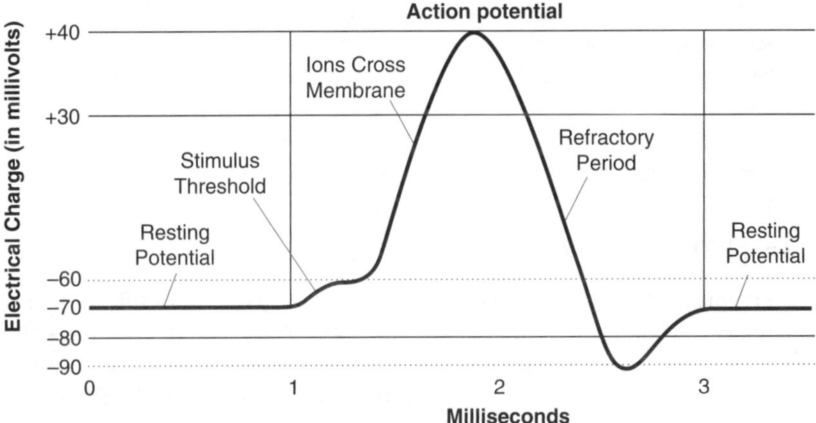

FIGURE 2.2 The Action Potential Over Time

Action Potential. The electrical component occurs within a neuron and is called the **action potential.** When a neuron is sufficiently stimulated, an action potential occurs, and the neuron is said to "fire" (see Figure 2.2). When a neuron is not being stimulated, it has a resting electrical charge of –70 mV (millivolts) with a number of negatively charged ions in the neuron's interior. When a neuron is stimulated, there is a depolarization. If this depolarization is sufficient, the electrical charge may reach –50 mV. At this point there will be a dramatic change in the charge of the neuron to +40 mV. This is the action potential. After a neuron fires, there is a recovery period where the neuron prepares itself to fire again and resets itself at the resting potential of –70 mV. It should be noted that the action potential operates on the all-or-none principle. That is, there is either an action potential, which is always the same, or there is no action potential.

Neurotransmitters and the Synapse. The other component of neural communication is chemical. This occurs at the **synapse** between two neurons. Although a single neuron may communicate with large numbers of other neurons, especially in the cortex, there is no direct physical connection between them, but there is a small gap between them, the synapse, which is 100 to 200 angstroms wide (1 angstrom = 1/10,000th of a millimeter). Neurons communicate across the synapse using chemicals called **neurotransmitters.** Neurotransmitters are forced into the synapse when there is an action potential, absorbed by the subsequent neuron, and altering its electrical potential. Some neurotransmitters are more important than others for memory. One of these is **acetylcholine (ACh).** When acetylcholine effects are enhanced, memory can improve, and it declines when acetylcholine effects are suppressed (Mishkin & Appenzellar, 1987). Acetylcholine may enhance the strength of synaptic potentials during long-term potentiation (see later). **Glutamate (Glu)** is a critical excitatory neurotransmitter involved in the formation of new synapses, and creating new memories. In comparison, gamma-amino butyric acid (**GABA**) is an inhibitory neurotransmitter, also critically involved in new memory formation. **Norepinephrine** is involved in memory consolidation, and **Dopamine** is also important to memory. Part of the problem with a condition like Parkinson's disease is the low level of dopamine available.

There are two classes of neurotransmitters. Excitatory neurotransmitters encourage the subsequent neuron to fire. In contrast, inhibitory neurotransmitters encourage the subsequent neuron to *not* fire. These both occur because information is coded in the nervous system as a pattern of activation across a set of neurons, with some neurons firing and others not, kind of like a computer code of 1s (on) and 0s (off), although there is much greater complexity and subtlety in the nervous system.

Neural Change in Learning

Communication between neurons occurs at the synapse, but how do these connections get altered as new things are encoded into memory? These connections must change in some way. The precise mechanisms for this are not well understood. One way is likely to be similar to a process known as **long-term potentiation**, or **LTP** (Bliss & Collingridge, 1993; Bliss & Lomo, 1973; Gustafsson & Wigstrom, 1988), often investigated using cells from the hippocampus (see later). LTP is a process that strengthens the connections between neurons by altering the ease with which postsynaptic neurons fire. LTP can last for days or weeks, but it eventually dissipates. Thus, it is a good model for the types of neural changes that occur in a memory. An important point to keep in mind is that LTP is not observed in living brains but is a phenomenon that is observed by sending rapid pulse trains to neurons in petri dishes (Eichenbaum, 2002). There is an analogous process called **long-term depression** or **LTD** that weakens connections between neurons, which can also be important for learning (e.g., Duffy, Labrie, & Roder, 2008).

Beyond the cellular consolidation in the hippocampus, there is a systemwide consolidation in larger brain systems (Abraham, 2006). This process, known as **consolidation**, takes a long time, on the order of days, weeks, and even years. This may be one function of sleep as memory consolidation is facilitated if people sleep during the retention interval than if they do not (Hu, Stylos-Allan, & Walker, 2006). So, new knowledge and experiences physically alter the structure of the brain. Our brains, and thus our memories, are in a constant state of flux as we encounter new events, thoughts, and experiences.

Synopsis

The fundamental building blocks of the nervous system, and hence of memory, are neurons. Having a working understanding of how neurons function and communicate provides better knowledge of how memory works. Neural communication occurs through electrical and chemical processes. The electrical component is captured in the action potential, and the chemical component is captured by neurotransmitters. Neurons form memories by altering their connections to one another. How the nervous system acts in a memory system is not completely understood.

LARGER STRUCTURES

Up to this point, we have been talking about low-level processes. Now we jump up to larger levels of neural organization. Those brain structures that have a more direct involvement can be classified into two broad categories: (1) the subcortical structures, which lie beneath the cerebral cortex, and (2) the various lobes of the cortex. In Chapters 16 and 17 we discuss various memory disorders that occur when one or more of these structures are damaged.

Subcortical Structures

Hippocampus. The subcortical structure that gets the most attention in memory is the **hippocampus** (see Figure 2.3). This is a seahorse-shaped structure (hence the name). The hippocampus, as well as the surrounding structures, is important for storing conscious memories (Mishkin & Appenzeller, 1987). It does not appear to be where long-term memories are actually stored, but it may help encode them in other parts of the brain. More simply, the hippocampus serves as a way station for the knowledge on the journey to permanent encoding (if it makes it that far). The hippocampus is divided into a number of regions including the *dentate gyrus*, regions *CA1* and *CA3*, and the *subiculum* that are implicated in different processes.

One type of information that the hippocampus is specialized in processing is memories for conjunctions of stimuli that appear together in the environment. The hippocampus is well designed for the rapid encoding of episode-specific conjunctions—that is, whatever is co-occurring at the moment. A slower, more generalized encoding of regular conjunctions is handled by the cortex (O'Reilly & Rudy, 2001). Damage to the hippocampus can cause severe declarative memory deficits (e.g., Mahut, Zola-Morgan, & Moss, 1982), such as anterograde amnesia, described in Chapter 16.

Other Structures. Another important structure for memory is the amygdala (see Figure 2.3). The **amygdala** is an almond-shaped structure located at the lower part of the hippocampus, toward the front of the brain. The amygdala is involved in processing emotional aspects of memories (Mishkin & Appenzeller, 1987).

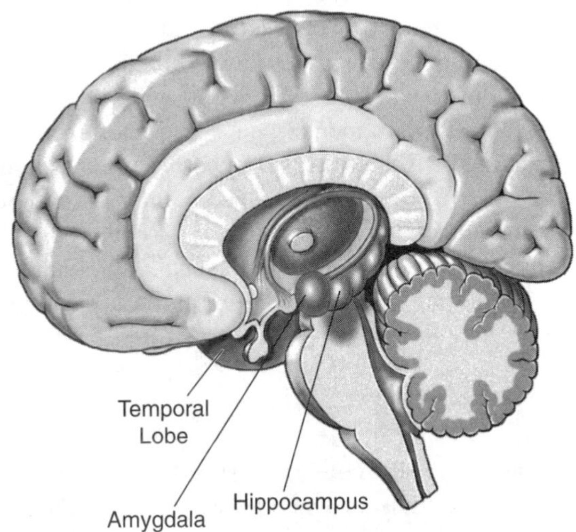

FIGURE 2.3 The Hippocampus and the Amygdala

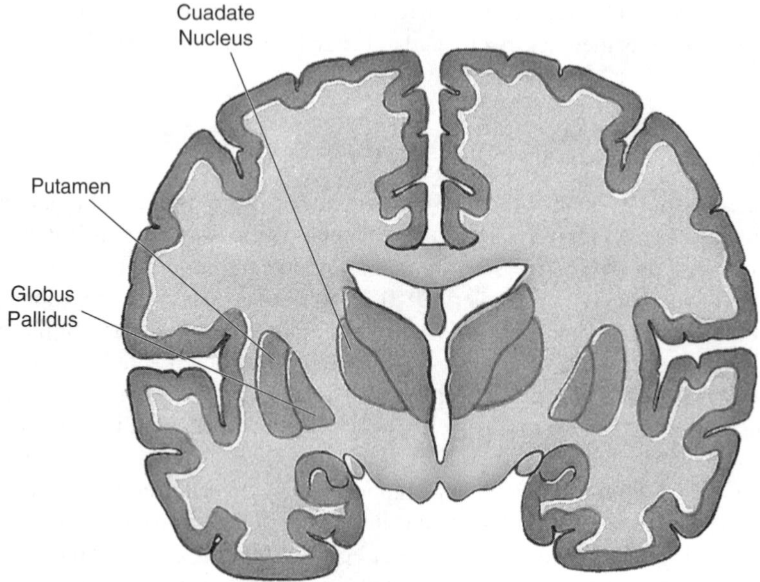

FIGURE 2.4 Basal Ganglia Structures

The **basal ganglia** are a collection of subcortical structures (including the caudate nucleus, the putamen, globus pallidus, and the subthalamic nucleus) located above and around the thalamus (see Figure 2.4). These structures are important for motor functioning—that is, the control of the voluntary muscle groups in the body. The basal ganglia is involved in memory for various unconscious types of memory processes, such as habits and motor skills. A related set of findings is observed with the **cerebellum.** This is a phylogenetically old structure located at the back of the brain (see Figure 2.5). Like the cerebral cortex, it has a convoluted surface structure, so it looks like a little brain underneath the larger one (and hence its name). The cerebellum is associated with complex motor control and coordination and is used in memory for procedural skills, such as walking. This is a more primitive form of memory but very important nonetheless.

The **diencephalon,** including the **thalamus** and **hypothalamus,** is a routing station for signals from different parts of the brain. It is involved in memory, although to not as great a degree as other structures. It is involved in memory for conscious, factual knowledge, such as storing information about the sequence of events. More indirectly, the diencephalon is involved in controlling the neurotransmitters in the nervous system at any given time.

Cortical Lobes

The most prominent part of the brain is the cerebral cortex. This is the wrinkly part that sits on top and is what most people think of when they picture a brain. The wrinkled appearance of the cortex is because there is so much surface area crammed into such a small volume. The brains of other animals, such as reptiles and amphibians, may be

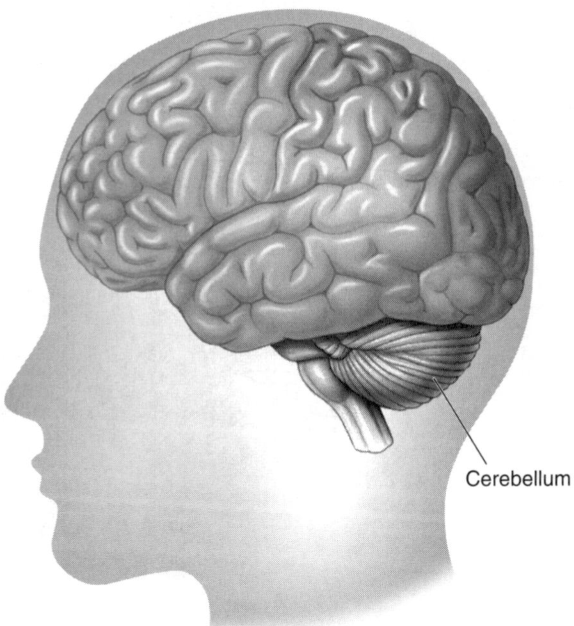

FIGURE 2.5 The Location of the Cerebellum

smooth in their entirety. In contrast, our brains are more powerful, so we need many more neurons. However, this increase in brain size brings with it an increase in head size. To keep the head reasonably small while increasing the number of neurons, the cortex has become folded and wrinkled. If you removed a person's cortex and lay it flat, you would see that it is very large. The average adult's cortex covers about 1,800 square cm (about 2 square feet) and is 2 to 3 mm thick. The wrinkling preserves the size of the surface area while reducing the volume occupied. An analogy is trying to get a sheet of paper into a coffee cup. The paper won't go in laying flat. But, if you wrinkle it up and stuff it in, you've taken a large surface area and enclosed it in a small volume.

The cortex is divided into a number of regions. First, it is divided into two hemispheres, a left and a right, and some memory functions are more dependent on one side than the other. This dominance of one hemisphere over the other is called **laterality.** In some cases laterality is important to memory, and we will look at these. For now, note that the left hemisphere is generally better at analytic processing, such as language and math, and the right hemisphere is better at holistic processing, such as spatial or music processing.

Each hemisphere is divided into four subsections called lobes (see Figure 2.6). Each lobe is associated with different functions. At the back is the **occipital lobe,** which is involved in visual processing. The occipital lobe detects features in the environment (Hubel & Wiesel, 1965), but the sensitivity to these features is based on experiences with the world. For example, if kittens are reared in an environment in which they see only horizontal lines, when they are adults, they will walk into a table leg because they cannot see vertical lines. They lack the feature detectors for vertical objects (Blakemore & Cooper, 1970). In front of the occipital lobe, on the top of the brain and just behind the central fissure, is the

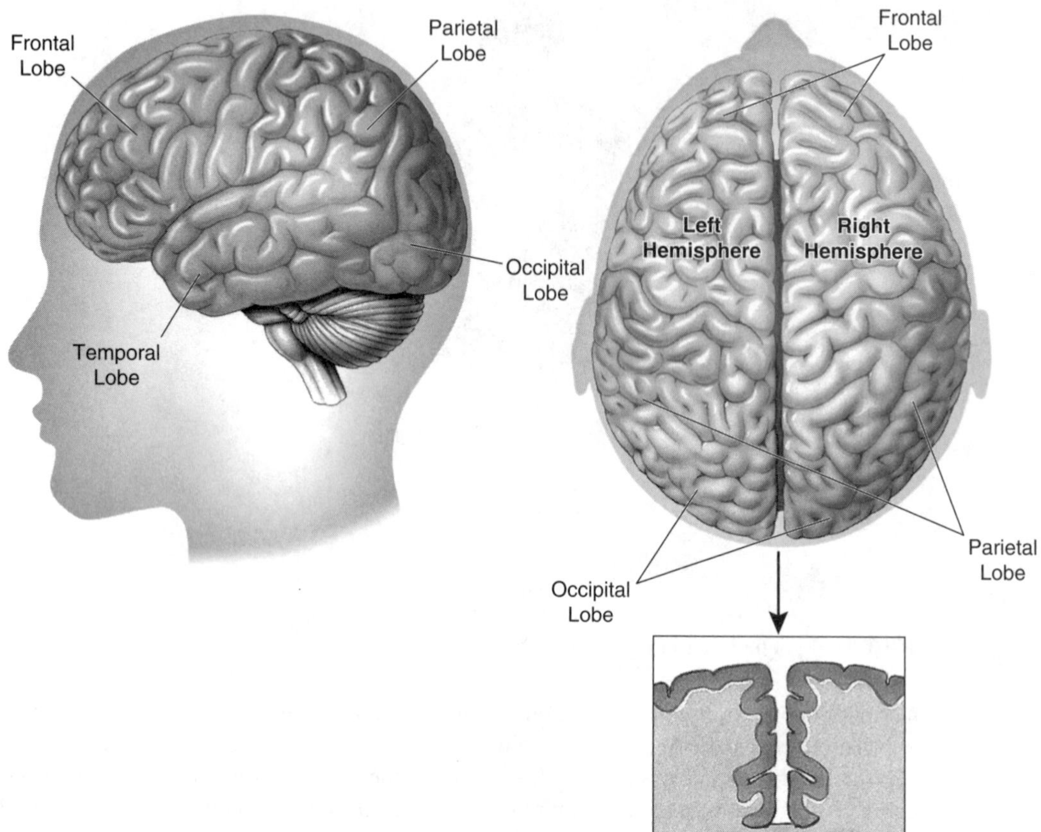

FIGURE 2.6 The Organization of the Cortical Lobes

parietal lobe. This is responsible for sensory processing from throughout the body, as well as spatial thinking, such as knowing where something is. Working memory processes for visual memory or the spatial manipulation of information (see Chapter 8) involve the parietal lobes (Mishkin & Appenzeller, 1987). For example, animals that have had their parietal lobes surgically removed have trouble remembering spatial relations. In front of the occipital lobe but below the parietal lobe and under the lateral fissure is the **temporal lobe.** This is responsible for auditory processing and retaining knowledge about the identity of things in the world. The temporal lobes surround the hippocampus, which, as we have already seen, is an important structure for memory. This is where our long-term memories for different types of information are believed to be stored. Damage to this part of the brain often results in memory loss. Finally, at the front of the brain, in front of the central fissure and above the lateral fissure is the **frontal lobe.** This is the most recently developed part of the cortex and is involved in the control of action, emotion, and thought. This makes them critical for working memory (see Chapter 5). The frontal lobes help a person select those memories that are most relevant on a given occasion. They also coordinate various types of information into a coherent memory trace. For example, knowledge of the information content, as well as knowing where it came from, must be put together using the process of source monitoring (see Chapter 12). The frontal lobes are also involved in the ability to remember what we need to do in the future, something called prospective memory (see Chapter 14). If you are trying to figure out how the names of the lobes correspond to a function or location in the brain, forget it! The lobes are named for the bones of the skull that overlay them.

To help you localize different parts of the cortex, throughout the text there will be verbal location descriptions as well as a number that refers to the Brodmann Area (e.g., B.A. 20). This is reference to a particular part of the cortex that has been identified on a Brodmann atlas. Copies of this are provided in the Appendix for your easy reference.

Synopsis

The brain is made up of several, specialized substructures. A number of these play some role in memory. More important for memory is a subcortical structure called the hippocampus. Other important subcortical structures include the amygdala, cerebellum, basal ganglia, and the diencephalon. The lobes of the cortex are also important to memory. The temporal lobe appears to play a prominent role, along with the frontal and parietal lobes, whereas the occipital lobe is the least involved in memory.

NEUROLOGICAL MEASURES

One of the most exciting areas of memory research is the development of methods and tools that allow us to look at how the brain works to encode, store, and retrieve memories. Some of these methods are described here.

Structural Measures

Sometimes clues to patterns in the way people think can be gained by understanding how their brains might be physically different from the norm. The brain's physical structure is not uniform; it differs from person to person, in much the same way that each person's face is unique. The best way to view the structure of a person's brain is to remove it from the skull (after death, of course). Another way to view the structure is to open up the skull of a living person and examine the brain, which can happen during surgery.

Computer-Assisted Tomography. Short of death and brain surgery, there are ways to examine the brain with little harm to a person. One way is to take a series of x-rays, each of them taking a different "slice" of the head, and then examine the brain structures revealed. This is known as a **computer-assisted tomography** scan, or CT scan. An example of a CT scan is shown in Figure 2.7. CT scans show the structure of a living person's brain, such as the location of a tumor, stroke damage, or just general condition.

Magnetic Resonance Imaging. A technique that has gained popularity is **magnetic resonance imaging,** or **MRI**. MRI works with the resonant frequencies of different molecules in the brain. When placed in a controlled magnetic field, the responses of those atoms can

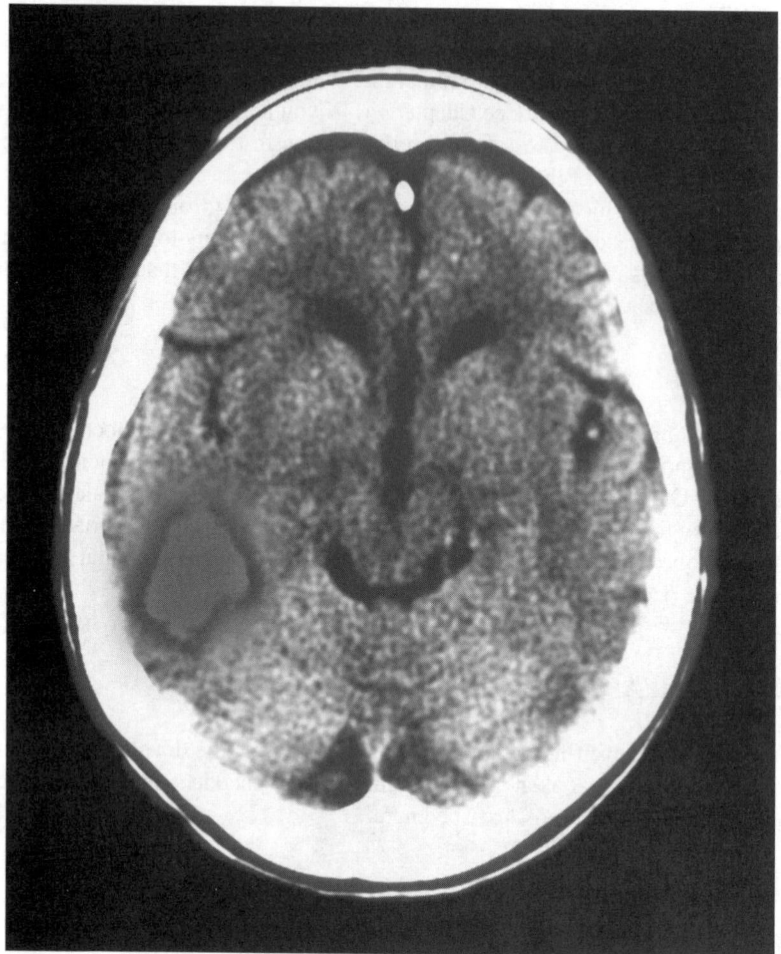

FIGURE 2.7 A CT Scan of the Brain

be detected and measured. An MRI scan is shown in Figure 2.8. Typically, the density of water molecules is used to determine structure, so it is not necessary to inject a chemical into the body, as with PET scans, or use harmful radiation, as with CT scans. A big advantage of MRI scans is their clarity, which are of much higher quality than CT scans.

Electrical Measures

This section examines measures of electrical activity generated by action potentials in the brain. Before covering modern methods, we look at some interesting reports by Wilder Penfield in the 1950s (Penfield, 1955).

Electrical Stimulation. Penfield was a Canadian neurosurgeon held in high regard for his mapping of the sensory and motor homunculi in the cortex. He did this by probing

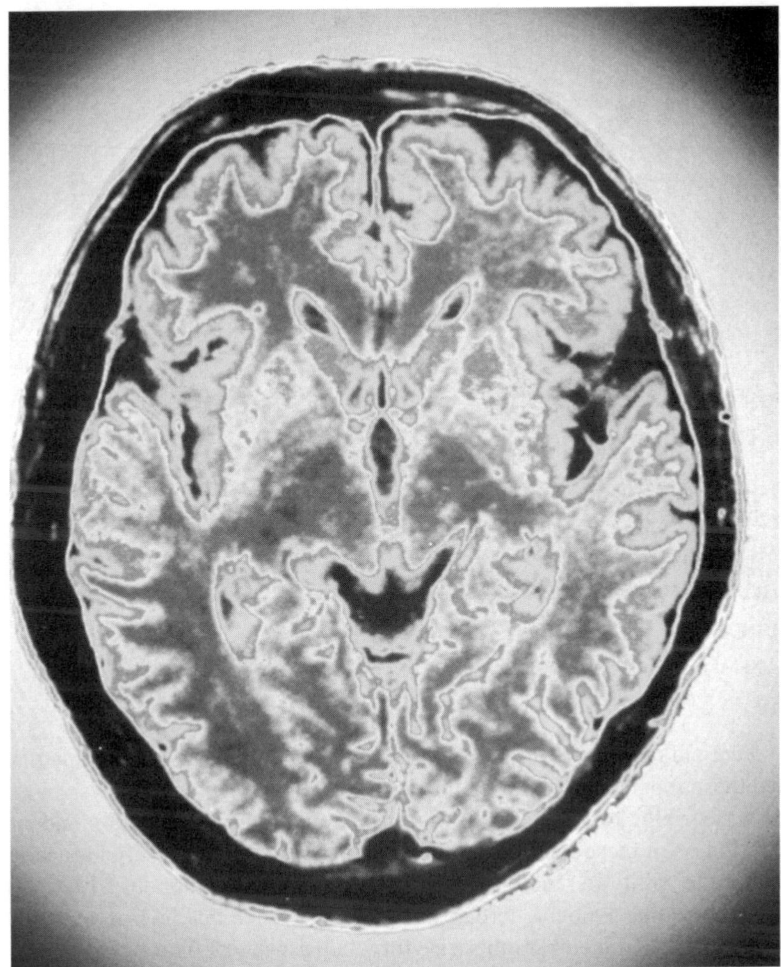

FIGURE 2.8 An MRI Scan of the Brain

people's brains with a mild electrical charge during surgery (see Figure 2.9). These people had some intractable condition, so parts of the cortex were removed in an attempt at a cure (and with a reasonable level of success). While the patient was awake, a section of skull was removed. Then the patient could report what effects the stimulations had. This allowed Penfield to identify those parts of the brain that were critically important. Although many functions rely on similar areas of different people's brains, there is some variability. While probing, Penfield would sometimes get interesting reports, usually for a portion of the temporal lobe. These reports were as if people were re-experiencing long-lost memories of their lives. Here is one example. The patient then said something about "street corner." The surgeon asked him, "Where?" and he replied "South Bend, Indiana, corner of Jacob and Washington." When asked to explain, he said he seemed to be looking at himself—at a younger age. (Penfield, 1955, p. 52)

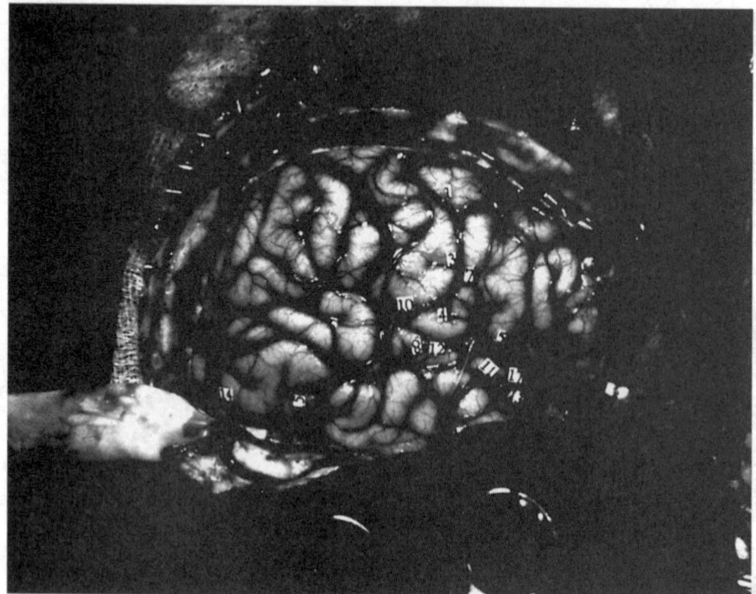

FIGURE 2.9 A Patient of Penfield's

Source: Penfield, W. (1958). *The excitable cortex in conscious man.* Liverpool, UK: Liverpool University Press.

Penfield reported several responses of this quality from different patients. He interpreted these reports as memories that the person had recovered or was re-experiencing. What was striking to Penfield was that they were rather boring and mundane memories. The vividness of these reports and their everyday quality led Penfield to suggest that the brain has the ability to record the stream of conscious throughout a lifetime. Long-term memory acted like a videorecorder. The electrical probe that he had applied to the cortex allowed people to remember otherwise forgotten aspects of their lives.

Although this characteristic is striking, there are some caveats, outlined by Loftus and Loftus (1980). First, it is unclear to what extent the reports were actually memories or were experiences generated at the time. These "memories" may be created in much the same way dreams are. According to the activation-synthesis theory (Hobson, 1988), during sleep, the cortex is stimulated with random electrical pulses. Because the brain does not like randomness, it imposes structure on the information it is receiving. To do so, it uses readily available information that is reasonably close to the stimulation it is receiving. This is information in long-term memory. Penfield's reports could be of the same quality. His patients were getting what amounted to random stimulation, and their brains were doing the best they could to make sense of this with whatever knowledge was available in memory.

Another problem is that there were very few of these reports. Of the 1,132 of Penfield patients, only 40 (3.5 percent) showed signs that he interpreted as memories, and most of these were not full-blown reports. Twenty-four had auditory experiences only (e.g., hearing voices or music), 19 had visual experiences only (seeing familiar people or objects), and only 12 gave what appeared to be complete memory re-experiences. Thus, there is very little evidence to work with.

Some of these reports could not possibly have been actual re-experiences of past events. For example, in the report just given, the person states that he can see himself standing on a street corner. If memories of experiences were faithfully recorded, this could not happen.

Event-Related Potentials. There are other methods for examining cortical processing that rely on the electrical component of neural communication. Studies of event-related potentials provide information about large groups of cells. Moreover, this approach is a noninvasive technique that can be used with ordinary people. In this procedure electrodes are attached to a person's scalp, so electrical activity in the underlying part of the brain can be recorded. These recordings are called electroencephalography, or EEG waves. There are several electrodes at regularly spaced locations over the skull to help localize what is being recorded.

EEG waves are used to measure **event-related potentials,** or **ERPs.** An ERP is a regular change in the pattern of electrical energy measured from the cortex at a given location as a function of the particular task or event that the person is thinking about (Coles, Gratton, & Fabiani, 1990). The memory researcher has a person engage in various tasks at predetermined points in time. These are the "events" of event-related potentials. Then the researcher looks at the EEG waves that were recorded at that time relative to when the events occurred. These electrical "potentials" in the EEG waves are what are "related" to the earlier "events"—hence the name ERPs.

One of the biggest advantages to ERPs is temporal resolution—that is, knowing when things happen. Recordings can be made at 1 ms time slices. Thus, it is relatively clear when certain processes are kicking in or when different regions of the brain are involved. People often talk about ERPs in terms of interesting components in the waveform and the nature of these components. For example, people might talk about a P300 wave, which refers to an electrically positive wave occurring about 300 ms after the beginning of an event. An N400 wave refers to an electrically negative wave occurring about 400 ms after the beginning of an event (Bentin, 1989).

There are some disadvantages to ERPs. One is that the spatial resolution—*where* things happen in the brain—is somewhat poor. One can get a general idea about what part of the brain is involved, but determining a precise location is difficult. Also, because there is so much activity going on in the brain at any given point in time, there is a lot of noise in addition to the signal one is interested in. This is further complicated by the fact that there is a lot of "stuff" between the electrodes and the brain activity they are recording—skin, blood vessels, meninges, and bone. Using EEG recordings to figure out what is going on in the brain is a lot like trying to figure out what is going on in a factory by listening through the wall.

Event-Related (De)Synchronization. While ERPs provide information about the mean level of positive or negative electrical charge at a point in time, there is other information that can be extracted from EEG signals. The nervous system has a tendency to have various oscillators throughout it. That is, groups of cells tend to fire together. This is called synchronization, and when this increases after an event, this is called **event-related synchronization,** or **ERS.** When a person is at rest, synchronization is stable. However, when a person is engaged in a mental activity, there is often a desynchronization. Thus, we can use **event-related desynchronization**, or **ERD**, as an indicator of processing. Furthermore, these oscillations can occur at a number of different frequency bands, depending on how fast the oscillations occur. For example, one way of dividing up the frequency bands is to have different regions separated by about 2 Hz each, using a person's based frequency as a reference point, defining the Delta band as –8 to –6 Hz, the Theta band as –6 to –4 Hz, the Lower 1 Alpha as –4 to –2 Hz, the Lower 2 Alpha as –2 to 0 Hz, and the Upper Alpha as 0 to +2 Hz (Dopplemayr, Klimesch, Pachinger, & Ripper, 1998). What can be done is then to look at changes in any of these bands as a function of the memory task.

ERD recordings are related to memory. For example, during effective memory processing, there is a decrease in alpha synchronization, and an increase in theta synchronization (Klimesch, 1999). Essentially, the resting alpha synchronization of the cortex is disrupted by activity of a particular type. The theta synchronization is associated with increased activity in the hippocampus and surrounding structures.

Transcranial Magnetic Stimulation. Another method is **Transcranial Magnetic Stimulation (TMS).** In TMS, a magnetic field is used to alter the electrical charges of the neurons in a part of the brain that the TMS device is placed over, thereby exciting them. This has a consequence of taking out that region of the brain as a kind of temporary lesion in a normal person's brain. The advantage of TMS is that it allows a memory researcher to explore how different parts of the brain are involved by selectively stimulating the neurons in various areas. As just one example of the use of TMS, Kirschen, Davis-Ratner, Jerde, Schraedley-Desmond, and Desmond (2006) used TMS to disrupt the phonological similarity effect in working memory (see Chapter 5).

Magnetoencephalography. Another development in neuroimaging is **Magnetoencephalography** or **MEG.** With MEG, magnetic fields are used to measure cortical electrical activity to help pinpoint which aspects of the brain may be active for various memory tasks. MEG scans have better spatial resolution than EEG measures, and have a good temporal resolution of about 10 ms. This is not as good as ERPs, but is still respectable. As one example of using MEG to study memory, Kim, Kim, and Chung (2008) tested recognition memory for individual words. The MEG scans revealed that medial temporal lobes are more involved when there is a delay prior to recognition compared to when it is more immediate.

Blood Flow Measures

Not all neuropsychological methods rely on electrical impulses. Some involve other measures of brain activity. One of these is cerebral blood flow. Collections of neurons that are working harder need more nutrients to be replenished and keep working. As a result, blood flow to those areas increases to compensate for this change.

Positron Emission Tomography. For **positron emission tomography,** or **PET,** people are injected with a radioactive isotope of oxygen called oxygen-15 or ^{15}O. This isotope decays to ^{16}O, which is reasonably stable. The level of radioactivity is very low and short-lived (it has a half-life of just over two minutes), so there is little harm to the body. Once the isotope is in the bloodstream, the person is placed into a scanner that measures the relative levels of the isotope in the brain. Recording levels in control conditions where the person is not doing much of anything are compared with experimental conditions where the person is engaging in the type of thought that is of interest for the study. Depending on the task, different parts of the brain are more or less active.

Compared to ERPs, the spatial resolution in PET scans is much better. However, there are some problems. One is that it takes a long time for a good image to be generated, typically no faster than 20 seconds. Think about how many different thoughts you could have if you were lying on your back in a scanner for 20 seconds. Thus, while the spatial resolution is better, the temporal resolution is relatively poor. So we can determine *where* something is occurring in the brain but not *when.* It should also be noted that an averaging process is used with PET images similar to what is done with ERP recordings. What is revealed in these sorts of scans is averaged over many actual events.

Functional Magnetic Resonance Imaging. The MRI technology discussed earlier can be adapted to look at function as well as structure. This approach is called **functional MRI** or **fMRI**. fMRI uses the detection of oxygen atoms as a measure of mental activity. The density of oxygen molecules is associated with the operation of neural assemblies and the flow of blood to fortify those cells. After all, the delivery of oxygen is one of the primary purposes of the bloodstream. An fMRI scan has an advantage over PET because no injection required, and the images can be taken in a shorter period of time, on the order of a few seconds. Still, fMRI scans cannot match the temporal accuracy of ERP measurements.

Altered Brains

Case Studies and Lesions. Another source of insight into neurological underpinnings of memory comes from studies of people who have suffered some damage or lesion to the brain. This might be from an external event, such as a car accident or a gunshot; an internal event, such as a stroke or a virus; or, in rare cases, from surgery. By examining the types of memory that are affected following brain damage, some inferences can be made about what role that structure plays. For example, if the damage leads a person to be able to remember very little in the short term, it suggests that short-term memory uses this structure. Because of their nature, it is not unusual for a single case to be studied in depth to help understand what happened, what went wrong, and what techniques can be used to improve the situation.

Although brain lesions provide valuable insights, it is an imperfect method. There are a number of reasons for this. One is that seldom is there a pure lesion, with one structure being completely affected but not other structures. Lesions are messy and affect a number of components. Another problem is that there are never two cases in which people have identical lesions. Thus, it cannot be determined whether the consequences of the damage that occurred are unique to that person or are a generalizable consequence. Finally, lesions are haphazard both in terms of where and when they occur. They do not afford the sort of control one would like in a systematic study.

Special Populations. Studies of people who have some altered neurological condition also provide pertinent data. For example, when we discuss amnesia (see Chapter 16), you'll see studies using chronic alcoholics who have a condition known as Korsakoff's Syndrome. Also, it is well known that as we age, there are systematic neurological changes that occur as a result of aging. Thus, age-related changes in memory can be viewed as neurological assessment of memory (see Chapter 15). Finally, some diseases, such as Alzheimer's, have systematic effects on the central nervous system (see Chapter 17). In these special populations, there is a high degree of regularity in the change that is a result of the condition, so we can observe a systematic change in neurological function that results in altered thoughts and behaviors.

Special populations are advantageous sources of information because there are a large number of people with a prespecified condition that has standard neurological changes associated with it. This allows for the removal of idiosyncratic aspects that occur and are often observed in case studies. Because these groups are large, it also allows for a better understanding of the condition and, hopefully, will lead to better treatments.

Synopsis

A number of methods have been developed to look at how brain function relates to memory. Some of these measures, like CT and MRI scans, look at structural characteristics, whereas others look at brain function. For example, TMS and EEG recordings examine electrical activity in the brain; PET and fMRI examine changes in blood flow as a function of mental work. Finally, some work has looked at how damage to the brain from disease or injury, as well as groups of people who have well-known changes in brain structure, such as the elderly, affect memory.

HEMIPHERIC DIFFERENCES, EMOTION, AND MULTIPLE MEMORY SOURCES

The HERA Model

We've covered a lot of territory, so let's start putting some ideas together. As a reminder, in Chapter 1 we discussed that there are different types of long-term declarative memories called episodic and semantic memories. Is there anything about the organization of the brain consistent with this difference? One such theory is the **Hemispheric Encoding/Retrieval Asymmetry** (or **HERA**) **model** (Habib, Nyberg, & Tulving, 2003; Nyberg, Cabeza, & Tulving, 1996), which focuses on the prefrontal lobes in the left and right hemispheres during episodic and semantic encoding and retrieval. The prefrontal cortex is the most forward part of the frontal lobes.

Data from PET studies show a greater involvement of the left frontal lobe in the retrieval of semantic information and the encoding of episodic information. Encoding new episodic memories involves semantic knowledge to interpret the current situation. Conversely, there is greater involvement of the right frontal lobe in the retrieval of episodic memories. This difference is even observed in behavioral data in which information is presented to either the left or right hemisphere (Blanchet et al., 2001). Thus, different parts of the brain are specialized for processing different types of information, and more precise studies of the prefrontal cortex show that smaller regions of the cortex are involved in more specific memory activities (Buckner, 1996; Shallice, Fletcher, & Dolan, 1998). This is further supported by ERD work that shows greater upper alpha de-synchronization during semantic memory performance, and increases theta band synchronization with episodic encoding (Klimesch, 1999).

An important point is that the HERA model does not state that episodic memories are stored in one hemisphere and semantic memories in the other. Nor is it the case that the frontal lobes are the brain regions where memory encoding and retrieval occur. For example, the temporal lobes seem to be most critical for memory encoding as evidenced by people with amnesia. We need to use the combination of information from both neuroimaging and brain lesion findings to better understand the facts (Mayes & Montaldi, 1999). What the HERA model does suggest is that different types of controlled processing are involved in different memory processes. Even researchers who have a different interpretation of how neurological structures relate to memory processing think that the brain handles semantic and episodic memories differently (e.g., Ranganath & Pallar, 1999; Wiggs, Wiesberg, & Martin, 1999).

Putting It All Together

The HERA model does not capture all of the relationships between neurological processes and memory. There are many others. As a sampler, while we are on the topic of left and right hemisphere differences, another is the idea that memory retrieval involves information from several different kinds of memories. Data from a study by Kensinger and Choi (2009) bring many ideas together. In this study, people were shown pictures that elicited neutral (a picture of a canoe), positive (a picture of a kitten), or negative (a picture of a snake) emotions. These pictures were briefly shown (for 250 ms) to either the right visual field (RVF), which projects to the left hemisphere (LH), or the left visual field (LVF), which projects to the right hemisphere (RH). Later, people were given a recognition test. They were to respond "same" if it was the same picture that had been seen before (the same picture of a snake), "similar" if it was a different picture of an item seen earlier (a different picture of a snake), and "new" if it was a picture of something they had not seen before (a picture of a scorpion).

As can be seen in Figure 2.10, when memory was assessed for visual detail ("same" responses), memory was better for information presented to the LVF/RH, particularly if it was emotionally negative, consistent with the idea that the right hemisphere is more involved in processing emotional information. However, when they assessed memory for more general gist ("similar" responses), memory was better for information presented to the RVF/LH, particularly if it was emotionally positive, consistent with the idea that the left hemisphere is more involved in processing general, conceptual, and abstract information. This illustrates how different aspects of theory and research can all be brought together to better understand our memories.

Synopsis

By understanding brain structure and function we can build theories that incorporate the results from the field of neuroscience. One example of this is the HERA model. This theory uses regularities emerging from neuroimaging studies—in this case hemispheric

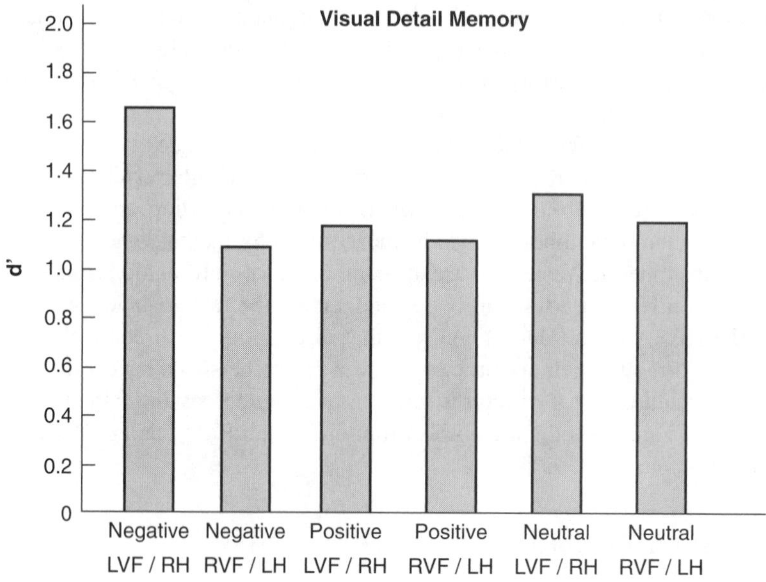

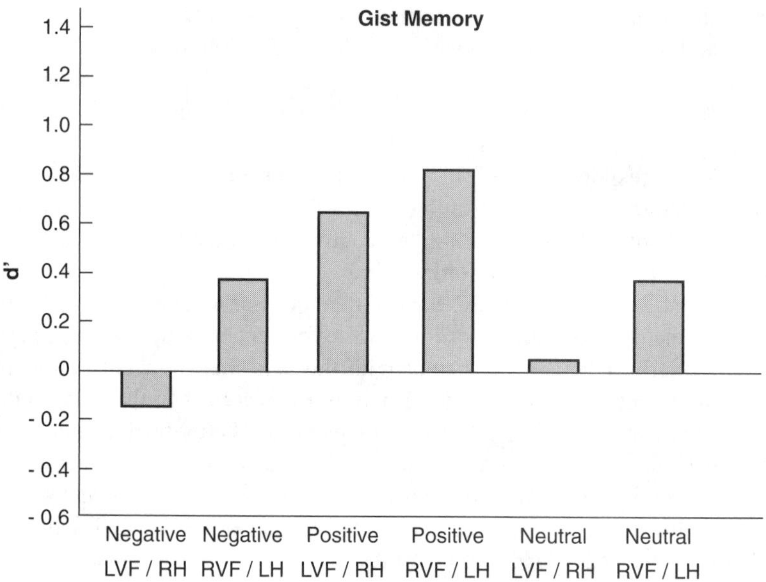

FIGURE 2.10 Memory for Visual Detail and Gist for Negative, Positive, and Neutral Emotion Pictures Presented to Either the Left Visual Field / Right Hemisphere (LVF/RH) or the Right Visual Field / Left Hemisphere (RVF/LH)

Source: Kensinger, E. A., & Choi, E. S. (2009). When side matters: Hemispheric processing and the visual specificity of emotional memories. *Journal of Experimental Psychology: Learning, Memory, and Cognition,* 35, 247–253.

asymmetries—and map them onto what is known about human memory. In addition, work in neuroscience can be brought together with other influences on memory, such as emotion and multiple memory traces, to get a better understanding of how memory works.

SUMMARY

Memory depends on the operation of the nervous system. At a basic level, we have covered the structure of the neuron and communication at a neural level. We have also surveyed some of the larger brain structures that play a role in memory. This includes both subcortical structures, like the hippocampus, as well as parts of the cortex, such as the temporal lobes. Finally, we have described a number of neuroimaging techniques. It is also possible to gain insights by looking at people whose brains have been altered by lesions, disease, or the developmental process. After all, all thought, including and especially memory, occurs as an operation of the nervous system.

STUDY QUESTIONS

1. What are the basic components of a neuron?
2. How does the nervous system communicate information? What is the electrical component? What is the chemical component?
3. How do neurons change in order to encode information into memory?
4. What are some of the various neuroimaging methods available? Which methods are good for assessing structure? Which methods are good for recording electrical activity? Which methods are good for recording blood flow?
5. In what ways can changes in brain structure be used to assess memory?
6. What are examples of a theory and research in memory that take into account findings from neuroscience?

KEY TERMS

acetylcholine (Ach), action potential, amygdala, axons, basal ganglia, cerebellum, computer-assisted tomography (CT), consolidation, dendrites, diencephalon, dopamine, emergent property, event-related desynchronization (ERD), event-related potentials (ERP), frontal lobes, functional magnetic resonance imaging (fMRI), GABA, glutamate (Glu), Hemispheric Encoding/Retrieval Asymmetry (HERA) model, hippocampus, hypothalamus, laterality, long-term depression (LTD), long-term potentiation (LTP), magnetic resonance imaging (MRI), magnetoencephalography (MEG), myelin sheath, neuron, neurotransmitters, nodes of Ranvier, norepinephrine, occipital lobes, parietal lobes, positron emission tomography (PET), soma, synapse, temporal lobes, terminal buttons, thalamus, transcranial magnetic stimulation (TMS)

CHAPTER THREE

METHODS AND PRINCIPLES

Memory is an intimate part of who we are. However, despite the fact that it permeates all mental processes (or perhaps because of this), we have little conscious awareness of it. Intuitively, memory seems very ethereal. As described in Chapter 1, for most of history, memory was thought to be beyond objective study. It wasn't until the late nineteenth century that it became sensible to think about systematically studying memory. Because it is so hard, if not impossible, to get a direct look at memory, we need good indirect methods. These often involve an experimenter manipulating what is to be remembered, recording an act of remembering, and then making inferences about memory based on what is observed. In this chapter we first address what an experiment is and how it compares to other types of data collection. Then we examine various methods of memory research. We first look at learning, followed by some tasks that can be used to test memory contents and structure. Finally, we consider issues of conscious introspections. Along with each method we also look at some basic principles of memory whose discovery can be attributed, at least in part, to the methods being presented. For those interested students, ways of calculating some memory measures, perhaps for a laboratory section or a research project, are provided in the Appendix.

COMPONENTS OF MEMORY RESEARCH

We approach memory from a scientific perspective to gain an objective understanding and minimize personal biases. As such, the ideas about memory discussed here reflect the work of scientists. To help you better understand how these people do their job, we first discuss what an experiment is and the different types of variables a researcher measures and controls.

What Is an Experiment?

Most of our knowledge of memory comes from experiments. So, what *is* an experiment? An *experiment* is a controlled situation in which a researcher manipulates variables of interest, measuring the effect of this manipulation, while keeping the irrelevant variables as consistent as possible. Furthermore, participants are randomly assigned to different conditions to reduce any unwanted systematicity. The variables being manipulated are the *independent variables*, such as how much a person has to remember, how long he or she has to remember it, and so forth. The active manipulation of these variables gives the researcher a great deal of control. The variables being measured are the *dependent variables*, such as how much is remembered, how accurate people are, how fast they remember, and so forth. Irrelevant aspects of the situation are known as *control variables.* This can include such things as the room lighting, the instructions, the apparatus used, and so forth.

For each experiment a researcher has a hypothesis about the outcome. A hypothesis is an educated guess or prediction about how the variation of the independent variables will be related to the outcome of the dependent variables. Often this is cast in some theoretical language about how memory is operating in the context of the experiment.

Other Types of Studies

The experiment is not the only way to study memory when experimental control is difficult or impossible. One alternative is a *correlation* study, where the performance of a dependent measure is assessed as a function of some preexisting variable. For example, one can look at memory as a function of age. Age cannot be experimentally controlled, but it is information that can be used to study memory. Alternatively, a researcher may do a quasi-experiment in which preexisting conditions are combined with the controlled assignment of the independent variables—for example, if one class of students memorized a set of 100 words and another class memorized a set of 100 pictures. Here, the assignment of students to conditions is not random but is based on the classes they are already in.

Finally, in some situations, it is not possible to study large numbers of people. Instead, the researcher can do a case study. When we look at the effects of brain damage, we can assess memory in specific individuals because they are the only ones available with a specific type of deficit.

Synopsis

There are various ways to study memory. The most common are experiments in which a researcher has control over the variables and can better assess what is affecting the observed outcome. The independent variables are manipulated, and the dependent variables are measured to see whether they conform to a hypothesis. In addition, it is also possible to use other methods, such as correlational, quasi-experimental, and case studies.

ASPECTS OF LEARNING

To test memory, some information first needs to be learned. How this happens is important. Was it something that was consciously learned, or was it something that was just picked up along the way? What kind of information was it, pictures or words?

Intentional versus Incidental Learning

Methods. An important factor is whether people explicitly *try* to learn. Explicit memorization is called **intentional learning.** The alternative is that a person just happens to learn something during the course of other activities. This is called **incidental learning.** An experimenter can explicitly alert a person that the information they are given is something that will be tested for later. These intentional learning instructions are direct, and they lead people to treat information more elaboratively. This elaborative processing can affect memory. Alternatively, if an experimenter gives incidental memory instructions, they have the person pay attention to and think about the information but not expend any extra effort memorizing it. In such cases, a cover task is given to orient people to the information. These cover tasks vary, and they can include things such as pleasantness ratings, sensibility ratings, or sorting information into categories.

Principles. In general, memory is better with intentional than incidental learning (see Block, 2009, for a review). This section outlines four principles that demonstrate the importance of the type of learning: levels of processing, mental imagery, the generation effect, and the automaticity of encoding.

Levels of Processing. An example of the influence of effort exerted during memorization is the **levels of processing** effect (Craik & Lockhart, 1972). This refers to the degree to which people elaborate on information during study. When people try to learn, they may simply repeat the information over and over. This is called **rote rehearsal.** In general, recall does not improve much with rote rehearsal, and recognition is only slightly improved (Glenberg, Smith, & Green, 1977). An example of the poor effectiveness of rote rehearsal is the results of a study by Nickerson and Adams (1979). Students at Brown University were shown individual drawings of pennies like those in Figure 3.1 and had to indicate whether it was correct. See if you can remember which one is correct. Students in this study were able to identify the correct drawing only 50 percent of the time. The penny with the highest rate of acceptance was incorrect version I (which 67 percent said was correct). Thus, repeated exposure does not improve memory.

In contrast, the more people think about the meaning of information, the more likely they are to use knowledge they already have, making inferences and elaborate on the to-be-learned information. This connecting of knowledge is called **elaborative rehearsal.**

Information that receives little elaboration is processed less. For example, suppose a task is to think about a set of words and only say whether the word is printed in upper-or lowercase

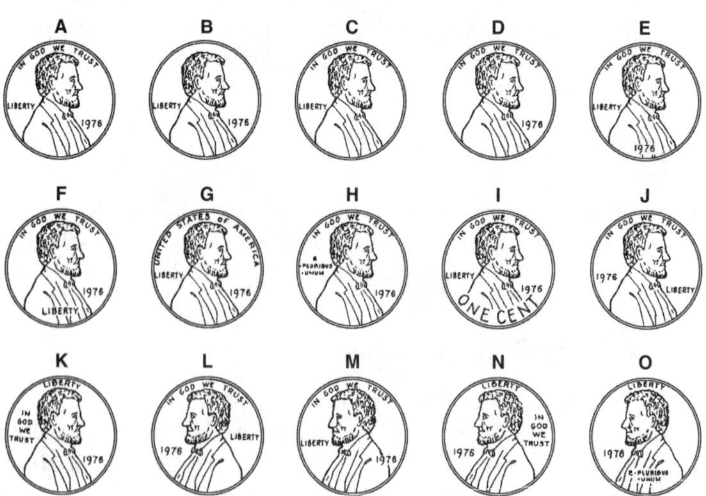

FIGURE 3.1 Which Penny Is Correct?

Source: Reprinted from *Cognitive Psychology,* 11, Nickerson, R.S., & Adams, M.J., Long-term memory for a common object, pp. 287–307, 1979, with permission from Elsevier.

letters. This is shallow processing because it requires little attention to meaning and prior knowledge. However, if the task is to determine whether the word makes sense in a sentence, this is deeper processing. The levels of processing effect can occur for both incidental and intentional encoding (Hyde & Jenkins, 1973), although it is more likely to be observed during intentional learning.

Imagery. One way to elaborate on information and improve memory is by creating a mental image of what is being learned (e.g., Schnorr & Atkinson, 1969), as shown in Figure 3.2. Memories were better when you made a concerted effort to form mental images than when you simply rehearsed the information. Mental images do not appear spontaneously.

The benefit to memory of mental images led to the development of **Dual Code Theory** (Pavio, 1969), which suggests that people store information in memory in at least two forms: a verbal/linguistic code and a mental image code. These two codes can be associated to each other if they refer to the same thing. Memory improves because with mental imagery, there are multiple memory retrieval pathways to the same information and more memory traces containing the desired information. This makes successful remembering more likely.

Generation. According to levels of processing, the more information is elaborated on, the better it is remembered. This is shown by the **generation effect:** Information that a person generates is remembered better than information that is simply read or heard (Slamecka & Graf, 1978; for a meta-analysis, see Bertsch, Pesta, Wiscott, & McDaniel, 2007). For example, suppose people are presented with a series of word stems, such as TAB_____, and asked to complete the word. This is a generation task because the person

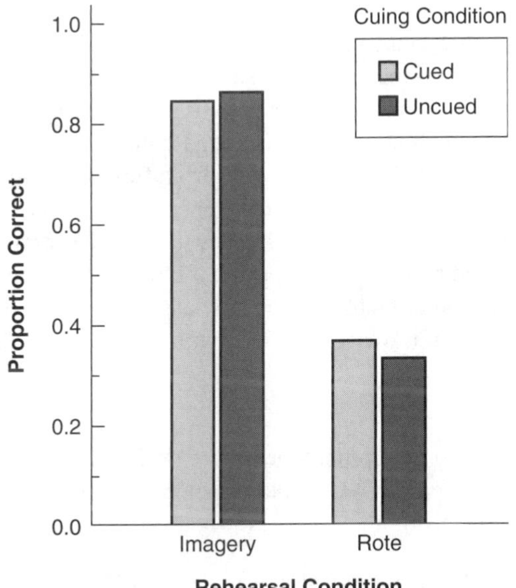

FIGURE 3.2 Impact of Mental Imagery on Memory

Source: Schnorr, J. A., & Atkinson, R. C. (1969). Repetition versus imagery instructions in the short- and long-term retention of paired-associates. *Psychonomic Science,* 15, 183–184. Permission granted upon citation of source.

is generating the rest of the information. Alternatively, if people are simply asked to read a series of complete words, this is not a generation task because nothing is being created. The generation effect extends to a wide variety of information, including memory for the context in which something was learned (Marsh, Edelman, & Bower, 2001).

A generation effect is also observed when people solve a puzzle or problem. This is called the **"aha" effect** (Auble, Franks, & Soraci, 1979). For example, a person may have trouble initially understanding a sentence like "The man's back ached because the ends were too large." At some point, there is an awareness that this sentence is about using barbells and the person has an "aha" experience. Because the person generated his or her own solution, memory is better. Similarly, if people complete a connect-the-dots puzzle, the picture is remembered better than if it was seen already assembled (Wills, Soraci, Chechile, & Taylor, 2000).

In addition to generating words and ideas, memory is better when people actually perform a task compared to watching someone else do it or reading about it. This is the **enactment effect** (Engelkamp & Zimmer, 1989). Like the generation and aha effects, this is a form of elaborative rehearsal (Senkfor, Van Petten, & Kutas, 2008). This seems to take advantage of embodied aspects of cognition. For example, people remember words better if they are signed (as with American Sign Language) than if they are printed (von Essen & Nilsson, 2003; Zimmer & Engelkamp, 2003). However, this memory benefit only occurs when a person enacts only some of the items, not all of them (Dodd & Shumborski, 2009). People mentally organize and structure information differently when they perform an action (Koriat & Pearlman-Avnion, 2003). This provides a better means of retrieving the information. It has also been suggested that the enactment emphasizes the processing of individual items, rather than the relations among the items in a series (Steffens, 2007).

Automaticity. It should be noted that under some conditions the type of learning does not matter much. Memory can be similar with incidental and intentional encoding, depending on how people think about the information at the time (Postman & Adams, 1956; Salzman, 1953, 1956) and may not be present on certain memory tests, such as recognition (Eagle & Leiter, 1964; Postman, Adams, & Philips, 1955). In some cases there is an **automaticity of encoding** (Hasher & Zacks, 1979; 1984) in which information is stored in memory with little effort. Information that is automatically encoded does not benefit from further efforts at learning. Some types of information that may be more automatically encoded are knowledge of event frequency, time, and location. For example, think of how many times in the past month you've eaten out. The answer comes to mind relatively easily, and it is unlikely that you deliberately learned this as it was occurring. If you think about the knowledge that you have, some of it was very easy to learn, whereas some of it was learned only with a great deal of effort.

Stimulus Characteristics

During learning, it is also possible to manipulate the nature of the information itself. As already mentioned, some things are easy to learn and remember, whereas others require more effort and are more likely to be forgotten.

Methods. When studying memory, it is important to take into consideration what research participants think about the experiment. An adequate *task analysis* must be done. If not, it is possible that the researcher and the participant may interpret the task in different ways. What an experimenter thinks the participant is memorizing is the **nominal stimulus.** The stimulus the participant identifies and thinks about is the **functional stimulus.** Usually, these are the same things, but in some cases, they are very different. For example, a researcher might give people a list of nonsense syllables, one of them "DAX." In the experimenter's mind, this is just a meaningless series of letters. However, if the participant is an avid *Star Trek* fan, he would recognize this as the name of a character in the series.

Principles.

Savings. Stimuli affect memory in a number of ways. One of these, discovered by Ebbinghaus, is the principle of **savings.** After information has been learned and forgotten, a person requires less effort to learn it a second time. This is important for two reasons. First, this illustrates that although we may not be conscious of knowledge from our past, it may still affect our ability to learn and remember. Second, information we already know something about, even if we're not conscious of it, is easier to remember than something we encounter for the first time. In general, the more information taps into prior knowledge, the easier it is to remember. Thus, the meaning of a stimulus varies from person to person depending on the individual's experiences with and knowledge of it.

Pictures and Concreteness. In general, pictures are remembered better than words (Shepard, 1967; Snodgrass, Volvovitz, & Walfish, 1972; Standing, 1973). This is the **picture superiority effect**. It occurs because we are better attuned to perceptual than linguistic information. Also, a picture is more likely to be unique and contain a higher degree of detail. However, how easily pictures are remembered can vary depending on how meaningful they are. For example, it is easier to remember pictures of faces than pictures of snowflakes or inkblots (Goldstein & Chance, 1970). The picture superiority effect can be magnified with dynamic images (e.g., video) over static images (Buratto, Matthews, & Lamberts, 2009; Matthews, Benjamin, & Osborne, 2007).

Pictures and words are treated differently, even at a neurological level. For example, the right part of the hippocampus is more active for pictures, whereas the left is more active for words (Papanicolaou, et al., 2002). Furthermore, fMRI scans show that during picture encoding there is bilateral activation of the fusiform area (BA 37), the lingual-middle occipital lobe (BA 18, 19), and the inferior temporal gyrus (BA 20) (Vaidya, Zhao, Desmond, & Gabrieli, 2002). Moreover, the fusiform area and inferior temporal gyrus, is also activated during memory retrieval of pictures, even if the memory probes are words. So, the picture superiority effect reflects an engagement of a broader range of brain regions.

It has also been found that concrete information—words like "car," "house," or "book"—are remembered better than abstract information—words like "truth," "betrayal," or "redemption." This is the **concreteness effect.** Concreteness may aid memory because it involves more perceptual qualities, consistent with dual code theory. This distinction between concrete and abstract information is supported neurologically. Concrete words involve more basal extrastriate activation (BA 19), suggesting more perceptual processing (although there is some involvement in abstract processing as well) (Martin-Loeches, Hinojosa, Fernandez-Frias, & Rubia, 2001). Finally, there is greater right hemisphere activation for concrete words, whereas abstract words tend to involve more left hemisphere processing (Holcomb, Kounios, Anderson, & West, 1999; Kounios & Holcomb, 1994; Nittono, Suehiro, & Hori, 2002; Swaab, Baynes, & Knight, 2002).

Emotion. Memory can also be influenced by emotions, with emotional memories often being better (e.g., Kensinger, 2009; Kleinsmith & Kaplan, 1963; Phelps, 2006) and more vivid (Kensinger & Corkin, 2003a). Less emotionally intense information tends to involve an influence of the frontal lobes (LaBar & Cabeza, 2006; Phelps, 2006). However, with more intense emotions, this superior memory involves an influence of the amygdala, which then affects memory functioning in the hippocampus and medial temporal lobes, perhaps because the amygdala helps direct attention and memory to more emotionally relevant aspects of the world (Easterbrook, 1959; Phelps, 2006), although this may come at a cost to less emotional details (see Mather, 2007 for a review). More emotional events may affect memory because of their more primitive-, visceral- and survival-based qualities.

In addition to emotional intensity, memory may be affected by the emotional valence. That is, whether something is emotionally positive (e.g., courage) or negative (e.g., ordeal). According to the **Pollyanna principle,** there is a tendency to better remember positive than negative information. For example, positive words are learned more quickly than negative words (Anisfeld & Lambert, 1966; Stagner, 1933). However, there are circumstances where negative information is remembered better (Ortony, Turner, & Antos, 1983), such as with flashbulb memories for surprising, and often negative, events (see Chapter 13). Also, negative words are learned more quickly than emotionally neutral words (like *wood,* for example) (Carter, 1936; Carter, Jones, & Shock, 1934). Finally, relative to neutral information, negative memories are more likely to benefit from the consolidating effects of sleep (Payne, Stickgold, Swanberg, & Kensinger, 2008).

Frequency. Another quality that can affect memory is **frequency.** Frequency is a bit odd in that memory is better for frequent information for recall tests (e.g., Taft, 1979), but better for rare information for recognition tests. Common things are easier to recall because there are more ways to get at them, making them more likely to be recalled. However, with recognition, less-frequent items have fewer competitor memories, so they are recognized more easily (see the following sections on recall and recognition).

Survival. Recent work has looked at the influence of evolutionary pressures on memory effectiveness (Nairne & Pandeirada, 2008b). People respond faster to words based on their subjective level of danger or usefulness (Wurm, 2006; Wurm & Seaman, 2008). Also, in some studies, people are given lists of words, and asked to rate each word on its survival value, such as locating food or avoiding predators. Focusing on the fitness-related value provides some of the best memory compared to other ways of boosting memory (Nairne, Thompson, & Pandeirada, 2007; see also Kang, McDermott, & Cohen, 2008; Nairne & Pandeirada, 2008a). Moreover, memory seems more attuned to grasslands survival than city survival (Weinstein, Bugg, & Roediger, 2008). Compared to other ways of boosting memory, including creating mental images, generating information, and intentional learning, as can be seen in Figure 3.3, recall memory is best when people learn the information by attending to its survival value (Nairne, Pandeirada, & Thompson, 2008).

Synopsis

How information is learned and the nature of that information can affect memory. Memory is usually better when people intentionally learn something than when they learn it incidentally, as reflected in the levels of processing framework, the influence of mental imagery, and the generation effect. However, some things are learned more automatically.

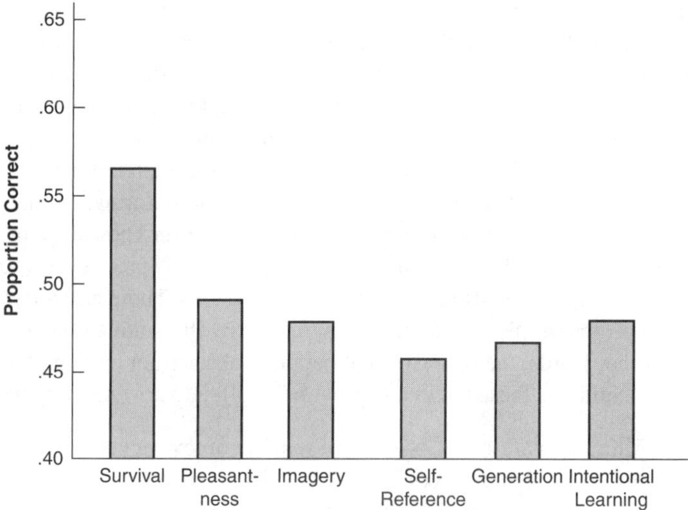

FIGURE 3.3 Influence of Survival Processing on Memory Compared to Other Standard Memory Improvement Methods

Source: Nairne, J. S., Pandeirada, J. N. S., & Thompson, S. R., & (2008). Adaptive memory: the comparative value of survival processing. *Psychological Science,* 19, 176–180. Reprinted by permission of John Wiley & Sons Ltd.

Memory is also influenced by what is remembered. Memory is better for things that a person already knows and for pictures, concrete information, and emotional things. Recent work suggests that information related to survival is remembered best.

ASSESSING THE CONTENTS OF MEMORY

Questions about memory often center around issues of what information is in memory, what can be remembered later, and how easily it is remembered. There are a number of ways of getting at the contents of memory, and each has its advantages and disadvantages.

Recall

Methods. A straightforward way to test memory is the **recall** test. For recall, a person needs to report whatever he or she can retrieve from memory. There are many types of recall tests.

Free Recall. The most basic recall test is **free recall,** in which people report as much information as they can. This is similar to answering an essay question on an exam. Because there is very little additional information provided, free recall is a good way to find out what a person knows very well. Presumably, this is what is reported. Information that a person knows, but not very well, is less likely to be reported because the person is less likely to successfully retrieve it.

Free recall data can also be used to study errors of omission (what people don't remember) and errors of commission (information that is reported as memories, but was not, in fact, part of the event). These are called **intrusions,** and they can be important when studying false memories (see Chapter 12). Studying **recall order** can give insight into how memories are structured. This is discussed in more detail in the section on cluster analyses.

Forced Recall. One problem with free recall is that there might be information that people remember, perhaps faintly, but that they are unwilling to report in case they might be wrong. Also, sometimes people report memories more generally when they actually have more precise knowledge (Goldsmith, Koriat, & Weinberg-Eliezer, 2002). One way to encourage people to report these weaker memories is to give a **forced recall** test. Unlike a free recall, where a person can report as much or as little as desired, in a forced recall test a person is forced to report a certain amount of information. Typically, this is more information than what would have been reported under free recall. Using this approach, weaker knowledge in memory can be assessed as being present. Typically, this weaker knowledge is provided toward the end of forced recall. Forced recall can also be used to elicit intrusions. These errors can be informative about the processes people use to recover memories by illustrating how that process can break down. In other words, the mistakes that people make are not random, but they follow certain principles. Studying these errors can provide insight into how memory works.

Cued Recall. Memories are often associated with a context or setting. There are many things in the environment that can serve as context. To get a better idea about how context influences memory retrieval, a **cued recall** test can be used. During memorization, people learn a set of information. The experimenter designates some of this information as target information to be recalled. Associated with this are other sets of information that serve as retrieval cues. Thus, the experimenter is controlling the context that will be relevant later. The paired associate learning tasks discussed in Chapter 1 are a good example of this sort of cue and target knowledge learning.

During retrieval, the experimenter provides a set of cues, and the task is to report the information that goes with those cues. Thus, the experimenter controls the context and can observe how it influences memory. Retrieval is more constrained than under free recall conditions. During cued recall, people respond to either as many cues as they can or to all of the cues, much like a forced recall test. Again, both accuracy and errors can help to understand the contents of memory.

Retrieval Plans. During recall, people need to mentally organize the information to be able to retrieve it later. This includes both recalling information that has not yet been reported as well as avoiding reporting something that has already been recalled. To monitor memory retrieval, people often develop a strategy known as a **retrieval plan.** This is a set of retrieval cues used to guide a person through the information. As we will see in Chapter 7, if this retrieval plan is thwarted or disrupted by external influences, performance declines. This is true even when the cues are some of the elements that must be remembered, which, on the face of it, should help memory.

Principles.

Forgetting Curve. Perhaps the clearest finding to come out of research using recall is that the more time that has passed, the less likely a person will remember a given piece of information. Or, to put it simply, people forget more as time passes. The way forgetting proceeds was one of the first things discovered using recall tests. In Ebbinghaus's studies he was able to track his performance at various time intervals. What he observed is the **forgetting curve,** shown in Figure 3.4. A forgetting curve is a negatively accelerating function. That is, the rate of forgetting is most rapid initially after the information was learned. As time passes, although the cumulative amount of knowledge loss grows larger, the rate of this accumulation slows

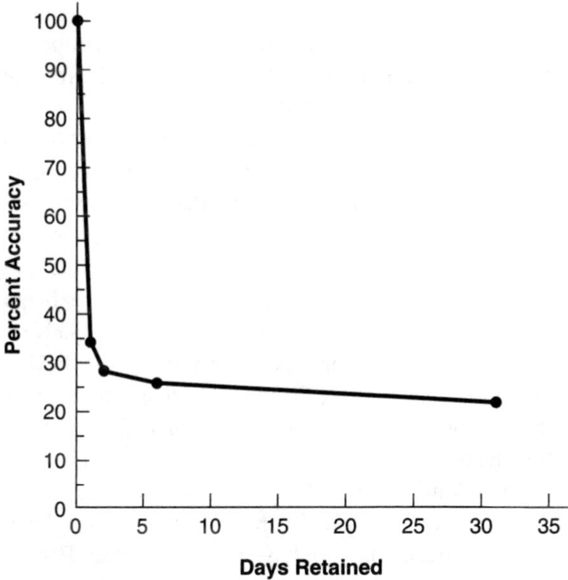

FIGURE 3.4 A Forgetting Curve

down accordingly. This forgetting function is captured by **Jost's Law** (1897; as cited in Wixted, 2004b) which states that for memories of a similar strength, the older memories will decay more slowly relative to the newer memories. Careful research has shown that the forgetting curve follows a power function (e.g., Anderson & Schooler, 1991; Rubin, 1982). However, it is unclear whether this is because of some fundamental exponential neurological process or because of some artifact of average across many trials (Anderson, 2001).

Forgetting curves are one of the most reliable observations in human memory and occur with all kinds of information. The rate of forgetting is similar across different levels of learning (Meeter, Murre, & Janssen, 2005). In other words, although people learn information to different degrees, they all forget the information at the same rate. So, the people who knew more initially almost always know more later on as well. Moreover, although we bring up the forgetting curve here in this section on recall tasks, forgetting curves are readily observed with other tasks as well, such as recognition.

Overlearning. The consistency of the forgetting curve is reassuring in its stability. Yet, at the same time, it is deeply disturbing in its suggestion that everything we've ever learned or known is fated to be forgotten at some point. While there is a truth in the forgetting curve, it is not always the case that forgetting inevitably occurs. Another principle that Ebbinghaus discovered using recall was overlearning. **Overlearning** occurs when a person continues to study information after it is already possible to recall it without errors. This continued practice causes the forgetting curve to lessen and possibly disappear altogether. In such cases, the information becomes chronically available and is greatly resistant to forgetting. Thus, many of the fundamentals you remember from your schooling, such as the "A, B, C" song, have been greatly overlearned, and you are unlikely to forget that knowledge. This is one reason why education emphasizes repetition and practice.

Reminiscence and Hypermnesia. Not only do we forget things all the time, but we can also remember things that were once forgotten. This principle of remembering previously forgotten information is called **reminiscence** (Ballard, 1913). Generally, reminiscence is observed with a recall task, particularly free recall. Although reminiscence occurs, so does forgetting. Thus, if the times that a person tries to remember are spread out, even though reminiscence is occurring, the person may be remembering less and less overall. However, if a person tries to recall information several times in a row, the rate of reminiscence may be greater than the rate of forgetting. Under such circumstances the person is cumulatively remembering more and more each time (Erdelyi & Becker, 1974; Wheeler & Roediger, 1992). This is called **hypermnesia** (the opposite of amnesia). Hypermnesia has been documented under a number of circumstances, but it is difficult to observe. It is more likely to be seen with pictures (Payne, 1987) and with shorter intervals between recall tests (Wheeler & Roediger, 1992). It is also more evident in free and cued recall situations than with recognition (Otani & Hodge, 1991). This may occur because the pieces of information in a set that are recalled earlier can serve as cues to assist the retrieval of the information that was previously forgotten.

It should also be noted that while shorter delays (e.g., a few minutes) are more likely to produce hypermnesia than longer ones (e.g., a few hours), at very short delays (e.g., a few seconds), whatever causes hypermnesia may not have time to operate. For example, using lists of words, hypermnesia does not occur if the delay is less than five seconds per word, but it does occur if more than five seconds per word is given (Payne, 1987).

The existence and operation of reminiscence and hypermnesia have practical significance. When it seems that you have completely forgotten a piece of information, putting it out of your mind for a period of time may help you remember it later. Of course, as with any type of memory, the more elaborately you think about the information during learning, such as forming mental images, the more successful later attempts to remember will be, even for reminiscence and hypermnesia.

Recognition

During recall, people need to generate the information, at least in part. However, in some cases, people need only to identify something already in their environment as being familiar or old, and thus recognized, or as being unfamiliar or new, and thus unrecognized. **Recognition** is a process in which the contents of the environment are compared with the contents of memory. If there is a match, then recognition occurs; otherwise it does not.

Methods.

Old-New Recognition. The simplest form of recognition testing is **old-new recognition.** In this method a person is given an item and is asked to indicate whether it is old or new. Memory is assessed based on the pattern of responses. This method simplifies the retrieval situation, making it easier to track and analyze. A great deal of information can be derived from such simple tasks. Sophisticated approaches can lead to penetrating insights into the contents and process of memory. Neurocognitive EEG recordings show that when items are recognized, there is an initial increase in synchronization of theta activity around the parietal lobe, followed by decreased synchronization in the upper and lower alpha bands around the temporal lobe (e.g., Burgess & Gruzelier, 2000).

Correction for Guessing. For simple old-new responses, some accurately reflect a person's memory, but others involve a degree of uncertainty, and are guesses. Suppose a person identified 50 items correctly on a memory test. If that person had no incorrect answers, then it would seem that his memory was very accurate. However, if that person got 50 wrong and 50 correct, then it would appear he was guessing. What is needed is some way to correct for guessing, to provide a more accurate estimate of memory.

A simple way to correct for guessing is to subtract the number of incorrect responses from the number of correct responses. And in some cases this is what is done. However, this is a rather crude adjustment, and it can miss more subtle aspects of performance. Guessing can be affected by two pieces of information. One is the degree to which old items can be distinguished from new ones in memory. This is called **discrimination.** Sometimes discrimination is relatively easy, such as identifying whether a person is a famous actor versus someone you've never heard of before.

The second piece of information is the degree to which a person is willing to accept what is remembered as new or old. This is called **bias.** Sometimes, people may adopt a strict criterion and have a "conservative" bias. In this situation, people accept only cases in which they are very sure that the information is old; so there are no false alarms. A **false alarm** is calling something old that is, in fact, new. A situation in which a person might be motivated to adopt a conservative bias would be in eyewitness identification. The eyewitness wants to be sure that the person he or she identifies is the criminal. Picking out the wrong person could lead to an innocent person being punished for a deed he or she did not commit and leaving the true guilty party at large, free to commit more crimes. In other cases, people may adopt a loose criterion and thus have a "liberal" bias. In this situation, people are more willing to accept a memory that has a more remote possibility of being old to avoid making any **miss** responses. A miss response is calling an item new that is in fact old. A situation in which a person might be motivated to adopt a liberal bias would be in looking for a lost set of keys. The searcher wants to be sure that all plausible locations are checked.

One method for estimating discrimination and bias is **signal detection theory** (Banks, 1970; Lockhart & Murdock, 1970). This approach has been adopted from psychophysicists, who, in turn, borrowed it from communications theory. By using this approach, one can derive a measure of discrimination, often called d', and of bias, often called β. (see Snodgrass & Corwin, 1988, for various measures of discrimination and bias.)

The basic idea is to assess the ability to detect the signal (an accurate memory) from the noise (inaccurate memories). The thinking in signal detection theory is illustrated in Figure 3.5. This approach assumes that there are two distributions: one for the old items and one for the new items along some dimension, such as familiarity. The farther apart these two distributions are, the easier it is to discriminate between them. Conversely, the more these two distributions overlap, the harder it is to discriminate between them. Keeping the distance between the two distributions constant, we can see how bias affects memory performance. The criterion a person uses to separate out what is identified as old and new is measured by β. If β is set very far to the right, the person has adopted a conservative criterion, and very few memories will be accepted as old. However, if β is set far to the left, the person has adopted a liberal criterion, and very few memories will be accepted as new.

Forced-Choice Recognition. Another form of recognition is when people are given several items and are asked to indicate which one is old. This is **forced choice recognition.** Typically, there are two, three, or four alternatives. Forced choice recognition allows a researcher to manipulate the incorrect items in terms of the degree to which they resemble the correct one. Such manipulations can provide insight into what sorts of knowledge

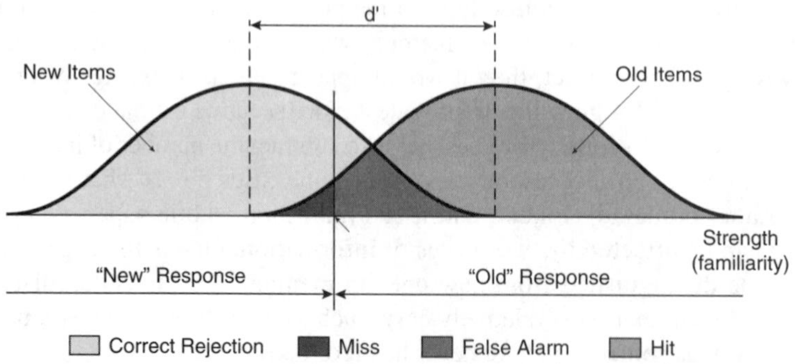

FIGURE 3.5 Illustration of the Underlying Logic for Signal Detection Theory

people are using when remembering something. The wrong items that are more often selected as "old" would more closely match the information in memory, thus lending some insight into the contents of memory.

Social Influences

Many of the studies discussed here have a person largely alone in the environment. However, in the real world, people are in social situations, interacting with others in complex ways. These other people can influence memory. For example, people remember events differently depending on who they are with (who they are telling their story to), which can then bias later memories for the event (Tversky & Marsh, 2000). Moreover, people who work with high-performing individuals will recall more later than people who work with low-performing individuals (Reysen, 2003), and people remember information better if they think it comes from another person as compared to a computer (Reysen & Adair, 2008). Even how well we remember someone's face depends on social influence. For example, people remember pictures of faces better when the person in the picture is looking at them versus when they are looking away (Mason, Hood, & Macrae, 2004). Thus, how well we remember is influenced by the people with whom we interact with. Now let us look at other social influences on memory.

Collaborative Inhibition. Is memory affected by whether people are remembering things alone or in a group? Studies have found that when people in groups try to recall something, they typically recall less than if they were separated, asked to recall information, and had their individual efforts pooled (Basden, Basden, Basden, Bryner, & Thomas, 1997; Weldon & Bellinger, 1997). This decline in memory when working in a group is **collaborative inhibition.**

Collaborative inhibition may seem to reflect some sort of social loafing. However, what is actually going on is that a person is encountering different ways that other people have structured the information. Each person's recalls are based on his or her own retrieval plan. When confronted with an organization that is inconsistent with one's own retrieval plan, the ability to recall becomes disrupted, and performance declines (Finlay, Hitch, & Meudell, 2000; Weldon, Blair, & Huebsch, 2000). This is related to the part-set cuing phenomenon (see Chapter 7). It should be noted that although people recall more as individuals than in groups, recalling in groups does increase the accuracy of the recalled information (Vollrath, Sheppard, Hinsz, & Davis, 1989).

Collaborative Facilitation. Although memory is worse on recall tests in groups than alone, the opposite is true for recognition (Hinsz, 1990; Rajaram & Pereira-Pararin, 2007; Vollrath, Sheppard, Hinsz, & Davis, 1989). This is **collaborative facilitation.** In recall, the retrieval plan plays an important role in performance. In contrast, in recognition there is no retrieval plan. Memory only requires that something seem familiar, and anything more is a bonus. When people do recognition in groups, they can pool their resources to arrive at some consensus about what happened, although this is more effective at accepting old items than rejecting new items (Clark, Abbe, & Larson, 2006; Clark, Hori, Putnam, & Martin, 2000). Issues of social influence on memory are discussed more prominently in Chapter 12 (Memory and Reality) and Chapter 13 (Memory and the Law).

Other People's Memories. In addition to the influence of other people on our own memories, we may also be called upon to evaluate the quality of other people's memories. While we can do this to some degree, there are some biases that can creep up. One is the *consensus bias* (Ross, Greene, & House, 1977), which is the idea that we often assume that other people know what we know. So, if we have some idea or information in memory, we implicitly expect other people to know this as well. Another bias is that people expect others to do better when the pressure is on to remember something. While motivation to remember can help when a person is first encoding something, it does not help much, if at all, during retrieval. However, other people expect a person to remember more when they are motivated at retrieval, even though this doesn't really help (Kassam, Gilbert, Swencionis, & Wilson, 2009). Imagine a high-profile court case in which a person is strongly motivated to remember something accurately. If he was trying to remember at the time the event occurred, then it is reasonable that memory will be better. However, if he was only motivated to try to remember at retrieval of something that did not seem particularly important at the time, then memory will be relatively poor in spite of the motivation. Despite this, other people will expect the person's memory to be better because of this lack of insight we have into how other people's memories work.

Synopsis

Two of the most common ways to test memory are recall and recognition. Recall involves producing information. Often people need a retrieval plan to help organize their recalls. Recall tests have helped illustrate such basic principles as the forgetting curve, overlearning, reminiscence, and hypermnesia. Recognition involves assessing whether something has been encountered before, such as with old-new recognition tests, although some correction for guessing may be needed. In more complex situations, people may be given forced-choice recognition tests in which they need to select one option from a set of alternatives. Finally, memory retrieval can be influenced by social circumstances. Sometimes other people can hinder memory, as with collaborative inhibition, whereas other times other people can augment memory, as with collaborative facilitation.

ASSESSING MEMORY STRUCTURE AND PROCESS

We have looked at methods that assess the contents of memory. In this section we cover ways of looking at memory structure and the processes that are used in retrieval. The structure of memories refers to both the organization of multiple pieces of information within a single memory trace or across multiple memory traces. The processes of memory refer to the mental activities that a person engages in when trying to retrieve a piece of knowledge. Basically, *how* do we remember?

Mental Chronometry

An important and frequently used source of information in memory research is the speed of responding. In many cases this **response time** is recorded on the order of milliseconds or seconds. The idea is that faster response times reflect simpler memory processes and/or more familiar memories, whereas slower response times reflect more complex memory processes and/or more unfamiliar memories.

Methods. Response time is measured from the onset of some stimulus. For example, when asked to identify whether a series of faces has been seen before, the time will be recorded from the moment the picture was shown to the time the person responds. The time recorded for any given memory is not very informative by itself. That time must be placed in some context of other times to understand whether it is fast or slow. While there are many variations on this idea, the use of response times can be classified into two broad categories.

The first description of mental chronometry was Donders's **subtractive factors logic.** This is outlined in Figure 3.6. The idea is to have at least two conditions that are identical except for the inclusion of one processing step. For example, both conditions include the same encoding (factor A) and response (factor B) processes. However, the condition of interest involves an extra step (factor X). After collecting the times, the time for the simpler process (A + B) is subtracted from the time for the more complex one (A + X + B). What is left over should be the time for the critical process. For example, in a simple condition one could have a person indicate whether a picture of a face is old or new. In a more complex condition the person would indicate whether a picture of a face is old or new and whether the person is living or dead. Based on subtractive factors logic, the difference between these two conditions would reflect the time it takes to remember a person's current health status.

While subtractive factors logic is appealing, it has a number of problems. For one, it is unclear whether the process of interest is being added in a way that does not disrupt or change others and that occurs at a time when these other processes are not taking place. Another approach to mental chronometry is **additive factors logic,** developed by Sternberg (and discussed in more detail in Chapter 4). This approach is outlined in Figure 3.7. Rather

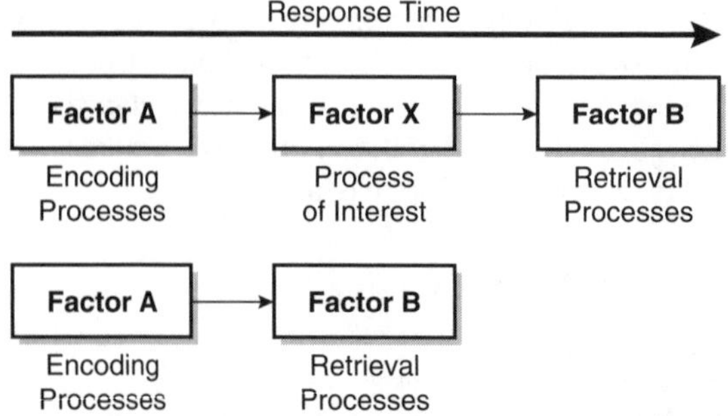

FIGURE 3.6 Donders's Subtractive Factors Logic for Response Times

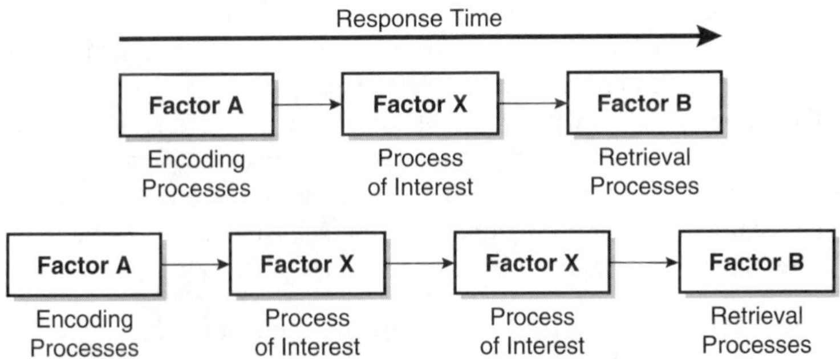

FIGURE 3.7 Sternberg's Additive Factors Logic for Response Times

than having two conditions that differ by the presence or absence of a mental stage, in additive factors logic the critical stage of interest (factor X) is always present. What varies is its degree of involvement—that is, how much of that process is added relative to a comparison condition. For example, it may be a stage that a person needs to go through many times or that it involves various numbers of memory traces. By looking at the differences among conditions, one can provide an estimate of the influence of each increment of complexity. This approach is more likely to preserve a greater array of mental processes across conditions, making the comparison more reliable and meaningful.

Principles. The analysis of response times has yielded a wealth of information about memory. One of the most prominent of these is priming. **Priming** is a speed up in response time to items that immediately follow related items. For example, when making lexical decision judgments (that is, deciding whether a string of letters is a word or not), people are faster to say that the string "doctor" is a word if it immediately follows "nurse" than if it follows "bread" (e.g., Meyer & Schvanevelt, 1971). The idea is that "nurse" activates or primes knowledge of nurses in long-term memory. The concept "doctor" is very related to "nurse," and so has been primed. So, information about doctors is retrieved faster than it would have been had the person just been thinking about something unrelated (like bread). This sort of unconscious, implicit influence on memory, while typically studied across brief periods of time (anywhere from a few milliseconds to several minutes), can last for years. One study reported significant priming 17 years after people initially had only 1–3 second exposures to pictures (Mitchell, 2006).

Cluster Analysis

Some methods of assessing memory are aimed at directly indicating how information is organized. Knowing this can provide insight into how things such as remindings occur and why our thoughts drift in some ways but not in others. There are a number of ways to approach this question. Looking at the data from priming studies is one way. Regardless of the method, what is going on in such studies is an attempt to look at clusters of memories. In fact, there is a special domain of statistics known as cluster analysis where the goal is to detect groups or clusters of information in a set of data.

Methods. There are a number of methods that can be used to look at clusters of information in memory. Here we focus on two relatively simple measures to give you a feel for how this approach works.

Inter-Item Delays. A time-based procedure for assessing memory organization with recall is if you keep track of the amount of time between each recalled item. What you'll find is that there is not a uniform pattern. Instead, people report a burst of a few items, then a pause, then a burst of a few more, and a pause, and so on (e.g., Patterson, Meltzer, & Mandler, 1971; Pollio, Richards, & Lucas, 1969). By using these **inter-item delays,** one can make inferences about memory structure. Memories that are structured together are likely to be recalled together during one of the bursts. However, information that is stored apart is more likely to be separated by a longer pause or delay.

ARC Scores. There are also methods of obtaining memory clusters by looking at the content of recall, specifically the order in which information was reported. Pieces of information that are stored together in memory are likely to be recalled together. In many cases you can make a reasonable guess about how a set of information could optimally be organized. For example, a set of words can be organized into categories. It then becomes possible to test whether people have adopted that organization. This can be done by calculating Adjusted Ratio of Clustering (ARC) scores (Roenker, Thompson, & Brown, 1971). ARC scores index the degree to which a recall sequence conforms to predetermined categories, taking into account how much organization would be expected by chance. The formula for calculating ARC scores is given in the Appendix.

There are many sorts of analyses that address the organization of information. For example, the ARC' score measures the degree to which a recall conforms to a predetermined sequential order (Pellegrino, 1971). (The method for calculating ARC' scores is also provided in the Appendix).

Subjective Organization. There are ways to get at subjective organization—that is, the organization imposed by the person himself or herself rather than the experimenter. This is useful when there is no clear a priori organization. One of these is a measure that produces an ordered cluster tree (e.g., Reitman & Rueter, 1980). Basically, people are asked to recall a complete set of information a number of times. What this measure then does is look for consistencies in these repeated recalls, both in terms of the clusters that might be present as well as any stable sequential orders that might be produced.

Another way to assess how people subjectively organize information is to have them indicate where breaks should occur when they are viewing continuous events. For example, people might watch a film in which they are asked to press a button every time they think there has been an important shift in the situation. The locations that people select as break points are thought to correspond to separation of different types of information in memory (Magliano, Miller, & Zwaan, 2001; Newtson, 1976; Zacks, Speer, & Reynolds, 2009).

Principles. Clustering methods have shown that memories are highly structured. This structure may take the form of a hierarchy. The more structure a person can impose on information, the better his or her recall will be (Mandler, 1967). When people are given a set of information, they often adopt that structure, which is seen in how they remember it. For example, in a study by Bousfield (1953), people were given a list of 60 words to memorize. These words were from four categories (i.e., animals, people's names, vegetables, and professions), but they were presented in a random order. When people later recalled those words, there was a strong tendency to recall them in clusters based on the four categories. Moreover, as time passes and people have more experience with a set of information, their memories become more organized (e.g., Bousfield & Bousfield, 1966). In fact, experts in a domain have highly organized knowledge bases.

Finally, even when given what appears to be a random set of information, people impose some subjective organization upon it (Tulving, 1962). This subjective organization takes into account the idiosyncratic interpretations people place on a set of items to create a structure that will help them remember. While space may abhor a vacuum, the human brain abhors randomness. It is always searching for regularities and structure.

Synopsis

There are a number of ways to look at the structure and function of memory. Mental chronometry allows us to look at how long it takes to remember something to help draw conclusions about memory structure, organization, and complexity. Priming is a classic example of the how mental chronometry can yield insights into memory. Cluster analyses assess more directly how knowledge is structured in memory.

CONSCIOUS EXPERIENCE OF MEMORY

Metamemory Measures

Another important characteristic is the phenomenological experience of memory. The awareness of one's own memory and memory processes is known as **metamemory** and is highlighted in Chapter 14. A brief coverage of metamemory issues is presented here to illustrate how to study the experience and awareness of memory.

Methods. Metamemory studies require people to report their own memory processes. This method of introspection has a long and checkered past dating back to the early days of experimental psychology, and many people are still cautious about using such **verbal reports** (e.g., Nisbett & Wilson, 1977) because many of our thought processes lie outside of conscious awareness. However, despite this, there are still cases where verbal reports can provide insights about cognition (e.g., Ericsson & Simon, 1980), especially if one is concerned with conscious mental states and their consequences.

There are a number of metamemory methods. A common one is remember vs. know judgments (Gardiner, 1988). With this approach, people are asked to recall or recognize a set of information. For those things that are recalled or identified as old, people then rate whether the information is something they consciously remember learning or something they know they encountered before but have no conscious memory of learning it. For example, if you can recollect where and when you learned of your acceptance into college, then you would say that you remember it. In contrast, if you have no conscious memory of this event, but you know it must have occurred, then you would say that you only know it.

Principles. A number of insights have been gained by looking at what people attribute to their own memory processes. People can be led astray and become biased when assessing their own memories. This is clearly illustrated by the hindsight bias (e.g., Fischhoff, 1975). The hindsight bias is a tendency to distort memories so they conform to one's goals or circumstances. For example, people might be asked to make predictions about how likely an event is to occur. Then some time afterward one group (the experimental group) is presented with information about the actual outcome. Another group (the control group) is not given this information. If everyone then reports his or her original estimates, those in the experimental group are more likely to "misremember" their original estimates as being much closer to the actual outcome. We'll discuss this more in Chapter 14.

Implicit Memory

Again, implicit memory refers to memories and memory processes that are unconscious. It is rare that memory uses only implicit or explicit processes. Performance almost always reflects a mixture of these two processes. However, there are methods that allow for the effects and influences of each of these to be separated.

Methods. Measures that are aimed more at implicit memory use tasks in which people are not aware that memory is being tested or when there is little to no conscious control over the process. In general, it is very difficult, if not impossible, to have a memory task that purely taps either implicit or explicit memory. As such, memory *tasks* are referred to as either **direct memory tasks**, which directly ask a person for a memory report (such as recall and recognition), or **indirect memory tasks**, which assess memory by focusing a person's attention on another aspect of the task. In general, direct memory tasks are thought to involve more explicit memory and indirect memory tasks are thought to involve more implicit memory. Indirect memory methods often either tap preexisting knowledge or present people with a set of information and then test memory some time afterward. In the latter case, the memory tests are given under the guise of being unrelated to what had been done previously so people are not motivated to consciously remember. Indirect memory measures include such things as word fragment completion, perceptual identification, and priming.

One method for separating out implicit and explicit memory processes is the **process dissociation procedure**. Because there are no "process pure" tasks, with almost any task including both conscious and unconscious components, this procedure can help estimate their relative influence (e.g., Jacoby, 1991). For example, suppose a person has read a list of words and then takes a word fragment completion test. This procedure works by having people recall information under two conditions. In the *inclusion* condition, the person completes a series of word fragments with whatever words he or she can think of, even if they were words from the prior list. In the *exclusion* condition, a person uses any word he or she can think of as long as they are *not* words that were on the previous list. Using performance in these two conditions, it is possible to arrive at estimates of explicit and implicit memories. The procedures for calculating these components using the process dissociation procedure are given in the Appendix.

Synopsis

It is important to know what it feels like to remember something. Awareness of one's own memory is known as metamemory. Studies of metamemory reveal our insights into our own memories as well as how these insights can be wrong. It is also important to realize that many memory processes occur outside of awareness in what is known as implicit memory.

SUMMARY

This chapter covered a number of methods for assessing memory and some basic principles that they illustrate. Each method has its strengths and limitations. To gain the most accurate picture of memory, it is important to use multiple methods. The more methods that point to the same answer, the more reliable that answer will be. However, if different methods lead to different answers, then something is wrong. For example, suppose there are two conditions. In one, people are more accurate. However, if they also are much slower, then this is known as a speed-accuracy tradeoff. Because people are making fewer errors and slowing down, it may just mean that they are being more careful, not that these data reflect anything about memory per se. More generally, multiple sources of data can be used in combination to provide a more complete picture of how memory operates (Meyer, Irwin, Osman, & Kounios, 1988). Because of our lack of direct access to memory, we need a variety of methods. Converging operations allow us the greatest level of certainty about one of the more elusive topics in science.

STUDY QUESTIONS

1. What is an experiment? What are the primary components of an experiment? Why is this a preferred way to study memory?
2. What are some ways to learn information so it can be better remembered later? Is this true of all kinds of information?
3. What kinds of information are easier to remember? What kinds are more difficult?
4. What are the various sorts of recall tests, and what can they reveal about memory?
5. What are the various sorts of recognition tests, and what can they reveal about memory?
6. What are some of the ways to correct for guessing on memory tests?
7. What are some of the ways in which social situations influence how well memory works?
8. How can mental chronometry be used to assess characteristics of memory? Give an example of some phenomenon of memory that is clearly shown using mental chronometry.
9. How are cluster analyses used to study memory?
10. What is metamemory, and what does it tell us about how people use their memories?
11. What is implicit memory, and, generally, why is it important to memory functioning?

KEY TERMS

additive factors logic, "aha" effect, automaticity of encoding, bias, collaborative facilitation, collaborative inhibition, concreteness effect, cued recall, direct memory tasks, discrimination, Dual Code Theory, elaborative rehearsal, enactment effect, false alarm, forced recall, forced choice recognition, forgetting curve, free recall, frequency, functional stimulus, generation effect, hypermnesia, incidental learning, indirect memory tasks, intentional learning, inter-item delays, intrusions, Jost's Law, levels of processing, nominal stimulus, metamemory, miss, old-new recognition, overlearning, picture superiority effect, Pollyanna principle, priming, process dissociation procedure, recall, recall order, recognition, reminiscence, response time, retrieval plan, rote rehearsal, savings, signal detection theory, subtractive factors logic, verbal reports

TRY IT OUT

In this chapter there are a number of basic ideas for research projects on memory. For many of these, you can create a list of 20 or so words and use these as your stimuli. When you generate these lists, try to keep the words similar in some way, such as all being from the same class of words (e.g., nouns or verbs), being similar in length (e.g., five to six letters long with two syllables), and so on. When you present the information to people, try to keep the presentation time constant in the different conditions. Typically, for word lists, people might see each word for one second each (you could write each word on an index card). To encourage some forgetting, have people do a distractor task, such as solve three-digit math problems (294 + 603 = ?) for two minutes. Ideally you should have at least 12 participants for each of these tasks, with at least 12 people in each group if you decide to vary things in your own experiment between groups. Now, with these basic ground rules, here are some things you could do:

- Test the difference between **incidental** and **intentional** learning by having one group of people (incidental) rate each word for pleasantness, and another group of people (intentional) study each word knowing that they will get a memory test later. After the distractor period, have people write down as many words as they can remember. If all goes well, people in the incidental learning group will remember less than people in the intentional learning group.
- Test the effectiveness of **imagery** by giving the list of words to two groups of people. Have one group (control) simply try to learn the words as effectively as possible. Have the other group (imagery) try to form mental images as they study each word. After the distractor period, have people write down as many words as they can remember. If all goes well, people in the imagery condition will remember more words than people in the control condition.
- To show the effectiveness of **concreteness**, have two groups of people. Keeping everything else the same, such as the length of the words, give one group a list of nouns that refer to concrete objects (e.g., truck), and give the other group a list of nouns that refer to abstract concepts (e.g., trust). After the distractor period, have people write down as many words as they can remember. If all goes well, people in the concrete word group will remember more words than people in the abstract word group.
- To demonstrate a **forgetting curve**, give your people four lists of words. Have them recall one list immediately, a second list after one hour, the third list after one day, and the fourth list after one week. If all goes well you should find that memory for the word lists will decline in a way that shows the greatest rate of forgetting soon after the list is read, and a slower rate of forgetting at longer periods of time.

CHAPTER FOUR

SENSORY AND SHORT-TERM MEMORY

When people think about memory, they typically think about retaining knowledge over long periods of time. When most people speak of short-term memory, they often refer to remembering over a few hours or days. However, for cognitive psychologists, memory in the short term means much briefer spans of time, often less than a minute. What is the point of studying such fleeting memories? Aren't changes in the world from one moment to the next rather trivial? Well, no. Without these short-term memories, we would live in the permanent, absolute present—the eternal now. Language as we know it would not be possible. You would not be able to watch a film. Much of the world involves events that are spread out over time. Take the example of hearing a word. If you think about it, all words are made up of strings of sounds that are occurring at different points in time. To hear this as a whole word, you need to integrate the sounds together. What allows you to do this is the memory of what occurred before, so the information you remember over time helps you link together the sounds to form the whole word.

Two types of brief memories are considered here. The first are very short-term memories: the sensory registers. These modality-specific systems allow us to do sensory identification and integration, such as the preceding example of word identification. The second is what is formally known as short-term memory. This type of memory stores ideas that are within or close to conscious awareness.

SENSORY MEMORY

The briefest memory systems are the **sensory registers.** These are modality-specific, such that each one retains information specific to a sensory modality. For example, the visual sensory register retains visual information. It is easy to see that these are relatively primitive memory systems. Their primary purpose is for processing sensory information. Because different sensory information has different physical properties, each sensory register has different qualities. As such, we consider three sensory registers: (1) The visual sensory register or iconic memory, (2) the auditory sensory register or echoic memory, and (3) the haptic sensory register for touch information. There are others, but these three provide a broad understanding of the sensory registers. The first two have been given a great deal of study. The third has received less attention, but is included to illustrate a sensory register in a modality for which humans are not well suited.

ICONIC MEMORY

The first sensory register considered is **iconic memory.** Humans are primarily visual animals. As such, iconic memory is the most extensively studied sensory register. Information in iconic memory is in a form that captures the visual stimulation from our retinas. The mental representation in iconic memory is called an **icon** (hence the name *iconic* memory). To understand the role iconic memory plays, we need to understand how much information it holds, how long an icon is retained, and how the icon is used to build up mental representation of the world, even though at any moment we only see a small bit of it.

Span and Duration of Iconic Memory

First, how much information can iconic memory hold and how long can it hold it? In one study, Averbach (1963) presented two people [himself (subject EA) and another (subject JP)] sets of 1 to 13 dots for 40 to 600 milliseconds. The task was to say how many dots there were. The results are shown in Figure 4.1. For the briefest display (40 ms), people were fairly accurate when there was one dot, but they were pretty lousy when there were more than one. For the longer two durations (150 and 600 ms), they were fairly accurate when there were four or five dots, with their performance declining gradually after that. Although there is a large time difference between the second and third conditions, the pattern of performance is roughly the same. The additional time did not provide much benefit.

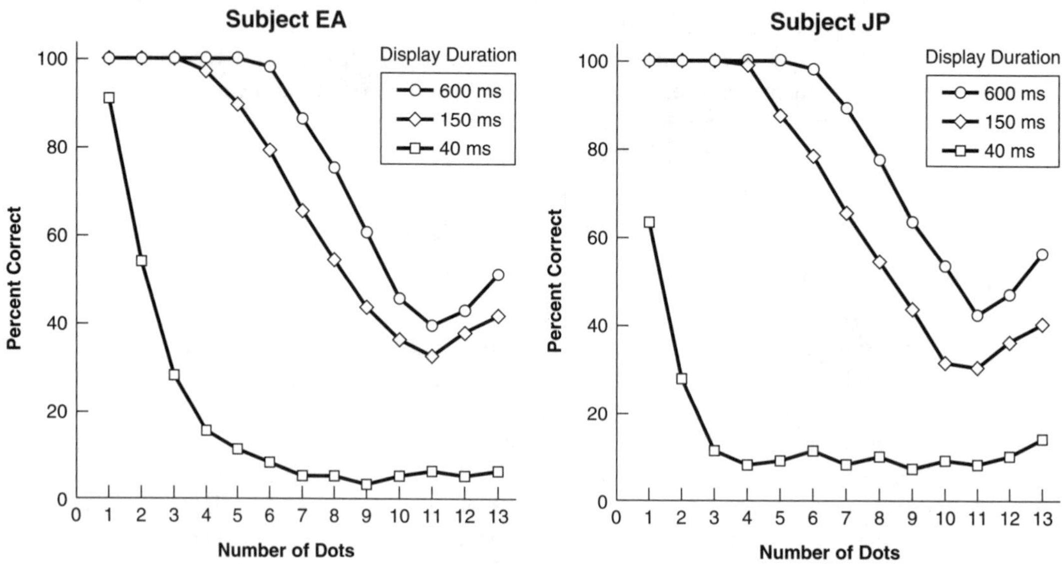

FIGURE 4.1 Span of Apprehension

Source: Reprinted from *Journal of Verbal Learning and Verbal Behavior,* 2, Averbach, E., The span of apprehension as a function of exposure duration, pp. 60–64, 1963, with permission from Elsevier.

Because this study looked at briefly presented displays, it is assessing iconic memory. From these data it is tempting to conclude that the amount of information held in iconic memory is four or five items. Any more is beyond a person's capacity. Within that range an accurate assessment can be made. However, this is an incorrect conclusion. In a study by Sperling (1960), people saw brief displays, similar to the Averbach (1963) study. People saw displays of letters instead of dots, and there were 12 of them (in a 3 × 4 matrix). The task was to recall as many letters as possible. This display was presented for 50 milliseconds. In the control condition (also called the whole report condition) people were simply asked to report as many of the letters as possible. In this case, people were typically able to name four or five. Again, by itself, this suggests that the number of items in iconic memory is four or five.

However, in an experimental condition in Sperling's (1960) study (also called the partial report condition), one of three tones was sounded to indicate which row people should report. A high tone for the top row, a medium tone was for the middle row, and a low tone was for the bottom row. Moreover, this tone occurred anywhere from just prior to the display being removed to 1 second after the display had disappeared. Sperling used the sum of the performance at each row to estimate what was available in iconic memory. If people could always report all four items in a cued row, this would indicate that all of the information was present but that it decayed quickly. Alternatively, if people could report all four items from the first row but very few, if any, from the others, this would suggest that iconic memory can hold only very few items.

The results are shown in Figure 4.2. Performance was near ceiling (very close to perfect) when the tone was presented at the time the display was removed. However, as the amount of time increased before the tone, there was a decline in performance. Nearing

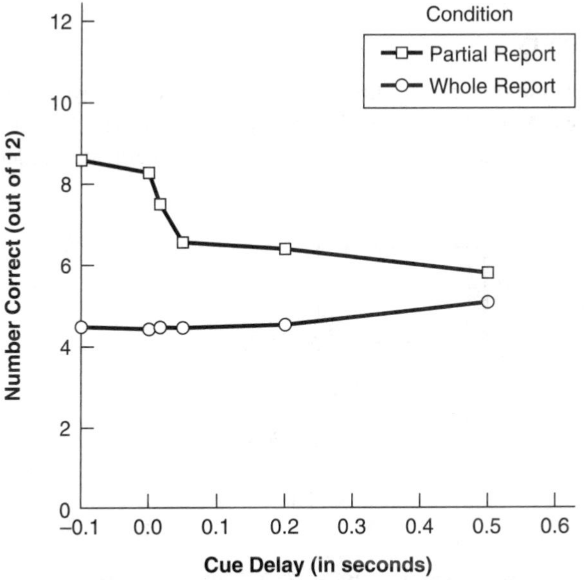

FIGURE 4.2 Availability of Information in Iconic Memory

Source: Sperling, G. (1960). The information available in brief visual presentations. *Psychological Monographs: General and Applied, 74 (11),* 1–29.

the 250 millisecond mark, people approached performance in the whole-report condition. This indicates that a large amount of information is held in iconic memor. However, iconic memory has a very brief duration. By about a one-quarter second, nearly everything has decayed (although this decay is not random, suggesting some influence of higher-order processing; Gold et al., 2005). Anything that is left was presumably transferred into short-term memory before it was lost.

Anorthoscopic Perception

The effects of iconic memory can be observed in the distortions it produces. For example, a lightning strike appears to last longer than it actually does because we hold onto a memory of it. Another example is **anorthoscopic perception,** or the seeing-more-than-is-there phenomenon (Parks, 1965). This is illustrated by passing a picture behind a slit, as shown in Figure 4.3. If the figure is passed through at a fast speed (e.g., 250–300 ms), then people report seeing more of it. This occurs because they are integrating information from different points in time in iconic memory to reconstruct the shape of the object.

Moreover, iconic memory is compressed to accommodate all that was seen in a small region of space (McCloskey & Watkins, 1978), as shown in Figure 4.4. Also, the faster the objects behind the slit move, the more compressed the perception is (Haber & Nathanson, 1968). This cannot be the result of a retinal afterimage because if lots of visual information was presented to the same retinal location, and this would be jumbled into the same space on the retina. Instead, there is an active construction based on memory of what was recently seen. There is a clear evolutionary advantage to having such a sensory register, such as trying to identify an object as it moves behind a cluster of branches. If you can quickly integrate the bits and pieces you do see, you can identify the creature more quickly.

Trans-Saccadic Memory

We do not view the world in one glance. Instead, we must move our eyes, head, and body to scan our surroundings. As such, we view different parts of the world and then integrate them to build a complete mental picture of it. A typical eye movement is called a *saccade*.

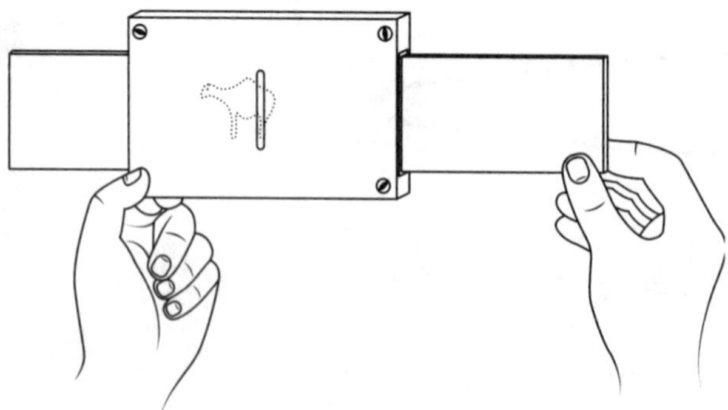

FIGURE 4.3 Example of a Device Used to Illustrate Anorthoscopic Perception

Source: Haber, R. N., & Nathanson, L. S. (1968). Post-retinal storage? Some further observations on Parks' camel as seem through the eye of a needle. *Perception & Psychophysics, 3,* 349–355. Permission granted upon citation of source.

FIGURE 4.4 Example of Stimuli and Response Generated by People in the Study of Anorthoscopic Perception

Source: Haber, R. N., & Nathanson, L. S. (1968). Post-retinal storage? Some further observations on Parks' camel as seem through the eye of a needle. *Perception & Psychophysics, 3,* 349–355. Permission granted upon citation of source.

When our eyes land on some point in space, it is a *fixation*. Fixations typically last around 300 milliseconds and saccadic eye movements typically take 30 ms. Moreover, we mostly perceptually process information during the fixations. This is important because it places demands on iconic memory. We need to integrate information across saccades to build up a picture of the world. We need a trans-saccadic memory (e.g., Irwin, 1996) in iconic memory to do this. How is this accomplished?

Research on this topic suggests that trans-saccadic memory does not use retinal or spatial coordinate (Irwin, Yantis, & Jonides, 1983). Instead, trans-saccadic memory uses representations of objects, called *object files* (Kahneman, Triesman, and Gibbs, 1992) to keep track of basic characteristics of an object. Evidence for this comes from studies in which people detect that something has been changed after an eye movement (Henderson & Anes, 1994). Moreover, change detection is more likely when the entity is at the focus of attention rather than in the background. This suggests that although we subjectively experience the world as stable and full of detail, this impression comes in part from our memories to fill in the gaps with what we have seen before or with what long-term memory assumes should be there (e.g., Henderson & Anes, 1994).

Although trans-saccadic memory seems fairly simple, it can have important influences on more complex processing. For example, if people need to mentally rotate an image (see Chapter 5), this takes longer if they have to concurrently make an eye movement (Irwin & Brockmole, 2000). The execution of an eye movement puts memory processes on hold while the eyes are doing their thing.

Change Blindness

The lack of accurate detail in iconic memory has interesting consequences. For example, there are often errors in feature films that go unnoticed by most audience members, such as objects appearing and disappearing across cuts, clothes changing, and so forth. These are called continuity errors. In a set of studies, people saw films in which objects changed across cuts. For example, dinner plates might change from red to white. However, people were very poor at detecting these changes and only did so less than 2 percent of the time (Levin & Simons, 1997).

In one study, people watched films in which the actor was changed across film cuts (the two people were of the same gender and ethnicity). Only 33 percent of the people noticed the change (Levin & Simons, 1997). Visual memory reflects our expectations. For example, for briefly presented scenes, people are more likely to detect a change in an object if it belongs in the scene (e.g., a blender in a kitchen) than if it does not (e.g., a live chicken in a kitchen) (Hollingworth & Henderson, 2003).

ECHOIC MEMORY

Echoic memory serves audition like iconic memory serves vision. The mental representation in echoic memory is the *echo*. However, echoic memory differs in important ways. Specifically, echoic memory must take into account the fleeting and temporary nature of sound.

Span and Duration of Echoic Memory

As a parallel to iconic memory, let's look at the capacity and duration of echoic memory. In an analog to Sperling's (1960) study, Darwin, Turvey, and Crowder (1972) presented people wearing headphones with three lists of three digits. One list was presented only to the right ear, a second to only the left ear, and a third to both ears (so that it sounded like it was in the middle of the listener's head). Afterward, the person was to report as many of the digits as possible (whole report control condition) or only one of the lists based on a visual cue that indicated left, right, or middle. The data are in Figure 4.5 Like Sperling's study, performance in the cued conditions indicated that more was available in echoic memory than was suggested by the whole report condition. Thus, echoic memory can retain a large amount of information.

Now consider the duration of echoic memory. As shown in Figure 4.5, echoic information is retained for a longer period of time, about 4 seconds. This makes sense given

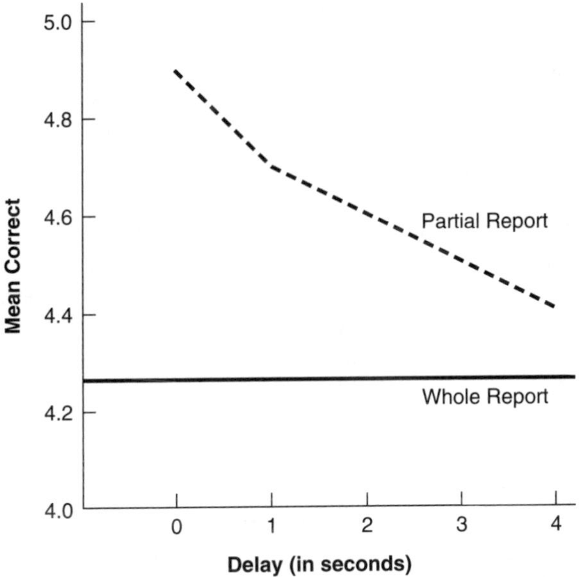

FIGURE 4.5 Assessment of Echoic Memory

Source: Darwin, C. J., Turvey, M. T., & Crowder, R. G. (1972). An auditory analogue of the Sperling partial report procedure: Evidence for brief auditory storage. *Cognitive Psychology, 3,* 255–267.

the nature of auditory information. Auditory information is stretched out over time and can typically only be heard only once. So, echoic memory needs to keep large chunks of information and retain it long enough so it can be properly analyzed.

HAPTIC SENSORY MEMORY

While iconic and echoic memories have received the most attention, each modality has its own memory store. For example, memory for touch, **haptic sensory memory,** must take into account qualities such as pressure and temperature. Moreover, it needs to account for both the spatial extent of what is in contact with the body, as well as how it changes over time. Thus, this sensory register is going to be more like iconic than echoic memory. Furthermore, different parts of the body are differentially sensitive to tactile information (e.g., the hands and face are more sensitive than the knees or back). Thus, the sensory register gives differential preference to touch information from different parts of the body.

Span and Duration of Haptic Sensory Memory

In terms of the capacity and duration of haptic sensory memory, in a study by Bliss, Crane, Mansfield, and Townsend (1966; Hill & Bliss, 1968), also modeled after the Sperling (1960) study, people received small jets of air at different locations their fingers. People gave whole reports of all of the stimulated locations or gave partial reports after a light or a tone indicated which parts of the fingers were relevant. Again, in the whole report condition people could report three or four skin locations, but in the partial report condition, performance was better, with people having access to nearly all of the locations. There was also a rapid decay of information such that by about 1.3 seconds, much of the information was lost.

Synopsis

Memory is needed even for brief periods of time. Each modality has a different dedicated sensory register. Iconic memory is for vision, echoic memory is for hearing, and haptic sensory memory for the sense of touch. Each of these stores holds a large amount of information for a short time. Although these memory stores interface with the world in different ways, they serve a common goal and use similar principles.

SHORT-TERM MEMORY

Short-term memory is the part of memory responsible for processing and retaining information beyond the sensory registers, but not much longer than a minute or so (without active processing). Short-term memory is unique in that its contents include consciousness. So, when a person is thinking, he or she is actively processing information in short-term memory. We'll examine the manipulation of information in Chapter 5 when we consider working memory.

Although it has been studied for years, the precise nature of short-term memory is unclear. Some researchers think that short-term memory is a qualitatively different part of human memory. In contrast, others view short-term memory as just a portion of long-term memory that is currently available. For the latter view, there is no clear distinction between short- and long-term memory, but a continuum of availability in a single memory system. Regardless of which view is closer to the truth, there are aspects of memory that are salient during short time periods. It is these aspects of memory that are of concern here.

Short-Term Memory Capacity

A striking aspect of short-term memory is its severely limited capacity. Only a small number of things can be actively held at once. This limited capacity is easily demonstrated. For a quick, at-home study, have a friend of yours read you lists of random digits at the rate of about one per second. At the end of the list, recall the digits in the order you heard them. Start with a short list, with only two or three digits, and then progress to longer lists. What you will find is that short-term memory capacity is very small. Although this task starts out easy, it quickly becomes difficult. Most people are able to remember between five and nine digits in the correct order. In everyday experience you may run up against this limit if a person rattles off a telephone number too fast, or too quickly gives you a list of things to buy at the grocery store.

A common idea is that a person's memory span is around seven items. This information processing bottleneck idea was first laid out in a classic paper by Miller (1956) entitled "The Magical Number Seven, Plus or Minus Two." Thus, memory span is often described as being 7 ± 2 chunks of information. The term *chunk* is important because what can serve as a unit of information is flexible.

Although this 7 ± 2 figure is often used, some researchers have argued that capacity is actually only about 4 ± 1 items (Cowan, 2000). People remember more information because they are using other resources to extend the functional size of short-term memory. For example, people may chunk the information or use long-term memories to augment short-term memory.

Chunking. Regardless of whether short-term memory capacity is seven or four units, this is still not a lot. Yet, we are capable of thinking about larger amounts of knowledge than this limit would imply. How do we do it? There are some ways to expand short-term memory capacity, including chunking. **Chunking** occurs when people take smaller units of information and group them into a larger unit. This functionally expands the capacity of short-term memory.

For example, if you were given a list of letters to remember, you may remember about seven of them. However, if those letters are grouped into words, then you can remember seven unrelated words, and the number of letters that you remember increases. A word is a chunk that organizes the letters. Every time there is an opportunity for chunking is an opportunity to hold more information in short-term memory. So when you are trying to learn something new, you are much more likely to be able to retain it if you can place it into some organization or structure.

So what guides chunking? Prior knowledge is a major influence. The more you know, the easier it is to form chunks, and the more efficient your application of that knowledge is, the greater your memory capacity will seem, even though it really stays about the same. Thus, memory can be improved by gaining expertise. So, expose yourself to a wide range of different kinds of experiences to improve your memory.

Very Large Capacity. The influence of expertise on short-term memory can be clearly seen in a study by Ericsson, Chase, and Faloon (1980). In this study at Carnegie-Mellon University, they had a person, known as S. F., come to the memory lab to assess his short-term memory span for digits. At the beginning of the study his digit span was about seven items. They continued to test him for over a year and a half. As shown in Figure 4.6, over time, his digit span grew larger and larger. At the end of the study he could repeat back, in the correct order, nearly 80 digits that he had just heard read to him at the rate of one per second. How did he achieve this superhuman feat?

Well, S. F. was a runner. He grouped the digits into chunks based on race lengths and running times, as well as using other devices, such as famous dates. For example, the sequence 3492 was recoded as "3 minutes, 49 point 2 seconds, near world-record mile time," and 1944 as "near the end of World War II." The increase in S. F.'s memory span was a result of his using long-term memory knowledge to organize information in short-term memory. This made his short-term memory capacity seem larger. Note that his chunks were often made up of three or four digits. S. F.'s short-term memory span did not actually grow larger as illustrated by the fact that after his digit span had grown to gargantuan proportions, when he was given a set of letters, his memory span dropped back down to six.

Another example of the influence of expertise is memory for chessboards. In one study people were shown a picture of a chessboard with pieces arranged on it. This was then removed and a person reconstructed the positions of the pieces. Chess experts are

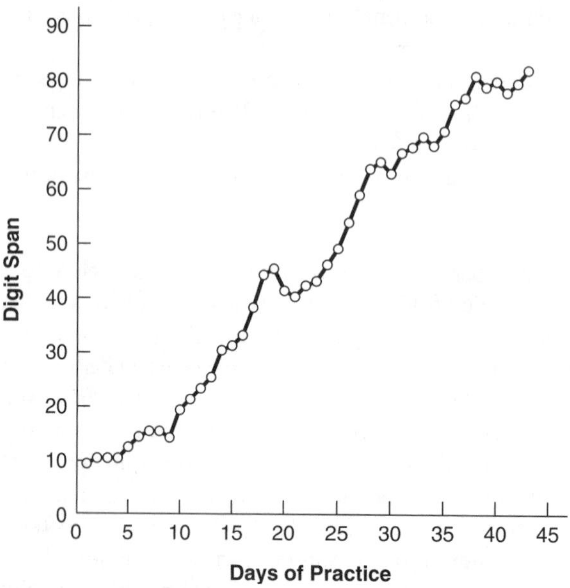

FIGURE 4.6 Example of Expertise Influences on Short-Term Memory Span. In this case, S. F.'s improved digit span with practice

Source: Ericsson, K. A., Chase, W. G., & Faloon, S. (1980). Acquisition of a memory skill. *Science, 208,* 1181–1182.

much better at this compared to novice chess players. The experts were drawing on their knowledge of the game to help them chunk the pieces and remember their original locations. This is highlighted by conditions in which people were given chessboards that were not from the middle of a game but had pieces randomly placed on the board. Here, everyone's memory declined, and the chess masters performed no better than the novices (Chase & Simon, 1973).

Duration of Short-Term Memory and Forgetting

Short-term memory is a bottleneck not only because of its small capacity; it also retains information for short periods of time. Without active attention, information in short-term memory is largely forgotten in 30 seconds. The trick in showing this is that a person must first think about something so that it enters short-term memory and then not think about it until memory is tested.

There are a number of problems with this. First, it is next to impossible to tell people *not* to think about anything and have them do it (Wegner, 1989). People's minds are always drifting around searching for something, anything, to think about. Second, whatever thoughts they have cannot be related to what you are trying to test. Otherwise, they are attending to it, and you cannot study how it is being forgotten.

Decay. In the study of short-term memory, a primary issue that has been whether forgetting is due to a decay or an interference process. For **decay**, the primary cause of forgetting is the passage of time. The more time that has passed, the more the memory trace has decayed and forgetting has occurred. An early piece of evidence to support a decay interpretation was reported more or less simultaneously by Brown (1958) and by Peterson and Peterson (1959). As such, it is known as the Brown–Peterson paradigm. In the Petersons' study, students at Indiana University were given consonant trigrams (e.g., TPZ) to remember. To keep students from actively rehearsing this, they gave them a three-digit number (e.g., 274) after the students had seen the trigram, with the task of saying the number aloud and then counting backward by threes (e.g., 274, 271, 268, 265) until they were told to stop, at which point they were to recall the trigram. This study varied the amount of time between the presentation of the trigram and the cue to recall it.

The data are shown in Figure 4.7 which is a nice forgetting curve. The more time that has elapsed, the less likely it was that the trigram was remembered. By 18 seconds, nearly all of the information was lost. Because the to-be-remembered information did not appear to be involved in the current stream of thought, the only mechanism that seemed a likely candidate for forgetting was decay.

Interference. While the decay theory has some intuitive appeal and is relatively simple (and science prefers simple explanations), there are serious challenges to it. Most of these challenges rest on the idea that forgetting is caused by interference. With **interference,** information in short-term memory interferes with or in some way blocks or hinders the retrieval of other information. Because short-term memory has a limited capacity, if new information is put into it, it will displace the information that is already there.

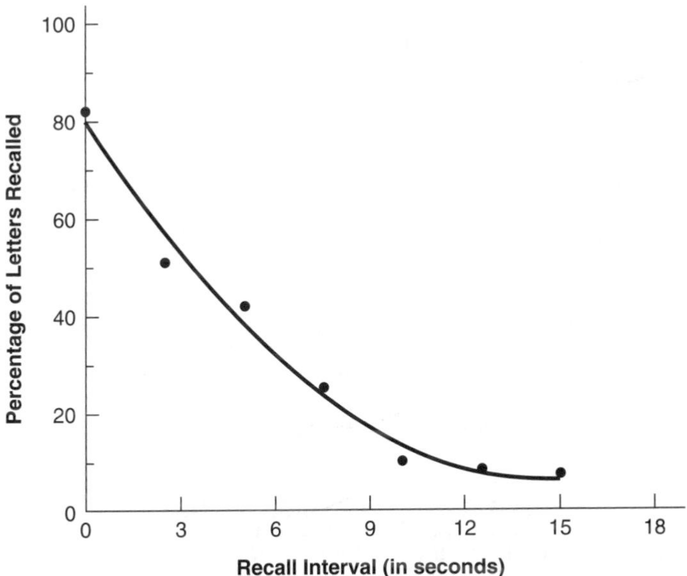

FIGURE 4.7 Results from Peterson and Peterson's Experiment

Source: Peterson, L. R., & Peterson, M. J. (1959). Short-term retention of individual verbal items. *Journal of Experimental Psychology, 58,* 193–198.

One study that supported the interference idea was done by Keppel and Underwood (1962). They suggested that some of the forgetting that was observed in the Brown–Peterson paradigm was due to interference from items learned on previous trials. What they did was to have only three trials. They found that there was virtually no forgetting on the first trial. Forgetting was observed only on the second and third trials. So, when there was no source of interference, there was no short-term memory forgetting.

Another study was by Waugh and Norman (1965). They gave people lists of 16 digits. At the end of each list was a probe digit. The task was to state what digit followed the earlier occurrence of the probe in the series that was just presented. This was a way to control how much interference people had experienced. The further back in the list the probe digit was, the more interference there was. To get at issues of decay, they presented the digits at either a slow rate (one per second) or a fast rate (four per second). The results are shown in Figure 4.8. The more intervening items between the probe and its prior occurrence—that is, the more interference there was—the greater the forgetting. The rate of forgetting is similar in the slow and fast presentation conditions. Thus, short-term memory forgetting is more a function of the amount of interference than the amount of time that has passed. Forgetting was observed in the Brown–Peterson studies because the task of counting backward produced interference and caused forgetting of the trigrams.

In sum, interference is the primary cause of forgetting in short-term memory (although this issue is not resolved, e.g., Berman, Jonides, & Lewis, 2009; Lewandowsky & Oberauer, 2009; Portrat, Barrouillet, & Camos, 2008). This limit of short-term memory has implications for everyday life. For example, if you are trying to keep information in mind, such as telephone number or a person's name, and are disrupted by something else, it is likely you will forget it. When you are reading or listening to something, you may need to keep track

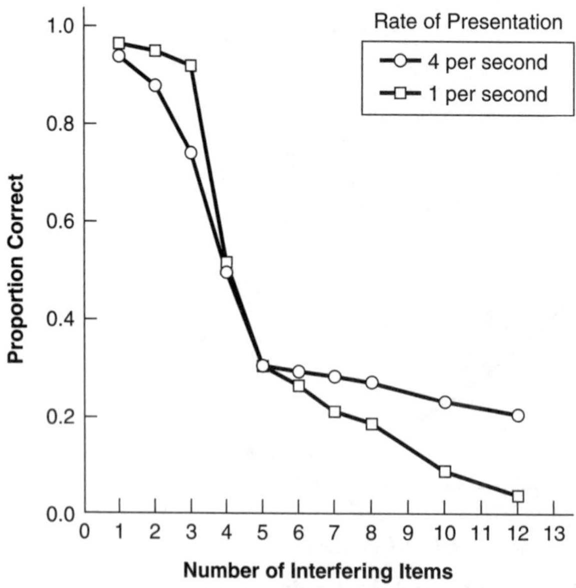

FIGURE 4.8 Results from Waugh and Norman Experiment

Source: Waugh, N. C., & Norman, D. A. (1965). Primary memory. *Psychological Review, 72,* 89–104.

of a number of ideas. If you are not able to do this effectively, then your comprehension, and your memory, will suffer. So, it is best to keep sources of interference to a minimum.

If there is interfering information in the environment during comprehension, this displaces the information that you need in short-term memory. For example, if you try to study with the television on, your ability to understand and remember is compromised. If you try to reason through something, you often need to consider various possibilities and outcomes. This places a strain on short-term memory. We all have been in situations in which there was a lot going on around us while we made a decision, and because we were not able to think clearly due to an interference, we were left with a choice we regretted.

Synopsis

Short-term memory can hold only a small amount of information for a few seconds. However, we can increase our capacity by chunking information into larger unit. When forgetting occurs, this is due not so much to the passage of time as to interference caused by the intrusion of new information entering short-term memory and displacing older information.

Retrieval in Short-Term Memory

If a person encodes information into the limited capacity of short-term memory and sufficiently avoids interference, it may become necessary to then use it. At that point it needs to be retrieved. For example, suppose someone tells you over the phone a list of names of people who will be attending a surprise party just as you are walking into a dining hall. There you see a friend, and now you need to remember if that person's name was in the set you just heard. Somehow, the contents of short-term memory must be searched to select the one name that is needed. How do you do this?

One of the most notable attempts to address this was a series of studies by Sternberg (1966, 1969, 1975). He used an experimental paradigm in which people were first given a list of one to six digits (e.g., 5, 2, 4, 3, 8, 0), well within the capacity of short-term memory. People were then given a memory probe (e.g., 4) with the task of saying whether the probe was in the list. Sternberg recorded how long it took to respond as a function of how many items were in the set and whether the probe was in the set.

Using this approach Sternberg tested three theories. The first is a **parallel search** theory in which all of the items in short-term memory are available more or less at once, and accessed in parallel. This makes sense if one assumes that the contents of short-term memory are either in or close to consciousness. If people search short-term memory in a parallel fashion, then the amount of information in the search set should not matter. All of the information is available at once regardless of the size of the search set. As a result, response times should not vary with set size, and there should be no difference between "yes" and "no" responses.

A second alternative is a **serial self-terminating search.** This involves going through items one at a time. Once people get to the target item, the search stops or terminates. Here there is an increase in response time with an increase in set size. By going through the items one by one, the larger the set, the longer it should take. There is also a difference in the slope of the response times for "yes" and "no" responses. For "no" responses, the function is relatively steep because the person always needs to go through the entire set to verify that the probe item is not there. However, for "yes" responses, there is an increasing response time slope, but it should be half that of "no" responses because on average people will get about halfway through the set before getting to the target item.

The final alternative is a **serial exhaustive search.** This would again involve people going through things one at a time. However, rather than stopping when they got to what they were looking for, people would continue until through the entire set. This search process would also result in an increasing response time function with increasing set size. However, if people searched in a serial exhaustive fashion, there is no difference in the response time slope for the "yes" and "no" responses. In both cases people are going through the entire set of information.

The results of one of Sternberg's studies are shown in Figure 4.9. As you can see, the data support a serial exhaustive search. This outcome is instructive in two ways. For one, it shows you information on how short-term memory is searched. The other lesson here is about our ability to report on our own memory processes. When I list out the three possible outcomes in my classes and ask students to state which one they think is true, most people pick serial self-terminating search. It may in some way be consistent with subjective experience. The fact that so many people get this wrong is important because we are talking about a simple process that occurs repeatedly throughout our lives in a portion of memory that is very close to conscious awareness. This is why memory researchers do so many studies trying to understand what may sometimes seem like a simple question to answer. It is not unusual for the results of experiments to produce counterintuitive results. We do not have much conscious awareness of how our own memories operate. We need objective measures to test our theories.

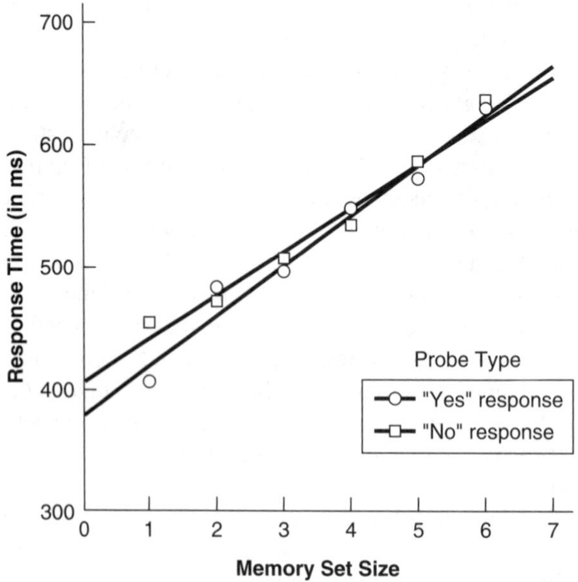

FIGURE 4.9 Results of Sternberg's Search of Short-Term Memory Task

Source: Sternberg, S. (1966). High-speed scanning in human memory. *Science, 153,* 652–654.

Serial versus Parallel Issues

An important point about the search of short-term memory is that not everyone agrees that a serial process is involved here. There are other possibilities that Sternberg did not consider. Specifically, it has been suggested that this pattern of data could result from a parallel process in which there are limited cognitive resources. When multiple elements are held in short-term memory, these resources are divided among them. This is like sending water down a pipe and then dividing the pipe into several smaller pipes, resulting in less water flowing down any one pipe. As a result, the more finely divided cognitive resources are, the less there is available to any one item, and thus the longer it takes for retrieval to occur.

This issue of serial versus parallel process has a long and tortuous history in memory research (e.g., Townsend, 1990). It is not unusual for one researcher to claim that a given process is either serial or parallel and then to have another researcher come along and demonstrate that the opposite could be true. For any process, both a serial and a parallel process can be derived to produce a certain outcome. As such, it is difficult to distinguish between the two.

For every complex memory process there are probably both parallel and serial components intermixed in *cascading* processes. The brain is composed of billions of neurons. Thus, because several neural assemblies are often simultaneously being used for memory, there is some element of parallel processing. For example, when people try to remember where they heard something, they need to know both the nature and source of the information. Memory processes can also involve stages in which latter steps simply cannot be done without the results of other, earlier steps.

Serial Position Curves

We now consider temporal influences on short-term memory. One of the most durable short-term memory effects is the **serial position curve**, shown in Figure 4.10. It has been studied since the early work of Mary Whiton Calkins in the late nineteenth century (Madigan & O'Hara, 1992). A serial position curve is a U-shaped function with memory being better for information at the beginning and end of a set compared to information in between (Murdock, 1962).

Primacy Effect. The superior memory for information at the beginning of a set is called the **primacy effect.** Traditionally, the primacy effect is not a short-term memory effect per se but is attributed to long-term memory. The idea is that items at the beginning of a set have more opportunity to be rehearsed and moved into long-term memory. For example, for the first item, all of the rehearsal effort can be devoted to it. As such, the first item has the highest probability of being transferred to long-term memory. For the second item, attention is now split between the first and second items, so it is less likely that the second item will make it to long-term memory. This logic can then be extended to the rest of the list. After a number of items, the amount of additional rehearsal benefit is negligible.

If people are given more time to rehearse information, then the primacy effect gets larger, as demonstrated in a study by Glanzer and Cunitz (1966), shown in Figure 4.11. Here, people were given information at different speeds. When the presentation rate was

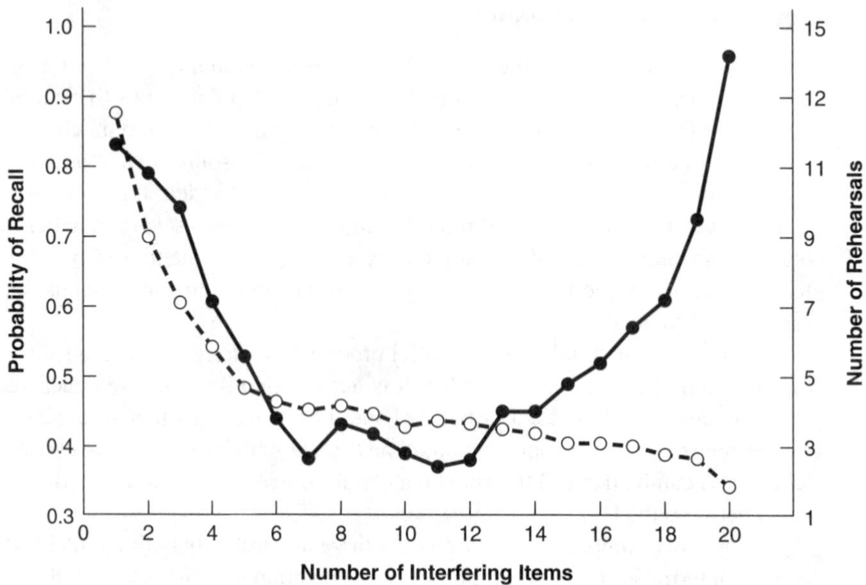

FIGURE 4.10 A Standard Serial Position Curve in Short-Term Memory. Solid dots show short-term memory, and open dots indicate the mean number of rehearsals per item

Source: Rundus, D. (1971). Analysis of rehearsal processes in free recall. *Journal of Experimental Psychology, 89,* 63–77.

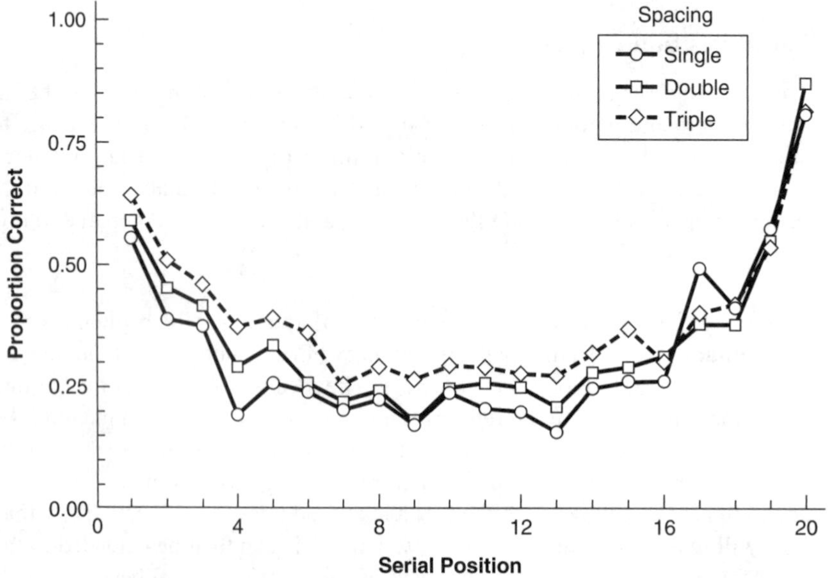

FIGURE 4.11 Effects of Additional Rehearsal Time on the Primacy Effect

Source: Glanzer, M., & Cunitz, A. R. (1966). Two storage mechanisms in free recall. *Journal of Verbal Learning and Verbal Behavior, 5,* 351–360.

slow, memory was better and the primacy effect was larger, but the recency effect was less affected. The idea that the primacy effect is dependent more on long-term than short-term memory is supported by fMRI data showing that early items (primacy effect) involve more activation of brain areas associated with long-term verbal memory, such as the left hippocampus and parts of the left temporal lobe (BA 36), whereas late items (recency effect) do not show increased activation of these areas, but show increased activation of parietal lobe areas, such as the right inferior portions (BA 39 & 40) (Talmi, Grady, Goshen-Gottstein, & Moscovitch, 2005).

Recency Effect. The other half of the serial position curve is the superior memory for information at the end of the set, which is called the **recency effect.** The recency effect can be attributed to short-term memory (Davelaar et al., 2005). These items have not been displaced by subsequent interfering information and so are less likely to be forgotten. As such, to maximize performance, it is best to try to recall the most recent things first, before you encounter potentially interfering information, and then move to whatever is stored in long-term memory. Glanzer and Cunitz's (1966) study also showed this aspect of the serial position curve. In a second experiment, people did a distractor task before they recalled the information. The results are shown in Figure 4.12. The longer the delay, the less pronounced the recency effect. However, the primacy portion of the curve, which is attributed to long-term memory, is unaffected.

More evidence to support the ideas about recency and primacy effects was found in a study by Rundus (1971).Here, people verbalized their rehearsals during memorization.

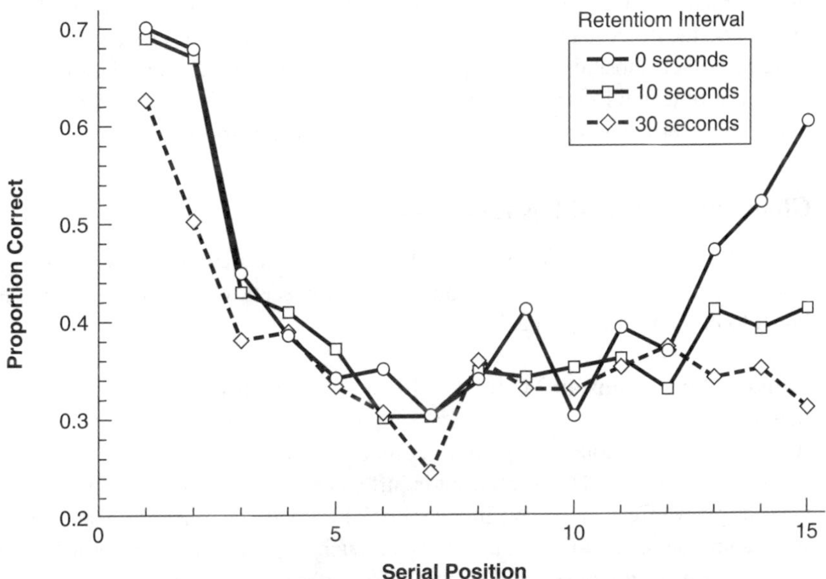

FIGURE 4.12 Effects of Different Filled Retention Intervals (in Seconds) on the Recency Effect

Source: Reprinted from *Journal of Verbal Learning and Verbal Behavior,* 5, Glanzer, M., & Cunitz, A. R., Two storage mechanisms in free recall, pp. 351–360, 1966, with permission from Elsevier.

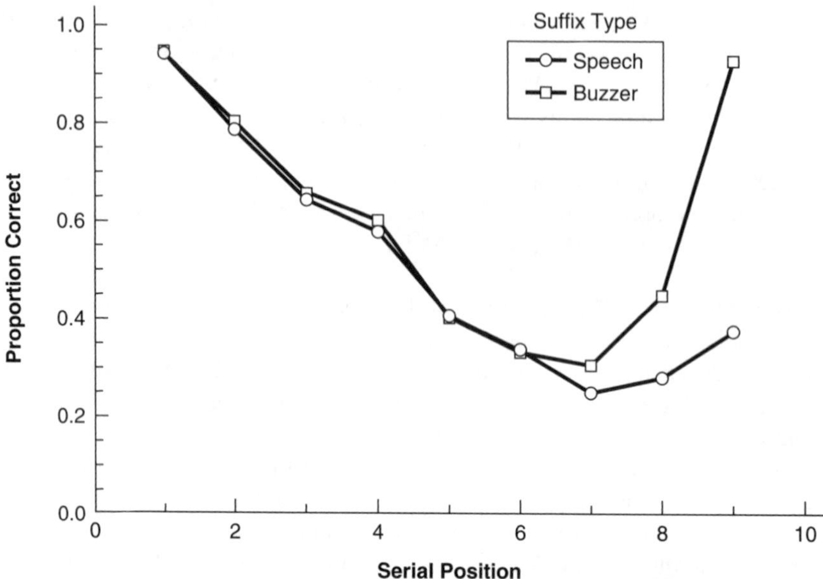

FIGURE 4.13 Suffix Effects with Human Speech and Nonhuman Nonspeech Sound

Source: Reprinted from *Journal of Verbal Learning and Verbal Behavior*, 5, Glanzer, M., & Cunitz, A. R., Two storage mechanisms in free recall, pp. 351–360, 1966, with permission from Elsevier.

What was observed was that people rehearse the earlier items a great deal. The influence of rehearsal on memory is seen in Figure 4.13. One line is the standard serial position curve, and the other is the amount of rehearsal of a given item. As can be seen, early items were rehearsed substantially and presumably they are in long-term storage. However, later items are rehearsed less. The end of the list items are remembered not because of how much they were rehearsed, but because they are still in short-term memory.

Changing the Serial Position Curve

While the serial position curve is a robust findings in memory, it is not always observed. There are things that can reduce the primacy or recency effect or eliminate it altogether. We'll look at examples of each.

Memory for Actions and Odors. Most research on serial position curves uses verbal materials, such as lists of words. In comparison, in terms of memories for recently performed actions, although they are remembered better than words (see Chapter 3), there is still some forgetting. This forgetting is influenced by serial position, but with actions there is no primacy effect (Seiler & Engelkamp, 2003). Doing something leads a person to focus more attention on the individual actions. As such, there is less opportunity to rehearse those that were done previously, and so this information is less likely to be transferred to long-term memory. As a result, no primacy effect is seen.

Also, when people are given a sequence various odors, they show a strong recency effect, but only a weak or absent primacy effect (Miles & Hodder, 2005). Items that are difficult to name tend to show recency effects, but not primacy effects, because it is more difficult to encode them into declarative long-term memory. Thus, the primacy effect, depends critically on the ability to effectively and quickly store information in long-term memory.

Suffix Effect. Another serial position phenomenon is the **suffix effect** in which the recency effect is diminished when extra information is presented at the end of a list (Conrad, 1960; Crowder & Morton, 1969). For example, suppose you heard a list of words. Then at the end of the list the experimenter either said nothing or said the word "go" to indicate that you should recall the list. In this case, the word "go" is a suffix. Memory is worse in the "go" condition than in the silence condition. The word "go" interferes with information in short-term memory, causing forgetting.

The size of the suffix effect is related to the nature of the suffix itself. The more the suffix is like the items on a list, the greater the interference and the greater the suffix effect (e.g., Ayers et al., 1979). For example, as illustrated in Figure 4.13, when the suffix was human speech, the recency effect was reduced, but not when it was an unrelated sound like that from a buzzer. It is also important what the person thinks the suffix is. For example, when people hear a list of words and then hear a "baa" sound, if they are told that the sound was made by a person, there is a larger suffix effect than if they are told it was made by a sheep, even though the same sound is used in both cases (Neath, Surprenant, & Crowder, 1993).

The suffix effect is heavily influenced by physical characteristics of a suffix, leading many researchers to consider it as part of echoic memory. This was hammered out in a marathon series of 15 experiments reported by Morton, Crowder, and Prussin (1971). They found that the suffix effect was unaffected by the suffix's meaning, its frequency, or its emotionality. However, the effect was reduced if the suffix came from a different location in space, was of a different timbre (human voice versus noise), or was from a different person, particularly one of a different gender. Thus, the suffix effect is influenced by both perceptual qualities and the conceptual understanding of what is being heard (see also Bloom, 2006).

The suffix effect occurs not only for auditory items, but also for visual information, lip reading, tactile stimuli, and odors (Campbell & Dodd, 1982; Mahrer & Miles, 1999; Miles & Jenkins, 2000; Parmentier, Tremblay, & Jones, 2004). This presence of a suffix effect in all these sensory modalities suggests that it is a general property of memory.

Memory for Serial Order

Short-term memory also retains serial order information. For example, if someone gave you a telephone number, remembering just the digits is not sufficient. You need to know the proper sequence as well. When people do forget the serial order, they do so in systematic ways. If people remember things out of order, the things they mix up are likely to be close to one another. For example, if you mess up the telephone number 123-4567, you are more likely to misremember it as 123-5467 than as 163-4527. Using an organization adopted by Henson (1998; although there are others, such as Brown, 1997 and Marshuetz, 1998), we look at the three classes of theories of memory for **serial order** (see Acheson & McDonald, 2009 and Perham, Marsh, & Jones, 2009, for the idea that serial order memory is supported by language processes).

Chaining Models. In **chaining models** (Ebbinghaus, 1913; Lewandowsky & Murdock, 1989) it is assumed that in short-term memory there are a series of associative links. Order information is recovered by moving along the associative chain. A problem with this view is that if people cannot remember an item, then the chain should be broken, and they should not be able to continue further. However, some approximation of the lost item could be used to pick up further along the chain.

Ordinal Models. In **ordinal models** order is captured by information about where a given item occurs along a dimension relative to the others. For example in the **perturbation model** (Estes, 1972) information in short-term memory is organized as a hierarchy of chunks regulated by control units. These control units themselves may be grouped together by higher-order control units. At the highest level is a control unit for the entire set. One such a hierarchy is given in Figure 4.14. The item-to-control unit associations convey order information. This can account for the fact that misorderings are more likely to occur at a local level and within chunks than across them. For example, a phone number, like 123–4567, is divided into two chunks: 123 and 4567. For the perturbation model, it is more likely that a person will misorder 4 and 5, because they are in the same chunk, than misorder 3 and 4, because they are in different chunks.

Other ordinal models are **inhibition models** (e.g., Burgess & Hitch, 1992) which suggests that inhibition, a mechanism of attention, is used to recover serial order. As a person proceeds through a list, the retrieval process selects the most active one, which is usually the first in the series. As each item is retrieved and reported, it is inhibited and then sends activation to the next item in the order, which is now the most active. Inhibition keeps that previous item from being recalled again. Serial order information then falls out of this process.

The inhibition of recently processed short-term memory information can be seen in the phenomenon of **repetition blindness** (e.g., Kanwisher, 1987), that is observed in studies in which people read sentences presented in a rapid serial visual presentation (RSVP)

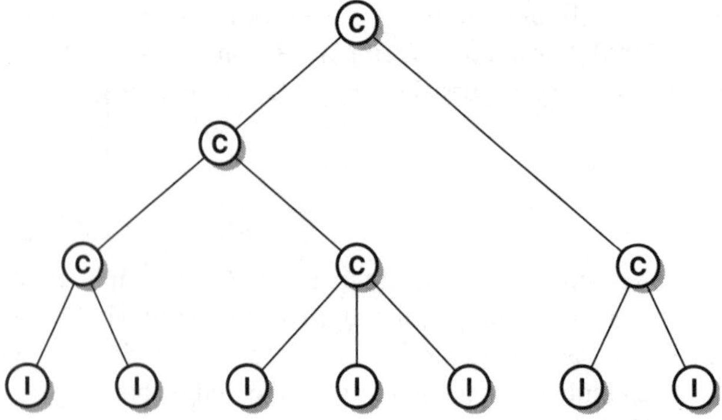

FIGURE 4.14 A Hierarchy of Control Units as Theorized by the Perturbation Model

Source: Crowder, R. G. (1972). Visual and auditory memory. In J. F. Kavanagh, & I. G. Mattingly (Eds.) Language by Ear and by Eye. Cambridge MA.: MIT Press.

format. Essentially words are presented one at a time in the same location on a computer screen in a rapid fashion but still slow enough that people can read what they are seeing. If the same word is repeated within a relatively short time span, people claim to not have seen the second occurrence of the word. For example, for the sentence "When she spilled the ink, there was ink all over" people are likely to not report the second "ink," even though this makes the sentence ungrammatical. This is because "ink" was recently processed and inhibited in short-term memory. As a result, people have trouble processing it again, even though they are looking right at it.

Positional Models. For **positional models**, serial order is conveyed by associating each item with its position in the sequence. The simplest versions of this are **slot-based models** (Conrad, 1965), which assume that short-term memory is a series of ordered slots (or boxes) and that information is dropped into each one as it is encountered. To convey order, one simply reads off what is in the slots. Here, item and order information are stored together because each item is put in a slot in a pre-determined order. However, there is little evidence to support such a simple view.

More sophisticated versions include **context-based models** (e.g., Brown, 1997; Burgess & Hitch, 1992) that exploit the fact that context is constantly in flux, even if at a very subtle level. This includes both what is going on in the environment as well as a person's internal context of their physiological, emotional, and cognitive states. This shifting context is not random but varies in regular ways, as with neural oscillators, which can then be used to identify positions in a series. It is also well known, as you will see in Chapter 7, that context information is stored in memory. This context can be used to determine order information by reconstructing the order of the context change. In this view, misorderings occur because the contexts were similar. Items that are close in time are likely to be associated with similar contexts than items farther apart. This is why local misorderings are more common than distant ones.

Finally, positional models can take into account salient positions in a series, such as the first and last positions (e.g., Henson, 1998). People are able to use these positions, and others defined in terms of them, to help reproduce a previously encountered order. An advantage of such theories is that they can account for the fact that sometimes people make errors in which an item from a previous series is misremembered in the current one. Such an error is called a *protrusion*. When protrusions occur, the incorrect item is remembered in the same position as it was in the prior series. This suggests that position information, in some way, is stored in short-term memory.

Neurological Support. The fact that there are different theories of serial order memory suggests that the way we figure out how to put things in the proper sequence is a complex process that may involve different types of information used in different ways. A review of the literature by Marshuetz (2005) showed that a number of cortical regions are involved, each playing a different role. The explicit need to remember order information requires the operation of the hippocampus, perhaps because the order itself becomes a source of content to be learned. Also, serial order memory involves increased activity in the prefrontal and parietal regions. The dorsolateral prefrontal cortex (B.A. 9 & 46) is involved in the allocation of the attention needed to encode and extract a sequence of items. Also, the portion of the parietal cortex used to code numerical magnitude (i.e., knowing that 8 is larger than 4) is also involved in tracking order information.

In addition, the premotor cortex (B.A. 6) is involved in chunking items into a sequence and its timing. Moreover, the motor cortex (B.A. 4) is involved in more detailed aspects of serial order. This makes sense from an embodied cognition perspective. Serial order is critical for many motor behaviors that would be impossible without doing things in the proper order (e.g., walking, eating, or tying your shoe laces).

Synopsis

Retrieval from short-term memory is affected by how much information is in memory, similar to what is expected from a serial exhaustive search, although there are other possibilities. Retrieval is also affected by various aspects of time. Serial position curves exhibit a primacy effect (better memory for things early on) and a recency effect (better memory for the most recent items), although the latter can be disrupted with a suffix. Finally, memory for a sequence in serial order memory is a complex process that is influenced by the associations formed between items, how the elements are chunked, and knowledge of where in a series a given item was encountered.

SUMMARY

This chapter examined issues of memory in the short term. Although the sensory registers retain large amounts of information, short-term memory has a surprisingly small capacity. This is a bottleneck in our memory. Moreover, short-term memory also loses information at an alarming rate due to interference. When we do retrieve information, our memory is better for things presented early on or near the end of a set. Also, we can reconstruct the order in which it was originally presented by chunking items, suppressing recently encountered information, and exploiting changes in context.

STUDY QUESTIONS

1. What is the point of having sensory registers as memory systems?
2. What are the characteristics of iconic, echoic, and haptic sensory memory, and why do they have these?
3. What does anorthoscopic perception tell us about sensory memory?
4. What is the capacity and duration of short-term memory? How can these be extended?
5. How does forgetting typically occur in short-term memory?
6. How is information retrieved from short-term memory?
7. What is a serial position curve, and what does it have to do with short-term memory?
8. How is short-term memory able to keep track of the order in which things are to occur?

KEY TERMS

anorthoscopic perception, chaining model, chunking, context-based models, decay, echoic memory, haptic sensory memory, icon, iconic memory, inhibition models, interference, ordinal models, parallel search, perturbation model, positional models, primacy effect, recency effect, repetition blindness, sensory registers, serial position curve, serial self-terminating search, serial exhaustive search, serial order, short-term memory, slot-based models, suffix effect

TRY IT OUT

In this chapter there are a number of ideas for research on short-term memory. Here we'll look at three ideas you can use to develop studies. These include studies of short-term memory capacity, serial position curves, and the suffix effect. Ideally you should have at least 12 participants for each task, with at least 12 people in each group if you decide to vary things in your own experiment between groups. Now, using these basic ground rules, here are some things you could do:

- Do an assessment of short-term memory **capacity** by giving a group of people progressively larger, randomly ordered sets of items to remember. These can be digits, letters, or even simple words. Start with small sets of items, such as two, and work up to larger set sizes, with five-item lists for each set size. Present one item at a time, for a 1 second each. At the end of the list, the person should write down the items in the order they were given. If a person cannot get any of the lists correct at a given level (e.g., none of the five-item lists), then you can stop. Afterward score each person in terms of the highest level that they could recall a list. If a person gets only one of the lists at the highest level, score that level as a half. If the person gets two or more, give him or her full credit. If all goes well, most people should have a highest recall level between five and nine.
- To demonstrate a **serial position curve** (see Zechmeister & Nyberg, 1982) read participants a list of 15 single-syllable words. At the end of the list have people write down as many as they can remember. If all goes well, what you should find is that people remember more words from the beginning and end of the list, but fewer from the middle. You can do a number of variations of this by altering list lengths, giving a second group of people a 30-second distractor task of math problems (e.g., 935 + 135 = ?) (to eliminate the recency effect), or have people verbalize their rehearsals to see the relationship of these and the primacy effect.
- To demonstrate a **suffix effect** you will need two groups of people. Before the study, set up 11 lists of digits (from 1 to 9) in which there are eight digits, in a random order, in each list. Make sure there are no repeats within a list, and no sequential runs (e.g., 7, 8, 9). Read people the list of digits. Their task will be to recall them, in order, after the end of a list. They can write their responses on a sheet of paper with a box for each of the eight digits. People can put an "X" in a box if they cannot

remember a digit at a given position. In the *control* group, people should start recalling when you have finished reading the eight digits. In the *suffix* group, at the end of each list give the digit 0. Tell those people to not start recalling until they hear the 0, and not to write down the 0. After all 11 lists, look at how people did. Throw out the first list as practice. Then, count up the number of errors. If all goes well, you should find that memory will be worse for people in the suffix group than for people in the control group (see Zechmeister & Nyberg, 1982).

CHAPTER FIVE

WORKING MEMORY

In Chapter 4 we dealt with the retention of information in the short term. We saw that short-term memory includes conscious experience, but conscious experience involves more than just retaining information over time. Things we are conscious of are being thought about. This "thinking" implies an active processing or manipulating of information. For example, when you are thinking about how to get to a mall you have never been to before, you combine various bits of knowledge you already have: the layout of the city, information from a map, knowledge of traffic patterns in that area, and conversations with your friends about the location of the mall. By actively using this information, you can determine the best route to take. This involves the controlled use of information in short-term memory. Because of the special nature of this kind of processing, this is referred to as **working memory**. The phrase *short-term memory* is reserved more for the brief retention of information. In fact, some researchers consider working memory and short-term memory to be different psychological constructs (e.g., Cantor, Engle, & Hamilton, 1991).

This chapter overviews some of the major issues involved with working memory. This overview adopts the perspective of one of the more popular theories of working memory. We examine the role of each part of working memory and some of the memory phenomena associated with it. Finally, we consider some applications of working memory to more complex levels of processing.

BADDELEY'S MULTICOMPONENT THEORY

The most prominent theory of working memory is **Baddeley's multicomponent model** (Baddeley, 1986, 2000; Baddeley & Hitch, 1974). This theory assumes that working memory is made up of several components: (1) the phonological loop, (2) the visuo-spatial sketchpad, (3) the episodic buffer, and (4) the central executive. An overview of this model is presented in Figure 5.1. The phonological loop, visuo-spatial sketchpad, and episodic buffer are specialized subsystems under the control of a generalized executive controller, which runs the operation. The phonological loop is part of working memory that is responsible for processing verbal and auditory information. The visuo-spatial sketchpad is responsible for processing visual and spatial knowledge. The episodic buffer is where multimodal information from different sources is combined or bound together.

The phonological loop and visuo-spatial sketchpad subsystems are relatively separate from each another and these different types of information tend not to influence

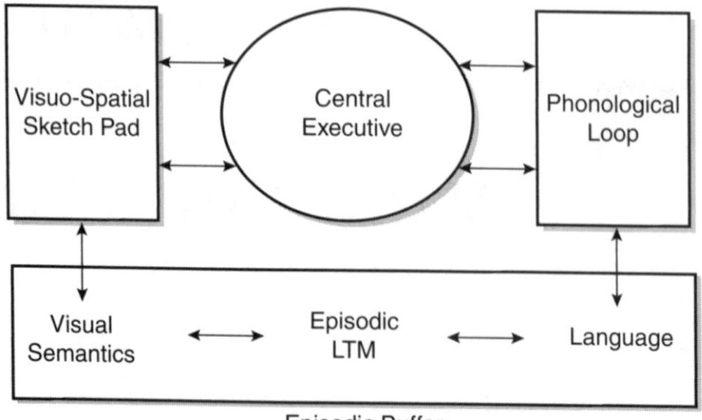

FIGURE 5.1 Baddeley Model of Working Memory

Source: Baddeley, A. D. (2000). The episodic buffer: A new component of working memory? *Trends in Cognitive Science*, 4, 417–423.

one another. For example, if you are trying to think about verbal information, such as reading a chapter in a book, you have more interference and distraction if you are exposed to other verbal or auditory information, such as listening to a radio. However, your reading is relatively unaffected by spatial tasks, such as tapping out a beat with your hand. Conversely, visual-spatial tasks, such as tracing a route on a map, are disrupted by other visual-spatial tasks but not by verbal tasks (Baddeley & Andrade, 2000). There is interference if two tasks require resources from the same part of working memory. For example, people have difficulty detecting visual and auditory signals if they are maintaining visual and auditory images, respectively (Segal & Fusella, 1970, 1971) or, conversely, evaluating mental images when viewing distracting pictures (Lloyd-Jones & Vernon, 2003). Across system deficits are typically observed only when executive controller processes are affected, such as when the tasks require relatively large loads (Morey & Cowan, 2005).

The episodic buffer is a newer part of Baddeley's theory. The episodic buffer integrates or binds information from different sources. Like the phonological loop and visuo-spatial sketchpad, the episodic buffer is a limited capacity, temporary storage system. There is only so much information it can handle at one time. What makes it unique is that it binds together information from the two subsystems, as well as information from long-term memory. The result is a unified episodic memory trace of an event. For example, your memory will include how things looked, the sound of a person's voice, where things were, what they meant, and so on, all integrated into a single memory trace.

The central executive is the control center of working memory. Although each subsystem has some degree of processing capacity, the central executive has additional capacity that it can devote to a subsystem if the demands on it become taxing. For example, if you are thinking about a difficult problem while walking, you may stop walking because the visual-spatial part of working memory that helps you navigate has some of its resources taken away by the central executive to be used elsewhere. One of the more important jobs of the central executive is to regulate the flow of information in the current stream of thought, which can be done in a number of ways. Some believe the suppression of irrelevant information is an important determinate in how effective the central executive is in controlling working memory (e.g., Kane, Bleckley, Conway, & Engle, 2001).

While Baddeley's theory is popular, it is not the only one. Other theories don't have separate subsystems, but assume a single working memory system (e.g., Guérard & Tremblay, 2008). These views account for the differential impact of verbal and visual-spatial interference based on information similarity. Other theories (e.g., Kane & Engle, 2002) assume that working memory is an attentional control system in which how effectively people process multiple pieces of information depends on the effectiveness with which people control the current stream of processing. Such theories can account for a broad range of findings, such as the fact that working memory processes can be disrupted by irrelevant tactile stimulation (i.e., feeling something on your skin that you don't expect) (e.g., Dalton, Lavie, & Spence, 2009).

There are also a number of aspects of thinking that it does not capture. For example, the idea of working memory is relatively isolated from the rest of what a person is doing. However, working memory is operating in a complex environment in meaningful ways that can influence performance. Take the example of people's body movements while they are thinking problems through. People who gesture when solving problems, such as math problems, have better memory for that information than those who do not gesture (Wagner, Nusbaum, & Goldin-Meadow, 2004). So, manipulating information in working memory is a complex and intricate process.

PHONOLOGICAL LOOP

Of the various parts of working memory, the **phonological loop** has received the most attention. This may be because much of the work on working memory follows from research in the Ebbinghaus/verbal learning tradition, and the phonological loop is concerned with processing verbal information. Studies of the phonological loop focus on linguistic materials, which are either read or heard, although other acoustic phenomena have been studied. As such, the parts of the brain often implicated in phonological loop processing include the more linguistic aspects of the temporal lobe (Jonides, Lacy, & Nee, 2005).

Components

The phonological loop has two parts: the **phonological store** and the **articulatory loop** (see Figure 5.2). The phonological store is a temporary storehouse, whereas the articulatory loop is for active rehearsal. A helpful analogy is that the phonological store is like an inner ear that listens to what we say to ourselves, and the articulatory loop is like our inner voice that says what we are thinking. The way the system works is that information first enters the phonological store. Over time, this information decays and is eventually lost. To prevent this, the articulatory loop can be engaged: By actively rehearsing the information in the phonological store, it is refreshed and preserved. The more information that is held in the phonological store, the harder the task of the articulatory loop and the more likely information will degrade to the point that it cannot be recovered and, so, is forgotten. This same basic process operates over language processing in general, including non-spoken languages, such as American Sign Language (Wilson & Fox, 2007).

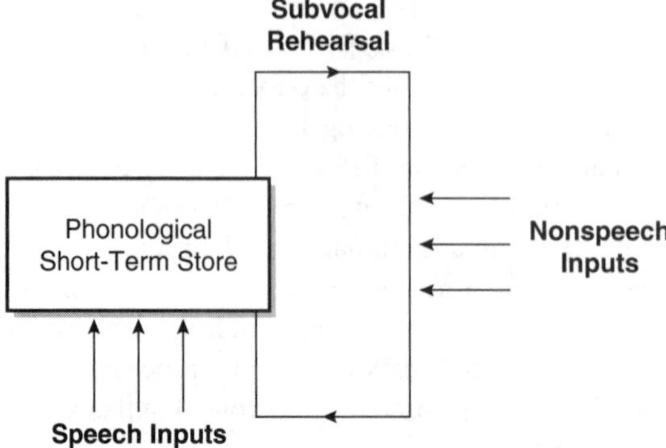

FIGURE 5.2 The Phonological Loop, with the Phonological Store and the Articulatory Loop

Source: Gathercole, S. E. (1997). Models of verbal short-term memory. In M. A. Conway (Ed.), *Cognitive Models of Memory*, pp. 13–45. Cambridge, MA: MIT Press.

Phenomena of the Phonological Loop

To illustrate the role of the phonological loop let's look at some major effects that have been observed (Gathercole, 1997). These provide insight into various characteristics of working memory.

Word Length Effect. The **word length effect** is the finding that a person's word span is smaller for longer words than for shorter words. This refers to articulation duration, not spelling or number of syllables (Baddeley, Thomson, & Buchanan, 1975). The longer it takes to say the words, the fewer that can be readily recalled. For example, keeping the number of syllables constant, more short-duration words, such as "wicket" and "bishop," can be remembered relative to long-duration words, such as "harpoon" and "Friday." Word length effects are even found in people who cannot speak (Baddeley & Wilson, 1985; Bishop & Robson, 1989), suggesting that the phonological loop captures the auditory properties of spoken language (, see Hulme et al., 2004 and Bireta, Neath, & Surprenant, 2006, for evidence that the word length effect disappears in mixed lists). The word length effect occurs because more time is needed to rehearse some items in a set, leading other items not to be refreshed, and more likely to be forgotten (Cowan, Baddeley, Elliott, & Norris, 2003).

A well-known finding is that Chinese speakers have larger digit spans than English speakers, who in turn have larger digit spans than Welsh speakers (Hoosain & Salili, 1988). This is related to the length of the digits words in the language. In Chinese, they are all monosyllables, whereas English has digit names that are multisyllabic, thereby lengthening articulation time. For example "seven" in English is "qi" in Chinese. Welsh has even longer digit names. Moreover, the digit span of Chinese-English bilinguals varies, depending on the language the person is speaking. A similar line of reasoning, in terms of "articulation time," has been used to explain the finding that memory spans are smaller with American Sign Language (ASL) than spoken language (Wilson & Emmorey, 2006). The signs take longer to produce.

Articulatory Suppression. The **articulatory suppression** effect is a reduced verbal span when a person is speaking while simultaneously trying to remember a set of items (Murray, 1967; Peterson & Johnson, 1971). For example, suppose a person is given a set of words to hold in memory. While the person receives the words, he or she says some word over and over—for example, "the" (i.e., "the", "the", "the", etc.). This results in a reduction in memory span. Talking about one thing makes it difficult to remember something else. For example, if someone tells you his or her name and college major at a party while you are engaged in conversation with someone else, this will impede your ability to rehearse and remember that particular name and major. In some sense, this is the suffix effect run amok. An articulatory suppression task, such as repeating the word "the," takes up resources from the articulatory loop, information in the phonological store cannot be adequately refreshed, and so it is lost.

Irrelevant Speech. The **irrelevant speech effect** is the finding that the phonological loop is less efficient when there is irrelevant speech in the background, even if it is in a language people don't understand (Colle & Welsh, 1976). You may have had the experience of trying to read in a room where other people are talking. It is difficult to concentrate on your reading because the background voices enter working memory and takes up some of the resources of the phonological loop, causing what you are reading to be forgotten.

This has implications for the best way to study. Salame and Baddeley (1989) had students try to remember information either in silence or while listening to instrumental music or music with vocals. The results, shown in Figure 5.3, reveal that memory was best

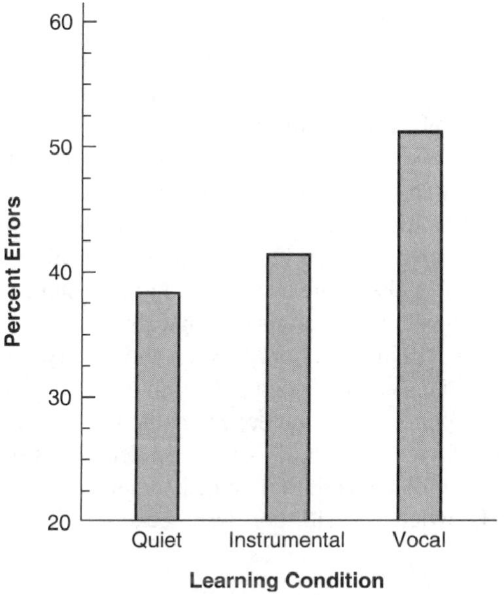

FIGURE 5.3 Working Memory Performance with Different Types of Background Music

Source: Salame, P., & Baddeley, A. (1989). Effects of background music on phonological short-term memory. *Quarterly Journal of Experimental Psychology, 41A,* 107–122. Reprinted by permission of the Experimental Psychology Society. http://www.psypress.co.uk/journals

when students were in quiet. When there was background noise that involved language, such as music with vocals, memory was worse. Listening to instrumental music had a moderate effect. The linguistic nature of the irrelevant speech of the music with vocals interfered with the operation of the phonological loop. Therefore, when you study, it is best to do so under quiet conditions. If you must have background noise, choose instrumental music rather than music with vocals or, even worse, television.

Phonological Similarity. The **phonological similarity effect** is the finding that more phonologically similar the items in a set are, the more memory errors that are made (Baddeley, 1966; Conrad & Hull, 1964). So, when the words share the same sounds (e.g., "whole," "bowl," "boat," "bone," and "phone") people forget more than when the words do not share the same sounds (e.g., "whole," "line," "milk," "fire," and "hunt"). Performance is not as bad when the words in the list rhyme (share the same ending sound), worse when they are alliterative (share the same beginning sound), and worst when both of these are occurring (Gupta, Lipinski, & Aktunc, 2005). Under these circumstances, people are more likely to misremember a similar sounding word. For example, if one of the words was "bowl," people might misremember it as "roll," which sounds similar but looks different, but not "fowl," which looks similar but sounds different. This is because information is degrading in the phonological store. When it is time for an item to be rehearsed, some reconstruction may be needed. Because phonological information is auditory, this reconstruction is based on the fragmentary phonological information. For phonologically similar items, it is difficult to keep track of which ones have and have not been rehearsed. This makes it more likely that an unrehearsed item is not refreshed, and forgetting occurs (Li, Schweickert, & Gandour, 2000).

Semantics. It should be noted that all of these effects do not take into account knowledge in long-term memory. However, working memory is influenced by prior knowledge. For example, memory spans are larger for lists of words than for nonwords. This is the **lexicality effect** (Hulme, Maughan, & Brown, 1991). People use long-term knowledge to support and reconstruct information in the phonological store. Information in long-term memory can even reverse some phonological loop effects. For example, for the phonological similarity effect, performance is worse when items are phonologically similar. However, if these words are embedded in the context of meaningful sentences, this effect reverses: performance is better for words which are phonologically similar rather than different (Copeland & Radvansky, 2001). This commonly occurs with poetry and song lyrics. People can draw on knowledge of the sentence along with memory of the rhyme scheme to come up with the appropriate response. For example, you could remember "pole" if you know that all of the words in a set rhyme with "hole" and the sentence was something like "The vaulter was surprised when he discovered that he had somehow broken his ____." Thus, people can use long-term knowledge to aid short-term recall.

Synopsis

The phonological loop is geared toward processing verbal/acoustic information. This is done using the phonological store and the articulatory loop. Evidence for the operation of the phonological loop comes from findings such as the word length effect, articulatory suppression, the irrelevant speech effect, the phonological similarity effect, and the lexicality effect. All of these generally hang together to provide a convincing story of how working memory handles verbal/linguistic information.

VISUO-SPATIAL SKETCHPAD

Another major working memory subsystem is the **visuo-spatial sketchpad**, which is responsible for visual information (e.g., size or color), and spatial information (e.g., orientations or spatially manipulation). Although some researchers suggest that there are separate spatial and visual components (Darling, Della Sala, & Logie, 2009; Klauer & Zhao, 2004) we will treat them together. As you read about different aspects of the visuo-spatial sketchpad, note how they often incorporate some element of embodied cognition.

It should be noted that the visuo-spatial sketchpad involves more of the right hemisphere than the left, consistent with the idea that the right hemisphere is dominant for spatial and holistic processing. More specifically, the premotor cortex (B.A. 6) is important for the visuo-spatial sketchpad's active processing (Smith, 2000), as well as portions of the parietal lobes involved in perception (Jonides, Lacy, & Nee, 2005).

Mental Images

One of the main tasks of the visuo-spatial sketchpad is the construction, maintenance, and manipulation of mental images. This is done by creating images that are isomorphically related to perceptual images. For example, mental images are sensitive to object size and viewer distance. People are better able to identify the components of an image if the image is large or the viewing distance is close (Kosslyn, 1975).

Mental images must be actively maintained in the visuo-spatial sketchpad, or they degrade. This is outlined in the CRT model of visual imagery (Kosslyn, 1975). For some televisions, the image you see on a screen (sometimes a cathode ray tube or CRT) is not projected all at once. Instead, it is continuously being refreshed, with a cathode ray constantly scanning from the top of the image to the bottom and then starting over. The speed at which this is done is the refresh rate. Even a static image is constantly decaying and being reconstructed. The CRT model assumes a similar process for the visuo-spatial sketchpad. A mental image is constantly decaying, and being refreshing, much like what goes on in the articulatory loop as described earlier.

In support of this, like the word length effect, people find it harder to maintain complex than simple images (Kosslyn, 1975). The more image components there are, the more elements the visuo-spatial sketchpad needs to refresh, and the greater the opportunity for forgetting to occur. Similarly, it has been found that larger images are harder to maintain than smaller images, for similar reasons.

Visual Scanning

How does the visuo-spatial sketchpad manipulate information, and toward what aim? One of its roles is as a surrogate for physical reality. A person might make decisions about objects at two different locations using working memory. A person may scan across his or her mental map of the area. Mental scanning increases proportionately with the distance that needs to be covered. Short distances are scanned in a short time, but longer distances require more mental effort and time. In one study, Kosslyn and his colleagues had people memorize a map of an island, like the one in Figure 5.4. The task was to verify some aspect of one of the island locations. The results shown in Figure 5.5 reveal that response time increased with increased distance from one location to another. Mental imagery processes in working memory rely on similar visual and spatial processes as those used during perception, except that a person needs to produce the images himself or herself. It is this constant image generation that can sometimes lead to errors in visuo-spatial working memory (Kosslyn & Pomerantz, 1977).

Thus, processing information in the visuo-spatial sketchpad has isomorphic perceptual qualities similar to what it would be in reality. A striking example of this was a study by Intons-Peterson and Roskos-Ewoldsen (1989) with students at Indiana University. In this study, students did mental scanning, as in the Kosslyn study. However, rather than a map of an island, the students used their knowledge of the Bloomington campus. More importantly, students were to imagine themselves going from one location to another, carrying either a balloon or a load of bricks. In both cases, response time increased with greater distances that needed to be mentally traveled. Moreover, the increase in response time was greater when the students imagined they were carrying the heavy load rather than the light one. Thus, the operation of working memory can capture aspects of the world in a direct fashion.

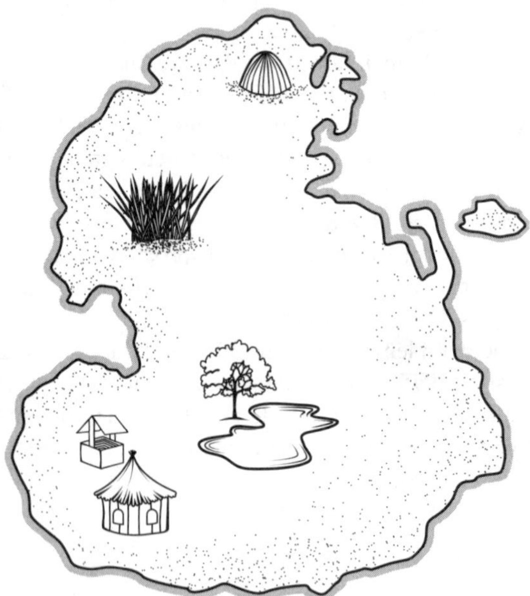

FIGURE 5.4 Map of an Island Used in Kosslyn's Mental Scanning Experiments

Source: Kosslyn, S. M. (1980). *Image and Mind.* Cambridge, MA: Harvard University Press.

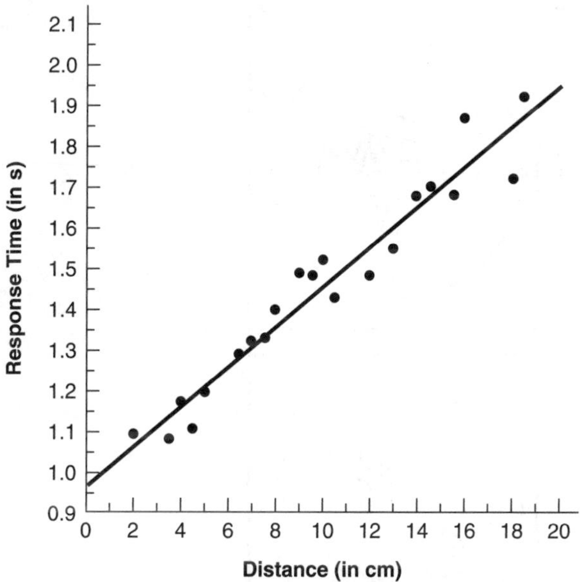

FIGURE 5.5 Response Time in Kosslyn's Mental Scanning Study as a Function of Distance on the Island Map

Source: Kosslyn, S. M. (1980). *Image and Mind.* Cambridge, MA: Harvard University Press.

Mental Rotation

Another visuo-spatial working memory process is **mental rotation,** in which a person needs to mentally turn some object. This might be done so that a person can make a decision, such as identifying it. For example, a sign that is upside down is difficult to read. You must mentally rotate the letters or numbers to decipher the message. Another possibility is that a person may need to compare two objects for some purpose. For example, a person working on a jigsaw puzzle may mentally rotate the pieces to see if they might fit together before actually picking up the pieces and trying them out.

Much like visual scanning, mental rotation has characteristics that mimic physical rotation. The greater the degree of rotation required, the longer it takes to do the task. In a study by Shepard and Metzler (1971), students saw pairs of three-dimensional figures, like the ones in Figure 5.6, with the task of saying whether the figures were the same or different. These figures could be rotated either in the picture plane (as is the case with the figure pair on the top) or in depth (as in the case with the figure pair in the middle). The results, as seen in Figure 5.7, showed that response time increased with the degree of rotation that was needed. The students were mentally turning the object about in their visuo-spatial sketchpad.

This mental rotation in working memory reflects embodied cognition. People perform the task mentally as if they were actually turning an object. This is reinforced by the finding that if there is unseen tactile feedback, such as feeling the actual object being turned in one's hand, then performance improves (Wraga, Creem, & Proffitt, 2000). This benefit is not observed if people feel the object and it is not rotated, if a different object is rotated, or if the rotation is in a different direction (Wraga, Swaby, & Flynn, 2008).

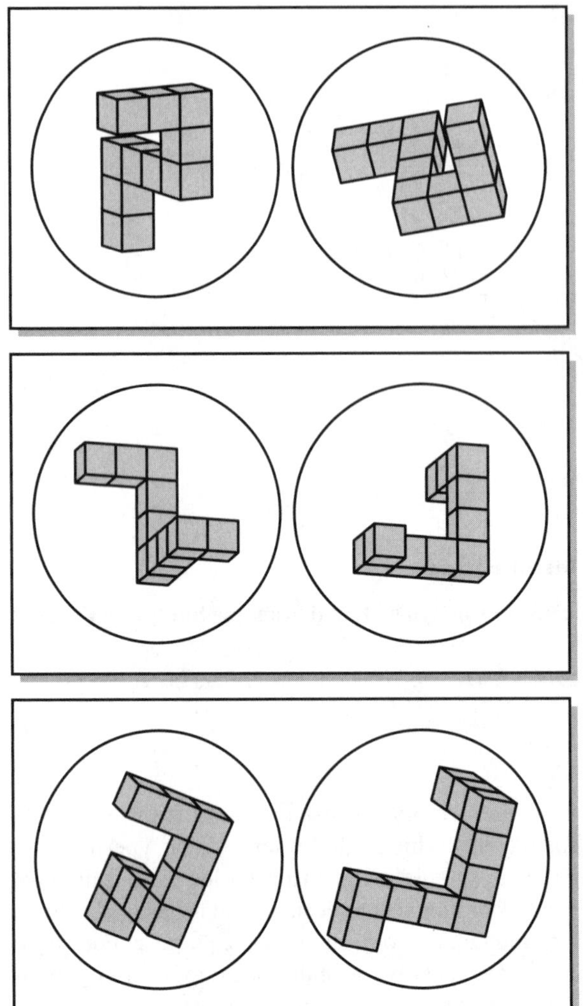

FIGURE 5.6 Object Pairs Used in Shepard and Metzler Mental Rotation Study

Source: Shepard, R. N., & Metzler, J. (1971). Mental rotation of three-dimensional objects. *Science, 171,* 701–703.

Like other visuo-spatial sketchpad tasks, mental rotation has neurological underpinnings. Here, the parietal lobes are more involved than other parts of the cortex, although there is some coordinating support from the frontal lobes. Furthermore, if mental rotation is particularly demanding, there may be more left hemisphere involvement, suggesting an increase in analytic processing (Just et al., 2001). Although many visuo-spatial processes involve more right hemisphere activity, when more holistic processing is needed—in cases where more analytical processing is needed—there might be more left hemisphere dominance.

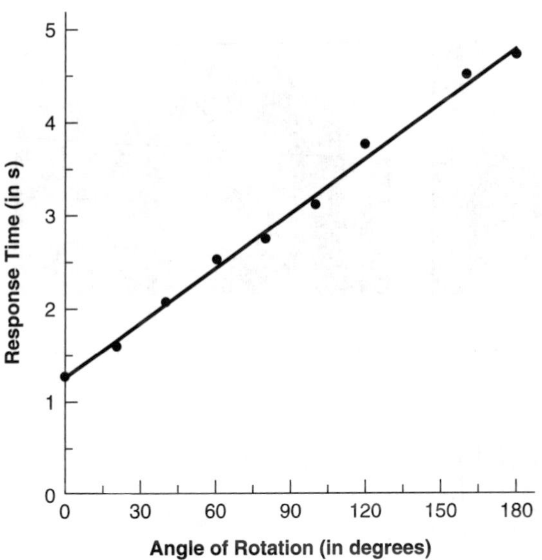

FIGURE 5.7 Response Time Results from Shepard and Metzler's Mental Rotation Study

Source: Shepard, R. N., & Metzler, J. (1971). Mental rotation of three-dimensional objects. *Science, 171,* 701–703.

Boundary Extension

The operation of the visuo-spatial sketchpad is also observed in the phenomenon of **boundary extension.** As noted in the discussion of iconic and trans-saccadic memory in Chapter 4, when we view the world, we are only getting bits and pieces of it at a time. What gives us the experience of being in a world filled with more visual information than is actually experienced? In part, we fill in beyond the edges with what we *think* should be there. This is especially striking in memory of pictures, television shows, or movies. For example, when you remember a movie, it is unlikely that your memory contains your experience of the edge of the screen and the theater beyond that. You remember more of the scene than you actually saw. This memory for details beyond what is seen is boundary extension (Intraub, Bender, & Mangels, 1992; Intraub & Berkowits, 1996; Intraub & Richardson, 1989).

In studies of boundary extension, people might see a series of photos, such as those in Figure 5.8. Then they would be see pictures with the task of identifying whether each was one seen before (old) or not (new). Some would be old, original versions. However, some shots would be closer up, and others would be taken from further back (and thereby extending the boundary of the original). People make more errors by selecting pictures that were taken from further out. Moreover, if people were asked to draw what they saw, their drawings tended to include information beyond the boundaries of the image. People fill in the surrounding space when the information is processed in the visuo-spatial sketchpad and then incorporated this into their memory of the scene. Boundary extension occurs even when images were viewed briefly (Intraub, Gottesman, Willey, & Zuk, 1996), even as short as 42 ms (Intraub & Dickinson, 2008) or when people were warned ahead of time that boundary extension could occur (Intraub & Bodamer, 1993).

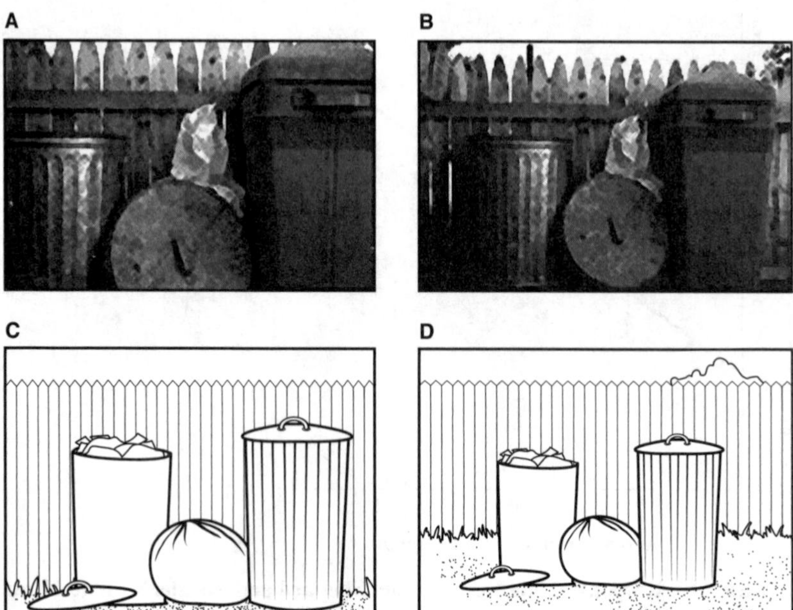

FIGURE 5.8 Example of Stimuli and Responses from a Study on Boundary Extension People tend to remember having seen a greater expanse of a scene than was shown in a photograph. For example, when drawing the close-up view in Panel A from memory, the person's drawing (Panel C) contained extended boundaries. Another person, shown a more wide-angle view of the same scene (Panel B), also drew the scene with extended boundaries (Panel D). (Note: To evaluate the drawings in the figure, it is important to study the boundaries of each drawing and its associated stimulus.)

Source: Intraub, H., & Richardson, M. (1989). Wide-angle memories of close-up scenes. *Journal of Experimental Psychology: Learning, Memory, and Cognition, 15,* 179–187.

Still, boundary extension is not an automatic, unconscious process. For it to occur, a person must think that what is being viewed is a scene from the world. There must be some sort of background, even if the background is only imagined (Intraub, Gottesman, & Bills, 1998). Pictures of objects without a background do not produce boundary extension (Gottesman & Intraub, 2002). Thus, the operation of the visuo-spatial sketchpad depends on knowledge in long-term memory. If a picture does not activate this knowledge, then no boundary extension occurs.

Dynamic Memory

There are other visuo-spatial sketchpad processes that alter perceptual experiences based on physical characteristics. These involve the interpretation of either the real or perceived motion. Because of this, it is called **dynamic memory** (see Hubbard, 1995b, 2005 for reviews).

Representational Momentum. When we watch moving objects and blink or look away briefly, they are likely to continue in motion. This idea of continued motion is captured in the visuo-spatial sketchpad. There is a bias for people to misremember the location or orientation of an object further along its path of motion than it actually was the last time it was seen (Freyd, 1987; Freyd & Finke, 1984, 1985). This is called **representational momentum.** It is as if people have difficulty stopping the object in their visuo-spatial sketchpad. An example of representational momentum is shown in Figure 5.9. Here, a box appears to be rotating across a series of displays, much like a cartoon. After the last display there is a delay, and people are given a test display. The task is to say whether the object is in the same orientation as it was when it was last seen. These test objects can be the actual last display, a box rotated slightly backward, or a box rotated slightly forward. The results, shown in Figure 5.10, reveal a tendency for people to misremember the box as being further along in its rotation than it actually was.

Representational momentum is observed along the path of the object's trajectory (Hubbard, 1990). For example, if you see a car moving along a street, and then it disappears behind a bush, you would misremember the car as being further along its path of travel when you last saw it than it actually was. Representational momentum is influenced by the apparent speed with which the object is moving, with faster objects exhibiting more representational momentum (Hubbard & Bharucha, 1988). This effect can take into account other regular properties of the world. For example, one may claim to remember a pendulum beginning its backswing when that has not yet occurred (Verfaillie & Y'dewalle, 1991) or remembering a ball bouncing off a wall before it happens (Hubbard & Bharucha, 1988).

Representational momentum can also reflect properties such as a centripetal force (Hubbard, 1996). This involves active processing in the visuo-spatial sketchpad because the amount of distortion observed is directly related to the speed of the mental rotation. The faster people mentally rotate, the greater the distortion (Munger, Solberg, & Horrocks, 1999). It should be noted that representational momentum tends to follow medieval impetus theories of motion rather than Newtonian or other modern views. This is true even for people who

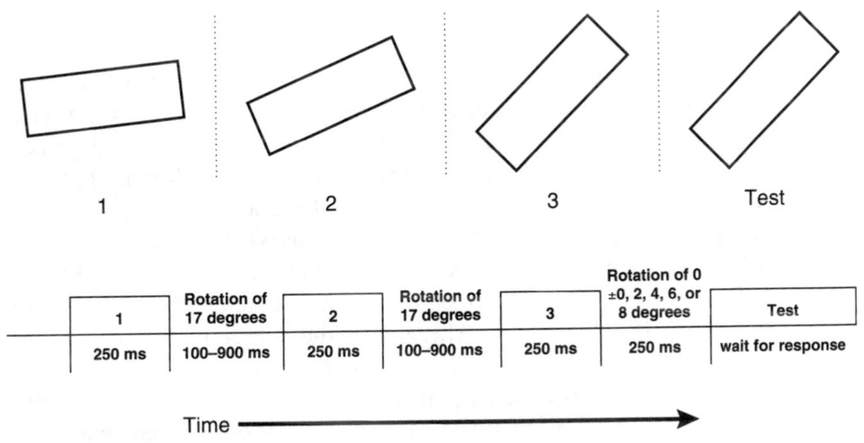

FIGURE 5.9 A Representational Momentum Display

Source: Freyd, J. J., & Finke, R. A. (1984). Representational momentum. *Journal of Experimental Psychology: Learning, Memory, and Cognition, 10,* 126–132.

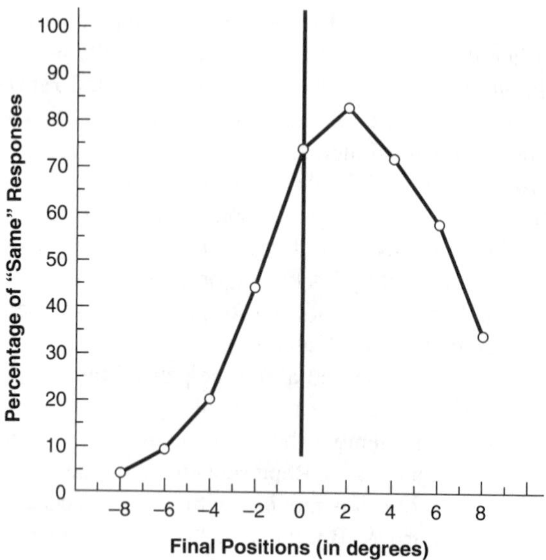

FIGURE 5.10 Results from a Study of Representational Momentum. Note that estimates of final position are distorted in the direction of the object's motion

Source: Reprinted from *Cognitive Psychology,* 19, Kelly, M. H., & Freyd, J. J., Explorations of Representational Momentum, pp. 369–401, 1987, with permission from Elsevier.

are experts in physics (Kozhevnikov & Hegarty, 2001), suggesting that this aspect of working memory is limited in terms of how it is influenced by knowledge in long-term memory (but see Courtney & Hubbard, 2008, for the insulating effects of training). It is important to note that this process may not be specific to visuo-spatial processing as representation momentum effects are also observed with music pitches moving up or down (Kelly & Freyd, 1987).

Representational Gravity. Representational gravity is the finding that memory for object tends to be distorted toward the earth, especially when the objects are not supported (Freyd, Pantzer, & Cheng, 1988; Hubbard, 1995a), as shown in Figure 5.11. Here, people viewed a plant that is initially on top of a table or suspended by a hook. Then in a later display, the table or hook was absent. People were then tested for their memory of the plant's location. People tend to remember it as being lower in the picture. This is consistent with the idea that representational gravity is influencing the visuo-spatial memory, moving the plant lower.

Similarly, if a circle is seen on an incline, it is remembered as being further down the incline, as if it had rolled. The greater the degree of the incline, the greater the distortion. Also, objects moving along in space may be remembered as being lower than they originally were, as if being pulled down by gravity (Hubbard, 1990). Larger, and presumably heavier, objects fall faster (greater effects of representational gravity) than do smaller ones (Hubbard, 1997). This is another example of visuo-spatial working memory taking into account physical principles to anticipate what will happen next. For example, if you see a paint can tipping off a ladder, you don't need to watch it fall to know that will

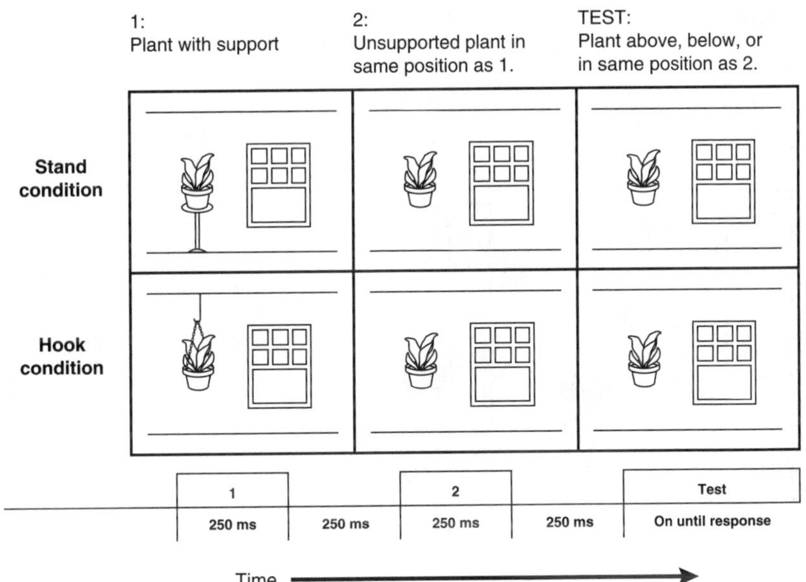

FIGURE 5.11 Representational Gravity Display

Source: Freyd, J. J., Pantzer, T. M., & Cheng, J. L. (1988). Representing statics as forces in equilibrium. *Journal of Experimental Psychology: General, 117,* 395–407.

be coming down, and you need to move out of the way. Although it seems similar to representational momentum, representational gravity appears to be a different mental process (Motes, Hubbard, Courtney, & Rypma, 2008).

Representational Friction. Representational friction is the finding that moving objects slow down more when moving along another object (such as the ground) that can produce friction (Hubbard, 1995). In some sense, representational friction puts the brakes on representational momentum. Overall, it is as if people unconsciously predict the outcome of events while processing them in the visuo-spatial sketchpad.

Context. A final thing to note about dynamic memory is that it exhibits context effects. The physical property that is exerted can vary depending on what that object is. In one study people saw an object moving up a computer screen. This was either a rocket or a church steeple. Rockets typically travel upward, whereas church steeples do not. As can be seen in Figure 5.12, there was greater upward displacement in working memory when it was a rocket than when it was a steeple (Reed & Vinson, 1996).

Synopsis

The visuo-spatial sketchpad is for processing visual and spatial information. It captures many qualities of the world in an analog and isomorphic format as illustrated by things such as mental scanning and rotation effects, as well as boundary extension. Its dynamic

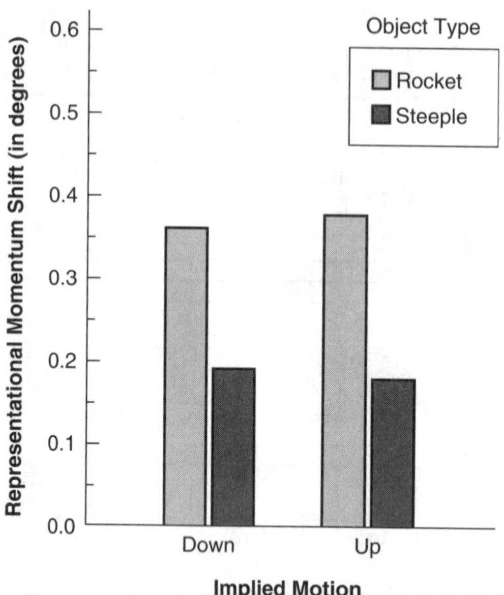

FIGURE 5.12 Influence of Object Context on Representational Momentum. Both a rocket and a church steeple were viewed moving upward across a computer screen. The representational momentum was greater in the rocket than in the steeple

Source: Reed, C. L., & Vinson, N. G. (1996). Conceptual effects on representational momentum. *Journal of Experimental Psychology: Human Perception and Performance, 22,* 839–850.

operation on information in working memory is seen in effects such as representational momentum, gravity, and friction. This aspect of working memory allows us to better function in a dynamic, fast-moving world.

EPISODIC BUFFER

The **episodic buffer** is a recent addition to the theory of working memory, so there is not as much to say about it here. As a reminder, the role of the episodic buffer is to bind together information from various sources to form episodic memory traces. These sources can include information in the phonological loop and visuo-spatial sketchpad, as well as long-term memory. This binding process uses attention, and can be disrupted by concurrent tasks (Elsley & Parmentier, 2009).

The operation of the episodic buffer integration was shown in a study by Jefferies, Lambon Ralph and Baddeley (2004). In this study, people were given either lists of words or sentences with the task of recalling them later. While they were holding these items in memory, people did a demanding spatial distractor task, which consumed central executive resources. What was found was that performance was disrupted on the sentence list task, but not the word list task. This is because for sentences people needed to bind together the words into a coherent sentence, but not in the word list task. With the heavy working memory load, people had difficulty doing this, and so performance was hampered.

The effective access and use of information from long-term memory is important for working memory. People who perform more poorly on tests of working memory generally have difficulty searching long-term memory, especially when there are sources of interference (Unsworth & Engle, 2007). Thus, they have difficulty with the episodic buffer. The resulting episodic memory representations are less complete, and less coherent. The net result is poorer memory overall.

An idea that is related to the episodic buffer is long-term working memory (Ericsson & Kintsch, 1995). *Long-term working memory* allows people to coordinate large amounts of information. Long-term working memory is composed of a set of retrieval cues held in working memory that reference information in long-term memory. By using these cues, people can quickly access the information as needed.

CENTRAL EXECUTIVE

The last component of working memory is the **central executive.** This is involved in the allocation of attention (i.e., deciding what and what not to think about), as well as dealing with any active processing that is not directly handled by the subsystems. As such, the central executive is critical for working memory, and it is given the lion's share of what we consider "thinking." The central executive does most of the work of working memory. If researchers are interested in studying working memory when this component is all tied up doing something else, they might give a person a task like generating random numbers (which is harder than it sounds). This causes people to do more poorly on tasks that require active thinking in which control over the flow of information is at a premium. The control of attention in working memory involves the frontal lobes, particularly the prefrontal cortex (Kane & Engle, 2002).

The central executive serves to distribute memory resources. Performance can be improved if there are more resources available. Activity that brings the body to a higher or optimal state of arousal has a positive effect on working memory. This is why you think more clearly when you've had enough sleep. Moreover, active executive processing is resource consuming, and can show deficits when resources are low, such as when there are low levels of blood glucose and/or low levels of brain glycogen (Gailliot, 2008). An interesting demonstration of the effect of activity and arousal was a study by Wilkinson, Scholey, and Wesnes (2002) in which people who were and were not chewing gum were given a number of working memory tasks. What was found was that the people who were chewing gum (a physical activity) performed better than those who weren't. Of course, this does not mean that gum chewing always enhances memory (and if you decide to try it, *please* chew with your mouth closed), nor will it automatically boost you to the next grade level. However, increasing physical activity does increase working memory performance. That said, after high levels of aerobic activity, such as running a marathon, explicit memory may be compromised, although implicit memory is largely unaffected (Eich & Metcalfe, 2009).

Suppression

One mechanism that the central executive controls is suppression. Suppression is used to keep irrelevant information out of working memory or to remove information that has become irrelevant or inappropriate (Conway & Engle, 1994). For example, in a reading span task in which people must remember the last word from each of a set of sentences, people with lower spans, and presumably less-efficient suppression, are more likely to get the word wrong (Chiappe, Hasher, & Siegel, 2000). The operation of suppression in the central executive is closely tied to that of the frontal lobes (Kane & Engle, 2000).

Dysexecutive Syndrome

The disruption of the central executive can be seen when there has been damage to the frontal lobes. This can result in a condition known as the **dysexecutive syndrome,** where people lose some central executive functions that help them control their thought processes. This is a disruption in the medial frontal lobes (B.A. 32), as revealed by EEG recordings (Gevins, Smith, McEvoy, & Yu, 1997). With this syndrome, people may exhibit two types of behavior: preseverations and distraction. Perseverations are when a person has been performing a task one way and needs to do it another way, but the switch is not made. For example, if a person is asked to sort a deck of cards by suit, he or she could do so easily. But if he or she were then asked to then sort the cards by value, he or she would continue to sort them by suit. There is a perseveration of the old mode of thinking, and the person cannot disengage from it to move on to the new way. What is especially odd is that people can report what the correct sorting strategy should be and may admit they are not following the new strategy even as they continue to follow the old one. Also, some behaviors may exhibit elements of distraction. For example, if they are not currently processing information at the moment, attention might drift and become locked on some other stimulus in the environment.

Overall, the dysexecutive syndrome illustrates the attentional control that has been attributed to the central executive. When this component has been damaged and is not operating properly, the flow of the stream of thought is disrupted, getting stuck on old processes and drifting out to unrelated areas.

Synopsis

The episodic buffer is the part of working memory where information is integrated from the other subsystems and from long-term memory to make new episodic memories. If central resources are disrupted, this can affect its operation. The central executive is probably the most active part of working memory. Still, we do have a good idea about what it is capable of. The central executive helps coordinate what is attended to and what is not. Part of this attentional control is achieved through suppression. Some people have problems with their central executive, producing the dysexecutive syndrome.

SPAN TESTS

In Chapter 4, we briefly examined measures of short-term memory span, including word span and digit span. These are **simple span** measures because they require a person to do one simple task—remembering something for a brief period of time and then reporting it back. However, this is a relatively poor measure of working memory because the person isn't doing anything complicated. To address this, a number of working memory span tests have been developed. These are **complex span** measures (see Conway et al., 2005, for their proper use) that have at least two components. One is a retention component, like the simple span measures, in which the person retains a set of information for a period of time. The other part is an active processing component, depending on the working memory process of interest. It should be noted that, although they are not discussed here, there have been some attempts to measures the capacity of the episodic buffer (e.g., Was & Woltz, 2007). Overall, this approach allows us to more closely measure working memory rather than short-term memory.

Complex span tests are important because they are often measures of fluid intelligence (I.Q.) (Engle, Tuholski, Laughlin, & Conway, 1999; Salthouse & Pink, 2008; Unsworth & Engle, 2006; but see Mogle, Lovett, Stawski, & Sliwinski, 2008) and even things like impulsive decision making, with people scoring lower on these tests being more likely to make impulsive decisions (Hinson, Jameson, & Whitney, 2003).There has been a suggestion that working memory processes have a strong genetic component (Friedman et al., 2008), although there are many ways a person can compensate or overcome such inherent limitations (e.g., Feng, Spence, & Pratt, 2007; Kozhevnikov, Louchakova, Josipovic, & Motes, 2009).

Reading Span. A widely used complex span tests is Daneman and Carpenter's (1980, 1981) **reading span** test. In this test, a person reads aloud a set of two to six sentences, such as "The taxi turned up Michigan Avenue, where they had a clear view of the lake." At the end of each set, the person must recall the last word in each of the sentences of that set. The largest set of words that can all be accurately recalled is the reading span score. The retention component here is remembering the final words. The processing component is thinking about the sentence in order to read it effectively. Sentence span is a good predictor of language processing (Daneman & Merikle, 1996), much better than simple span measures. Language processing requires an active manipulation of knowledge, much like the processing component of the reading span task, which is absent in the simple span tests.

Comprehension Span. There are a number of other verbal span tests. One is the **comprehension span** test (Waters & Caplan, 1996) in which a person reads sentences and then recalls the last word of each one in a given set size from 2 to 6. Unlike the reading span, the person makes sensibility judgments. Some of the sentences are sensible, such as "It was the gangsters that broke into the warehouse," whereas others are not, such as "It was the warehouse that broke into the gangsters." These sensibility judgments require thinking more deeply about the meaning of the sentences, providing a better measure of higher-level working memory processes, such as those operating at the mental model level (see Chapter 7).

Operation Span. Another measure of working memory is the **operation span** test (Turner & Engle, 1989). In this test, a person reads aloud a two-step math problem, such as $(2 \times 4) + 1 = 8$, and then indicates whether the solution is correct. After this, a word is presented. These math operation–word combinations are presented in set sizes from 2 to 6. At the end of each set the person recalls as many words from that set as he or she can. The largest set size that can be accurately recalled is the operation span score. The retention component is remembering the words from a set, and the processing component is solving the math problems. This complex span test have been suggested to be a more domain-independent measure of working memory span.

Spatial Span. A final complex span test is Shah and Miyake's (1996) **spatial span** test which taps into spatial working memory. In this test, a series of letters are presented that have been rotated from the normal upright position. The initial task is to indicate whether the letters are normal or mirror reversed. This is the active processing component. Then, after a set of letters, people indicate where the tops of the letters were by pointing to a predetermined set of locations. This is the retention component.

Synopsis There are a number of ways to assess working memory capacity, known as span tests. Some, such as word span and digit span, are simple span tests that only measure retention capacity. Complex span tests, such as reading span, comprehension span, operation span, and spatial span, have people to hold a set of items in mind while some other task is done simultaneously. This shows an influence of the working part of working memory. Performance on these span tests is often related to more complex types of thinking.

WORKING MEMORY AND COMPLEX PROCESSING

Working memory influences other, more complex mental processes. For example, long-term memory retrieval is not automatic, but requires working memory resources and can be disrupted by other thoughts (Carrier & Pashler, 1995; Rohrer & Pashler, 2003). The effect of working memory on long-term memory retrieval is also seen when comparing people with different working memory capacities. People with larger capacities are better able to retrieve information than people with smaller capacities. Cantor and Engle (1993; Radvansky & Copeland, 2006) reported that people with larger working memory span scores showed less associative interference, or fan effects (see Chapter 7), than people with smaller scores. Similarly, Kane and Engle (2000) found that people with larger span scores showed less proactive interference. In general, more working memory capacity reduces the effect of irrelevant, interfering information. This additional information may be more easily managed and worked around if a person has more capacity. Put another way, people with smaller working memory capacities search through a larger set of information during memory retrieval, making their retrieval less efficient (Unsworth, 2007).

Working memory span scores may reflect, not necessarily the amount of capacity or "size" of working memory per se, but the ability to coordinate working memory contents, such as by removing irrelevant information and preventing irrelevant information from entering working memory and mucking up the works (Hasher & Zacks, 1988). People with larger working memory spans are better able to coordinate information and show smaller interference effects in long-term memory retrieval because they are better at keeping the irrelevant information out of working memory (Cantor & Engle, 1993).

Although having more working memory capacity is typically more desirable, there are cases when the reverse is true. For example, in a study by Beilock and DeCaro (2007;

see also Beilock & Carr, 2005 and Beilock, Kulp, Holt, & Carr, 2004) students were given a series of math problems that required a complex solution at first. However, later problems could be solved more efficiently with a simple solution (Some students may remember this as the Luchin's water jug problem). What was found was that people with greater working memory spans were more likely to miss the simpler solution, and continued using a more complex formula. In comparison, people with lower working memory spans, because they prefer simpler solutions (as a result of their smaller capacity) were more likely to notice and use the simpler solution. So, people with more working memory capacity were better able to construct more complex solutions, but they continued to use them even when a simpler process made itself available.

Synopsis

Working memory span has implications for other mental tasks, such as the effectiveness of long-term memory retrieval. What is important for effective thinking is keeping the contents of working memory filled with relevant information and keeping irrelevant information out.

SUMMARY

This chapter covered ways that information is actively manipulated in working memory. A prevalent view of working memory is Baddeley's multicomponent model involving a phonological loop for verbal/acoustic information, a visuo-spatial sketchpad for visual and spatial information, an episodic buffer for binding multimodal information together, and a central executive for actively manipulating information, and guiding the focus of attention. The active manipulation of information is influenced by the skill with which a person can process information, as well as unconscious factors, such as how knowledge of physical reality alters memory of perceived scenes. Finally, working memory is critically involved in any sort of complex processing. Thus, by gaining an understanding of how working memory operates, we can learn something about how memory is involved at more complex levels of thinking.

STUDY QUESTIONS

1. What are the primary components of the Baddeley's working memory theory?
2. What are the primary components of the phonological loop?
3. What are some of the major findings that support the idea of a phonological loop?
4. What is the nature of the information in the visuo-spatial sketchpad?
5. What is the evidence that the visuo-spatial sketchpad captures real-world, physical processes?
6. What is the purpose of the episodic buffer?

7. What is the role of the central executive in working memory?
8. What are the different types of span tests? What are the properties of each span test?
9. What are some of the ways in which working memory capacity influences other types of thought?

KEY TERMS

articulatory loop, articulatory suppression, Baddeley's multicomponent model, boundary extension, central executive, complex span, comprehension span, dynamic memory, dysexecutive syndrome, episodic buffer, irrelevant speech effect, lexicality effect, mental rotation, operation span, phonological loop, phonological similarity effect, phonological store, reading span, representational friction, representational gravity, representational momentum, simple span, spatial span, visuo-spatial sketchpad, word length effect, working memory

TRY IT OUT

The most straightforward ways to assess working memory is to look at aspects of the phonological loop using verbal materials. In this section we'll look at two ways to manipulate phonological loop processing, namely, the word length effect and articulatory suppression. Ideally you should have at least 24 people for each of these tasks.

- **Word length effect.** For this task, create two lists of eight nouns. For one list, the words should all be one syllable long. The words in the other list should all be three or four syllables long. For each person, pick out five words at random. Read them at the rate of one per second. At the end of the list, have the person write down the words in the order that they heard them. After a person is done recalling the first list, read the second list and have the person recall that one. Have half of the people get the short words list first, and the other half get the long words list first. Score performance by counting up the number of words correctly recalled on each list. If all goes well, there will be better recall for the list of short words than for the list of long words (see Neath, 1998).
- **Articulatory suppression.** For this task, create ten similar lists of five two-syllable words each. For each person, read a list of words at the rate of one per second. For five of the lists have people simply listen and then write down the words in the order that they heard them. For the other five lists have the people say the word "the" over and over from the time you start reading to the time they finish recalling the words. If all goes well, you should find is that people remember fewer words when they were articulating than when they were not.

CHAPTER SIX

NONDECLARATIVE MEMORY

When we think about "remembering," we usually think about times when we are consciously aware of using our memories, such as trying to remember a person's name, the answer to an exam question, or where we left the car keys. This conscious, explicit use of memory is readily understood and is apparent. It is not difficult to talk about such experiences, the content of these memories, and our awareness of them. This is part of what makes them declarative memories. However, as prominent as this type of memory may seem, much of human memory operates at an unconscious level. Some of these unconscious memories are so far removed from awareness that it is very difficult, if not impossible, to accurately talk about them. These are **nondeclarative memories.** An interesting thing about nondeclarative memories is that they are often spared in amnesia, consistent with the idea that this is a distinctly different way to remember something.

This chapter covers a number of aspects of nondeclarative memory. We start with some basic forms of memory. One of these is classical conditioning, in which an organism learns to respond to signals that are predictive of future outcomes, thereby showing memory for previous environmental contingencies. We also examine how procedural and implicit memories influence our behaviors without conscious awareness.

CLASSICAL CONDITIONING

Classical conditioning is one of the simplest forms of memory. Its formal discovery is credited to Ivan Pavlov (1849–1936), a famous Russian physiologist (see Chapter 1). As such, it is sometimes called **Pavlovian conditioning.** In classical conditioning, an organism learns that certain stimuli are reliable predictors of the imminent onset of other important stimuli (Pavlov, 1923). We examine classical conditioning in three forms: abstract; concrete, with the experimental situation used by Pavlov; and an example that is more in line with understanding human memory.

Abstract Structure

The basic classical conditioning paradigm is shown in Figure 6.1. It starts out with a stimulus that elicits a response. This is the unconditioned stimulus, or US, and the response it elicits is the unconditioned response, or UR. Both are unconditioned because no learning is needed; it is prewired in the organism. Another stimulus is introduced that initially

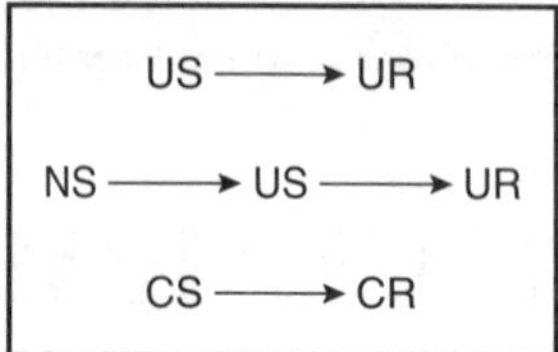

FIGURE 6.1 The Basic Classical Conditioning Paradigm

elicits no response. It is a neutral stimulus, or NS. During learning, the NS is presented prior to the US in a reliable and consistent way. Over time, the organism associates the NS with the oncoming US. As a result, the organism makes a preparatory response, as if the US were about to occur. The NS is now the conditioned stimulus, or CS, and the response that is made in the presence of the CS is the conditioned response, or CR.

Pavlov

For an example of classical conditioning, let's look at Pavlov's experiment. Pavlov received a Nobel Prize for his work on digestion. After getting his prize, he was studying the initial stage of digestion, salivation. Pavlov collected saliva from dogs by surgically inserting tubes into their mouths and feeding them. To his annoyance, Pavlov found that the dogs sometimes salivated when they weren't fed. Pavlov noticed that the additional salivation occurred with some regularity: It often preceded the actual food. Pavlov suspected that the dogs had made a mental connection between the person who gave them the food and food itself, so the dogs would salivate at the sight of the person. Pavlov decided to test his idea.

In his study he used meat as the US and the dogs' salivation as the UR. The dogs did not need to learn to salivate to the meat. As an NS, he used a bell. He rang the bell before he gave the meat. Over time, the dogs learned that the bell meant food. The dogs began to salivate when the bell rang but before they were fed. The bell was now a CS, and the salivation was a CR.

Examples with Humans

Another example of classical conditioning that relates more to humans is the development of phobias, which are irrational fears, such as a fear of elevators, open spaces, and public speaking. It is not unusual for phobias to develop through a classical conditioning process of nondeclarative memory, which the person is unaware. A person may have an initial experience that comes to elicit the phobia. For example, a person may have a negative public speaking experience, the anxiety experienced prior to public speaking is classically conditioned, and the person begins to avoid that situation, creating the phobia.

Happily, classical conditioning can be used to get rid of phobias. This can be done through the clinical process of systematic desensitization (Wolpe, 1958). In this method, people first think of situations that are remotely related to the one that elicits the phobia.

Over time, the person is brought closer and closer to the phobic situation. At each step the person remains at that stage until he or she does not feel disturbed. When a feeling of calm is associated with the situation at each stage, the person moves on to the next one. This process continues until a person finally reaches the phobia situation, which is classically conditioned to a relaxed feeling. At this point the phobia is conquered.

Associative Structure

What sort of association is learned in classical conditioning? There are two general possibilities, shown in Figure 6.2. The first is that the CS is directly associated with the CR. That is, the CS directly causes the CR to occur. This is a **stimulus-response association.** The other is that the CS is directly associated with a memory representation of the US, which then leads to the production of the CR. In other words, the CS is interpreted as predicting the onset of the US, so this elicits a CR in preparation for the CS. This is a **stimulus-stimulus association.** This is one of those few cases where both possibilities are true. Both types of conditioning can occur. However, in any given learning situation, only one type of association is stored. In the vast majority of the cases, it is stimulus-stimulus associations that are learned.

Because of the prominence of stimulus-stimulus associations, what is important in classical conditioning is not contiguity but contingency. **Contiguity learning** is the idea that learning occurs when an NS and a US occur near each other in time. However, while timing is important to a degree, it is not the critical factor. Instead, learning is driven by deriving some cause-effect relationship (however primitive).**Contingency learning** involves a sensitivity to the underlying causal structure.

Important Phenomenon

Initial Learning. There are many important features of classical conditioning. First there is an acquisition period, or **learning curve.** It takes a period of time for an association to be learned. For example, it takes a while for a dog to learn that the sound of a bell is a signal for the presentation of food. Not all co-occurrences in the environment are meaningful over the long term. Most are not. An organism has only a limited number of resources, such as a short-term memory capacity, so those resources must be used wisely. By encoding and using only those relationships that are stable and meaningful, classical conditioning allows one to more effectively direct preparation for events in the environment.

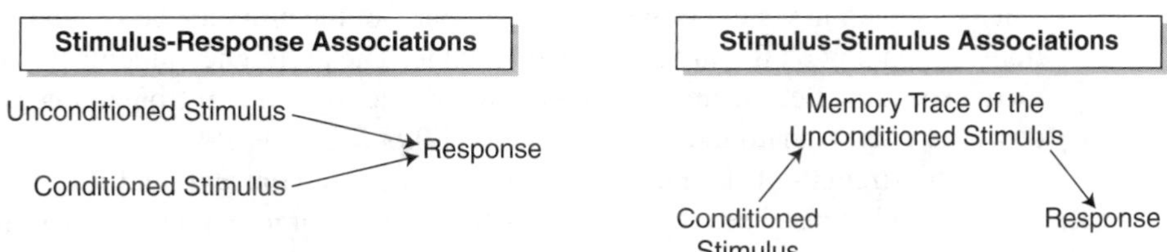

FIGURE 6.2 The Difference between Stimulus-Response and Stimulus-Stimulus Associations in Classical Conditioning

Forgetting. Of course, the environment is not always stable, and one needs to adapt to change not only by learning new associations but also by ceasing to respond to ones that are no longer relevant. When a CS is presented many times without a US, responses to that CS will stop. This is **extinction.** For example, if a bell rings but no food is offered, the dog will stop salivating when it hears the bell. Note that even when extinction has occurred, forgetting is not complete. This fact is revealed by two phenomena. The first is **spontaneous recovery.** This occurs when, after extinction, there is a long delay, and then the CS is presented again. The CR, which was extinct, reemerges, but it is not as strong as before. The organism remembers the original association and forgets that it is no longer predictive and useful. This may be advantageous because environmental conditions might be present that make the CS meaningful again after an absence. The other phenomenon is **savings.** This is similar to the savings described in the discussion of Ebbinghaus in Chapter 3. Savings shows that after extinction has occurred, when relearning a previous association, less time is required to do so than the first time it was learned. This suggests that some memory for that association remains, even though it appears to be forgotten.

Mere Exposure Effect

The operation of classical conditioning at an unconscious level can influence our preferences. This is illustrated by the **mere exposure effect** (Harrison & Zajonc, 1970; Zajonc, 1968, 2001), in which people prefer things they already have been exposed to one or more times. When we are exposed to something, we register that information, even if only at a subconscious level. As long as there are no negative connotations associated with it, a mild positive association is established. That is, the absence of negative associations in nondeclarative memory is interpreted, at some level, as something we have experienced that will not hurt us. So, in general, we prefer things we have been exposed to before, even if we don't remember them.

The effects of mere exposure influences on our lives and our culture. As an example of this, James Cutting (2003) showed that the development of the standard Western canon of French Impressionist paintings (the set of works that are identified by experts as the core or most important ones) is highly related to exposure. Adults' preference judgments were related to frequency of exposure in the culture rather than whether the adults consciously recognized a painting, its complexity, or its prototypicality. Importantly, children who have not had this sort of exposure do not show such a bias. So, there is nothing special about the paintings at the core of the canon. What puts these paintings at the core is their frequency of exposure influencing people's ratings of preference.

This influence of memory on preferences is different from explicit memory of whether something is old or new. Different parts of the brain are activated in these situations, depending on the judgments being made. The preference judgments that drive the mere exposure effect seem to uniquely involve the right lateral frontal lobe, which is not observed with standard memory judgments (Elliot & Dolan, 1998).

The strength of the mere exposure effect is not constant, and it can vary under a number of circumstances (Bornstein, 1989). It grows larger with more exposures, up to a point. With large numbers of exposures (e.g., over 100), the effect starts to decline. The effect is also more likely to occur when something is presented in multiple contexts rather than the same context over and over. Similarly, the mere exposure effect is greater with a delay between the time the information was received and the preference ratings. Finally, there is even an embodied aspect to mere exposure. If people are chewing gum when they are briefly exposed to stimuli, they show a mere exposure effect if the items are Chinese ideographs, but not for words (Topolinski & Strack, 2009). This is because the words could be spoken, but the mental and neural machinery that would simulate this is taken up by the action of moving the mouth to chew the gum. This suggests that some change in context makes the information more distinct and, therefore, more preferable.

CAUSAL LEARNING

More recently, work on conditioning has been extended to understanding of human causal learning. That is, how does a person figure out cause and effect relations in the world? Learning causal relations is needed to understand how technology works, what causes diseases, or how to find food. In essence, this is what goes on in conditioning. An organism learns events predict other events (often some sort of causal relation) so that it can prepare for it. Many of the same principles that are observed in conditioning are also observed in causal learning (e.g., Mitchell, Lovibond, Minard, & Lavis, 2006; Vandorpe & De Houwer, 2005).

At this point is unclear the extent to which the memory principles that underlie conditioning are also driving causal learning. A number of theories have been proposed (Perales & Shanks, 2007). Some of these are based on theories of conditioning, such as associative models (e.g., Shanks & Dickenson, 1987) that involve the Rescorla-Wagner (1972) model of classical conditioning. In comparison, some are based on normative information about event probabilities, such as the Power PC theory (Cheng, 1997). Still other theories assume a rule-based approach with the idea that people are drawing inferences (Mitchell, Lovibond, & Gan, 2005). It should be noted that causal learning is more effective when people have an opportunity to interact with the system, although it can occur to some degree with simple passive observation (Enkvist, Newell, Juslin, & Olsson, 2006), suggesting a further influence of embodied factors.

Synopsis

A fundamental form of nondeclarative memory is conditioning. In most cases, this involves learning a predictive association between two stimuli, one that is already important and one that is a predictor of the occurrence of the first. What is learned is often stimulus-to-stimulus associations, not stimulus-to-response associations. These associations take some time to be learned, but they can be forgotten, at least on the surface, through extinction. Phenomena like spontaneous recovery and savings illustrate that even after extinction/forgetting has occurred, there is still some memory for the association. One example of an effect of conditioning in human memory is the mere exposure effect. More recent work has investigated how people learn cause and effect relationships.

PROCEDURAL MEMORY

Knowledge of how to do things, such as play the piano, throw a ball, or walk, is part of nondeclarative memory. People have skills and do not know exactly how they acquired them. For example, just because someone is a skilled athlete does not *necessarily* mean that he or she will make a good coach because much of his or her knowledge is unconscious and procedural. We now look at the acquisition of procedural skills and the influence of expertise on procedural memory.

Skill Acquisition

Many tasks we do improve with practice. These **skills** include activities where expertise is widely recognized, such as being able to play a sport, play a musical instrument, or craft a best-selling novel. Most skills, however, are very mundane, and you may not consider them "skills." These include activities like walking, reading, riding a bicycle, driving a car, and having a conversation.

Stages of Skill Acquisition

Although a range of skills are stored in nondeclarative memory, the process of skill memory development is similar to them all. There are three levels or stages of skill acquisition: the cognitive stage, the associative stage, and the autonomous stage. This reflects a transition from arduous and clumsy execution of a skill to its easy and fluid execution. The idea that there are three stages does not mean a person is necessarily in one particular stage. An expert in a certain skill spends most of his or her time at the autonomous stage but still has nondeclarative memory for the associative and cognitive stages for aspects of that skill. As skills develop people make choices about which strategy to use (Bajic & Rickard, 2009).

Cognitive Stage. The skill beginning is the cognitive stage in which a person consciously and deliberately does the skill actions. For example, when learning to play chess, a person exerts a great deal of cognitive effort to keep the game progressing by trying to consciously assess what is going on in the attempt to defeat the opponent. The cognitive stage often involves comparing the current state with the desired state and taking those actions that bring one closer to the desired state.

Associative Stage. After spending some time in the cognitive stage, a person moves on to the associative stage. At this stage a person more quickly retrieves the knowledge needed for the task. Different memories are directly associated with different aspects of the skill. The need to mentally verbalize to think things through is less necessary. Information is quickly and easily retrieved into consciousness, although some deliberate and conscious effort is still needed. For example, a chess player would directly retrieve information about what a set of moves would entail, and different alignments on the board begin to be viewed as offensive or defensive.

Autonomous Stage. After more practice with a skill, a person moves to the final, autonomous stage. At this stage that skill execution becomes more proceduralized and becomes largely unconscious. A person's memories and knowledge have moved from being dominated by declarative knowledge to being dominated by nondeclarative knowledge. This is clearly seen in cases where a person is learning a motor skill, such as learning to play an instrument. When a person becomes an expert, the execution of various components is done with little conscious involvement other than the desire to execute a particular series of moves. There is very little overt, conscious involvement in the execution of the smaller steps of the skill.

In most cases skill automation is helpful. However, there are cases where it has the opposite effect. This occurs when people consciously think about what they are doing in cases where the skill is highly developed. An example of this is when players choke under pressure. The athlete's conscious thoughts about what he or she is doing intrude on and conflict with information automatically retrieved from procedural memory (Beilock & Carr, 2001). People with a low level of skill (novices) do better if they focus on accuracy, whereas those at a high level of skill (experts) do better if they focus on speed (Beilock, Bertenthal, McCoy, & Carr, 2004). This difference between experts and novices is shown in Figure 6.3.

Synopsis

Procedural memory is nondeclarative memory for how to do things and can be seen in skill development. Skills start out in memory as conscious, declarative memories, but with practice, they develop more and more into automatic procedural memories that are not open to conscious awareness. In fact, conscious awareness can actually disrupt this system.

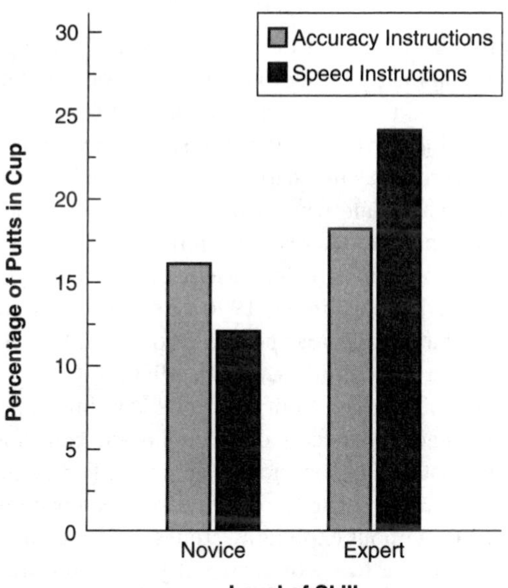

FIGURE 6.3 Mean Percentage of Putts Made for Novices and Experts as a Function of Whether They Were Instructed to Focus on Accuracy or Speed

Source: Beilock, S. L., Bertenthal, B. I., McCoy, A. M., & Carr, T. H. (2004). Haste does not always make waste: Expertise, direction of attention, and speed versus accuracy in performing sensorimotor skills. *Psychonomic Bulletin & Review, 11,* 373–379.

IMPLICIT MEMORY

The last form of nondeclarative memory examined here is implicit memory. **Implicit memory** is any form of memory that does not require consciousness and can potentially operate without a person being aware that memory is being used. For example, some accounts of the déjà vu experience attribute the odd feeling of familiarity one has with a new situation to unconscious, implicit memories of different, but similar experiences (Brown, 2003; Cleary, 2008). Also, the idea of intuition appears to rely heavily on implicit memory as intuition is an unconscious feeling about something. For example, suppose people are given word triads, such as "dream" "ball" and "book" or "salt" "deep" and "foam." People intuitively know that the first three do not go together, but the second three do because they all relate to a fourth concept (e.g., sea), even if the person cannot consciously report that concept (Topolinski & Strack, 2009).

In some sense, the other forms of memory can manifest themselves as implicit memory. For example, procedural memories can be implicit, such as a person's knowledge of how to walk. The concept of savings, originally described by Ebbinghaus, is a form of implicit memory in which a person is unaware of how previous, unconscious memories are influencing later learning (Nelson, 1978). This section considers how knowledge gets into memory without our awareness, how implicit memory is assessed using indirect memory tasks, the effects of data-driven and conceptually driven processes on implicit memory, and the unconscious learning of sequential orders.

Incidental Learning

We have already discussed implicit memory in terms of encoding in Chapter 3. People learn things either explicitly—intentionally trying to learn them—or implicitly—incidentally learning. Incidental learning is a form of implicit memory because a person is not consciously aware at the time that the knowledge is being stored in memory. Although it is difficult to observe incidental learning as it is happening (because it's incidental), neurological measures provide some insight into what will and will not be remembered later. EEG recordings show what is remembered later shows up in different wavebands. There is increased theta band synchronization and decreased alpha band synchronization (Klimesch, Doppelmayr, Russegger, & Pachinger, 1996). People who remember more show a greater lower alpha band change, whereas people who remember less show more desynchronization in the upper alpha band (Klimesch et al., 1996).

Much of the tacitly acquired information from incidental learning makes up the contents of implicit memory. The influences exerted on our thoughts and behaviors by implicit memory retrieval use knowledge that was unconsciously acquired. For example, a person moving to a new part of a country may start altering his or her speech patterns to conform to the local accent. This may occur without explicit awareness of speaking with the new accent. You may have noticed this in your own experience. If you've gone away to college, how you speak when you are at school may differ from how you speak at home.

Indirect Tests of Memory

It is difficult to clearly understand what implicit memory is and does because its operations and effects are largely unconscious. To see its effects, a person must show an influence of prior experience (memory) without consciously being aware of doing so. That is, we need an indirect way of testing memory. A number of indirect memory tests have been developed, some of which we examine here.

Priming. An extensively studied form of indirect memory testing is **priming.** Priming occurs when a person is faster and/or more accurate at retrieving target information that has been facilitated by an earlier prime trial (Tulving & Schacter, 1990). There are different types of priming, but here we focus on the most basic: repetition priming. **Repetition priming** is priming of an item that was encountered recently. For example, if you saw the word *assassin* earlier, you recognize it faster and more accurately when you see it again later. Repetition priming is better when the information is presented in the same way it was encountered. For example, people have a better memory for rotating objects if the objects are rotating in the same direction as the first time they saw them (Liu & Cooper, 2003). This suggests that even seemingly irrelevant details can influence the ability to remember them later.

The amount of benefit a person gets from repetition priming varies depending on how information was learned in the first place. Let's look at memory for information read in a book (see Raney, 2003). If repetition priming is operating, people will show a benefit by reading the text faster the second time. However, the nature of this priming can vary. Suppose a reader is relying primarily on memory of the text itself (like surface form or textbase memory), such as when people do not try to comprehend what they are reading (perhaps because they are looking for spelling errors) and so do not build adequate mental models of what is being described. Under these conditions, repetition priming is more affected by perceptual characteristics, such as the handwriting that was used, the font used, or the word order. In contrast, if readers fully understood what is being read and are able to build adequate mental models, repetition priming extends to other texts that refer to the same state of affairs. Moreover, this repetition priming is less influenced by the perceptual properties of the text. In another domain, it has also been found that repetition priming does not occur for musical chords (Bigand, Tillmann, Pulin-Charronnat, & Manderlier, 2005). This is likely due to the fact that musical elements, such as chords, are often repeated as part of the structure of a larger musical piece.

An interesting thing about priming is that it can involve a decrease in neural activity (Schacter & Badgaiyan, 2001). Repetition priming is associated with decreased activity in the visual cortex, whereas semantic priming is associated with decreased activity in the frontal lobes. This decreased neural activity reflects the lower amount of work that must be done because those memory engrams are already at a heightened level of availability based on the recent experience.

Indirect memory tests, such as repetition priming, influence multiple levels of representation (see Chapter 7). For example, people respond faster to words that were seen in a word list than a paragraph. However, people read a text faster if that same text had been read earlier but not if they see the same words out of context, such as in a word list (Levy & Kirsner, 1989). This suggests that in order to have repetition priming, the appropriate level of representation (in this case either the word level or the text level) needs to be retrieved. Retrieving the wrong sort of memory is less helpful.

In a profound demonstration of indirect tests using reading, Kolers (1976) had people read a series of texts. These texts were presented either in a normal font or had inverted the letters. An example of an inverted text is shown in Figure 6.4. People then read the same texts again more than a year later. It was found that people read these texts faster the

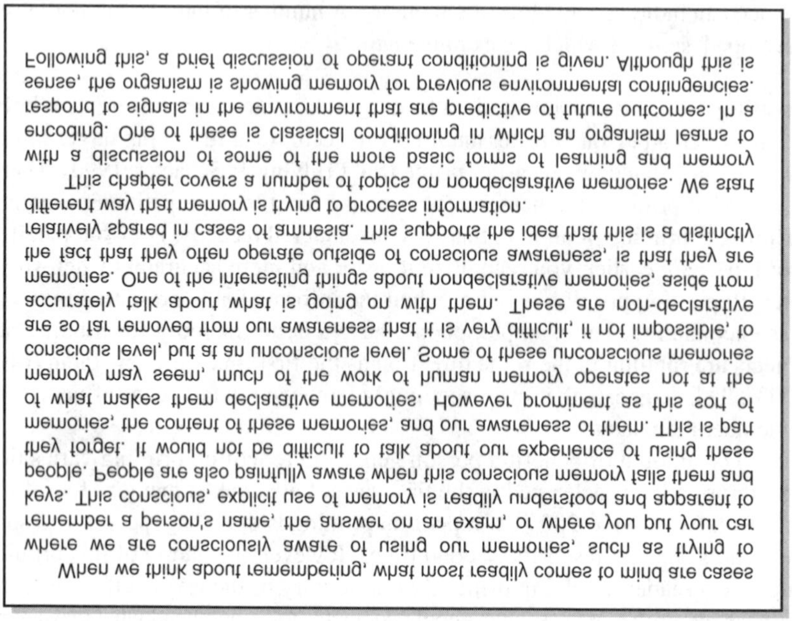

When we think about remembering, what most readily comes to mind are cases where we are consciously aware of using our memories, such as trying to remember a person's name, the answer on an exam, or where you put your car keys. This conscious, explicit use of memory is readily understood and apparent to people. People are also painfully aware when this conscious memory fails them and they forget. It would not be difficult to talk about our experience of using these memories, the content of these memories, and our awareness of them. This is part of what makes them declarative memories. However prominent as this sort of memory may seem, much of the work of human memory operates not at the conscious level, but at an unconscious level. Some of these unconscious memories are so far removed from our awareness that it is very difficult, if not impossible, to accurately talk about what is going on with them. These are non-declarative memories. One of the interesting things about nondeclarative memories, aside from the fact that they often operate outside of conscious awareness, is that they are relatively spared in cases of amnesia. This supports the idea that this is a distinctly different way that memory is trying to process information.

This chapter covers a number of topics on nondeclarative memories. We start with a discussion of some of the more basic forms of learning and memory encoding. One of these is classical conditioning in which an organism learns to respond to signals in the environment that are predictive of future outcomes. In a sense, the organism is showing memory for previous environmental contingencies. Following this, a brief discussion of operant conditioning is given. Although this is

FIGURE 6.4 Inverted Text

Source: Kolers, P. A. (1976). Reading a year later. *Journal of Experimental Psychology: Human Learning and Memory, 2,* 554–565.

second time, both for normal and inverted texts, even after a substantial forgetting had occurred. Thus, not only were the words and ideas of the text remembered, but even superficial characteristics, such as the orientation of the letters, were stored in memory, producing a savings that made later reading easier.

While repetition priming is a pervasive, it is not always observed. A clear illustration of this is a study by Oliphant (1982). First occurrences of repeated words were presented either in the context of the study (as is normally done) or as part of the instructions. Repetition priming was observed when the first occurrence of a word was in the study itself (the standard condition), but not when it was in the instructions. This suggests that memory is compartmentalized and the processing of information is based on how we parse up the world, even at an unconscious level.

Other Verbal Tasks. Many indirect memory tasks involve reconstructing partial or degraded information in some way. The idea is that if people have information in memory, even at an unconscious level, they should find it easier to reconstruct it. One example of this is a **word-stem completion** task (e.g., Graf, Mandler, & Haden, 1982). In this task people are given the initial few letters of a word (the word "stem"), with the task of completing it with the first word that comes to mind. Here, people are more likely to complete these stems with words they had seen previously, even though they are unaware that they are using prior knowledge. This isolation of implicit memory processes can be shown by using methodologies such as the process-dissociation procedure (see Chapter 3 [Toth, Reingold, & Jacoby, 1994]).

Another indirect memory task is **word-fragment completion** in which people are given words with missing letters, such as A _ _ A _ _ IN, and are to complete the words. Again, people do better if they saw the words before (Tulving, Schacter, & Stark, 1982). Moreover, as shown in Figure 6.5, this ability remains stable even after a long delay, whereas more conscious and explicit recognition memory continues to decline over time.

Another indirect memory test is anagram solution (Srivinas & Roediger, 1990) in which people are given anagrams, such as "tderhun" for the word "thunder." People are better at solving the anagrams if they were exposed to the word recently than if they were not. Again, people are not consciously using memory to help them solve the anagrams.

Yet another verbal indirect memory task is **lexical decision** (e.g., Duchek & Neely, 1989) in which a person is given a string of letters as is to indicate whether it is a word or not (hence the term *lexical decision*). What is often of interest is how fast people respond to words depending on what occurred earlier. People respond faster when they have been exposed to them recently or to words that are related to ideas they have been thinking about recently. Similar effects can be observed with a **naming** task in which people simply name aloud, as quickly as possible, visually presented words (e.g., Hashtroudi, Ferguson, Rappold, & Chrosniak, 1988). Words are named faster if they were seen before, or were unconsciously activated by a person thinking about related concepts.

Some Nonverbal Tasks. Indirect memory is also seen when perceptual clarity is compromised. Imagine that a word is shown for only 35 ms and it is very difficult to consciously identify the word. However, if a person was previously exposed to it, this **perceptual identification** is greatly enhanced (Crabb & Dark, 2003; Jacoby & Dallas, 1981)

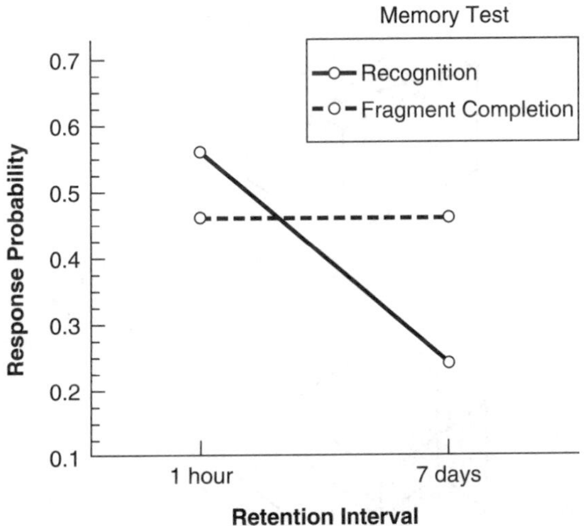

FIGURE 6.5 The Enduring Influence of Implicit Memory (Word-Fragment Completion) Relative to Explicit Memory (Recognition)

Source: Tulving, E., Schacter, D. L., & Stark, H. A. (1982). Priming effects in word-fragment completion are independent of recognition memory. *Journal of Experimental Psychology: Learning, Memory and Cognition, 8,* 336–342.

and it is easier for people to identify what they see. This process is also seen in pop music. Often lyrics are unclear, and you have to guess what a person is singing. However, if you *read* the lyrics, you can easily follow them the next time you hear the song.

Indirect memory tasks can assess implicit memory for all types of information. An example of a nonverbal indirect memory task is priming for pictures of possible and impossible objects (see Figure 6.6). What happens is that people first view a set of objects as part of some task, such as judging whether an object faces left or right. Then they are to make possible-impossible decisions. Some of the objects in the second test are the same as the first test. The degree to which people respond faster and more accurately to old objects relative to new objects is an indicator of priming. Nonverbal priming for these pictures occurs only for possible objects and not for impossible objects (Liu & Cooper, 2001; Schacter, Cooper, & Delaney, 1990). Thus memory takes into account an understanding of the object as a whole and not just the parts that make up the image.

Implicit memory influences can also occur with odors. Holland, Hendriks, and Aarts (2005) had students at Radboud University take a lexical decision task in a room with or without a citrus-scented cleaner in a cupboard (out of sight), or no cleaner (control condition). This odor prime led people to respond faster to cleaning-related words (e.g., "poetsen," the Dutch word for "cleaning") on a lexical decision task. So, implicit memory very much has a multimodal influence on how we think.

Implicit memory works on us in many ways. Even information that we are unaware of initially can have an influence. For example, Kunst-Wilson and Zajonc (1980) had subconsciously presented a set of randomly generated geometric shapes by displaying them for only 1 ms. Some time later, people got a forced-choice recognition test and selected which objects were seen earlier. Despite having no conscious memory, people performed

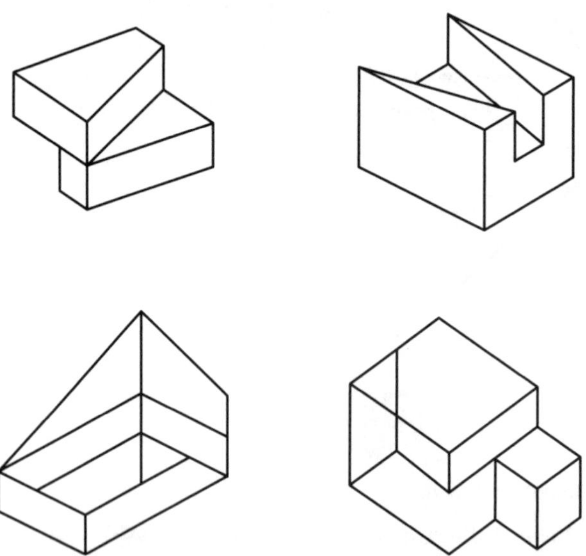

FIGURE 6.6 Examples of Possible and Impossible Objects

Source: Liu, T., & Cooper, L. A. (2001). The influence of task requirements on priming in object decision and matching. *Memory & Cognition, 29,* 874–882.

above chance. That is, they selected the previously seen shapes more often than would be expected if they were just guessing.

Data-Driven and Conceptually Driven Processes

Although the distinction between explicit and implicit memory is complex, a number of attempts have been made to describe the differences between them. One of these is the idea that implicit memory tends to be driven more by the perceptual characteristics. This is referred to as data-driven processing because the mental activity is driven more by information in the environment than the contents of a person's thoughts. In contrast, explicit memory is driven more by the conceptual characteristics. This is referred to as conceptually driven, because the mental activity is driven more by a person's knowledge, expectations, and goals. As an illustration, seeing a cloud in the sky as a cloud is an example of data-driven processing, but seeing shapes in the clouds is an example of conceptually driven processing (e.g., Blaxton, 1989).

Sequence Learning

Another type of information that is encoded into nondeclarative, implicit memory is the order of events. These are repeating patterns of events in the world that we may not be consciously aware of, but to which our implicit memory has become attuned. This was clearly shown in a study by Nissen and Bullemer (1987; see also Fu, Fu, & Dienes, 2008). In this study, students saw a row of four lights, with a button below each one. The task was to press the button below a light *after* it lit up. There were two groups in this study. In the random order, control group, the lights came on in a random order throughout the study. In the experimental group, the lights came on in a consistent ten-light sequence. The speed with which people pushed the buttons dramatically increased (i.e., response time decreased), with even very little exposure in the experimental group (see Figure 6.7). It is even possible to see eye movements anticipating the next item in a series (Tremblay & Saint-Aubin, 2009). People used their memories of the sequence before they were consciously aware of doing so. Moreover, when people are asked to explicitly report the sequence, they cannot (but see Wilkinson & Shanks, 2004). Similar results occur in visual search tasks (looking for an object in a display) when the response sequence is repeated (Jiménez & Vázquez, 2008). While sequence learning can occur in various modalities, such as touch and vision, knowledge of the sequence does not transfer well across modalities, suggesting that there is perceptual component to the memory—it is not completely action-based (Abrahamse, van der Lubbe, & Verway, 2008).

A more complex type of sequence learning involves implicit learning of **artificial grammars** (for a review, see Pothos, 2007). In these studies, people are shown sequences of letters. These sequences are created using an algorithm such as the one shown in Figure 6.8. For example, in this case, the sequences VXVPS, TPPTS, and VXXXS are valid or "grammatical" sequences, whereas the sequences XVSPV, PPTTS, and SXXXV are not. During a learning phase, people are shown a series of letter strings that were generated using the algorithm and are asked to simply copy the sequence. It has been found that even in the absence of explicit memorization, people learn not just the sequences that were presented but the "grammar" or production algorithm used to generate them. This implicit memory shows itself in people's ability to also accept (at above chance rates) valid sequences that were never seen before and to accept

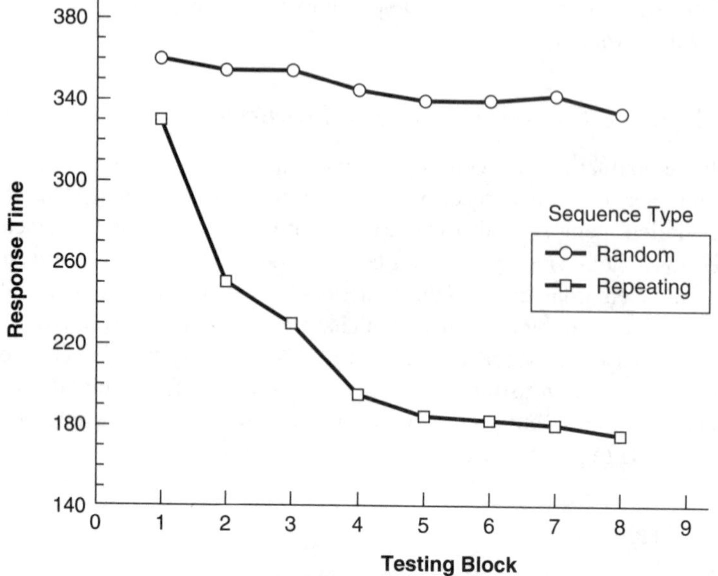

FIGURE 6.7 Improvement on a Serial Order Task with Random and Repeating Sequences

Source: Reprinted from *Cognitive Psychology,* 19, Nissen, M. J., & Bullemer, P., Attentional requirements of learning: Evidence from performance measures, pp. 1–32, 1987, with permission from Elsevier.

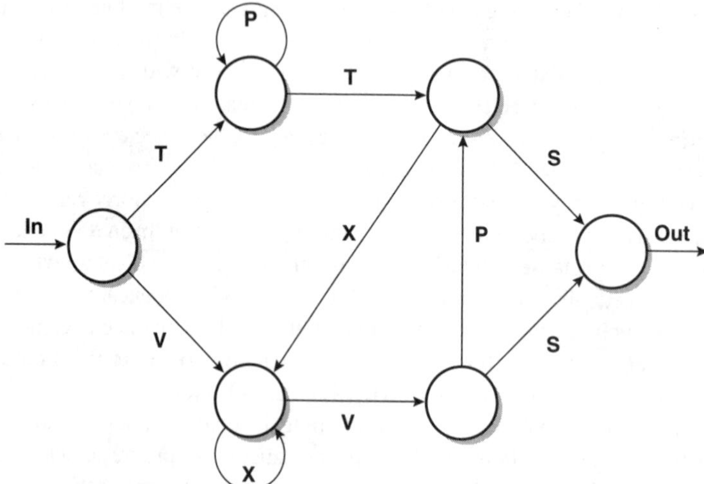

FIGURE 6.8 Algorithm Used to Generate Artificial Grammar

Source: Reprinted from *Journal of Verbal Learning and Verbal Behavior,* 6, Reber, A. S., Implicit learning of artificial grammars, pp. 855–863, 1967, with permission from Elsevier.

new sequences that used different letter sets but that followed the same rules (Reber, 1967; 1969; Vokey & Highham, 2005). However, people do develop expectations based on the structure of individual stimuli (Pothos, 2005), which suggests that there is some learning of bigram probabilities (i.e., the probability that a given letter will follow another) rather than an entire grammar (Poletiek & Wolters, 2009). Overall, this is a general memory process and not only applies to letters, but even to other types of information, such as sequences of modern dance movements (Opacic, Stevens, & Tillmann, 2009). People make grammaticality judgments based on how familiar an item seems, and this familiarity is related to an item's similarity to others that a person was trained on (Scott & Dienes, 2008). Although this is a largely unconscious process, conscious influences also play a role if a person becomes aware of the structure (Dulany, Carlson, & Dewey, 1984; Eitam, Schul, & Hassin, 2009; Sallas, Mathews, Lane, & Sun, 2007).

Memory under Anesthesia

Most of the memory that we have seen so far in this chapter has involved information presented when people are conscious and aware of their surroundings. One way that learning can occur when a person is unconscious is to look at things learned during anesthesia. One purpose of anesthesia is to make sure a person does not remember what happened during surgery (such as feeling the incision being made). The brain is not completely dormant under anesthesia. The question is whether it is active enough to learn.

In some cases, people read information while they are anesthetized for surgery. It might be a list of words or sentences, or a story. After surgery, memory is tested for what was heard while a person was unconscious. Based on an extensive review by Andrade (1995), many cases have shown evidence of learning under anesthesia. This has been shown a number of ways, including a greater likelihood of producing words heard during anesthesia on category generation, free association, stem completion, ratings of familiarity, recognition, and preference ratings tasks. Some tests have also looked at more complex forms of learning, such as providing people with answers to general knowledge questions, false fame effects (Chapter 12), classical conditioning, behavioral suggestion (such as touching one's ear or chin), and therapeutic suggestions. In one study, Schwender et al. (1993) had 15 patients listen to a tape of *Robinson Crusoe* while they were anesthetized and undergoing surgery. After surgery, when asked to free associate to the word *Friday,* 10 of these patients responded with "Robinson Crusoe." In contrast, none of another group of 15 patients who did not hear the novel gave this response.

What people learn under anesthesia is important because it can impact recovery. It has been suggested that derogatory comments made about a patient, such as commenting on an obese patient's weight, can cause the person to recover more slowly. This is known as "fat lady syndrome." Some surgeons make a point of speaking about how well things are going during the surgery, even if it's not true, to facilitate recovery.

Most of the effects of learning under anesthesia are at an unconscious, implicit level. People have very little, and more often no, conscious awareness of having learned this information. While this is all very interesting, it should also be pointed out that it has been very difficult to replicate many of these findings. In almost every case where studies have found evidence of memory, there are similar studies that have not. There are many reasons for this. In some cases, it may be that the data just happened to fall in such a way that an effect was observed and reported. Researchers are less likely to report not finding an effect. Alternatively, it could be that these are often very weak memory effects that are difficult to measure in the first place, so it is not surprising if they are difficult to replicate. Finally, it is hard to control many factors that could influence the results. These include the type of anesthesia used, how deeply the patients go under, the extent of the surgery, and so forth. So, as it stands, there is an intriguing possibility that there may be some nondeclarative learning going on when a person is under anesthesia, but at this point it is unclear when this happens and to what extent.

Synopsis

Implicit memory is memory that is largely outside of conscious awareness, although we may occasionally be made aware of its outcomes. Incidental learning is a form of implicit memory. To test implicit memory, a number of methods have been developed to look at the influence of memory without making people aware that they are using their memories. These tasks include priming, word-stem completion, lexical decision, word naming, and perceptual identification. The operation of implicit memory not only involves memory for specific content but can also be seen in memory for how things fit together in the world, such as in sequence learning. Finally, implicit memory can be seen in cases where conscious awareness is not present and general neurological functioning should be absent, as well as when a person in under anesthesia. This illustrates the durability and pervasiveness of unconscious, nondeclarative forms of memory.

SUMMARY

This chapter covered a number of forms of nondeclarative memory. These memories are difficult to articulate and may fall outside of conscious awareness. Nondeclarative memories include primitive forms of memory, such as classical conditioning. Nondeclarative memories can also be involved in the development of skills, as with procedural memories. This type of knowledge allows us to perform many activities, such as walking and chewing gum at the same time without using much conscious mental effort. Finally, the operation of implicit memory was discussed. Although implicit memories operate and influence us below the radar screen of awareness, a number of methods have been developed for assessing this important component of our memories.

STUDY QUESTIONS

1. What are the primary components of classical conditioning, and how does learning occur?
2. What are some of the important phenomena of classical conditioning?
3. How is the mere exposure effect a nondeclarative memory phenomenon?
4. In what way are studies of causal learning examples of nondeclarative memory?
5. What are the stages that knowledge goes through to develop skilled procedural memories?
6. What is implicit memory, and how is it measured?
7. What are some sorts of effects of implicit memory that can be observed?
8. What sort of knowledge can be learned and can influence later behavior with implicit memory?

KEY TERMS

artificial grammars, classical conditioning, contiguity learning, contingency learning, extinction, implicit memory, indirect memory tasks, lexical decision, long-term working memory, mere exposure effect, naming, nondeclarative memory, Pavlovian conditioning, perceptual identification, priming, repetition priming, savings, skills, spontaneous recovery, stimulus-response association, stimulus-stimulus association, word-fragment completion, word-stem completion

TRY IT OUT

For this Try It Out section, we focus on a task that exhibits the effects of unconscious nondeclarative memory, namely priming on a **word-fragment completion** task (see Neath, 1998). Ideally you should have at least 24 participants for this task. This project is broken down into two parts. For the first part have half of the people go through a list of 20 words printed on index cards. This list of words was used in the original study by Tulving et al. (1982):

AGNOSTIC	ANTENNA	ANTIQUE	ASSASSIN	BASILICA	BAYONET
BOURBON	BROCCOLI	CASHMERE	CHASSIS	CHIMNEY	CHIPMUNK
CONIFER	CUTLERY	DELIRIUM	DINOSAUR	ELECTRON	ELLIPSE
EPITAPH	FASCISM	GAZELLE	GRANARY	HAYLOFT	HORIZON
HYDRANT	INFERNO	ISTHMUS	JAMBOREE	KEROSENE	LACROSSE
LECTERN	LEPROSY	LETTUCE	LINEAGE	MARTINI	MASCARA
MYSTERY	NIRVANA	NOCTURNE	OBELISK	OCTOPUS	PARANOIA
PHOENIX	POLLIWOG	QUARTET	RAINBOW	RHOMBUS	ROTUNDA
SAPPHIRE	SEQUOIA	SHERIFF	SURGEON	THEOREM	TWILIGHT
UNIVERSE	VENDETTA	VERMOUTH	WARRANTY	YOGURT	ZEPPELIN

Pick 20 of these. Be sure to include all of the letters in a word, and do not include the underlining shown here. Ask people rate each word for pleasantness. That is, how pleasant the words are to them. After going through the entire list of 20 words, have people spend 10 minutes doing a distractor task. This should be any task that does not refer to the words that they just rated (such as solving math problems, sorting decks of cards, and circling the letter "h" each time it appears on a page from a magazine article).

The second half of the study involves both groups. Present people a list of 60 word fragments. Use the same list, except remove the letters that are underlined and replace them with blank spaces. The task is for the people to complete those words. It is important that you *do not* tell the first group that these words are related to the ones they rated earlier. These words should be presented in a random order; the only constraint is that the 20 words you had in the first half of the study do not appear as any of the first 10 fragments. If all goes well, people who rated the words for pleasantness should complete more of the 20 fragments than those people who did not see those words.

CHAPTER SEVEN

EPISODIC MEMORY

Memories help define who we are. Our opinions, attitudes, likes, and dislikes are a result of our previous experiences. Memory is the repository of those experiences and the shaper of our future actions. Thus, it is important to understand our memories of the events and episodes of our lives. It has been found that memories of personally experienced events are stored and remembered in ways that have unique characteristics. Memories for events that we experienced are **episodic memories**, whereas memories for general world knowledge are **semantic memories**. An example of this distinction is the difference between remembering the last movie you saw (episodic) versus remembering what a movie is (semantic). This chapter covers episodic memories. Semantic memories are covered in Chapter 9.

Several aspects of episodic memory are covered here. We first look at the information that makes up episodic memories and then examine how they can compete with one another or combine to form composite memories of different events. Although episodic memories are of specific events, we can have repeated exposure to the same and similar information. We look at how different types of practice influence memory. Finally, some attention is given to how we either separate out information in memory or integrate several pieces of experience and the effects this has on later memory.

THE CONTENTS OF EPISODIC MEMORY

Like most long-term memories, episodic memories are amalgams of various types of information. These different components can be used either as whole units or as separate pieces. For example, when you remember a birthday party, you may recall the people, food, music, and gifts. Alternatively, you may remember a conversation you had with someone at the party but have no memory of songs that were sung, what other guests were wearing, or the party decorations.

Serial Position Effects

The discussion of short-term memory in Chapter 4 introduced serial position curves. These are also seen in long-term memory, such as memories of going to the theater (Sehulster, 1989), although the recency effects are larger (Hitch & Ferguson, 1991). The explanations for serial position curves in episodic memory are different from those for short-term memory. Primacy and recency effects can more clearly be attributed to the distinctiveness of those positions (Healy, Havas, & Parker, 2000). In addition, the primacy effect reflects a novelty process. The first item is unusually relative to the context that preceded it, and so it is remembered better. The recency effect reflects a standard forgetting curve, with more recent events being remembered better than older events. Finally, events at the beginning and end of a sequence are less susceptible to interference (see later in the chapter). The primacy effect reflects less proactive interference, and the recency effect reflects less retroactive interference.

Levels of Representation

When we experience an event, we process it at multiple levels. Each of these levels leaves a memory trace. An illustration of this is memory for text, where there are three levels of representation: the surface form, the textbase, and the mental model (van Dijk & Kintsch, 1983). The surface form captures the verbatim text. This is important initially but is usually quickly forgotten (Hayes-Roth & Hayes-Roth, 1977; Sachs, 1967, 1974). The textbase is an abstract representation. For example, the sentences "The girl hit the boy" and "The boy was hit by the girl" have different surface forms but the same underlying meaning, which is captured by the textbase. At the highest level is the mental model (Johnson-Laird, 1983; Zwaan & Radvansky, 1998), which represents the state of affairs described by the text rather than the text itself (Glenberg, Meyer, & Lindem, 1987). The mental model is a mental simulation of the described events.

In general, mental models are remembered over long periods of time. People use knowledge at this level to make memory decisions about what was encountered before (Bransford, Barclay, & Franks, 1972; Garnham, 1981; Jahn, 2004; Rinck, Hähnel, & Becker, 2001). For example, people who read "The turtles sat on a log, and the fish swam beneath them" are more likely to say later that they read the sentence "The turtles sat on a log, and the fish swam beneath it" because this sentence describes the same situation.

In a study by Kintsch, Welsch, Schmalhofer, and Zimny (1990), people read a text and then took a recognition test either immediately, 40 minutes, 2 days, or 4 days later. The results, shown in Figure 7.1, reveal that the surface form memory decays rapidly. The textbase memory, although better than the surface form, continues to decline. However, memory for the mental model was relatively durable and did not show much change. As a real-life example, when you read a newspaper article, you quickly forget the exact wording, but remember the basic ideas for a while, at least. However, your memory for the event described in the article (what the article was about) is more enduring and is what you remember over the long term.

Cuing. When we recall an event, we sometimes need a prompt. This is called **cuing.** Memory cues generally improve retrieval (e.g., Tulving & Pearlstone, 1966). The retrieval cue helps a person access memory traces that contain the same information (Bransford & Stein, 1984). Long-term memory is content addressable, so we can access information using the components that make it up.

Types of Cues. There are two types of episodic retrieval cues: feature cues and context cues. Feature cues involve components of the memory itself. One of the best feature cues is yourself. If you can relate things to aspects of who you are, then your memory will be

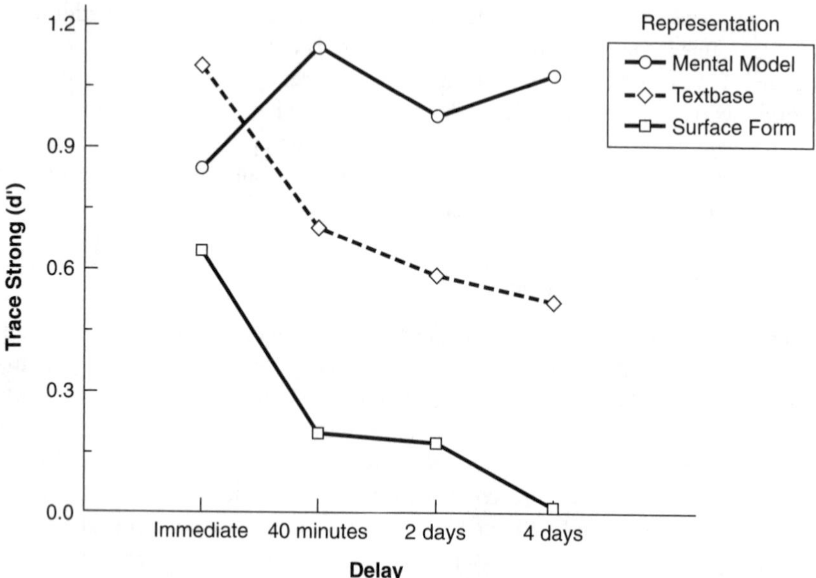

FIGURE 7.1 Episodic Memory Retention for Information at the Surface Form, Textbase, and Mental Model Levels

Source: Reprinted from *Journal of Memory and Language,* 29, Kintsch, W., Welsch, D., Schmalhofer, F., & Simny, S., Sentence memory: A theoretical analysis, pp. 133–159, 1990, with permission from Elsevier.

better (e.g., Bellezza, 1992; Symons & Johnson, 1997). In contrast, context cues involve the setting or environment. For example, one sentence from the list may remind you of the others, because each sentence was part of the context of the others.

A particularly powerful type of memory cue is odors, which can be either a feature or a context cue. The smell of things is a good memory cue because of the ease with which odors tap into emotional aspects of memories (Herz & Engen, 1996). This is why some odors are strongly associated with certain emotions (think flowers and perfumes). This may be because of the strong neurological connection between olfactory parts of the cortex and the amygdala and hippocampus (only two or three synapses).

Context

Context can be a powerful memory cue. A variety of contexts can influence memory. Two important ones are external and internal context. External context is the environment outside a person, such as the room he or she is in, the lighting level, or the objects and people present. Internal context is the environment inside a person, such as physiological state, emotions, and his or her thoughts at the time.

Encoding Specificity. A well-known influence of context on memory is the **encoding specificity** principle (Thompson & Tulving, 1970). This is the superior ability to remember when retrieval occurs in the same context as information that was learned as compared to a different context. For example, if you learn something in one room, it is easier to recall it when you are in the same room. It is not unusual to fail to remember something until you return to the room where you got the information in the first place. Smith (1988) provides a clear account of the power of encoding specificity.

> Having lived most of his life in St. Louis, Missouri, except for 2 years at the University of Texas at Austin, and 4 years in the military service during the Second World War, my father returned to Texas after 42 long years of forgetting. Although previously certain that he could recall only a few disembodied fragments of memories of his college days, he became increasingly amazed, upon his return, at the freshness and detail of his newly remembered experiences. Strolling along the streets of Austin, my father suddenly stopped and animatedly described the house in which he lived in a location now occupied by a parking lot. He recalled in vivid detail, for example, how an armadillo had climbed up the drainpipe one night and became his pet, and how the woman who had cooked for the residents of his house had informed them of the attack on Pearl Harbor, abruptly ending his college career. Not until he returned to the setting in which those long-past events had occurred had my father thought or spoken of them. (p. 13)

The encoding specificity principle is illustrated nicely in a study in which scuba divers learned lists of words. Some lists were learned on land, and others were learned underwater. Later the divers were tested in either the same or a different context. As shown in Figure 7.2, memory was better when the words were recalled in the same context than in the different one (Godden & Baddeley, 1975).

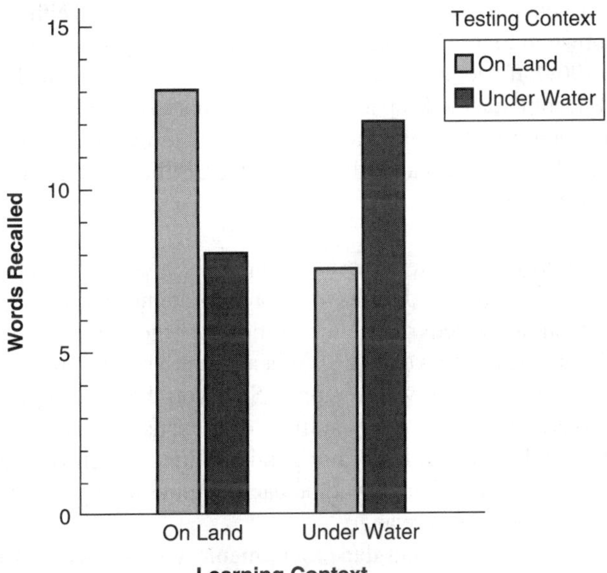

FIGURE 7.2 Results of Study Illustrating the Effect of Encoding Specificity on Memory for Word Lists

Source: Reproduced with permission from the Journal of Neuropsychology, © The British Psychological Society.

The effects of encoding specificity are quite reliable. They occur when an environment is actually present or only thought about (Smith, 1979, 1984). Also, although it initially seemed that encoding specificity was stronger with recall than with recognition (Smith, Glenberg, & Bjork, 1978), it actually operates in both (Smith & Vela, 2001). However, the influence of context during recognition benefits from conscious recollection (Macken, 2002). If people distract themselves from the immediate environment during learning (Smith & Vela, 2001), then encoding specificity may not be apparent.

As a student, you may think encoding specificity means that it is better to study in the same room where you will take an exam. However, this applies encoding specificity in a suboptimal way. Memories are strongly associated with a context when things are always presented in the same one. Something that is learned in many different contexts—if you study in different places—does not have a strong encoding specificity influence. The information is more context independent (Smith, Glenberg, & Bjork, 1978). You can use your knowledge when you need it, not just when you happen to be in the right place. Another concern is that being in a familiar context can make incorrect information on a recognition test seem like it is remembered just because of an increased feeling of familiarity (Hockley, 2008; Ngo, Sargent, & Dopkins, 2007).

State-Dependent Memory. Encoding specificity may refer to external contexts, such as a room. However, there are internal contexts, such as a person's physiological state (e.g., being sleepy, drunk, or excited), which is also stored in memory. Memory is better remembered when people are in a similar physiological state during recall as they were during learning. This is **state-dependent memory.** An example of this is seen in a study in which people learned while they were sober or drunk. They then took a memory test in either the same or a different state. As shown in Figure 7.3, memory was better when people were in the same state (Goodwin et al., 1969). If people studied while drunk, they did better on the test if they took it while drunk. (It is important to keep in mind that memory is worse overall if a person is drunk during learning or testing.) Similar state-dependent memory effects occur with nicotine (Peters & McGee, 1982), marijuana (Eich, Weingartner, Stillman, & Gillin, 1975), and Ritalin (Swanson & Kinsbourne, 1976).

Mood-Dependent Memory. Another internal context is mood or emotion. We are always in some mood. These emotional states are stored in memory, allowing for **mood-dependent memory.** Memory is better if we are in the same mood we were in when we learned something (Blaney, 1986; Bower, 1981). When you are happy, you better remember things you learned when you were happy. Say you have a fight with your boyfriend/girlfriend. While you are angry, you think of reasons why he or she is a jerk. Later, you calm down and think about his or her good qualities. When you have another fight weeks later, all those negative thoughts come back to mind more easily because you initially thought of them while you were angry.

A case for the importance of mood-dependent memory was made by Eich (1995), who suggested that encoding specificity and state-dependent memory are simply forms of mood-dependent memory. Different environments elicit different emotions. If two different places elicit similar emotions, they lead to better memory. A similar argument is made for state-dependent memory. Different physiological states tend to produce different affective states, which then influence memory.

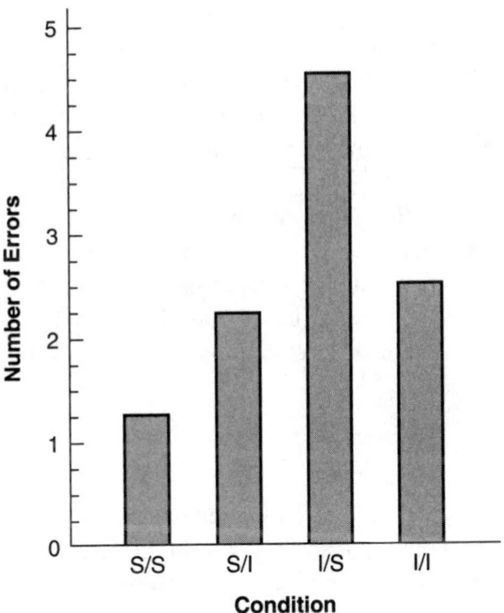

FIGURE 7.3 Results of a Study on State-Dependent Memory. The various condition labels represent "Study state" / "Test state" with S = sober and I = intoxicated

Source: Goodwin et al., (1969). Alcohol and recall: State-dependent effects in man. *Science, 163,* 2358–2360.

A related concept is **mood-congruent memory** in which it is easier to think of things that are congruent with one's current mood, such as a depressed mood makes it more likely that depressing ideas will be retrieved. Mood-congruent memory is supported by neurological work. Maratos et al. (2001) tested memory for words that were read in emotionally positive, emotionally negative, or neutral sentences. Later, a recognition test was given during an fMRI scan. Words that were read in emotionally positive or negative contexts were accompanied by more activation in brain regions associated with emotion processing, such as the amygdala and oribitofrontal cortex (B.A. 11).

Context has wide-ranging influences on episodic memory. As noted by Terry (2000), other types of context that influence memory include music (Smith, 1985), odors (Cann & Ross, 1989), temperature (Richardson, Guanowsky, Ahlers, & Riccio, 1984), time of day (Holloway, 1978), body position (lying down or standing up) (Rand & Wapner, 1967), phone calls (Canas & Nelson, 1986), and pain (Pearse et al., 1990). Even the sound of a person's voice can be a context and can influence memory (Goh, 2005).

Transfer Appropriate Processing. Memory is also influenced by a person's thought processes during learning. Memory is better when retrieval uses mental processes that are more in tune with those used at learning, a principle called **transfer appropriate processing** (Kolers & Roediger, 1984; Roediger & Blaxton, 1987; but see, e.g., Mulligan & Lozito, 2006). This principle is related to the idea of depth of processing discussed in Chapter 3. When learning uses processing that emphasize meaning, this has a greater positive impact on direct memory tests such as recall or recognition. In contrast, when learning emphasizes shallow surface characteristics, this has a greater impact on indirect memory tests, possibly because similar neural structures are activated when transfer appropriate processing occurs (Schendan & Kutas, 2007). In a study by Morris, Bransford, and Franks (1977), students responded to words using either a meaning-based (deep-level) task, such as whether the word "plane" made sense in the sentence "The ________ had a silver engine" or a rhyme-based (shallow-level) task, such as whether the word "eagle" made sense in the sentence "________ rhymes with legal." Later, students took either a standard recognition test (a direct memory test) or a rhyming recognition test (an indirect test) in which they indicated whether a new word rhymed with one that they had heard earlier (e.g., "regal"). The results, shown in Figure 7.4 reveal that memory is better when the encoding and retrieval processes match than when they do not. Thus, depth of processing is not a clear guide to future memory. Instead, how successful memory is in the future depends on how people think about information.

Synopsis

Episodic memory is for individual experiences. These memories are influenced by the order in which things were learned, showing a serial position curve. They also contain both content information as well as the context in which things were learned. Both content and context can be used as cues to aid remembering. Context can refer to the external environment, or a person's physiological or emotional state. Finally, episodic memories also contain information about how they were created, as illustrated by transfer appropriate processing. It is easier to remember when people use the same mental processes that they used when they first learned the information.

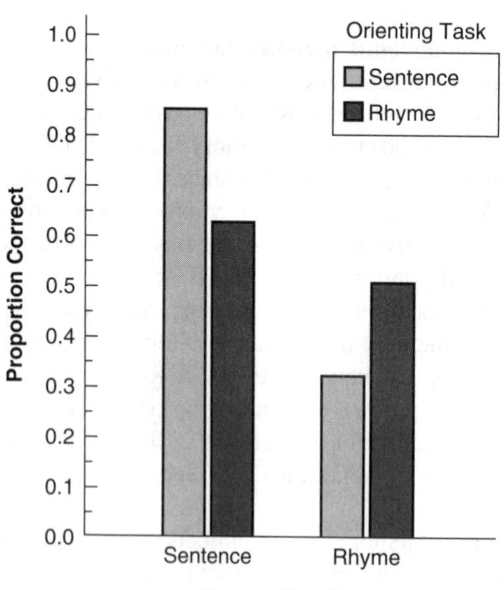

FIGURE 7.4 Results of a Study of Transfer Appropriate Processing

Source: Reprinted from *Journal of Verbal Learning and Verbal Behavior,* 16, Morris, C.D., Bransford, J. D., & Franks, J. J., Levels of processing versus transfer appropriate processing, pp. 519–533, 1977, with permission from Elsevier.

IRRELEVANT MEMORIES

Each experience that we have alters what is stored as a memory. Even the act of remembering alters memory because the *experience* of remembering gets stored. A consequence of this multiplication of memory traces is that episodic memories compete with one another. This competition is **interference**. Interference, rather than decay or disuse, is a primary mechanism of forgetting in long-term memory (McGeoch, 1932). There are ways to control interference, such as the process of **inhibition**.

Interference

Interference occurs in memory retrieval when there is competition between traces. When there are two or more traces that have overlapping information, and you only want one of them, interference develops. For example, suppose you are trying to remember your friend Mary's phone number. You remember getting the number when you met Mary for lunch, but Susan was there, too, and you also got her number. These two memories compete because they both contain phone numbers and the element of having lunch. Here, several kinds of interference are covered, including negative transfer, proactive interference, retroactive interference, associative, and general interference.

Negative Transfer. **Negative transfer** is a kind of interference in which prior knowledge impedes the learning of new information (Anderson, 2000). For example, if a person has learned to drive a standard-shift car and then drives one with an automatic transmission, there may be negative transfer and the person tries to press on the clutch (which isn't there). The memory traces for old information are well established when new information is encountered. Because these older memories are so strong, they are activated when a person tries to learn something new, and they block the acquisition of the new information.

The amount of negative transfer experienced is a function of the degree of overlap between the old and new information. In a study by Postman and Stark (1969), students at Berkeley memorized lists of paired associates. After learning an A-B list, negative transfer was observed in the ability to learn a second list when the old responses were paired with new cues (C-B), new responses were paired with old cues (A-C), the pair items were recombined (A-Br), or synonyms were used (A-B') relative to a control condition using new lists (C-D). When the new information overlapped with the old, learning was impeded. The amount of negative transfer was greater when memory was tested using recall than recognition (Postman & Stark, 1969). This is because there are more traces that can get involved and compete for output during recall, whereas for recognition, the memory search is more targeted on a few, or one, memory trace(s).

The impact of negative transfer can be profound. In a classic study by Kay (1955; see also Fritz et al., 2000) students at Cambridgeshire Technical College were given two stories to read for later recall. They then recalled the stories immediately and five more times over the next 4 months. Importantly, students were given opportunities to reread the stories after each recall attempt. What was striking was that when students made an error in story recall, the error often persisted through additional recall attempts, even though there was an opportunity to correct each mistake after each rereading. There was negative transfer of the old incorrect knowledge blocking the ability to acquire the newer correct information. This negative transfer is more profound for emotional information (Novak & Mather, 2009). So, it is best to try to understand something correctly the first time, to as great a degree as possible.

Proactive Interference. **Proactive interference** occurs when old knowledge causes an increase in the forgetting of new knowledge (Underwood, 1957). For example, if a person studies psychology and then studies sociology, there is greater forgetting and worse performance on a subsequent sociology test. Although proactive interference and negative transfer seem alike because they both involve older information impeding memory for newer information, negative transfer applies to learning new information, whereas proactive interference refers to forgetting of memory traces for new information.

The degree of proactive interference experienced depends on the amount of overlap between different sets of information, (Postman & Keppel, 1977). The more related the information a person has memorized, the more proactive interference there is. The difficulty differentiating between memory traces because of their content leads to proactive interference. This is why sociology and psychology interfere with one another. Any effort that you can make to distinguish and differentiate sets of information reduces the amount of interference, and memory improves accordingly. Proactive interference is resolved by processes using the left lateral prefrontal cortex (B.A. 46), although the right dorsolateral prefrontal cortex (B.A. 8) and parietal regions (B.A. 7) may be involved as well (Nee & Jonides, 2008).

There is a buildup of proactive interference over time that continues until people are given information that differs from the old knowledge. At that point, memory improves, and there is release from proactive interference. A study by Wickens (1972) illustrates release from proactive interference. In this study, people were given lists of words to remember (see Table 7.1). The words in the first three lists were all fruits. If the fourth list were fruits again, then memory continued to decline, as shown in Figure 7.5. However, if the words in the fourth list belonged to a new category, *release from proactive interference* occurs. The greater the difference, the greater the release. For example, vegetables are different from fruits, but they still have some traits in common, whereas professions are quite distinct from fruits.

Retroactive Interference. **Retroactive interference** occurs when new knowledge makes it difficult to remember old knowledge (Melton & Irwin, 1940). A classic demonstration of this is a study by Jenkins and Dallenbach (1924) in which students at Cornell University learned lists of ten nonsense syllables. They were then tested 1, 2, 4, and 8 hours later. What is important is what they did during this time. Half of the time, they were given the lists early in the day, so they were awake the whole time. The rest of the time they were given the lists at night, so they were asleep during the retention period. The results in Figure 7.6 show less forgetting when the students slept than when they were awake. When people are awake, there is a continuous stream of new information (including thoughts). This new information produces retroactive interference, making the older information harder to remember. However, if people are asleep, there is not as much new information, so there is less retroactive interference and less forgetting.

As another example of retroactive interference, if you study psychology and then study sociology, you forget some of the psychology you studied because the newer sociology memory traces interfere with the retrieval of older psychology information.

TABLE 7.1 Stimulus Lists from Proactive Interference Study

CONDITION	TRIAL 1	TRIAL 2	TRIAL 3	TRIAL 4
Fruits (control)	banana peach apple	plum apricot lime	melon lemon grape	orange cherry pineapple
Vegetables	banana peach apple	plum apricot lime	melon lemon grape	onion radish potato
Flowers	banana peach apple	plum apricot lime	melon lemon grape	daisy violet tulip
Meats	banana peach apple	plum apricot lime	melon lemon grape	salami bacon hamburger
Professions	banana peach apple	plum apricot lime	melon lemon grape	doctor teacher lawyer

Source: Wickens, 1972.

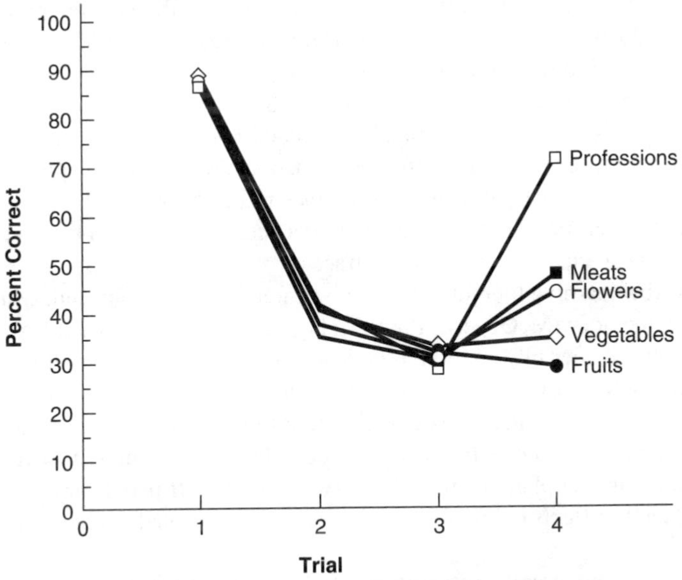

FIGURE 7.5 Results from a Study of Release from Proactive Interference

Source: Wickens, D. D. (1972). Characteristics of word encoding. In A. W. Melton & E. Martin (Eds.) *Coding Processes in Human Memory*, pp. 191–215. New York: Wiley.

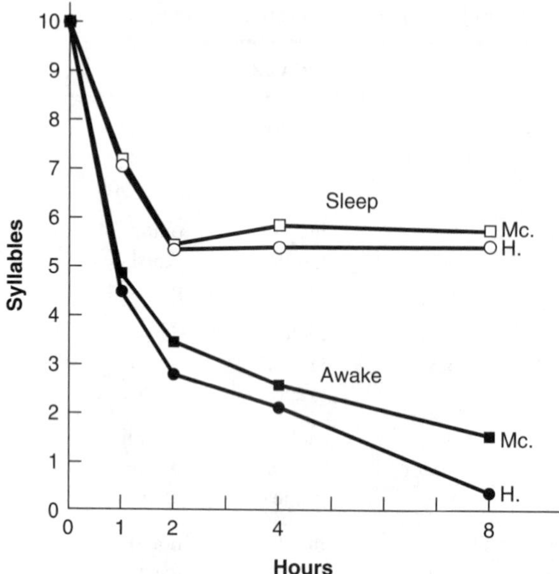

FIGURE 7.6 Results from a Study of Long-Term Memory Interference. Mc. and H. are the initials of the two subjects used in this study

Source: Jenkins, J. G., & Dallenbach, K. M. (1924). Oblivescence during sleep and waking. *American Journal of Psychology, 35,* 605–622.

Alternatively, if you move to a new city, your memory for the new telephone numbers, street names, and stores cause retroactive interference, making it harder for you to remember the city you used to live in. In a study by Postman and Stark (1969) retroactive interference was observed in a variety of cases when there was overlap between two sets of paired associate lists. Like negative transfer, retroactive interference is more pronounced with recall than with recognition. During recall people try to sort through a large number of competing memory traces, allowing interference to be observed, whereas during recognition there are fewer memory traces involved because a more direct match can be made between the retrieval cue and an individual trace.

In the verbal learning literature, retroactive interference was an "unlearning" of prior associations in memory (McGovern, 1964; Melton & Irwin, 1940). The idea was that new information causes older information to be lost or disrupted. However, this "unlearning" idea is not completely correct. There are cases where retroactive interference can subsequently be reduced or eliminated, suggesting that the original memories are still intact, even if they are difficult to use. Instead, retroactive interference may involve a disruption of the set of the retrieval plan that would otherwise be used. If people are given the appropriate cues, then the effects of retroactive inhibition are attenuated or eliminated (Tulving & Psotka, 1971).

Sleep can help overcome retroactive interference. One way is by avoiding sources of retroactive interference, as in the Jenkins and Dallenbach (1924) study. Another way is by strengthening weaker associations among information brought about by retroactive interference. For example, memory for A-B paired associate lists, after learning A-C lists, is better following sleep, with memory for the A-C lists being unaffected (Drosopoulos, Schulze, Fischer, & Born, 2007; Ekstrand, 1967).

Associative Interference. **Associative interference** reflects the associative complexity of newly learned information. The disruption of memory is not based on a temporal sequence (as is the case with the other forms of interference), but on the associations with a concept. For example, if you have just learned five things about Jenny, you will be slower to verify any one of these than if you had learned only one thing.

Often, associative interference is described in terms of the **fan effect.** The term *fan effect* assumes that information is stored in a memory network with nodes for individual concepts and links representing the associations among them (see Chapter 10). During retrieval, the more links "fanning" off of a concept, the greater the interference from the competing associations, and retrieval time increases accordingly. In a study of associative interference, Anderson (1974) gave students lists of sentences to memorize, such as "The doctor is in the park" or "The lawyer is in the museum." The number of associations with the person and location concepts (e.g., doctor or park) was varied from one to three. Thus, there were one to three places that a person could be in and one to three people in a location. After memorization, a recognition test was given in which students indicated whether the sentence was studied. Nonstudied sentences were recombinations of people and locations, such as "The doctor is in the museum." The results showed that as the number of associations increased, response time also increased, as seen in Figure 7.7. Like other types of interference, associative interference is reduced by practice (Pirolli & Anderson, 1985). Repeated exposure continues to make facts distinct relative to the others, thereby reducing competition at retrieval.

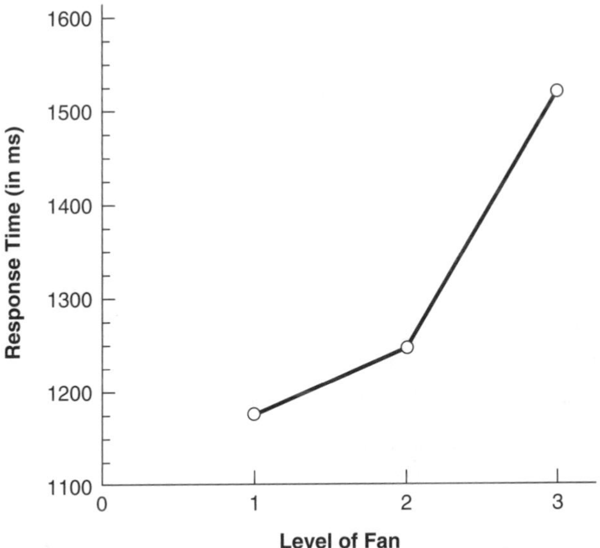

FIGURE 7.7 Results from a Study of Associative Interference Producing a Fan Effect

Source: Reprinted from Cognitive Psychology, 6, Anderson, J. R., Retrieval of propositional information from long-term memory, pp. 451–474, 1974, with permission from Elsevier.

An implication of associative interference is that the more you know, the harder it should be to remember. However, experts actually learn more information than novices with no deficit in remembering. This is "the paradox of the expert" (Smith, Adams, & Schorr, 1978). A way out of this paradox is to use chunking. Information that is integrated into a common memory trace reduces interference because there are fewer traces to compete with one another. Chunking can be done around a common theme, causal structure, ownership relations, locations, time frames, or people (Kole & Healy, 2007; Myers, O'Brien, Balota, & Toyofuku, 1984; Radvansky, Spieler, & Zacks, 1993; Radvansky, Wyer, Curiel, & Lutz, 1997; Radvansky & Zacks, 1991; Radvansky, Zwaan, Federico, & Franklin, 1998; Smith, Adams, & Schorr, 1978).

Let's look at chunking in detail. Suppose a person memorizes sentences about objects in locations. For some sentences, a single object is in several locations, such as "The potted palm is in the hotel," "The potted palm is in the barbershop," and "The potted palm is in the airport." In these cases, multiple mental models are created, because each sentence refers to a different situation. So, there are three memory traces that compete at retrieval. In contrast, for other sentences, multiple objects are in a single location, such as "The pay phone is in the laundromat," "The oak counter is in the laundromat," and "The ceiling fan is in the laundromat." In these cases, a single mental model is created that includes all of this information because it all refers to a single event. As such, there is only one memory trace, and thus no interference (Radvansky & Zacks, 1991). These differential interference effects are shown in Figure 7.8. This outcome is also observed when people retrieve information from maps that have been studied (Bower & Rinck, 2001) or make metamemory judgments of learning (McGuire & Maki, 2001).

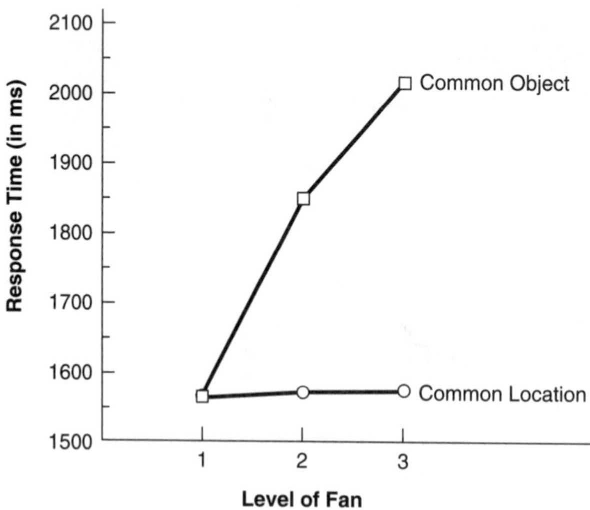

FIGURE 7.8 Differential Interference Effects When Information Can and Cannot Be Integrated Into Mental Models

Source: Radvansky, G. A., Spieler, D. H., & Zacks, R. T. (1993). Mental model organization. *Journal of Experimental Psychology: Learning, Memory, and Cognition, 19,* 95–114.

General Interference and Consolidation. As noted earlier, the more information overlaps in terms of content, the greater the degree of interference. However, there is more to interference than just overlapping content. Think again of the study by Jenkins and Dallenbach (1924). In this study when people slept they experienced less interference than when they did not. However, the information they learned were nonsense syllables. It is unlikely that people encountered many other nonsense syllables during their daily interaction with the world. So, what must be happening is that there is some kind of general interference that occurs when people are processing lots of different types of information in their daily activities.

General interference is reflected in *Jost's Law* (see Chapter 3) and the process of consolidation (Wixted, 2004, 2005). Memories are first held in a limited capacity short-term system, such as the hippocampus. When new things are learned, there is LTP as new memories are created, which displaces the older memories. This is why there is less retroactive interference following sleep or the disruption of new memories by some substance, such as alcohol (see Chapter 17). In general, the older a memory is, the more consolidated it is, and the less susceptible it is to general interference. Overall, if the formation of new memories is prevented, **retroactive facilitation** can occur in which older memories are remembered better.

Inhibition

Interference in memory is a problem if you want to remember accurately and quickly. One way to reduce or control it is by using **inhibition** to actively reduce the activation of interfering information. There are a number of ways that inhibition influences memory (Anderson, 2003, but see MacLeod et al., 2003).

Part-Set Cuing. As you learned, providing retrieval cues can aid memory. However, there are exceptions. If a person tries to remember a set of things, such as the names of sports teams, the probability of recalling any one of them is higher if a simple recall test is used than if some of the names are given as cues to help a person get started. This poorer memory when provided with partial information is **part-set cuing** (Nickerson, 1984; Slamecka, 1968). There are two mechanisms that can influence the part-set cuing effect (Bäuml & Aslan, 2006). One is that giving people part of the set disrupts their retrieval plan (Basden, Basden, & Galloway, 1977; Basden, Basden, & Stephens, 2002; Sloman, Bower, & Rohrer, 1991), similar to the collaborative inhibition discussed in Chapter 3.

Another explanation involves inhibition (e.g., Aslan, Bäuml, & Grudbeiger, 2007). When people recall an item from a set, it is at a higher level of activation than the rest, and it blocks access to others (Roediger, Stellon, & Tulving, 1977). This occurs in part because, to reduce the interference from the other items, they are inhibited (Anderson & Neely, 1996). As a person gets further and further into the set, the unrecalled traces get more and more inhibited, making it harder to recall or recognize them (Oswald, Serra, & Krishna, 2006). So, for part-set cuing, providing people with part of the set leads them to inhibit memory traces that might otherwise have been more available if they had been left alone.

Negative Priming. Inhibition is also observed with associative interference. When people need interfering memories immediately after they have been inhibited, they are less available (Radvansky, 1999). The decreased availability of memory traces that were recently inhibited is **negative priming.** It is the opposite of what is seen in normal (positive) priming, in which related information becomes more available (see Anderson, Garavan, Rivardo, & Chadwick, 1997, for an example of negative priming in working memory). More generally, this is a case of **retrieval-induced inhibition,** because remembering one thing makes remembering related things more difficult. In other words, remembering causes forgetting. This inhibition is effortful in that it declines when there are demands on the working memory (Radvansky & Copeland, 2006) or when a person is in a negative mood (Gunther, Ferraro, & Kirchner, 1996).

Repeated Practice. Finally, inhibition occurs when people repeatedly retrieve part of a set of items (Anderson, Bjork, & Bjork, 1994) (note that, like part-set cuing, this could also be a disruption of a person's retrieval plan; see Dodd, Castel, & Roberts, 2006). Repeated retrieval or practice causes competing traces to be inhibited (Bäuml & Kuhbandner, 2003; but see Perfect et al., 2004; Williams & Zacks, 2001). As a result, the probability of recalling the nonpracticed memories decreases (Tulving & Hastie, 1972). It is as though people are forgetting that information faster. This retrieval-induced inhibition for related but unpracticed memories is the **repeated practice effect** (Anderson & Spellman, 1995). This phenomenon occurs only when memory retrieval actually occurs, even if it is only by creating a mental image of the information (Saunders, Fernandes, & Kosnes, 2009). Merely exposing people to information is insufficient (Ciranni & Shimamura, 1999). Furthermore, there must be some competition or interference during retrieval (Anderson, Bjork, & Bjork, 2000), even if people think that this retrieval was part of some other task (Bäuml, 2002).

Here's an example of how to produce a repeated practice effect, using the diagram in Figure 7.9 as a guide. Suppose a person is given categories to learn, such as "red things," like "blood" and "tomato," and "foods," like "strawberry" and "crackers." Now if a person practices some items, such as "red-blood" and not others, the effects of inhibition are observed. The repeated rehearsal of certain items makes them easier to remember (not surprising). What is interesting is that, compared to a control condition, such as practicing "tool-pliers," this repeated practice makes unpracticed items less available because they are inhibited each time the "red-blood" item is rehearsed (because they are interfering competitors). This is also true for other items learned in that category, such as "tomato," but, more importantly, for other things that are part of that category in the real world, like "strawberry." The repeated practice effect occurs when the competitors share categories, like "red things" or "foods" (Anderson & Spellman, 1995), or syntactic class, like "nouns" (Dopkins & Ngo, 2002), sentences with similar concepts (Anderson & Bell, 2001; Gómez-Ariza, Lechuga, Pelegrina, & Bajo, 2005), or even elements of prose (Saunders & MacLeod, 2006).

The repeated practice effect is observed with both recall and recognition (Hicks & Starns 2004; Veling & van Knippenberg, 2004; Verde, 2004), as well as with indirect memory tests (Camp, Pecher, & Schmidt, 2005), so it is a pervasive phenomenon. Note that this retrieval-induced inhibition is only seen in indirect memory tests that tap into conceptual knowledge (such as generating category members) but not perceptually based knowledge (such as completing word stems) (Perfect, Moulin, Conway, & Perry, 2002).

The repeated practice effect can be modified depending on how people think about information. If people can integrate information, then the effect is reduced or eliminated (Anderson & McCulloch, 1999) because there are fewer competitors, no interference, and

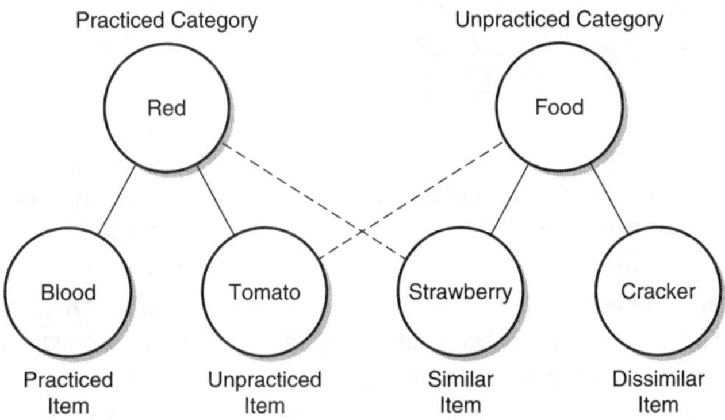

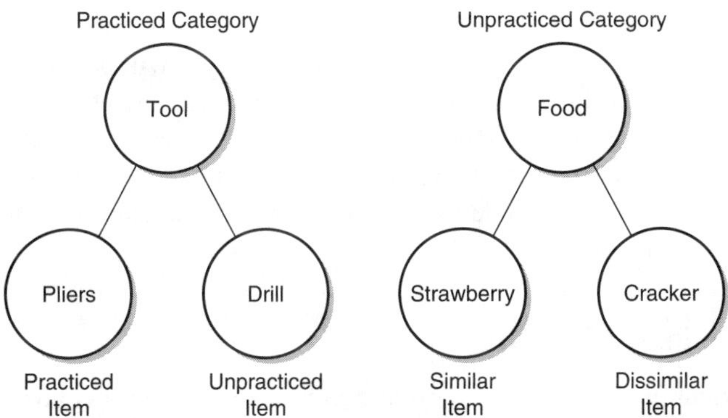

FIGURE 7.9 Operation of Retrieval-Induced Inhibition in a Repeated Practice Paradigm

Source: Anderson, M. C., & Spellman, B. A. (1995). On the status of inhibitory mechanisms in cognition: Memory retrieval as a model case. *Psychological Review, 102,* 68–100.

so no need for inhibition. Alternatively, if memory traces are made distinct from one another, this can also reduce the effect by reducing interference (Anderson, Green, & McCulloch, 2000; Smith & Hunt, 2000). Note that unretrieved and *highly* related traces may actually be facilitated rather than inhibited (Anderson, Green, & McCulloch, 2000; Bäuml & Hartinger, 2002; Chan, 2009; Chan, McDermott, & Roediger, 2006), perhaps because the information has been integrated, reducing the effects of interference. Also, note that for highly salient information, such as knowledge of one's self, this retrieval-induced forgetting is not observed (Macrae & Roseveare, 2002).

Inhibition, Working Memory, and Episodic Memory

The idea that memory retrieval uses inhibition is a claim that attention is needed to remember (Anderson & Neely, 1996). In Chapter 5, we saw that one role of working memory is to regulate attention. Thus, people who are better at working memory inhibition should also be better at long-term memory retrieval. In fact, people who do better on working memory span tests show less proactive interference (Kane & Engle, 2000) and less associative interference (Bunting, Conway & Heitz, 2004; Radvansky & Copeland, 2006).

Synopsis

Part of effective retrieval in episodic memory is sorting out relevant and irrelevant memories. When there are multiple, related episodic memories, this can produce interference, including proactive interference, retroactive interference, and associative interference. To regulate this, inhibition may be used to keep unwanted memories from entering the current memory process. This inhibition can make later retrieval of the inhibited memories difficult as seen with the part-set cuing, negative priming, and repeated practice effects. The operation of inhibition in episodic memory may be similar to that found in working memory.

REPETITION AND PRACTICE

The more a person is exposed to information, the more likely it will be remembered. This is called a **repetition effect.** For example, information that is studied twice is more likely to be remembered than that studied only once. However, repeated exposures vary in their effectiveness. For example, the effects of interference can be dramatically reduced for well-practiced material (Pirolli & Anderson, 1985). How information is practiced can have a profound impact on memory.

Massed and Distributed Practice

Practice at memorization can affect memory depending on whether it is grouped together or spread out over many sessions. This is a distinction between massed and distributed practice. **Massed practice** is when there is a single, lengthy study session. For example, if a person decides to spend 5 hours studying, massed practice would be a single 5-hour session. In contrast, **distributed practice** (also called *spaced practice*) occurs when effort is spread out across multiple study sessions. For example, a person studies for 5 hours, 1 hour per day for 5 days. In other words, massed practice is like cramming, and distributed practice is like consistently studying across a term. The difference between massed and distributed practice is important because, in general, memory is better following distributed practice than massed practice, and the longer the spacing between the distributed practices, the better the memory (Glenberg & Lehmann, 1980).

For example, in the results of a study shown in Figure 7.10, memory improved at a greater rate for distributed practice compared to massed practice. Distributed practice improves memory, even a year later (Pashler, Rohrer, Cepeda, & Carpenter, 2007). What is odd is that people are generally unaware of the impact of different kinds of practice. In a study by Zechmeister and Shaughnessy (1980), students thought that memory was better after massed practice than after distributed practice. This is the opposite of reality. There are three explanations for why this difference in practice types occurs (Greene, 1989; Toppino & Bloom, 2002). These are deficient-processing, encoding-variability, and two-process accounts.

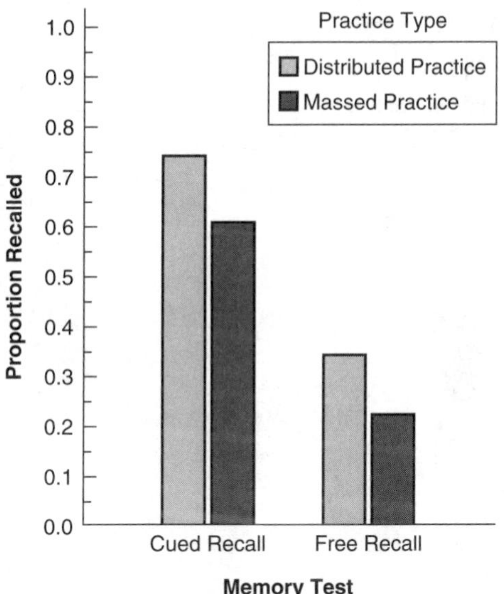

FIGURE 7.10 Effects of Massed Versus Spaced Practice on Subsequent Memory (with a Constant Context)

Source: Glenberg, A. M. (1979). Component-levels theory of the effects of spacing of repetitions on recall and recognition. *Memory & Cognition, 7,* 95–112. Permission granted upon citation of source.

Deficient Processing. For deficient-processing accounts massed practice reflects a processing deficiency for a number of reasons. Neurologically, massed practice may be inferior because in consolidation has not run its course, whereas with distributed practice, there is more consolidation, and better memory (Landauer, 1969). In terms of habituation/attention, people may habituate to information during massed practice and not actively attend to it, leading to poorer memory (Rundus, 1971; Zechmeister & Shaughnessy, 1980). Finally, there may be accessibility/reconstruction issues in that with massed practice less effort is needed to retrieve it because it is so fresh. As a result, people assume it is learned and do not devote the needed amount of time and effort to it.

Encoding Variability. For encoding-variability accounts, differences in the contextual information stored in memory traces account for massed and distributed practice differences (Glenberg, 1976, 1979). For distributed practice, the contexts (both internal and external) of each session are more distinct from one another, whereas in massed practice, they are roughly the same. A wider variety of learning contexts provide more retrieval pathways, making it more likely information will be remembered when needed.

An illustration of this is a study by Verkoeijen, Rikers, and Schmidt (2004) in which people had either massed or distributed practice, with all the items shown on the same or different backgrounds (context) each time. The results are shown in Figure 7.11. For massed practice, showing items on different backgrounds helped memory because, even though repetitions occurred close in time, each presentation was in a different context, thereby facilitating retrieval. In contrast, for distributed practice, the information was

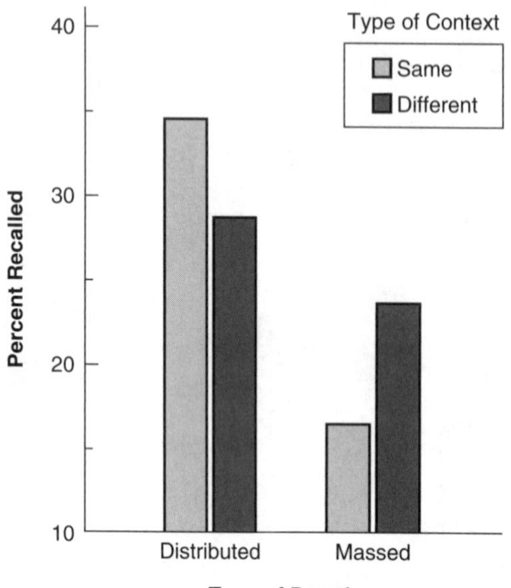

FIGURE 7.11 Effects of Massed Versus Spaced Practice on Subsequent Memory (with Varying Context)

Source: Verkoeijen, P. P. J. L., Rikers, R. M. J. P., & Schmidt, H. G. (2004). Detrimental influence of contextual change on spacing effects. *Journal of Experimental Psychology: Learning, Memory, and Cognition, 30,* 796–800.

already distinct, and so having each presentation of an item on a different background actually made things worse. Here, changing the context made it harder to remember previous study experiences, so memory was poorer. However, when the background was the same in distributed practice, this reminded a person of the previous experiences and facilitated memory.

Dual Processes. For dual process accounts, there are two processes that operate during retrieval, both deficient-processing and encoding variability (Greene, 1989; Russo, Parkin, Taylor, & Wilks, 1998; but see Toppino & Bloom, 2002). The encoding-variability component is more automatic because it involves the context, which has a largely unconscious effect on memory. In contrast, the deficient-processing component is more controlled and involves conscious, deliberate thinking.

Overlearning and Permastore

If a person continues to practice memorized information, then **overlearning** occurs. As reported by Ebbinghaus, overlearning strengthens memories, and increases resistance to forgetting. For example, actors and musicians continue to rehearse their parts even after they are flawless. Continued rehearsal strengthens memory, making forgetting less likely during a performance.

What about things that you learn in school? You are in college right now. What is the fate of the information you are learning? Is it subject to the forgetting curve? What is the point of learning if you're only going to forget it all later? Why try to get an A when, after a few years, the natural process of forgetting will more or less even everyone out? Well, although there is an initial period of forgetting, a great deal of what is learned in school is retained throughout life.

Harry Bahrick, a researcher at Ohio Wesleyan University, has addressed these issues. His method is to get people attending college reunions and test their memories for college course material, such as Spanish, from 3 months to 50 years after graduation. He discovered that, although there is an initial period of forgetting of about 3 years, there is little forgetting after that (Bahrick, 1984, 2000; Bahrick, Bahrick, & Wittlinger, 1975; Conway, Cohen, & Stanhope, 1991). Similar effects have been found in actors' memory for play lines (Noice & Noice, 2002). Whatever memory remains after 3 years is stable for the rest of your life and is said to be in **permastore** as a consequence of distributed practice and overlearning.

It is important to note that forgetting occurs at the same rate for everyone. So, people who learn more forget at the same rate as people who learn less. Even after the initial forgetting period, the same difference in knowledge levels persists. The people who got A's always know more than the people who got C's (Bahrick, 1984; Conway, Cohen, & Stanhope, 1991). So, study hard.

Still, for some information, there is no clear permastore benefit; it continues to be forgotten. These are generally things that have some isolated status and are difficult to relate to other things. This includes campus and town landmarks, things that a person is unlikely to have interacted with directly.

To Study or To Test

This part of the chapter has covered how distributed and massed practice affect memory. Now let's consider another important way to practice, namely by taking tests. Intuitively, it seems that studying would lead to better memory than testing. After all, studying is what gets the information in memory in the first place. However, the opposite is true. People typically learn more by taking a test than engaging in further study (Roediger & Karpicke, 2006; Pashler et al., 2007).

So, why does testing help memory? One thing testing does is reduce the rate of forgetting. In a study by Carpenter, Pashler, Wixted, and Vul (2008) people were assessed at delays from 5 minutes to 42 days. People practiced either by studying the material more or by taking tests. The forgetting curves from one experiment are shown in Figure 7.12. Note that the forgetting curve is shallower for material that was tested as compared to when it was only studied. Testing causes a person to engage in deeper processing (Carpenter, 2009). Moreover, testing reduces the effects of proactive interference that are observed with studying by itself (Szupnar, McDermott, & Roediger, 2008). Finally, taking a test may reveal to a person what is not yet known, and so any subsequent study efforts can be focused on that unknown material (Kornell, Hays, & Bjork, 2009). So, bottom line, a good way to improve learning, such as for the stuff you are trying to learn in your classes, is to take quizzes and tests that are either provided by the instructor, or that you make up to give to each other in a study group. In fact, the act of creating such tests will also boost memory because of the generation effect (see Chapter 3).

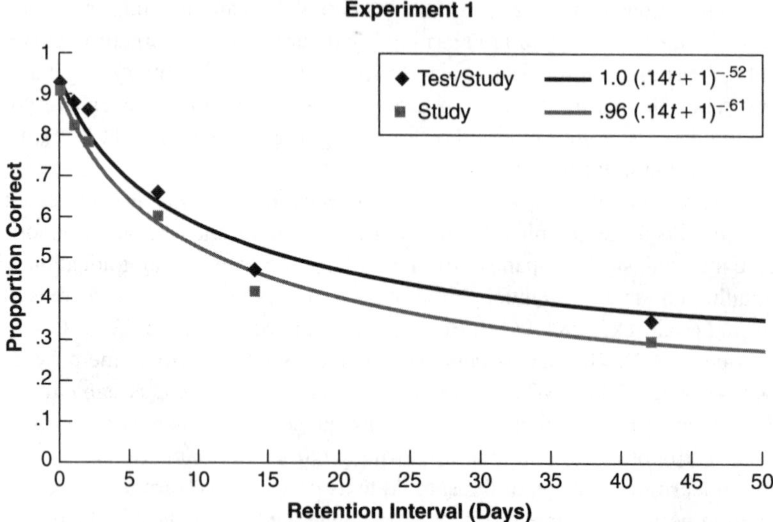

FIGURE 7.12 Forgetting Curves as a Function of Whether People Simply Studied Material, or Took a Test

Source: Carpenter, S. K., Pashler, H., Wixted, J. T., & Vul, E. (2008). The effects of tests on learning and forgetting. *Memory & Cognition, 36,* 438–448. Reprinted by permission.

Synopsis

A major factor that influences episodic memory is how information is practiced. Memory is better with distributed than massed practice because with massed practice some items are not processed well, and there are not as much contextual variety. Continued practice after information is well learned causes overlearning and leads information to be placed in permastore, where it is unlikely to be forgotten. Finally, the testing effect shows that there is better memory when practice takes the form of a test rather than simply studying.

ORGANIZATION AND DISTINCTIVENESS

Organization

Episodic memory improves if people use **organization**. Figure 7.13 shows data for a study across a number of study sessions when a set of words was presented in either an organized (i.e., based on categories) or random manner. Thus, the effects of chunking also work in long-term memory. An example of a pre-established structure that can aid memory is shown in Figure 7.14. Here, a hierarchical organization categorizes 18 words into groups of 3 or 4 items. Each of these sets is chunked, and some of the chunks are chunked. As described in Chapter 3, when people are not given an explicit organization, they use a subjective one (Bousfield, 1953) and impose a structure. When people subjectively cluster, it often takes some time for the organization to develop, but it still aids memory.

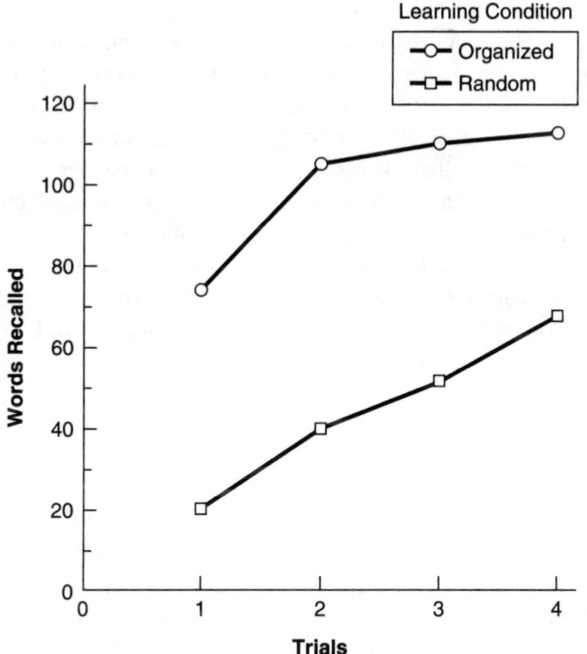

FIGURE 7.13 Forgetting Curves as a Function of Whether People Simply Studied Material, or Took a Test

Source: Reprinted from *Journal of Verbal Learning and Verbal Behavior,* 8, Bower, G. H., Clark, M. C., Lesgold, A, M., & Winzenze, D., Hierarchical retrieval schemes in recall of categorized word lists, pp. 323–343, 1969, with permission from Elsevier.

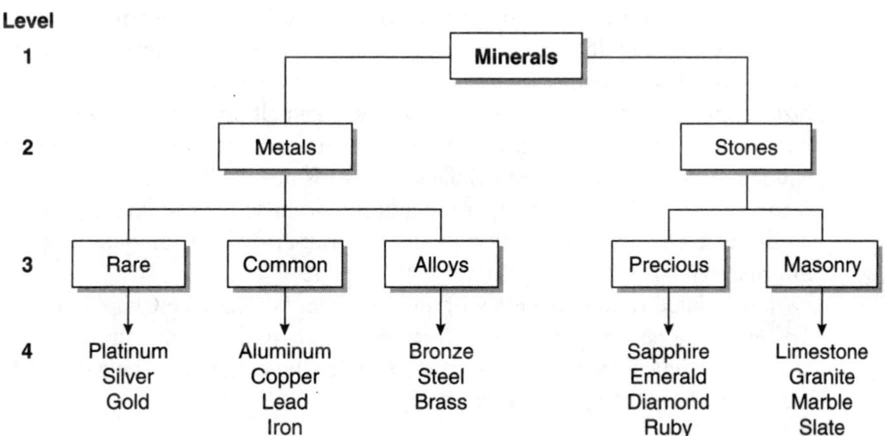

FIGURE 7.14 Example of a Hierarchical Structure That Can Be Used to Help Organize Memory

Source: Reprinted from *Journal of Verbal Learning and Verbal Behavior,* 8, Bower, G. H., Clark, M. C., Lesgold, A, M., & Winzenze, D., Hierarchical retrieval schemes in recall of categorized word lists, pp. 323–343, 1969, with permission from Elsevier.

The influence of organization and elaboration on memory is seen in actors' memories for scripts. Actors learn scripts in amazingly fast periods of time if one assumes that they are rote learning a series of sentences. However, they are doing much more than this. What they do is organize the material based not only on the semantic information, but also by creating integrated perceptually based images, self-referencing the information by taking the perspective of the character, generating the lines themselves as well as the manner in which they are delivered, and generating emotional states to match the mood of the character (Noice & Noice, 2006). These processes serve to organize the material into a larger whole.

More generally, almost everything you say is a *speech act*. That is, you are trying to accomplish something by your utterance (such as bragging, instructing, warning, etc.). Speech acts can then serve as organizational principles, allowing people to remember larger sets of language (Holtgraves, 2008).

Distinctiveness

Episodic memory is also enhanced when a memory trace is separated out from competitors that produce interference. Thus, memory is better for distinct items. For example, if one word is printed in red in a list of black words, the word in red is remembered better. Similarly, if the word *tulip* appears in a list of vehicle names, the word *tulip* will be remembered better. Memory for the unique item is better than memory for any one of the others. This is called the **von Restorff effect,** after the woman who discovered it (Hunt, 1995). This is also the reason why emotional information is remembered better than neutral information (Schmidt & Saari, 2007; Talmi, Luk, McGarry, & Moscovitch, 2007). Emotional events are distinct against a background of more common events.

Another example of distinctive processing is the effect of **bizarre imagery.** Here, people form mental images of something they are trying to remember. The very act of forming a mental image is a lot of work, so it improves memory (see Chapter 3). However, we can go a step further by creating bizarre images that are more distinctive. For example, to remember to buy ice cream, tomatoes, and carrots at the grocery store, you might imagine a bowl of ice cream with a face made with slices of tomatoes and carrots. However, bizarre imagery only improves memory when a small portion of the information gets this treatment. If more than half or everything is bizarre, none of the information is distinct, and memory is not improved (McDaniel & Einstein, 1986). This effect is seen with free recall and not with cued recall or recognition because bizarre imagery effects reflect the ability to access the information at retrieval rather than the amount of attention paid to information during learning (Riefer & Rouder, 1992).

A related finding occurs with the enactment effect (see Chapter 3). As a reminder, actions that a person performs are remembered better. The enactment effect is observed when only some actions are performed. People who enact everything do not have superior memories (Engelkamp & Zimmer, 1997).

Relational and Item-Specific Processing

At this point there may seem to be a contradiction. On the one hand, organization helps memory, but on the other hand, distinctiveness helps memory. These processes seem to be working in opposition. The more organized information is, the less distinctive the elements are, because similarities are emphasized. Conversely, the more distinct informa less organized it is, because differences are emphasized. However, it is also clear that both of these are at work (Hunt & Einstein, 1981; Hunt & McDaniel, 1993; Rawson & Van Overschelde, 2008). On the one hand, relational processing is helpful in generating a retrieval plan for later recall. On the other hand, item-specific processing helps reduce sources of interference. Each of these has an impact on memory (Einstein & Hunt, 1980). The degree to which each of these aids memory is a function of the current set of information.

An illustration of the differential effects of organization and distinctiveness is a study by Hunt and Seta (1984; see also McDaniel, Einstein, & Lollis, 1988) in which people learned items from categories of different sizes. People learned by emphasizing either relational processing (sorting items into categories) or distinctive, item-specific processing (rating items for pleasantness). The results, shown in Figure 7.15, illustrate that memory was better for small categories when relational processing was emphasized (helping identify the interrelations among the few members of a category) but was better for larger categories when distinctiveness processing was emphasized (helping people contend with larger amounts of interference).

Material Appropriate Processing. The distinction between item-specific and relational processing has implications for learning. Memory is better if the type of learning emphasizes the information for which memory is likely to be weak. For example, with descriptive texts, such as a college textbook, the emphasis is on sets of facts, or item-specific information. Thus, memory is better if people engage in learning that emphasizes relational information. In contrast, with narrative texts, such as a novel, the emphasis is on the narrative

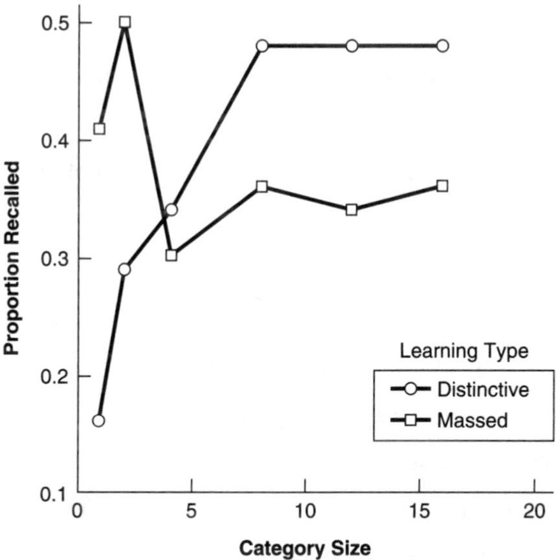

FIGURE 7.15 Effects of Learning Emphasizing Distinctiveness and Relational Processing as a Function of Category Size

Source: Hunt, R. R., & Seta, C. E. (1984). Category size effects in recall: The roles of relational and individual item information. *Journal of Experimental Psychology: Learning, Memory, and Cognition, 10,* 454–464.

flow and the interrelations among the events or relational information. Thus, memory is better in this case if people engage in learning that emphasizes item-specific information. This distinction between types of learning and memory for different types of texts is called **material appropriate processing** (Einstein, McDaniel, Owen, & Cote, 1990; McDaniel, Einstein, Dunay, & Cobb, 1986).

The distinction between item-specific and relational processing has a broad range of applications. For instance, it can help explain generation effects, which involve an increase in relational processing for the generated item (Burns, 1992; McDaniel & Bugg, 2008; McDaniel & Waddill, 1990; Mulligan, 2001).

Synopsis

Episodic memory effectiveness is influenced by how information relates to other memories that share some affinity with it. Memory is improved by putting the information into some organizational structure, and by making new information distinct from other memories. While these two seem to be at odds, both are effective under the right circumstances. Relational processing improves memory for information for which a person does not have a large knowledge base, and it is unclear how it relates to what is already known. Conversely, item-specific processing improves memory when a person already has a well-developed organization, thereby helping make this knowledge stand out and be less affected by interference.

SUMMARY

This chapter covered a number of issues about episodic memory. Episodic memories represent individual events, including knowledge of both content and context. Their retrieval is aided by cuing with either content or context information. In episodic memory forgetting is largely caused by interference with other memory traces. People can reduce the effects of interference through organization and the use of inhibition. Finally, memory effectiveness reflects the type of practice used, and the employment of both organization and distinctiveness processes.

STUDY QUESTIONS

1. What is the influence of serial order of event types on episodic memory?
2. What are kinds of knowledge that are stored in episodic memories?
3. What kind of information can be used to cue episodic memory?
4. How does context influence episodic memory? What are the different types of contexts?
5. What does transfer appropriate processing tell us about what information is stored in episodic memory and how it is remembered later?
6. What are the different ways in which interference disrupts memory retrieval?
7. What is the role of inhibition in episodic memory retrieval? What effects are produced by inhibition?

8. How does organization help episodic memory? How does distinctiveness help? How are they opposites? How can this puzzle be resolved?

9. How do different types of practice influence long-term episodic memory? Why is taking a test a better form of practice than simply studying?

KEY TERMS

associative interference, bizarre imagery, cuing, distributed practice, encoding specificity, episodic memories, fan effect, inhibition, interference, massed practice, material appropriate processing, mood-congruent memory, mood-dependent memory, negative priming, negative transfer, organization, overlearning, part-set cuing, permastore, proactive interference, repeated practice effect, repetition effect, retrieval-induced inhibition, retroactive facilitation, retroactive interference, semantic memories, state-dependent memory, transfer appropriate processing, von Restorff effect

TRY IT OUT

There are a number of principles of episodic memory that can be demonstrated as research projects. In this section, we consider three: cuing, proactive interference (and release from it), and part-set cuing. For each of these you need at least 12 people, with at least 12 in each group if there is to be more than one group.

- To demonstrate the effectiveness of **cuing**, we'll borrow from a study by Bransford and Stein (1984). First, read the list of sentences in the box to a group of people. Then, wait a minute, and have people try recall as many as they can by writing the sentences down on a sheet of paper.

A brick can be used as a doorstop.
A wine bottle can be used as a candle holder.
A record can be used to serve potato chips.
A leaf can be used as a bookmark.
A newspaper can be used to swat flies.
A sheet can be used as a sail.
A bathtub can be used as a punch bowl.
A rock can be used as a paperweight.
A pen can be used as an arrow.
A rug can be used as a bedspread.
A scissors can be used to cut grass.
A balloon can be used as a pillow.
A dime can be used as a screwdriver.
A ladder can be used as a bookshelf.
A pan can be used as a drum.
A guitar can be used as a canoe paddle.
An orange can be used to play catch.
A TV antenna can be used as a clothes rack.
A boat can be used as a shelter.
A flashlight can be used to hold water.
A knife can be used to stir paint.
A barrel can be used as a chair.
A telephone can be used as an alarm clock.
A board can be used as a ruler.
A shoe can be used to pound nails.
A lampshade can be used as a hat.

- When the people are done, have them draw a line under the last one they recalled. Then read these words:

Brick	Rock	Pan	Barrel
Wine bottle	Pen	Guitar	Telephone
Record	Rug	Orange	Board
Leaf	Scissors	TV antenna	Shoe
Newspaper	Balloon	Boat	Lampshade
Sheet	Dime	Flashlight	
Bathtub	Ladder	Knife	

If everything works out right, people will now be able to remember more sentences because the words in the list serve as retrieval cues for the sentences read earlier, and help people access otherwise forgotten memory traces.

- To illustrate the effect of **proactive interference**, and the subsequent **release from proactive interference,** we will use the example from Table 7.1. Give two or more groups of people the lists of fruit names. Have them recall the words at the end of each list. For all groups, the first three lists should be the same. However, on the fourth list, vary the nature of the list depending on the condition a person is in. Give one group another list of fruit names. However, give other groups lists of words that are more and more removed from fruits, namely, vegetables, flowers, meats, and professions. You don't need all of the groups to do this demonstration, but you need at least the first group and one other. If all goes well, everyone's memory gets worse from list 1 to 3, and that at list 4, the recall of the fruit group continues to get worse, but the recall of the other groups gets better, with the amount of improvement being related to how different the words are from fruits.
- Another memory phenomena that you can demonstrate is **part-set cuing** in which the probability of recalling an item is worse if you give people half of the list first than if you do nothing. For this you need two groups of people. First, for both groups, read everyone a list of 20 words. Then, have people recall the words. For the control group, have people try to recall all 20 words. For the experimental group, first give people ten of the words from the original list, and then have them try to recall the other ten. Then, score the recall of both groups only for the ten words that were not provided for the experimental group. If all goes well, the rate of recalling these words will be worse in the experimental group than in the control group.

CHAPTER EIGHT

MEMORY FOR SPACE AND TIME

Space and time. According to physicists, this is the fabric that makes up our reality. They also provide the framework for the events that we experience and remember. Spatial information allows us to navigate, locate objects, estimate distances, and so on. In this chapter we look at how memory for spatial configurations corresponds to physical layouts and the influences that distort memory for space. In general, space is a relatively static dimension of reality. We can move from one location to another and back again with ease and with little change in the spaces themselves. In contrast, temporal information allows us to understand when events occurred, with respect to the present, to other events in the past, or even to a standard time scale, such as a calendar. Unlike spatial location, our current place in time is always, inexorably, being pushed forward. We can't go back. This chapter addresses how time information is stored and retrieved from memory, influencing how accurate people are in locating memories in time.

MEMORY FOR SPACE

Although space may be the final frontier in science fiction, it is far from that in memory research. There have been many studies of memory for spatial information. In fact, the study of memory and space was one of the research areas with rats that helped bring an end to radical behaviorist views in psychology (Tolman, 1948). One of the appeals of spatial knowledge is that it is easy to understand exactly what was present in the world. We can get precise measurements of spatial reality. We can measure distances, areas, curvatures, and so forth. We can then directly compare these measurements to memory of these qualities. Also, there are parts of the brain dedicated to processing spatial knowledge. Single-cell recordings have shown that certain parts of the hippocampus are important for knowing spatial locations (e.g., Muller, Kuble, & Ranck, 1987; Muzzio, Kentros, & Kandel, 2009; O'Keefe & Dostrovsky, 1971; Shapiro, Tanila, & Eichenbaum, 1997; for a review, see Burgess, 2002), and there is a region of the cortex, the parahippocampal place area (B.A. 36), that fMRI studies have shown to be critical to understanding the local space (Epstein & Kanwisher, 1998) and can disrupt spatial memory encoding if it is damaged in humans (Epstein et al., 2001). This part of the chapter discusses how actual spatial information relates to one's memory for a space by looking at memory psychophysics, memory for information learned from maps, and how our interaction with the world affects our spatial memory.

Memory Psychophysics

How well do our memories for space correspond to actual spaces? The part of psychology that deals with how experience of the world corresponds to physical properties is **psychophysics.** Many psychophysicists study issues of sensation and perception and have established some consistent "laws" of psychophysical relations. A prominent one is **Steven's Law** of psychological magnitude (Stevens & Galantner, 1957). According to this law, the relation between actual and perceived magnitudes is a power function that is captured by the formula $\Psi = k\Phi^n$. Here, Ψ corresponds to psychological magnitude, the mental experience of an actual physical magnitude, Φ, raised to a power, *n*, and modified by a constant, *k*. The same principles can be used to study memory. This is memory psychophysics (e.g., Algom, 1992; Björkman, Lundberg, & Tärnblom, 1960; Moyer, Sklarew, & Whiting, 1982). Memory psychophysics has been applied to a number of domains, including memory for size, area, loudness, and labor pains (Algom & Lubel, 1994; Algom, Wolf, & Bergman, 1985; Chew & Richardson, 1980; Kerst & Howard, 1978, 1983; Moyer et al., 1977). Here, we consider memory psychophysics for spatial properties, such as distance and area.

The relation between actual and perceived spatial distance is fairly good. The exponent in Steven's Law is close to 1, which means that our perceptual experience of space is a near perfect one-to-one relationship. As for our memory of space, such as distance, the relation is still good, but there are noticeable distortions (Wiest & Bell, 1985). The amount of distortion is less when the space was originally viewed all at once compared to when it is inferred from memory from separate experiences (e.g., estimating distances between buildings in a city that are separated by other buildings, so the actual distance cannot be viewed directly).

Category Adjustment Theory. Category Adjustment Theory (Huttenlocher, Hedges, & Duncan, 1991; Newcombe et al., 1999) is a fuzzy trace account of memory for space. According to this view, performance reflects a combination of both fine-grained and coarse-grained memories. Objects in space are located within regions that serve as categories or schemas. Thus, a person remembers the object itself as well as the category to which it belongs. For example, if you are trying to remember where a certain city is located in the country, you may have a fine-grained memory of the actual location of the city on a map, as well a coarse-grained categorical memory of the area it is in, such as which state it is in. Memory for space is always a combination of these two influences. However, these sources vary in their relative contribution at any given occasion. The more influence the fine-grained memories have during retrieval, the weaker the influence of the coarse-grained memories (Radvansky et al., 1995; Sampaio & Wang, 2008), and vice-versa (Kemp, 1988).

Mental Maps

Of course, memory for space is more complex than just remembering distances. People create complex mental representations to help guide their travels around the house, through town, and across the country. We carry around mental maps of the environments we encounter to help us navigate and do other kinds of spatial thinking. This section looks at how mental maps are represented and used in memory.

Spatial Theories. The first class of theories is *spatial* because these theories assume that mental maps are structured according to the same structure as space. Here, mental maps are second-order isomorphs (Shepard & Chipman, 1970) that functionally capture the structure of a real map, although, neurologically, there is no one-to-one relationship between the two (which would be a first-order isomorph). For example, a clock is a second-order isomorph of the daily rotation of the Earth (by capturing that regular temporal quality), but a model of the solar system in which the Earth spins each day is a first-order isomorph.

The simplest version of a spatial theory is that a mental map corresponds directly to the space it represents, called a **metric view.** Given the results in memory psychophysics studies, this seems reasonable. However, there have been few serious metric theories (e.g., Kosslyn, Ball, & Reisser, 1978; Levine, Jankovic, & Palij, 1982), because mental maps are almost always distorted in some way.

One major influence is areas or regions. Space is not uniform. The world is divided into continents, continents are (often) divided into countries, countries are divided into states or provinces, and so on. There are many ways that we chop up space. Locations are often assigned to superordinate locations, or regions. The **hierarchical view** (Stevens & Coupe, 1978) is that mental maps are organized the same way. Figure 8.1 gives an example of a hierarchical representation for cities in Colorado and Ohio. This spatial hierarchy reflects the organization of smaller areas into larger ones, and can lead people to make errors. For example, when people estimate the direction between two locations, these estimates may be in error if the actual direction between the two places is different from the relation between the hierarchical regions, as shown in Figure 8.2. People often mistakenly report that San Diego, CA, is west of Reno, NV, because California is generally west of Nevada. However, Reno is actually farther west than San Diego. Thus, the direction of the superordinate regions influences spatial memory.

A mental map that was based strictly on spatial regions would be categorical. All of the locations within a region could be considered more or less the same, but this is not the case. More complex mental map theories, like the partially hierarchical view (McNamara, 1986), use a combination of metric and region information. Some of the best evidence for this

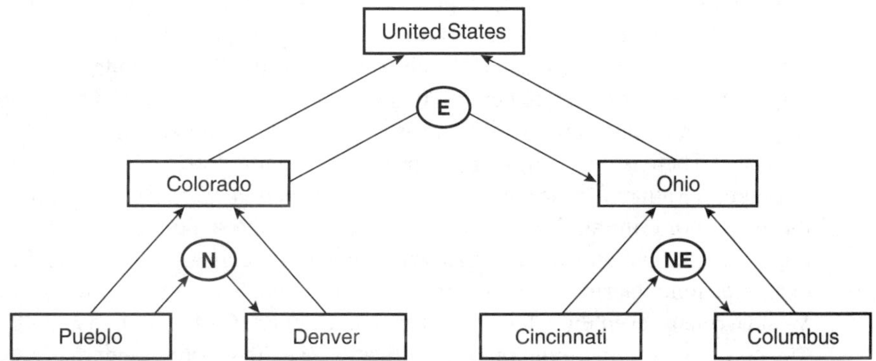

FIGURE 8.1 Hierarchical Representation of Space

Source: Reprinted from *Cognitive Psychology,* 10, Stevens, A., & Coupe, P., Distortions in judged spatial relations, pp. 422–437, 1978, with permission from Elsevier.

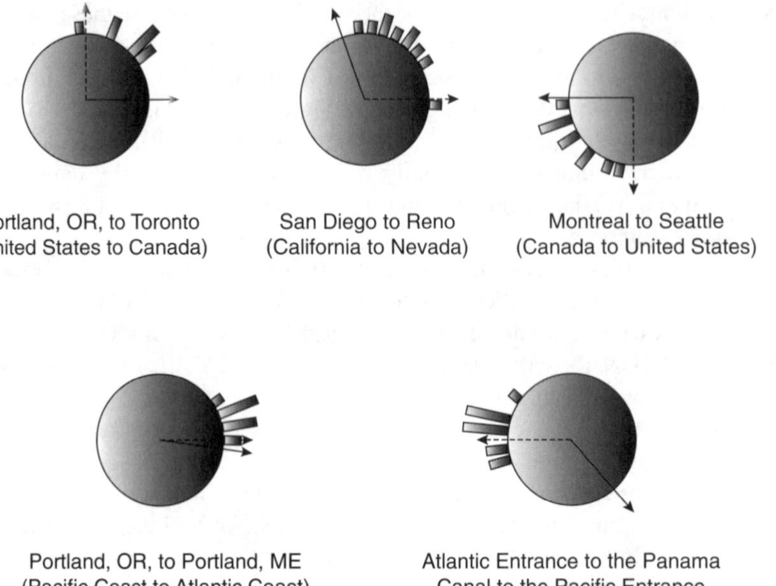

FIGURE 8.2 Distortion of Direction Judgments as Influenced by Superordinate Regions. The bars indicate the number of responses given for a certain direction

Source: Reprinted from *Cognitive Psychology,* 10, Stevens, A., & Coupe, P., Distortions in judged spatial relations, pp. 422–437, 1978, with permission from Elsevier.

view comes from spatial priming studies in which people first memorized a map that was divided into regions. Within each region were a set of locations, such as cities or objects (see Figure 8.3). After memorization, people were given a primed recognition test (see Chapter 3) in which a series of location names is given, and the people indicate whether those names were on the map. Priming was measured by looking for any speedup in response times for target object as a function of the spatial proximity of the prime object. In general, mental map locations prime one another (McNamara, 1986), as shown in Table 8.1. There is more priming (people are faster) for close locations (e.g., *key* and *spool* in Figure 8.3) than for far locations (e.g., *candle* and *needle*). Moreover, regions mediate the amount of priming. Keeping Euclidean distance the same, there is less priming across regions (e.g., *boat* and *stapler*) than within a region (e.g., *key* and *spool*). In a real-world example, some Germans overestimate distances between cities in the former East and West Germany, even though the country is now united (Carbon & Leder, 2005). Moreover, the more negative their opinion of reunification (i.e., the more salient the East-West differences are in their mind), the greater the overestimation (see Maddox, Rapp, Brion, & Taylor, 2008 for a related account involving social relations). Thus, this partially hierarchical influence is seen even when the region divisions are subjective rather than objective (McNamara, Hardy, & Hirtle, 1989).

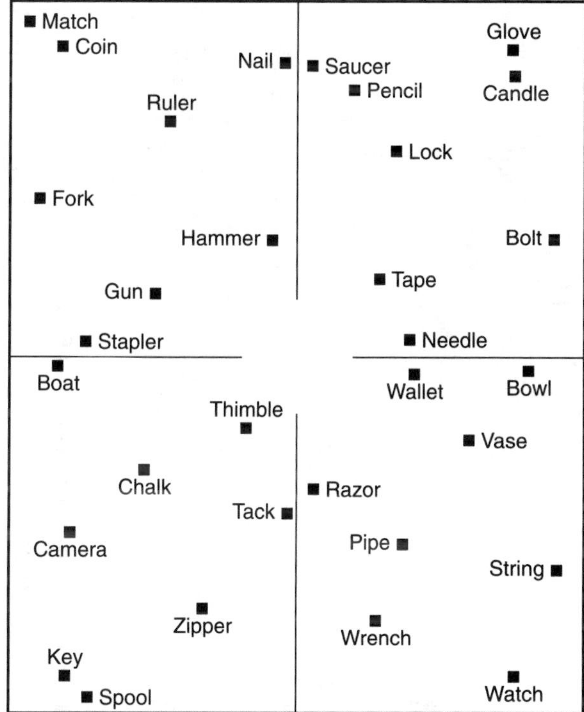

FIGURE 8.3 Map Used in Spatial Priming Studies

Source: Reprinted from *Cognitive Psychology,* 18, McNamara, T.P., Mental representations of spatial relations, pp. 87–121, 1986, with permission from Elsevier.

Additional Mental Map Phenomena. Consistent with a partially hierarchical view is geographical knowledge of the locations of cities (e.g., Friedman & Brown, 2000a; Friedman, Brown, & McGaffey, 2002), which is often clustered based on political/climatic regions, even when people are given supporting information, such as an outline map of the North American continent (Friedman, 2009). As shown in Figure 8.4, when Canadian students were asked to estimate the latitude of North American cities, four categories emerged: Canada, the northern United States, the southern United States, and Mexico

TABLE 8.1 Response Times (in ms) Used to Assess Spatial Priming, Both Within and Across Spatial Regions

SAME REGION		DIFFERENT REGIONS	
Close	*Far*	*Close*	*Far*
705	768	763	790

Source: Reprinted from *Cognitive Psychology,* 18, McNamara, T.P., Mental representations of spatial relations, pp. 87–121, 1986, with permission from Elsevier.

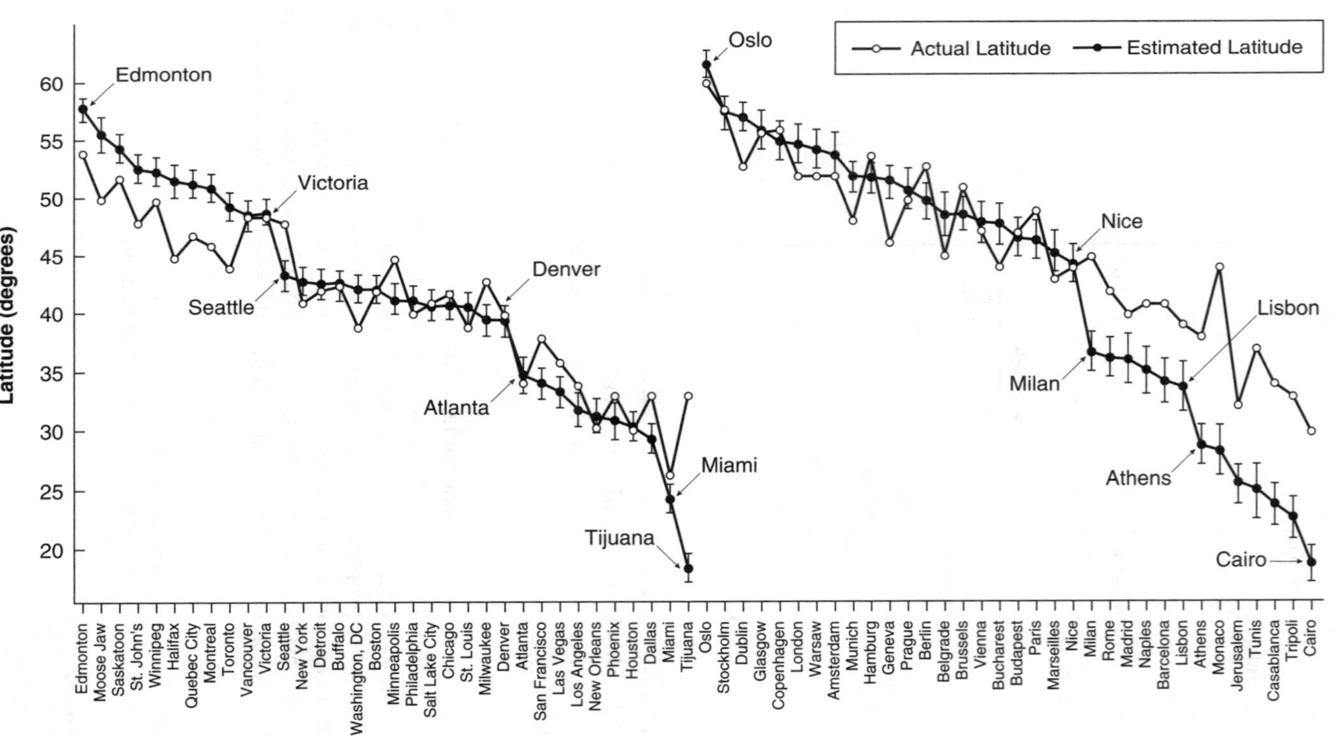

FIGURE 8.4 Influence of Geographical Regions on Latitude Estimations in North America and Europe/Africa

Source: Friedman, A., & Brown, N. R. (2000a). Reasoning about geography. *Journal of Experimental Psychology: General, 129,* 193–219.

(with Miami floating in between the United States and Mexico). Similar results were found with students from Texas (Friedman, Kerkman, & Brown, 2002) and Mexico (Friedman, Kerkman, Brown, & Stea, 2005), so where people live is less important than how they mentally divide up the world. Figure 8.4 also shows a similar categorical grouping for European cities. This prior knowledge of the world is important as these biases are not observed if maps of imaginary places are used (Newcombe & Chiang, 2007).

When accurate information about the correct latitudes or longitudes is provided as seed knowledge, people do make adjustments (Friedman & Brown, 2000a; 2000b), with the greatest adjustments occurring for those regions in which the seeds are provided. The amount of adjustment for other regions varies depending on their relation to the seeded region. If the regions are not directly adjoining, adjustment may be limited. For example, when European seed cities are provided, although there is adjustment of the European cities northward, there is little change in the locations of the African cities. People just increased their idea of the size of the Mediterranean Sea.

Other spatial characteristics can influence mental maps in memory, including the number of intervening locations on a route between two locations. The more locations along a route, the longer the estimated distances (Thorndyke, 1981). This increased crowding causes that part of the mental map to "expand" to accommodate all of the places. In one study people memorized a map like the one in Figure 8.5. In this map there are varying numbers of intervening locations between two cities. When memory is tested by having people estimate the distances between pairs of cities, the more intervening cities there are, the greater the distance estimates (see Figure 8.6).

Route distance can also influence memory (McNamara, Ratcliff, & McKoon, 1984). Given the same Euclidean distance, priming is reduced if there is a long circuitous route between two locations compared to if there is a short and direct route. In one study, students memorized maps like the one in Figure 8.7. The primed recognition test that followed had conditions in which map locations were close in both Euclidean and route

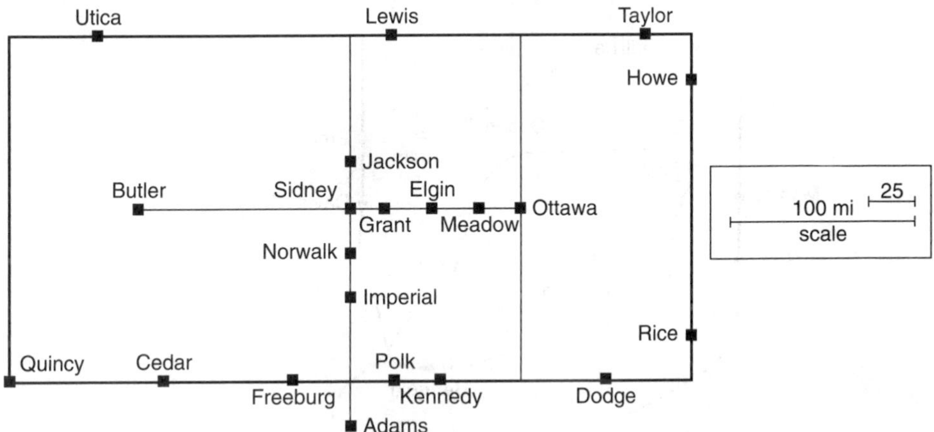

FIGURE 8.5 Map of Fictitious Area That Varies the Number of Intervening Locations Between Cities But Keeps the Distance Relatively Constant

Source: Reprinted from *Cognitive Psychology,* 13, Thorndyke, P.W., Distance estimation from cognitive maps, pp. 526–550, 1981, with permission from Elsevier.

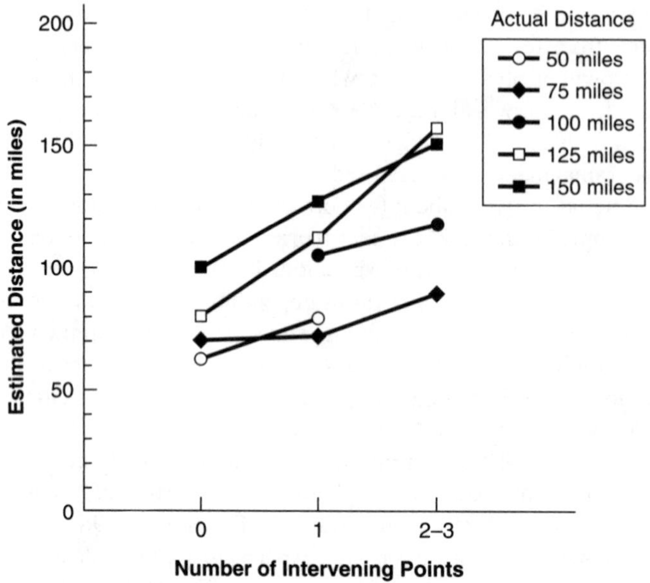

FIGURE 8.6 Distance Estimate Results as a Function of the Number of Intervening Cities

Source: Reprinted from *Cognitive Psychology,* 13, Thorndyke, P.W., Distance estimation from cognitive maps, pp. 526–550, 1981, with permission from Elsevier.

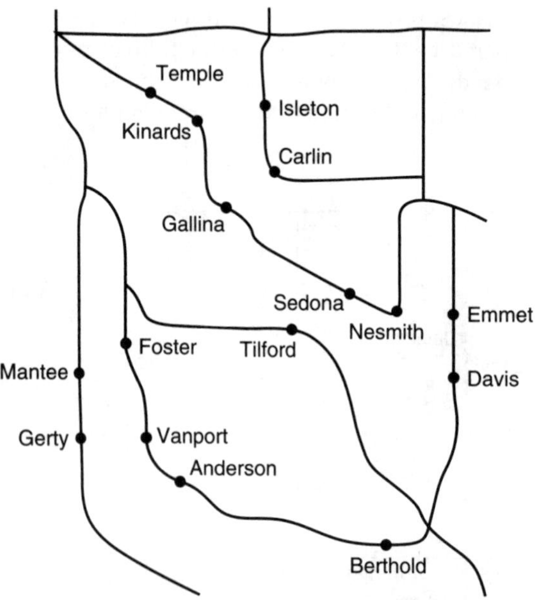

FIGURE 8.7 Map Used to Study the Effects of Spatial and Route Distance on Spatial Memory

Source: McNamara, T. P., Ratcliff, R., & McKoon, G. (1984). The mental representation of knowledge acquired from maps. *Journal of Experimental Psychology: Learning, Memory and Cognition, 10,* 723–732.

TABLE 8.2 Spatial Priming as Affected by Both Euclidean and Route Distance. CE = close Euclidean, CR = close route, FE = far Euclidean, and FR = far route.

CONDITION	RESPONSE TIME
Close Euclidean—close route	627
Close Euclidean—far route	682
Far Euclidean—far route	627

Source: McNamara, Ratcliff, & McKoon, 1984.

distance (e.g., Emmet & Davis), far in both Euclidean and route distance (e.g., Gallina & Sedona), or close in Euclidean distance but far in route distance (e.g., Mantee & Foster). As seen in Table 8.2, if the two map locations were far along the route, even if they were spatially close, the two places were handled as if they were spatially far apart.

Finally, spatial memories are distorted by *landmarks*, such as prominent buildings, natural features, like lakes, or salient objects, like statues. Landmarks help define spatial regions and people distort their memory for nonlandmark locations toward the landmarks (Sadalla, Burroughs, & Staplin, 1980), although this may be mediated by the way they are thought about (Bugmann, Coventry, & Newstead, 2007), such as whether people think about how important they are (larger influences) versus how often they are visited (smaller influence). Landmark influences are observed even when spatial memories are acquired verbally rather than through a map (Ferguson & Hegarty, 1994). The influence of landmarks has been explained using the Category Adjustment Theory (Newcombe et al., 1999), which we saw in the section on memory psychophysics. Essentially, people store landmark information as categorical information, along with fine-grained information about the locations themselves. Memory reflects a combination of these two, which results in nonlandmark locations being mentally drawn to the landmarks.

Temporal and Hybrid Theories. While mental maps can be affected by spatial characteristics, they may also be affected by nonspatial information, such as the temporal order in which map items are learned. Thus, places can be either close or far in temporal proximity in much the same way that they can be close or far in spatial proximity. Often spatial and temporal proximity are confounded during learning. Locations that are close in space are also studied close in time. However, these two dimensions can be disassociated. For example, imagine a person learns the map in Figure 8.8 in the order indicated by the arrows. Although people can derive spatial qualities (such as direction and distance) from their mental map, evidence from priming studies suggests that temporal structure can underlie a mental map's structure (Clayton & Habibi, 1991; Curiel & Radvansky, 1998; Sherman & Lim, 1991).

This dominance of temporal structure can vary. **Hybrid theories** assume a contribution of both spatial and temporal information. In a study by Curiel and Radvansky (1998; see also Kelly & McNamara, 2008), during memorization people either named indicated locations (focusing on identity information) or pointed to named locations (focusing on

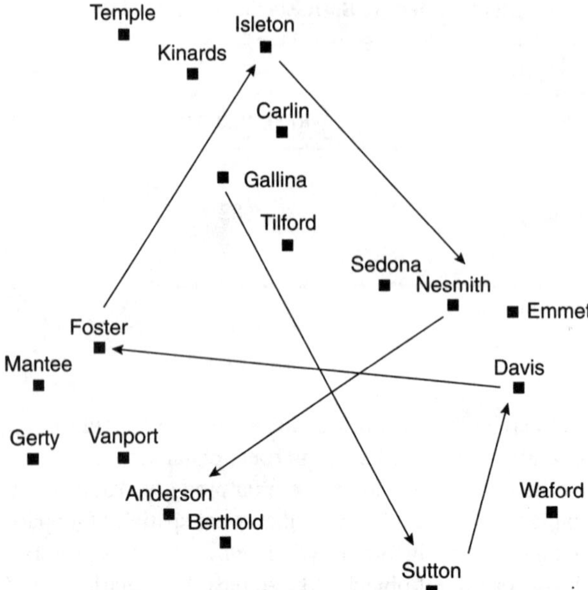

FIGURE 8.8 Fictitious Map Illustrating the Deconfounding of Spatial and Temporal Proximity with a Partial Temporal Order Indicated by the Arrows

Source: Clayton, K., & Habibi, A. (1991). Contributions of temporal contiguity to the spatial priming effect. *Journal of Experimental Psychology: Learning, Memory, & Cognition, 17,* 263–271.

spatial information). As shown in Table 8.3, there was more temporal priming when people named locations but greater spatial priming when they pointed to locations. How people encode the information into memory had a dramatic influence. Note that spatial and temporal information can work together to influence mental map structure (McNamara, Halpin, & Hardy, 1992). Learning map locations that are close together in both time and space provides the greatest benefit to memory.

Hybrid theories of mental maps are supported by neurological evidence. The parallel map theory (Jacobs & Schenk, 2003) suggests two types of information are used in making mental maps using two different neurological structures. A *bearing map* is a representation of the current heading in an environment, and corresponds to a coarse-grained representation of space based on the relative position to certain environmental locations. The bearing map involves the dentate gyrus and area CA3 of the hippocampus. This type of map tends to be more developed in males, who are better at dead reckoning sorts of navigation. This type of representation is also more sensitive to temporal order information. A *sketch map* is a representation of salient landmarks, and corresponds to a fine-grained representation of space based on the known landmark positions The sketch map involves area CA1 of the hippocampus. This type of map tends to be more developed in females, and is more sensitive to spatial structure information. The information from both the bearing and sketch maps are used to form an integrated map that includes both types of information, depending on what is available.

TABLE 8.3 Differences in Spatial and Temporal Priming
Whether people name map locations during learning in response to location cues or point to map locations in response to name cues.

CONDITION	NAMING	POINTING
Spatial	690	681
Close	714	730
Far	24	49
Priming		
Temporal	669	721
Close	709	718
Far	40	–3
Priming		

Source: Curiel & Radvansky, 1998.

Semantic Effects. Mental maps also reflect semantic relationships. Meaningful similarities across locations can accentuate priming, particularly if those places are already near one another (McNamara, Halpin, & Hardy, 1992; McNamara & LeSueur, 1989; Merrill & Baird, 1987). For example, memory of a college campus is somewhat semantically structured. In priming studies, buildings prime one another more if they serve the same function (e.g., dorms, administration buildings, sports facilities).

In memory psychophysics, mental map memories reflect a mixture of fine-grained and coarse-grained information. Consider maps in the real world; there may be portions that are not quite straight but are at an angle with respect to a larger frame of reference. For example, on a city map, the streets may not be at 90-degree angles to one another, or the orientation of a town may not square with the standard compass points. Research by Tversky (1981) has shown that when these deviations are present, memories are distorted to smooth out these irregularities. For example, streets are remembered as intersecting at something more closely approximating 90 degrees. A demonstration of this is the tendency of many North Americans to assume that South America is more directly south of North America, while it is actually more to the east. The western shore of South America is around the same longitude as the eastern shore of North America.

Mental Maps and Thinking. The structure of mental maps influences more than just memory for the map itself. It also influences other types of thinking. For example when someone memorizes a map and then reads a story about events that occur in that area (e.g., Morrow, Greenspan, & Bower, 1987). In a series of studies people memorized a map of the research center shown in Figure 8.9 and then read a series of stories about events that happened there. While reading, people use their mental maps, and this influenced their comprehension. For example, if a story character is described as thinking about an object in the building, the time it takes a person to read that sentence varies as a function of the distance between the character's current location and the object he or she is thinking about

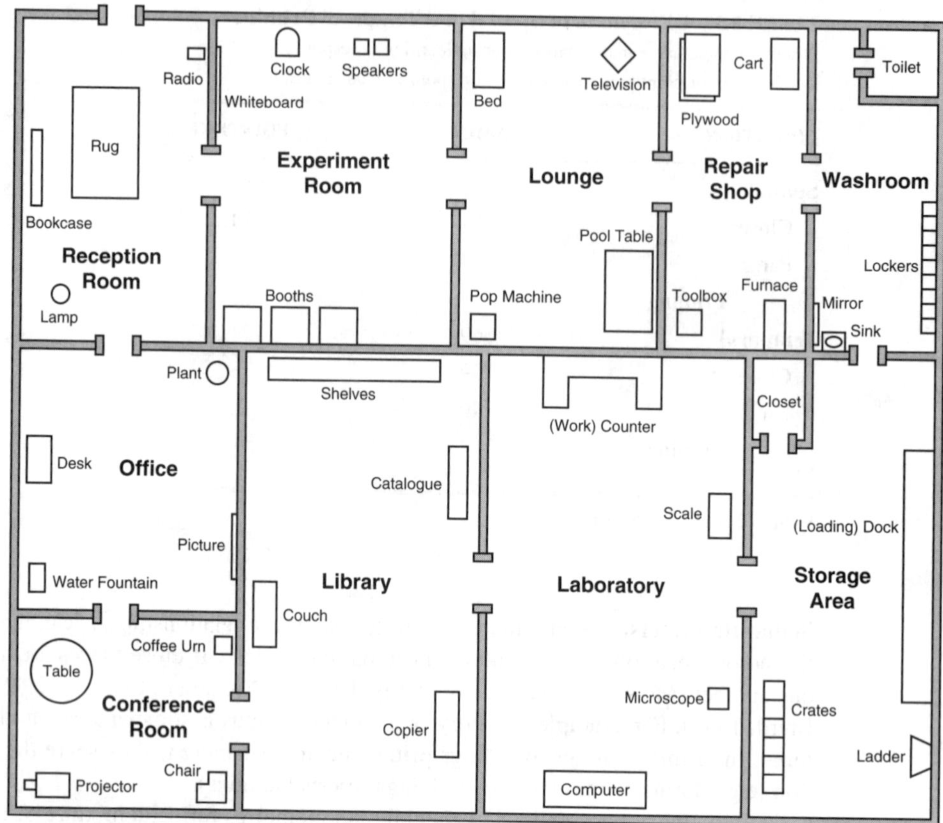

FIGURE 8.9 Map of the Research Center

Source: Morrow, D. G., Greenspan, S. L., & Bower, G. H. (1987). Accessibility and situation models in narrative comprehension. *Journal of Memory and Language, 26,* 165–187.

(Rinck & Bower, 1995). The greater the distance, the longer it takes people to read. This is the **spatial gradient of availability.** The mental map captures spatial characteristics of the building, and this spills over into comprehension.

This search of a mental map during comprehension also shows the importance of map regions. People treat each room as a chunk of information. Thus, the spatial gradient of availability is influenced by the number of rooms between the character and the object, not by Euclidean distance (Rinck, Hähnel, Bower, & Glowalla, 1997).

Spatial Frameworks

We spend our time in spaces and regions that are defined in particular ways—a kitchen, a mall, a highway, and so on. These regions are **spatial frameworks,** and how we interact with them affects our memories for them.

When we learn about a location, especially large ones that we cannot see all at once, such as a mall or a town, we may derive our understanding from a physical map

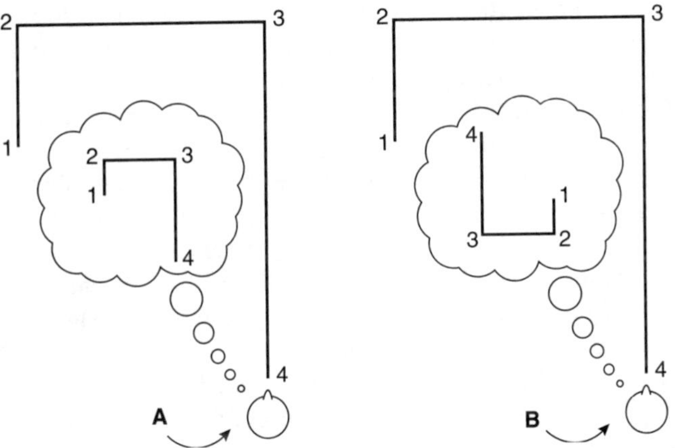

FIGURE 8.10 Direction Judgment When the Memorized Map Is Aligned or Misaligned with the Current Orientation

Source: Levine, M., Jankovic, I. N., & Palij, M. (1982). Principles of spatial problem solving. *Journal of Experimental Psychology: General, 111,* 157–175.

that we study to create our own mental map. One consequence of this is that the orientation that the map was in during learning becomes ingrained in the mental map. So when a person estimates directions when facing a direction other than the original map orientation, he or she is slower to respond and may make mistakes (Evans & Pezdek, 1980; Levine et al., 1982; Waller, Montello, Richardson, & Hegarty, 2002). It is as if the mental map were being viewed as a mental image. The greater the deviation from the orientation the map was learned in, the more likely a direction error will be made. For example, in Figure 8.10 a person who has his or her mental map aligned with his or her current orientation is less likely to make errors than someone who has his or her mental map misaligned. This **orientation effect** is shown in Table 8.4. This even extends to memory for observed spatial layouts (not just maps) that are either static or dynamic (like a soccer game [Diwadkar & McNamara, 1997; Garsoffky, Schwan, & Hesse, 2002; Shelton & McNamara, 1997]). It can also occur when a space is viewed from multiple perspectives. Each perspective can be stored as an orientation-specific viewpoint

TABLE 8.4 Influence of Orientation on Mental Map Retrieval

This expresses error rates (in degrees) from the correct orientation, depending on whether the orientation during retrieval either matched or was counteraligned with the original orientation.

CONDITION	ALIGNED	COUNTERALIGNED
Small map	15.2	43.3
Large map	22.7	31.7
Path	20.2	28.3

Source: Levine, Jankovic, & Palij, 1982.

(McNamara, Rump, & Werner, 2003; Valiquette, McNamara, & Smith, 2003). However, it is not observed when people are active participants in the situation but only when they view it passively (Sun, Chan, & Campos, 2004; Waller, Loomis, & Haun, 2004).

It appears that people can be broadly categorized into two types (Rossano, Warren, & Kenan, 1995), as shown in Figure 8.11. One type is relatively unaffected by how much their mental maps must be rotated, whereas another type is susceptible to such errors. (e.g., some people need to rotate a road map to their current driving orientation.) Thus, there are individual differences in the ability to rotate a mental map. This may be related to how well a person is able to use the visuospatial sketchpad in working memory.

However, if people learn an area, such as a college campus, through experience, and not a map, there may not be an influence of orientation (Evans & Pezdek, 1980; Presson, DeLange, & Hazelrigg, 1989; see also McNamara et al., 1989), although there may be effects of a larger spatial framework, such as the walls of a room (Valiquette et al., 2003). Natural exploration exposes a person to a variety of perspectives, and the resulting mental map does not have a preferred orientation. Figure 8.12 shows data from a study in which students made distance judgments for their own campus or for a map of an unfamiliar campus. An orientation effect was observed only for the unfamiliar campus.

A person's current perspective can have other influences. People often overestimate distances to locations near their current location but underestimate distances to places far away. A demonstration of this influence of perspective is a study by Holyoak and Mah (1982; see also Sholl, 1987) in which students at the University of Michigan estimated the relative east-west locations of cities in the United States. They were asked to make these

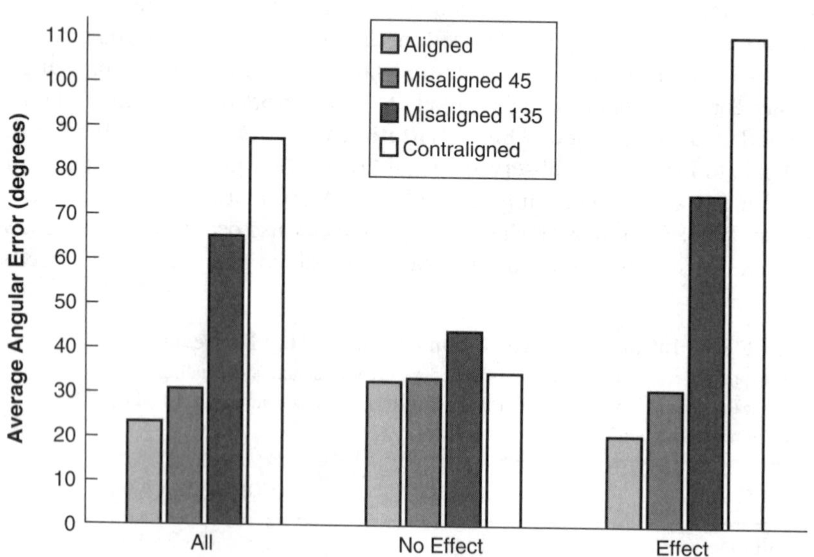

FIGURE 8.11 Performance of Good and Poor Misaligned Map Populations

Source: Rossano, M. J., Warren, D. H, & Kenan, A. (1995). Orientation specificity: How general is it? *American Journal of Psychology, 108,* 359–380. Used with permission of the University of Illinois Press.

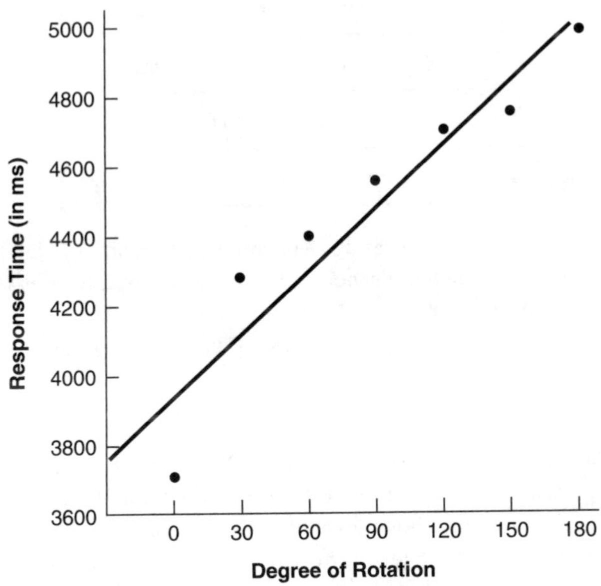

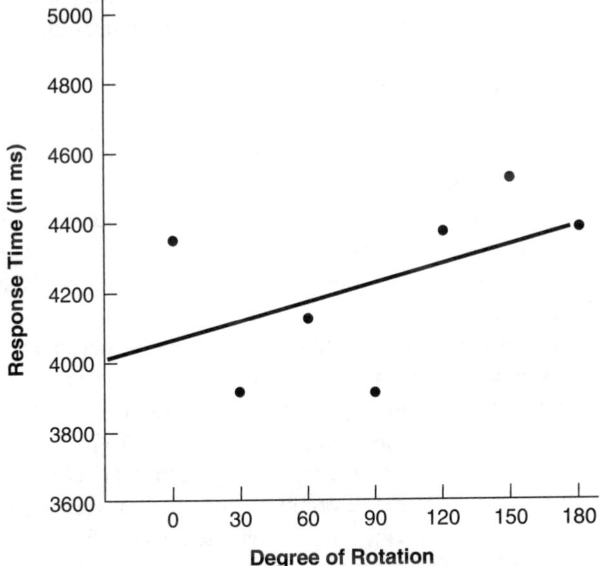

FIGURE 8.12 Mental Rotation Effects for Unknown and Known Campus Layouts. Mental rotation effects only observed for the unknown (map) campus condition

Source: Evans, G. W., & Pezdek, K. (1980). Cognitive mapping: Knowledge of real-world distance and location information. *Journal of Experimental Psychology: Human Learning and Memory, 6,* 13–24.

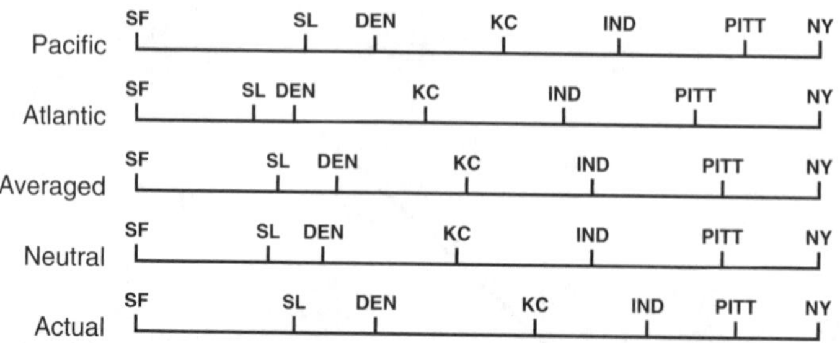

FIGURE 8.13 Effects of Relative City Locating Depending on the Point of View Taken at Retrieval. The cities tested here were San Francisco, Salt Lake, Denver, Kansas City, Indianapolis, Pittsburgh, and New York

Source: From *American Journal of Psychology*. Copyright 1995 by the Board of Trustees of the University of Illinois. Used with permission of the University of Illinois Press.

judgments by imagining that they were standing on the West Coast looking eastward or on the East Coast looking westward, or to simply estimate (keep in mind the students were in Ann Arbor, Michigan). The results, shown in Figure 8.13, reveal that location estimates were biased based on the perspective taken. Students who imagined themselves on the Pacific Coast reported the western cities being farther apart and the eastern cities being closer together, whereas the opposite was true when they imagined they were standing on the Atlantic Coast. Finally, students who were simply asked to estimate the distances imposed a mid-Westerner's bias by spreading out the distance among cities in the middle of the United States.

Sometimes people can create mental maps from language—for example, giving oral directions (e.g., "Go west on Cleveland until you get to Swanson. Turn north. Then turn right at the third stop sign"). People can navigate using only this type of information. How the information is given may not have a major effect on the resulting mental maps in memory (Taylor & Tversky, 1992), although performance is better when people learn from maps (e.g., Fields & Shelton, 2006). Where maps are learned and tested visually, there is a preference for the map orientation present during learned (Shelton & McNamara, 2004; Wildber & Wilson, 2008).

For verbal learning, in some cases people are given a **route perspective,** in which spatial information is present as if a person were walking through an area. In other cases people are given a **survey perspective**, in which the spatial layout is presented as if it were being viewed from high overhead, such as from a helicopter. When people verify spatial inferences (spatial information derived from a mental map), they are able to make inferences similarly in the two cases (Taylor & Tversky, 1992). If they verify pictures of the area (walking perspectives or overhead views), however, memory is better for the perspective from which the information was originally learned (Shelton & McNamara, 2004). Overall, people who are better at remembering orientations, as with the spatial span task (see Chapter 5), do better with route learning, whereas people who are better at perspective tasks, such as mental rotation (also see Chapter 5), do better at survey learning (Fields & Shelton, 2006). Thus, how information represented in a mental map is influenced by how that information got into memory in the first place.

Synopsis

Memory for space is generally pretty good. People's estimates of spatial qualities, such as distance, are very similar when made from memory as when people are looking right at something. People create memories of spaces called mental maps. The organization and structure of mental maps are influenced by various qualities of the spaces they represent, such as the influences of regions, routes, landmarks, semantic relations, and how the map information was originally learned. People's uses of mental maps are influenced by the perspective taken when remembering, and can be biased toward a certain orientation, especially for areas that are less familiar.

MEMORY FOR TIME

The other major physical property we deal with is time. In particular, how do people remember *when* things happened, and what sorts of distortions in this kind of memory occur? First, note that there are three ways people can use memory for time (Friedman, 1993). The first is **temporal distance,** or knowing how long in the past an event occurred. The second is **temporal location,** or knowing when an event took place, such as knowing a date. Finally, there is **relative time,** or knowing the order of two or more events, such as which came first. Friedman uses the analogy of an archeologist to explain these three aspects of temporal memory. Temporal distance is like radiocarbon dating used to determine the age of an artifact. Temporal location is like looking at the characteristics of an artifact to determine to what time it belongs, perhaps by comparing it to similar artifacts. Finally, relative time is used to place an artifact before or after others, perhaps based on the primitiveness or sophistication of one artifact relative to the others.

Phenomena

Using these three ways of thinking about time, we'll look at a number of phenomena that characterizes memory for time and some of the theories that have been proposed to account for distortions in it.

Basic Memory Effects. People have difficulty placing events in time. It is not unusual to misremember events as having occurred even several years before or after when they actually happened. This distortion is more likely to occur with older memories. That is, the further back in time an event was, the more likely it is that a mistake will be made in remembering when it happened. This is the **memory age effect**.

The forgetting of older memories is not that surprising. However, as with other memories, there are serial position curves in the accuracy of temporal memories (Toglia & Kimble, 1976; Zimmerman & Underwood, 1968). There is a **primacy effect.** People have better memory for the time of the first event of a certain type. For example, it is easy to remember when you got your first speeding ticket, but it is harder to remember when subsequent tickets were earned (I've had only one, so this is easy for me). There is also a **recency effect**. People have superior memory for the time of recent events.

The ability to locate memories in time improves as memory for content gets better. An illustration of this **accuracy effect** is a study in which people heard either the melodies or titles of songs that were popular from 2 to 56 years before. Although people could locate a song in time at better than chance level when they did not consciously remember it (25 percent accuracy), temporal memory was better if either the melody or the title was recognized (38 percent accuracy), and was best if the lyrics were also remembered (60 percent accuracy [Bartlett & Snelus, 1980]). Thus, the more information that was remembered, the more accurately people knew when the song was popular.

Shifting in Time. Another temporal memory phenomenon is the **scale effect** in which memory for when an event occurred may be accurate at one scale of time but be distorted at another. For example, a person may remember that an event occurred on a Monday but misremember the week it happened. A scale effect is shown in Figure 8.14 with data taken from a study by Thompson, Skowronski, Larsen, and Betz (1996). They had students at Kansas State University record their experiences during a semester. At the end of the term they tested students' memories for those events. Notice that along with the gradual shift in memory for the time of events, there are peaks at regular intervals. Thus, as memory for the time of an event became distorted in terms of what week it occurred, there was some memory for the correct day.

Memories for when events occurred can also be distorted by **forward telescoping** in which memory is placed more recently than when it actually occurred (Bradburn, Rips, & Shevell, 1985; Thompson, Skowronski, & Lee, 1988). For example, you might think something happened 2 years ago when it actually happened 3 years ago. Forward

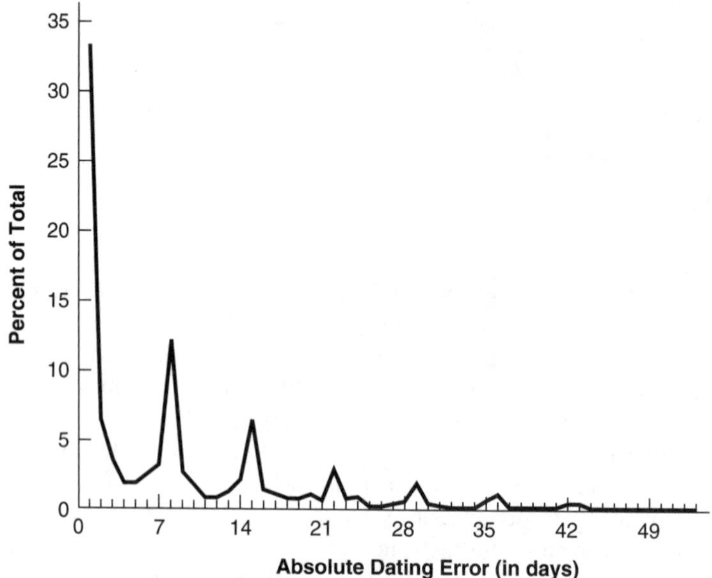

FIGURE 8.14 Results Showing a Scale Effect in Temporal Estimation

Source: Thompson, C. P., Skowronski, J. J., Larsen, S. F., & Betz, A. L. (1996). Autobiographical memory: Remembering what and remembering when. Mahwah, New Jersey: Erlbaum.

telescoping is likely to begin 2 months after the original event, when sufficient forgetting has had an opportunity to set in. The primary cause of telescoping is how long it has been since the event.

A related phenomenon is **backward telescoping** when recent events are placed further back in time than they actually occurred. Backward telescoping is largely confined to recent memories (Rubin & Baddeley, 1989; Zacks et al., 1984) in which very recent events can seem like they occurred longer ago than they actually did. For example, in the evening, it may seem that the morning's events didn't even happen that day.

Telescoping effects reflect uncertainty in memory for time and may be a form of regression to the mean (Rubin & Baddeley, 1989). Forward and backward telescoping can be assessed using memory psychophysics by looking at which component of the memory processes is affected. Psychophysical functions using Stevens's Law show slopes that are less than 1 and y-intercepts that are greater than 0 (Ferguson & Martin, 1983), meaning that there is a shift in memory for temporal events away from the extremes and more toward an average amount of time. Looking at memory for events, both in the news and personal events, for events less than 100 days ago, memory is quite accurate. However, for events between 100 and 1,000 days ago, there is backwards telescoping, whereas for events older than 1,000 days, there is forward telescoping, with older events showing more distortion (Janssen, Chessa, & Murre, 2006).

Ordering. Finally, memory is good for **order information** about the sequence in which events occurred. As a consequence, people can locate events in time by considering event order, either a forward or backward order. Anderson and Conway (1993) found that people better recall a sequence of events in their lives if they are recalled in a forward order. In contrast, Whitten and Leonard (1981) found that students recall their precollege teachers best when they try to remember them in a backward order. Thus, in some way, temporal information is encoded as a part of memory.

Processing Factors

A number of accounts of temporal memory have been suggested. Following Friedman (1993), here are some prominent ones broadly based on distance-based, location-based, and relative time factors.

Distance-Based Factors. Distance-based factors produce time estimates based on how far in the past an original event is from the present. The simplest way is to use the strength of the memory trace (e.g., Brown et al., 1985). The longer it has been since a trace was accessed, the weaker it will be. In contrast, stronger traces refer to more recent events. Thus, the strength of a memory can be used to determine its age. This can explain the memory age, recency, and relative ordering effects, as well as why events that have been thought about frequently are remembered as being closer to the present which gain strength each time they are retrieved (Brown et al., 1985).

Also, people can use context (e.g., Glenberg et al., 1980). Two events close in time are likely to be associated with similar contexts, but events that are distant in time have more distinct contexts associated with them. Again, contexts can be either external or internal. Your present situation is more similar to what it was last week, compared to a year ago, or even 10 years ago. So, the greater the difference between the current context and the one associated with a memory, the older that trace is assumed to be.

It should be noted that, overall, distance-based factors have difficulty with the primacy and accuracy effects. There is little evaluation of the nature of the content of the memory, only its age.

Location-Based Factors. Location-based factors involve locating a memory in time based on information stored in the memory trace. The simplest way is if people store a tag with the memory for the event that would convey the hour, day, month, year, or whatever was relevant. All a person would need to do is read this information off. For example, I know that I officially started my current job on August 23, 1993. This is directly stored in my memory. Although some people have suggested that time tags may be associated with a biological clock (Tzeng, 1976), most memories do not have this sort of detailed information.

Another way is for people to locate a memory in time based on the knowledge in the trace. People figure out the time of an event using information they know, as well as similar events whose time is known. For example, I remember an event that happened on May 1, 1983. I remember seeing some people in old convertibles driving through Cleveland's near west side, shouting and waving signs. It was late afternoon and I was on my way home from school. I know it was May 1 because these people were members of the local Communist party, and there was also a brief segment about them on the news that night. They were shouting about how there should be a revolt of the workers and that communism should replace the current political system (it didn't happen). I know it was May 1 because this is an important date in communism, and I know it was 1983 because I was coming home from high school, which would have made it 1980, 1981, 1982, or 1983. I also remember discussing this with a girl I was dating at the time, and I did not date her until my senior year, so it must have been 1983. Thus, using my knowledge of the event along with the circumstances of my life at the time, I can infer the date.

Location-based factors can account for the memory age effect due to a loss of either a time tag or context information. As for serial position curves, primacy effects are attributed to both the superior memory for the event itself and any temporal information associated with it. This is assisted by the fact that the early occurrence of events of a type makes those events more temporally distinct, and makes them better remembered. Scale effects are accounted for by the loss of a time tag or being able to use information in the memory to reconstruct only part of the time accurately. For example, remembering an event that occurred at church could be easily reconstructed to be one that occurred on a Sunday, which is very likely to be accurate, but the memory is vague enough that the year cannot be reconstructed. Telescoping effects are explained by reconstructive processes by assuming that memory traces may be distorted based on the amount of content recovered. Relative ordering effects can be accounted for by time tags and reconstruction processes, although not as well. Finally, accuracy effects are easily accounted for in that the more that is retained in a memory, the more accurate the time tag or the more reliable the information used for reconstruction.

Relative Time Factors. For relative time factors, temporal order information is stored directly in memory. This could happen by an associative chaining of memories (e.g., Lewandowsky & Murdock, 1989): along with an event are stored associations of prior occurrences of events of the same type. To locate an event in time, one assesses how it is associated with other related events. Did it occur before or after these other events? Thus, by determining where the event is in a sequence, one can figure out its temporal location.

Also, every time an event occurs, all of the related events are activated in memory (e.g., Hintzman, Summers, & Block, 1975). These activated events are then associated with the memory for the current event. So the more recently an event has occurred, the more events that are associated with it. Of course, the first event of that type has no additional associated memories. Thus, a person is able to locate an event in time, at least relatively, by using information about other activated and associated events.

Such processes can directly account for relative order effects. They can also explain the memory age effect in that older memories are more likely to have lost the needed associations. For serial position effects, older memories have the fewest number of associations, so they are easier to locate. Conversely, a recency effect occurs because newer memories have had the least amount of forgetting and a large number of associations. Forward telescoping is explained as a loss of associations, making the memory seem not so old.

Evidence also suggests that while people may use this sort of information in restricted settings, it does not appear to be a major factor. Friedman (2007) gave people pairs of events, such as movies or class announcements, which may or may not be related (such as having the same major actor) and asked them to judge the temporal order of the two. If they were related, then people should make relative time associations. However, the results revealed no such process, suggesting that people do not necessarily draw these temporal associations as they experience events.

Category Adjustment Model of Time. Using an approach similar to understanding spatial memory, Huttenlocher and colleagues (Huttenlocher, Hedges, & Bradburn, 1990; Huttenlocher, Hedges, & Prohaska, 1988) developed a theory of temporal memory assuming that memories are stored at a fine-grained and a coarse-grained level. The coarse-grained level would include large categories of time, such as 7, 10, 14, 21, 30, and 60 days. Estimates of when events occurred reflect a combination of both the detailed and categorical information. The temporal categories serve to both placing limits on which events could have occurred (such as knowing that a lecture must have happened sometime between the beginning and the end of a semester), as well as a basis for rounding estimates when there is uncertainty at a fine-grained level.

This fuzzy trace approach accounts for memory age and accuracy effects because forgetting at the fine-grained level is more likely to occur as memories get older. Serial position effects are also explained with recency effects occurring due to a relatively small amount of forgetting, and primacy effects reflecting memories that are more likely to occur at a temporal border and so can be easily located within that category. The use of coarse-grained information explains scale effects because the scales often correspond to categorical values. Finally, both forward and backward telescoping are explained as tendencies to use categorical prototypes when fine-grained information is forgotten.

How well people locate memories in time is also affected by how the information is reported, such as whether it is an absolute or relative time format (Janssen et al., 2006). People prefer absolute time formats (exact dates) for more recent events, and relative time formats for more remote events, consistent with the idea that more recent events are likely to have more details. Moreover, people prefer absolute time formats for personal events compared to news events, consistent with the idea that personal events are more likely to be well encoded and have sufficient details available for absolute dating.

Synopsis

Memory for time is worse than memory for space. Memories for when things happened are fraught with distortions and errors. In addition to general memory errors due to the age and serial position, a number of other factors can distort memories of time. Temporal memories show scale effects, involving categories of time, as well as consistent telescoping that shift memories in time in a regular fashion. Despite these errors, people are able to remember the proper sequence or order in which events occurred, even if they cannot place them properly in time. Various processes are used for temporal memory. These include distance factors based on the age of the memory, location-based processes based on knowing when the information occurred in time, and relative time–based factors that derive estimates of time based on memory for the order of events. These multiple processes are reflected in mixture models, such as the Category Adjustment Theory, that take into account a number of mental processes acting on memory for time.

SUMMARY

In this chapter we looked at memory for time and space. Memory for spatial information is fairly reliable. When distortions in memory occur, they are systematic to the point of obeying psychophysical laws. The mental maps stored in memory are rarely metric representations that capture the Euclidean information in a spatial layout. Instead, they are hierarchically distorted by spatial regions and the temporal order in which information was learned. The organization of mental maps is also influenced by semantic knowledge and important landmarks. When using a mental map from memory, accuracy is influenced by the initial orientation of the map, as well as the perspective a person takes on a space being thought about.

Memory for time is less reliable than memory for space. Memory is influenced by how old the memories are, when they occurred in a sequence, the particular time period in which they occurred, and how well the memory is remembered in general. A number of factors were looked at in terms of how temporal memories were derived by using the age of the memory itself, information in memory that can be used to determine time, and the relative position of that memory with respect to others.

STUDY QUESTIONS

1. How can psychophysical principles be applied to memory?
2. To what degree and how are memories for space distorted with respect to actually perceiving a space? Why?

3. What are some of the major factors about a space that can influence the organization of a mental map?
4. What are the different ways of experiencing or learning the information that will go into a mental map, and how do they influence the final nature of that mental map?
5. How good is a person's memory for time?
6. What are some of the characteristics of memory that affect the ability to remember when something happened?
7. In what ways does memory for time get distorted?
8. What are the major processing factors that account for people's ability to remember when things happened?
9. How does the category adjustment model account for people's ability to location memories in time?

KEY TERMS

accuracy effect, backward telescoping, Category Adjustment Theory, forward telescoping, hierarchical view, hybrid theories, memory age effect, metric view, order information, orientation effect, partially hierarchical view, primacy effect, psychophysics, recency effect, relative time, route perspective, scale effect, spatial frameworks, spatial gradient of availability, Steven's Law, survey perspective, temporal distance, temporal location

TRY IT OUT

For this Try It Out we'll look at the accuracy of memory for distances using memory psychophysics. First set up 12–36 objects at different distances (although you can study areas, angles, or something else if you want). For example, you can have pairs of small pictures of objects on pieces of paper. Another way is to have a variety of objects at different distances from a person. Have people estimate those distances. If you have objects on pieces of paper, have people estimate the distances between the objects. It does not matter how accurate people are in terms of what they think an inch, meter, or whatever is, so long as they are consistent with themselves. Collect this data under two conditions. In one condition have the people estimate the distances from *perception* with a person is directly looking at the distance. In another condition have the people estimate the distances from *memory* by looking at the distance, then either removing it or having them turn away, and then estimate the distance. The objects for the perception and memory conditions should be different. Ideally have at least 12 participants. After you have collected the data, plot people's estimates against the actual distances. For each person, derive an estimate of the slope for the function that best fits the points for each condition. If all goes well, the slope of the function will be smaller in the memory than the perception condition, illustrating the distance compression that can occur in memory.

CHAPTER NINE

SEMANTIC MEMORY

Sometimes memories do not refer to specific events but are more encyclopedic. This general knowledge is **semantic memory**, which takes advantage of regularities in the world to make more accurate predictions about what will happen next. For example, if all you had to go on were episodic memories of specific events, then every time you encountered a dog you would have to start all over again figuring out the safety of the situation and how you should react. Every time you saw a new chair, you would need to determine what it was. Every time you went to a restaurant, you would have to learn the procedure how to get some food. Semantic memories are generalizations that apply to a variety of similar but different circumstances.

In this chapter we cover a number of aspects of semantic memory. We first address semantic memory organization and how it provides not only information we may need at the time, but also other related information that is likely to be relevant. This is semantic priming. We then examine two classes of semantic memories. One is how categories are structured and used. We also will see how ordered relations are represented and how they influence memory. The second type of semantic memory is scripts and schemas for commonly experienced aspects of life. Finally, we spend some time looking at cases where semantic memory falls short of our expectations and desires.

SEMANTIC PRIMING

A salient characteristic of semantic memory is its organized and regular structure. Remembering one concept brings related memories closer to awareness. This facilitation of related ideas is **priming** (Meyer & Schvaneveldt, 1971). When a concept is activated, this activation spreads to related concepts such that if there is then a need to use them, they are now closer to awareness and can be used more quickly.

In a typical priming study people are given a lexical decision task in which they need to indicate whether strings of letters are words. For example, "doctor" is a word, but "dohter" is not. In these studies there are pairs of words: a critical trial, called a *prime*, followed by a *target*. What is of interest is how fast people respond to the target (such as by pressing a button). If the prime is unrelated to the target, this is a baseline, *control* condition—for example, if the target "nurse" is preceded by the prime "potato." If the prime is semantically related to the target, this is the experimental condition—for example, if the target "nurse" is preceded by the prime "doctor." Generally, people are faster to respond to the target in the *experimental* condition relative to the control. Priming is even observed in ERP recordings as early as 250 ms after the target word is presented (Bentin, McCarthy, & Wood, 1985). It should also be noted that there is less brain activity when there are richer semantic representations (Pexman et al., 2007) because it is easier for the brain to activate that information. It doesn't need to work as hard.

Semantic priming occurs because concepts are not understood in isolation but in terms of how they relate to other ideas. By activating related concepts, people bring to bear a larger set of knowledge to help them understand. For example, when you listen to a lecture, you need a broad understanding of what is being discussed, and not just narrowly think about the specific words and concepts being said. Priming also helps people detect inconsistencies. When people encounter semantically anomalous information, such as a sentence like "The doctor listened with his carrot," ERP recordings show increased negativity in electrical potential around 400 ms after encountering it (Kutas & Hillyard, 1980). This semantic inconsistency detection is called the N400.

Semantic memory is structured based on shared aspects of meaning (Thompson-Schill, Kurtz, & Gabrieli, 1998). Similar concepts are metaphorically stored closer in semantic memory. This includes emotional states. People respond faster to happy words such as "peace" when in a happy mood and faster to sad words such as "die" when in a sad mood (Olafson & Ferraro, 2001).

Semantic memory can be aided by information that shares the same general abstract structure as prior information, even if they are not superficially related. For example, in a study by Bassok, Pedigo, and Oskarsson (2008) the targets were simple addition facts. The primes were word pairs. Priming was observed when the two things were in the same category and could be added together (e.g., *apples – oranges*), but not when there was a superordinate relationship that was less consistent with addition (e.g., *dressers – drawers*). Thus, semantic memory incorporates abstract structural relations into how it uses information, and this abstract structure can prime other knowledge that has a similar structure.

Controlled Priming

In general, priming is a more or less automatic, implicit process. Still, it is possible for it to be affected and redirected by conscious effort. In a study by Neely (1977), people were given category names followed by a lexical decision task. The lexical decision trials came 250, 400, or 700 ms after the category name. The difference between the onset of the category name and the lexical decision is called the stimulus onset asynchrony (SOA). There were five conditions of interest, and the pattern of results for each of these is shown in Figure 9.1. The first was *Nonshift-Expected-Related* in which people expected that if a word followed the category name, it would be a member of that category, and it was—for example, seeing the category "BIRD" followed by the word "robin." As can be seen, positive priming was found at all SOAs.

A second condition was *Nonshift-Unexpected-Unrelated*, in which people expected that if a word followed the category name, it would be a member of that category, but it was not—for example, seeing "BIRD" followed by "arm." Looking at Figure 9.1, there is initially no effect on response time, but later people are slower to respond to "arm" because the activation has all been directed to the "BIRD" portion. Thus, it takes time to disengage from this part of semantic memory and move it to another one.

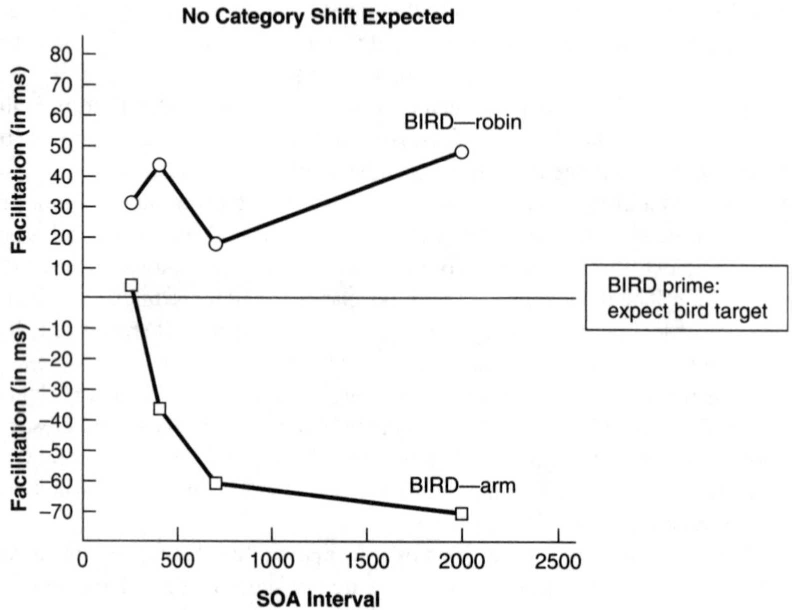

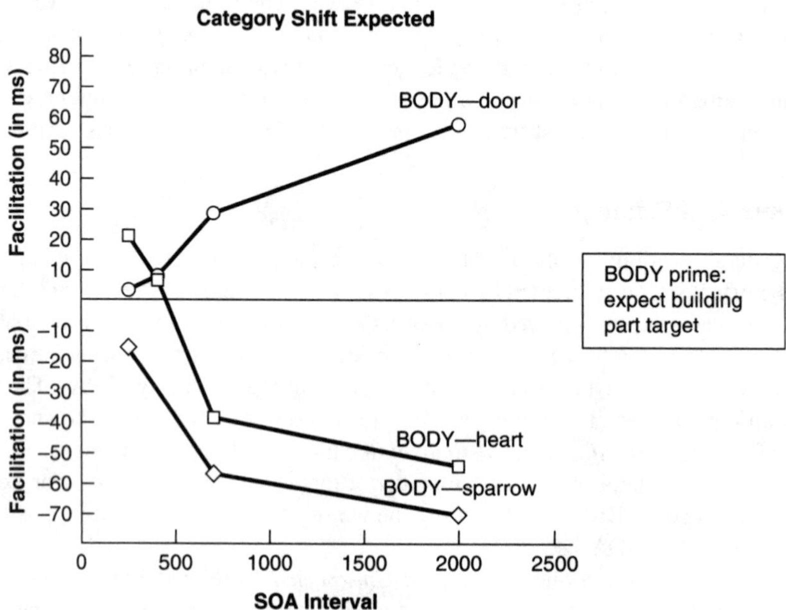

FIGURE 9.1 Automatic and Controlled Priming in Semantic Memory

Source: Neely, J. H. (1977). Semantic priming and retrieval from lexical memory: Roles of inhibitionless spreading activation and limited-capacity attention. *Journal of Experimental Psychology: General, 106,* 226–254.

The third condition was *Shift-Expected-Unrelated*, in which people expected that when a word followed a category name, it would be a member of a certain unrelated category, and it was. An example of this would be seeing "BODY" followed by "door" when a building part was expected. As seen in Figure 9.1, positive priming develops over time. If people expect a BUILDING part when they get "BODY," they can consciously activate that portion of semantic memory, but this takes time.

The fourth condition, *Shift-Unexpected-Unrelated*, was similar to the third, except the word was a member of an unrelated category—for example, seeing "BODY" followed by "sparrow." As shown in Figure 9.1, there is initially some negative priming, and this gets larger over time. Because people expect a BUILDING part when they get "BODY," they consciously activate the BUILDING part of semantic memory, and it requires effort to disengage this activation and move it to another portion.

The fifth condition, *Shift-Unexpected-Related*, is similar to the previous two except that the word is a member of the same category as the prime—for example, seeing "BODY" followed by "heart." As shown in Figure 9.1, there is initially some positive priming. An automatic process activates the portion of semantic memory associated with the probe. However, over time, people have consciously shifted away activation to another part of semantic memory. They needed to engage in more effort to disengage from the part that is expected and move back to the original portion. This pattern of response times is supported by EEG recordings showing that automatic activation emphasizes the parieto-temporal cortex, whereas conscious evaluation emphasizes the frontal lobes (e.g., Krause, Gibbons, & Schack, 1998).

Mediated Priming

The theory behind semantic priming is that when a concept is activated, this activation spreads to related concepts. From this perspective, one question is, how far does this spread go? Do only those concepts that are directly related to the first receive spreading activation, or does it go beyond that? For example, when retrieving the concept "lion," it is likely that the concept "tiger" is activated because these are both large, predatory cats. If "tiger" is primed, concepts related to it are also activated, such as the concept "stripes." To test this, a memory researcher would have a person retrieve the concept "lion" and then look at how the retrieval of "stripes" is affected. This is **mediated priming** because the connection between "lion" and "stripes" is mediated by "tiger."

In general, mediated priming does occur (Balota & Lorch, 1986; McNamara & Altarriba, 1988), as shown by both response times and ERP data (particularly the N400 component) (Chwilla, Kolk, & Mulder, 2000; Hill, Strube, Roesch-Ely, & Weisbrod, 2002). However, mediated priming is smaller in magnitude than regular priming, and it is sometimes not observed (De Groot, 1983). The further away concepts are from the original, the less likely that meaningful priming occurs.

Semantic Interconnectivity

In episodic memory, more associations with a concept can slow down retrieval, as with the fan effect. Semantic memory is made up of very large numbers of associations among concepts. This interconnectivity can be thought of as a complex network of concepts and associations (as described in Chapter 10). And so, based on the fan effect, one would expect that it should be difficult to retrieve semantic information.

However, the opposite is true. Concepts in semantic memory that have more interconnections are retrieved faster (Ashcraft, 1978; Kroll & Klimesch, 1992) and allow people to make responses based on partial information (Kounios, Montgomery, & Smith, 1994). This is because in semantic memory these associations provide both direct and indirect connections among concepts. Two concepts might be directly associated but also share a number of intermediate concepts, which increases the number of retrieval pathways between them. As a result, there are many ways that concepts can prime one another. The more indirect connections there are, the more likely any one of those pathways will be activated after a given period of time. Think of this as a horse race. If there are lots of horses running, the race will be over faster than if only a few horses are racing because it is more likely that there will be a fast horse in the bunch.

Inhibition

Like episodic memory, inhibition helps narrow the semantic memory search. During active retrieval, related concepts may be inhibited, such as when a person generates information, but not when it is passively heard or read (Blaxton & Neely, 1983; Johnson & Anderson, 2004; Roediger, Neely, & Blaxton, 1983). For example, people retrieve the concept "salmon" for the category "FISH" more slowly if they had recently retrieved several other examples of fish. The same applies for semantic memory of mathematical problems (Campbell & Phenix, 2009). The need to select a specific semantic memory causes the inhibition of related competitors that could produce interference.

Nature of Semantic Information

The nature of semantic memories is complex because they capture our general knowledge about the world. Information requires a great deal of time to move it from episodic to semantic memory. In a study by Dagenbach, Horst, and Carr (1990), college students did not show significant priming of newly learned words until after five weeks of practice. Thus, the conversion of knowledge from episodic to semantic memory is a long process. That said, even early in learning, the acquisition and stabilization of semantic memories can be aided by the consolidation processes that occur during sleep (Dumay & Gaskell, 2007).

Although some theories give the impression that semantic memory has a clear structure, like a computer database, keep in mind that this is a memory system with a human face. Semantic memory certainly captures such distributional information, but it also captures more experiential, embodied aspects as well (Andrews, Vigliocco, & Vinson, 2009). When people process abstract concepts (e.g., barrier) they rely more on associative information (what words tend to occur together), but when they are concrete concepts (e.g., mushroom) people rely more on similarity information (Crutch Connell, & Warrington, 2009). As an example, right-handers tend to associate positive concepts with the right half of space, whereas left-handers do the opposite (Casasanto, 2009). Moreover, even simple things like how we represent nouns and verbs reflect different aspects of semantic memory. ERP recordings show that nouns, particularly concrete nouns of objects that you can see, activate more of the sensory cortex in the parietal lobe (B.A. 1, 2, & 3), whereas verbs of action activate more of the motor cortex in the frontal lobe (B.A. 4) (Andres, Olivier, & Badets, 2008; Pulvermüller, Lutzenberger, & Preissl, 1999).

Another embodied influence is that information retrieval reflects perceptual qualities (Solomon & Barsalou, 2004), such as the visual area taken up by a property. For example, for the concept "fish," the property "scales" is relatively easy to retrieve, whereas the property "eye" is more difficult. This embodied influence on semantic memories also applies to emotional responses (Olafson & Ferraro, 2001). In a compelling demonstration of embodied cognition on semantic memory, Pecher, Zeelenberg, and Barsalou (2003) gave students a property identification task in which they were given with pairs of words, such as "BLENDER-loud". The task was to indicate whether the second word was a property of the first. They found that students were faster when the property was from the same sensory modality as the previous trial. For example, people were faster to respond to "BLENDER-loud" if it immediately followed "LEAVES-rustling" (which also involves sound) than if it followed "CRANBERRIES-tart" (which involves taste). Thus, semantic knowledge, although abstract in the sense that it does not refer to specific events, is still very much influenced by how we physically interact with the world.

Synopsis

The activation of knowledge in semantic memory causes the priming of related concepts. After an initial, automatic process, a person may also engage in a more consciously controlled search. Priming can extend beyond immediately related concepts, as with mediated priming. Semantic memory retrieval, generally, is facilitated by more connections among concepts, in contrast to episodic memory. However, priming does have its limits, and people can actually be slowed if they have recently actively selected related concepts. Finally, semantic information, although seemingly abstract, clearly captures embodied qualities of thought.

CATEGORIES

An important job of semantic memory is the organization of categories. Rather than remember lots of bits and pieces of information, we group knowledge together. This similarity-based grouping is **categorization,** in which two or more entities are treated as though they are equivalent. Categorization allows us to draw on prior experience in a regular and reliable fashion in new situations to avoid spending too much time thinking about how to act. Some assumptions can be made of aspects of the new situation are like those that were observed previously. For example, the category "dog" allows one to treat members of that category as being more or less the same, such as knowing that all dogs eat dog food, may bite, and like to run.

In this section we look at how semantic memory categorizes information. We first look at some properties of human categories, followed by some theories of categorization (Medin, 1989; Medin & Smith, 1984). After this, we look at cases of categorization in social situations, namely stereotypes and prejudice.

Properties of Categories

Human categories are complex. One way that people use categories is seen in the **levels of categorization.** There are three levels of categorization: basic, subordinate, and superordinate (Rosch & Mervis, 1975). The basic level is the one we operate at most often. At this level categories are defined by features that provide enough detail to allow us to treat different members as similar, but without more detail than is often necessary. Examples of basic categories are things like saw, dogs, chair, or drum. The subordinate level provides detailed information about specific portions of a basic category. Examples of subordinate categories are things like camping saw, miniature poodle, leather recliner, and kettle drum. Finally, the superordinate level provides general information that captures a wide range of basic categories. Examples of superordinate categories are tool, pet, furniture, and musical instrument.

This distinction is important because it reflects how people use categories. Basic level category information is retrieved better than the other two (Rosch et al., 1976). People can retrieve more attributes that are particular to basic level categories and can retrieve the names of basic level categories more quickly than the others (Tversky & Hemenway, 1984). This difference in retrieval speed is shown in Figure 9.2. This suggests that the basic level has some kind of primacy in semantic memory.

Categories have many members. Their combined influence gives rise to a category and manifests itself in several ways. First, there is a **central tendency,** or averaged category ideal. Second, categories have **graded membership.** Some members are thought of as being better members of the category than are others. For example, "robin" is often

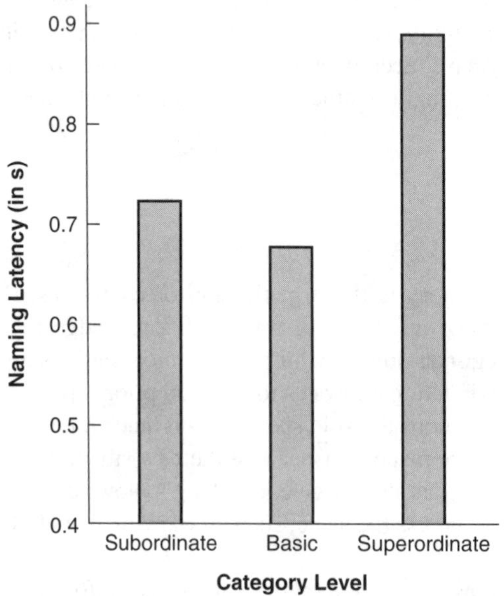

FIGURE 9.2 Naming Time for Concepts at Different Category Levels

Source: Tversky, B., & Hemenway, K. (1984). Objects, parts, and categories. *Journal of Experimental Psychology: General, 113,* 169–193.

thought of as being a better member of the category "bird" than is "penguin." Alternatively, some things are ambiguous category members that may be marked with linguistic hedges—for example, statements like "technically, a tomato is a fruit" or "loosely speaking, a bat is a bird."

Finally, category members might not be defined by a single set of features but different features may be shared among several members. This is **family resemblance** (Rosch & Mervis, 1975). An example of this is that for the category "furniture," many members have legs, are made of wood, are intended to be used indoors, but this is not true of all types of furniture. Overall, people are sensitive to the correlations among features that define categories—for example, the idea that flying tends to go with birds and tires tends to go with bicycles. This is true both in terms of how categories are distinguished from one another, as well as the features that create a family resemblance within categories (Chin-Parker & Ross, 2002).

An important distinction is made between *artifact categories*, things people make, and *natural kind* categories, things found in nature. These category types are served by different brain regions (Martin & Chao, 2001). Natural kinds, such as animals, involve more of the *medial* fusiform gyrus (B. A. 37) and superior temporal gyrus (B.A. 41), whereas artifacts involve more of the *lateral* fusiform gyrus (B. A. 37), the posterior middle temporal gyrus (B. A. 21), near brain regions important for verbs and action (consistent with an embodied cognition view that artifacts are understood by how we interact with them). While both types of categories have graded membership, this is more evident in artifact categories (Estes, 2004). This is because people have more certainty about natural kinds (e.g., what makes something a bird), whereas there is more ambiguity about artifacts (e.g., what makes something a tool). Also, people make perceptual decisions faster for natural kind of objects (what something looks like tells you what it is), but make manipulability (how you use it) decisions faster for artifacts (Kalénine & Bonthoux, 2008).

Classical Theory of Categorization

You might think that people use rules to define categories—for example, knowing that a "bachelor" is an unmarried adult male, that an "even number" is divisible by two, and that "speeding" is going faster than the posted limit. The idea that categories are defined by necessary and sufficient features is the **classical view of categorization.** They are *necessary* in that those features must be present. They are *sufficient* in that as long as they are present, something is a member of a category, and additional features are irrelevant. A study by Bruner, Goodnow, and Austin (1956) supported this view. Here, people saw figures like those in Figure 9.3 where items varied along four dimensions: the type of objects, their number, their color, and the number of borders. When given subsets of items, along with an indication of whether each was in a category, people had little difficulty deriving category rules (see three examples in Figures 9.4, 9.5, & 9.6).

Although people can derive rules of necessity and sufficiency for some categories, it does not appear that this is how humans typically derive and use categories. The classical view cannot explain the ideas of central tendency, graded membership, and family resemblance. This is clearly seen when one looks at categories that have simple and clear defining rules. For example, the categories "even numbers" and "odd numbers" are very simply defined. However, they show graded membership (Armstrong, Gleitman, & Gleitman, 1983).

FIGURE 9.3 Set of Stimuli Used to Illustrate the Classical View of Categorization

Source: Bruner, J. S., Goodnow, J. J., & Austin, G. A. (1956). *A study of thinking*. Oxford, England: Wiley. Reprinted with permission from author.

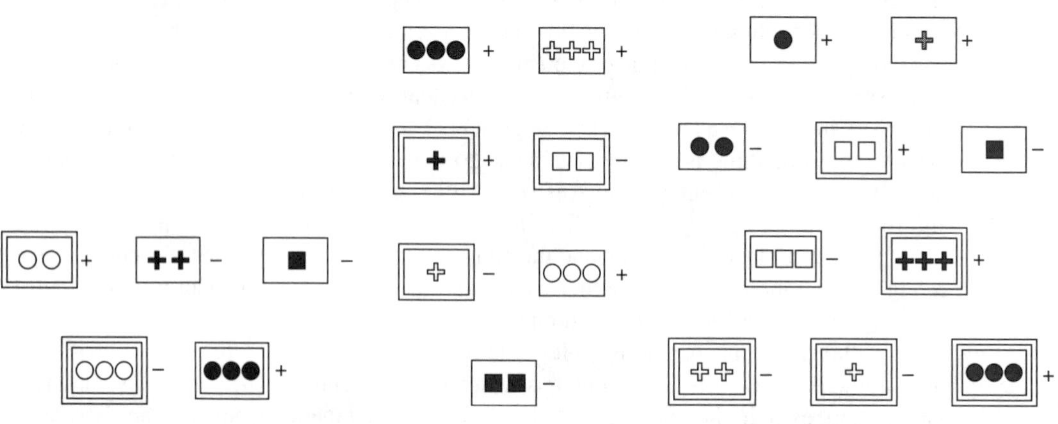

FIGURE 9.4 Simple Set of Items Used to Derive a Category

FIGURE 9.5 Moderately Complex Set of Items Used to Derive a Category

FIGURE 9.6 More Complex Set of Items Used to Derive a Category

TABLE 9.1 Ratings of Items (Out of 6) for a Well-Defined Category—in This Case, Odd and Even Numbers

EVEN NUMBER	RATING	ODD NUMBER	RATING
4	5.9	3	5.4
8	5.5	7	5.1
10	5.3	23	4.6
18	4.4	57	4.4
34	3.6	501	3.5
106	3.1	447	3.3

Source: Reprinted from *Cognition*, 13, Armstrong, S.L., Gleitman, L.R., & Gleitman, H., What some concepts might not be, pp. 263–308, 1983, with permission from Elsevier.

In the data, shown in Table 9.1, "4" is rated as a better example of the category "even number" than is "106," even though they both equally follow the defining rule. Also, the properties that define category members can vary in their importance (Ashcraft, 1978), with rarer features being more diagnostic (e.g., has a trunk) than common features (e.g., breathes) (Mirman & Magnuson, 2009).

Prototype Theory

Categories are organized, in part, using unconscious mental statistics. One approach to capture this is the **prototype model**. From this view, categories are determined by a mental representation that is an average of all category members called a *prototype* (Rosch, 1975), which may or may not correspond to an actual entity in the world. For example, the prototype for "dog" would be an average of all dogs ever encountered and may not correspond to any particular breed of dog. When photographs of faces are used for making preference judgments along with morphed composites of faces, people prefer and rate the composite faces which are closer to the prototype face as more attractive (Langlois & Roggman, 1990; Langlois, Roggman, & Musselman, 1994; Rhodes et al., 2003; but see Alley & Cunningham, 1991). People prefer faces that are averages of others. Because they are averages, they have fewer unusual and distinguishing characteristics, and so are easier to mentally process (Winkielman, Halberstadt, Fazendeiro, & Catty, 2006). A pretty face is a boring face. This is one reason why attractive faces are more difficult to remember (Light, Hollander, & Kayra-Stuart, 1981). Similarly, high attractiveness for more prototypical instances is also observed for dogs, cats, watches, birds, fish, and automobiles (Halberstadt & Rhodes, 2000, 2003).

The nice thing about prototypes is that they provide a clear explanation for the central tendencies of a category (which would be the prototype itself) and graded category structure. The closer a given instance is to the prototype, the better it is a member of the category.

However, there are important aspects not accounted for. For example, people are often aware of the size of a category. For example, we know that "types of insects" is a large category, but "types of elephants" is a small one. With a prototype there is also no information about variability among category members. It is only an average. Also, a caricature (a category member with exaggerated features) is thought to better represent a category than a prototype when a category is considered in the context of other, related categories (Goldstone, Steyvers, & Rogosky, 2003). This is because the caricature captures distinctive features and emphasizes them. This helps distinguish a category from other, similar categories. However, although caricatures are better representatives of a category, at least for faces, they are rated as less attractive than the prototype (Rhodes & Tremewan, 1996).

Exemplar Theory

Another approach to understand categorization is **exemplar theory** (Medin & Shaffer, 1978; Nosofsky, 1988). In this view, people use all the category members to make memory decisions. This captures central tendency, graded membership, and family resemblance, as well as information about category size, variability, correlated attributes, and any new information about it. Because categorization is always using all of the memory traces, any new experiences have an influence.

Another plus of exemplar theories is that they can explain the context sensitivity of categories. For example, the color gray is more similar to white in the context of hair color but is more similar to black in the context of clouds (Medin & Shoben, 1988). The selection of exemplars constantly changes, depending on the particular memory traces that happen to be used. Also, more priming is experienced when the contexts are experienced similarly. For example, people are primed more for a pony *mane* after verifying a horse *mane* than a lion's *mane*. This is because a pony mane is more perceptually similar to a horse's than a lion's (Solomon & Barsalou, 2001). Finally, previously activated semantic meanings can bias how new information is interpreted (Gagne & Shoben, 2002). A phrase like "adolescent doctor" is easier to interpret if it follows "animal doctor" than if it follows "country doctor." Both "adolescent doctor" and "animal doctor" refer to the kind of patient treated, whereas "country doctor" refers to where the doctor lives.

A serious problem with both prototype and exemplar theories is an inherent circularity. Categories are defined by experiences with members of that category. However, the memory traces that are selected are those that conform to the criteria of the category. In short, how can memory traces be selected to define a category if the category is needed to select them in the first place?

Explanation-Based Theory

Another view of categorization is that people try to provide reasons why things should be grouped together. For **explanation-based views**, categories are theories or explanations for why things tend to go together. For example, feathers and wings go together because feathers are well suited for flying. People seek out and use prior knowledge to understand how entities form a coherent group to allow us to create categories (Rehder & Ross, 2001). Examples of this are social groups, political events (e.g., revolutions), and social institutions (e.g., governments), which may not share physical features but that overlap thematically.

People place a greater emphasis on causal factors rather than the effects (Ahn, Kim, Lassaline, & Dennis, 2000), because they are creating explanations for what makes something a category. For example, knowing that an animal swims is a more fundamental characteristic than knowing that an animal has webbed feet (presumably they have webbed feet because they swim). Also, categories are defined, in part, by how people interact with things (Markman & Ross, 2003), not just statistical regularities. For example, what makes something a chair has more to do with your sitting in it than with the materials that make it up as different chairs are made of different types of materials. This captures the more general idea that causal relations help define semantic memories (Fenker, Waldmann, & Holyoak, 2005).

An important point is that people can create new categories on the fly, called **ad hoc categories** (Barsalou, 1983). For example, coffee, perfume, leather, and skunks are all members of the category "things with a distinctive smell." Ad hoc categories are interesting because people generate them off the cuff, but they have many of the properties as standard categories, such as having a central tendency, graded structures, and family resemblance. Thus some semantic memory structures can be easily generated, and this raises questions about the stability of semantic memory in general.

One idea from explanation-based theories of categories is **psychological essentialism.** This is the idea that all the members of a category have an underlying essence that people may or may not be aware of. This usually applies to natural kind categories, which can be defined by chemical structure or DNA, such as "water" or "skunk," respectively. However, some artifact categories, such as "scientific instruments," are treated as if they have essential qualities, and some natural kind categories, like "humans," do not (Kalish, 2002). People create categories pragmatically, as is needed (Kalish, 2002), to serve a purpose. The degree to which members fit a category is a function how well they serve that purpose. Overall, causal relations among category attributes for the derivation of such explanations (Rehder & Hastie, 2001).

Stereotypes and Prejudice

There is no question that categorization is a valuable aspect of semantic memory. However, it can cause problems, such as when we engage in stereotyping. Stereotypes are categories for groups of people. When you stereotype people, you treat them as if they are essentially the same as any other members of that group. Stereotypes are activated automatically (Oakhill, Garnham, & Reynolds, 2005) and we use them to make assumptions about people, and are surprised when these assumptions are violated (e.g., Duffy & Keir, 2004). When a stereotype leads one person to treat another in an inappropriate manner, this is prejudice. So, overall, while categorization is useful, we must be careful to ensure that any categories we form about people are accurate and fair. Although categorization is a very human way to think about things, we need to exert some effort to monitor our thoughts and behavior.

Synopsis

A central role of semantic memory is to create and use categories. People's categories are oriented around a basic level and show evidence of central tendency and graded membership with family resemblance among the members. Human categorization does not follow the rules of the classical categorization model. Instead, it operates using probabilistic information, as in prototype and exemplar theories. Moreover, it also exhibits characteristics to suggest that people are problem solving their way through category creation, with the use of explanation-based categories. Overall, human categorization reflects both environmental (probabilistic theories) and goal-oriented (explanation-based theories) influences (Love, 2005; Rouder & Ratcliff, 2006). This categorization process can go awry when inappropriately extended to people.

ORDERED RELATIONS

Another characteristic of semantic memory is the influence of knowledge ordered along some dimension, such as size, intelligence, or age. These influences are linear order effects (Banks, 1977).

One ordering effect is the **semantic distance effect,** in which people make quicker judgments about the relative order of two items as the distance between them increases (Potts, 1972; Rips, Shoben, & Smith, 1973). For example, it is easier to judge that an elephant is bigger than a rabbit than to judge that a dog is bigger than a rabbit. The farther two concepts are along a dimension, the easier it is to discriminate between them, and so people retrieve and compute this information quickly. However, concepts that are relatively close in memory are harder to discriminate, so judgments are slower and more error prone.

With the **semantic congruity effect** people are faster to make judgments about two items if the valence of the comparison term matches the end of the dimension they are on (Banks, Clark, & Lucy, 1975). For example, it is easier to judge that Jefferson was president before Monroe than to judge that Monroe was president after Jefferson because both are at the "early" end of the dimension. Dimensional information is stored in semantic memory along with the concepts. For example, Jefferson and Monroe are both thought of as early U.S. presidents. As a result, the attribute "early" is stored directly with them. When this information is needed, if the attributes match the judgment, people respond quicker than if there is a mismatch, in which case people need to do more thinking to get the information lined up properly.

Finally, with the **serial position effect** people are faster to make judgments about two or more items at the extremes of an ordered dimension than those in the middle (Shoben, Čech, Schwanenflugel, & Sailor, 1989). For example, it is easier to judge that Rhode Island is smaller than Connecticut than to judge that Indiana is smaller than Ohio. Items that are at the ends of a dimension are more distinct and, so, are easier to discriminate, and semantic decisions can be made quickly. However, to some extent, people make such semantic decisions on the fly. For example, if, during the course of a study, semantic memories, such as animal sizes, are broken down into two categories—large animals (e.g., horse, whale, rhino) and small ones (e.g., flea, rat, snail)—people show serial position effects for both subsets, not just for the extreme ends of the entire set (Čech, Shoben, & Love, 1990). More generally, serial position effects, such as primacy and recency effects, are also observed in semantic memory as with memories for U.S. presidents (Roediger & Crowder, 1976) and church hymns (Maylor, 2002). These serial position curves are due to the frequency of exposure to information, with people encountering the names of the very early and the very recent presidents more so than others (Healy, Havas, & Parker, 2000). This also accounts for the fact that Lincoln is remembered much better than he should be. Thus, there are a number of influences of ordered relations in semantic memory on the ability to retrieve knowledge.

Embodied Influences on Ordered Relations

How we use our bodies can influence semantic order knowledge, as with the Spatial-Numerical Association of Response Codes or **SNARC effect** (Dehaene, Bossini, & Giraux, 1993). When people make judgments about numbers, such as if they are odd or even, judgments about smaller numbers were made faster with the left hand. The reverse was true for the larger numbers. The SNARC effect is consistent with the idea that people have a mental number line in semantic memory going from left to right with small numbers on the left and large numbers appear as one moves to the right (but see, Santens & Gevers, 2008), although this may be due to relative, rather than absolute, magnitudes (Nathan, Shaki, Salti, & Algom, 2009).

The SNARC effect is also observed in blind people (Castronovo & Seron, 2007), reinforcing the idea that it is not strictly visual. It is also more prominent in people who speak languages that are read left to right rather than right to left (Dehaene, Bossini, & Giroux, 1993; Shaki & Fischer, 2008). Furthermore, the SNARC effect is not limited to numbers. Lidji, Kolinsky, Lochy, and Morais (2007) found a similar pattern with musical pitches. People respond faster to lower tones with the left hand and higher tones with the right, similar to the arrangement of notes on a piano or guitar (see also Gevers, Reynvoet, & Fias, 2004, for a day of the week effect, and Prado, van der Henst, & Noveck, 2008 for a linear order effect).

Another example of embodied influences is the finding that the closer an object is to a person, in space, time, or social relations, the more effectively it is processed. Although knowledge of an object should be abstract, the more likely we are to interact with it, the more it influences the availability of knowledge about it (Amit, Algom, & Trope, 2009). Also, people are faster to identify words that refer to large objects (e.g., bookcase) than to small objects (e.g., teaspoon) (Sereno, O'Donnell, & Sereno, 2009). So, people incorporate their perceptual experiences in their more abstract conceptual knowledge.

Synopsis

Semantic memories can capture order relations in the world, with the availability of knowledge being influenced by relative positions in an order, as with the semantic distance and congruity effects. Ordered semantic memories also reveal serial position effects. Moreover, semantic memories of ordered information can even show embodied influences, as with the SNARC effect.

SCHEMAS AND SCRIPTS

In life, there are many events that are fairly regular in how they unfold and operate and how we react to them. That is, commonly experienced aspects of life have some shared framework that unites them. We are able to capitalize on this to help us understand new situations, much as we use categories to understand new objects or creatures. A semantic memory that captures commonly encountered aspects of life is called a *schema*, an idea that was originally developed by Bartlett (1932). (If you have more than one schema, it is called either schemas or schemata. Both plurals are acceptable.)

The schema concept is found in many areas of psychology, and you may have come across them in another course. For those of you who haven't, schemas contain the basic information about components of a certain aspect of life and how these parts interact with one another. A schema is a kind of blueprint for events that a person can draw upon to understand specific cases. In some sense, schemas are types of theory-based categories. As you will see, schemas can help memory, but they can also hurt memory.

Primary Schema Processes

There are five primary processes that are involved in using schemas (Alba & Hasher, 1983). Four of them are for encoding information, and the fifth is important during retrieval.

Selection. When people have a schema, they can tell which things are likely to be important and which are peripheral. For example, when watching a football game, it is important to understand how much time has elapsed. Thus, your schema for football tells you to pay attention to the clock. In contrast, if you were watching a baseball game, the amount of time that has elapsed is less important. Thus, your schema for baseball would select out information about the time. Information that is important in the schemas is more likely to be encoded and remembered.

Knowing which schema is relevant can greatly influence performance. For example, in a study by Bransford and Johnson (1972), people read an ambiguous passage (see Table 9.2). If people are told ahead of time that the passage is entitled "Washing Clothes," then they remember more of it later. The title allows them to activate the appropriate schema and they can then select what is relevant in the passage and interpret it. This helps out at encoding because if the title is given afterward, when a person is trying to recall the text, then there is no benefit (Summers, Horton, & Diehl, 1985).

TABLE 9.2 Ambiguous Passage that Is Clarified by Activating the Appropriate Schema

The procedure is actually quite simple. First arrange items into different groups. Of course, one pile may be sufficient depending on how much there is to do. If you have to go somewhere else due to a lack of facilities, that is the next step; otherwise, you are pretty well set. It is important not to overdo things. That is, it is better to do too few things at once than too many. In the short run this may not seem important, but complications can easily arise. A mistake can be expensive as well. At first, the whole procedure will seem complicated. Soon, however, it will become just another facet of life. It is difficult to foresee any end to necessity for this task in the immediate future, but then, one never can tell. After the procedure is completed one arranges the material into different groups again. Then they can be put into their appropriate places. Eventually they will be used once more and the whole cycle will then have to be repeated. However, that is part of life.

Source: Reprinted from *Journal of Verbal Learning and Verbal Behavior,* 11, Bransford, J.D., & Johnson, M.K., Contextual prerequisites for understanding: Some investigations of comprehension and recall, pp. 717–726, 1972, with permission from Elsevier.

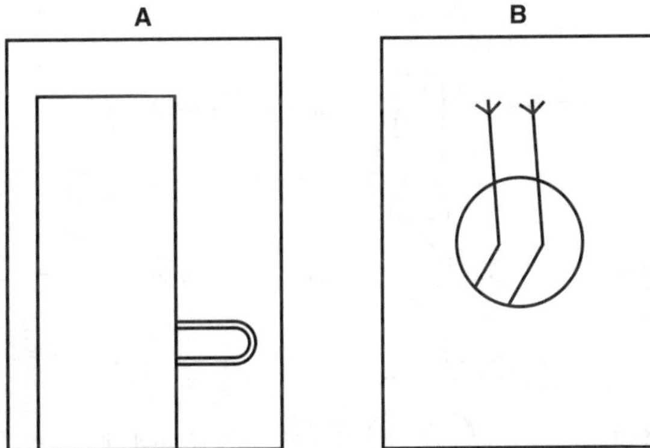

FIGURE 9.7 Droodles Used in a Study to Assess the Influence of Labeling and Schema on the Ability to Remember. Droodle A could be described as a very short person playing a trombone in a telephone booth. Droodle B could be described as an early bird who caught a very strong worm

Source: Bower, G. H., Karlin, M. B., & Dueck, A. (1975). Comprehension and memory for pictures. *Memory & Cognition, 3,* 216–220.

A similar outcome is seen with pictures. Bower, Karlin, and Dueck (1975) used droodles such as those shown in Figure 9.7 that people saw either with or without labels indicating what they were. The labels helped people's memories.

Abstraction. Abstraction involves converting the surface form of information (e.g., verbatim wording) into a more abstract representation that captures the underlying meaning. For example, when people hear a list of sentences and try to comprehend them, within a few minutes they are not able to distinguish the verbatim sentence from a paraphrase (Sachs, 1967, 1974). Similarly, if people see a picture, they are less likely to notice a change if the same basic situation is present, such as changing a specific instance of an entity (e.g., one type of car for another), moving the relative position of two entities, or even zooming in or out of the picture (Mandler & Ritchey, 1977). However, people are more likely to notice changes that alter the meaning of what they saw.

This effect of schemas is not always a case of making things more general, but it can sometimes be the opposite if a person goes from a superordinate to a basic level category (Pansky & Koriat, 2004). For example, if one person hears "vehicle" (superordinate) and another hears "sports car" (subordinate), both will abstract this to the basic level "car."

An example of abstraction is shown in Figure 9.8. In a study by Carmichael, Hogan, and Walter (1932), people saw the line drawings in the middle column with one of two labels. Each of these labels is placed next to the drawing. After a period of time, people drew what they remember seeing. Examples of the types of drawings people produced are on the right and left sides of Figure 9.9. People tended to distort their drawings to have them conform to the label that was provided. People used their schemas to abstract away and lose the ambiguous information. Thus, what is remembered is more schema consistent.

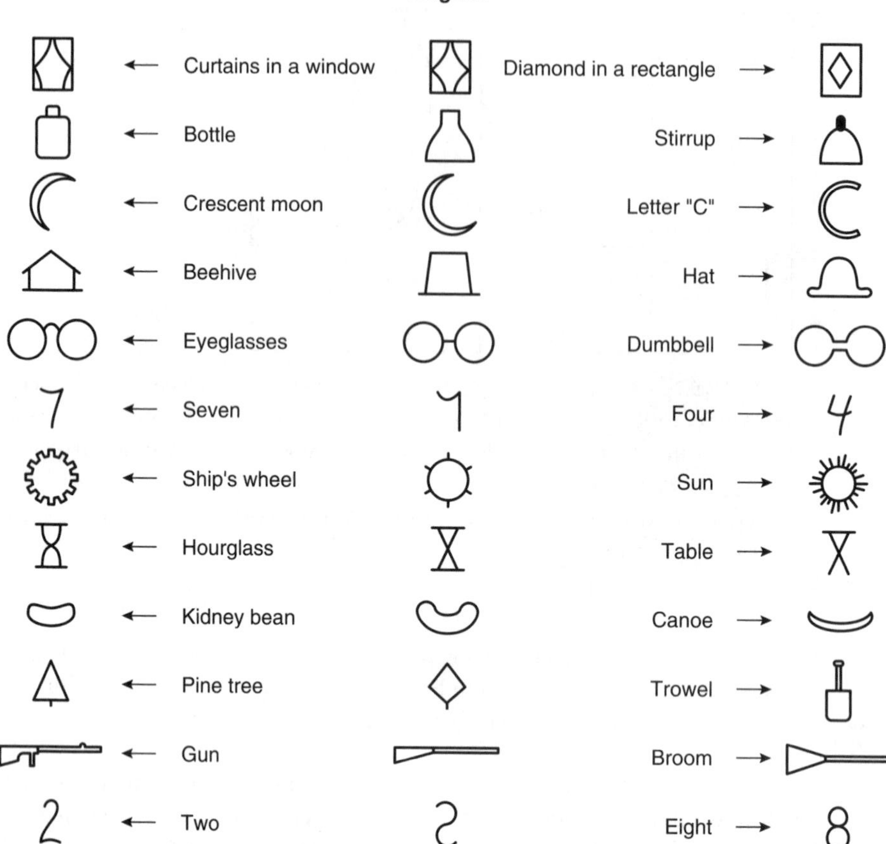

FIGURE 9.8 Ambiguous Line Drawings in the Middle Were Given One of Two Labels. Later reproductions by people, on the left and right, conform to the schema activated by the label

Source: Carmichael, L., Hogan, H. P., & Walter, A. A. (1932). An experimental study of the effect of language on the reproductions of visually perceived forms. *Journal of Experimental Psychology, 15,* 73–86. Permission granted upon citation of source.

Interpretation. When we read a book, watch television, or experience events, there is a lot that we miss. For example, when you see a movie, many things happen off-camera, but you easily infer them. If you watch a person boarding an airplane one moment and getting off the next, you don't think that the person got onto the plane and then immediately turned around. Instead, you infer that there was a flight in between, although only a few seconds elapsed in the theater. The interpretation process has a powerful effect on memory. People may misremember having encountered things that they only inferred from a schema. For example, people who view a sequence of events in which they see the effect are likely to claim to remember seeing an unpresented schema-consistent cause (Hannigan & Reinitz, 2001). For example, people who saw a picture of a person pulling an orange from the bottom of a pile (cause) are less likely to misremember seeing the pile fall (effect), but people who saw a picture of the oranges on the floor (effect) are more likely to misremember seeing a person pulling an orange from the bottom of the pile (cause).

Integration. In life we usually get information about an event all at once. However, we do come across event descriptions that are given out piecemeal. For example, when reading a mystery novel, the author may give different aspects of the murder at different points in the story. If the reader has any hope of figuring out what happened and who the guilty party is before the end, these pieces of information must be integrated into a common mental representation of the event. This is done using schemas.

Reconstruction. Up to now we have seen how schemas influence encoding. However, schemas also affect retrieval. Memories are incomplete fragmentary records. As such, only bits and pieces of the original experience make it into consciousness. Sometimes there are a lot of fragments, enough to recover almost the entire memory, whereas in other cases the fragments are few and far between. In either case, some reconstruction is needed. In reconstruction, people fill in the gaps in the memory traces with information that has a good chance of being accurate if those gaps contained information that is generally true. This is like a paleontologist reconstructing an entire creature from fossilized bits and pieces.

There is a lot of evidence for the operation of reconstruction in memory. Some of this comes from Bartlett's (1932) work. In one set of experiments, he gave British college students a Native American folktale called "The War of the Ghosts" to read. This tale is shown in Table 9.3. Some time after reading—often several days, weeks, or months later—a person was asked to recall it. During recall, people not only forgot parts of the story, but they added new elements. Often this new information was less consistent with the original story but more consistent with typical English folktales. One recall is shown in Table 9.4. Schema-based reconstruction is reflected in the idea that if the warrior had been shot, he would have fallen unconscious and been carried off the battlefield. However, this did not occur in the original story.

People also show schematic reconstruction with nonverbal information. In one study, students at the University of Illinois waited in a graduate student's office before an experiment began. However, what they did not realize was that the experiment had begun. After spending a few minutes in the "office," they were taken to another room, where their memory for the "office" was tested. What was found was that people tended to misremember items as being in the "office" when they were not. These were consistent with a schema of an office. For example, many people remembered seeing books, when there were none (Brewer & Treyens, 1981; see also Hemmer & Steyvers, 2009). In general, people use a combination of detailed memories and schemas to remember, just as in fuzzy trace theory. People are more likely to falsely remember schema-consistent information after longer delays (e.g., 48 hours) than if tested immediately (Lampinen, Copeland, & Neuscatz, 2001). The detailed memories are rapidly forgotten, leaving people more dependent on their schemas.

Forgetting leads people to rely more on schemas rather than memories of particular instances (Gilovich, 1981). Memory reports become more schematic. Information that is falsely recalled but is central to a schema is often accompanied by a feeling of familiarity (see Chapter 14).

TABLE 9.3 "The War of the Ghosts," a Native American Folktale

One night two young men from Egulac went down to the river to hunt seals, and while they were there it became foggy and calm. Then they heard war-cries, and they thought: "Maybe this is a war party." They escaped to the shore, and hid behind a log. Now canoes came up, and they heard the noise of paddles, and saw one canoe coming up to them. There were five men in the canoe, and they said:

"What do you think? We wish to take you along. We are going up the river to make war on the people."

One of the young men said: "I have no arrows."

"Arrows are in the canoe," they said.

"I will not go along. I might be killed. My relatives do not know where I have gone. But you," he said turning to the other, "may go with them."

So one of the young men went, but the other returned home.

And the warriors went on up the river to a town on the other side of Kalama. The people came down to the water, and they began to fight, and many were killed. But presently the young man heard one of the warriors say: "Quick, let us go home: that Indian has been hit." Now he thought: "Oh, they are ghosts." He did not feel sick, but they said he had been shot.

So the canoes went back to Egulac, and the young man went ashore to his house, and made a fire. And he told everybody and said: "Behold I accompanied the ghosts, and we went to fight. Many of our fellows were killed, and many of those who attacked us were killed. They said I was hit, and I did not feel sick."

He told it all, and then he became quiet. When the sun rose he fell down. Something black came out of his mouth. His face became contorted. The people jumped up and cried.

He was dead.

Source: Bartlett, 1932. Reprinted with permission of Cambridge University Press.

TABLE 9.4 Recall Attempt for "The War of the Ghosts" Four Months Later

There were two men in a boat, sailing toward an island. When they approached the island, some natives came running toward them, and informed them that there was fighting going on the island, and invited them to join. One said to the other, "You had better go. I cannot fight very well, because I have relatives expecting me, and they will not know what has happened to me. But you have no one expecting you." So one accompanied the natives, but the other returned.

Here there is a part I can't remember. What I don't know is how the man got to the fight. However, anyhow the man was in the midst of the fighting, and was wounded. The natives endeavored to persuade the man to return, but he assured them that he had not been wounded.

I have an idea that his fighting won the admiration of the natives.

The wounded man ultimately fell unconscious. He was taken from the fighting by the natives.

Then, I think it is, the natives described what happened, and they seem to have imagined seeing a ghost coming out of his mouth. Really it was a kind of materialization of his breath. I know this phrase was not in the story, but that is the idea I have. Ultimately the man dies at dawn the next day.

Source: Bartlett, 1932. Reprinted with permission of Cambridge University Press.

Scripts

When knowledge refers to a common *sequence* of events, a type of schema called a **script** is used (Abbot, Black, & Smith, 1985; Barsalou & Sewell, 1985). In general, people prefer using script information in a forward order (Haberlandt & Bingham, 1984), although more central components may be more available (Galambos & Rips, 1982). People have good memories for the order of common events. When people are asked to list script components, such as what happens at a restaurant, many of the lists have the same entries (Bower, Black, & Turner, 1979), suggesting that there is a great deal of regularity in this type of semantic memory. A typical list for what to do in a restaurant is shown in Table 9.5.

Scripts influence how information is retrieved and used. For example, when people read a text of a scripted event, they take longer to read a sentence when the action is further along in the script from the prior sentence than if it is closer (Bower, Black, & Turner, 1979). For a story about going to a restaurant, if people had just read a sentence about waiting to be seated, they would read the next sentence faster if it was about looking at the menu than if it was about finishing the meal. The idea is that people are scanning their scripts to help make sense of what they are reading. When the information is close in the script, less effort is required. However, when the information is far in the script, more effort is required because more knowledge must be inferred.

The influence of scripts is also seen when people are given pieces of information about a scripted event in a random order. During later recall, there is a tendency to report those fragments in an order that more closely approximates the script (Bower, Black, & Turner, 1979). Moreover, if people give summaries of normal and scrambled texts, their summaries are similar (Kintsch, Mandel, & Kozminsky, 1977). Thus, people use scripts to organize information to help them both understand it and remember it better.

Limits on Schema Usage

While schemas and scripts strongly influence memory, they are not always used. There are constraints on when memories do or do not conform to schemas. It is also possible to get people to disregard schema-generated information when the schema has been discredited. In a study by Hasher and Griffin (1978; see also Anderson & Pichert, 1978)

TABLE 9.5 A Typical Script for What to Do in a Restaurant

Open door	Meal arrives	Pay bill
Wait to be seated	Eat food	Leave tip
Go to table	Finish meal	Get coat
Be seated	Order dessert	Leave
Look at menu	Ask for bill	
Order meal	Bill arrives	

Source: Reprinted from *Cognitive Psychology,* 11, Bower, G.H., Black, J.B., & Turner, T.J., Scripts in memory for text, pp. 117–220, 1979, with permission from Elsevier.

TABLE 9.6 Ambiguous Story Consistent with Two Schemas—an Escaped Convict Or a Deer Hunter

The man walked carefully through the forest. Several times he looked over his shoulder and scrutinized the woods behind him. He trod carefully, trying to avoid snapping twigs and small branches that lay in his path, for he did not want to create excess noise. The chirping of the birds in the trees almost annoyed him, their loud calls serving to distract him. He did not want to confuse those sounds with the type he was listening for.

Source: Hasher & Griffin, 1976.

students were given ambiguous texts, such as the one in Table 9.6. It is ambiguous because it could be either about an escaped convict or a deer hunter. Students were first asked to read this text from one of these perspectives. After a brief delay, the students were asked to recall the story. Some did this from the same perspective as they read it. In contrast, others were led to believe that the experimenter had given them the wrong title initially. They were then given the "correct" other title. The results are shown in Table 9.7. Overall, people recalled the same amount of information when there was a title switch as when there was not. However, when there was a title switch, people made fewer schema-consistent intrusions. Thus, people can disregard schemas to use more detailed, verbatim memories.

Synopsis

Schemas are semantic memories for commonly experienced aspects of life. During encoding, schemas can select relevant ideas, abstract away the critical ideas, draw inferences through a process of interpretation, and integrate otherwise separate bits of information. During retrieval schemas help reconstruct details that were forgotten. For sequences of events, people can use scripts. While schemas and scripts powerfully influence memory, under some circumstances people can disregard them and remember more accurately.

TABLE 9.7 Influence of a Schema Shift on Later Memory for Schema Consistent Inferences. The data are for the percentage of idea units recalled from an ambiguous story and the number of intrusions based on the initial theme, the alternate theme, or some other theme

CONDITION	IDEA UNITS	FIRST THEME	SECOND THEME	NEUTRAL
Same schema	35%	2.58	0.17	0.92
Schema shift	35%	0.54	0.08	1.33

Source: Hasher & Griffin, 1976.

PROBLEMS WITH SEMANTIC MEMORY

Semantic Illusions

How many animals of each kind did Moses take on the ark? Many people respond with the answer "two," but this is incorrect. Moses did not take any animals on the ark, Noah did. In the original study of this type of memory error, Erickson and Mattson (1981) found that 81 percent of students at the University of California, San Diego, responded with the answer "two" even though they all knew the correct answer. So why do so many people make this mistake? Semantic memory, like other types of memory, is prone to error. In addition to forgetting, errors occur that involve the inappropriate retrieval of information.

One semantic memory error is the **Moses Illusion.** This illusion does not appear to be due to people mentally correcting the question or making rushed responses (Reder & Cleermans, 1990; Reder & Kusbit, 1991). Instead, there are three accounts of it. First, semantic processing is very general unless people focus on the information of interest (Barton & Sanford, 1993; Erickson & Mattson, 1981). Second, people engage in only a partial assessment of semantic information (Bohan & Sanford, 2008; Reder & Cleermans, 1990; Reder & Kusbit, 1991). Third, similar language elements, such as a similar name, can inappropriately activate information in semantic memory, giving the illusion that it is known (Shafto & MacKay, 2000). Thus, information in semantic memory is accessed in a less than precise way and can lead to errors that would not be made if people were being more deliberate and careful.

Naïve Physics

Semantic memory illusions also apply to nonverbal knowledge. As was shown in Chapter 5, memory can incorporate physical principles and properties of the world, such as gravity and friction. This **naïve physics** of how objects move is stored, to some degree, in semantic memory. However, when we consciously try to apply this knowledge, semantic memory errors can be revealed. This is seen in the mental models people use when asked to make predictions about the movement of objects. In some studies, students at Johns Hopkins University were given diagrams, such as those shown in Figure 9.9. The task was to indicate (1) the trajectory of a ball shot out of the tube, (2) the trajectory of the ball when the string broke, and (3) the path of the bomb when the plane dropped it. The responses are shown in Figure 9.10.

Although people do give the correct responses in some cases, they also give incorrect responses based on incorrect knowledge in semantic memory (McCloskey, Caramazza, & Green, 1980). What is interesting is that people are responding as if they are holding medieval impetus theories of motion (but see Cooke & Breedin, 1994). Such responses are more likely when people are viewing static diagrams, and are less likely when they are viewing moving displays (Kaiser, Proffitt, & Anderson, 1985; McCloskey & Kohl, 1983), although not always (Rohrer, 2003). It should also be noted that while education can improve performance (Donley & Ashcraft, 1992), it can get in the way as well. Oberle, McBeath, Madigan, and Sugar (2005) reported what they called the *Galileo bias*. Specifically, people mistakenly believe that two balls of different weights dropped

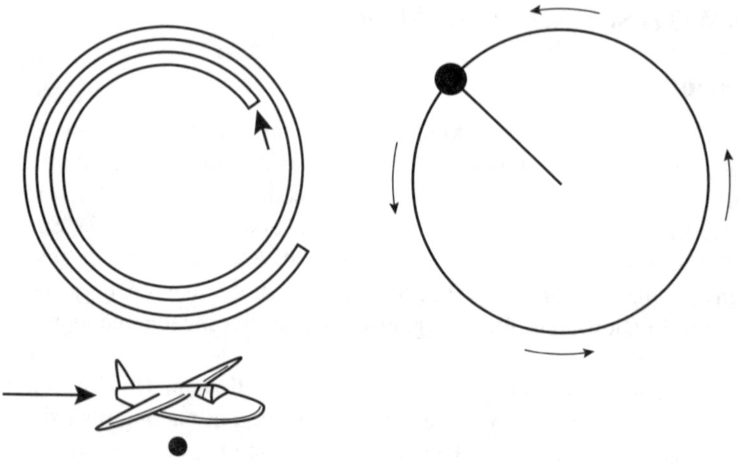

FIGURE 9.9 Stimuli Used to Illustrate Principles of Naïve Physics. A person's task is to show the path of the ball once it leaves the tube or is released.

Source: McCloskey, M. (1983). Naïve theories of motion. In D. Gentner & A. L. Stevens (Eds.), *Mental models* (pp. 299–324). Hillsdale, NJ: Erlbaum.

from 10 meters will hit the ground simultaneously if they are released at the same time. However, this does not take into account wind resistance. Even with extensive practice dropping these balls, students at Arizona State University continued to make errors based on their prior semantic knowledge of what they had learned in elementary school about Galileo and gravity.

This incorrect understanding can be extended to semantic models of device—for example, many people treat a thermostat not as a device for setting the ideal temperature but as a heat accelerator, setting the temperature much higher in the mistaken belief that the house will get warmer faster (it doesn't).

Another source of misinformation in semantic memory is people's understanding of how vision works. Vision works by light energy entering the eye and being absorbed by the photoreceptors (rods and cones) in the retina. However, a large number (33–86 percent, depending on the measure) of college-educated people mistakenly believe that vision involves emissions from the eye (Winer et al., 2002). This is the *extramission view of vision.* This is reflected in people's responses when talking about or depictions of vision, such as imagining rays coming out of the eyes or the belief that you can "feel" when a person behind you is looking at you. This semantic misunderstanding of an intimate part of our human experience illustrates the degree to which our knowledge may be completely erroneous.

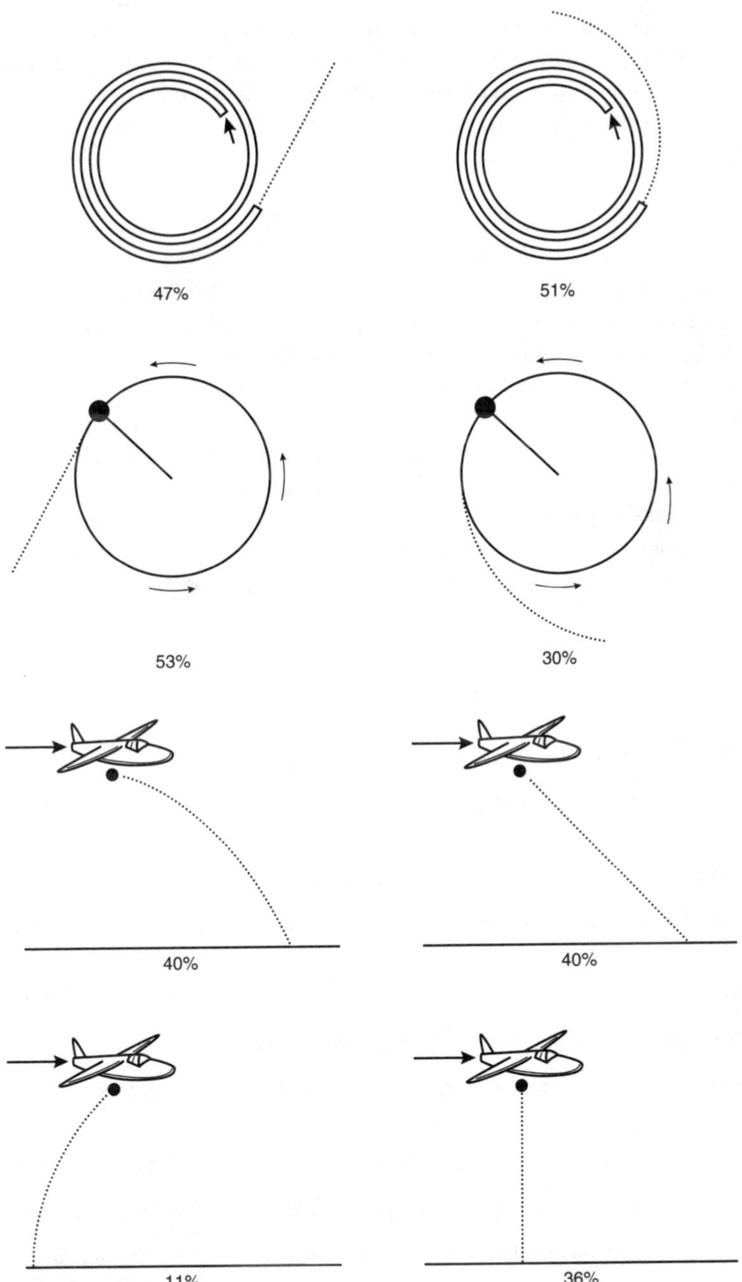

FIGURE 9.10 Responses Given in Naïve Physics Studies

Source: McCloskey, M. (1983). Naïve theories of motion. In D. Gentner & A. L. Stevens (Eds.), *Mental models* (pp. 299–324). Hillsdale, NJ: Erlbaum.

Synopsis

Semantic memory is only as accurate as the information in it or how it is used. While most knowledge in semantic memory is accurate, it can break down, such as when knowledge is only superficially accessed, as in the Moses Illusion. Breakdowns can also occur when semantic memories, although based on experience, have somehow been stored incorrectly, such as the errors people make on naïve physics tasks.

SUMMARY

This chapter looked at how people use general world knowledge in semantic memory. Semantic memory is highly structured. This organization brings related concepts to mind through the process of priming. Although priming is largely automatic, it can be controlled to some extent. The organization of knowledge is clearest when people use categories. The process of categorization is less dependent on rules of necessary and sufficient features and more on information about overlapping properties or causal relationships among category members. We also looked at how ordered relationships can influence the use of semantic memory. We explored the operation of schemas and scripts during learning and retrieval. Although their use is quite pervasive, it does have its limits. Finally, we looked at cases where semantic memory can be in error, leading people to look at the world in ways that are incorrect.

STUDY QUESTIONS

1. What is semantic priming? What sorts of information get primed? How far does it extend?
2. How long does it take for information to be established in semantic memory?
3. To what degree can semantic priming be consciously controlled? When are semantic memories inhibited?
4. What are the basic properties of categories formed in semantic memory?
5. What are some of the major theories of how people form categories?
6. How is semantic memory retrieval affected by the order of information along a dimension?
7. What are the primary ways that schemas influence memory at encoding and at retrieval?
8. What are schemas for sequential event knowledge called? How do they operate?
9. How can a person avoid the influence of schemas and remember more accurately?
10. What sorts of problems can occur when semantic memory is used? How do these errors arise?
11. How is semantic memory influenced by embodied/perceptual aspects of experience?

KEY TERMS

ad hoc categories, categorization, central tendency, classical view of categorization, exemplar theory, explanation-based views, family resemblance, graded membership, levels of categorization, mediated priming, Moses Illusion, naïve physics, priming, prototype model, psychological essentialism, scripts, semantic memory, semantic distance effect, semantic congruity effect, serial position effect, SNARC effect

TRY IT OUT

For this Try It Out section, two examples are provided of studies you could do to illustrate basic principles in semantic memory involving categories and schemas.

- Here is a study that can illustrate the influence of **categories** on thought (see Neath, 1998). For this task, give people a list of eight animal names, such as, goose, duck, robin, sparrow, hawk, eagle, ostrich, and bat. Give each person a list, preferably in a different random order for each person. Tell people that they need to estimate how many animals of the other species are infected with a disease, given that a particular animal has that disease. You will need 36 people. Tell six of each of them that the infected species is either the goose, duck, robin, sparrow, hawk, or eagle (leave out ostrich and bat), and have them estimate what percentage of the other animals are likely to be infected as well. Tell people to assume that these animals live in close proximity to one another, such as on an island. If all goes well, the more typical the infected animal is of the category BIRD, the higher the percentage of other animals infected, and the less typical the animal, the lower the percentage.
- Here is a study that can assess whether **schemas** are activated in semantic memory (Zechmeister & Nyberg, 1982). For this study you need two passages. One should be the *washing clothes* passage on page 186. The other is about running a pizza parlor and is shown below. For one group of people, read them one passages with the title, and the other passage without the title. If you test people individually, counterbalance the order that people get the passages and the order that they either do or do not get the passage titles. After reading each passage, have people write down as much as they can remember. You will need at least 12 people. If all goes well people remember more from the passage for which you gave the title. The title activates the appropriate schema, making it easier to remember.

Generally the atmosphere is not conducive to street clothing. Proper attire lessens the worry. It may also facilitate dexterity. Awe-filled spectators surely provide extra motivation. Hopefully they don't cause distractions. Finesse and enthusiasm add a lot to the performance, however, the final results constitute the true measure of achievement. Experiment with ways of throwing. Making the think pellets into thin skins is the aim. You usually cannot select all the constituents. Customers choose much themselves. Your task is to integrate the raw material. Careful engineering of embellishment placement guarantees consistency of quality. Once heated, no changes can be made. Consumption is imminent. Quantity ultimately secures survival.

CHAPTER TEN

FORMAL MODELS OF MEMORY

Verbal descriptions of memory are nice. They give us a feel for how memory operates, but they can be vague. Worse, alone they may not distinguish among different ideas about how memory works. A more precise language is needed to capture the subtle flavors and nuances of human memory, and that language is mathematics. By casting ideas in a mathematical language, thereby creating a formal model, we can look at finer qualities of memory than is not possible with verbal descriptions. This mathematical expression is often done using computer models. Creating a formal model of memory forces us to be explicit about how everything works and our assumptions are laid bare. With verbal descriptions it's easy to fudge things and make assumptions without realizing it. Also, formal models allow for more accurate predictions about how memory works. If psychology is to continue to succeed as a science, there should be a reasonable level of predictability. This does not mean that the goal of psychology is to predict every little behavior or thought, but it at least must provide a general description of what will happen on average, such as knowing that people remember more if they spread studying out over several short sessions rather than a single long one.

Formal models provide a degree of precision and accuracy that is not possible with verbal descriptions and play an important role of explicitly pointing out errors in a theory. Hintzman (1990) has stated the following.

> The common strategy of trying to reason backward from behavior to underlying process (analysis) has drawbacks that become painfully apparent to those who work with simulation models (synthesis). To have one's hunches about how a simple combination of processes will behave repeatedly dashed by one's own computer program is a humbling experience that no experimental psychologist should miss. (p. 111)

In this chapter we look at a number of formal models of memory. We first look at two simple models of recognition and recall and how a formal comparison about these simple models has led to some interesting and unexpected insights. Next, we cover four classes of theories: (1) network models, in which memory has a highly integrated, associative structure; (2) global matching models, which assume that memory is accessed as a whole, and structure emerges from this process; (3) parallel distributed models of memory, which use the nervous system as their inspiration; and (4) dual process models, which assume there are two fundamentally different types of memory processes.

Before turning to the models themselves, you should be aware that these mathematical models rely heavily on quantitative descriptions. However, this chapter has relatively few formulas. The intent is to provide you with a general overview of how these models characterize memory while not assuming a degree of mathematical sophistication nor the ability to apply that knowledge.

SIMPLE MODELS OF MEMORY

We first examine a couple of relatively simple models and then move on to more developed ideas. The first theory is the threshold model of recognition, followed by the generate-recognize model of recall.

Threshold Model

The first simple model of memory, the **threshold model** (Murdock, 1974; see Anderson, 2000, for descriptions), is the idea that there is a threshold of activation for a memory trace to exceed for it to be identified as "old" (or recognized). This threshold is a subjective level that a person uses (in some way, consciously or unconsciously) to evaluate items as new or old. Now, not all memories that people think are old have, in fact, been seen before. Some are new, but for some reason, people recognize them as old. For the threshold model, these incorrect responses are essentially guesses. We must be able to account for how much guessing is going on to better understand how memory is operating. For example, if a person answers "yes" to all of the old items on a memory test, but never says "yes" to a new item, then we can assume that memory is very good. However, if a person answers "yes" to all of the old items, and all of the new items, this is a much less impressive feat. So, to get at the true state of memory, we need to correct for guessing.

To correct for guessing in the threshold model we need both the probability of correctly recognizing something and the probability of incorrectly identifying something as old (a guess). Here p is the probability of correct recognition, and g is the probability of guessing correctly. The "|" sign stands for "given that." Therefore, the probability of giving a correct "yes" response on a recognition test can be written as follows.

$$P(\text{“yes”} \mid \text{old item}) = p + (1 - p)g$$

Using this formula and logic, the terms can be rearranged to allow us to gain an estimate of the likelihood that a person is actually recognizing rather than guessing.

$$p = \frac{P(\text{“yes”} \mid \text{old item}) - P(\text{“yes”} \mid \text{new item})}{1 - P(\text{“yes”} \mid \text{new item})}$$

This is related to ideas in **signal detection theory** (see Chapter 3), which are more sophisticated. When a memory of an old item exceeds threshold, a person correctly recognizes it. This is called a *hit*. When an old item's activation level fails to reach the threshold, it is rejected. This is called a *miss*. When a new item is rejected because the memory does not exceed threshold (because it is new), then this is called a *correct rejection*. Finally, if a new item has a representation in memory that exceeds threshold, a person inappropriately identifies it as old. This is called a *false alarm*. Signal detection approaches play a larger and more obvious role in the global matching models discussed later in the chapter.

Generate-Recognize Model

The other simple formal model considered here is the **generate-recognize model** of recall (Kintsch, 1970), which assumes that recall, particularly free recall, is a two-stage process. Here, recall is just recognition except with a higher threshold before a person can report the information. The generate-recognize model takes a more elaborate view. Instead, recall involves a search of memory, whereas recognition simply involves indicating whether an item is familiar. Still, it would be nice if the retrieval involved in recall were not completely different from recognition. The generate-recognize model tries to accomplish both of these.

The first stage of the model is the generate component, which is unique to recall. During this phase a person takes the available retrieval cues and begins to generate a set of memory traces whose contents can be reported. This is done by the activation of information in memory that is associated with the cues, followed by the information that is associated with that, and so on. This information is cross-referenced to generate a set of possible responses. In the second stage, the person then applies the standard recognition processes to the information generated in the first stage.

This model, although relatively simple, makes clear predictions about how retrieval operates. One is that recall is more difficult than recognition, which is true, because there are more steps involved. Another is that recall should be more influenced by associations between items in memory, which is also true, although recognition can also be influenced, as in priming paradigms. Finally, the model also predicts that everything that affects recognition should also affect recall because recognition is a subprocess of recall.

Modeling Recognition and Recall. As described in Chapter 3, recall and recognition are popular ways to assess memory. Here is a formal assessment of the relationship between them. In some ways they seem similar—for example, they are both direct memory measures—but there are important differences. For example, they differ in the degree to which they are influenced by the organization of information during learning, such as whether items are grouped by categories (organized) or are presented randomly (unorganized). In general, the organized list is recalled better than the unorganized list. However, recognition is much less affected by this, if at all (Kintsch, 1968). This is consistent with the generate-recognize model.

However, there is a problem. In many experiments of reasonable scope, a number of items may be recalled but not recognized (see Starns, Hicks, Brown, & Martin, 2008, for an account of memories where people can identify the sources, but not recognize them). This is called **recognition failure,** and it is a serious problem for the generate-recognize theory. If all of the processes that operate during recognition also operate during recall, then anything that is recalled should be recognized. However, recognition failure is a regular occurrence. This consistency is shown in Figure 10.1. In this graph, if everything that could be recognized was also recalled, then the data points should all fall along the diagonal (with some accommodation for random error), but this does not occur. There is a systematic deviation, with points regularly falling above the diagonal, indicating recognition failure. The first formal description of this phenomenon, the **Tulving-Wiseman function** (Tulving & Wiseman, 1975), conveys this mathematical relationship. In this function, Rn stands for recognition, and Rc stands for recall. (And as a refresher, *p* stands for "probability that," and "|" stands for "given that.")

$$p(\text{Rn} \mid \text{Rc}) = p\,(\text{Rn}) + .5[p(\text{Rn}) - \text{p}(\text{Rn})^2]$$

An explanation for this function is that recall and recognition use different types of retrieval cues (Flexser & Tulving, 1975; see Hintzman, 1987, 1992; Tulving & Watkins, 1977, for different interpretations). Recall uses cues to prompt retrieval, whereas recognition uses the item itself. For example, if someone asks for the last four digits of your phone number there is mild difficulty as you may need to silently recall the first three digits (the exchange) first. In this case, a phone number is stored so that the retrieval of the

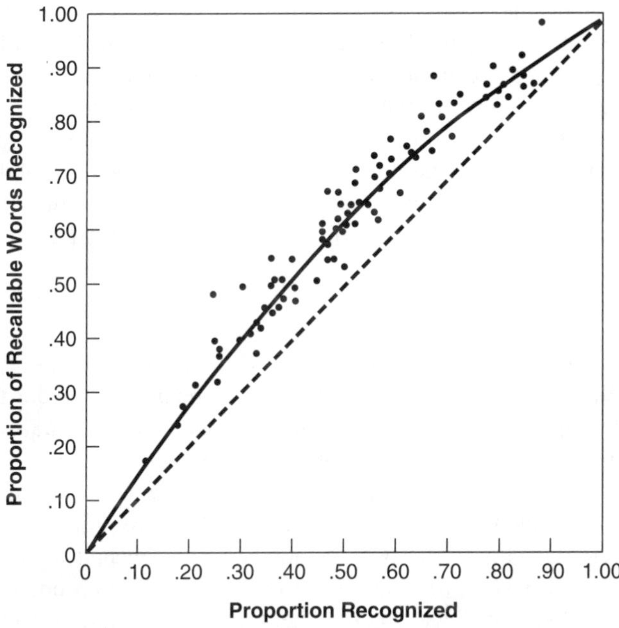

FIGURE 10.1 Data Plot Illustrating Recognition Failure and the Tulving-Wiseman Function

Source: Flexser, A. J., & Tulving, E. (1975). Retrieval independence in recognition and recall. *Psychological Review, 85,* 153–171.

last four digits is highly associated with the context of the first three. If presented with only the last four digits without such a context, people may not immediately recognize it as part of their phone number. This differentially based retrieval that uses different memory cues, with relative independence between recall and recognition, is at odds with the generate-recognize model and was brought to light only with a formal analysis of the data.

Synopsis

Simple models can capture basic aspects of memory, as well as reveal where simple-minded thinking, which may be intuitively plausible, is actually in error. The threshold model of recognition assumes that memories are retrieved when activation exceeds a threshold, similar to signal detection models. The generate-recognize model is a theory of recall that incorporates all of the essential characteristics of recognition. As appealing as the generate-recognize model might be for its simplicity, consistent findings such as recognition failure indicate that it is in error.

NETWORK THEORIES

Chapter 1 mentioned that the work of Aristotle has had a profound influence on psychological theories through his ideas about associations. The influence of associations on the structure and function of memory has been seen in Chapters 6 through 9 with phenomena such as priming, encoding specificity, the organization of mental maps, and the structure of semantic memory. Many formal models have taken this idea of associative structure and used it as the fundamental basis for their account of memory. The clearest ways to see this is in terms of the complexes of associations in network models. These are mental representations in which there are large numbers of smaller units, often called nodes, joined together in a tangled web of associations by an even larger number of links.

Semantic Networks

The first major **network theory** of memory was by Collins and Quillian (1969, 1972; elaborated on by Collins & Loftus, 1975), to capture semantic memory in the service of a computer program to hopefully be able to use human language in a natural way (a goal that is still far off). In **Collins and Quillian's network model** of semantic memory, the nodes were concepts, like "bird" or "canary," and the links were of several types. For example, in Figure 10.2, which shows part of a network, there are property associations and categorical associations. For property associations, some concepts are properties of other concepts they are associated with. For example, "feathers" is a property of "bird," "yellow" is a property of "canary," and so on. Other types of associations were category relations—for example, "A canary is a bird."

Spreading Activation. When a person accesses a concept in memory, like "canary," a search process begins by having activation move along all the links associated with that concept. This is **spreading activation**. A simple way to think about spreading activation

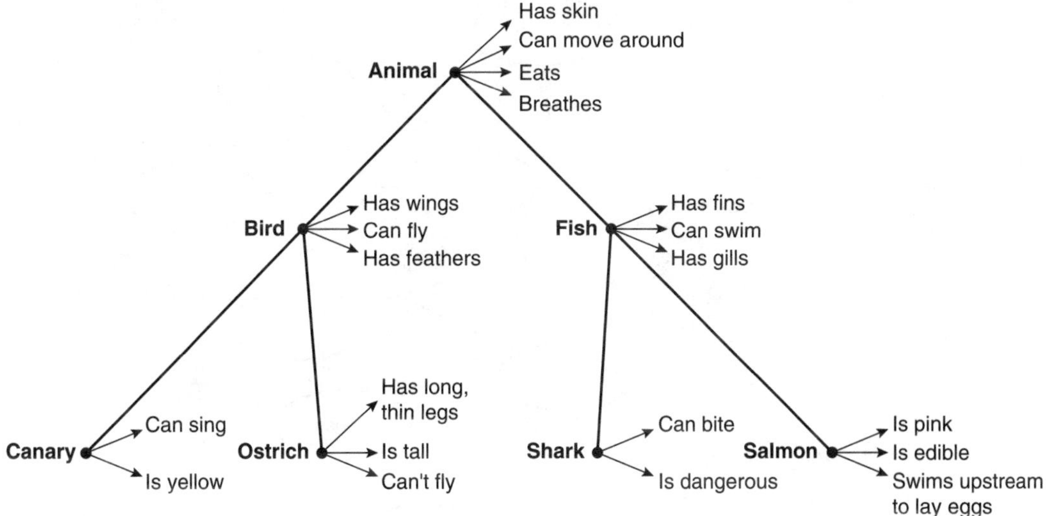

FIGURE 10.2 Portion of a Network in Collins and Quillian's (1969, 1972) Model of Memory

Source: Reprinted from *Journal of Verbal Learning and Verbal Behavior,* 8, Collins, A. M., & Loftus, E. F., Retrieval time from semantic memory, pp. 153–171, 1975, with permission from Elsevier.

is as electricity flowing through the wires of a circuit. Through spreading activation, if the concept "feathers" were also accessed, the links associated with it would be searched, too. When two search paths meet to create an intersection, the person can verify that the concepts are associated and stored in memory. If the two searches do not form an intersection, because they are not connected in memory, then the information is not something that is known.

A prediction of this model is that the speed with which information is retrieved is a function of the distance between two nodes in the network. For example, people should be faster to verify that "A canary is yellow" than "A canary has feathers." This can be defined in terms of hierarchical category representations, or degree of relatedness (Ashcraft, 1976). Figure 10.3 illustrates a memory network to capture this idea of relatedness. Here, red is more closely associated with colors because there are more links to other colors. Red is less associated with vehicles because, in this network, there is only a single link from red to the vehicles cluster. Also, the relative strength of associations is captured by the length of the links connecting the concepts, with shorter links standing for stronger associations. For example, while "sunsets" is associated with both "red" and "sunrises," it is more closely associated with "sunrises."

Although initial studies supported this idea (Collins & Quillian, 1969), subsequent work revealed some problems. For example, if nodes in a hierarchical structure are far from one another, it should take longer to verify one of those facts. However, some facts are verified quicker than should be possible according to these network models (Rips, Shoben, & Smith, 1973). For example, people verify that "A pig is an animal" faster than "A pig is a mammal," even though the opposite is predicted. Still, the formal model made predictions that can be easily and directly tested.

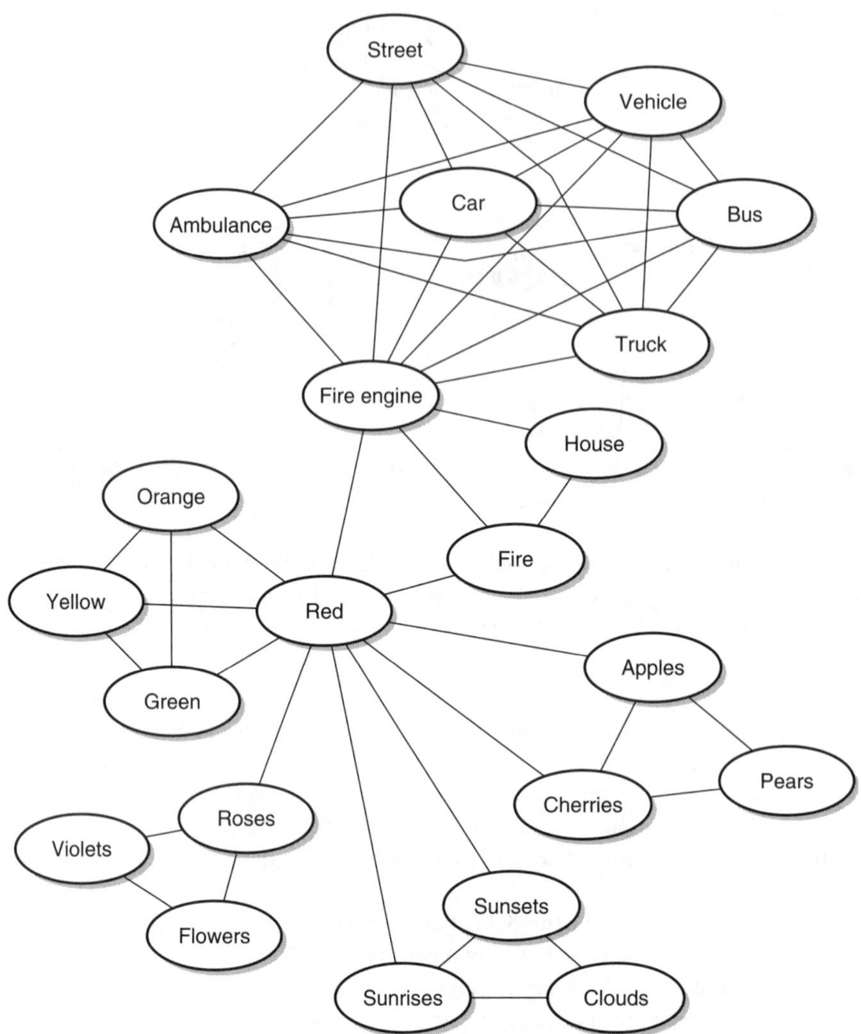

FIGURE 10.3 Portion of a Network in Collins and Loftus's (1975) Model of Memory

Source: Collins, A. M., & Loftus, E. F. (1975). A spreading activation theory of semantic processing. *Psychological Review, 82,* 407–428.

Priming. An attractive idea behind network theories of memory is that everything is defined in terms of everything else, much like a dictionary (but see Johnson-Laird, Hermann, & Chaffin, 1984). Network models provide nice, simple accounts of priming effects. As a reminder, when people encounter information, this not only activates those particular concepts in memory, but related concepts as well. For network models, priming occurs because a concept is activated in memory, and this activation then spreads along the associative links to related concepts. This is why it is easy to shift your thinking to related ideas (because they are already activated to some degree) rather than to something completely different.

ACT

Another network model of memory is the **ACT** (Adaptive Control of Thought) model (Anderson, 1976, 1983, 1990). Of all the models discussed in this chapter, this is probably the most advanced in the sense that it tries to be a model of many aspects of cognition rather than just memory.

ACT Network. For the ACT model, information is stored in a propositional network. A proposition is a simple idea unit. In the network a proposition is defined as two nodes and a link. Information is retrieved by nodes being activated and the activation spreading along the links, similar to the semantic networks just discussed. An example of a propositional network for the sentence "The sleepy student is in the old classroom" is given in Figure 10.4. This sentence is made up of a number of propositions that are organized by the network. A number of other aspects of ACT make it different from semantic networks.

An important property of ACT is the distinction between type nodes and token nodes. **Type nodes** correspond to general concepts, like those seen in the semantic networks. For example, a "bird" type node would stand for birds in general. In addition, **token nodes** correspond to specific instances. For example, a "bird" token node would stand for a specific bird, such as "that robin over there."

The ACT model also has the idea that there is a limited amount of activation available. Not all concept associations in memory are searched equally well, simultaneously, and to a high degree. Instead, activation is a limited resource. The more associations with a concept, the more finely divided the activation becomes, and retrieval time slows down accordingly. This is the ACT model's explanation for the fan effect (described in

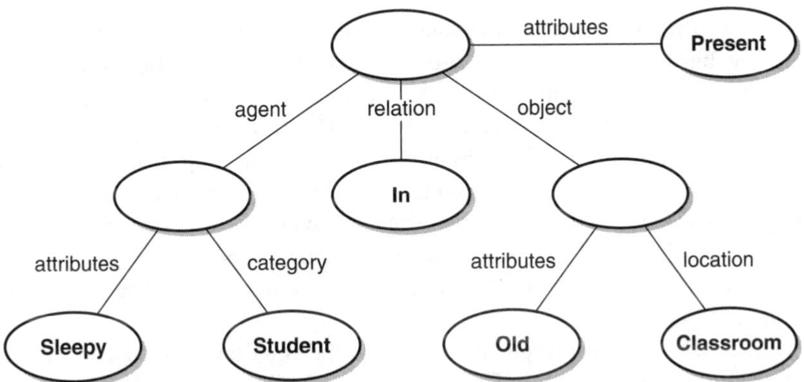

FIGURE 10.4 ACT Model Propositional Network for the Sentence "The sleepy student is in the old classroom."

Chapter 7). In essence, the more facts a person learns about a concept, the more associations that are linked to it. When a person needs to verify any one of those facts, the number of associations divides up the activation, and retrieval along any one of those associative pathways is slowed down (Anderson, 1974).

Memory Systems. Another characteristic of ACT is the distinction between production and declarative memory and how they interact in working memory. What has been discussed up to now is the declarative memory part of the model. The other part is production memories, which are the mental steps a person proceeds through to go from one state of knowing to another. These productions actually manipulate information. Production memories are executed when the appropriate conditions in working memory match the relevance of the production. They are basically, "if. . . then" statements in long-term memory. If a condition is present, then the information is manipulated in a specified way. For example, when you learned addition in your elementary school math class, you were developing production memories for how to manipulate the number information as it was encountered in problems you were given.

Productions are initially slow and cumbersome to execute. However, they become more automatized and subconscious with more practice. For example, when you solve a math problem—such as "574 × 63 = ?"—you invoke the appropriate mental procedures to arrive at the correct answer. The more practice you have, the stronger the productions become, and the easier it is to solve the problems. At some point, your ability to solve such math problems is nearly automatic.

Production memories interact with declarative memory through working memory. Working memory is that part of the declarative network that is currently active along with the productions that are operating on it. The addition of a production memory makes ACT a powerful tool and allows for explanations of memory based not only on how information is structured but how people actively manipulate it and the consequences this has for long-term memory.

LSA

The idea of relating concepts to one another, the essence of most network models of memory, has been incorporated into other theories of semantic knowledge, even if the models themselves are not strictly network models. One of these is *Latent Semantic Analysis*, or **LSA** (Landauer & Dumais, 1997). In LSA, a very large number of texts (nearly a million) are fed into the program. From that input, it creates a high-dimensional space (over 300 dimensions) to evaluate the co-occurrences of words in the language. Meaning is determined by assessing which words occur in similar contexts. Thus, if two words are perfect synonyms of each other, they would occur in the same contexts, although they would rarely ever occur together (because that would be redundant).

Knowledge is represented in LSA as the relations among concepts in the high-dimensional semantic space. The model "acquires" knowledge in a way that can mimic human performance and without a programmer directly hardcoding the relations among concepts. This is the latent part of latent semantic analysis. These relations just fall out of the high-dimensional structure. This model has been successfully applied to a number of tasks including grading essay exams (Steinhart, 2001), metaphor comprehension (Kintsch & Bowles, 2002), and problem solving (Quesada, Kintsch, & Gomez, 2001).

Synopsis

Network theories of memory have been very influential. The Collins and Quillian semantic memory model was the first to provide clearly testable predictions that were, at least initially, verified in studies with people. Network models of memory have continued to develop over the years. The concept of spreading activation pervades a great deal of thinking about memory retrieval, especially in accounts of priming. One of the most prominent theories of memory, the ACT models, has a propositional network for how it stores information in long-term memory. LSA is a more recent development that uses co-occurrences in a sophisticated manner to automatically derive contextualized meanings.

GLOBAL MATCHING MODELS

According to network models of memory, knowledge is stored in a complex, highly organized, and highly integrated structure, in which portions of the network become activated to meet the demands of the current task. In comparison, for **global matching models** of memory, information is accessed through processes that consider the entire set of traces. In such views, any relation between different memories occurs at retrieval, depending on the nature of the cues to the probe. That is, structure in memory emerges out of the process of retrieval rather than being a part of long-term storage.

In these models, information is either stored in separate memory records, in what are called **multiple trace models**, or it is patterns of information imposed on a common framework, in what are called **distributed storage models** of memory. In global matching theories, multiple memory traces are activated in parallel. What is retrieved is a function of (1) the familiarity of the memory probe, (2) the degree of overlap between the probe and the memory traces, and (3) the amount of activation of the memory traces related to the probe (Clark & Gronlund, 1996).

In general, global matching models have evolved out of signal detection theories of retrieval (see Chapter 3). The availability of memory traces is a function of their familiarity (discrimination), and successful retrieval involves activation reaching a given threshold (bias). Two multiple trace models, SAM and MINERVA 2, are considered here. We also examine two distributed storage models, TODAM and CHARM.

SAM

One successful multiple trace model is the Search of Associative Memory, or **SAM** model (Gillund & Shiffrin, 1984; Raaijmakers & Shiffrin, 1980, 1981, 1992). According to SAM, memories are stored in traces that contain content, associative, and contextual information. Remembering occurs when a cue (something in the world or a thought) overlaps with information in a trace. This causes the trace to be activated and potentially be retrieved. Memory retrieval is probabilistic—that is, the probability that a given trace is remembered is a function of its relation to the memory probe and its strength relative to other traces. The greater the strength, the higher the probability of retrieval.

Recall. The recall process for SAM is illustrated in Figure 10.5. Initially, a person is given a recall cue, such as a question. To organize the information to be recalled, even if it is a modestly complex set, a person creates a retrieval plan to keep track of the information. This retrieval plan generates a series of probe cues to access memory traces using a global matching process. During the memory search, the model first restricts itself to a subset of traces that are more likely to be relevant. It then searches through those traces, starting with the stronger ones and moving to the weaker ones. These are recovered into short-term memory, where they are evaluated and either reported (output) or not (similar to what happens in the generate-recognize model). Then a person either continues to search memory for more information or quits.

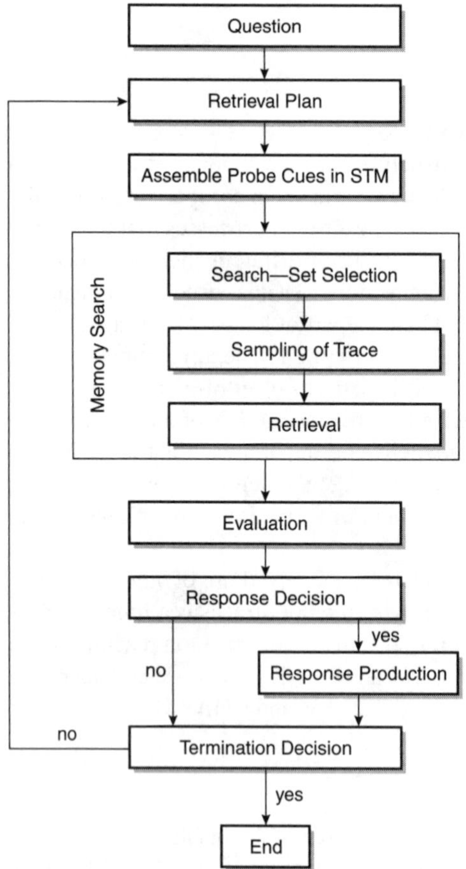

FIGURE 10.5 The Processes Involved in Recall in the SAM Model of Memory

Source: Reprinted from *Psychology of Learning and Motivation,* 14, Raajmakers, J. G., & Shiffrin, R. M., A theory of probabilistic search of associative memory, pp. 207–262, 1980, with permission from Elsevier.

So, information is retrieved through a sampling process that is influenced, but not completely determined, by how much memory traces are related to a retrieval cue. Traces that more closely match the cue are more likely to be retrieved and reported; otherwise, they are not. After each recall, the person goes back to search for more information that could be recalled until a point is reached when a decision is made to stop.

Recognition. In comparison, in recognition, whether an item is recognized is a function of the sum of all of the memory traces related to a probe, as illustrated in Figure 10.6. First, information in both the recognition item and the context in which it is embedded are used to sample memory. This makes contact with all of those traces that share those features. The addition of the context helps narrow down the set of traces, thereby making it more accurate. If the familiarity value that is returned by this sampling process is above threshold, then a person accepts the information as old (it is recognized). Otherwise, it is classified as something new (it is not recognized). Thus, something may be recognized because a person has a large number of weak memories for that information, not just a single strong memory.

Minerva 2

Another multiple trace model is **MINERVA 2** (Hintzman, 1986, 1988) (MINERVA 1 didn't last long) in which memory traces are strings of features that comprise the original event. Each feature, either content or context information, is represented by a value indicating its presence or absence. For MINERVA 2, during remembering, what is retrieved is not a single trace (as in the threshold model) or a level of familiarity (as in SAM), but is a new memory

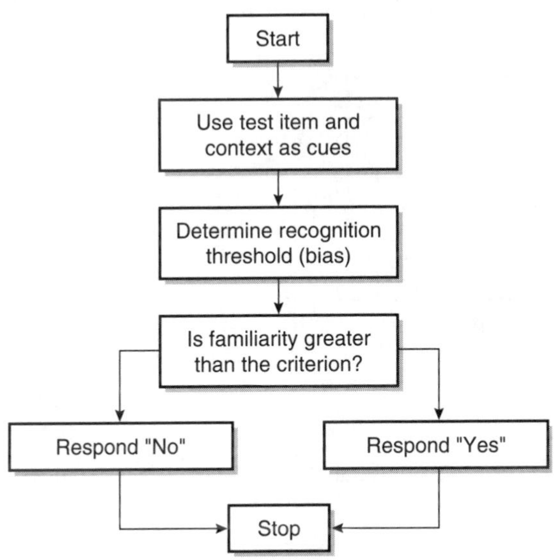

FIGURE 10.6 Processes Involved in Recognition in the SAM Model of Memory

Source: Gillund, G., & Shiffrin, R. M. (1984). A retrieval model for both recognition and recall. *Psychological Review, 91,* 1–67.

trace called an *echo*, which is a weighted composite of all the traces that were activated. We examine two characteristics of the echo in detail: echo intensity and echo content.

Echo Intensity. Echo intensity is the activation strength of the echo that is returned by retrieval. This is a function of the intensity of the memory traces that were tapped by retrieval (see Figure 10.7) and is analogous to the familiarity value returned in SAM. The amount of overlap of the memory probe with a trace allows this to vary. The greater the overlap, the greater the activation. So if a memory probe activates traces with a high degree of overlap, then the echo intensity is greater. For example, you have many memories of people speaking your name. Thus, if your name were a memory probe, the echo would have a high level of intensity because of the high degree of overlap. In contrast, you are likely to have very few to no memory traces about St. Ignatius High School football during the early 1980s. Although this information makes contact with some memories—such as those about football, high school, and the 1980s—there is likely little overlap with this memory probe as a whole, and the echo intensity is weak, thereby indicating that this information is not known. Echo intensity is also useful in determining event frequency (e.g., how often have you been to the grocery store in the past 2 weeks?). More high-intensity echoes reflect frequent events, whereas low-intensity echoes reflect rare events (Hintzman, 1988).

Echo Content. The other aspect of the echo is echo content, which in MINERVA 2 is a weighted average of the contents of all of the traces activated by the probe. Those memory traces with a greater overlap carry greater weight and have a greater influence over the content of the echo. This is illustrated in Figure 10.8. Thus, what is returned during retrieval is a composite or blending of many traces. As a result, MINERVA 2 can produce generalized effects in memory, such as the influence of schemas (Hintzman, 1986). This is because specific features get averaged out, and what is left are the general abstract

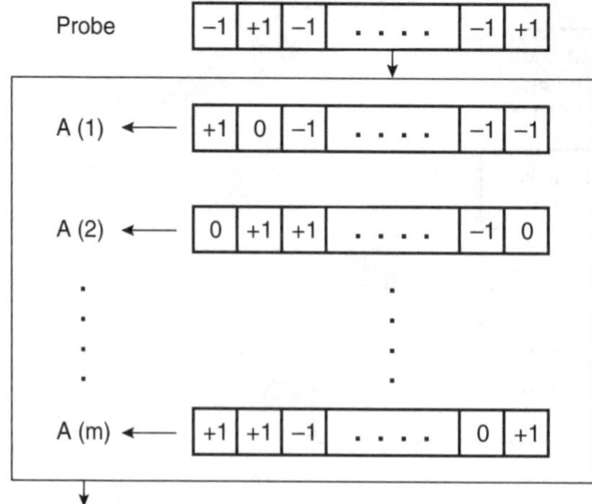

FIGURE 10.7 Echo Intensity in MINERVA 2

Source: Hintzman, D. L. (1986). "Schema abstraction" in a multiple-trace memory model. *Psychological Review, 93,* 411–428.

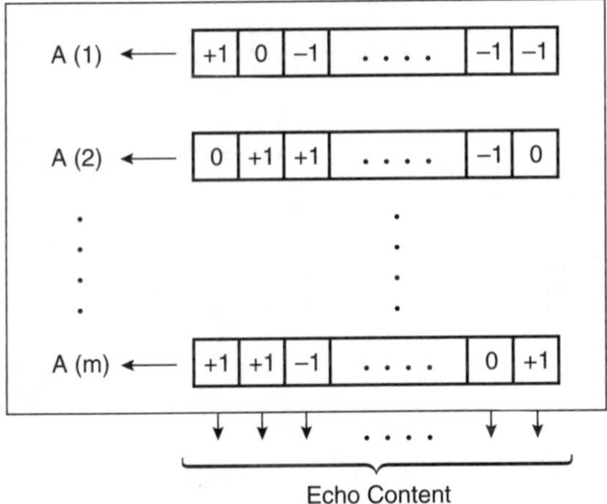

FIGURE 10.8 Echo Content in MINERVA 2

Source: Hintzman, D. L. (1986). "Schema abstraction" in a multiple-trace memory model. *Psychological Review, 93,* 411–428.

components. For example, if you are given the concept "grocery store," this activates all the memory traces about grocery stores that you have in long-term memory. What you experience when you remember is a weighted average of all grocery store experiences you have ever had, with the individual contexts averaged out.

Specific and General Retrieval. When a person is interested in remembering a single event, the precision of the memory cue is important. The more closely a trace corresponds to the memory cue, the larger the role it plays in the structure of the echo. But there is always some contribution of other overlapping traces, even if that contribution is weak. In this way, memory retrieval is always a distorting process because what is remembered is always a composite of several memories. To compound this distortion further, the echo that is returned is itself then stored as a memory trace. In this way, MINERVA 2 captures the idea that our memories are constantly changing as a result of experience and even by the act of remembering.

Although the MINERVA 2 retrieval process has this constantly distorting property, this same process also helps it narrow in on a memory trace. By using the echo that was returned to help focus the memory search, thereby activating a smaller and smaller set of memory traces, a person can have more accurate memory retrieval compared to getting only the first returned, most averaged, memory trace. This process is illustrated in Figure 10.9. Initially, the echo only remotely resembles the information that is being searched for. However, over time, by using the echoes that were generated previously as part of the memory search process, the correspondence gets better and better.

Further Work

Work continues on more sophisticated models of memory. A more recent model is **REM** (Retrieving Effectively from Memory) (Malmberg, Steyvers, Stephens, & Shiffrin, 2002; Shiffrin & Steyvers, 1997), which combines properties of SAM and MINERVA 2, as well

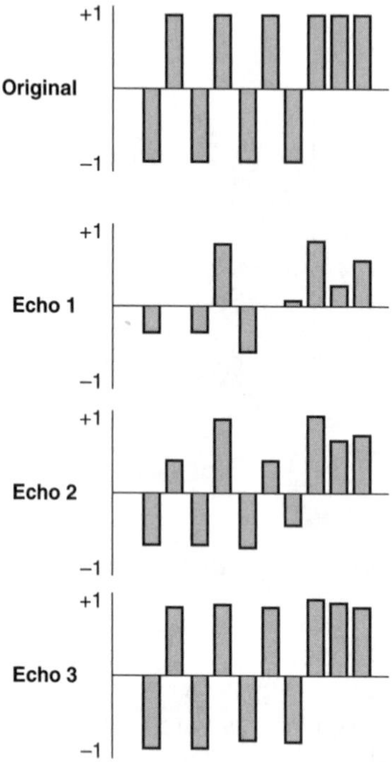

FIGURE 10.9 Echo Improvement in MINERVA 2

Source: Hintzman, D. L. (1986). "Schema abstraction" in a multiple-trace memory model. *Psychological Review, 93,* 411–428.

as other sources, to provide a wider-ranging, more effective account of memory. Like SAM, REM assumes that information is stored in multiple traces, and that memory is searched in a trace-by-trace, probabilistic fashion. Moreover, information is represented as a set of features, like MINERVA 2. In addition, unlike other models, REM assumes that there is a probability of an error in the information stored in a memory trace.

TODAM and CHARM

SAM and MINERVA 2 are multiple trace models that store each experience separately in memory. Any blending of information occurs during retrieval. Now we consider a pair of global matching models that involve distributed storage. This is sensible if one thinks about how the brain works. It is probably not a system where each experience is stored at a separate location in the cortex. Instead, many memories are imposed on the same neural structure, and the information is distributed throughout this structure.

Two of these models are the Theory of Distributed Associative Memory, or **TODAM** (Murdock, 1982a, 1982b, 1983, 1993, 1995), and the Composite Holographic Associative Retrieval Model, or **CHARM** (Eich, 1982, 1985). These models were developed to account for memory for item and associative information, as well as serial order information. This largely reflects their development out of a verbal learning tradition. In that research, emphasis was on memory for paired associates.

These models, like MINERVA 2, assume that memories are vectors of features, with a different memory trace for each item. However, associative information is stored as a memory trace that is a convolution of the two memory vectors. So what's a convolution? The convolution process is illustrated in Figure 10.10. Each item vector is combined with every element of the vector of another memory trace to create the composite vector trace. Thus, information from both items is distributed across a shared set of elements. This is actually an efficient way of encoding a set of information about items and associations, using a relatively small number of resources. Because of the regular structure of these convoluted vectors, the original information can be extracted using a correlation process. In this case, the properties of the convoluted vector are correlated with the values of a memory probe, thereby allowing for the extraction of the previous information.

One metaphor that has been used to describe this model is that of ripples on a pond (Murdock, 1982a). Different objects, such as a textbook or a computer, make different types of waves when thrown in the water. If a number of objects are thrown in the pond, all of the waves are superimposed on the same surface. With enough sophistication, one could examine the wave patterns to determine what objects were thrown in.

Synopsis

Unlike network models, global matching models do not make strong assumptions about how information is organized in memory. Instead, the structures that are observed is more a result of the retrieval process. The SAM model is a very successful theory of recall and recognition that is based on probabilistic access of memory traces as a function of the match with the retrieval cue. Other models, such as MINERVA 2, provide accounts of how memory is changed by the act of remembering. Still other global matching models, such as CHARM and TODAM, demonstrate how multiple memory traces can be superimposed on a limited representational structure, as would be expected to be seen in the neurons of the brain.

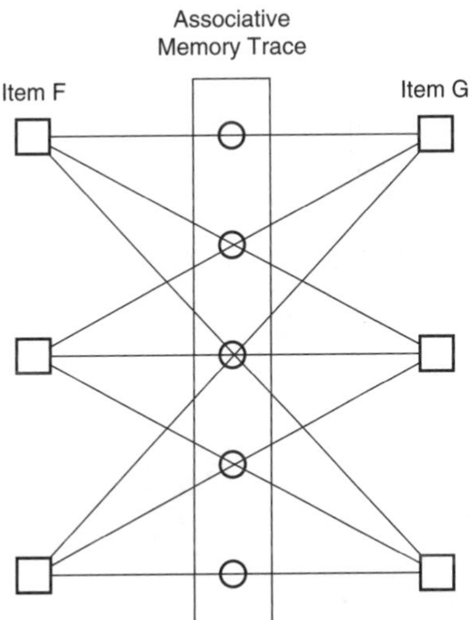

FIGURE 10.10 Process of Convolution in Models like TODAM and CHARM

Source: Eich, J. M. (1982). A composite holographic associative recall model. *Psychological Review, 89,* 627–661.

PARALLEL DISTRIBUTED PROCESSING MODELS

Another class of models is **parallel distributed processing**, or PDP, models. In these models information is stored in a single structure with multiple memories being superimposed on one another in a common representational framework in which each node is massively interconnected with a large number of other nodes. In many cases, memory representations are distributed across a number of shared components. That is, it is the pattern of activation, not the particular nodes that are activated, that produces the representation, learning, and memory in a PDP model.

Perhaps the most prevalent types of PDP models are **connectionist models** (McClelland, 2000) or **neural networks**. These theories use the structure of the nervous system as the inspiration for trying to capture memory. The brain is, in a real sense, a distributed representation. Information is not stored in individual neurons. Instead, it is captured by the pattern of neural firing over large sets of neurons. As a result, any given neuron participates in the representation of a very large number of different memories, along with what other neurons are doing.

Connectionist models take a similar approach. An example of a connectionist network is shown in Figure 10.11. First, there is a network of nodes and links. The model is a collection of "units" that are interconnected to other units (and possibly to themselves as well). The units in these models could correspond to neurons, and the connections to axonal connections with other neurons. This is different from network models in that a given node does not stand for a particular concept. It is just a node. These nodes are massively interconnected with other nodes, forming layers of nodes, similar to the layers of cells in the brain for processing some types of information. Information is represented in the pattern of activation in the nodes of the network. These patterns are established by shifting the weights of the connections among the nodes. Thus, learning is a shift in connection strengths, which allows new patterns to emerge.

As noted, these units are divided into "layers", consistent with the fact that brain cells are often grouped into layers along some path of information processing. A typical connectionist model might contain three layers: an input layer, an output layer, and a "hidden" layer, whose presence allows for a great deal of flexibility and power to learn and retain information.

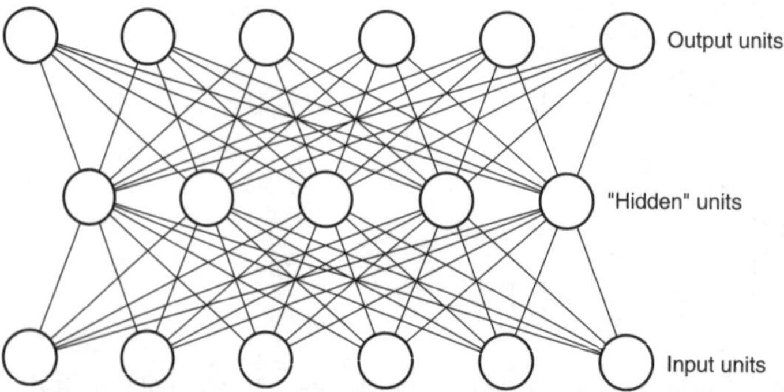

FIGURE 10.11 Sample Parallel Distributed Processing Network

Learning

Information is represented in a connectionist model in terms of the "strength" of the connections between the units. These strengths are called *connection weights*. Some connections are excitatory and some are inhibitory. Information is represented as the pattern of activated units. A model is operating well when the pattern of activity at the output stages bears a stable and consistent relationship to the pattern of information at the input stage.

Shifting of connection weights during learning is a gradual process. Furthermore, every experience alters the neural connections in some way. Those that correspond to an experience become stronger, whereas the others may be weakened or not be affected at all. Over time, there is evidence of differences in the representation of different types of knowledge. Figure 10.12 shows shifts in the activation levels of a number of output nodes in a network that has been trained on a number of concepts. The more training there has been, the more differentiated the representations. Moreover, notice that concepts that have similar meanings are represented by similar activation patterns. Thus, a PDP model is able to capture memory characteristics such as semantic similarity.

Retrieval

After a representation is established in a PDP network, at some point it may be necessary to retrieve this information. As one example of the use of PDP models to simulate memory retrieval, Norman, Newman, and Detre (2007) reported a PDP model that simulated the retrieval inhibition observed in the repeated practice paradigm (see Chapter 7). This is a complex model in which there are separate networks for hippocampal (episodic) and

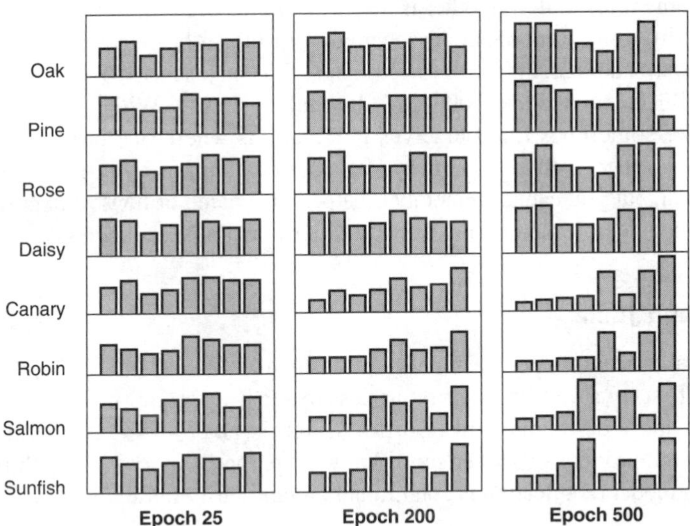

FIGURE 10.12 Representational Improvement Across Various Epochs (Training Cycles) in a Parallel Distributed Processing Model. The height of the bars correspond to the activation level of a set of output nodes for each of the concepts.

Source: McClelland, J. L. (2000). Connectionist models of memory. In E. Tulving & F. I. M. Craik (Eds.), *The Oxford Handbook of Memory*, pp. 583–596. New York: Oxford University Press.

cortical (semantic) memory systems, with (direct or indirect) connections among network elements for learning, and which uses oscillating patterns of activity (akin to the cortical synchronization of theta waves). Using this model, Norman et al. were able to simulate the pattern of results that are observed with humans in a repeated practice study. So, PDP models can be effectively used to simulate, model, and understand how the act of retrieval occurs and how it affects other memories.

Synopsis

PDP models are some of the most advanced and complex models of memory. They are inspired by the organization and processing of neurons in the brain. Information is encoded in a complex of massively interconnected units by changing the pattern of connection weights between them. This is in contrast to other models, such as network models, where individual concepts are represented by single nodes. In PDP networks, there is a great deal of flexibility because any individual unit does not stand for anything. Instead, information is represented and processed in a distributed fashion across the entire network.

DUAL PROCESS THEORIES

One characteristic of the models we have seen so far is that retrieval is a single process, possibly involving some version of a signal detection theory. However, other theories take the view that retrieval involves **dual processes.** One is a *familiarity* process that uses a signal detection-like principle in which information is identified as old (remembered) when it exceeds some threshold. The other is a *recollection* process that involves the conscious retrieval of different components associated with the to-be-retrieved information (see Mandler, 2008; Yonelinas, 2002, for reviews; but see Donaldson 1996; LeBoe & Whittlesea, 2002; Rotello & McMillan, 2006 for alternative views). While both processes are operating, we sometimes find ourselves in situations where one process produces one result and the other produces another. For example, suppose you meet someone who seems familiar, but you cannot remember the person's name or how you know the person. This is an example of remembering using familiarity but not recollection.

Atkinson and Juola

An early dual process model was one by Atkinson and Juola (1973, 1974) that suggested that people first try a fast, familiarity process to see if information is recognized. If this fails, then a more deliberate and effortful search is made of long-term memory. This effortful search produces a richer set of knowledge that is associated with recollection. Thus, in this model recollection is conditional on familiarity failure.

Recent Views

Subsequent dual process theories assume that recollection and familiarity operate concurrently (e.g., Mandler, 1980). Because familiarity uses less information, it often finishes before recollection. Moreover, the familiarity processes are more unconscious and automatic, whereas the recollection processes are more conscious and effortful (Jacoby, 1991). Also, familiarity can be thought of as providing more quantitative information about the strength of the memory trace(s), whereas recollection provides more qualitative information about what are associated with the information (e.g., who? what? where? when? why? [Yonelinas, 2002]). There has also been the suggestion that there may be three processes, namely familiarity, recollection, and reconstruction (Brainerd, Reyna, & Howe, 2009).

One Process or Two?

One of the rules of thumb in science is, when all else is equal, accept the simplest solution. This is Occam's Razor. The idea is to trim out all of the irrelevant stuff. So why have a dual process theory of memory if a single process model will do just fine? Well, one reason is that that recollection is much more influenced than familiarity by (1) levels of processing, (2) generation effects, and (3) full versus divided attention during learning or retrieval. In contrast, familiarity is more affected than recollection by (1) changes in modality (e.g., first hearing something and then later reading it), (2) perceptual priming, (3) changing response bias (i.e., more liberal or conservative), (4) the speed of forgetting (Yonelinas, 2002), and (5) the influence of novelty (Kishiyama & Yonelinas, 2003). So, a number of factors have a stronger influence on certain of these memory processes but not the others, suggesting that both may be needed.

Familiarity and recollection involve different neurological structures. Familiarity depends more on the temporal cortex surrounding the hippocampus and on the operations of the cortex as a whole; thus brain damage typically has a smaller effect on familiarity than on recollection. In contrast, recollection depends more on the hippocampus itself and the frontal lobes. The influence of the hippocampus is seen in amnesiacs who have suffered damage to it. The influence of the frontal lobes on recollection is also seen in older adults who have age-related changes in frontal lobe functioning. Similar results are observed in people who have sustained frontal lobe damage (Yonelinas, 2002). So, again, this suggests that there are two retrieval processes.

Synopsis

While most of the models are single-process theories, memory may involve dual processes. In dual-process models there is usually a simpler, automatic, familiarity-based process and a more complex, deliberative, conscious recollection–based process. Evidence for dual processes comes from work showing double dissociations. That is, something is changed that affects one process but not the other, and vice versa, or even that affects the two processes in opposite ways. This is discussed more in Chapter 14.

SUMMARY

This chapter covered a number of formal models of memory. The importance of formal models is that they allow for a level of precision in description and prediction that is not available with verbal descriptions. We began with a pair of simple models: the threshold theory and the generate-recognize model, and how they relate to the recognition failure function and how this analysis of memory performance can reveal inadequacies in a formal theory. Four classes of models of memory were discussed. The first were network models that describe the structure of memory using associative relations among concepts. The second class of models was global matching models, which address memory as a whole rather than acting only on a few select traces or components. Many of these global matching models have some form of signal detection theory as the basis for their explanation of memory. The third class of models was parallel distributed processing models. These theories use the structure of the nervous system as an inspiration for how they account for memory. They assume a high degree of interconnectivity among sets of primitive elements, with the pattern of connection strengths and activation levels corresponding to memories in the system. Finally, the fourth class of theories discussed was dual process models of memory. These theories assume that there are at least two memory processes operating during retrieval: a familiarity component and a recollection component. Overall, there is great value to developing precise and well-articulated formal models because they allow us to more closely capture and understand the workings of our memories.

STUDY QUESTIONS

1. What are two simple models of recognition and recall? What evidence suggests that they may be in error?
2. What were some of the first network models of memory, and how did they structure information?
3. By what processes are memories retrieved from or activated in a network model of memory?
4. In what ways is LSA similar to and different from more tradition network models of memory?
5. What are the primary characteristics of global matching models of memory?
6. What are some of the ways that information is thought to be stored and retrieved in global matching models?
7. What are some of the major features of PDP models of memory?
8. What are the two types of processes operating in dual process models? What evidence supports this idea?

KEY TERMS

ACT, CHARM, Collins and Quillian's network model, connectionist models, distributed storage models, dual process, generate-recognize model, global matching models, LSA, MINERVA 2, multiple trace models, network theory, neural networks, parallel distributed processing model, recognition failure, SAM, signal detection theory, spreading activation, threshold model, TODAM, token node, Tulving-Wiseman function, type node

CHAPTER ELEVEN

AUTOBIOGRAPHICAL MEMORY

Many of the issues presented in other chapters covered aspects of human memory, such as knowing how to ride a bike, remembering whether a word has been seen before, or knowing what a bird is. While these are important, there are other factors that are important to who we are as people. These are the memories that make us unique. They help form our identities and give structure to our lives. When we meet new people, an important part of getting to know one another is to exchange memories, often by providing excerpts from our life story. The memory of our life story is **autobiographical memory,** and it is the focus of this chapter. Autobiographical memory covers events and other knowledge about your life. This chapter covers general characteristics of autobiographical memories and the various levels of detail in them. We consider how autobiographical memory has a narrative character and how it changes over time and develops, including infantile amnesia for our earliest memories and a reminiscence bump for central portions of our lives. Finally, we cover issues involved with flashbulb memories for surprising events.

CHARACTERISTICS OF AUTOBIOGRAPHICAL MEMORIES

In this section we examine what autobiographical memories are. This includes their relationship to episodic and semantic memories, their nature, and the ease with which they are retrieved.

Episodic or Semantic?

Because autobiographical memories are about a person's own life, are they a kind of episodic memory? In a way, they are. However, they are much more than that. Autobiographical memories go beyond the information found in episodic memory alone. They are far more constructive and integrative, often spanning multiple events. In contrast, episodic memories are each confined to a single event.

Autobiographical memory also contains generic information, such as your address, phone number, your job, and so on. Much of your life story involves relatively stable, semantic-like information. Still, autobiographical memories differ from semantic memories in that they are unique about our lives. There is an intimate relationship between semantic and autobiographical memories. Not only does autobiographical memory have semantic aspects, but semantic memories are influenced by autobiographical memories. For example, semantic knowledge of famous people is more available if they are autobiographically significant, such as a personal hero, even when you account for frequency and recency of exposure (Westmacott & Moscovitch, 2003).

Varieties of Information. Autobiographical memories are about events in our lives and how they are interrelated. This may involve integrating events separated by long periods of time. They are amalgams of all kinds of information about our everyday experiences, including knowledge of sensory experiences (what things looked, sounded, smelled like, etc.), where things happened, how people acted, what people said, and what emotions were felt (Rubin, 2006). Moreover, autobiographical memories contain many interpretive inferences about how an event relates to others and what it means to us.

We gain some insight into autobiographical memories by looking at retrieval. Typically, people report general information followed by specific details (Anderson & Conway, 1997). For example, a person may report something like "I remember when I was in high school back in Cleveland Ohio. I had this Latin teacher. He used to constantly terrorize our class. It was horrible. I remember one day he gave a really hard exam. To make sure we didn't cheat, he put a chair up on his desk at the front of the class. He then sat on the chair, staring at us all, making us more nervous and tense than we already were." It is more unusual for people to report information in the reverse order, starting with the details and working out to general information. This suggests that autobiographical memories are organized around general themes. Within these more generalized chunks are the details of our lives.

This organizational structure suggests that autobiographical memories are complex. They contain information at a variety of levels of detail and span broad periods of time. This complexity causes people to take longer in retrieving an autobiographical memory (2–15 seconds) than a typical episodic or semantic memory (1 or 2 seconds) (Anderson & Conway, 1997). This slower processing time reflects a need to access more information and to sort through the autobiographical structure to locate specific memories.

Synopsis

Autobiographical memory is a complex form of memory with components borrowed from episodic and semantic memories. Autobiographical memories are woven out of basic knowledge about the events in our lives, along with the inferences and interpretations of these events.

LEVELS OF AUTOBIOGRAPHICAL MEMORY

Autobiographical memory is hard to simply and easily describe because it is made up of different types of information. One way to parse this type of knowledge is by the length of time covered (e.g., Conway, 1996). There are three levels that can be addressed: (1) the *event level*, for specific, individual events; (2) *general events*, for extended sequences or repeated series of events, often sharing a common component (as compared to a strict temporal sequence); and (3) *lifetime periods*, for theme-based parts of a person's life.

An example of the organization of these different levels is shown in Figure 11.1 (Conway, 1996; Conway & Pleydell-Pearce, 2000). At the top are two lifetime periods, which happen to overlap: the relationship and work themes. Within each of these are a number of components. Each of these components is associated with a collection of general events. For example, in the work theme, "working at A" is associated with a number of general events, such as "first day at work," "working in the C office," and "drinks in the evening with W." Each general event is also associated with memories of specific episodes at the lowest level of the hierarchy. While this organization shows some structural stability, it can be altered to some degree by the cues used at retrieval (e.g., Odegard, Lampinen, & Wirth-Beaumont, 2004).

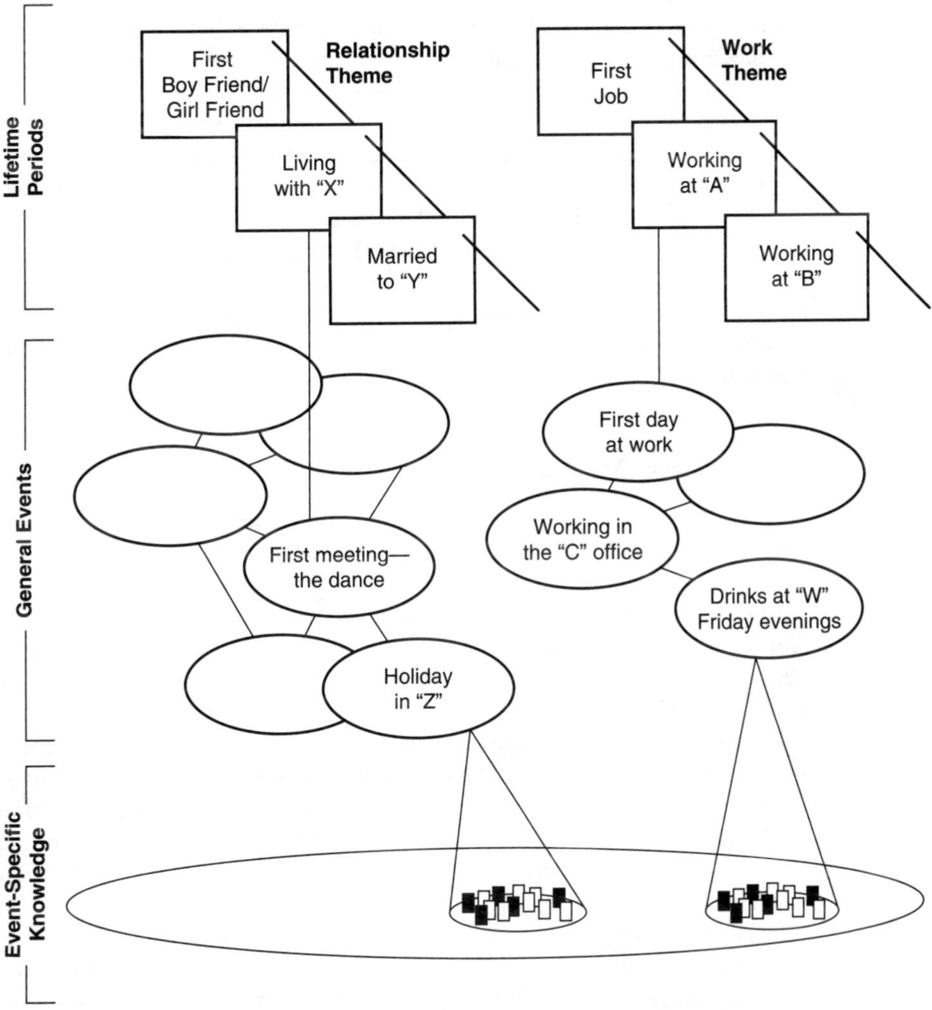

FIGURE 11.1 Hierarchy of Autobiographical Memories

Source: Reprinted from Bjork et al., *Memory,* Conway, M.A., Autobiographical memory, 1996, with permission from Elsevier.

Event-Specific Memories

The **event-specific** level closely corresponds to episodic memories. These are memories for specific, periods of time that involve a common activity occurring at a particular place. For example, the Latin teacher sitting on his or her chair while perched on his or her desk is an event memory. Event memories contain many perceptual and contextual details about what things looked or sounded like, as well as details about time and space. Finally, event memories contain internal context information, such as the person's emotional reaction to the event or physiological state at the time.

While most event-specific memories are lost over time, others endure and become important singular memories. This is the opposite of many memory processes that make things more semantic and schematic (Pillemer, 2001). For an event-specific memory to be retained as a single event, it needs to have a special quality. Pillemer outlined four ways of doing this. First, they can be memories of initial events that have many goal-relevant memories that follow them—for example, a memory of a childhood experience of going to the hospital for an injury sets a person on the path toward becoming a doctor. Second, they can be memories of turning points when a person's life plan is redirected—for example, being injured in a car accident. Third, they can be memories of anchoring events that serve as a basis for a major belief system—for example, having a religious experience. Finally, they can be memories of anomalous events that are used to guide future behavior—for example, remembering an embarrassing incident at work when a person got caught goofing off when the temptation arises to do that again. These qualities of event-specific memories make them easy to remember and hard to forget.

General Event Memories

At an intermediate level are **general events**, which are of two types. One type is a sequence of events that forms a larger episode. For example, the first day on the job is a general event composed of the various specific events of that day, such as being given a tour of the building, assigned a desk, given literature on company policies and benefits, and so on. The extension of an event across time and space occurs because people unify smaller events by one or more common themes (Burt, Kemp, & Conway, 2003).

The other type is a repeating event. For example, your memory for a class taken last year is a general event. The different class sessions are not a sequence of events because they were separated by large periods of time. Still, the repeated event quality of the class can organize experiences into a general event of being in that class. For both types of general events, there is often a personal goal that is affected by the extended event.

The creation and storage of general event memories require integrative and interpretive thinking. They are integrative because different events are brought together into a common memory. This is particularly clear for recurring situations. They are interpretative because a person must understand how the sub-events go together. For example, in a memory of a class, the memory for receiving an exam grade must be related to the memory for taking the exam and those for studying before that.

Lifetime Period Memories

At the highest level of the hierarchy are **lifetime periods.** These are periods of life organized along a common theme, such as "early childhood," "education," or "career." Lifetime periods give a sense of the progression and development of life in the service of various goals or preferences. When people recall autobiographical memories, if they go beyond a single general event, they are likely to confine their retrieval to a given theme (Barsalou, 1988). For example, when recalling information about previous work experience, they are unlikely to recall information about the various relationships they were involved in, unless those relationships in some way overlapped with their work experiences (such as dating a coworker).

Evidence for the Hierarchy

This autobiographical memory hierarchy is more of a heuristic than a hard-and-fast categorization. There are many cases where it is unclear at what level a given memory belongs. Also, information may be divided into subcomponents at the different levels. For example, a general event may be broken down into other general events, such as a memory for a class being broken down into different parts of a semester. Thus, autobiographical memories have a recursive quality in which smaller and smaller parts can be nested in larger description (Barsalou, 1988). An example of this recursive decomposition is shown in Figure 11.2

People typically have different aspects of their lives going on concurrently. Thus, there is some overlap of extended life events. Thus, there are a number of ways that autobiographical memories relate to one another (Barsalou, 1988). For example, Figure 11.3 illustrates events from different lifespan periods overlapping in time.

Neurological Evidence. Despite the fuzzy nature of this division of autobiographical memory, it has some neurological support. Some people with dense amnesia can recall lifetime period and general event information but not specific episodes. One patient, S. S. became amnesic after a case of herpes simplex encephalitis when he was about 40 years old (Cermak & O'Connor, 1983; McCarthy & Warrington, 1992). The virus damaged part of

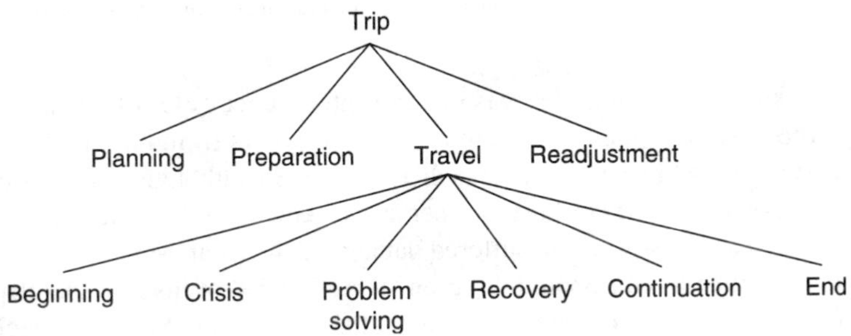

FIGURE 11.2 The Recursive Process of Breaking Down an Autobiographical Memory into Smaller and Smaller Parts—In This Case, a Memory of a Trip

Source: Barsalou, L. W. (1988). The contents and organization of autobiographical memories. In U. Neisser & E. Winograd (Eds.) *Remembering Reconsidered: Ecological and Traditional Approaches to the Study of Memory.* New York: Cambridge University Press. Reprinted with the permission of Cambridge University Press.

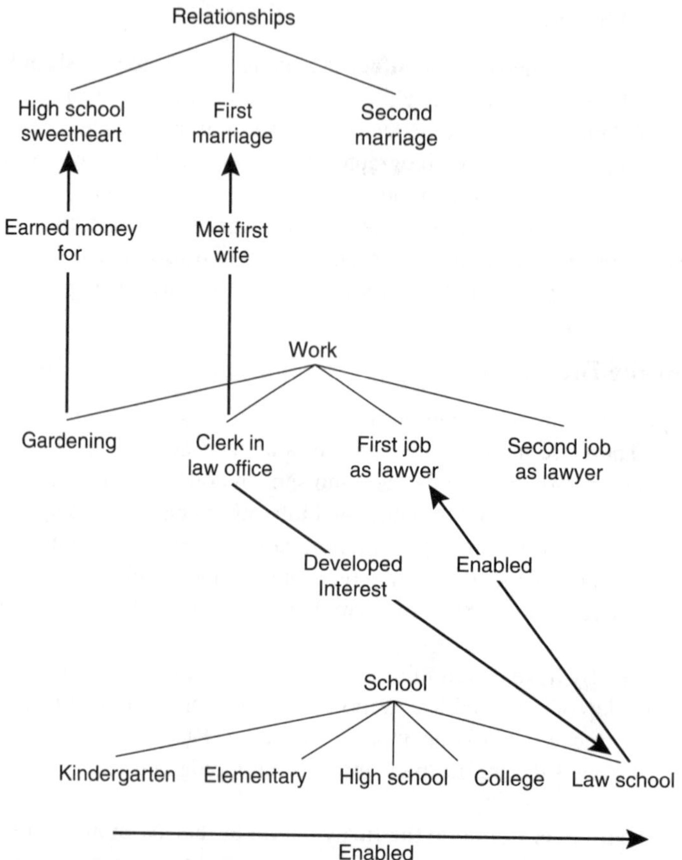

FIGURE 11.3 Temporal Overlapping of Various Lifetime Periods with Different Themes Based on Common, Shared Specific, and General Events

Source: Barsalou, L. W. (1988). The contents and organization of autobiographical memories. In U. Neisser & E. Winograd (Eds.) *Remembering Reconsidered: Ecological and Traditional Approaches to the Study of Memory.* New York: Cambridge University Press. Reprinted with the permission of Cambridge University Press.

his left hemisphere. Although he was of high intelligence (I.Q. of 133), he had severe memory problems. S. S. cannot remember specific events from his life, but can recount general aspects of his life experiences, such as his job. So, although he had trouble remembering at the event level, he could remember at the general and lifetime period levels.

A similar case is K. C., who suffered damage to the frontal-parietal region of his left hemisphere and the parietal-occipital region (B.A. 7 & 39) of his right hemisphere as the result of a motorcycle accident at the age of 30 (Tulving, Schacter, McLachlan, & Moscovitch, 1988). He cannot remember any life events. For example, he cannot remember the circumstances of his brother's tragic drowning death ten years before. However, he does remember semantic knowledge including knowledge of his job, which he had recently begun, and even personally relevant information, such as the floor plan of the house he grew up in (although he can't say which room was his), the names of his school classmates, and places where he has vacationed. This distinction between what is and what is not remembered reinforces the idea that autobiographical memory for events is a separate form of memory from more general knowledge.

In contrast, K. S., who had a right anterior temporal lobectomy to control her epileptic seizures, could recall specific life events but not general knowledge about the people involved (Ellis, Young, & Critchley, 1989). She also had trouble with the names of famous people and product brands. Thus, in a sense, she had the ability to store memories at the event-specific level but not more general information.

Another person with autobiographical memory trouble was P.S., a man in his late 60s with bilateral damage to his thalamus. This condition led to profound anterograde amnesia as well as extensive retrograde amnesia for autobiographical memories, but not semantic, non-personal information (Hodges & McCarthy, 1993; McCarthy & Hodges, 1995). For instance, although he is married, he cannot recall any details of his wedding. He also knows that he has three sons but cannot provide any details about their births. He also does not recognize photos of family events. However, he can recognize famous faces accurately, and can place them in chronological order for when they were famous, but cannot remember public events (e.g., the Watergate scandal). Thus, P.S. has lost the ability to remember autobiographical events, as well as the people involved in the events, and this deficit extends to memory for other types of events.

Synopsis

Autobiographical memory has three levels. At the event-specific level are memories of individual events, which is closest to episodic memory. At the general event level are memories for extended and repeating events. Finally, at the lifetime period level are memories that span broad, thematically related parts of our lives. This hierarchy is supported by studies of the effectiveness with which people retrieve memories as well as neurological evidence from brain damaged patients who have selective deficits.

AUTOBIOGRAPHICAL MEMORY AS LIFE NARRATIVE

Autobiographical memories are **life narrative** memories (McAdams, 2001). This follows a general human tendency to organize our experiences into narrative structures (Bruner, 1991), rather than simply a structure based on semantic information (Conway & Berkerian, 1987). Because autobiographical memory is a kind of story, it should reveal such characteristics. People often access information in autobiographical memory using event components that are found in narratives, such as people, places, activities, and other thematic information (e.g., Barsalou, 1988; Burt, 1992; Burt et al., 1995; Conway 1990; Lancaster & Barsalou, 1997; Wagenaar, 1986).

When people are probed for autobiographical memories, they tend to retrieve them in clusters of other events from a similar time (Brown & Schopflocher, 1998b), as is expected if they are part of a story. Moreover, people are most often reminded of events that are causally related (either as a cause or as an effect), and are reminded of events that share the same person, place, or activity (Brown & Schopflocher, 1998a), similar to how people organize their memories of actual stories (Zwaan & Radvansky, 1998).

To give autobiographical memories a narrative style, people may draw on semantic memory. As is discussed in Chapter 9, people have scripts of common events. These are used to structure autobiographical memories, giving them the temporal order of the script. In fact, people are better at recalling life events in a forward order and are faster at recognizing the first and more important details of the event (Anderson & Conway, 1993). For example, if you remember a trip to a restaurant, you are more likely to replay it back in your mind in a forward order, as it was experienced. However, if you were just thinking about one or two important details, such as a marriage proposal, you would to be able to retrieve it quickly without the need to start at the beginning.

While narrative structure is important, it is not always observed and information about temporal order may be missing. In a study by Burt, Watt, Mitchell, and Conway (1998), people took photos during the course of their daily lives. Later, they were shown the pictures for the first time with the task of putting the pictures in the correct temporal order. Performance on this task was terrible. People were correct only 9 percent of the time, although they did better if less than a week had passed, in which case they were 35 percent correct. This may have occurred because the snapshots were random bits that did not create well-defined narratives and so were difficult to correctly structure and order.

Perspectives in Autobiographical Memory

Narrative structure also shows itself in our experience of autobiographical memories. When you think about your life events, there may be an accompanying mental image. The thing is that these images vary in their perspective. Sometimes we experience a memory from our original perspective, with the same perceptual field of view. These are called **field memories.** In contrast, at other times, we view the event from outside of ourselves and may see ourselves in it. These are called **observer memories** (Nigro & Neisser, 1983). The very fact that we have observer memories emphasizes the constructed nature of autobiographical memory.

There are three factors that influence how a memory is experienced (see Table 11.1). One is the age of the memory with older memories being more likely to be observer memories. Second is the emotionality of the memory, with more emotional memories being more likely to be experienced as field memories. Finally, the greater one's self-awareness in a situation the more likely he or she is trying to understand his or her role in the larger event, and so this tends to lead to more observer memories. For example, an observer memory is more likely to be generated when one remembers giving a speech.

TABLE 11.1 Dimensions and Criteria for Field and Observer Memories

DIMENSION	FIELD MEMORY	OBSERVER MEMORY
Age of memory	Newer	Older
Emotionality	More emotional	Less emotional
Self-awareness	Less self-aware	More self-aware

Schema-Copy-Plus-Tag Model

People use schemas and scripts to help reconstruct incomplete autobiographical memories. The older autobiographical memories are, the more schema-consistent people's reports are likely to be (Eldridge, Barnard, & Bekerian, 1994). Thus, in an important sense, schemas guide the formation of our memories and strongly influence how and what we remember. However, if you think about your life, it does not feel like you have a memory full of generic, stereotypical events. Instead, you tend to remember the parts that are unusual. Memory is heavily schematic, but what is schema-inconsistent tends to be more memorable.

So what is the solution here? One idea is that our memories represent both schematic and unique aspects of an event. This is the **schema-copy-plus-tag model** (e.g., Graesser, Gordon, & Sawyer, 1979; Graesser & Nakamura, 1982; Graesser, Woll, Kolwalski, & Smith, 1980; Nakamura & Graesser, 1985; Trafimow & Wyer, 1993). When you encounter a new event, you first activate the appropriate schema. That schema, or at least the more relevant parts of it, will be the basis for your event memory. This schema helps reduce the need to actively think about and process every little detail. One can simply assume that most of them are about the same as they usually are.

In addition, people associate "tags" with a memory trace to denote the important things that are inconsistent with the schema, thereby making the memory unique. For example, if you go to a restaurant and the manager tells you that you do not have to pay, this is going to be represented by a tag in memory. Because autobiographical information is focused on the self, people show a greater benefit for tagged information when the memory involves themselves or another familiar person (Colcombe & Wyer, 2002).

Item-Specific and Relational Processing. This use of schemas and tags is in line with the distinction between item-specific and relational processing (see Chapter 7). Schemas provide relational processing, whereas the tags serve as item-specific processing. Memory for event information can further be influenced by how information is learned. Learning that emphasizes the structure of the event, such as sorting things based on themes, facilitates the schematic aspect, whereas learning that emphasizes item-specific processing, such as filling in missing letters in words, facilitates the tag aspect (Hunt, Ausley, & Schultz, 1986). This distinction between the schemas and the tags also parallels fuzzy trace theories.

Representing autobiographical knowledge this way has two consequences. First, because trivial details are less likely to be directly represented in a memory, it is difficult for people to distinguish between schema-consistent parts that were actually present and those that were not. Second, because the tag is part of the memory, it is easy for a person to remember what was odd about an event. This has some unfortunate consequences for education. Students' memories for what happened during class is often better for unusual things that happened during lecture, such as spilling coffee or jokes that were told, as compared to the content of the lectures (Kintsch & Bates, 1977; Nakamura, Graesser, Zimmerman, & Riha, 1985).

Synopsis

Autobiographical memory is structured as a life narrative, paralleling the structure seen for actual stories. This is seen in the distinction between field and observer perspectives. Although autobiographical memory construction and retrieval is guided by schemas, people use tags to help remember odd and unusual but important aspects of an event.

EMOTION AND AUTOBIOGRAPHICAL MEMORY

A central aspect of our experience is the emotions we feel during events, as well as our emotional reactions when we remember. Like most memories, autobiographical memory has a forgetting curve. People better remember more recent events than older ones (Whitten & Leonard, 1981). However, emotion adds some complexity. First, consistent with the Pollyanna principle, over time there is a tendency to remember pleasant events better than unpleasant ones (e.g., Wagenaar, 1986), which are forgotten more rapidly (Holmes, 1970; Meltzer, 1930), and with the emotional intensity of negative events being tempered more so than positive events (Walker, Skowronski, & Thompson, 2003; Walker, Vogl, & Thompson, 1997).

Although there is a bias to remember more positive things, we do have many clear, well-remembered negative emotional events such as those involving anger, shame, and depression. These negative autobiographical memories differ in some ways from positive ones. For instance, people tend to focus more on central details, and less on peripheral details, of negative memories (Berntsen, 2002), leading to better detailed memory for things in the focus of attention (Kensinger, 2007). This is likely brought on by increased activity in the amygdala during negative events.

The increased focus on details in emotional memories is called **tunnel memory** (Safer, Christianson, Autry, & Österlund, 1998). Tunnel memories also alter other memory phenomena. For example, they are less likely to exhibit boundary extension (see Chapter 5), perhaps because these central details are more critical in a negative event (e.g., an automobile accident), whereas positive events are less likely to hinge on a single critical detail (e.g., falling in love). In general, the influence of emotion on memory is driven more by the intensity of the emotion, than by whether it is positive or negative (Talarico, LaBar, & Rubin, 2004).

Olfactory cues (the smell of things) are special for autobiographical memory. Odors are particularly effective at helping people remember events from their lives (Chu & Downes, 2002), are more likely to elicit memories that people rarely think about (Rubin, Groth, & Goldsmith, 1984), and are more likely to elicit memories from the first decade of life than are words or pictures (Willander & Larsson, 2006, 2007). The autobiographical memories elicited by odors tend to be more emotional than those elicited by other memory cues (Herz, 2004; Herz & Cupchik, 1995; Herz & Schooler, 2002). This may be because the olfactory nerves are more directly connected to the amygdala, which, in turn, is critically important for emotion processing. In essence, smells are more directly connected to emotional experience, and so are more likely to call emotional memories to mind.

Involuntary Memories

While the retrieval of autobiographical memories may require additional time and effort, there are occasions when they are retrieved spontaneously and involuntarily (Ball & Little, 2006; Berntsen, 1996; 2001; see Kvavilashvili & Mandler, 2004, for a similar idea for semantic memories). Such spontaneous memories, especially negative ones, are a symptom of post-traumatic stress disorder (PTSD) in which a person has involuntary flashbacks to a negative, aversive event, which can be quite persistent (Berntsen, 2001), and may be one of the driving forces behind PTSD (Rubin, Berntsen, & Bohni, 2008; Rubin, Boals, & Berntsen, 2008).

With PTSD, these traumatic memories are often quite accurate (Alexander, et al., 2005), even after a long period of time (Porter & Peace, 2007). That said, involuntary memories occur in unaffected people as well (Berntsen & Rubin, 2008), although most ordinary involuntary memories are about positive, rather than negative, events (Berntsen, 1996, 2001).

For traumatic memories, as with PTSD, steps can be taken to lessen their severity using what is known about autobiographical memory. When people with PTSD remember traumatic events, they feel more stress and anxiety when they recall them from a field memory than from an observer memory perspective (McIsaac & Eich, 2004). Taking the view one had during an event is more likely to reinstate the emotional and physiological states of the time. However, taking an outsider's perspective helps detach the person from the event and reduces the anxiety that comes from remembering it. That said, observer memories may also contribute to the perseveration of PTSD symptoms over the long term (Kenny et al., 2009). Also, although there can be directed forgetting (see Chapter 14) of autobiographical memories (Joslyn & Oakes, 2005), salient negative involuntary memories, such as those associated with PTSD, are responded to very emotionally (Berntsen & Hall, 2004), and attempts to use directed forgetting may have opposite effect of making them more prominent (Dalgleish, Hauer, & Kuyken, 2008).

Synopsis

With autobiographical memory the general bias is to remember positive memories. When people remember negative events, they may be tunnel memories that focus on the central details. More generally, autobiographical memory characteristics are guided more by the intensity of the emotions than their valence. Finally, although most involuntary memories are emotionally positive, in some cases, they are negative, and may take a pathological bent when they are associated with PTSD.

AUTOBIOGRAPHICAL MEMORY OVER TIME

Like most memories, autobiographical memory shows a forgetting curve. People remember recent events better than older ones (Whitten & Leonard, 1981). Oddly enough, this forgetting curve extends to events that happened prior to birth (Rubin, 1998), which reflects an interest in historical events that led up to the current situation (Brown, 1990). There are two major deviations to the forgetting curve. The first is the poor memory for very early life experiences, called infantile amnesia. The second is the very good memory for life experiences around the age of 20, called the reminiscence bump.

Infantile Amnesia

Let's look at our memories from when we were infants. But wait. Where *are* they? Most adults, if they think about it, find that their earliest memory is not from infancy but from when they were between the ages of 2 and 4. (It is possible to have autobiographical memories from as early as ages 18 to 24 months, but not earlier [Howe, 2003)]. These earliest memories are often fragmented, such as a memory of standing in a room, whereas more episodic memories are regularly reported about a year later (Bruce et al., 2005).

Occasionally, people report memories from even earlier ages. However, many of these "memories" were generated in response to seeing pictures, hearing stories told by older relatives, or other sources. Thus, they are not memories of the event itself.

My earliest memory is from when I was 2½ years old. My parents had just moved to Wisconsin, and we were living in a trailer until they could find a house. It was late December, and I remember ice creeping in underneath the door. Because my family was new in town, some of my father's new coworkers wanted to help out. So one of them came to the trailer one evening dressed as Santa Claus to give me a thrill. (He already had a Santa suit because he had discovered that when he wore it to a bar, someone always wanted to buy Santa a drink.) When he walked into the trailer, I was terrified. I remember crying and screaming and running into my bedroom to get away from this big, red, creepy-looking guy who had burst into my home and started ho hoing at me.

So what happens to memories of a person's life before the age of 2 or so? Clearly there is a lot of learning during this time, and information is being stored in memory, such as learning how to walk and talk. However, this learning does not have a quality that allows us to remember those events. They are forgotten. This absence of early childhood memories is **infantile amnesia.** So, why does infantile amnesia occur?

Psychodynamic View. One of the first people to take note of infantile amnesia was Sigmund Freud (1899/1938), whose explanation was integrated into his psychodynamic theories. In Freud's scheme, many psychological problems involved sexual thoughts and desires. Infantile amnesia was no exception. For Freud, infants go through a period of sexual thinking and wishing. Part of this is a desire to be sexually intimate with our opposite-sexed parent. As we mature, we take on the rules and norms of our culture in the development of the superego. At this time we learn that our incestual thoughts are taboo. To protect ourselves from this threatening and horrible knowledge about ourselves, our subconscious blocks from consciousness all memories from this time. This grand scale repression is so successful that people have no memory of when they were infants. Freud's theory makes interesting reading, and it fits well into his broader theories. However, there are few people today who accept this view of infantile amnesia.

Modern Views

There are several plausible modern ideas about the cause of infantile amnesia, and there are multiple factors that contribute to it.

Neurological Development. A neurological account is based on the state of neural structures in the course of development. For example, the hippocampus, an important structure in creating new memories (see Chapter 2), and whose damage can lead to severe amnesia (see Chapter 16), is undeveloped at birth. It does not reach adult form until a child is a few years old (Nadel & Zola-Morgan, 1984). Also, infants have less developed frontal lobes. This part of the brain is important for binding contextual factors in memory, allowing for such things as source monitoring (see Chapter 12). This inability to link different aspects of experience leads to an inability to form autobiographical memories (Newcombe et al., 2000). Finally, during infancy and early childhood, the ability to consolidate memories is underdeveloped, leaving the memories more prone to interference from later events (Bauer, Burch, Scholin, & Güler, 2007), thereby contributing to infantile amnesia. In general, infantile amnesia reflects a period of time when infants are acquiring but not retaining, complex and neurologically sophisticated episodic memories (see Chapter 15).

Schema Organization. Another idea is that infants are trying to understand how the world works and are still developing their schemas. For example, a child might remember what typically happens on a trip to McDonald's but not remember the details from a given trip. Relatedly, young children tend to focus more on inappropriate aspects of an event. As schemas become more developed, people have difficulty retrieving the prior memories that were formed with the old schemas.

Language Development. An important thing to note is that the time when infantile amnesia lifts is also the time when language acquisition is making significant strides (Nelson, 1993). Infantile amnesia may reflect an inability to organize information into a coherent life narrative, which can then be used to help retrieval. Early on, infant memory has two roles: either as a generic schema-driven memory or as a repository for temporary episodic memories. With the advent of language, and the need to share experiences with others in a social context, autobiographical memory develops. So the chaotic jumble of memories, that is infantile amnesia, is displaced with the organization of a new autobiographical memory. This is supported by work showing that preverbal children do not translate nonverbal knowledge into verbal information after they learn how to talk about those events. The memories appear to stay nonverbal (Simcock & Hayne, 2002), which makes them more difficult to retrieve (Richardson & Hayne, 2007).

Emergent Self. Infantile amnesia is also related to a development in how people think about themselves. From this view, the removal of infantile amnesia is a function of a person developing a sense of self as a unique and an identifiable entity. Newborn infants lack a clear sense of self as a separate entity from the environment. The development of the self is divided into the acquisition of the "I' and the "me." The "I" is the subjective sense of self as a causal agent, whereas the "me" is the objective sense of self, such as your personal features. This latter sense of self emerges around 18 months and is fairly well established by 24 months. Once this concept of self is established, autobiographical memory can be constructed around it. Again, the offset of infantile amnesia corresponds to the onset of autobiographical memory.

Multicomponent Development. The **multicomponent development theory** (Nelson & Fivush, 2004) is the idea that there are a number of memory abilities that emerge to bring about autobiographical memory. These components include the development of an adequate episodic memory system, the development of language and narrative skills, an understanding of how adults think and talk about the world and the passage of time, as well as how the person understands himself or herself. The interaction of these multiple influences is reflected in the fact that people in different cultures experience different offset ages for infantile amnesia. For example, people in Western cultures, such as the United States, come out of infantile amnesia six months earlier than people living in Asian cultures (Wang, 2004). This may be because in these cultures children interact differently with adults, with a greater focus on the self in Western cultures.

Reminiscence Bump

Another influence of autobiographical memory on the standard forgetting curve is something that is easier to observe as a person ages. Memories of a person's life tend to be dominated by events from around the age of 20 (between 15 and 25). In these studies, the Galton-Crovitz method is used. This is a free association paradigm in which people are given lists of words—such as "bird," "chair," "apple"—and are asked to recall the first memory from their life that comes to mind. Most of the memories are from the recent past, and the further back in time one goes, the fewer memories there are, just as in a standard forgetting curve. However, the oddity is that there is a bump in the curve around the age of 20, with people recalling more information from this period than would be expected in a normal forgetting curve (see Rubin, Rahhal, & Poon, 1998). This is the **reminiscence bump** (see Figure 11.4). This phenomenon is so pervasive that it even influences the life periods from which we derive the topics of our dreams (Grenier et al., 2005). There are a number of explanations for this finding.

Cognitive Mechanisms. A general serial position effect exists in long-term memory. Part of this is an autobiographical memory primacy effect for first experiences of a certain type (e.g., your first kiss). One of the things about the age around which the reminiscence bump is centered is that this is a time when there is a great deal of change and a number of experiences are occurring for the first time, such as one's first kiss, first car, first apartment, first job, and so forth. Because there are so many firsts, it is not surprising that these memories are easier to recall. Thus, the reminiscence bump is partially due to a large number of primacy effects. For example, people who immigrated to the United States from Spanish-speaking

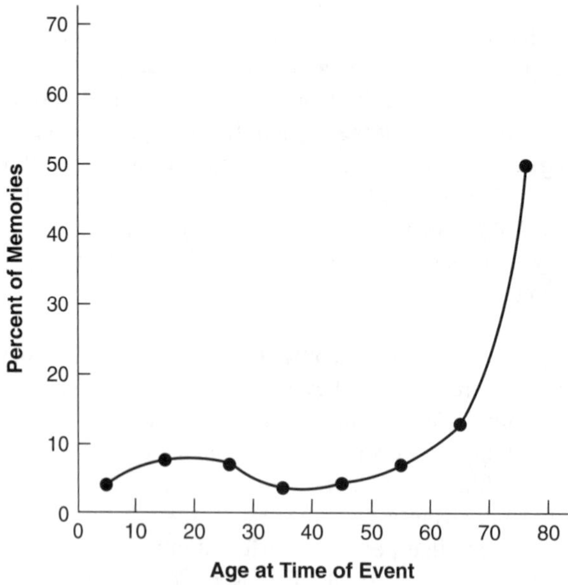

FIGURE 11.4 The Reminiscence Bump

Source: Rubin, D. C., Rahhal, T. A., & Poon, L. W. (1998). Things learned in early adulthood are remembered best. *Memory & Cognition, 26,* 3–19. Permission granted upon citation of source.

countries show reminiscence bumps at different times, depending on when they moved. The later they moved, the later the reminiscence bump. Moving to a new country with a new language provides a lot of novel first experiences (Schrauf & Rubin, 1998).

Neurological Changes. Another explanation for the reminiscence bump is neurological. This period of time is when a person is at his or her neurological and cognitive peak, when his or her nervous system is neither maturing nor declining. As such, people are at their best capacity to encode and store memories. Thus, memory should be more efficient at this time. Prior to this, people have difficulty encoding information into long-term memory. After this, beginning in the late 20s, one begins to see declines in memory.

Identity Formation. Another account of the reminiscence bump is that this is a time a person is making decisions about who he or she is with regard to preferences, ideologies, vocation, and so on (Rathbone, Moulin, & Conway, 2008). Although we can make these decisions at any time, more decisions are made at this time of life. These are decisions that shape our future choices and actions and become associated with them. A result of this increased interconnectivity is that, memories from this time are more available.

Cultural Schemas. A final explanation for the reminiscence bump is that people have schemas or "life scripts" for the important periods and major transition points of their life (Berntsen & Rubin, 2004). In American culture this would be things like graduating from school, getting married, buying a house, having a child, and so on. People then organize their autobiographical memories using these schemas. Then, when retrieving information, they use these schemas as a guide, thereby producing the reminiscence bump. In a study by Rubin and Berntsen (2003), college students estimated the likelihood that a typical 70-year-old would remember various life events. These students' estimates were very close to the actual pattern shown by older adults. Thus cultural expectations may guide the retrieval of autobiographical memories.

Because most of the events in cultural life schemas are positive (e.g., going to college, getting married, having a baby), this may also contribute to the bias for remembering more positive life events as time goes on (Berntsen & Rubin, 2002; Collins, Pillemer, Ivcevic, & Gooze, 2007), as well as those events that a person has a perceived sense of control (Glück & Bluck, 2007).

Also, in support of this view, a study by Copeland, Radvansky, and Goodwin (2009) had people read a novel (*The Stone Diaries*, by Carol Shields, which describe a person's entire life) and then were tested for their memory for the novel. Interestingly, a reminiscence bump was found, even though this was a story about someone else's life. Retrieval was guided by a cultural schema, and not by first events, neurological development, or a people's development of their self identity, all of which are impossible in this case.

Summary. There are several explanations for the reminiscence bump. The cognitive theory focuses on the uniqueness of initial experiences. The neurological theory focuses on the neurological peak. The identity formation account focuses on the development of one's self-identity. Finally, the cultural schemas account focuses on prior knowledge of how life is supposed to go. None of these explanations has a clear advantage over the others, and it seems likely that each of them plays a role in producing the reminiscence bump.

Flashbulb Memories

So far, our discussion of autobiographical memory has focused on relatively mundane aspects of life. However, we also have memories for surprising and important events that are very vivid, have a great deal of detail, and are relatively resistant to forgetting. For example, many people remember where they were and how they heard about the assassination of President Kennedy. A generation later, people can tell you detailed information about hearing about the explosion of the space shuttle *Challenger.* People are also likely to have such detailed memories for the news of Princess Diana's death (Hornstein, Brown, & Mulligan, 2003) or the terrorist attacks on September 11, 2001 (Lee & Brown, 2003; Schmidt, 2004; Tekcan, Ece, Gülgöz, & Er, 2003; Weaver & Krug, 2004), although such memories are better if they were personally experienced rather than simply heard about (Pillemer, 2009).

Highly detailed memories for surprising events are called **flashbulb memories** (Brown & Kulik, 1977) because it is as if the mind had taken a picture of the events that were occurring when the surprising information was learned. What is striking about flashbulb memories is that they contain detailed information for not only the event itself but also for the context in which it was learned. It is not unusual to find people who remember who told them the news, what the weather conditions were, whom they were with, where they were, what they were wearing, and so on. This contextual information is not directly relevant to what was learned. Still, it is stored at a high level of detail.

Flashbulb Memories Are Special. The original explanation for flashbulb memories was that there is a special memory process, called the "Now Print!" mechanism, somewhere in the neural coding of long-term memory (Brown & Kulik, 1977). This mechanism is triggered when something of great importance occurs to encode a great deal of detail. By storing all these details, a person can later sort out and identify the important components. This is especially critical for rare events because another experience of this type is unlikely. Thus, this would have some survival value. People are more likely to remember locations and from whom they heard the news (McKay & Ahmetzanov, 2005), although, interestingly, memory for the emotions experienced at the time is not well remembered (Hirst et al., 2009).

Flashbulb Memories Are Not So Special. Some researchers have suggested that flashbulb memories are just normal memories for important events because they can contain errors, become distorted, and are forgotten over time (Christianson, 1989; Lee & Brown, 2003; McCloskey, Wible, & Cohen, 1988; Schmolck, Buffalo, & Squire, 2000; Talarico & Rubin, 2003). They can also include misinformation from hearing other people's accounts of the event (Niedźwieńska, 2003). It may be that people are creating autobiographical stories for themselves that then remain relatively stable over long periods of time (Weaver & Krug, 2004). As an example of forgetting and distortion of flashbulb memories, a person might remember that he or she was having lunch with a friend when he or she heard the news, but in truth, the person he or she remembers having lunch with was somewhere else that day. Flashbulb memories may reflect a belief in the accuracy of the memories that emerges out of the emotional reaction to learning surprising news rather than the actual accuracy of the memory. The stronger the emotional reaction, the more a memory is believed (Talarico & Rubin, 2003). A clear example of how wrong a flashbulb memory can be is seen in the following quote from memory researcher Ulric Neisser (1982).

> For many years I have remembered how I heard the news of the Japanese attack on Pearl Harbor, which occurred on the day before my thirteenth birthday. I recall sitting in the living room of our house—we only lived in that house for one year, but I remember it well—listening to a baseball game on the radio. The game was interrupted by an announcement of the attack, and I rushed upstairs to tell my mother. This memory has been so clear for so long that I never confronted its inherent absurdity until last year: no one broadcasts baseball games in December! (It can't have been a football game either: professional football barely existed in 1941, and the college season ended by Thanksgiving.) (p. 45)

Criteria for Flashbulb Memories. Flashbulb memories differ from normal memories, even if they are created through normal mechanisms and are subject to forgetting. Flashbulb memories may be better records of the experience of a surprising event (our reaction) than of the event itself (Talarico & Rubin, 2009; Tekcan et al., 2003). Although they are not perfect, flashbulb memories do have distinguishing qualities, at least phenomenologically. It is only under rare circumstances when all of the relevant factors are present that a flashbulb memory is created (Conway et al., 1994).

So, when are flashbulb memories more likely to be formed? An outline of the more important criteria was provided by Finkenhauer et al. (1998), one of the best accounts of flashbulb memories (Luminet, 2009), and is shown in Figure 11.5. The first criterion is that the event be novel. That is, it should be a rare and, most likely, a new occurrence. For example, seeing the World Trade Center towers being attacked was a new event, but hearing about a murder on the evening news, sadly, is not. This novelty can lead to a feeling of surprise. This uniqueness and unexpectedness help it stand out in memory and be less likely to be influenced by interference. Also, because the event is surprising, people are likely to dedicate more effort in elaborative processing trying to make sense of the event and its consequences. This makes a flashbulb memory more complex and detailed as well as more enduring.

Also flashbulb memory creation requires that events be important and have significant consequences for the person witnessing or hearing about it. We better remember information that had an impact on our lives compared to more trivial information. For example, the events of September 11, 2001, were important and consequential, but a penny found in a parking lot is not.

The degree to which the events are surprising and important affects the person's emotional reaction. The more intense the reaction, the more likely a flashbulb memory will be formed. Emotionally intense events raise a person's arousal level, which aids memorization (Bradley, Greenwald, Petry, & Lang, 1992), perhaps influencing much of the effect of surprise (Hornstein et al., 2003). Note that not all flashbulb memories are formed from negative events, but can also be formed from very positive events, such as the positive flashbulb memories that some Germans have for when the Berlin Wall came down (Bonn & Berntsen, 2007), although these positive flashbulb memories tend to be less accurate than the negative ones. Emotion can lead to more attention to an event, more elaborative processing, and more remindings as subsequent consequences are encountered. All these facilitate the creation of a flashbulb memory. An emotional reaction can

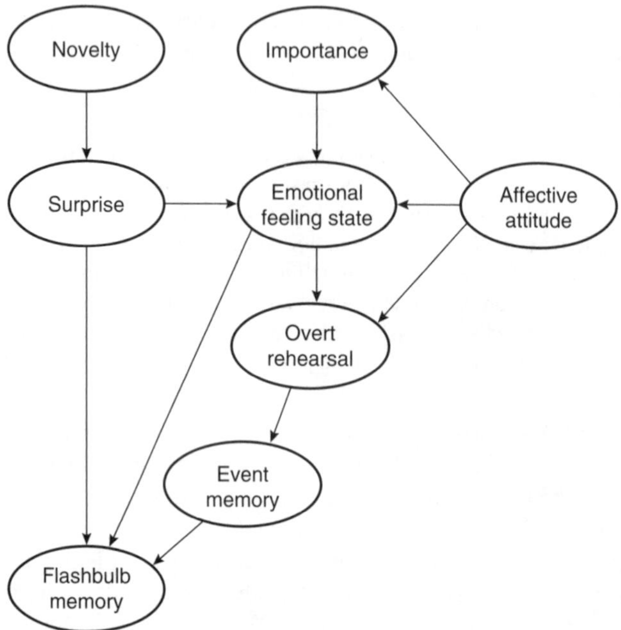

FIGURE 11.5 Outline of Major Factors in the Creation of Flashbulb Memories

Source: Finkenhauer, C., Luminet, O., Gisle, L., El-ahmadi, A., van der Linden, M., & Philipott, P. (1998). Flashbulb memories and the underlying mechanisms of their formation: Toward an emotional-integrative model. *Memory & Cognition, 26,* 516–531. Permission granted upon citation of source.

even override the novelty and surprise components for events that are expected, even if they are repeated, but which are emotionally intense. For example, a survey of gay men in the New York City area found that although there were repeated experiences of loved ones dying of AIDS, and the death was expected with the progression of the disease, the emotional intensity of each experience was sufficient to create lasting memories of hearing of the death (Mahmood, Manier, & Hirst, 2004). Thus, emotional reaction plays a pivotal role in forming flashbulb memories.

Another factor that influences flashbulb memory formation is affective attitude. These are the person's opinions and beliefs prior to the event that can provide the basis for later elaborative processing. If a person lacks the requisite knowledge to understand or think deeply about an event, a flashbulb memory is less likely to occur. For example, if a popular sports figure suddenly retires, people who are not fans of that sport will consider that news insignificant and will not form a flashbulb memory. In contrast, a person who is an avid fan may form a flashbulb memory.

Finally, people engage in more rehearsal of a flashbulb memory event by discussing it with others. When these events occur, people spend a great deal of time thinking about it and how they heard about it, including discussing with others how they heard about it and their reactions to it. If it is a public event, the news media repeatedly devotes intense coverage to it. This dwelling on and sharing of the information affects memory. The memory traces are reinforced and strengthened, decreasing the likelihood that forgetting will occur, and are a form of overlearning.

Synopsis

Autobiographical memories are affected by the passage of time and other influences that are unique to this type of memory. The inability to produce autobiographical memories from the first few years of life is infantile amnesia. Also, as we age, there is a change in the forgetting curve, such that there is better memory for events around the age of 20 as with the reminiscence bump. Finally, memories of surprising and emotionally engaging events can lead to flashbulb memories that are remarkably resistant to forgetting.

SUMMARY

Autobiographical memory is memory for the events of one's life. This life narrative can be examined at a number of different levels, including specific events, repeating or extended general events, and thematically organized lifetime periods. This distinction is supported by evidence from people with brain damage, who remember information at one level but not another. Many autobiographical memories are reconstructed as a person tries to remember, using scripts and schemas. The parts of an event that are most likely to be accurately remembered are the unexpected and important parts, not the mundane and trivial ones, with emotion having an especially large impact. Autobiographical memory changes over the life span. Adults have almost no memories for the first few years of life. Moreover, although a person continues to lose memories due to forgetting, the time from 15 to 25 years of age tends to be better remembered. Finally, some events that have such a profound impact on our lives in that relatively few details are forgotten.

STUDY QUESTIONS

1. In what ways are autobiographical memories like episodic memories? Like semantic memories?
2. How quickly can people retrieve autobiographical information? How does this compare to information learned in the lab? What does this tell us about autobiographical memories?
3. What are the three levels of autobiographical memory? What are their characteristics?
4. What neurological evidence supports the idea that there are different levels of autobiographical memories?
5. How is autobiographical memory like a story or narrative? How does this affect how memories are remembered?
6. What are the two types of perspectives that one can take on an autobiographical memory? What sorts of factors influence which of these two occur?
7. What is better remembered from autobiographical memories, the schema consistent or inconsistent details? What theory accounts for this and how?
8. What role does emotion play in the creation and maintenance of autobiographical memories?
9. During what period of a person's life does infantile amnesia occur?

10. What are some of the causes of infantile amnesia? How credible is each of these?
11. What is the reminiscence bump? Why does it occur?
12. What are flashbulb memories? What causes them? How much are they like or dislike regular memories?

KEY TERMS

autobiographical memory, event-specific memories, field memories, flashbulb memories, general events, infantile amnesia, life narrative, lifetime periods, observer memories, tunnel memories, reminiscence bump

TRY IT OUT

One aspect of autobiographical memory is that is has a strong **temporal order bias.** For the most part, people prefer remembering events from the beginning to the end. This can be illustrated by asking people to recall 10 details from a set of 12 events. Have people recall the details of four events in a forward order (from the beginning to the end), four in a backward order (from the end to the beginning), and four events in an importance order, starting with the most important detail and then proceeding to the least important. Have at least 12 people write these details down on a sheet of paper, for each event, numbered from 1 to 10. You should also time how long people take to do each one. Here are 12 life events you can use, although you can think of your own if you wish: "going to a birthday party," "getting an important message," "visiting relatives," "going on a shopping trip," "playing a game," "getting a job," "moving to a new home," "learning to drive," "coming home from school," "taking a trip," "meeting a new friend," and "attending a sporting event." You should mix up which events get assigned to which condition for each person, as well as the order of the conditions. When you are done, if all goes well, people will recall more details and/or be fastest for details recalled in a forward order compared to a backward or based on importance, thereby illustrating the sequential nature of autobiographical memories.

CHAPTER TWELVE

MEMORY AND REALITY

Our memory is our contact with the world beyond the present. We make assessments about the nature of the reality, how it works, and what has happened in the past, based on what we remember. Most of the time our memories are fairly accurate and we get along fine. However, other times, what we remember and what actually happened may differ. For example, if you misremember that you turned off the oven before you left for vacation when in reality you left it on, you risk burning down your house, or at least a very large gas bill. It is important to understand when our memories can betray us and when they can be trusted. What are the circumstances that cause memory and reality to part ways?

In this chapter we discuss issues of how memory and reality square up and how our ideas of the past may be faulty. The first issue is how we keep track of where our memories come from, or source monitoring, which includes situations of unconscious plagiarism, or cryptomnesia, and false fame effects. We also examine the sleeper effect and how this affects our attitudes and opinions. We look at cases where people remember things that never happened, called false memories. This includes implanted memories and memories recovered under hypnosis. Finally, we look at how the normal use of memory can change it, as with verbal overshadowing and the revelation effect.

SOURCE MONITORING

Many of the issues that we have seen so far have been on what a memory is about. Although this is important, another critical factor is knowing *where* a memory came from. For example, was a story heard on the news or from a friend? Was it all just a dream? The ability to keep track of where memories come from is **source monitoring** (Johnson, Hashstroudi, & Lindsay, 1993), and it involves processes over and above those used to assess whether something is old or new (Johnson, Kounios, & Reeder, 1994; Lindsay & Johnson, 1991). However, as complex as it is, source monitoring does not necessarily require complete conscious awareness of a source. Accurate judgments are regularly made using vague and partial information associated with less conscious feelings of familiarity (Hicks, Marsh, & Ritschel, 2002; Meissner, Brigham, & Kelley, 2002).

Source monitoring requires people to take source and content information and integrate them into a common memory trace. Later there is an active search of memory for source information. Each of these stages involves a different part of the brain. The integration of different types of information involves the hippocampus, whereas the search for source information, being a controlled memory process, involves the frontal lobes, and the actual retrieval of information emphasizes the temporal lobes (Senkfor & Van Petten, 1998), as well as the parietal lobes when there is conscious recollection (Leynes & Phillips, 2008).

Types of Source Information

Different types of information are used to evaluate the source of a memory. One criterion is *perceptual detail*. This is perceptual information that is encoded into the memory, such as what a person was looking at or hearing when the memory was created. Memories of events that were actually experienced often have more perceptual detail than those generated by hearing about an event from someone else or imagining it. For example, people find it easier to discriminate between words they actually said versus words they only imagined saying. The difference in perceptual experiences in these two cases is relatively pronounced. However, people find it harder to remember words that another person actually said versus "hearing" in their mind the words being said in that person's voice (Johnson, Foley, & Leach, 1988). This is because they have similar perceptual or pseudoperceptual qualities.

Another criterion is *contextual information* about the context in which a memory was acquired. For example, if people remember seeing a plane crash while they were at an airport, it is more likely that the event was witnessed. However, if people remember seeing the plane crash while they were sitting in their living room, it is more likely they saw it on the local news. Thus, people use expectancies based on the context to help make source monitoring decisions (Bayen, Nakamura, Dupuis, & Yang, 2000).

People remember source information better when the source is consistent with expectations than if a memory is from an unexpected source, suggesting that some guessing is involved (Bayen, Nakamura, Dupuis, & Yang, 2000). These expectancies are more likely to be operating at retrieval than at encoding (Hicks & Cockman, 2003). For example, it is easier to recall that a reminder to call your mother came from your sister than from your professor because the first is more expected, even if the second were true. People can also be swayed by what others say. For example, if you know that other people claimed to have witnessed something, you are more likely to mistakenly claim to have seen something you only imagined (Hoffman, Granhag, See, & Loftus, 2001).

A third criterion is the amount of *semantic detail and/or affective information*. This is how much a person was mentally and emotionally involved in the events. This can include thoughts that a person had (e.g., "Man, Bob must really be stupid to ask if gravity's getting heavier") or emotional reactions (e.g., "I remember feeling really queasy when I saw what the car accident had done to that girl's face"). This information helps us figure out where a memory came from. It should be noted that source information is less likely to be bound to an emotional memory (Cook, Hicks, & Marsh, 2007), perhaps because emotional responses tend to focus our attention on the central object, and less on the context or source.

A final criterion is *cognitive operations*, the mental processes done are encoding, including retrieving information from memory, manipulating it, trying to generate a mental image, and so on. This is more likely to be found in memories of things that were only thought about. When we think things through, we not only remember what we were thinking about, but also the mental activity that we used to generate those thoughts. Source memory may sometimes show a generation effect (see Chapter 3) and be better for information that a person actually generated (because of the stored cognitive operations) compared to something that was simply read (Geghman & Multhaup, 2004).

Types of Source Monitoring

There are three types of source monitoring (Johnson, Hashstroudi, & Lindsay, 1993): internal source monitoring, external source monitoring, and reality monitoring. Table 12.1 provides a summary of these.

Internal Source Monitoring involves distinguishing between actions a person either thought about or actually did. The person who is trying to remember if he or she locked the back door before going on vacation is engaged in internal source monitoring. Perceptual detail is important for these decisions because actions actually taken have more perceptual details in memory (e.g., remembering seeing the key turning in the lock), whereas events that were only thought about will have fewer perceptual details. A similar point can be made for context. Semantic detail and emotional reactions are likely to be low because these actions were generated by the person and so are unlikely to be reacted to. Finally, cognitive operations are likely to be high in both because the person is planning to carry out the action. The question is whether it was done.

A second type of source monitoring is **external source monitoring,** in which a person distinguishes between two external sources. Who told you this, Susie or Jane? Did you read about this in a newspaper or a supermarket tabloid? Perceptual detail is important because different external sources have different perceptual details (e.g., a man's voice or a woman's voice). Contextual information is also informative. For example, when deciding which of two people told you something, and you always see one person in your neighborhood and the other on campus, then knowing where you heard something can help you narrow it down. Semantic detail and emotional reactions can be used similarly. Finally, because the information is coming from outside the person, cognitive operations are likely to be low and uninformative about source.

Reality Monitoring (Johnson & Raye, 1981) involves distinguishing among memories of events that actually happened and those that were only imagined. For example, did a witness to a car accident actually see broken glass, or did he or she only hear someone speak of

TABLE 12.1 Types of Source Monitoring and How They Relate to Different Types of Source Information

TYPE	PERCEPTUAL DETAIL	CONTEXTUAL INFORMATION	SEMANTIC DETAIL	EMOTIONAL REACTIONS	COGNITIVE OPERATIONS
Internal	+	+	–	–	–
External	+	+	+	+	–
Reality	+	+	+	+	+

broken glass later? It is more common for people to mistakenly think they saw things that were only read or heard about, and less common to think that something that was seen was only read or heard about (Belli, Lindsay, Gales, & McCarthy, 1994). Also reality monitoring errors are less likely for emotional information (Kensinger & Schacter, 2006).

Perceptual detail is important in reality monitoring. Real events have more perceptual details than imagined events. Moreover, real event memories have more contextual information than memories of imagined events. Semantic detail and emotional reactions are more developed in memories of real events. Last, knowledge about cognitive operations is scarcer for real events but plentiful for imagined events. Still, reality monitoring errors do occur, even when it would seem a person could easily discriminate between what was only thought about and what actually happened. For example, a week after viewing photographs and reading descriptions of scenes, people made frequent mistakes in identifying pictures of scenes they had only read about but made fewer mistakes when identifying scenes they had viewed photographs of (Intraub & Hoffman, 1992).

Source Monitoring Errors

Source monitoring is pertinent for the topic of memory and reality because source information grounds memories in reality. Often, people are accurate about where their knowledge came from. However, errors can be made. For example, repeated attempts to remember, which can produce reminiscence and hypermnesia, can also increase the likelihood of confusing an imagined event for a real one (Henkel, 2004). This is because the repeated memory retrievals of imagined information may introduce more perception-like qualities to the memory (through the process of imagination) and make a memory seem more like something that actually happened. As a result, people claim that imagined events actually happened.

When source monitoring errors occur, a person's understanding of the world and what actually happened are at odds. For example, an internal source monitoring error can cause a person to believe he or she had done something that was not done. An external source monitoring error can cause a person to think that he or she had gotten information from one source when it was from another. Finally, a reality monitoring error can cause people to think that events had actually happened when they were only imagined.

Source misattributions can be biased to make ourselves look good. In a study of choice making (Mather, Shafir, & Johnson, 2000), people chose between two alternatives—for example, which of two people they would go on a blind date with. A number of characteristics of each person were given. Some were positive, such as "always interesting to talk to," and others were negative, such as "awkward in social situations such as parties." Some time after picking someone, people identified which characteristics belonged to which person. In general, people tended to misremember positive characteristics of the other choice as belonging to the person they picked and, to a lesser extent, tended to misremember the negative attributes of the person they picked as belonging to the person they rejected. This does not occur when options are assigned rather than chosen (Mather, Shafir, & Johnson, 2003). So our choices can distort our memories. We have a tendency to think of the things we choose as being more positive than they are and the things we do not choose as being more negative than they are.

Source Cuing

Source information can also be used for retrieval and help a person remember. This is **source cuing** (Radvansky & Potter, 2000; see also Dodson & Shimamura, 2000; Jacoby, Shimzu, Daniels, & Rhodes, 2005). In contrast to engaging in source discrimination, which involves determining the source of a retrieved memory, in source cuing, knowledge of a source is used to narrow down or access traces in memory. For example, in music, the timbre on which a melody is played (e.g., piano, guitar, trumpet, etc.) may be source information because different timbres are associated with different instruments and so would be different entities in the world. If you hear a melody on one instrument, you are more accurate at identifying it later if it is played on the same instrument than if it is played on a different one (Radvansky, Fleming, & Simmons, 1995). The source information is a memory cue. The separation of source and content information is also seen in the surprising fact that people can correctly identify, at above chance levels, the source of an item, even if they can't remember the item itself (Cook, Marsh, & Hicks, 2006).

Cryptomnesia

Knowing where information comes from can have important consequences. For example, it is important to know whether an idea is one's own or someone else's. When we present someone else's idea as our own, it is plagiarism, but not all plagiarism is intentional. Some plagiarism is unconscious and unintentional. This occurs when people come up with ideas they believe are their own but in fact were encountered in the past. This memory of the previous encounter has an unconscious, implicit effect, in the absence of knowledge of the information's original source. This unconscious plagiarism is **cryptomnesia** (but see Brown & Halliday, 1991, for a different account).

Why does cryptomnesia occur? One idea is that it is a reality monitoring error. A person retains the information in memory, but because of the amount of time that has passed and/or because little attention was paid during the original encoding, the memory is weak, and the source information has little or no influence later. The feeling of familiarity produced only boosts a person's confidence in the idea. Also, memories of plagiarized ideas have many of the same phenomenological characteristics as accurate memories (Brédart, Lampinen, & Defeldre, 2003), such as confidence in these memories.

Another way that source monitoring errors produce cryptomnesia is by having people take existing ideas and elaborate or improve on them (Stark & Perfect, 2006; 2007). For example, people might try to think of novel uses for an object, like a brick. Then during an elaboration phase, people try to improve on the ideas, both their own and other people's. By elaborating on the information, there are now memories for cognitive operations associated with that idea, and so it seems more like something a person would have thought of, rather than something that was heard from someone else. This cryptomnesia gets worse the more times people elaborate on the ideas (Stark & Perfect, 2008). This is why people working in groups where everyone is generating ideas and trying to improve on each other's ideas may later misremember which ideas were generated by other people, and thus experience cryptomnesia.

False Fame

A powerful way to manipulate memory is to influence the frequency that something is encountered. For example, information that is repeatedly encountered is more likely to be remembered, may become overlearned, and subsequently be chronically available (see Chapter 7). However, different components of a memory are forgotten at different rates. Information content may be remembered for a long time, but source knowledge may be lost. Alternatively, source knowledge may never have been learned or learned very poorly. In either case, a person may need to reconstruct the missing information perhaps by using how familiar the memory seems. Familiarity is related to how frequently something has been encountered.

One source monitoring error that is familiarity based is the **false fame effect** (Jacoby, Kelley, Brown, & Jasechko, 1989). This is the tendency to think that someone is famous or more famous than he or she really is because his or her name is familiar. For example, you may think that your favorite musicians or actors are more widely known because they are well known to you. The false fame effect is even more dramatic in that it may be possible to take a person who has utterly no fame whatsoever and make him "famous" overnight. This is done using the principle of mere exposure (see Chapter 6).

In a study, a memory researcher might give people a list of names. Some names are of people who were mildly famous for a time, such as Roger Bannister, Minnie Pearl, and Christopher Wren. These are names that most students might recognize but not quite remember who they were. The other names on the list are people who are not famous, such as Sebastian Wiesdorf, Larry Jacoby, and Gabriel Radvansky. The task is to go through the list and pick out who is famous and who is not. Later, people are given a new list of names of famous people, nonfamous people whose names were seen before, and new nonfamous names. Half of the people are given this new list immediately after the first, but the other half are given this the next day. People who got the second list the next day are twice as likely to call nonfamous people famous simply because they had seen those names earlier. Thus, those names became famous overnight!

This false fame effect can occur if a person is distracted by another task (such as listening to a series of numbers, waiting for three odd numbers in a row) while they are first learning the names (Jacoby, Woloshyn, & Kelley, 1989). In such cases, because the name was familiar, the person said that it was somebody famous. Thus, the link between memory content and source is disconnected (Steffens, Buchner, Martensen, & Erdfelder, 2000). There is an unconscious influence of previous memories (this name was encountered before) on conscious efforts to make a decision (is this name famous?). This is one reason why some people say that there is no such thing as bad publicity. People may remember that they've encountered a name before but not why. The more times a name is seen or heard, the more familiar it is, and the more famous that person seems. (It's not a good idea to overdo it. Eventually people connect unflattering information with a name, as with the name Hitler.)

Another consequence of increased frequency is that people prefer things that are familiar. This has some survival value. We are not tempted to try new things, which could be dangerous. If we stick to familiar things, we are more likely to survive because we've survived encounters with them before. This is why publicists for actors, musicians, or politicians try to get their client's name heard as often as possible. The more the name is heard, the more familiar it is, the more famous the person is, and the more people like them. This is also why advertisers try to get their commercials played as often as possible. The more familiar the product's name, the more people like it, and the more they are going to buy it.

Social Influences and the Sleeper Effect

Source memory can also be affected by social factor, such as the influence of social stereotypes. When asked to remember from whom a set of statements came from, people who forget the appropriate source misattribute statements to people based on social stereotypes (e.g., Bayen, Nakamura, DuPuis, & Yang, 2000; Dodson, Darragh, & Williams, 2008). For example, people are more likely to attribute the statement "I'll come talk to you as soon as I wash up." to a doctor and the statement "I had a deposition yesterday." to a lawyer, even if the opposite were true.

A phenomenon in social psychology that involves source monitoring is the **sleeper effect** (see Kumkale & Albarracin, 2003, for a review). This occurs when people get propaganda from a source of either high or low credibility. If the source has low credibility, then people initially discount it. However, after a few days, weeks, or months, people still remember the information but now consider it more credible than before. What previously seemed unreasonable has, with the simple passage of time, become reasonable (Hovland & Weiss, 1951; Weiss, 1953). The sleeper effect is shown in Figure 12.1.

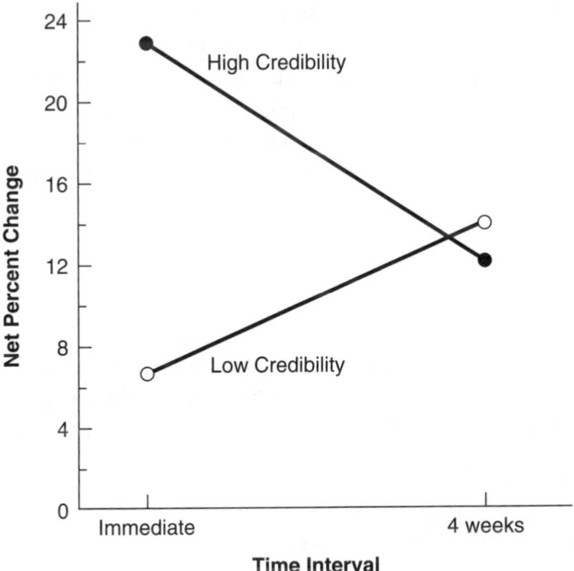

FIGURE 12.1 An Illustration of the Sleeper Effect

Source: Hovland, C. I., & Weiss, W. (1951). The influence of source credibility on communication effectiveness. *Public Opinion Quarterly, 15,* 635–650. Reprinted by permission of Oxford University Press.

The sleeper effect occurs because people remember the content of a message but forget the source, or at least, the source is disconnected from the memory content. Thus, people accept ideas as credible because they no longer have the source information that would make it suspect (Underwood & Pezdek, 1998). Several components must be in place to get a sleeper effect. First, people must pay attention to the message to set up a memory trace of the content. Second, the message source should be discounted after the message was given, preventing people from discounting the message from the outset and not learning it. Finally, the person should rate the trustworthiness of the source immediately afterward. This provides more time for the source information to be forgotten (Pretkanis, Greenwald, Leippe, & Baumgarder, 1988).

A related finding is the **wishful thinking bias,** which is a tendency to misremember desirable information as having come from reliable sources, and undesirable information as having come from unreliable sources (Gordon, Franklin, & Beck, 2005), especially for information about yourself (Barber, Gordon, & Franklin, 2009). For example, if you hear someone say about you "Boy, she is really smart" you are more likely to misremember this as having been said by a reliable source, such as your professor, as compared to a less reliable source, such as your bus driver. This is more likely here because it is a positive statement about you, and not someone else. The opposite is true for negative statements.

Synopsis

In addition to remembering information content, it is also helpful to remember where information came from. This is source monitoring, and it can include discriminating between external sources, whether one thought something or actually did it, or some event actually happened or was just thought about. Information about source can also be used as a memory cue. Although people are reasonably accurate at source monitoring, errors can occur and manifest themselves in unconscious plagiarism (cryptomnesia), false fame, and sleeper effects. In all of these cases, people remember content information but forget where it came from. As a result, they handle it differently than if they accurately remembered the source.

FALSE MEMORIES

One intensively studied aspect of memory is the question of when and how people "remember" things that never happened. These are **false memories.** Their occurrence is especially important when our memories are the only source of information, as with eyewitness testimony.

Deese–Roediger–McDermott (DRM) Paradigm

A simple way to create false memories is to use the **DRM paradigm**. First, people hear a list of words, such as those in Table 12.2. Soon after, they try to recall as many of those words as possible. Of course, people are able to recall only part of the list. The interesting thing here is that people often systematically misremember words that

TABLE 12.2 Words That May Lead to a False Memory for the Word "Sleep"

bed	dream	doze	peace
rest	wake	slumber	yawn
awake	snooze	snore	drowsy
tired	blanket	nap	

Source: Roediger & McDermott, 1995.

were not on the list. For example, for the list in Table 12.2, people often mistakenly say that they heard the word "sleep" even though it was not there (Deese, 1959; Read, 1996; Roediger & McDermott, 1995). Interestingly, over time people tend to forget false memories *less* than the true memories, even over periods as long as 2 months (Seamon et al., 2002).

False memories occur more frequently when there is a plausible context. People are likely to misremember the word "sleep" because all the other words in the list refer to things having to do with sleep. In fact, these words were selected because of their strong association with that word. The process of activating information and creating false memories occurs in as little as 4 seconds (Atkins & Reuter-Lorenz, 2008) suggesting that we create false memories as we actively comprehend the world around us.

In general, false memories are guided by how many associations there are between the words that were actually seen (the more the better), as well as the general recallability of the actual words (the fewer the better) (Roediger, Watson, McDermott, & Gallo, 2001). The larger number of associations makes it more likely that a false memory word will be primed or unconsciously activated. The less recallable the actual items are, the more likely a person will do some guessing or memory reconstruction, making it more likely that a false item will be "remembered." These false memories are based on partial information (Heit, Brockdorff, & Lamberts, 2004). For example, a person may misremember the source (it was thought about but not heard) or use more gist than verbatim memories (Brainerd, Payne, Wright, & Reyna, 2003; Brainerd, Wright, Reyna, & Mojardin, 2001). Because memories for pictures are much more detailed and less gist oriented, they are less likely to show this effect (e.g., Hege & Dodson, 2004).

The DRM false memory effect is supported by ERP measures. At encoding, in conditions that lead to false memories, there is greater neural positivity in the ERP signal compared to when people remember accurately (Urbach, Windmann, Payne, & Kutas, 2005). This can be seen in Figure 12.2. This suggests that when a false memory occurs, during encoding, people are not paying as much attention to the details of the real information, as revealed by the weaker ERP signals. fMRI recordings have found that false memories are associated with more activity in those the brain used for creating mental images (see the description of imagery inflation later in this chapter), particularly the anterior cingulate cortex (B.A. 24), precuneus medial parietal lobes (B.A. 7), and right inferior parietal lobe (B.A. 40) (Gonsalves et al., 2004).

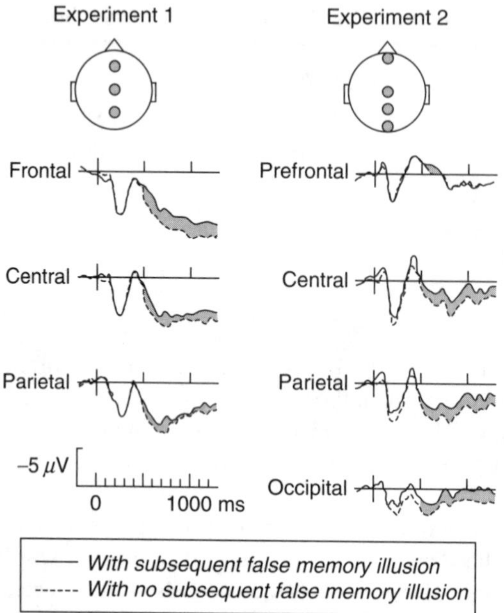

FIGURE 12.2 ERPs for Correctly Recognized Studied Words That Either Did or Did Not Result in a Later False Memory

Source: Urbach, T. P., Windmann, S. S., Payne, D. G., & Kutas, M. (1971). Mismaking memories: Neural precursors of memory illusions in electrical brain activity. *Psychological Science, 16,* 19–24.

The P300 component of an ERP signal reliably occurs *about* 300 ms after people are given a memory probe, and is associated with recognition. With false memories, the P300 is observed earlier than with true recognition (Miller, Baratta, Wynveen, & Rosenfeld, 2001). Also, there is less gamma activity during the recall of false memories, particularly in the hippocampus and left temporal lobe (Sederberg et al., 2007). This suggests that people are making these memory decisions faster perhaps because they are being less thorough and using less information.

This creation of a false memory can be influenced by a number of factors. One is the operation of inhibition, which was described in Chapter 7. Two memory processes that are thought to use inhibition are directed forgetting and part-list cuing (Kimball & Bjork, 2002; Kimball Bjork, Bjork, & Smith, 2008). When people are asked to forget a set of words that regularly elicits a false memory, the rate of producing false memories goes up. Apparently, the instruction to forget inhibits the memory for that list, thereby making access to the memories for the entire list harder. As a result, people have trouble discriminating between what was actually heard and what was not, so more false memories are produced.

In contrast, if people are given part of the original set of items, the part-set cuing effect is extended to the critical unpresented word, as well as those that were actually heard. Because all the other information is suppressed by the cued-for information, the

TABLE 12.3 Sentences Used in the Bransford and Franks (1971) Study

The ants ate the sweet jelly, which was on the table.	The ants ate what?
The ants in the kitchen ate the jelly, which was on the table.	The ants were where?
The ants in the kitchen ate the jelly.	What was in the kitchen?
The ants ate the sweet jelly.	The jelly was what?
The ants were in the kitchen	What was in the kitchen?
The jelly was on the table.	What was on the table?

Source: Reprinted from *Cognitive Psychology,* 2, Bransford, J.D., & Franks, J.J., The abstraction of linguistic ideas, pp. 331–350, 1971, with permission from Elsevier.

false memories rate declines. In other words, not only are the words that were actually heard suppressed, but so are the ones that would have been false memories.

False Memories from Integration

Another way people misremember is when items that were presented at different times are integrated into a single memory trace. Thus, with integration, what were actually several events are misremembered as one. This is similar to the schema integration processes discussed in Chapter 9. So, people may misremember different pieces of information as being part of the same event if they "seem" like they should go together.

An example of integration is a study by Bransford and Franks (1971) in which people read a list of sentences, as shown in Table 12.3. During study, people had to answer simple questions, also shown in the table. (Go ahead and read the sentences and answer the questions now.) Afterward, people identified which sentences they had seen before. In addition, they rated their confidence in their answers. An example recognition test is shown in Table 12.4. Try to identify which sentences you remember seeing. Also, rate how confident you are. After you are done, look at Table 12.3 to see which sentences were actually there.

The important result was that memory did not simply reflect whether a sentence was seen before. The study and test sentences varied in the number of simple idea units (called propositions) they had, which could be 1, 2, 3, or all 4 propositions from a given theme. For example, in one theme the sentence "The ants were in the kitchen" is a one-proposition sentence, "The ants in the kitchen ate the jelly" is two, "The ants in the kitchen ate the jelly, which was on the table" is three, and "The ants in the kitchen ate the sweet jelly, which was on the table" has all four propositions. On the memory test, the more propositions a test sentence had, the more likely people "remembered" it. A sentence with four propositions that was not read was more likely to be "recognized" than a sentence with only one proposition that was actually read. Moreover, confidence ratings showed the same pattern and increased with the number of propositions, as shown in Figure 12.3.

When people read the sentences, because there is overlap in content, they are interpreted as referring to a common situation (see also Chapter 7). This makes integration easy. This integrated representation is then used to make memory judgments. Items that contain more propositions more closely match the memory trace, and so are more likely

TABLE 12.4 Recognition Test from the Bransford and Franks (1971) Study

The ants in the kitchen ate the sweet jelly, which was on the table.
The ants in the kitchen ate the sweet jelly.
The ants ate the sweet jelly.
The sweet jelly was on the table.
The ants ate the jelly, which was on the table.
The jelly was sweet.
The ants ate the jelly.

Source: Reprinted from *Cognitive Psychology,* 2, Bransford, J.D., & Franks, J.J., The abstraction of linguistic ideas, pp. 331–350, 1971, with permission from Elsevier.

to be recognized and given higher confidence ratings. People use memories of entire events that they created, not memories for what they actually experienced.

This integration process is also seen with normal reading. When people read fictional stories about real people, they may misremember fiction as fact. The fictional knowledge is integrated with the real knowledge. Although people are aware that the story had some fictional information, they also think that they knew some of the fictional information *before* reading the story (Marsh, Meade, & Roediger, 2003). What's more, if people are warned about this memory distortion, even before they read, they still incorporate inaccurate information into semantic memory (Marsh & Fazio, 2006).

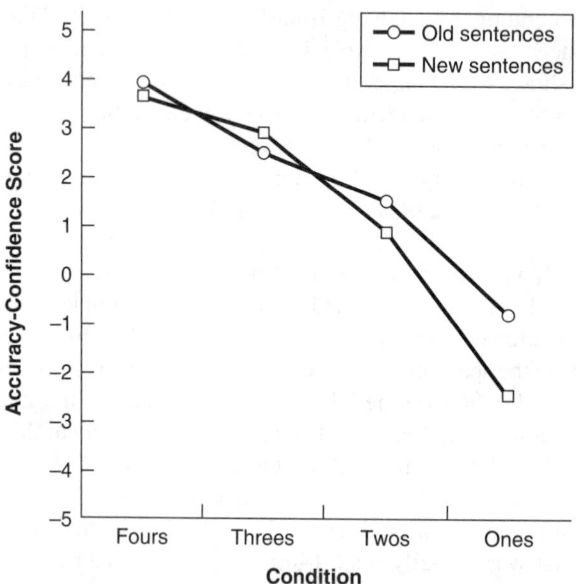

FIGURE 12.3 Recognition Test Data from the Bransford and Franks (1971) Study
The accuracy score reflects the combined influences of people's selection on items along with their confidence in having heard items before.

Source: Reprinted from *Cognitive Psychology,* 2, Bransford, J. D., & Franks, J. J., The abstraction of linguistic ideas, pp. 331–350, 1971, with permission from Elsevier.

Implanted Memories

In the preceding examples, false memories were created almost as a natural consequence of thinking about information. The false information is never explicitly conveyed. However, it is possible to explicitly implant false memories (Loftus, 2004). One way this occurs is if people overtly question whether someone remembers something. For example, if someone tells you that your mother says that when you were 8-years old, you got lost in a mall, and then repeatedly asks if you remember that incident. Another way to implant memories is if a person overhears or reads another person's report. For example, if you hear me say that I remember a story about whales on the news, you might later misremember reading the story yourself (Meade & Roediger, 2002). Finally, people who are told that, as a child, they had an unpleasant experience with a food they don't eat often (e.g., egg salad), they will avoid that food in the future, as if they had a real taste aversion experience (Bernstein & Loftus, 2009; Geraerts et al., 2008). These implanted memories are delivered in such a way that people believe that they are real. This sounds strange, but it's true.

Implanted false memories are observed for autobiographical memories, not just word lists. Again, the likelihood of creating a false memory is a function of how plausible it is (Pezdek, Finger, & Hodge, 1997). In one study, students were asked about events to see if their memories corresponded with those of their parents. The researchers relayed a description of an event that was presumably described by the student's mother but that had never happened. This event was one that was consistent with being raised either Jewish or Catholic. Jewish students were more likely to have a false memory for the Jewish event than the Catholic event, and vice versa, as shown in Table 12.5. Thus, the probability of having a false memory is a function of the event plausibility. However, it is possible for people to have false memories of implausible events, such as witnessing a demonic possession, if the event is made to seem more plausible, such as reading articles about possession. Increased plausibility makes it more likely that people will claim that the event actually occurred to them (Mazzoni, Loftus, & Kirsch, 2001; Pezdek et al., 2006).

In some unfortunate cases, people inadvertently get implanted memories from overzealous and substandard therapists looking for repressed memories (Loftus, 1993). The suggestion that these "memories" were repressed makes it more likely that a person will accept them as real. The normal scrutinization of the memory content and source does not take place.

A technique that makes the creation of implanted false memories more likely is visualization or imagination, which also increases the confidence that people feel about them. This is **imagination inflation** (Garry & Polaschek, 2000; Mazzoni & Memon, 2003). Imagination makes memory traces richer in detail and gives them pseudoperceptual

TABLE 12.5 Number of People Reporting False Memories for Catholic and Jewish Events

PARTICIPANTS	NEITHER EVENT	CATHOLIC EVENT ONLY	JEWISH EVENT ONLY	BOTH EVENTS
Catholic	19	7	1	2
Jewish	19	0	3	0

Source: Pezdek, Finger, & Hodge, 1997.

qualities, making them more like real memories. Moreover, imagination inflation is greater if people already have some experience of the event, and it is plausible (Pezdek, Blandon-Gitlin, & Gabbay, 2006). For example, if people heard about something but did not see it, if they also imagined that they saw it, they are more likely to come to believe that it was seen (Henkel, Franklin, & Johnson, 2000). Imagination inflation has a greater influence when people take a first-person perspective (Libby, 2003) or with repeated imaginings (Thomas & Loftus, 2002). In general, false memories can be as much as twice as more likely when the details are relevant to yourself (Desjardnis & Scoboria, 2007). Over time, people claim to consciously "remember" actually doing imagined events, even if they are bizarre activities, such as sitting on dice (Thomas, Bulevich, & Loftus, 2003; Thomas & Loftus, 2002).

Given the power of imagination inflation, it is not surprising that actually viewing pictures makes false memories even more likely (Garry & Gerrie, 2005; although narratives have a bigger effect, Garry & Wade, 2005). If people see photos of themselves at the age that an event was supposed to have occurred, they create false memories at a higher rate (Lindsay et al., 2004). Viewing old family photos gives memory concrete perceptual information to put into the false memories, along with any additional memories that are triggered by seeing the pictures. Similarly, if people see pictures of places under divided attention, they may later misremember having been to those locations (Brown & Marsh, 2008).

Although it seems unlikely, it is possible for people to implant false memories in themselves. In a study by Zaragoza et al. (2001; see also Chrobak & Zaragoza, 2008), students at Kent State University first watched a film. Afterward, they were asked a number of questions about the movie. Some people were told to answer all of the questions, even if the described event did not occur in the movie. For example, a question might be "The chair broke and Delaney fell on the floor. Where was Delaney bleeding?" when the character did not bleed. That is, the students manufactured an answer that they knew to be false. What is interesting is that during memory tests a week later, students who knowingly confabulated answers during the first part of the study now accepted many (32 percent) of these answers as truth. Moreover, if the experimenter had provided supportive feedback during the made-up response (such as "Yes, that's right"), then the rate of accepting these self-implanted false memories was higher (38 percent) than if only neutral feedback (such as "Okay") had been given (26 percent). Thus, even minimal external support of self-implanted false memories boosts their credibility (see also Thomas, Bulevich, & Loftus, 2003).

Although people can falsely remember implanted information, there are some qualities that distinguish true from false memories. True memories are often richer in detail, are more emotional, and are more likely to be "recollected" and to be field memories. In contrast, false memories are more likely to be stereotypical events, to be "known," and to be observer memories (Frost, 2000; Heaps & Nash, 2001). However, these are not defining criteria because true and false memories overlap on all of these qualities. These are only trends that characterize the set of false memories as a whole from the set of true memories. This is like saying men are taller than women. While this is true in general, there is a great deal of overlap between these two distributions. Just as you cannot make any clear judgments about the sex of a person given their height, you cannot use such qualities of a memory to determine if it is true or false.

False Memories: A Social Contagion

As with source monitoring, false memories are influenced by social factors. As a reminder, people are more willing to say that they "remember" events that were only imagined if other people also claim they saw them (Roediger, Meade, & Bergman, 2001; Reysen, 2007). This is memory as a "social contagion." Just hearing other people relate events may cause us to remember them as if we experienced them.

That said, working with other people does not always lead to more false memories. For example, with the DRM paradigm, people working in actual groups recall more actually presented words than people working in nominal groups or alone; however, the rate of recalling false memories does not change (Maki, Weigold, & Arellano, 2008).

The social influence of implanted false memories is also affected by the people involved. False memories are more likely to occur in people who are prone to dissociative experiences (e.g., driving and not remembering what happened the past few miles). These people may have a harder time distinguishing between what was real and what was plausible but imagined. Furthermore, false memories are more likely when the person who provides the implanted information is extroverted. This influence is particularly strong when the person who is remembering is more introverted (Porter, Birt, Yuille, & Lehman, 2000).

Emotional Consequences

The influence of emotion on false memories is complicated. In the DRM paradigm, compared to emotionally neutral items, false memories are more likely if a set of words is emotionally negative, but less likely if it is emotionally positive (Brainerd et al., 2008). Negative emotional content encourages more gist-based processing, causing people to be more willing to remember something that is generally consistent with the actual information, producing a false memory. However, positive information encourages more item-specific, verbatim memories, which decreases the likelihood of false memories.

In comparison to emotional content, the emotional mood of the person also influences the creation of false memories. In the DRM paradigm, relative to people who are in a neutral mood, false memories are more likely in people who are in a positive mood and less likely in people who are in a negative mood (Storbeck & Clore, 2005), although this may due to emotional intensity rather than negativity (Corson & Verrier, 2007; Kensinger & Schacter, 2006). Positive moods encourage relational processing, which would encourage the activation of a common associate concept, whereas negative moods encourage item-specific processing, which discourages the activation of what would become the false memory.

Hypnosis and Memory

If you are not familiar with **hypnosis,** you should be aware that this is a real thing. It is an altered state of consciousness in which a person is more willing to accept and follow the suggestions of the hypnotist. People vary in the degree to which they can be hypnotized. Some people are not at all susceptible, whereas others are highly susceptible to the point of being able to experience auditory, visual, or tactile illusions.

While there are many interesting topics that can be explored with hypnosis, the issue at hand is how hypnosis influences memory. Does hypnosis make memory better, worse, or have no appreciable effect? At first blush, it seems that hypnosis has a beneficial effect on memory. If you put people under hypnosis and ask them to recall things, they report more than if they are not under hypnosis.

However, there are problems. For one thing, there is a larger risk that the memories people report are inaccurate (Scoboria, Mazzoni, Kirsch, & Milling, 2002; Smith, 1983). The new accurate information that is reported under hypnosis is no different from the hypermnesia that one would normally see with repeated recall (see Chapter 3). Anything beyond that are often false memories. In a study by Dinges et al. (1992), people were given 40 line drawings to look at and memorize. People were then asked repeatedly to report what they had seen either when they were hypnotized, or not. A forced recall test (see Chapter 3) was used, in which the people had to recall 40 things. Thus, hypnotized and unhypnotized people were equated for the amount of information reported. What was found was that there was no difference in how much was recalled when people were hypnotized or not. Consistent hypermnesia was observed in all cases. Thus, hypnosis adds little to the ability to remember more than what is normally seen.

Synopsis

The separation between memory and reality is most salient when people have false memories of events that never occurred. These false memories come from different sources and take several forms. For example, people can mistakenly think a word that is closely related to other words on a list was actually heard earlier. Other times, false memories come from our natural impulse to integrate several pieces of information into a single, coherent memory, and we misremember what individual pieces were learned apart from the whole. More disturbing are situations where false memories are created by a failure to resist the implanting of false information from outside sources. These implanted false memories are even more likely when the information comes from a trusted source, including when that trusted source is a hypnotist. However, it should be noted that while we are easily misled in some circumstances, our grip on reality is fairly firm, and do not create false memories wildly but create them for things that are likely to have occurred anyway. Thus, with most false memories, little if any harm is done.

FALSE MEMORIES THROUGH NORMAL MEMORY USE

Every time we use our memories we change them in some way. Different things that we do with the information alter memories' content. In this section we look at two examples of normal ways of using memory that can lead to false memories. These are verbal overshadowing and the revelation effect.

Verbal Overshadowing

When we talk about things we've seen, our memories are changed by this verbalization. This is **verbal overshadowing.** When we describe an event, we create a verbal memory of our description. Because verbal information differs from visual information, our memory for what we said alters our memory for what we saw. This is consistent with fuzzy trace views that suggest that memory is a mixture of various traces. Overall, somehow our more recent verbal memories overshadow our older visual memories.

As an example of this, students at the University of Washington, in a study by Schooler and Engstler-Schooler (1990), watched a videotape of a bank robbery. Afterward, some people spent 5 minutes verbally describing the robber's face. Everyone was then shown eight pictures of similar faces and asked to pick out which one was the robber. It was found that students who produced a verbal description correctly picked the robber's face out 38 percent of the time, whereas students who did not provide a description picked out the robber 64 percent of the time. Thus, memory was worsened by talking about the experience. Verbal overshadowing is so powerful that even naming pictures of simple objects (e.g., saying "chair" to a picture of a chair) can make memory worse (Lupyan, 2008). It should be noted that verbal overshadowing does not occur if people only read a description—only when they actually generated a description does it occur (Dodson, Johnson, & Schooler, 1997).

Verbal overshadowing occurs even when the target face is not described. In a study by Dodson, Johnson, and Schooler (1997), verbal overshadowing was present when people described another face. Moreover, in a study by Westerman and Larsen (1997), when people described a car that was in a videotaped scene, memory for the target face still became more difficult. Thus, verbal overshadowing influences memory for the entire event, not just what was described. In these cases, there was a shift from visual to verbal information. Alternatively, verbalizing may alter the recognition process and make people more conservative, because verbal overshadowing is less likely to occur when people are forced to make a choice between several alternatives (Clare & Lewandowsky, 2004). Either way, talking about things can sometimes make memory worse. Finally, it should be noted that verbalization can act as a form of repeated practice in that details that are not talked about are more likely to be forgotten, even for emotionally intense events, such as hearing of the September 11th, 2001 terrorist attacks (Coman, Manier, & Hirst, 2009).

While verbal overshadowing occurs, providing a verbal description does not always make memory worse. In some cases, *verbal facilitation* occurs (e.g., Brown & Llyod-Jones, 2005, 2006; Lyle & Johnson, 2004). For example, if people are presented with a series of faces, and provide a description of each one as it is seen (in a control condition, no description is provided), people adopt strategies of encoding faces to memory. They can then take advantage of these verbal descriptions.

Revelation Effect

When we interact with the world, sometimes information is revealed slowly over time. At such times we may be trying to figure out what we are dealing with. As a consequence of this revelation process, people are more likely to recognize information as old, for both old and new information. This is the **revelation effect** (Luo, 1993; Peynircioğlu & Tekcan, 1993; Watkins & Peynircioğlu, 1990). It can also occur when people make frequency judgments (how often something occurred) in addition to recognition judgments (Bornstein & Neely, 2001). There are several ways that the revelation effect is studied. For example, a word might be revealed one letter at a time until the person can make a recognition judgment (e.g., M _ _ _ _ _, M _ _ O _ _, M _ _ O _ Y, etc.). The revelation effect occurs only when people think they are remembering a prior event. It does not occur if people either know that no such episode occurred or if they engage in semantic memory retrieval (Frigo, Reas, & LeCompte, 1999; Watkins & Peynircioğlu, 1990).

The revelation effect appears because people are using memory familiarity (Cameron & Hockley, 2000; LeCompte, 1995; Westerman & Greene, 1996; but see Hicks & Marsh, 1998, and Niewiadomski & Hockley, 2001, for a response criteria account). As people go through the revelation process, the information feels more familiar, so they are more willing to claim it was seen before. This occurs even when people have not heard something before but were subjected to subliminal suggestions that they had (Frigo, Reas, & LeCompte, 1999). ERP recordings show that there is greater frontal lobe activity for information that was revealed (see Figure 12.4), consistent with the idea that people are relying on memory familiarity (Azimian-Faridani & Wilding, 2004).

Also consistent with this familiarity idea, the revelation effect is more likely when people are less able to consciously recollect the circumstances in which information was learned and need to rely on feelings of familiarity. So, having a longer delay between the original presentation and the memory test or presenting the information faster makes it

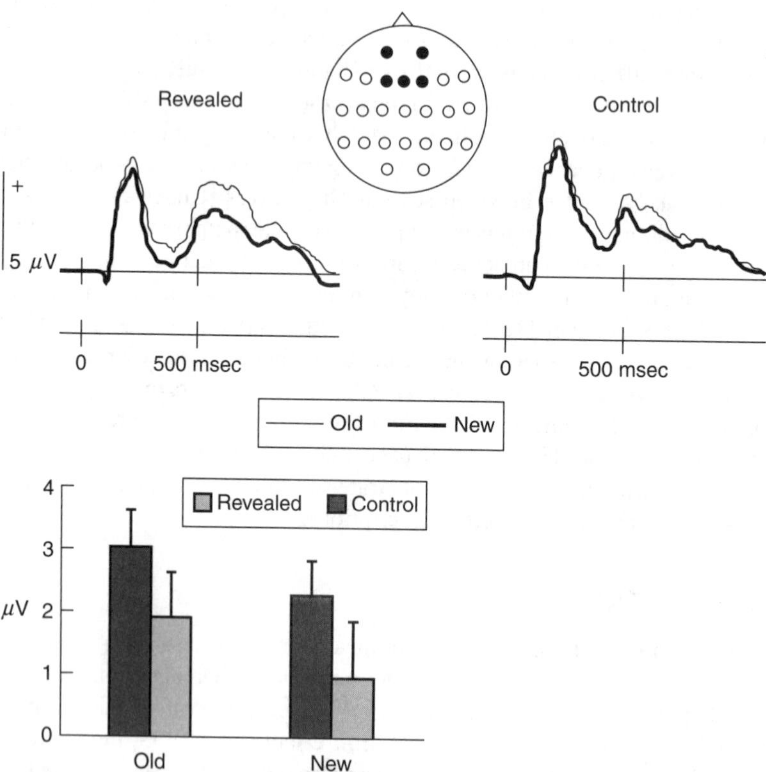

FIGURE 12.4 ERP Data Showing That There is Less Cortical Activity Revealed Items Relative to Control Items That are Not Slowly Revealed

Source: Azimian-Faridani, N., & Wilding, E. L. (2004). An event-related potential study of the revelation effect. *Psychonomic Bulletin & Review, 11,* 926–931. Reprinted with permission.

harder for people to encode it in a way to make conscious recollection possible (Landau, 2001). This feeling of familiarity may even come in the form of general activation by a presumably unrelated prior task, rather than revelation itself, such as doing a working memory span task prior to recognition (Westerman & Greene, 1998), or by solving a problem such as an anagram (Dougal & Schooler, 2007). However, when retrieval emphasizes conscious recollection, the revelation effect may not be observed (Westerman, 2000).

The revelation effect not only applies to simple items, like words, but also to complex events (Bernstein, Godfrey, Davidson, & Loftus, 2004; Bernstein, Rudd, Erdfelder, Godfrey, & Loftus, 2009; Bernstein, Whittlesea, & Loftus, 2002). If people go through a process of trying to uncover their memories, this very uncovering process can increase the likelihood that a person will falsely claim that a memory is real. Thus, efforts at recovering previously hidden memories can lead a person to believe in false memories.

The revelation effect is similar to other phenomena, including the mere exposure effect (Chapter 6), and the false fame effect, in that memory is altered by prior encounters. More false memory reports occur if people are exposed to a brief preview of something, such as a word, face, or scene. This preview makes something seem more familiar, and people are more likely to report that they had encountered it earlier (other than the preview) (Brown & Marsh, 2009; Jacoby & Whitehouse, 1989; Titchener, 1928). This may partially explain a déjà vu experience. Sometimes people get an initial glace of something, and then later when they look at it more carefully, it seems oddly familiar.

Synopsis

False memories can be created through what would seem to be the normal use of memory. For example, the seemly benign act of describing a witnessed event can lead to memory distortions. This occurs even when the part of the event being described is not the one that is tested later. Also, the gradual recovery of information during the memory search can create false memories. In this case, the build-up of partial memories during the revelation process leads to greater feelings of familiarity and the mistaken impression that the information was encountered before.

SUMMARY

In this chapter we saw a number of ways that memory can depart from reality. An important aspect that is needed to help determine whether a memory is real is knowing its source. Source monitoring draws from different types of information to assess where a memory came from. While source monitoring is usually accurate, from time to time there can be errors in which a person either loses the source information or misattributes something to a wrong source. One example of a source monitoring error is cryptomnesia, the inappropriate attribution of others' ideas to one's self. Other source monitoring problems include the false fame effect and the sleeper effect, in which people forget the source of information and then accept information as more credible than they previously thought.

Another way memory can be disconnected from reality is by creating false memories. Sometimes false memories are for things that are likely to have occurred. False memories may also be implanted from outside sources by suggestion, especially repeated suggestion. Implanted memories are more likely to occur if people engage in visual imagery and are encouraged by other people. Finally, the incidence of source monitoring errors and false memories is heightened by hypnosis in which a person wants to cooperate with the hypnotist, leading to the acceptance of information as being real memories that would have otherwise been rejected as imaginary.

Finally, we looked at instances of where problems in memory can occur through its normal use. In one case, memory for witnessed events became worse after people talked about the events. This is verbal overshadowing. Also, information that is revealed slowly is more likely to be falsely remembered, as with the revelation effect. Overall, while memories often correspond well to reality, there are exceptions.

STUDY QUESTIONS

1. What is source monitoring? What are the different types of source monitoring?
2. Generally speaking, what happens when a source monitoring error occurs? More specifically, what are some of the ways that source monitoring errors produce problems?
3. What is source cuing and how can this help memory retrieval?
4. What are cryptomnesia, the false fame effect, and the sleeper effect? How are each of these related to the process of source monitoring?
5. How can false memories be created by hearing related sets of information?
6. How are false memories implanted? What influences the probability that a false memory will be created?
7. What is the best way to describe the effect of hypnosis on attempts to remember?
8. What is the influence of providing a verbal description of a witnessed event on memory?
9. Does slowly revealing information to people make memory more or less accurate? Why?

KEY TERMS

cryptomnesia, DRM paradigm, external source monitoring, false fame effect, false memories, hypnosis, imagination inflation, internal source monitoring, reality monitoring, revelation effect, sleeper effect, source cuing, source monitoring, verbal overshadowing, wishful thinking bias

TRY IT OUT

There are a number of ways that memory can be inconsistent with reality. This Try It Out section outlines two ways to find such differences, namely the processes of source monitoring and the creation of false memories.

- As a reminder, **source monitoring** is the ability to tell where a memory came from. There are also three types of source monitoring: internal, external, and reality monitoring. You can do whichever version you find the most interesting. First, create a list of 40 five- to seven-letter two-syllable nouns. Then randomly assign these words to two conditions. Have people go through the list, presenting the words in one of these three ways:
    - For **internal source monitoring**, have people read 20 words out loud, and have them read 20 other words silently (mix up the aloud and silent reading). For the memory test, have people indicate whether the words were actually said or just imagined. If all goes well, most of the source monitoring errors should occur where people say that words they only imagined were actually said.
    - For **external source monitoring,** you need two experimenters (if they are of the same gender, that is even better). Have the experimenters take alternating turns reading the words aloud, with one person reading 20 words and the other reading the rest. For the memory test, have people indicate which words were said by which experimenter.
    - For **reality monitoring**, read 20 of the words aloud to people, and have them imagine the other 20 words being said in your voice. For the memory test, have people indicate whether the words were actually said or just imagined. If all goes well, most of the source monitoring errors will be where people say that words they imagined were actually said by you.

At the end of the list, give people a distractor task, such as solving math problems, to occupy their time for 5 or 10 minutes. At the end of the distractor period, give people the entire list of 40 words and have them indicate from which source the word came from.

- To assess **false memories**, you can use the DRM paradigm described earlier. Read people lists of 15 words that are strongly related to a target word, which will become a false memory. You can use the list in Table 12.2, or one of these three lists:

  Bread: butter, food, eat, sandwich, rye, jam, milk, flour, jelly, dough, crust, slice, wine, loaf, toast

  Needle: thread, pin, eye, sewing, sharp, point, prick, thimble, haystack, thorn, hurt, injection, syringe, cloth, knitting

  Soft: hard, light, pillow, plush, loud, cotton, fur, touch, fluffy, feather, furry, downy, kitten, skin, tender

- Read the words to people one at a time at a rate of about 1 second per word. When you are done, have people recall as many words as they can remember on a sheet of paper. This can be done individually or in groups, but you should have at least 24 people. After they are done with recalling, collect their response sheets and tabulate how many false memories occurred.

CHAPTER THIRTEEN

MEMORY AND THE LAW

Memory has practical and important applications even outside of the classroom. One of the more salient of these is how memory works, and how forgetting occurs, in the legal arena. There are many situations in which arriving at a just legal outcome involves people using their memories effectively. When memory is more accurate, police, judges, and juries can come to more appropriate conclusions. However, as we have seen, there are cases where memory reports may be inaccurate, even though a person is doing the best he or she can. Such memory errors can lead to serious miscarriages of justice, with guilty individuals not being held accountable and still at large or innocent people being punished for things they did not do.

This chapter looks at five ways that memory can influence legal matters. The first is the accuracy of eyewitness memory. The second is the confidence eyewitnesses have in their memories. The third is the development of a cognitive interview used to gather information in a way to get the most out of memory. The fourth is the ability to identify a perpetrator from a lineup. And for the fifth, we consider how memory processes influence the effectiveness of juries.

EYEWITNESS TESTIMONY

When an accident occurs or a crime is committed, one important source of evidence is **eyewitness testimony**. Eyewitnesses can provide information that cannot be obtained any other way. Moreover, if it is a serious enough case to warrant a jury trial, eyewitnesses can provide convincing evidence. Thus, the accuracy and stability of eyewitnesses' memories are critically important. It is vital to understand how accurate such accounts are, even in the absence of any desire to mislead on the part of a witness. We approach the accuracy of eyewitness reports by looking at how some things can affect memory, such as the wording of a question, the influence of misleading information, the witness's emotional state at the time of the event, and other aspects of the event that may influence later memory.

Wording Effects

To get information from a witness, questions must be asked. It is critical to understand that the way questions are worded can influence what is remembered. People reconstruct their memories of an event based on the questions they are asked. Take the example of an automobile accident involving two cars. People vary their estimates of the speed at which the cars were traveling, depending on the wording of a question. In a study by Loftus and Palmer (1974), people watched a film of a car accident. After the film, they were asked, "How fast were the cars going when they smashed/collided/bumped/hit/contacted each other?" with each person receiving a different verb. What was found was that the speed estimation varied, by nearly ten miles per hour, depending on which verb was used (see Table 13.1).

Furthermore, in the car accident film, there was no broken glass. However, after the question about speed, people were asked if they had seen any broken glass (there was none). Only the verbs "smashed" and "hit" were used. Loftus and Palmer found that the more severe the verb, the more likely people claimed to have seen broken glass. People reported seeing broken glass 16 percent of the time when they heard "smashed" but only 7 percent of the time when they heard "hit." People who were not asked the speed question said "yes" to the broken glass question only 6 percent of the time.

This influence of wording even occurs with seemingly subtle differences, such as whether a question contains the article "a" or "the." In one study (Loftus & Zanni, 1975), people saw a car accident film. They then wrote a summary of what they saw and answered some questions. One question was either "Did you see a broken headlight?" or "Did you see the broken headlight?" The difference between the articles "a" and "the" is important because "a" doesn't presuppose the existence of a broken headlight, whereas "the" does. Half the time the questioned item was in the film, and half the time it was not. When the item was not in the film (e.g., no broken headlight), people claimed they saw the (nonexistent) item 7 percent of the time when "a" was used but 18 percent of the time when "the" was used. The error rate is more than twice as large following a change in a seemingly small article.

Misleading Postevent Information

Not only is it easy to alter memory reports based on the wording of a question, it is also alarmingly easy to alter memory by giving misleading information afterward, whether intentionally or not. This is called **misleading postevent information.** This misinformation enters memory, and people have difficulty distinguishing it from accurate memories.

TABLE 13.1 Speed Estimates as a Function of the Severity of the Verb Used in the Question "How fast were the cars going when they _________ each other?"

VERB	SPEED ESTIMATE (MPH)
smashed	40.8
collided	39.3
bumped	38.1
hit	34.0
contacted	31.8

Source: Reprinted from *Journal of Verbal Learning and Verbal Behavior,* 13, Loftus, E.G., & Palmer, J.C., Reconstruction of automobile destruction: An example of the interaction between language and memory, pp. 585–589, 1974, with permission from Elsevier.

These memory distortions come from hearing other people describe the event, with memory being distorted in the direction of what other people report (Gabbert, Memon, & Wright, 2006; Wright, Memon, Skagerberg, & Gabbert, 2009). We first look at how to assess the influence of misleading postevent information and then consider some theories of how this happens.

Methods. A standard approach for assessing the influence of misleading postevent information on memory was first used by Loftus, Miller, and Burns (1978). First, people watch an accident or a crime on video. For example, a person might see an accident in which a driver goes past a yield sign. Then the person is asked a question about the video. In some cases, the question refers to an object that was in the scene, such as "Did another car pass the red Datsun when it was stopped at the yield sign?" Because the sign mentioned in the question is consistent with the video, this is the *consistent* condition. In other cases, this question refers to an object that was not in the scene, such as "Did another car pass the red Datsun when it was stopped at the stop sign?" Because no stop sign was in the video, this is the *misleading* condition. Finally, in a third *neutral* control condition, the question is neutral, such as "Did another car pass the red Datsun when it was stopped at the intersection?"

After viewing the event and answering the critical question (among others), people make a decision about what they saw, such as whether the car had stopped at a stop sign or a yield sign. Although memory is better in the consistent condition (relative to the neutral condition), it is worse in the misleading condition. The results of one study are shown in Table 13.2. The misleading postevent information effect is fairly stable and occurs in a variety of situations. It is more pronounced the greater the delay between witnessing the event and the time the misleading information is encountered (Loftus, Miller, & Burns, 1978). It also occurs when the misleading information is presented prior to witnessing the event (Eakin, Schreiber, & Sergent-Marshall, 2003). People can even mislead themselves. Witnesses who provide false information (i.e., lie) after witnessing an event have a poorer memory when they later try to remember accurately. They retrieve less true information and are more likely to have their lies intrude on their attempts to remember (Pickel, 2004). In their minds, their lies have become truths.

Theories. There are a number of explanations for why misleading postevent information alters memory. Three of them are the memory replacement theory, memory coexistence theory, and source monitoring theory.

TABLE 13.2 Proportion Correct for Selecting the Correct Item after Consistent, Misleading, or Neutral Information

QUESTION TYPE	PROPORTION CORRECT
Consistent	70
Misleading	43
Neutral	63

Source: Loftus, Miller, & Burns, 1978.

For *memory replacement theory* (Loftus, 1979), misleading information replaces or overwrites the original memory, which is permanently lost. In support of this in some studies people are given three alternatives on the memory test, the original item (e.g., yield sign), the misleading item (e.g., stop sign), and a new item (e.g., no parking sign). After the initial response, people selected their best second-guess. If people initially selected the misleading item, the probability of selecting the correct item on the second-guess is at chance. If the original memory were still present, then performance should have been better because it would have had some small effect.

A second view is that the original and misleading information coexist in memory. This is *blocking theory*. Because the misleading information is more recent, it obscures the original memory. If people are asked to recall an event prior to being exposed to misinformation, they are more likely to accept the misinformation (Chan, Thomas, & Bulevich, 2009). Recalling the event may make it easier to bind and integrate the misinformation into memory, blocking access to the original memory. It may even be that the original memory is inhibited, similar to what happens in the repeated practice paradigm (MacLeod & Saunders, 2005, 2008). Berkerian and Bowers (1983) found that if the context is adequately reinstated at the time the questions are asked, then the effect of misleading postevent information is reduced or eliminated. Also, if people are warned before the memory test that some of the questions contained misleading information, then people can disregard some information and perform more like people who were not misled (Christiaansen & Ochalek, 1983). Thus, they were able to remove the memory traces containing the misleading information and focus only on traces from the original event. Similarly, if people are provided misleading information, but not provided the misleading item on the memory test, but only the original item and some new distractors, then performance is comparable to people who were not misled (McCloskey & Zaragoza, 1985). Finally, even when there appears to be no memory for the original event on a direct memory test, like recognition, there is evidence that the information is still present when an indirect memory test is used, like lexical decision (Dodson & Reisberg, 1991).

A third view, *source monitoring theory*, suggests that there is a source monitoring problem (see Chapter 12). Witnesses generally remember where misinformation came from (Zaragoza & Koshmider, 1989). However, errors do occur. These source monitoring errors are more likely for people who are more dissociative thinkers (they also show a lower correspondence between their accuracy and their confidence [Cann & Katz, 2005]). Witnesses are less likely to fall prey to misinformation if it is presented as a narrative (Zaragoza & Lane, 1994), although creating such descriptions makes memory even worse (Lane & Zaragoza, 2007) by bringing together the misinformation, generation, and verbal overshadowing effects to work against source monitoring. Finally, the more thematically similar misleading information is to the witnessed event, the more likely errors that are made. Errors can also occur for more thematically distant information, but at a lower rate (Lindsay, Allen, Chan, & Dahl, 2004).

Note that just because a person encounters misleading information does not mean that memory is altered. It depends on the source. For example, misleading information about an accident is more likely to have an effect if people think it came from a bystander than if it came from a driver involved in the wreck, in which case, people are more likely to disregard the misinformation (Dodd & Bradshaw, 1980; Echterhoff, Hirst, & Hussy, 2005). In an interesting twist, Assefi and Garry (2003) found that people were more

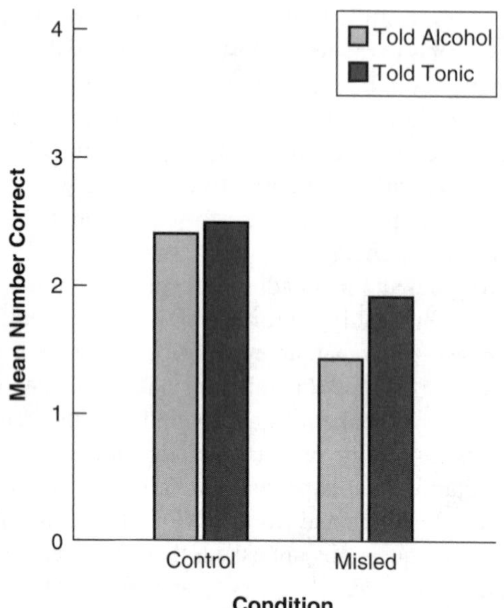

FIGURE 13.1 Influence of Perceived Alcohol Consumption on Memory Performance

Source: Assefi, S. L., & Garry, M. (2003). Absolute memory distortions: Alcohol placebos influence the misinformation effect. *Psychological Science, 14,* 77–80.

susceptible to misinformation if they thought they had recently consumed alcohol (even though they hadn't because the experiments gave them drinks that only tasted like alcohol, but weren't), as seen in Figure 13.1. Thus, even implicit social demands can influence eyewitness memory. What was even more disconcerting was that not only did people who *thought* they had consumed alcohol make more errors, but they were also more confident in their answers.

Arousal Influences

Events involving eyewitnesses are often not standard and mundane. Instead, they are emotion arousing, as when someone witnesses a violent car accident or is a victim of a serious crime. How do intense emotions affect an eyewitness's memory? Do emotions make it better? Do they make it worse? Well, the picture is somewhat complicated. Although, there is no doubt that memory is affected by emotion. This relationship is outlined well by Christianson (1992).

Yerkes-Dodson Law. One early view was that emotion and memory followed the **Yerkes-Dodson law** (Yerkes & Dodson, 1908). According to this view, arousal is a continuum, with memory performance being an inverted-U-shaped function, as shown in Figure 13.2. At low levels of arousal, a person does not encode information into memory very well. This is like trying to study when you are tired (not that you've ever done that). As arousal increases, performance increases as well, up to a point. There is a certain level

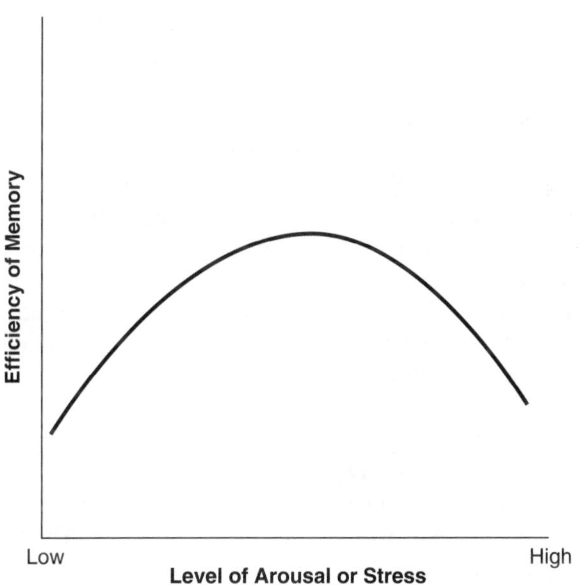

FIGURE 13.2 The Yerkes-Dodson Law

where memory encoding is maximized. Beyond that point, a person is overaroused, and memory worsens. This is like trying to study when you are preparing to go out on a hot date. So, people who are bystanders to a violent crime are likely to remember more than a person who is the victim. The bystander would be closer to the optimum level, whereas the victim would be too highly aroused.

Easterbrook Hypothesis. There is evidence that overall memory does follow this basic pattern. However, the situation is more complicated. Specifically, the ability to remember details under different levels of emotional stress depends on the type of details. At high levels of emotion, memory for peripheral details (e.g., the color of a car, someone's clothing, the actions of bystanders) is worse. However, memory for central details (e.g., what a robber said) is better. This contradicts the Yerkes-Dodson law, but it is consistent with another account called the Easterbrook hypothesis.

For the **Easterbrook hypothesis** (Easterbrook, 1959), at higher levels of emotional intensity, people restrict their attention to a narrower range of details. Attention is more focused (see also Kensinger, Garoff-Easton & Schacter, 2007; but see Laney, Campbell, Heuer, & Reisberg, 2005, for an alternative take), a process called cue utilization. Under normal emotional stress levels, people notice a variety of aspects of their environment, giving a more balanced amount of attention to various details. However, during an emotional event, people focus their attention on the principal parts of that event and less on other irrelevant details. Thus, peripheral details are less well remembered, whereas the central details are better remembered. For example, if you encountered people in a non-stressful event, you might remember their faces equally well. However, if you met them as part of a stressful event, where one was a bank robber and another was a person in line, the cue utilization that occurs as a result of narrowing your attention to the critical part of the event would lead you to pay more attention to, and thus better remember, the robber's face relative to the other customer's face.

Although high levels of emotion can lead to more accurate memory for a narrower range of information, this does not mean that people do not report remembering a wide range of things. Although accurate memory is present for the details focused on, people can still fill in their memories with what they *expect* to be present in the rest of the situation based on their schemas and scripts. For example, people who see both emotional and neutral pictures show boundary extension effects (see Chapter 5) of similar magnitudes (Candel, Merckelbach, & Zandbergen, 2003). In effect, they are still interpreting their memories of the pictures they have viewed using their expectations of what likely extended beyond the boundaries of the pictures.

Weapon Focus. A good example of the influence of emotional intensity is the **weapon focus effect**, which is an increase in memory for a weapon (such as a gun, knife, cleaver) along with a decline in memory for other details (Maass & Köhnken, 1989; Steblay, 1992). Recordings of eye movements while watching pictures that depict a crime show that people spend more time looking at what a person is holding if it is a weapon than if it is a neutral object (Loftus, Loftus, & Messo, 1987). This even occurs when a weapon is present but not involved in a violent action (Kramer, Buckout, & Eugenio, 1990). The barrel of a gun or the blade of a knife is a point of great interest to people, and they spend a lot of time looking at such things. At some level people want to know whether the weapon will be used against them. This increased attention to a weapon increases memory for it, and decreases memory for other aspects of the event, such as a perpetrator's face. While some of the weapon focus effect is due to the unusualness of a weapon (Pickel, 1998), there is also added memory disruption because it is a source of danger (see also, tunnel memories in Chapter 11).

John Dean's Memory

A famous case of memory in legal proceedings is John Dean's memory for the coverup of the Watergate break-in during President Nixon's administration. This incident led to the president's resignation. John Dean, one of the White House advisors, testified before Congress about the coverup in terms of what was going on in the White House. John Dean testified against President Nixon and the other coconspirators. What was remarkable about Dean's testimony was the number of conversations he claimed to remember and the degree of accuracy with which he remembered them. (His initial statement to Congress was 245 pages.) His memory was so remarkable that reporters nicknamed him "the human tape recorder."

The interesting thing is that soon after John Dean had given his testimony, real tape recordings emerged that Nixon had secretly made of White House conversations. At that point, it was possible to compare Dean's memory with the recordings and a scientific study of memory for conversations that had legal implications. And this is just what was done (Neisser, 1981).

In comparing the initial testimony concerning things that were claimed to have been said and the actual conversation on the tapes, John Dean hardly ever got it right. Many of the things that he claimed were said were never actually said. For example, with regard to one of the White House meetings, Dean claimed that Nixon had asked him to sit down, had asked Halderman (another aid) to keep him posted, and praised Dean for doing a good job. Also, John Dean claimed that he himself had made statements about not really wanting to take credit for his efforts and that the coverup would eventually unravel. The tapes revealed that none of these statements were made during the meeting in question.

However, a comparison of Dean's statements and the tapes also indicated no attempt to lie on Dean's part. The tapes do corroborate important points in Dean's testimony, such as the fact that the White House was aware of and was involved in the coverup. Often the distortions in Dean's testimony reflected a schematization of his prior memory. His memory reflected the events in a cleaned-up fashion. Also, Dean misremembers himself as playing a more central role in the conversations than was the case. This self-centered bias is an expected aspect of anyone's memory of an event. This is because our memory includes both the things that objectively occurred and our own subjective thoughts and emotions. Any act of remembering will involve these components.

Synopsis

While eyewitness testimony is generally accurate, it can be altered. The way a question is worded can lead people to misremember an event in the direction implied by the wording. People also incorporate misleading information into their reports. Finally, eyewitness memory is affected by the level of arousal that a person experiences. At high levels of arousal, memory is worse. This seems to be because attention during encoding is focused on a few smaller, critical details, such as a weapon.

EYEWITNESS CONFIDENCE

Is there any way to assess how accurate eyewitness reports are, especially when there are few to no other sources of corroborating evidence? Intuitively it seems that as the **confidence** of a witness increases, the more accurate the information is. Conversely, a memory that a witness is unsure about is less likely to be accurate. However, metamemory, the monitoring of one's own memory performance, is imperfect (see Chapter 14). The same principle applies to eyewitness accounts. It is quite possible to have people who are very confident that an innocent person committed a crime. In the case of eyewitness identification, the average overall correlation between accuracy and reported confidence is quite low: $r = .29$. If only people who actually select someone are considered (leaving out people who say that they do not see the offender in a lineup), the correlation improves somewhat: $r = .41$ (Sporer, Penrod, Read, & Cutler, 1995). Still, the relation is far from perfect. In terms of memory for details, confidence is more reliable for central as compared to peripheral aspects of the event (Roberts & Higham, 2002).

Eyewitness confidence is influenced by postidentification feedback, which is information about the quality of an eyewitness's report. For example, if positive feedback is given to a witness, such as "Good. You identified the suspect," the witness's confidence in his or her memory increases, compared to when no feedback is given. This can also make the witness embellish claims about the quality of his or her view of the crime, the clarity of his or her memory of the event, and the speed with which he or she remembers identifying the person (Wells & Bradfield, 1998, 1999). Of course, there is no way for such a comment to actually improve any of these qualities of memory.

Also, telling a witness what other witnesses reported increases confidence. For example, after lineup identification for an offender, if a witness is told that another witness picked the same person, he or she feels more confident about his or her choice. However, if the person hears that another witness picked someone else, confidence decreases (Luus & Wells, 1994). Thus, the relation between a person's identification accuracy and confidence can be distorted by subsequent information.

Witness confidence is also influenced by how many times questions are asked. The more times a person is asked about an aspect of a crime or an accident, the greater confidence will be in the memory. This is noteworthy in that, by and large, from what you know about memory already, the passage of time typically makes memories worse, not better, even though confidence is increasing over time with more retellings. This increase in confidence even occurs for misleading postevent information (Shaw & McClure, 1996). Again, this increase in confidence as a result of repeated questioning is unrelated to the accuracy of the memory for the event.

Repeated questioning makes information easier to access and more salient in memory (remember it is impossible to probe memory without changing it). Increased retrieval fluency may lead a person to be more confident in its accuracy (Shaw, 1996). Judges and juries are often swayed by the confidence a witness has in the memories that are reported. By the time a witness gets to trial, the same questions have been answered many times, thereby increasing confidence without a corresponding increase in accuracy. To make matters worse, efforts to make a person aware of the relationship between level of confidence and memory accuracy may either have no effect or actually worsen the relationship (Robinson & Johnson, 1998).

Finally, eyewitness confidence is influenced by external motivation to remember. In a study by Shaw and Kerr (2003), students at Lafayette College received extra motivation to remember accurately (a possibility of winning money for being the most accurate). People witnessed an event in their classroom and were given a memory test 5 days later, with or without the additional motivation. In this study, extra motivation did not alter the accuracy of the memory reports and confidence ratings. However, motivation did affect the relationship between accuracy and confidence. For the unmotivated students, the correlation between accuracy and confidence was relatively good: $r = .44$. However, for motivated people, the correlation was horrible: $r = .05$. Essentially, by encouraging people to try harder, more effort is associated with each retrieval attempt. Thus, it becomes harder for people to identify what was easy and what was difficult to remember, and the usefulness of the confidence ratings drops tremendously. This is important because a witness is often motivated to try hard to remember.

Synopsis

Although eyewitness confidence is often used as an indicator of accuracy, the real relationship between them is imperfect. Moreover, this relationship is worsened by a number of factors, including reinforcing feedback, even from someone who did not know what really happened. Eyewitness confidence can also be affected by repeated attempts to remember and external encouragement to try to remember accurately.

COGNITIVE INTERVIEW

Given the problems with eyewitness memory, can anything be done to improve these reports? Research has led to information gathering methods to increase accuracy, such as the **cognitive interview**. This technique uses basic memory principles to maximize the amount of correct information and minimize the amount of incorrect information from a witness (Geiselman et al., 1984; Geiselman, Fisher, MacKinnon, & Holland, 1985). The cognitive interview does this by focusing on five retrieval processes.

First, it uses the principles of encoding specificity and mood-dependent learning (see Chapter 7). There should be some attempt to reinstate the external and internal contexts of the event. This can include having people imagine being back at the scene and feeling how they felt at the time. Reinstating the context serves as a retrieval cue, making it more likely that people can access information in memory. As a reminder, context is most likely to have an effect on memory retrieval during recall with weaker memory traces—just as in the case of police interviews.

Second, because people sometimes retrieve only partial information, as with the tip-of-the-tongue state (see Chapter 9), witnesses are encouraged to report whatever they can, however partial or insignificant it may seem to them at the time. For example, if a witness cannot remember someone's name but can remember how many syllables it had or what letter it began with, then it should be reported. Information, even in a fragmentary state, can potentially be useful to investigators.

Third, there are often many retrieval pathways to a given piece of information. When we forget information, we may be able to retrieve it later if we take a different approach (see Chapters 7 and 9). This retrieval can be accomplished by reporting an event in a variety of orders. By starting at different points, this emphasizes different types of information, and different details are reported. This enhances eyewitness reports.

Fourth, a person may report information from a different perspective (see Chapter 9) to make some information more salient and more likely to be reported and the witness's report is more complete. Alternative perspectives provide alternative retrieval pathways, allowing information to be remembered that might otherwise have been missed.

Finally, questioners are discouraged from interrupting a witness's report, when possible. By disrupting a person, the flow of the natural retrieval plan is disturbed, and some of the more weakly stored information might not be reported. This is similar to the part-set cuing effect (see Chapter 9).

The cognitive interview is an effective eyewitness memory tool. Using it can boost the reports of accurate information by more than 50 percent without noticeable changes in how much incorrect information that may be reported (Fisher, Geiselman, & Amador, 1989). The cognitive interview takes more time to administer than the standard interview. However, given the amount of extra work that might be required without that information, the cost is well worth it.

Synopsis

Although eyewitness memory can be imperfect, by using what we know about memory, we can develop techniques that are less likely to disrupt memories and are more likely to increase accuracy. The cognitive interview does this by taking into account what is known about the influences of learning context, partial retrieval, hypermnesia, and part-set cuing on memory.

EYEWITNESS IDENTIFICATION

An important thing an eyewitness can do is to identify the people involved, particularly criminal suspects. An eyewitness must remember the features of individuals to identify them later. However, as we have seen, people are prone to forgetting, which can cause errors. For eyewitness identification, this forgetfulness can lead to two undesirable outcomes: (1) failing to identify a perpetrator and (2) misidentifying an innocent person as the perpetrator. The second of these is worse because it leads to the prosecution of an innocent person, leaving the culprit free to commit further crimes. In cases of DNA exoneration of previous convictions, erroneous eyewitness identification was the primary cause of the imprisonment of innocent people. A number of things can influence a witness's memory of a person involved in a crime. Some of these are beyond the control of the legal system, such as whether a perpetrator was carrying a weapon (which reduces identification accuracy). However, steps can be taken to increase identification accuracy (see Clark & Godfrey, 2009; Wells et al., 2000; Wells, Memon, & Penrod, 2006, for reviews).

Mugshots

Mugshots are a standard device used to help identify perpetrators of crimes. Essentially, an eyewitness is shown a series of photographs of people who have been involved in previous crimes. If the witness can identify the perpetrator from this set of faces, the police can more quickly solve the crime. However, mugshots also have negative effects on memory. If people are shown a series of mugshots, and the perpetrator is not among them, the eyewitness may sometimes pick out another person as the criminal. When people incorrectly identify someone from mugshots, their ability to identify the perpetrator later is lower than for people who do not incorrectly identify someone (Brigham & Cairns, 1988; Davis, Shepherd, & Ellis, 1979; Gorenstein & Ellsworth, 1980). Essentially, memory for the selected mugshot interferes with, and makes it harder to retrieve the memory of the face of the perpetrator. However, this occurs only if people commit to identifying a face in the mugshots as the perpetrator (Dysart, Lindsay, Hammond, & Dupuis, 2001). No memory deficit comes from just viewing the pictures.

When the perpetrator was not among the mugshots, witnesses may later pick out a person whose mugshots were viewed, even if they were not the one who was initially picked (Memon, Hope, Bartlett, & Bull, 2002). Witnesses may pick these people because they seem "familiar," not realizing it was because they were among the mugshots. People have better memory for having seen a face before than remembering *where* they had seen that face (Brown, Deffenbacher, & Sturgill, 1977). So, problems in source monitoring with mugshot viewings can lead to errors in eyewitness identification.

A procedure that also focuses on face memory is to have a sketch artist generate a composite drawing of a perpetrator. This is a form of recall memory. Unfortunately, the individual drawings created using this method are poorer than one would hope, although morphing the drawings from several witnesses can produce a more accurate image

(Wells & Hasel, 2007). The poor recall observed here is likely due to the fact that people do not encode faces as sets of features, but in a more holistic fashion.

Lineups

One way to improve eyewitness identification is proper lineup procedure. With memory, there is always some forgetting of details, and eyewitness memory is not perfect. Identification of a suspect is a recognition process. A person is comparing his or her memory with what is presented in the environment, such as faces in a police lineup. During identification, people make judgments based not only on how well a given person matches their memory, but also how well the different people in the lineup compare to one another in terms of how much they resemble the offender. This is the **relative judgment principle** (Wells, 1984). According to this principle, people may select someone from a lineup not because this was the person the witness saw, but because compared to the others, that person most resembles the criminal.

So, **lineup similarity**—the physical resemblances of others in the lineup—is important. Lineups created with fillers who do not resemble a suspect much are biased in favor of the witness choosing the person who most closely resembles the memory of the offender. However, when lineup fillers at least fit the basic description given by the witness, people need to use memory more carefully, and their selections are more diagnostic (Wells, Rydell, & Seelau, 1993). With similar lineup fillers, the identification of guilty suspects is roughly the same, but the identification of innocent suspects decreases considerably (Lindsay & Wells, 1980).

Another factor that can influence eyewitness identification is the instructions given to a witness. A critical factor is whether the instructions include a statement telling the witness that the perpetrator might not be present. This explicitly opens up the possibility of the witness not identifying anyone. Without this simple instruction, there is a strong compulsion to select *someone.* As a result, an innocent person in the lineup may be identified just because he or she closely resembles the perpetrator. With this instruction, people are less likely to feel compelled to pick someone, and the false identification rate drops dramatically (Malpass & Devine, 1981). In general, the rate of false identification drops by about 42 percent when this instruction is included. The rate of not selecting a perpetrator drops by only about 2 percent (Steblay, 1997).

Finally, eyewitness identification is influenced by how the lineup is presented. The traditional lineup—what you see in movies and cop shows—is a *simultaneous* lineup, where all of the alternatives are shown together and the witness is asked to select one. Another type is a *sequential* lineup, where the witness sees one person at a time. Keeping in mind that people make decisions using a relative judgment principle, witness identification errors are more likely with a simultaneous lineup than with a sequential lineup (Lindsay & Wells, 1985). It is easier for a witness to make relative comparisons among people when they are presented simultaneously. However, with sequential lineups, people are forced to compare the person they are seeing at the moment with their memory of the perpetrator. This is because a witness does not know whom he or she will be seeing next or how many people he or she will see altogether. Using a sequential as opposed to a simultaneous lineup greatly lowers false identifications, with little to no effect on positive identifications of actual offenders.

Unconscious Transference. In addition to aspects of identification that investigators can control, such as the way a lineup is presented, there are other aspects that are not under their control. One of these is **unconscious transference**, which is when a person mistakenly identifies an innocent bystander as the perpetrator (Ross, Ceci, Dunning, & Toglia, 1994). In such cases, a witness remembers seeing the offender, but then becomes confused. So an innocent bystander is incorrectly remembered as being the one who committed the crime. According to a memory blending theory of unconscious transference (Ross et al., 1994) during memory retrieval, the assumption is made that these two individuals are one and the same. However, if people are aware prior to witnessing an event that these are two different people, then they are less likely to make this error.

Another view is a source monitoring theory of unconscious transference (Read, 1994) in which witnesses remember a person but fail to remember the situation in which they interacted with that person. As a result, they may be more likely to misattribute the source of that memory and misremember the person as the perpetrator of a crime.

Synopsis

Understanding how memory works is important for eyewitness identification. As with other memories, the act of using a memory can change it. Having seen a face previously in a set of mugshots can mistakenly lead people to think that was the face of the perpetrator. Also, because people are prone to use relative judgments, it is better to use sequential lineups rather than simultaneous ones. This forces people to compare each person with their memory of the perpetrator rather than with one another. In addition, lineup accuracy is increased if people are reminded that they can say "not present" to the lineup. While some techniques can be used to reduce memory errors, it is still possible for things to occur that cannot be controlled. For example, an eyewitness may make a blending error and misremember a bystander as the perpetrator because the witness remembers that person's face as part of the event.

JURIES

The influence of memory on legal matters affects areas other than gathering testimony from eyewitnesses. Another legal setting that the operation of memory is important is in juries. In this section we look at two ways that memory can influence jury decisions. These are the order in which information is encountered and the ability of juries to disregard inappropriate information.

Information Order

When jurors hear evidence, they try to mentally construct an understanding of the event in the form of a coherent story, much like what occurs for autobiographical memory (see Chapter 11), only in this case the memory is for other people's experiences (Pennington & Hastie, 1986; 1988). The juror memories are affected by the order that they learn information, just like other settings, and this order influences the decisions rendered later. There are two ways to assess how information order affects jury decisions. The first is a step-by-step process in which people render preliminary decisions after each piece of information is given. Under these circumstances, people show a recency effect (Furnham, 1986; Pennington & Hastie, 1992). That is, their decisions are more influenced by the information they learned most recently. The most recent information is most available in memory, so people are more likely to rely on it.

The other way to assess the influence of information order is to have people make decisions after all of the information is given. Here, one of two things can happen. If people are given background information, such as the motive for a killing, then decisions show a recency effect. However, if people are not given background information but are presented only with reports from various witnesses, then people show a primacy effect (Kerstholt & Jackson, 1998). Background information gives people a starting point, and they are more willing to adjust their opinions based on new information. However, without background information, people try to make a coherent story with the information they have. As a result, they need to keep more information of their own creation active in working memory, and are more reluctant to alter their prior understanding of the events.

In addition, jurors may hear contradictory testimony, sometimes from a single witness. How is memory affected by these inconsistencies? Are jurors more affected by the initial statement or the later, contradictory statement? As it turns out, jurors are affected by both. For inconsistent testimony from a single witness, jurors remember and note both statements and place less emphasis on such testimony when making decisions (Berman & Cutler, 1996).

Inadmissible Evidence

One problem that can arise before a jury trial (as with pretrial publicity) or during the trial itself is when jury members are exposed to evidence that a judge deems inadmissible. If this happens, the judge has a couple of choices. One is to declare a mistrial, and the other is to instruct the jurors to disregard or ignore the inadmissible evidence. Clearly, the second alternative is preferable if the jury can be trusted to do so because it would make the process quicker.

The instruction to disregard evidence is essentially a directed forgetting instruction (see Chapter 14). In directed forgetting, people are given a set of information. At some point, they are told to remember some of the information but to forget the rest. In general, people are fairly efficient at doing this. Information that is designated as to-be-forgotten is recalled less well compared to information designated as to-be-remembered (Bjork, 1970). The question here is how well does the instruction to forget work in a real-world setting that have serious implications for a defendant on trial?

When memory for inadmissible evidence is tested for using a directed forgetting paradigm, jurors' memories for the inadmissible evidence are poorer than for admissible evidence. So, there is some success in forgetting the information. However, when looking at assessments of a defendant's attributes (e.g., friendly, dishonest) and decisions to convict or acquit, there is a clear influence of the inadmissible evidence. The presence of damaging inadmissible evidence biases jurors toward a guilty verdict, whereas supporting inadmissible evidence biases jurors toward a not guilty verdict (Golding & Hauselt, 1994; Thompson, Fong, & Rosenhan, 1981). Generally, people continue to use information they were supposed to disregard and use it to make attributions about a person (Wyer & Unverzagt, 1985).

This is because the memories for inadmissible information may have been suppressed, and people have difficulty accessing the source information in long-term memory (Bjork & Bjork, 2003). Thus, jurors may remember the information but not where it came from. Thus they forget that they are supposed to disregard it. In essence, this is also a form of the sleeper effect.

To-be-forgotten information also influences decision making about what jurors think about the nature of the information. Directed forgetting is less efficient, and the opinions are more biased when the jurors believe that information is accurate and relevant to the defendant, such as when the information is described as confidential but inadvertently presented. However, directed forgetting is more efficient and opinions much less biased when the jurors believe that the information is inaccurate and irrelevant to the defendant (Golding, Fowler, Long, & Latta, 1990), such as if the jurors were told that the information actually referred to another person in a different case. Alternatively, if the jurors are suspicious of the source of the inadmissible evidence, it will not affect their decision making (Fein, McCloskey, & Tomlinson, 1997), such as when people are exposed to pretrial publicity that is damaging to the defendant and then later learn that this information was leaked by a source trying to unfairly discredit the defendant.

There are clear influences of inadmissible evidence on the decisions of individual jurors. When the evidence is deemed relevant and comes from a reliable source, people have a hard time forgetting it so that it does not influence their subsequent decisions. It is still in long-term memory and has an implicit effect on thinking. While this may sound depressing, the impact of this ineffective forgetting can be mediated or softened during the deliberation process where the jurors discuss the case with each other and come to a consensus about what verdict to render (London & Nunez, 2000). Here, the collective memory efforts of the jury help dampen the implicit influences of supposedly to-be-forgotten and inappropriate information. This information is so weak to begin with that it cannot compete with the stronger, explicit knowledge that is being openly discussed.

As a final point, it should be noted that not all inadmissible evidence comes from external sources. Sometimes it comes from the jurors themselves. When people think about events, they may think about the way things might have been different. This is called counterfactual thinking. When people engage in counterfactual thinking, they are likely to focus on behaviors that are outside of a person's normal routine. Jurors are more likely to award a victim a larger compensation if the defendant did something out of the ordinary because it is easier to imagine that person doing something different. However, if the victim did something outside of his or her normal routine, then the juries tended to award a smaller compensation. It is as if they are, in part, unconsciously blaming the victim. Moreover, the smaller people's working memory spans, the less likely they are to suppress these irrelevant thoughts when making these decisions (Goldinger, Kleider, Azuma, & Beike, 2003).

Synopsis

Memory is important for juries. Their decisions are influenced by the order in which information was encountered. Thus, there is a serial position curve influence in this real-world setting. Also, juries vary in their effectiveness at suppressing, or forgetting, inadmissible evidence. Even when they try to conform to instructions to disregard irrelevant information, decisions can be biased in the direction of the inappropriate information due to unconscious memory processes. Finally, the collective deliberation process can mitigate the distorting effects of memory.

SUMMARY

In this chapter we looked at how memory can influence on legal issues. Memory reports of eyewitnesses can be altered by how questions are worded or by being exposed to misinformation after the original event. These inaccurate memory reports reflect biases in how information is encoded or problems in the monitoring source information, and are less likely to involve an actual change or loss of the original memory. Eyewitness memory is further complicated by the influences of emotional arousal. In general, memory encoding becomes more selective and focused on a relatively few critical details at the high levels of arousal, such as when a weapon is present. However, it was also noted that although distortions in memory reports from witnesses can occur, as was seen with John Dean's memory of the Watergate scandal, the gist of eyewitness memory is fairly accurate. Also, unfortunately, it is difficult to detect discrepancies between an actual event and a person's memory based on the confidence of a witness. To get around such difficulties, the cognitive interview is available to help safeguard the investigative processes. Also, memory biases in eyewitness identification are known, and there was ways to better conduct identifications so that such errors do not complicate and damage the legal process. Finally, the influence of memory on juror decision making was considered. While jurors can forget information that was deemed inadmissible, this is less likely to be successful when the information is thought to be relevant. It was also noted that the jury deliberation process corrects for some of these memory biases.

STUDY QUESTIONS

1. How can an eyewitness's memory be altered by what he or she hears after witnessing an event?
2. What are some likely effects of misleading postevent information?
3. How does an eyewitness's arousal level at the time of an event affect memory? What theory best captures this?
4. How does the presence of a weapon during a crime affect memory?
5. What is the relationship between eyewitness confidence and accuracy? How can this be altered, and with what outcome?
6. How does the cognitive interview work to produce more accurate memory reports?
7. How is eyewitness identification affected by the use of mugshots? By different types of lineups? By things that are said by an investigator? By the presence of bystanders?
8. How does the order in which they hear things affect jurors' memories?

9. What happens in the memories of jurors when they are instructed to disregard inadmissible evidence? How does this influence their decision making?

KEY TERMS

cognitive interview, confidence, Easterbrook hypothesis, eyewitness testimony, lineup similarity, misleading postevent information, relative judgment principle, weapon focus effect, wording effects, unconscious transference, Yerkes-Dodson law

CHAPTER FOURTEEN

METAMEMORY

Much of how our memories affect thinking and behavior occurs out of conscious awareness. Still, we do have conscious insights. There are instances in which we are very much aware of our efforts to remember and, more painfully, instances when we fail to do so. To remember effectively, we need some conscious awareness and control of our own memories. This is **metamemory**—the awareness of one's own memory. This refers to both the contents of memory as well as how to control it. There are a number of ways to look at metamemory. First, we examine theories of metamemory, and then we look at a number of phenomena, including our ability to judge when we have learned something or whether we will later remember things that are currently forgotten. We also look at how we know that we *don't* know something. After this we look at issues involved in the phenomenology of memory, such as the experience of an act of remembering, and how what we currently know biases what we remember of the past. After this we address the monitoring and control of one's own memory with prospective memory, which is remembering to do things in the future, and directed forgetting. Finally, we look at how to use what we know about our own memory to improve it, including the use of mnemonics and some people who have exceptional memories.

GENERAL PROPERTIES AND THEORIES OF METAMEMORY

Before addressing various aspects of metamemory, let's go over the difference between cues and targets. Then we'll look at some theories on how metamemory judgments are made—namely, the cue familiarity, accessibility, and competition hypotheses.

Cues and Targets

As a point of terminology, the memory traces that people make judgments about are called *targets*, and the questions or prompts are called *cues*. So, if someone were to ask you if you remember your 13th birthday, the memory for the birthday would be the target, and the question would be the cue.

In his review of metamemory, Schwartz (1994) outlined two types of information that are used to make judgments. Target-based sources are information from the memory trace about which the judgment is made, including information retrieved from memory, as well as the ease with which it is recovered. Target-based sources are especially important in judgments of learning. In comparison, cue-based sources are information gleaned from a memory cue, such as a question. Metamemory judgments are better in proportion to the familiarity of the cue information. For example, if someone asks you a question about a topic you are relatively familiar with, you are more inclined to say that you know the answer based on how familiar the information in the question is. Now, let's look at three general theories of metamemory.

Cue Familiarity Hypothesis

According to the **cue familiarity hypothesis** (Metcalfe, 2000; Reder, 1987), metamemory judgments are based on the familiarity of the information in a cue. The more familiar it is, the more likely people will judge that the knowledge is in memory. Imagine if someone asked you if you know your grandmother's maiden name. If you know a lot about your family, you might recognize this as a familiar topic and say to yourself, "This is something I know." However, if you are not all wrapped up in your family's history, you might recognize this as a topic you know little about and say to yourself, "I have no clue."

Accessibility Hypothesis

According to the **accessibility hypothesis** (Koriat, 1993, 1995), people infer what is in memory based on information at hand, including partial retrievals. Two sources of information are used to make these inferences. One is the amount of information activated when a judgment is made. The more that is activated, the more likely that the information is known. For example, if you can't think of someone's name, but you know what letter it begins with, how many syllables it has, and so on, then that is a lot of information, and you judge that the name is in memory. The other source of information is the intensity of the activated memory traces, including the ease of access, how specific the information is, and so on. The stronger the retrieved information, the more likely the knowledge is in memory. For example, if you are asked what your best friend's mother's maiden name was, a number of names might be activated in memory, but only very weakly. As a result, you decide that you do not know that. Comparing the cue familiarity and accessibility hypotheses, the first is more apt for metamemory decisions are made under time pressure; otherwise the second is more appropriate (Benjamin, 2005; Metcalfe & Finn, 2008b).

Competition Hypothesis

According to the **competition hypothesis** (Schreiber, 1998; Schreiber & Nelson, 1998), metamemory judgments are influenced by the number of memory trace competitors involved in retrieval. Metamemory judgments are greater with less competition. When only a few traces are involved, people can assume that the search process is fairly targeted and is likely to produce the desired information. In contrast, if a large number of traces are involved, then it is less likely that the knowledge is going to be retrieved. The more competition among the relevant traces, the more difficult retrieval will be.

Synopsis

There are a number of theories of metamemory. They suggest that decisions are based on the familiarity of the cues, on a partial memory search, or on how much interference is experienced.

KNOWING WHAT IS KNOWN

The first type of metamemory we tackle is how well people know their own memories, including assessments of how well information has been learned, whether information that has been forgotten is still known, and how we know that we don't know something.

Judgments of Learning

When learning, it is helpful to know how well new information is stored in memory. Information that is poorly learned should be studied more, and information that is well learned does not need much further study. Estimates people make for how well they have learned something are called **judgments of learning** (JOLs) (Arbuckle & Cuddy, 1969). Studies of JOLs have shown that they are between poor and horrible assessments of how much has actually been learned. The question is, why?

Theories of JOLs. One idea is the *inability hypothesis,* which states that JOLs are poor because people have little conscious awareness of their own mental processes (Nisbett & Wilson, 1977). We lack the ability to assess our own learning. An alternative is the *monitoring-retrieval hypothesis*, which states that JOLs are poor because people are assessing whether they can retrieve information. When JOLs are made soon after the information was encountered, that knowledge is still in working memory. As such, people think that the information is better learned than it actually is.

These theories were tested by Nelson and Dunlosky (1991; Dunlosky & Nelson, 1994; Scheck, Meeter, & Nelson, 2004). They elicited JOLs either immediately or after a delay. If the inability hypothesis is correct, then a delay should not matter. However, if the monitoring-retrieval hypothesis is correct, then after a delay, working memory will be cleared out, and people will depend more on long-term memory and judge their future performance more accurately. In one study (Dunlosky & Nelson, 1994), people learned a set of words either through rote rehearsal or by forming mental images. As discussed in Chapter 3, memory is better when people use imagery. As shown in Figure 14.1, when JOLs made immediately after studying showed little to no distinction between how well the information was actually learned. However, with a delay, the difference between the JOLs in these conditions was the same as that is revealed by actual memory performance (see Kimball & Metcalfe, 2003, for an explanation based on distributed practice).

These JOL improvements are consistent with Koriat's (1993) accessibility hypothesis. The low correspondence between immediate JOLs and later memory may be due to the mismatched conditions when a person is studying (the information is present) versus at test (the information is absent), making it difficult to predict future performance (Koriat & Bjork, 2006). JOLs are more accurate the closer the conditions at the time the judgments

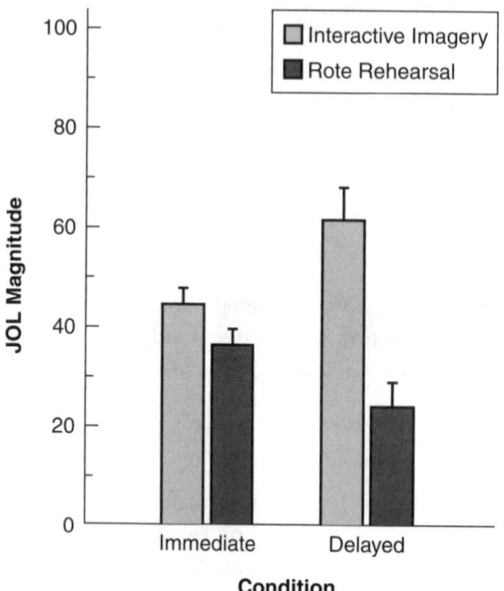

FIGURE 14.1 Judgments of Learning. Words were learned under imagery or rote memorization instructions, given either immediately or after a delay

Source: Reprinted from *Journal of Memory and Language,* 33, Dunlosky, J., & Nelson, T.O., Does the sensitivity of judgments of leanring (JOLs) to the effects of various activities depend on when the JOLs occur?, pp. 545–565, 1994, with permission from Elsevier.

are made to those at memory retrieval. When people can properly assess what is available in long-term memory, JOL estimates are more accurate.

JOL Cues. JOLs are affected by three types of cues: extrinsic, intrinsic, and mnemonic (Koriat, 1997). Extrinsic cues concern aspects of the learning situation, such as massed or distributed practice, or presentation times. People are not attuned to how external characteristics influence learning, and JOLs are not affected by extrinsic cues. Intrinsic cues are aspects of the material being learned, such as the perceived ease of learning each item. In contrast to extrinsic cues, JOLs are sensitive to intrinsic cues, in line with the cue familiarity hypothesis. Finally, mnemonic cues are memory-based sources of information, such as assessments of how a person has done on previous judgments. Over time, if people continue to make JOLs, they shift from using intrinsic cues to using mnemonic cues, in line with the accessibility hypothesis.

Additional information does not always improve JOLs. In some cases, JOLs can actually worsen. For example, multiple study–test cycles can worsen JOLs over time (Koriat, 2002). Declines in JOLs also occur when there is competition among memory traces. In the fan effect (see Chapter 7) retrieval is more difficult with an increased number of associations with a concept. This also lowers JOLs (McGuire & Maki, 2001). When additional memory traces compete with a desired memory trace, people judge that they do not know information, so JOL estimates are decreased. This is in line with the competition hypothesis.

Allocation of Study Time. Although JOLs can be inaccurate, people do have some sense of their own learning. These JOLs impact how people allocate their study time (Metcalfe & Finn, 2008a). Ideally, study time should maximize the amount of new knowledge that is learned. Spending all your time on material you know well is less effective. It may increase overlearning, but it does not help you learn new things.

Although people can allocate study time based on a goal to learn certain items over others (Ariel, Dunlosky, & Bailey, 2009), in general, they regulate study time based on how easy they think pieces of information are to learn. However, this allocation is not always effective. People may choose distributed practice for easy items and massed practice for hard items, which is ineffective (Son, 2004; but see Benjamin & Bird, 2006, for an alternative account). When people first encounter information, they tend to focus more effort on the difficult items, often using massed practice (and also gives the illusion of harder studying). Moreover, because these items are so difficult, people have trouble learning anything new. They spend most of their effort on things that are far from being learned. As a result, there is little gain of new knowledge. This is the **labor-in-vain effect** (Nelson & Leonesio, 1988).

However, the picture is not completely dismal. As people gain experience with the new material, study time allocation becomes more effective. People shift to spending more time on items that are just beyond their current ability level. This is called the *region of proximal learning* (Metcalfe, 2002, 2009; Metcalfe & Kornell, 2003). This method is more efficient because people spend less time on knowledge that is way beyond their ability, but focus on things that can help them ratchet up to the next level.

Feeling of Knowing

When you forget things, it does not always feel the same. Sometimes you don't know something and it seems like you never learned it. Other times, you don't know the answer, but you feel that it is somewhere in memory, and if you heard or saw it, you would be able to identify it. These forgetting differences are revealed by **feeling of knowing** (FOK) judgments (Hart, 1965).

To get FOK judgments, people are asked a series of moderately difficult questions, such as "Who was Richard Nixon's vice president before Gerald Ford?" Some things were never learned, but others were learned but are no longer prominent. After failing to recall an answer, people make an FOK judgment by rating how likely it was that they would identify the answer on a later recognition test. Then, at the end, people are given an actual recognition test to see how well their FOK judgments corresponded to actual memory. In general, FOK judgments are reasonable predictors of future memory, although there are some deviations (Hart, 1965).

According to the cue-familiarity hypothesis (Reder, 1987), FOK judgments are based on the familiarity of information in the question or cue. One way to test this is by using the "game show" method (Reder, 1987), in which people are given a question and then either answer it (control condition) or indicate that they know the answer (game show condition). This is called the game show method because it is like a game show in which the contestants are asked a question and the one who hits the buzzer first gets to answer. This technique reveals that people know whether they have information in memory before they actually retrieve it (Reder, 1987), as shown in Figure 14.2. Moreover, the rate at which people indicate that they know an answer is related to the familiarity of the information in the question and not necessarily what is in memory (Reder & Ritter, 1987). Similarly, people give higher FOK ratings to things they think they ought to know, rather than what they actually do know (Costermans, Lories, & Ansay, 1992). In general, FOK involved a controlled assessment of memory as people with frontal lobe damage are much less accurate on FOK tasks (Janowski, Shimamura, & Squire, 1989).

FOK judgments are related to how much partial information is retrieved (Koriat, 1993, 1995). Most of this partial bits are semantic attributes of what people are trying to remember (Koriat, Levy-Sadot, Edry, & de Marcas, 2003), such as failing to recall a name, but knowing that the person was a nineteenth-century composer who lived in Germany. However, metamemory judgments can be tricked. FOK increases when information is revealed slowly rather than presented all at once, showing a revelation effect (Chapter 12) (Young, Peynircioğlu, & Hohman, 2009). With a large amount of accurate partial information, there is a high correspondence between FOK ratings and future memory. However, if the partial information is incorrect, the correspondence is lower. This is why the overall relation between FOK ratings and actual memory is not ideal. Partial information also predicts whether what is eventually retrieved is "remembered" or is just "known" (Hicks & Marsh, 2002; see the remember-know section later in this chapter). A cue-familiarity account applies more to the early stages of the processing, which is related to "known" information. However, an accessibility account applies more to later stages, when cue familiarity is high and people have gone past the initial evaluation stage (Koriat & Levy-Sadot, 2001), which is related to "remembered" information. Finally, FOK judgments are affected by the number

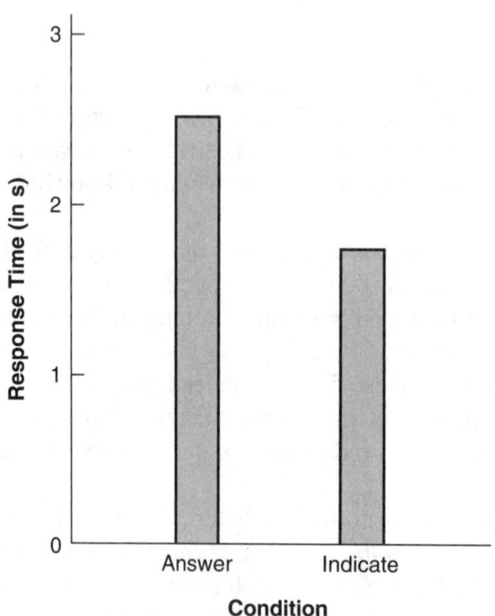

FIGURE 14.2 Difference in Response Times. People either had to answer a question (control) or indicate that they knew the answer (game show)

Source: Reprinted from *Cognitive Psychology,* 19, Reder, L.M., Strategy selection in question answering, pp. 90–138, 1987, with permission from Elsevier.

of competitors involved. If people are trying to remember something, FOK ratings are higher if it has a smaller set of competitors (Schreiber, 1998; Schreiber & Nelson, 1998), in line with the competition hypothesis.

Tip-of-the-Tongue State

A **tip-of-the-tongue (TOT) state** is when people fail to recall information but feel that they are about to retrieve it. It is on the tip of their tongues [Brown & McNeill, 1966; see Thompson, Emmorey, & Gollan, 2005 for an account of a tip-of-the-fingers (TOF) state for deaf signers]. This seems like a FOK judgment. However, a FOK judgment assesses whether a person thinks information can be remembered, whereas a TOT state indicates that remembering is imminent (Brown, 1991; Schwartz, 2001). Also, FOK and TOT judgments are differentially affected by a working memory load (e.g., remembering sets of digits), with FOK judgments increasing or unaffected, but TOT rates decreasing (Schwartz, 2008). With a higher working memory load, it is harder to evaluate partial information being retrieved for FOK judgments. However, TOT rates are lower because less partial information is retrieved into working memory because it is being blocked by the information that is being actively maintained as part of the dual task.

There are a number of characteristics of TOT states (Brown, 1991). First, people experience them about once a week on average. Second, there is often some information available. People typically can think of words that are similar to the one that is needed, either in terms of meaning, sound, or both. Third, people in a TOT state often have trouble with proper nouns, such as names. Fourth, people in a TOT state may be aware of the first letter or sound, and perhaps the last one as well, of the word, along with the number of syllables. Finally, the occurrence of TOT states is not related to feelings of stress or anxiety.

One theory of the TOT state is the *incomplete activation view* (e.g., Brown & McNeill, 1966). A TOT state occurs when the search range has not been sufficiently narrowed. There are too many possibilities, so the person cannot retrieve the desired word. Another theory is a *blocking view*, in which TOT states occur when related but inappropriate competitors are activated to a greater degree and block access to the appropriate information. These blocking memories, rather than the appropriate one, are being retrieved, making it harder to access the target memory. People keep retrieving the wrong one. Moreover, because these wrong traces have been retrieved recently, they are more available and so are more likely to be retrieved again. This starts a vicious cycle, resulting in the TOT state.

Knowing That You Don't Know

Sometimes we feel like we know something, even if we can't remember it at the moment. Other times, we know that we just **don't know** something. No matter how long we search, we know that the information can never be remembered. For example, if I asked you "When was the city of Lakewood, Ohio, founded?," "Is *scissel* a word?," or "Does President Obama use an electric toothbrush?," most of you know immediately that you do not know the answer. What is interesting about these "don't know" judgments is that people make them as rapidly, if not more rapidly, as they do about knowledge that is actually in memory (Kolers & Palef, 1976). Why does this occur?

Feeling that you don't know something is different from feeling that you do know something (Liu, Su, Xu, & Chan, 2007).When people are asked about very unfamiliar topics, they can rapidly make a judgment based on the information in the question, consistent with the cue-familiarity hypothesis (Reder, 1987). For a question with very unfamiliar information, because memory retrieval does not get very far in starting, people can quickly identify the information as unknown.

In support of this, in a study by Glucksberg and McCloskey (1981), people first explicitly learned that they did not know certain items, such as "It is unknown whether John has a pencil" (*explicit don't know*) along with items that were known, such as "John has a shovel" (*true*) and "John does not have a chair" (*false*). After learning, people made "yes," "no," and "don't know" responses to these items, as well as to new items that they would not have known about. People were slower and less accurate in saying that they did not know something if they had previously learned that they did not know it than if they had never studied it (see Figure 14.3). Thus, by having something in memory for the "don't know" facts that were learned, there is now something for memory to access, so retrieval time slows down. However, when nothing was learned, there is nothing in memory, so rapid "don't know" responses are made.

Finally, when asked questions about things people don't have in memory, if the information is distinctive, it will not make contact with many memory traces. This is a failure to retrieve any information in a very short period of time. Based on this lack

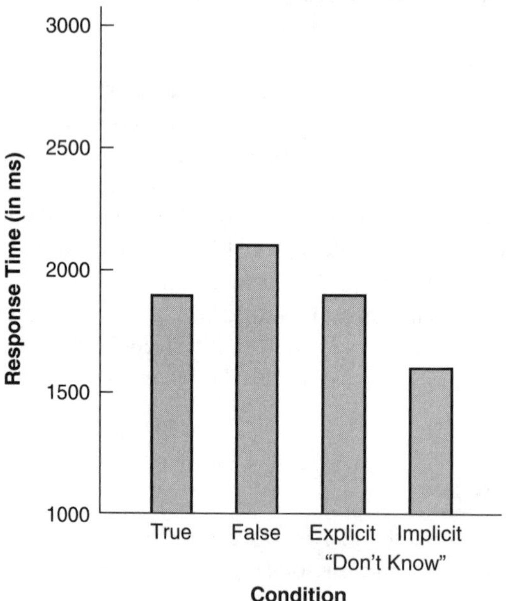

FIGURE 14.3 Difference in Response Times. Questions were true, false, or unknown. "Don't know" responses were for facts that were either learned earlier as "don't know" (explicit) or not (implicit)

Source: Glucksberg, S., & McCloskey, M. (1981). Decisions about ignorance: knowing that you don't know. *Journal of Experimental Psychology: Human Learning and Memory, 7,* 311–325.

of retrieval, a person can judge that the information is not known (Ghetti, 2003), consistent with the accessibility hypothesis.

Synopsis

Judgments of learning are important for learning. Unfortunately, the relationship between JOLs and later accuracy is often low. Part of this is because people make JOLs before clearing out what is in working memory. People use their JOLs to manage their study time in inefficient ways and may spend too much effort studying things that are too hard. With more experience, however, a person learns to use what is already known as a springboard for learning new things. When people forget something, they can estimate whether they know it, even if it is not currently available, as with feeling-of-knowing judgments. These judgments are fairly accurate, but not perfect. FOK judgments are based on either partial information or an assessment of the familiarity of a cue. When remembering seems imminent, it is a tip-of-the-tongue state. FOK inaccuracies often occur because the information is in a domain that the person has substantial knowledge of, so they inappropriately judge that the item is known, or because it is in a domain that they have little knowledge of, so they judge that it is not known. Finally, when there is no information in memory, people can quickly say that they do not know something.

MEMORY PHENOMENOLOGY

In this section we look at the phenomenology or conscious experience of remembering. We first look at the difference between conscious and unconscious memories as outlined by the remember-know distinction. Then we cover how errors in recollection lead us to misunderstand what we were like in the past, as with the hindsight bias.

Remember Versus Know

At this point let's consider where people rate the quality of what they do remember by making a **remember-know judgment** (Gardiner, 1988; Tulving, 1985b). If the remembering is accompanied by a conscious recollection of the circumstances in which the information was learned, this is a "remember" experience (although Rubin, Schrauf, & Greenberg, 2003, suggest that "remember" responses reflect a *belief* that an event occurred). In contrast, if people do not consciously recollect but only have a feeling of familiarity, this is a "know" experience. This distinction between "remember" and "know" parallels issues discussed in Chapters 6 and 10, such as the difference between autonoetic (remember) and noetic and anoetic (know) knowledge in Tulving's (1985b) Triarchic Theory, and the dual trace models of memory.

The "Remember" and "Know" Distinction. A great deal of research has been done on the remember-know distinction (Gardner & Java, 1990, 1991; Gardiner & Parkin, 1990) and how it reflects memory processes and experience (summarized by Gardiner & Java, 1993, and Gardiner & Richardson-Klavehn, 2000). "Remember" and "know" responses reflect distinct qualities of memory (Dudukovic & Knowlton, 2006). Research has shown a double dissociation between these types of responses, such that things that affect one type of response do not affect the other, and vice versa. Thus, remembering and knowing reflect different ways of using memory and are not just after-the-fact labels that people apply to their experiences.

"Remember" but not "know" responses are affected by depth of processing, generation effects, frequency of occurrence, divided attention at learning, the retention interval (if less than a day), reading silently or aloud, intentional versus incidental learning, serial position, and external context (Gruppuso, Lindsay, & Masson, 2007). As an example, if you read something aloud, you are more likely to have a "remember" experience than if you read it silently. However, the probability of giving a "know" judgment would be the same, regardless of how you read the text.

In contrast, "know" but not "remember" responses are affected by repetition priming, stimulus modality (e.g., visual or auditory), amount of maintenance rehearsal, and suppression of focal attention. For example, if you engage in maintenance rehearsal and repeat a word over and over, this does not alter the degree that you later recollect it. However, you are more likely to say that you "know" that you learned it.

Also, "remember" and "know" responses can both affect but in opposite ways, such as "remember" responses being more common and "know" responses being rarer. Cases of this type are word versus nonword memory, massed versus distributed practice, gradual versus abrupt presentations, and learning that emphasizes similarities or differences (e.g., Cook, Marsh, & Hicks, 2006a,b). For example, with massed practice, "remember" responses are less likely and "know" responses are more likely.

These "remember" and "know" metamemory responses correspond to memory differences. For example, "remember" responses correspond to knowledge-based, conceptually driven processing, and "know" responses correspond to perceptually based, data-driven processing (Rajaram, 1993). This distinction is also supported neurologically. For example, relative to "know" responses, "remember" responses involve greater parietal lobe activity (Curran, 2000; Wilding, 2000), greater EEG activity (Burgess & Ali, 2002), and more hippocampus activity, whereas "know" responses reflect more parahippocampus (around the hipposcampus) activity (Meeter, Myers, & Gluck, 2005).

This "remember" and "know" distinction reveals differences between expert's and novice's memories. The influence of prior knowledge, such as schemas, on retrieval is often observed with recall but less frequently with recognition. Experts almost always recall more accurately than novices, but these two groups do not differ on recognition tests. This is related to the fact that experts are more likely to give "remember" reports, whereas novices are more likely to just say that they "know" it. In a study at the University of California, Davis, Long, and Prat (2002) had students read stories based on the television series *Star Trek*. Some of the students were experts (people who watch the show a lot), and some were novices (people who watched the show only occasionally). The two groups performed similarly on a recognition test of the stories. However, the experts were more likely to report that they remembered reading the items, whereas the novices were more likely to say that they knew it. The experts' prior knowledge allowed them to spend more time making inferences and elaborating on the memory traces they were creating, which made it more likely that they would have an experience of remembering it.

Hindsight Bias

One characteristic of human thought is that people tend to think of events as being more deterministic after the fact. This is the **hindsight bias,** and this increased deterministic thought is called "creeping determinism" (Fischhoff, 1975). For memory, the hindsight bias is seen when people misremember their mental state as being different from what it really was and being more like their current knowledge state.

In a study by Safer, Bonanno, and Field (2001), bereaved spouses rated their grief 6 months after the death and then 4 1/2 years later. At the second rating, people also rated how much grief they felt at the 6-month period. Although most people said they felt more grief at the 6-month period, their memory of their experience was positively related to their current level of grief. Thus, they misremembered their emotional states in hindsight based on their current state (see also Levine et al., 2001).

Other examples of the hindsight bias are memories for people's predictions of outcomes of the Rodney King civil rights trial (Gilbertson, Dietrich, Olson, & Guenther, 1994), the Clarence Thomas Supreme Court Justice confirmation vote (Dietrich & Olson, 1993), the probability of a medical diagnoses being correct (Arkes, Wortman, Saville, & Harkness, 1981; Detmer, Fryback, & Gasser, 1978), the results of political elections (Blank, Fischer, & Erdfelder, 2003; Leary, 1982; Powell, 1988), the outcome of sporting events (Leary, 1981), the inevitability of a work layoff (Mark & Mellor, 1991), and memory for faces (Harley, Carlsen, & Loftus, 2004). This reinforces the point that our memory is in a constant state of flux and that what we currently remember is in part due to our experiences and current state.

The hindsight bias also applies to romantic relationships. People's relationship memories are biased in the direction of their current opinion. People who are pleased remember events more positively than people who are unhappy (McFarland & Ross, 1987). Moreover, even when relationship satisfaction is constant, people misremember it as improving over time (Sprecher, 1999). This leads to an unusual idea that people in satisfactory relationships, even for marriages over 20 years, are biased to remember the past as worse than it was, although they remember the relationship positively overall. This bias is a trick that makes the relationship seem to be improving more than it actually is (Karney & Coombs, 2000). So, people have a more positive attitude toward their relationship than if memory were accurate.

The hindsight bias is driven by a need to reconcile one's current view with memory for the past. For example, people show a larger hindsight bias when outcome information is surprising than if it is more congruent with what one knows (Ash, 2009). The act of trying to make sense of a surprising outcome leads people to think more about the information, reconciling it with what is already known, thereby leading to the false impression that the information was better known than it actually was.

The Knew-It-All-Along Effect. A variant of the hindsight bias is the **knew-it-all-along effect** (Fischhoff, 1977; Wood, 1978) in which people evaluate information in some way at Stage 1—for example, judging whether a series of statements are true or false, such as "Lhasa is the capital of Nepal." Then, at Stage 2, people are given feedback about the information encountered at Stage 1, such as learning that Kathmandu is the capital of Nepal. This feedback is likely to be knowledge that the person did not have at Stage 1.

Finally, in Stage 3, people indicate their memory for what they knew at Stage 1. Compared to people who got no feedback at Stage 2, metamemory reports of prior knowledge are biased toward the information learned during Stage 2. After Stage 2, people have a hard time remembering what it was like not knowing something, as if they knew it all along.

The knew-it-all-along effect can be reversed if the more recent learning is discredited in some way. For example, if you didn't know the capital of Nepal originally, were then told the capital name, you might show a knew-it-all-along effect and state that you knew this information before. However, if you were then told that this information was wrong, this would reverse the bias, and there would be a more accurate assessment of what was and was not known (Erdfelder & Bechner, 1998; see also Hasher, Attig, & Alba, 1981). A similar knew-it-all-along effect reduction can occur if people retrieve information that was only recently learned, rather than what they remember knowing before the new knowledge (Begg et al., 1996). People who monitor source information are better able to assess whether knowledge is recent. Just encouraging people to try harder has no influence (Fischhoff, 1977). Asking people to try to remember something, even after it becomes hard to think of other alternatives, may increase the potency of a hindsight bias because additional retrieval attempts make the outcome seem more like it was known (Sanna & Schwartz, 2004; Sanna, Schwartz, & Small, 2002).

In general, it is difficult for us to remember what it was like when we did not know something. College professors are no exception. If you have ever felt that one of your instructors was talking over your head, it may not be because he or she was arrogant, or uncaring. The problem may have been that, because of the knew-it-all-along effect, he or she was having trouble remembering what it was like to learn the course material for the first time.

Remembering Forgetting. Another illustration of the hindsight bias is people's memories for their own memory. Specifically, how well do people remember whether they had remembered or forgotten something previously? In a study by Joslyn, Loftus, McNoughton, and Powers (2001), people were tested 1 day and 6 weeks after originally learning information. At the 6-week session, people were also asked whether they had remembered or forgotten specific items at the first session. People were more accurate at remembering their previous memory successes but were less accurate at remembering their previous instances of forgetting. About half the time a person had originally forgotten an item, it was later reported that it had been remembered. Thus, there is a metamemory bias to think that we have better memories than we do.

Remembering Beliefs. Memory can be affected more globally as well. In a study by Winkielman and Schwartz (2001), some people were told that sad events fade quicker from memory, whereas others were told that happy events fade quicker. People who were told that sad memories are forgotten quicker were more likely to rate their childhood as less happy, especially following a difficult autobiographical memory task. It is as if people think that if they have forgotten many sad memories, then their childhood must have been less happy than they would have otherwise rated it.

Another influence of beliefs on memory and the hindsight bias, people misremember their features of options to be more consistent with their own choices (Henkel & Mather, 2007). For example, people might be given descriptions of both positive and negative features of cars (e.g., comfortable seats, good handling, has dents, not much trunk space) and are then asked to choose which car they prefer. Later, when those people are asked to assign the various features to the original choices, they are more likely to misremember the positive features as being ones for the choice they selected, and the negative features for the choice they did not select. So, people show a memory bias to think that things that are consistent with their own beliefs have more positive and fewer negative characteristics than they actually do.

Synopsis

Remembering is accompanied by different conscious experiences, as seen with the difference between "remember" responses (associated with conscious recollection) and "know" responses (associated with unconscious feelings of familiarity). This distinction is supported by neurological and behavioral dissociations. Metamemory awareness sometimes leads people astray, as with the hindsight bias. Essentially, people assess the past in a way that is more consistent with the present.

MEMORY MONITORING AND CONTROL

In this section we look at the conscious monitoring and control of memory. This involves how we use our memories to remember to do something in the future, which is called prospective memory. In addition we look at the ability to consciously remove information from memory through the direct forgetting procedure.

Prospective Memory

Prospective memory is used to remember to do things in the future (Loftus, 1971). Remembering to give your roommate a message or take the pizza out of the oven in 20 minutes are both examples of prospective memory. This is in contrast to **retrospective memory**, or memory for things learned in the past. Prospective memory is covered in this section on metamemory because one must monitor one's own memory to know when some action is to be taken in the future. Like other memory monitoring abilities, this is disrupted by damage to the frontal lobes (Burgess & Shallice, 1997; Cockburn, 1995).

Prospective memory has been tested in a number of ways. Some of these are naturalistic, such as having people remember to make a call at certain times (West, 1988). Others are laboratory-based, such as having people press a button when they see a certain word (Einstein & McDaniel, 1990) or after a certain amount of time has elapsed. This gives the researcher more control over what people use to help them remember. For example, in naturalistic studies, people could write reminders on a calendar or a sticky note.

Components of Prospective Memory. There are many differences between prospective and retrospective memory. For example, as we will see in Chapter 15, while aging has a profound effect on retrospective memory, the changes to prospective memory are more subtle (Burgess & Shallice, 1997; Einstein & McDaniel, 1990). In general, prospective memory performance has relation to retrospective memory performance on tasks such as recall and recognition.

Prospective memory involves several components: (1) monitoring the environment for a cue to do something, (2) remembering what to do in the future, (3) retrieving the memory of what to do, and (4) actually doing it. Number 2 is similar to retrospective memory. Thus, prospective memory depends on retrospective memory, not vice-versa. The other parts are unique to prospective memory. The monitoring the environment for a cue to remember is an element that is absent in retrospective memory. This is supported by neurological findings, such as an MEG study by Martin et al. (2007) that revealed that prospective memory monitoring involved activation of posterior parietal lobe areas, whereas the later remembering of what to do involved activation of the hippocampus, similar to a retrospective memory task. This constant monitoring of the environment comes at a cost as people then have fewer memory resources for other tasks, especially if they have a relatively large number of things that they need to remember to do (Cohen, Jaudas, & Gollwitzer, 2008; Hicks, Marsh & Cook, 2005). So, when you have a lot to do, you are more likely to make a prospective memory error, and forget to do something.

The importance of control over memory in prospective memory is evidenced by the link with the frontal lobes and conscious awareness. Prospective memory requires some conscious control of thought, and so people are more aware of their prospective than their retrospective memory errors. People who complain about memory problems are more likely to have prospective memory problems (Mäntylä, 2003).

Types of Prospective Memory. There are two types of prospective memory: event based and time based (Einstein & McDaniel, 1990). Event-based prospective memory occurs when people need to remember to do something when some event occurs—for example, remembering to give a person a message when you see him or her. Event-based prospective memories differ from retrospective memories in that while increased retention intervals make retrospective memory worse (the forgetting curve), prospective memory actually may get better (Hicks, Marsh, & Russell, 2000). This may be because, as time passes, people repeatedly remind themselves of what they need to do, thereby improving their performance.

Event-based prospective memory is complicated. It can be influenced by the relation between the event that is supposed to signal people to remember and the action that is to be done (McDaniel, Guynn, Einstein, & Breneiser, 2004). When the event and the action are semantically related (e.g., write down the word "needle" when you hear the word "thread"), prospective memory is more automatic and is less influenced by divided attention. However, if the event and action are not related (e.g., write down the word "needle" when you hear the word "parasol"), prospective memory is more deliberative and is more disrupted by divided attention. Event-based prospective memory is also more difficult when there are multiple cues as opposed to one, and even more difficult if these cues are unrelated to one another (Marsh et al., 2003). In essence, as attention is drawn further away from the prospective memory task by different things in the environment, memory worsens. Event-based prospective memory can be improved if a person makes a clear public statement of the intention to do something in the future (McDaniel, Howard, & Butler, 2008). This may be driven by a desire to fulfill social commitments and be viewed positively by others, thereby giving the prospective memory task higher priority in cognition, making it more likely to be done.

Time-based prospective memory occurs when people need to remember to do something at a certain time or after a certain time interval. Remembering to call home on

Mother's Day or to take another pill in 4 hours are examples of time-based prospective memory. Time-based prospective memory is harder than event-based (Einstein et al., 1995) because with event-based prospective memory, there is something in the environment to remind the person. With time-based prospective memory, it is up to the person alone. We can improve time-based prospective memory by making it more event based. For example, you could set a timer and wait for it to go off (an event) to remind you to take your pill.

With time-based prospective memory, people make more errors if the tasks are repetitive—for example, taking medications after certain time intervals. The more a person has done the task, the more likely an error will be made and the person will forget. Part of what is going on is that source monitoring errors occur, which then cause problems with prospective memory (Einstein, McDaniel, Smith, & Shaw, 1998; Marsh, Hicks, Hancock, & Munsayac, 2002). For example, a person is confused and thinks he or she has just taken the medication, when in fact he or she is remembering another time that it was done. This is a case where doing something frequently actually makes memory worse, not better.

Directed Forgetting

Most of the metamemory topics covered here are about how people try to remember. However, there are times when we do not want to remember, and want to forget. An everyday example of this is if someone was telling you his or her phone number, and then realized he or she gave you the wrong one and said "Oh, wait, that's not the number, the number is . . ." Clearly you want to forget the incorrect number. This process is **directed forgetting** (Bjork, 1970; Geiselman, 1974), the metamemory action of removing information from memory. In an experiment people might be given a list of words, told to forget them, and then be asked to remember a new set of words. Here, memory for the to-be-remembered (TBR) words is the same as if the participant had never been given the to-be-forgotten (TBF) words (Epstein, Wilder, & Robertson, 1975). There is no proactive interference from the TBF words. This is the directed forgetting effect. Interestingly, information that precedes an instruction to forget may experience greater retroactive interference as the effects of the forgetting extend further back in time than it should (Sahakyan, 2004; see Delaney, Nghiem, & Waldum, 2009, for directed forgetting of information related to narrative characters).

Part of the explanation for directed forgetting is that people inhibit the irrelevant TBF memory traces (Bjork, 1989) to keep them out of the current stream of processing does not disrupt the practice of the TBR information (Basden, Basden, & Morales, 2003). This is also consistent with the finding that people with higher working memory spans are better at directed forgetting (Delaney & Sahakyan, 2007), and the idea that working memory span reflects the ability to effectively control mental processing.

This inhibition of the TBF information is pervasive. It occurs both for direct memory tests, like recognition and recall, and indirect tests, like word fragment completion and repetition priming (MacLeod, 1989; but see Racsmány & Conway, 2006, and Racsmány, Conway, Garab, & Nagmáté, 2008 for evidence that directed forgetting primary influences conscious "remember" not unconscious "know" responses, and does not disrupt semantic priming). For autobiographical memories its effectiveness is unrelated to emotional quality (Barnier et al., 2007). For enacted tasks (things that you do rather than only think of or watch somebody else do), it occurs although to not as great a degree for verbal information (Sahakyan & Foster, 2009). Moreover, inhibiting irrelevant memories is effortful, even if we are not aware of it. When people are disrupted by an unrelated secondary task, the inhibition of TBF items is reduced or eliminated (Conway et al., 2000).

Directed forgetting may not occur if people believe that the information they are told to forget will be relevant later (Golding, Fowler, Long, & Latta, 1990), or if the TBF information is meaningfully (semantically) related to TBR information (Golding, Long, & MacLeod, 1994). Presumably, the automatic priming of TBF items by TBR items keeps it from being effectively forgotten. Directed forgetting is also reduced if the TBF information is consistent with a person's beliefs. For example, during the 2003 Iraq war, misinformation was sometimes reported by news outlets, such as a report that Iraqi forces were executing coalition prisoners of war. After misinformation was denied or corrected by the news agencies, people who were more suspicious of the motives for the war were more successful at forgetting and discounting the misinformation than people for whom it was consistent with their beliefs about the reasons for the war (Lewandowsky, Stritzke, Oberauer, & Morales, 2005).

Synopsis

People need to know what to do in the future and when to do it. This is prospective memory. Although it shares some aspects with retrospective memory, it is also guided by some of its own processes. Prospective memory tasks can be either event based or time based. Event-based prospective memory is generally easier and may improve with the passage of time. In comparison, time-based prospective memory is harder and is more susceptible to source monitoring errors. With directed forgetting, people can exert conscious control over their memories by deliberately removing traces that are deemed to be irrelevant.

MNEMONICS

When we are aware of the limitations of our own memory, we can take steps to address this. One thing we can do is to use metamemory techniques, known as mnemonics. **Mnemonics** are mental or physical devices used to help people remember. There are a number of ready-made mnemonic devices that can be used as structured cue sets to help remember larger sets of information. One example is the *peg-word mnemonic*, in which people use a known sequence of items, or "pegs," on which to "hang" other pieces of information. For example, people might memorize the sequence "One is a bun, two is a shoe, three is a tree, (and so on)." This structure can then be used as a set of pegs for other information. For example, suppose you needed to go to the grocery store to buy onions, milk, and watermelon. You could use the peg word mnemonic by forming a mental image of sliced onions on a bun, a shoe full of milk, and watermelons hanging from a tree. When you get to the store, your sequence of pegs will help you remember the images you formed, which will help you remember what you need to buy.

Another common mnemonic is the *method of loci*. In this mnemonic a person first has a set of well-known locations. These can be rooms in a house, locations along a familiar path, and so on. A person then imagines things at each location. To use our grocery shopping example, a person might mentally place the onions in the living room, cartons of milk at the foot of the stairs, and watermelons in the dining room. Then, to remember, the person takes a little mental tour of his or her home.

Other mnemonics take advantage of the information itself. A *rhyming mnemonic* takes all the information and forms a rhyme from it. For example, "Thirty days hath September, April, June, and November" is a rhyming mnemonic for the number of days in the months. *Acronyms* are a mnemonic in which the first letters of phrase help people remember. For example, the word HOMES is an acronym for the names of the five great lakes: Huron, Ontario, Michigan, Erie, and Superior. Finally, *acrostics* are a mnemonic, in which the first letters of the items are used as the basis of forming some new memorable phrase. For example, the phrase "On Old Olympus' Towering Top, A Finn And German Vault And Hop" can be used to help a person remember the names of the twelve cranial nerves in their correct order: olfactory, optic, oculomotor, trochlear, trigemenal, abducens, facial, auditory, glossopharyngal, vagus, accessory, and hypoglossal (premed students take note!). Remembering the phrase provides the cues to the appropriate names as well as preserving the correct sequence of the information.

There are many mnemonics people can use. Sometimes a mnemonic is a simple cue, like tying a string around your finger. Other times, the structure of the mnemonic helps a person remember the information itself, such as the knuckle mnemonic, which is another way of remembering how many days there are in each month (see Figure 14.4) with the knuckles being the months with 31 days and the valleys standing for months with 30 days or fewer. Regardless of the specific mnemonic, in all cases, the ability to cue memory is at work, in much the same way as the other sorts of cues we've talked about (see Chapter 7).

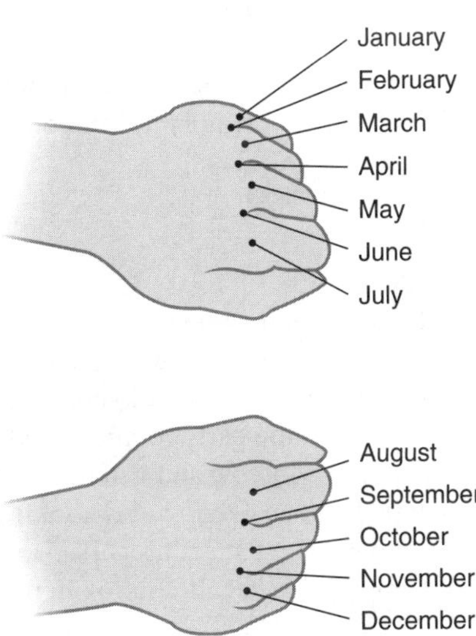

FIGURE 14.4 The Knuckle Mnemonic

Synopsis

People can use their metamemory knowledge to help them remember better, such as with mnemonics. Most mnemonics rely on some well-known or readily available, consistent structure that can then be used as a guide to help a person remember what they are interested in retrieving.

EXCEPTIONAL MEMORY

Having an awareness of one's own memory can help improve how it is used. Further improvements can occur as the range of knowledge is broadened. The more you know, the easier it is to remember because it is easier to organize and chunk information. Thus, expertise can cause a person to have what would otherwise seem an exceptional memory for certain types of information.

We saw some of this in Chapter 4 when discussing how to improve the capacity of short-term memory and still have 7 ± 2 chunks of information, as with the case of S. F., a runner who extended his digit span up to over 80 items (Ericsson, Chase, & Faloon, 1980). Another example of this is that taxi drivers' memories for street names are better than most people's. This superior memory is not due to their intelligence, but to both the large amount of knowledge they have about streets in their city and the highly organized way this information is represented. For taxi drivers, this information is chunked based on routes through the city (how they use this knowledge), rather than spatial proximity, semantic relatedness, or alphabetical order (Kalakoski & Saariluoma, 2001).

Other studies of exceptional memory are cases when the knowledge people are using is implicit. Speakers of tonal languages, such as Mandarin Chinese and Vietnamese, are better at memory for musical pitches and are more likely to have perfect pitch than speakers of nontonal languages, such as English (Deutsch, 2002). Because those languages place a greater demand on remembering pitch information, this knowledge can then be applied, at an unconscious level, to memory for the pitches of tones used in music.

Memorists

There are cases of people with exceptional memories, people are called mnemonists or **memorists.** We use the term *memorist* because they are not relying on mnemonics as described previously (Neisser, 1982). A well-known memorist was Solomon V. Shereshevsky, better known as S., who lived in the Soviet Union in the early to mid-twentieth century (Luria, 1968). S. worked as a newspaper reporter in Moscow and had the uncanny ability to accurately remembering large sets of details from an event without taking any notes. S. had a short-term memory span of over 70 items, with the additional amazing ability of recalling them in any order requested. He could also recall lists of items years after hearing them only once.

A major contributor to S.'s ability was the fact that he had synesthesia. This is a condition in which sensory qualities from different modalities intrude on one another.

For example, different sounds may also be experienced as colors. S. had a particularly strong case of this. This made his memory traces very rich and detailed, allowing them to endure, be highly structured in memory, and be recalled accurately. While S.'s condition allowed him to remember exceptionally large sets of items, there were some drawbacks. For one, because he was so dependent on sensory and perceptual qualities, he found it difficult to comprehend and think about abstract ideas.

Not all memorists have an unusual neurological condition. Let's look at three, who were all in the *Guinness Book of World Records* for reciting pi from memory. The first is Rajan Mahadevan (Biederman, Cooper, Fox, & Mahadevan, 1992; Thompson, Cowan, & Frieman, 1993; Thompson et al., 1991) who set the record on July 5, 1981 by reciting pi out to 31,811 digits in 3 hours and 49 minutes. His memory ability was first observed at the age of 5 when his parents hosted a dinner party for 50 people. To occupy himself, Rajan memorized, in just a few minutes, the license plate numbers of all of the guests' cars and then reported them to the guests. Rajan has a letter span of 13, a visual digit span of 28, and an auditory digit span of 43. One strategy he uses is keeping track of the position of an item in a sequence. The sequence, with its various positions, serves as a mnemonic encoding and retrieval device. When he makes errors, they are often for digits at adjoining locations. This use of position as a memory aid makes Rajan treat information differently. For example, when given a list of words, Rajan is less likely to use semantic relations to help him remember. His performance on more complex information, such as stories and spatial information, is well within the normal range. So, his exceptional memory is confined to digits and similar information. Rajan earned a master's degree in clinical psychology from the University of Mysore in 1986 and a master's degree in cognitive psychology from Kansas State University in 1991. While he had good memory for digits, he had normal memory for other types of information. He sometimes tried to extend his memorization approach to other types of information but not always with the same level of success. He had a tendency to memorize information from a text or lectures. However, as many professors will tell you, while memorization is important, what is as important is the ability to apply and use that knowledge.

The second memorist is Hideaki Tomoyori who set his record on March 9, 1987 by reciting pi out to 40,000 digits in 13 hours and 6 minutes (Takahashi, Shimizu, Saito, & Tomoyori, 2006). Tomoyori has good skills for memorizing long lists of numbers, but his memory for word lists and stories is no different than everyone else (Takahashi, et al., 2006). Tomoyori accomplished his task by using a digit-symbol mnemonic in which the Japanese symbols for digits were combined to form words, and then images. The digit symbol mnemonic is like assigning letters to numbers in English, (e.g., 1 = t, d or th; 2 = n; 3 = m; etc.). Thus, his approach was very different from Rajan's. He also had large, but not far from normal, digit spans of ten for auditory digits and eight for visual digits, and his word and story memories were not meaningfully different from standard controls. Thus, Tomoyori achieved his feat not through an inherent talent, but through the persistent application of a particular strategy and a lot of effort.

Tomoyori's record was bettered by Chao Lu, who, on November 20, 2005, recalled pi out to 67,890 digits in 24 hours and 4 minutes (Hu, Ericsson, Yang, & Lu, 2009). Lu did this by relying on the phonology, or word sounds, of the various digits to recode the information linguistically, much like Tomoyori, and then develop stories for himself out of this information. However, he also developed techniques based on the shapes of the characters for the digits and their meanings. Lu has a normal digit span of about nine digits. Overall, these three memorists accomplished similar tasks using different talents and strategies to achieve a similar effect.

Eidetic Imagery

Some people think they have photographic memories—the ability to use mental images in a way that resembles perceptually viewing an image. This is **eidetic imagery** (De Beni et al., 2007; Gray & Gummerman, 1975). Someone with this ability would have an extraordinary memory for information that was seen earlier, showing little to no distortion. In general, there is little support for the existence of eidetic imagery, and if it does exist it is very rare. For the most part, people who appear to have eidetic imagery are instead using other memory skills to a high degree. This is often restricted to a limited type of knowledge. If eidetic imagery does exist, it is present in some young children, but gradually disappears as a person ages (Haber, 1979), although there are reported exceptions (Stromeyer & Psotka, 1970).

Synopsis

Some people have exceptional memories. In some cases, this comes with expertise. More exceptional cases are memorists who have memory skills that seem to defy the imagination. Often these memorists have exceptional memory for certain types of information but normal memory for other types. Finally, there is little evidence to suggest that there is something akin to a photographic memory. People who make this claim often have special strategies for handling certain types of information, and do not have memories that are highly detailed visual representations of what was seen earlier.

SUMMARY

In this chapter we looked at metamemory, the awareness, monitoring, and control of one's own memory processes and content. There are a number of theories of metamemory. The cue-familiarity hypothesis focuses on the familiarity of external memory cues. The accessibility hypothesis focuses on information that is actually retrieved from memory. A number of metamemory processes were considered, including judgments of learning, feelings of knowing, and tip-of-the-tongue states. We have seen how one's current state of knowledge influences how we remember our own previous memories, as with the knew-it-all-along effect. We have also seen how memory can reach forward in time to allow us to plan and do things in the future (prospective memory). Many of these metamemory processes critically involve the frontal lobes, which control patterns of thinking in general. Finally, we discussed some mnemonic devices, as well as cases of people with exceptionally good memories, even if only for certain types of information. Being more accurately aware of your own memory abilities can serve you well.

STUDY QUESTIONS

1. What are the sources of information available to people when making metamemory judgments? How do these relate to the major theories of metamemory?
2. How accurate are judgments of learning and how are they made? What can be done to improve judgments of learning?
3. How effective are people at allocating their study time, and why? In what ways are people ineffective? What are more effective ways to allocate study time?
4. What are feeling-of-knowing judgments? When are they given? How accurate are they?
5. What is the difference between feeling-of-knowing judgments and the tip-of-the-tongue state? What are some of the unique characteristics of the tip-of-the-tongue state?
6. How do people assess that they do not know something?
7. What is the difference between "remember" and "know" responses?
8. What are the hindsight bias and the knew-it-all-along effect? How can they be avoided?
9. What are the types of prospective memory? What influences their effectiveness?
10. What is directed forgetting? How is it accomplished? How does deliberately forgotten information affect memories of other information?
11. What neurological structures are strongly associated with metamemory performance?
12. How do mnemonics work? What are some examples of mnemonics?
13. What are some of the ways that people can exhibit exceptional memory performance?

KEY TERMS

accessibility hypothesis, competition hypothesis, cue-familiarity hypothesis, directed forgetting, don't know, eidetic imagery, feeling of knowing, hindsight bias, judgments of learning, knew-it-all-along effect, labor-in-vain effect, memorists, metamemory, mnemonics, prospective memory, remember-know judgment, retrospective memory, tip-of-the-tongue (TOT) state

TRY IT OUT

An important feature of metamemory is the ability to exert some control over your own learning and memory. For this Try It Out section, two types of studies are outlined to illustrate this. These are tests of directed forgetting and mental imagery, and their influence on the ability to remember. Ideally you should have at least 16 participants for each of these tasks, with at least 16 people in each group if you vary things in your own experiment between groups.

- To assess the influence of **directed forgetting**, you should create a list of 30 words, divided into two lists of 15 words, such as five- to seven-letter two-syllable nouns. Read this list to two groups of people. For the first group (the control group), label the first list as "List A" and then read the words to them. In all cases, read the words at a rate of one word per second. When you get to the end of the first list say "O.K., try to remember List A. Now I am going to read you List B, which you also need to remember" or something similar. Then read them the second list. For the second group (the directed forgetting group), after you read the first list say "O.K., try to forget List A. Now I am going to read you List B, which you do need to remember" or something similar. At the end of the second list, have the people in both groups try to recall as many words from List B as they can. If all goes well, because of continued proactive interference, people in the control group should recall fewer List B words than the directed forgetting group. If you want, you can also then have people try to recall the List A words. People should recall fewer List A words in the directed forgetting group.
- Here is how you can show the effectiveness of **imagery** and **mnemonics** to improve memory (Neath, 1998). First, create a list of 40 concrete nouns (things like dog, house, rope, etc., and not truth, justice, or hope). Give people 20 random pairings of these words. Tell them that they will later need to be able to recall the second word when given the first. For one group of people (the control group) simply tell them to memorize the word pairs as efficiently as possible. For the second group (the imagery group) tell them to try to form a mental image in their mind that involves the two words represented as objects interacting in some way (they don't need to tell you what their images are). Give people in both groups 5 seconds per word pair during the study portion. Then, at the end of the study portion, give people the first words of each word pair and see if they can recall the second. You can do this by giving them a sheet of paper with the first words in a column and have them write down the other word next to the appropriate first word. If all goes well, people who use imagery as a mnemonic technique will remember more words than the control group.

CHAPTER FIFTEEN

MEMORY AND DEVELOPMENT

As we have seen repeatedly, memory is not stable and static. Our every experience alters our memories, making some things easier and some things harder to remember, distorting some things, and clarifying others. To further complicate this, people are in a constant state of development. These developmental changes have profound implications for how memory functions. This chapter examines some of the major issues in memory and development, but rather than covering the entire life span, we look at three regions of development and the major changes in memory that occur within them. These are infancy and childhood at one end and old age at the other. By looking at infancy and childhood, we can see how our memory and memory skills became more and more sophisticated and efficient. By looking at the effect of aging on memory, we can get some idea of how our own memories are going to change as we enter into old age, which usually means some decline in our memory abilities. However, as you will see, there are some things that remain the same, or even improve.

INFANCY

The development of memory begins as soon as the nervous system is capable of retaining information. However, not all types of memory are available at the same time or for the same reasons. Here we consider the very early memories of infants. We first consider issues about how to test preverbal humans to give you an idea of the challenges faced by memory researchers. After this we look at some findings for different types of memories and memory processes of infants (0–2 years of age).

Testing the Very Young

Testing infant memory is exceedingly difficult. The biggest challenge is that infants neither understand nor produce language, which is the medium of most studies of memory. Thus, researchers who study infant memory are immediately faced with the problem of how to study such nonverbal primates to provide meaningful information. A number of techniques have been created to do this (see also Rovee-Collier & Cuevas, 2009). Each of these methods uses something that is already available to the infant—that is, some activity that the infant already does. What the memory researcher does is look to see how this behavior changes as a function of whether something is remembered or not.

One way to study infants is to use a gaze duration/direction or **looking method** (Friedman, 1972). Infants spend a lot of time looking around the world in a constant effort to understand it. Infants spend more time looking at things that interest them, which are more likely to be new things than old things. In essence, things that are looked at less are things that are recognized, and thus are in memory. There is some evidence that increased looking times reflect an unconscious, implicit memory novelty preference than an explicit memory recognition of old items (Snyder, Blank, & Marsolek, 2008).

Another way to determine what infants remember is to use the infants' natural sucking behavior. Babies love to suck on things. This is important because it helps the infant to eat, but they also suck on lots of other things that do not provide any nutritional value, such as pacifiers. We can take advantage of **nonnutritive sucking** as a tool to study memory because the rate of sucking changes as a function of whether the infant is seeing or hearing something old (in memory) or new. This can be measured using high-tech pacifiers that record the sucking rate. When something is old, infants suck at a slower rate. However, when something new is introduced, infants suck faster (Cowan, Suomi, & Morae, 1982).

A third task that has been used is a **conjugate reinforcement** paradigm (Rovee-Collier & Fagan, 1981). With this technique, infants lay on their backs in a crib. One end of a ribbon is tied around one of the baby's ankles, and the other end is attached to a mobile. Whenever the baby kicks, the mobile moves, which is a very cool thing for infants. They soon pick up on the kicking–mobile movement relationship and spend a good deal of time kicking. Memory for this event can be tested by varying any number of things, such as the amount of time that has passed or the context that can serve as a cue.

Researchers have found that young children can recall information using techniques such as **elicited imitation** (Bauer, 1996, 2002). In these studies, an experimenter does some task, such as assembling a simple toy, while the child watches. Then after a delay, such as a month later, it is observed whether the child also does the task. This is evidence of recall because it requires the child to deliberately bring to mind a mental representation of the steps needed. It has been found that some form of memory recall begins in infants as young as 9 months and becomes stable by 2 years of age.

Memory and Infancy

Human memory is composed of several components that develop at different rates. This development is guided by neurological changes, as well as the acquisition of abilities that greatly increase memory, including the ability to crawl (around 9 months) and the acquisition of language (starting around 10 months and increasing rapidly from there) (Hayne & Simcock, 2009). Here, we look at different types of memory, and how they are progressing during infancy.

Different types of memory development are associated with various **neurological development** rates. For example, the thalamus and some medial temporal structures, which are important for more primitive types of memory, are nearly developed at birth, whereas the frontal lobes, which are important for controlling the flow of processing in memory are not completely functional until the age of 1 year or older (Chugani, Phelps, & Mazziotta, 1986). The prefrontal cortex and hippocampus continue to develop through infancy and into childhood (Bauer, 2007). Importantly, there is a slow development of the dentate gyrus, the part of the hippocampus that receives information from other parts of the brain. So, because the hippocampus is important to memory, if neural signals are not effectively getting into it, then declarative memories are not going to be as reliable as they are in adults. Thus, infant memory abilities are, to some degree, influenced by the readiness of their nervous systems.

It is clear that infants have various forms of **nondeclarative memory**, such as the ability to learn new motor skills, associate the sights and sounds of their parents with care and comfort, and acquire a large array of unconscious influences on behavior. Almost immediately, people start developing skills to help their children get along in the world (e.g., teaching them to eat). Thus, implicit memory is well on its way at an early age. There is even evidence that infants prefer familiar sounds that they heard while in the womb, such as the sound of their mother's voice. Although nondeclarative memory is present at birth, if not before, it still must also go through a period of development (Rovee-Collier, 1997).

Complex forms of **episodic memory** are present in even at very young ages. For instance, using the conjugate reinforcement paradigm, it has been found that even 3-month-old infants remember to kick 5 days later (Butler & Rovee-Collier, 1989; see also Cuevas, Rovee-Collier, & Learmonth, 2006). This is episodic memory, because the kicking is context dependent. When the crib liner is the same during the second session as it was during the first, the kicking rate is higher when compared to the usage of a different liner. The crib liner is an episodic memory retrieval cue (see Chapter 7).

The ability to explicitly remember information over long periods increases in accuracy and duration as the infant matures. For example, using the elicited imitation paradigm, Carver and Bauer (2001) have found that 9-month-old infants can remember and reproduce a previously viewed action up to 4 weeks later. In contrast, 10-month-old infants are able to reproduce the action up to 6 months later. The pattern of forgetting curves for infants from 2 to 18 months of age in a variety of tasks is shown in Figure 15.1 (Hartshorn et al., 1998), and the pattern of retention durations is shown in Figure 15.2 (Bauer, 2007). This remembering is even evidenced in ERP recordings (Bauer et al., 2003).

Infant **semantic memory** is advanced enough to abstract away from the original information (Mandler, 1988), although early schemas are grounded in perceptual experience (Mandler, 1992). Infants also appear to create and use categories. As early as 3 or 4 months, they make basic-level category distinctions, such as dogs and cats (Eimas & Quinn, 1994; Quinn, Eimas, & Rosenkrantz, 1993), and subordinate category distinctions by 6 or 7 months (Quinn & Tanaka, 2007). However, it isn't until about 14 months that infants make distinctions based on superordinate category relations, such as knowing that "drinking" and "sleeping" belong to the superordinate category of "animals" and that "needs keys" and "giving a ride" belong to the superordinate category of "vehicles" (Mandler, Fivush, & Reznick, 1987; Mandler & McDonough, 1996). Knowledge of finer basic level categories remains elusive until over 2 years old (Mandler, Bauer, & McDonough, 1991).

Semantic memory also involves the identification of drawings and pictures. To do this, one must match a more abstract picture with a memory of a real object, which is not as simple as it sounds. To test this ability, Hochberg and Brooks (1962) raised a child from birth to age 19 months in an environment in which objects in pictures were never named

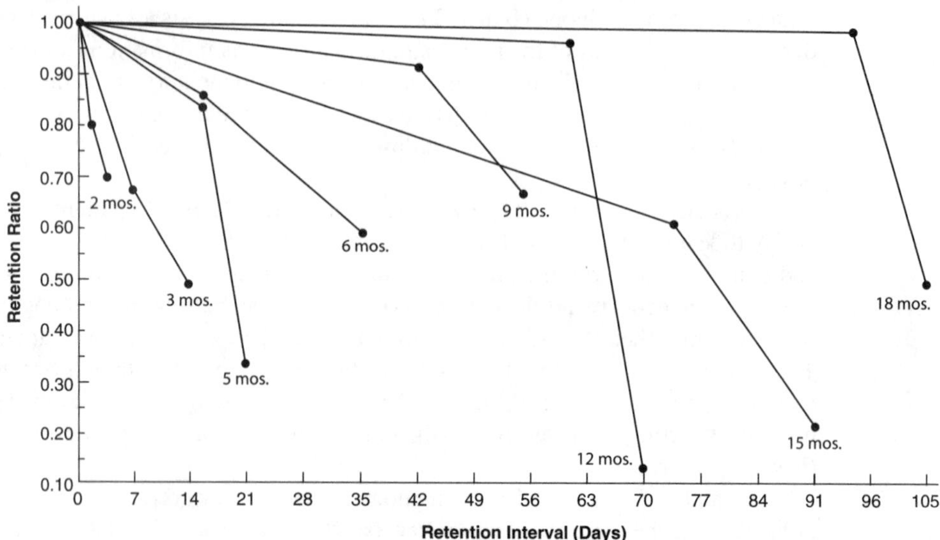

FIGURE 15.1 Forgetting Curves for Children 2 to 18 months Old from a Number of Studies

Source: Hartshorn, K., Rovee-Collier, C., Gerhardstein, P., Bhatt, R. S., Wondoloski, T. L., Klein, P., Gilch, J., Wurtzel, N., & Campos-de-Carvalho, M. (1998). The ontogeny of long-term memory over the first year-and-a-half of life. *Developmental Psychobiology, 32,* 69–89.

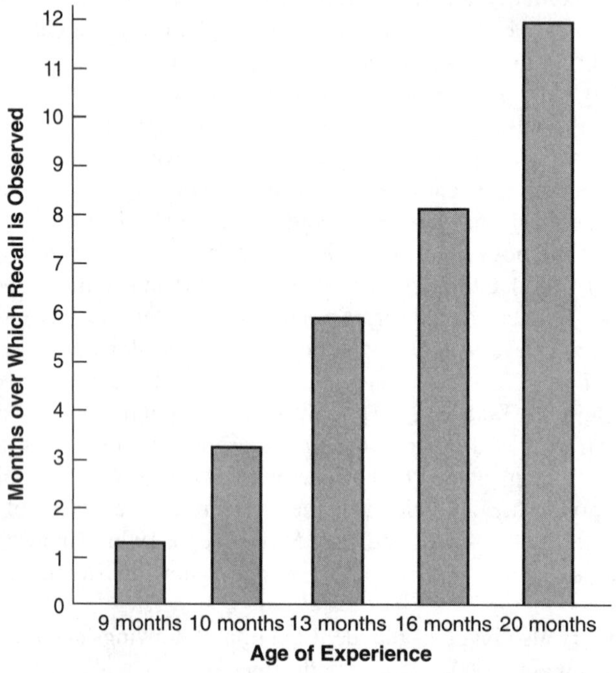

FIGURE 15.2 Recall Intervals for Children 9 to 20 Months Old from a Number of Studies

Source: Bauer, P. J. (2007). Recall in infancy. *Current Directions in Psychological Science, 16,* 142–146.

and where pictures were relatively unavailable, to the point of not letting the child see picture books and removing labels from baby food jars. Despite this, at 19 months, the child was able to identify pictures and drawings with no problem.

Synopsis

To test infants, researchers have derived some clever methods. These include the looking method, nonnutritive sucking, conjugate reinforcement, and elicited imitation. Using these methods, it has been found that infants have developed a variety of nondeclarative, episodic, and semantic memories. The lag in development of these memories can be attributed, in part, to the developmental trajectories of neurological structures such as the frontal lobes and hippocampus.

CHILDHOOD

As a person leaves infancy and moves into childhood, memory continues to develop and progress. For our purposes, childhood is that period of time from ages 2 to 17, although much of what we have to say here applies to children under the age of 12. During this time the nervous system continues to develop well until a person reaches early adulthood. These changes, of course, influence memory. For example, the speed with which children can execute memory processing increases exponentially until the mid to late teens (Kail, 1991). The nervous system becomes much more efficient.

Memory and Childhood

As a person progresses through childhood, neurological development continues. The dentate gyrus of the hippocampus continues its progress toward adult levels until the age of 5. Moreover, there is a pruning of neural connections, with adults having fewer connections than children, although there is an overall increase in brain size (Bauer, 2009).

Although the sensory registers are well developed by childhood (Engle, Fidler, & Reynolds, 1981), the ability to use **short-term working memory** consistently improves. For instance, there is an increase in the rate and effectiveness of rehearsing information to keep it in memory (Flavell, Beach, & Chinsky, 1966). There is a consistent increase in the amount of information that is being rehearsed (Case, 1972; Ornstein, Naus, & Liberty, 1975)—that is, memory span is getting larger. With the larger memory span, overall performance increases. Another factor is the speed with which children articulate information. As a reminder, the word length effect is the finding that people remember fewer words as their articulation length increases. This is because longer words are more likely to decay in the phonological loop (see Chapter 5). As children age, they can pronounce words more quickly. This increased speech rate results in older children having larger memory spans (Hulme, Thomson, Muir, & Lawrence, 1984). This relation between rehearsal speed and span is shown in Figure 15.3.

Another factor that influences working memory is a child's interests. A study by Lindberg (1980) showed that when children were given words pertaining to topics that interested them, such as the names of cartoon characters, memory spans improved to

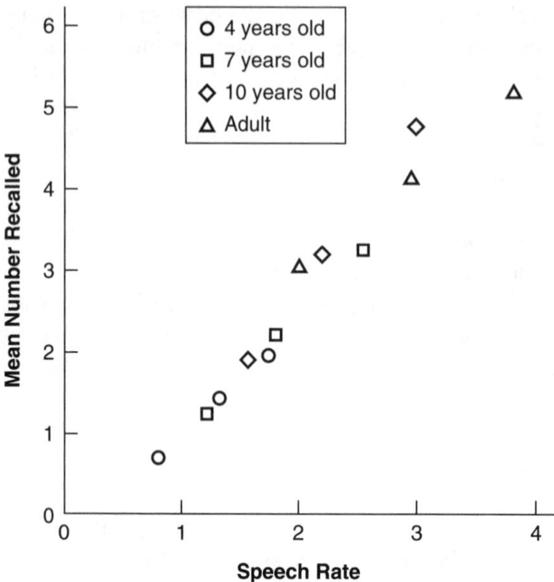

FIGURE 15.3 Relation between Person's Speech Rate and Working Memory Span Scores Broken Down by Different Age Groups

Source: Hulme, C., Thomson, N., Muir, C., & Lawrence, A. (1984). Speech rate and the development of short-term memory span. *Journal of Experimental Child Psychology, 38,* 241–253.

that of a college student, but college students' memories were better for categorized lists of words, as shown in Figure 15.4. In other words, the ability to remember a set of words is at least partially a function of the person's knowledge base. If a set of items is drawn from a child's knowledge base, his or her performance is much better.

Another thing that contributes to increased working memory capacity is an increase in processing speed (Kail, 1991) and this influences both verbal and visual-spatial working memory (Kail, 1997). As children increase the speed with which they process information, they maintain information more effectively for whatever memory process is operating.

In childhood there is an increase in the degree of information structure and organization, and this is reflected in **episodic memory** retrieval success (Bjorklund & Zeman, 1982). For example, when remembering furniture at home, younger children (around age 10) tend to organize memory based on furniture category (e.g., chairs, tables, etc.), whereas by age 16 children have switched over to organizing around spatial categories (e.g., living room, dining room, etc.) (Plumert, 1994). At retrieval, children show similar interference effects, such as a fan effect, as adults, and they can also organize information to eliminate that interference (Gómez-Ariza & Bajo, 2003). Moreover, inhibition appears to be helping children to the same degree as adults, and children show repeated practice and part-set cuing effects that are similar to those of adults (Zellner & Bäuml, 2005).

As children acquire more knowledge about the world, **semantic memory** becomes more complex. At young ages, a child can have a complex semantic network of a particular domain. For example, the portion of a 4 1/2-year-old boy's semantic knowledge

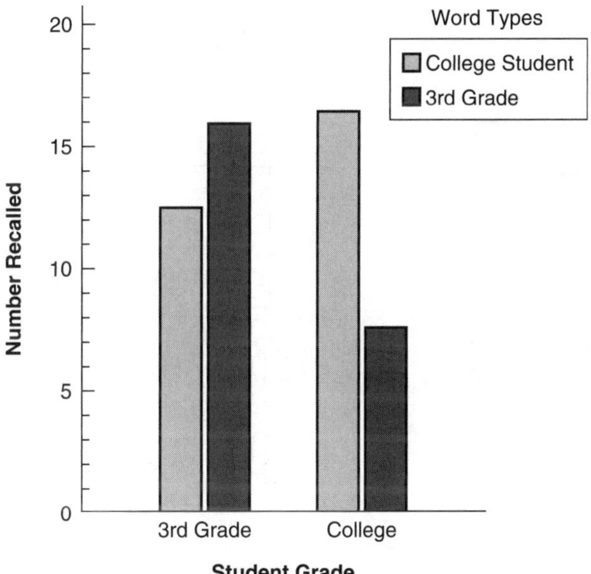

FIGURE 15.4 Influence of Domain of Interest Words on Memory Span in Children and Adults

Source: Reprinted from *Journal of Experimental Child Psychology,* 38, Hulme, C., Thomson, N., Muir, C., & Lawrence, A., Speech rate and the development of short-term memory span, pp. 241–253, 1984, with permission from Elsevier.

of dinosaurs is shown in Figure 15.5 (from Chi & Koeske, 1983). This boy's memory is fairly complex and well organized. Many of the armored dinosaurs are in a cluster and so are the large plant-eaters. When the boy recalled the names of dinosaurs, the ones he recalled most often were those with the greatest number of semantic links.

Children also start to develop schemas and scripts for common aspects of the world around the age of 3 (Nelson & Gruendel, 1988). These become more numerous and developed as a child ages. As children mature, scripts include more details and minor steps in whatever the process might be. The prevalent use of scripts and schemas by young children can be clearly seen in their desire to cling to set routines where they can predict and understand what is happening.

For categorization, even relatively young children show some proficiency. However, there are some changes that occur in development. For example, preschool children are likely to assume that members of the same basic level category have a similar internal structure (same kind of stuff inside) but do not do this for superordinate level categories until second grade (Gelman & O'Reilly, 1988). Another thing that changes is how natural kind and artifact categories develop (Gelman, 1988). Natural kind categories are for objects that exist in nature, such as animals and plants. These are often defined by adults based on characteristics such as mating practice and genetic structure. Members of a natural kind category are often superficially similar. Artifact categories are made of items created by people for various uses and are defined by how objects are used, not its

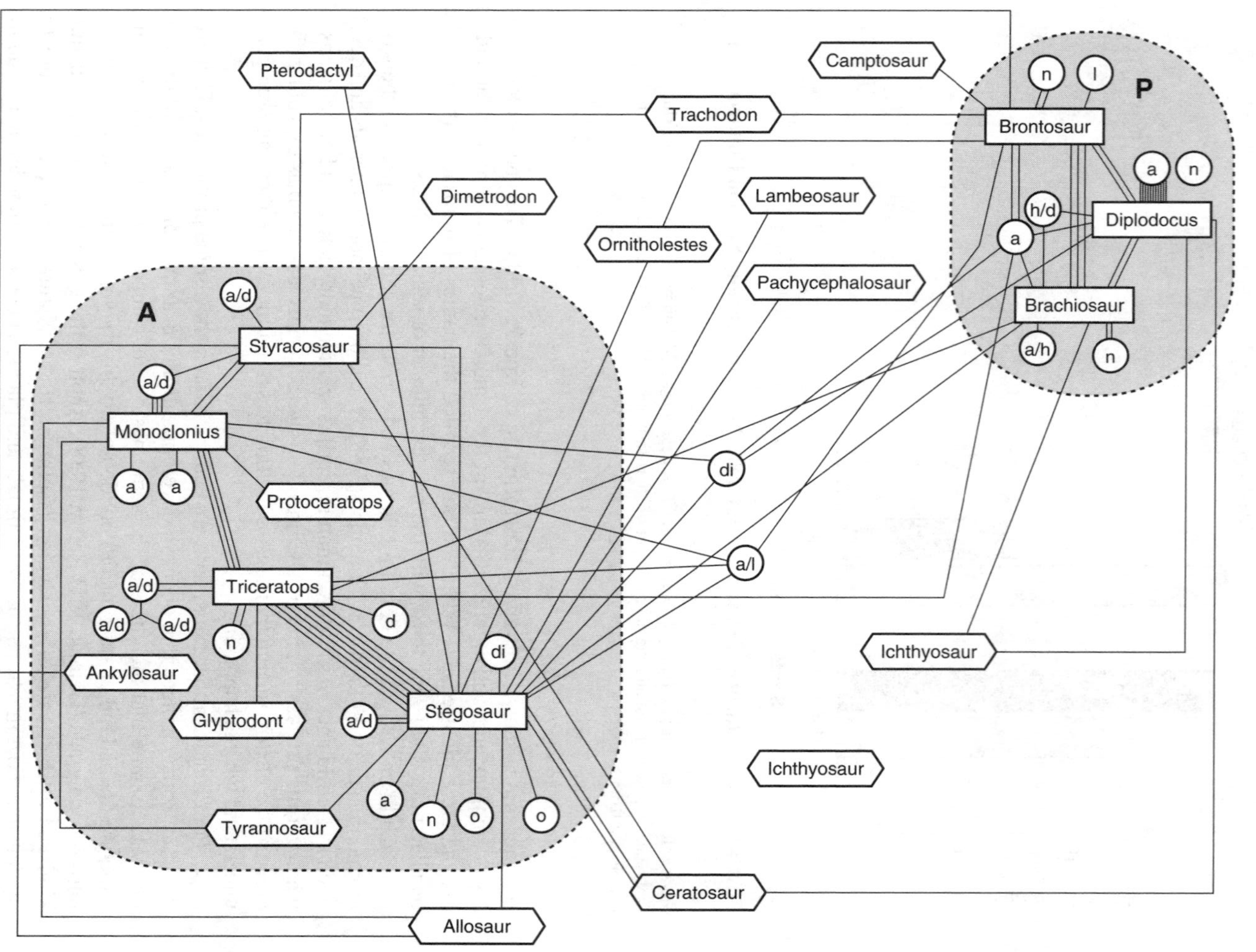

FIGURE 15.5 A Boy's Semantic Memory Network for Dinosaur Concepts

Source: Reprinted from *Journal of Experimental Child Psychology,* 30, Lindberg, M.A., Is knowledge base development a necessary and sufficient condition for memory development?, pp. 404-410, 1980, with permission from Elsevier.

appearance. For example, a screwdriver is more similar in appearance to a butter knife, but the knife is more likely to be classified with a fork. Categories are driven largely by appearance for young, preschool children but not by older children.

Given developmental changes, how does this affect **memory and reality** judgments in children? An important aspect of this is source monitoring. In general, children are not as effective as adults at source monitoring, particularly for internal and external source monitoring as compared to reality monitoring (Lindsay, Johnson, & Kwon, 1991; Parker, 1995; Roberts & Blades, 2000). However, these skills do improve with age. For false memories, such as in the DRM paradigm (see Chapter 12), the illusion is absent in 5-year-olds. Eight-year-old children show a small effect and 11-year-old children show larger effect, but still smaller than adults (Brainerd, Reyna, & Forrest, 2002), and the effect is more pronounced for emotional than neutral materials (Howe, 2007). In general, the false memory effect grows larger over time. This is likely related to the fact that children's semantic memories, which are behind the generation of this effect, are still developing.

An important **memory and the law** situation where childhood may be involved is eyewitness testimony. As we saw (see Chapter 13), eyewitness memory is easily distorted when a witness has been exposed to misleading information. How reliable are children's eyewitness accounts? The facts are a bit mixed up and complicated; however, some simple points can be made (Ceci & Bruck, 1993). First, children can provide accurate eyewitness testimony. In the absence of external influences, a child's memory is similar to an adult's, provided that a child understands the event. Also, unfortunately, children are more susceptible to misinformation than adults (Poole & Lindsay, 2001), even with a single instance of misinformation (Bruck & Cici, 2004). This may occur because adults are more likely to serve as authority figures, making children less able to resist and discount inappropriate information heard from adults. This can be mitigated to some degree by repeated interviews (La Rooy, Pipe, & Murray, 2005). Children may even benefit from repeated interviewing and avoid the influence of misleading post-event information, but only when their prior memories are fairly strong (Goodman & Quas, 2008).

Another important change is in **metamemory**, which gets better with age (Bjorklund, Dukes, & Brown, 2009). For example, in a short-term memory serial position curve (see Chapter 4), to get the most out of the recency effect, people should recall the last items first before they are displaced out of short-term memory. People develop an implicit understanding of this, and adults often do recall this way. However, young children lack this awareness and are less likely to start with the final items, reducing overall retrieval. For example, Samuel (1978) found that this strategy was used infrequently by first graders, but it became progressively more used as people moved into the college years. Metamemory strategies also develop in an increased awareness of the need to rehearse information to maintain it, which emerges in 2-year-old children (DeLoache, Cassidy, & Brown, 1985). For example, a toy might be hidden under an object, and children will continue to glance or point in that direction, suggesting an active attempt to maintain this information in memory.

The ability to organize and structure information continues to mature (Paris & Lindaur, 1976). An example of this is inferring that a spoon is used when reading the sentence "The truck driver stirred the coffee in his cup." If this inference is made, then the word "spoon" is an effective memory cue for this sentence. Older children are more likely to make implicit associations to help organize the information and improve memory. This also assists in the emergence and development of autobiographical memory.

Changes in metamemory can also been seen with prospective memory, which children around the ages of 4 to 6 are less effective at. However, by the ages of 13 or 14, prospective memory abilities are at adult levels (Zimmermann & Meier, 2006). Finally, metacognitive control increases as the ability to inhibit irrelevant information as with directed forgetting. As an illustration, Harnishfeger and Pope (1996) tested 6-, 8-, and 10-year-olds, along with college students (see Chapter 14). They found that the ability to inhibit information increased with age, with 10-year-olds doing as well as the adults.

Synopsis

Memory continues to develop in childhood, along with neurological changes, particularly in the hippocampus. Short-term/working memory processes are more efficient, along with faster processing speed, and better inhibition of irrelevant information. Episodic memories are more structured, along with more developed categories, schemas, and scripts. Although children can be effective eyewitnesses, they may also be more prone to distortion from misleading information. Finally, children make strides in the awareness of the limits and abilities of their own memories and how well they can control them.

OLD AGE

Memory is an area of our lives in which we expect to see changes in as we progress into old age. The stereotype is that old people are more forgetful, and there is some degree of truth to this. However, the natural aging process does not negatively affect all types of memory. There are some things that stay the same or even improve. So, here, we will first look at things that change and then look at things that stay the same or improve with aging.

Some Things Change

This section focuses on changes that occur as a result of the natural aging process.

Age-related **neurological change** in memory is a universal phenomenon seen across a variety of cultures (Park, Nisbett, & Heeden, 1999). This is a result of fundamental changes in the nervous system. A basic change is in the rate or speed of neural firing, which is slower in older adults. As a consequence, older adults take longer to engage in any cognitive process than younger adults. The more complex the task is, the more noticeable is the slowdown.

Age-related changes in neural processing have led to theories of memory and aging that center on this, known as **speed theories.** Changes in processing speed can affect memory in many ways. One is that, during processing, it is more likely that forgetting will occur for some of the information in the stream of thought, and performance declines (Myerson et al., 1990; Myerson, Ferraro, Hale, & Lima, 1992; Salthouse, 1996), leading to more problems.

In addition to neural speed, other parts of the brain are changing. The frontal lobes undergo the greatest change (Albert & Kaplan, 1980) and are less effective in older adults (Rypma, Prabhakaran, Desmond, & Gabriei, 2001; Stebbins et al., 2002). This reduces the ability to control the flow of information in memory. The part of the frontal lobes that is most affected is the dorsolateral prefrontal lobe (on the top and sides in the front) rather than the ventromedial prefrontal lobe (on the bottom and middle) (MacPherson, Phillips, & Sala, 2002). The dorsolateral prefrontal lobe is more responsible for the central executive part of working memory, controlling the flow of thought. In contrast, the ventromedial prefrontal lobe is more involved in emotional and social tasks, such as regulating one's feelings. Finally, this decline is accompanied by a decline in the dopamine system (Braver et al., 2001).

The age-related decline in the frontal lobes leads to a decline in the ability to inhibit irrelevant information (Dempster, 1992; Hasher & Zacks, 1988) as captured by **inhibition theory.** When older adults are trying to remember information, related but irrelevant information is activated, thereby clogging the stream of thought. In a sense, one reason that older adults have trouble with memory is not that they are remembering too little but that they are remembering too much.

With aging, there are also problems with temporal lobe processing. As described earlier (see Chapter 2), the temporal lobes are important for different types of memory. There are also problems with the hippocampus, which shows declines with aging in the ability to engage in LTP (Jessberger & Gage, 2008). As such, older adults show global problems with learning and retrieving information.

One way older adults compensate for a decline in function is to decrease lateralization (Colcombe, Kramer, Erickson, & Scalf, 2005) in which one hemisphere of the brain (left or right) becomes more dominant or does more of the processing than the other. Lateralization may occur initially because a group of nearby cells can make the necessary computations faster than groups that are spread out and need to pass information along the corpus callosum. However, in older adults, there is less lateralization (Cabeza, 2002; Reuter-Lorenz & Cappell, 2008) because older adults need to recruit a larger array of cells across the cortex to do the same job that a more localized portion would handle in younger adults.

Older adults have reduced **short-term/working memory** capacity (Craik & Byrd, 1982). Because they are less efficient at keeping information active, they are less able to coordinate information to the degree necessary for efficient thinking. One example of this decline can be seen in story comprehension. In a study by Light and Capps (1986), people heard brief three- to five-sentence stories in which the final sentence contained a pronoun that referred back to a story character. What was manipulated was the distance between the characters and the pronoun by varying the number of sentences between them. The greater the distance, the more performance declined, especially in older adults. An example of one of these stories, along with some data, is shown in Table 15.1. Because older adults have less memory capacity, they have a greater difficulty holding on to the name and are more likely to forget it. As a result, when the pronoun is heard, they have a harder time determining to whom it referred.

One of the most noticeable age-related changes in **episodic memory** that occurs is a decline in the ability to recall and recognize information (e.g., Zacks, Hasher, & Li, 2000; Zelinski & Stewart, 1998). Part of the difficulty is with binding different units of information together. Thus, certain characteristics, such as context and features, may not be stored as effectively. So, older adults show smaller von Restorff effects (Bireta, Surprenant, & Neath, 2008; Geraci, McDaniel, Manzano, & Roediger, 2009; but see Gallo, Cotel, Moore, & Schacter, 2007), somewhat smaller bizarre imagery effects (Nicolas & Worthen, 2009), and encoding specificity effects (Duchek, 1984; Luo & Craik, 2009).

TABLE 15.1 Effects of Age-Positive and Age-Negative Words on Memory in Terms of Percentages of Accurate Resolutions of Anaphors. Difference in pre- and postexposure conditions.

	YOUNG	OLD
Number of intervening sentences		
Zero	65.1	64.1
One	61.8	58.3
Number of intervening sentences		
Zero	64.9	63.4
Two	61.3	54.7

Source: Light & Capps, 1986.

Because of an age-related increase in forgetting rates, it is harder to observe hypermnesia, although the rate of reminiscence is the same for younger and older adults. There is so little hypermnesia because the faster rate of forgetting for older adults outpaces any reminiscence benefit (Henkel, 2007; Widner, Otani, & Smith, 2000).

Finally, older adults have trouble regulating the retrieval of information from long-term memory. For example, older adults are more susceptible to associative interference and show larger fan effects than do younger adults (Cohen, 1990; Gerard, Zacks, Hasher, & Radvansky, 1991). So, what this means is that as older adults are trying to remember something, they experience more interference from related memories, thereby making their retrieval slower, and more likely to not succeed.

It appears that the **autobiographical memory** found in older adults is dominated more by salient landmark events, self-relevant information, and emotionally positive events (Dijkstra & Kaup, 2005). They also become more generic (Piolino et al., 2006). However, this appears to be more true for voluntary autobiographical memories than for spontaneous ones (Schlagman, Kliegel, Schulz, & Kvavilashvili, 2009), although spontaneous memories are more emotionally positive, overall. Older adults also focus more on the semantic than the episodic aspects of autobiographical memory and these memories are experienced more from an observer than a field perspective, and are more likely to be classified as "known" rather than "recollected."

In terms of **memory and reality,** older adults show several declines. First, older adults are less effective at source monitoring and are more likely to make reality monitoring errors, confusing perceived and imagined events, perhaps because of declines in memory for perceptual and contextual information (Hashtroudi, Johnson, & Chrosniak, 1990). Older adults are also more likely to have source monitoring errors for perceptually similar sources (e.g., two women) (e.g., Ferguson, Hashtroudi & Johnson, 1992; Simons, Dodson, Bell, & Schacter, 2004). Older adults are also less able to integrate different types of source information (e.g., perceptual and conceptual) (Dodson, Bawa, & Slotnik, 2007; Johnson, De Leonardis, Hashtroudi, & Ferguson, 1995). This leads to increased likelihood of exhibiting cryptomnesia (McCabe, Smith, & Parks, 2007) and false fame effects (Dywan & Jacoby, 1990). Older adults are more likely to have errors if their attention is focused elsewhere, such as when negative emotions play a larger role in a situation (Hashtroudi, Johnson, Vnek, & Ferguson, 1994; Kensinger et al., 2007). This can be seen in ERPs recorded during source monitoring, with younger adults' ERP waves showing greater discrimination than older adults' (Dywan, Segalowitz, & Webster, 1998).

As noted earlier, older adults place more emphasis on semantic memories, such as categories and schemas. A consequence of this is that they may be more likely to report false memories, such as the DRM false memory effect (see Chapter 12) (e.g., Norman & Schacter, 1997; Smith, Lozito, & Bayen, 2005). This is attributed to declines in the ability to reality monitor (being more likely to mistake words they just thought of for words that were heard) (Dehon & Brédart, 2004), inhibitory processing (not suppressing related competitors) (Butler, et al., 2004; Lövdén, 2003; but see Chan & McDermott, 2007). Moreover, older adults are more likely to create false *event* memories (Gallo & Roediger, 2003), which may involve script-consistent information that was not actually encountered (LaVoie & Malmstrom, 1998). Older adults are also more likely to misidentify positive attributes as corresponding to the choices they selected (Mather & Johnson, 2000), perhaps because of insufficient binding of source information (Lyle, Bloise, & Johnson, 2006), or by relying more on stereotypes (Mather, Johnson, & De Leonardis, 1999). Some of the increase in false memories is due to older adults being less able to use conscious-based recollections of prior events, and relying more on familiarity (Jacoby & Rhodes, 2006; McDermott & Chan, 2006). That said, it should also be noted that age-related changes in source monitoring do not always occur. When two sources are defined based on value characteristics, such as being told that John always tells the truth and Mary always tells lies, older and younger adults do equally well at correctly identifying source (Rahhal, May, & Hasher, 2002).

For **memory and the law,** aging affects eyewitness memory, with older adults being just as likely as younger adults to have memory influenced by misleading post-event suggestions. However, older adults are more confident in these memory errors (Dodson & Krueger, 2006). These misinformation errors are caused by source monitoring problems. For example, older adults are more likely to pick a person from a police lineup even if the person was not the perpetrator but had only been seen in a series of mugshots (Memon, Hope, Bartlett, & Bull, 2002). These errors in eyewitness accounts and identification are driven by declines in frontal lobe functioning (Roediger & Geraci, 2007).

There are age-related changes in **metamemory** (see Chapter 14). Older adults are less accurate in their JOLs than younger adults (Bieman-Copland & Charness, 1994), which may be due to declines in conscious recollection processes (Daniels, Toth, & Hertzog, 2009). However, older adults do effectively use relative accuracy and they use JOLs to guide study time (Dunlosky, Baker, Rawson, & Hertzog, 2006; Dunlosky & Hertzog, 2000; Hines, Touron, & Hertzog, 2009; Miles & Stine-Morrow, 2004). They adjust their JOLs based on the nature of the information being learned, such as whether the information is difficult or easy to learn. Older adults may be providing JOLs based for the entire set of information, rather than for individual items (Matvey et al., 2002).

Another difficulty older adults have is with feeling of knowing judgments. Older adults' FOK ratings are poorer than younger adults' (Souchey, Isingrini, & Espagnet, 2000), and they may experience greater problems in a tip-of-the-tongue state (White & Abrams, 2002). Relatedly, older adults are more confident in their recognition errors, perhaps due to declines in medial temporal lobe activity, and their increased reliance on overall cortical activity (Chua, Schacter, & Sperling, 2009). Overall, older adults show a decline in conscious recollective experiences, but with little evidence for declines in more unconscious familiarity-based memory processes (e.g., Prull et al., 2006).

For prospective memory (remembering to do something in the future), there are some declines in old age (e.g., Einstein & McDaniel, 1990; Logie & Maylor, 2009; Maylor, 1993; Smith & Bayen, 2006), depending on the type of prospective memory. Older adults show declines for both time-based and event-based prospective memory, but more so for time-based prospective memory (Einstein et al., 1995; Henry, MacLeod, Philips, & Crawford, 2004; Park et al., 1997). That said, older adults actually tend to do better in naturalistic settings (such as remembering appointments) (Bailey et al., in press; Henry, Macleod, Philips, & Crawford, 2004). This may reflect better time management and developing strategies that more than compensate for other declines in prospective memory. For example, time-based prospective memory in older adults is better when they lay out a plan (e.g., taking medication) ahead of time rather than just rehearsing information (Chasteen, Park, & Schwarz, 2001; Liu & Park, 2004). The difficulty older adults have with prospective memory reflects difficulties with the ability to self-initiate some memory processes as needed (Craik & Byrd, 1982). As a result, older adults are less able to monitor themselves, and so, are more likely to not start something when it is needed. That said, those aspects of prospective memory that are affected by aging are not related to other age-related memory changes (Salthouse, Berish, & Siedlecki, 2004).

Another part of metamemory that declines with age is directed forgetting (Andrés, Van der Linden, & Parmentier, 2004; Zacks, Radvansky, & Hasher, 1996). This is more likely when people are told to remember or forget after each item (item method) than for an entire set of information (list method) (Zellner & Bäuml, 2006). This decline in directed forgetting has been attributed to declines in inhibitory processes (but see Sahakyan, Delaney, & Goodmon, 2008, for an alternative account). For example, if later asked to recall items that they were previously told to forget, older adults recall more than younger adults because this information was not sufficiently inhibited.

Up to now, we have seen that older adults have more trouble with memory. However, memory does not inevitably get worse. In the next section we highlight some things that stay the same or even improve. Before that, it is important to understand that one's attitude is very important. If a person *thinks* memory gets worse, then performance will be worse. This occurs at a subconscious level. In a study by Levy (1996; see also Hess & Hinson, 2006), older adults were given a series of memory tests. Prior to this they were then subliminally exposed to a number of age-positive words, such as "wisdom," "sage," or "guidance," or age-negative words, such as "senile," "dementia," and "decrepit." Although the older adults were not aware that they had seen the words, their performance was greatly affected. Data from this study are shown in Table 15.2. Older adults did worse following age-negative words but better following age-positive words. There was no influence on the younger adults. Thus, the implicit age-related stereotypes that are activated can impact on how well memory actually works.

When goals are set for people to improve memory, both younger and older adults respond well. However, this is sometimes greater for the older adults (West, Thorn, & Bagwell, 2003), suggesting that older adults may be more prone to discounting their abilities and may be making their situation worse by having self-handicapping thoughts.

TABLE 15.2 Effects of Age-Positive and Age-Negative Words on Memory. Difference in pre- and postexposure conditions.

	OLDER ADULTS		YOUNGER ADULTS	
	Negative	*Positive*	*Negative*	*Positive*
Immediate recall	−1.77	0.98	−0.36	−0.10
Learned recall	−0.46	0.49	0.43	0.07
Delayed recall	−1.11	0.20	0.33	−0.07
Photo recall	0.14	1.50	0.77	0.24
Auditory recall	−0.64	−0.20	−0.47	−0.60

Source: Levy, 1996.

Some Things Stay the Same

While aging is associated with a decline in memory, there are some aspects that do not suffer. Instead, these memory abilities remain constant and may even improve. This follows on ideas outlined by Hess (2005) that note that traditional views of memory and aging may overemphasize age-related declines, miss areas of stability or improvement, do not take into account adaptive developmental changes, and that there is a greater degree of variability between people when older adults are considered.

Nondeclarative memories is one area that shows some stability with age, perhaps because they are neurologically more foundational and robust. For example, other than an overall change in processing speed, there is little in the way of age-related changes in priming (Fleishman et al., 2004; Laver, 2009).

There is no doubt that **episodic** and **autobiographical memories** decline with age, but this decline has limits. Some aspects stay at a high level and may even improve. It has been suggested that distinction between what is and is not remembered is a distinction between quantitative and qualitative aspects of memory (Small, Dixon, Hultsch, & Hertzog, 1999). There is a near uniform quantitative decline in episodic memory, with older adults generally remembering less. However, qualitative aspects of memory are preserved. That is, the way information is remembered stays the same. For example, older adults show as much information organization and structure during remembering as do younger adults and may even shown an increase. The degree to which people have information organized stays about the same (Kahana & Wingfield, 2000). For example, older adults show similar flashbulb memory effects as younger adults (Berntsen & Rubin, 2006). Overall, older adults may be more dependent on the organization of information in memory, leading them to be more susceptible to things such as part-set cuing (Marsh, Dolan, Balota, & Roediger, 2004).

There is also some evidence that although there are declines in inhibitory processes in other aspects of memory retrieval, older adults do not show declines in the suppression of irrelevant concepts in the repeated practice paradigm (Aslan, Bäuml, & Pastötter, 2007). This suggests that not all types of inhibitory memory processes are compromised in old age.

Overall, there is relatively little age-related decline in **semantic memory** (e.g., Rönnlund, Nyberg, Bäckman, & Nilsson, 2005; Spaniol, Madden, & Voss, 2006). Over time, people are exposed to a broader range of information, and this knowledge continues to accumulate. Older adults often outperform younger adults on measures of semantic knowledge, such as vocabulary tests. This is not related to educational factors, such as the older adults getting a "better" education.

As noted above, semantic priming effects remain stable (Balota & Duchek, 1988; Lavaer & Burke, 1993), including both automatic (Howard, McAndrews, & Lasaga, 1981), more consciously controlled priming (Burke, White, & Diaz, 1987), and even mediated priming (Bennett & McEvoy, 1999). This means that older adults can reliably draw on a broader range of real-world knowledge than younger adults.

As episodic memory declines, there is a greater reliance on schemas in semantic memory, which are well preserved (Arbuckle, Vanderleck, Harsany, & Lapidus, 1990; Hess & Flannagan, 1992; Light & Anderson, 1983; Zelinski & Miura, 1988). As such, older adults perform well in their ability to focus on more important (relative to less important) information (Castel, Farb, & Craik, 2007). Older adults rely on their schemas so much that they may have trouble suppressing them when they are irrelevant (Arbuckle, Cooney, Milne, & Melchior, 1994).

The information that is more readily forgotten, and most likely to suffer as a consequence of aging, is memory for details. Keeping in mind fuzzy trace theories, memory is composed of detailed, specific memories and more general, gist-related memories. As the aging process proceeds, episodic memory declines, but semantic memory is more stable and might even improve (Nyberg et al., 2003). As a result, older adults' memories are more likely to be influenced by general information about the past, rather than memory for details (Koutstaal, 2006; Koutstaal & Schacter, 1997; Reder, Wible, & Martin, 1986), which is not observed when older adults do not have prior knowledge (Koutstaal et al., 2003).

This differential use of semantic and episodic memory can also be seen in social judgments. Older adults are more likely to make predictions of other people's future behavior based on a general, schematic understanding, rather than specific episodic information about the person (Hess & Follett, 1994; Hess, Follett, & McGee, 1998). However, not all social judgments are biased toward schematic information. For example, if people are asked to rate how likable a person is, younger and older adults use schematic and specific information similarly (Hess & Bolstad, 1998).

At times, semantic knowledge may be activated, even though we don't want it to be, as is with social stereotypes. Older adults are in a position in which their semantic knowledge is intact, but their ability to suppress unwanted information is compromised. As a consequence older adults are more likely to activate stereotypes and have them influence them, even when they are trying to be egalitarian (Radvansky, Copeland, & von Hippel, 2009; Stewart, von Hippel, & Radvansky, 2009; von Hippel, Silver, & Lynch, 2000). Thus, older adults may be prejudiced against their will. That said, it is also possible for older adults to deactivate the influence of stereotypes if they are discounted in some way (such as explicitly noting that a baby sitter was male) (Radvansky, Lynchard, & von Hippel, 2009).

Another area of memory that is less affected by aging is **higher-level memory**, such as the mental model level (Radvansky & Dijkstra, 2007). Younger and older adults use mental models similarly in memory (Radvansky, Gerard, Zacks, & Hasher, 1990). In some cases, while older adults show memory problems at lower levels, such as remembering verbatim or propositional information, their ability to remember information at higher levels, such as the mental model level, are unaffected (Radvansky, Zwaan, Curiel, & Copeland, 2001). This preserved memory at higher levels of thought is seen in more everyday tasks, such as remembering news events (Frieske & Park, 1999). Compared to younger adults, older adults better remember the content of news stories and the sources of those stories.

Although there are age-related changes in **memory and reality** processing, such as source monitoring, cryptomnesia, false fame, and false memories, this is not always found. Work by Thapar and Sniezek (2008; see also Thapar & Westerman, 2009) has shown that older adults are like younger adults in exhibiting the revelation effect. They are similarly likely to give more positive responses to items that are revealed gradually as compared to those that are revealed all at once, especially when this relies on conceptual process, such as word fragment completion and anagram solving, because semantic processes are better preserved in aging. However, when the revelation process is more perceptual, such as revealing words slowly, pixel by pixel, on a computer, then age-related differences may be observed, with older adults not showing a revelation effect (Prull, Light, Collett, & Kennison, 1998).

While there are a number of age-related changes in **metamemory**, Bayen, Erdfelder, Bearden, and Lozito (2006) found no overall effect of aging on the hindsight bias. Here, people were asked for a set of obscure facts, and were then given the correct answers. Hindsight judgments are similar in younger and older adults. In fact, if people were told that they do not need to remember the correct information for a later memory test, younger adults actually show a larger hindsight bias than the older adults.

Aging and Emotion

A popular issue in recent years is the role of emotion in aging, specifically, a tendency to emphasize positive information over negative information as one grows older (e.g., Mather & Knight, 2005; but see Murphy & Isaacowitz, 2008). This reflects a greater interest in close interpersonal relationships and a desire to control emotions as one ages. As a consequence, older adults show poorer memory for negative information than do younger adults (Charles, Mather, & Carstensen, 2003; Kennedy, Mather, & Carstensen, 2004; Thomas & Hasher, 2006; but see Gruhn, Smith & Baltes, 2005). This is consistent with fMRI work that shows that while there are preserved connections between the dorsolateral prefrontal cortex (B.A. 9 & 46) and the amygdala, preserving emotional control, the connections from the amygdala to the hippocampus are weakened, suggesting a decline in emotional influences on memory (St. Jacques, Dolcos, & Cabeza, 2009). Another consequence is that, younger adults show greater tunnel memory effects than do older adults (Waring & Kenisnger, 2009). Fernandes, Ross, Wiegand, and Schryer (2008) suggest that the positivity effect is not due to remembering more positive memories, but to more positive false memories. Alternatively, Petrician, Moscovitch, and Schimmack (2008) suggest that the positivity effect is due to older adults placing more of a positive spin on the memories.

Overall, older adults are more sensitive to emotional information. They more often show mood congruency effects in memory (Knight, Maines, & Robinson, 2002) and although they are less efficient at source monitoring, but this age difference disappears if the information is emotional (May, Rahhal, Berry, & Leighton, 2005). A similar age-invariant finding is observed for emotional information in working memory, particularly for positive materials (Mikels, Larkin, Reuter-Lorenz, & Carstensen, 2005). It should be noted that this emotional influence is observed only if a person is thinking about the emotional aspects of an event at the time. It does not occur automatically (Emery & Hess, 2008).

Good Advice

So, while some parts of memory remain stable or improve with age, is there anything that can be done about those things that show some sort of decline? There is a paper by Hertzog, Kramer, Wilson, and Lindenberger (2008) that outlines some steps that can be taken to address age-related changes in memory. They cover the intellectual, social, and physical activities a person can engage in. In short, the more a person can stay actively engaged in a number of complex intellectual, social, and physical activities, the more successfully they will age, and the smaller their deficits will be. So, be active in a wide variety of things throughout your life, and you will have fewer problems as you grow older.

Synopsis

Several changes occur in memory as a result of old age. Some of these are due to neurological declines, such as in the speed of neural firing and cortical functioning, particularly the frontal lobes. A number of cognitive changes also occur, including reductions in working memory span and decreases in inhibitory and self-initiated processes. There are also declines in some episodic memory processes, such as free recall and source monitoring, as well as changes in metamemory tasks such as prospective memory. Importantly, some aspects of memory are relatively unchanged, including much of semantic memory, the organization of episodic information, and the retention of information at higher levels of thought. There is also a shift in the role that emotions play which then has consequences for memory and aging, with older adults having greater control over some aspects of emotional processing than younger adults.

SUMMARY

In this chapter we looked at the consequences of development on memory. We saw that some memory abilities are present at birth, whereas others, such as episodic and autobiographical memories, require some time for them to function adequately. As a person moves from infancy to childhood, memory continues to develop. During childhood, much of this development is related to increases in the speed of processing, as well as a greater self-knowledge of how memory works. This helps a person devise and implement strategies, such as rehearsal, that can result in better memory later. Near the other end of life, memory changes as a result of natural aging. There are a number of declines in memory including declines in the speed of processing, a reduction in working memory capacity, and a decline in controlled memory processes, such as suppression and the self-initiation of various memory processes. Despite these changes, there are some parts of memory that are less affected by aging. These include memory at higher levels of processing, semantic memory, and more control over emotional processing.

STUDY QUESTIONS

1. What are some of the various ways of testing infants' memories, and how do they work?
2. Which memory systems are well developed in infancy, and which are still immature?
3. What are some of the major changes in memory that are observed during childhood?
4. What important role does metamemory play in changes in memory during childhood?
5. What are some major neurological changes that occur with old age that can affect memory?
6. What are the dominant theories of age-related changes in memory? In what ways do they overlap? In what ways are they different?
7. What are the major changes in memory that occur as a result of the normal aging process?
8. What aspects of memory remain relatively unchanged, or even improve, with old age?
9. What are the changes in emotional processing that occur with aging? What are the impacts of these changes on aging and memory?
10. What can you do to help preserve your memory ability when you move into old age?

KEY TERMS

autobiographical memory, conjugate reinforcement, elicited imitation, episodic memory, higher-level memory, inhibition theory, looking method, memory and the law, memory and reality, metamemory, neurological change, neurological development, nondeclarative memory, nonnutritive sucking, semantic memory, short-term working memory, speed theories

CHAPTER SIXTEEN

AMNESIA

As we have seen, one of the most important issues in memory is not how much people remember but how much they forget. In this chapter we consider forgetting on a grand scale, to the extent that it is pathological. **Amnesia** is the catastrophic loss of memories or memory abilities beyond what is expected with normal forgetting, along with otherwise normal intelligence and attention span (O'Connor, Verfaellie, & Cermak, 1995). There are various types of amnesia. While they vary in their scope and content, they all cripple memory in systematic ways, damaging some memories but leaving others more intact. Most amnesias are a result of organic brain damage. However, some may be a result of some psychological trauma. In such cases, the loss of memory functioning may be due to exclusively mental processes and not a problem with the underlying neurophysiology per se. Such amnesias are psychogenic amnesias. In this chapter we first cover issues of organic amnesias with regard to retrograde and anterograde amnesia, followed by a consideration of the various types of psychogenic amnesia.

LONG-TERM MEMORY AMNESIA

First we consider amnesias that are the result of organic disturbance: retrograde and anterograde. Retrograde amnesia is a loss of long-term memories prior to a traumatic incident, backward in time. In contrast, anterograde amnesia is a loss of the ability to store new long-term memories, forward in time. Although we consider them separately, it is rare to find a pure case of either one or the other. Whenever there is a trauma dramatic enough to produce amnesia, typically both are present to some degree. Some traumas result in much more retrograde amnesia than anterograde, whereas others have the opposite effect. The conditions described here are situations in which one type of amnesia is dominant. A clear case of a mixing of the two is considered after the section on anterograde amnesia.

Retrograde Amnesia

Retrograde amnesia is a loss in the ability to access long-term memories that were previously available (see Kapur, 1999, for a review). Typically, with retrograde amnesia, the personal past is lost. This is the sort of amnesia that people in soap operas tend to get. Usually, in those scenarios, people get hit on the head, and then they can't remember who they are, where they are, whether they're married, and so forth. In real life, the situation is more complex, and retrograde amnesia has specific defining characteristics.

There are a number of things that can cause retrograde amnesia but each involves trauma to the brain that disrupts the **consolidation** (see Chapter 2) of long-term memories (McGaugh, 1966; but see Riccio, Millin, & Gisquet-Verrier, 2003, for an alternative view). Consolidation is a relatively slow process that makes memories more permanent. The easiest memories to disrupt are those that are less consolidated. In severe cases, more stable memories might be disrupted. This may occur either when there has been a disruption to the parts of the brain where the information is held or to the neural mechanisms that are used to retrieve and reconstruct that knowledge.

What can bring about retrograde amnesia? Severe blows to the head are a common way (and consistent with accounts provided by the entertainment industry). This physical trauma can affect the brain in a number of ways depending on the nature of the blow, such as its location and intensity. Another thing is a cardiovascular incident, such as a stroke. During a stroke there is a disruption of oxygen and nutrients to parts of the brain. If this disruption is brief, many of the cells will recover, and memory loss will be temporary. However, with longer periods of time, it is more likely that permanent cell damage and death will occur. With cell death, the patterns of neural information are disrupted, and there is a permanent memory loss. This is why stroke victims may need to relearn to speak and walk.

Characteristics of Retrograde Amnesia. One characteristic of retrograde amnesia is a graded loss of memory in which more recent memories are more easily disrupted. In contrast, older memories are more firmly established and difficult to disrupt. Memory loss is greater as the age of the memory approaches the time of the incident. This graded pattern of memory loss and retention is **Ribot's Law,** and it reflects the consolidation of memories in the nervous system. Basically, the older a memory is, the more consolidated it is and the less susceptible it is to disruption (Brown, 2002).

Much of what is lost in retrograde amnesia are autobiographical memories—memories that refer to events of one's own life, as well as personal semantic information, such as addresses and jobs, and public events, such as news stories. Nondeclarative memories are largely preserved, as well as semantic knowledge, although a person may not be aware of acquiring this knowledge and may deny having it.

Another interesting aspect of retrograde amnesia is that the memory loss may not be immediate. There may be a delay of a minute or two between the time of the injury and the onset of the amnesia. In a study by Lynch and Yarnell (1973), University of Colorado football players were tested after a concussive injury. When tested immediately (within 30 seconds) after coming off the field, all of the players remembered the play that had just occurred. However, 3–5 minutes later, or longer, players who suffered a concussion could no longer remember the play that led to their injury. This suggests that retrograde amnesia may take time to establish itself.

When there has not been permanent brain damage, the recovery of memories follows a regular pattern. Because older memories are more stable, they are the first to return. As time goes on, more memories are recovered, with the older memories being recovered sooner. It is not unusual for many memories to be recovered at or close to their level prior to the incident. However, there is also a period of time just prior to the trauma that is never recovered. This is because these memories have been permanently destroyed. The disruption hits them while they are in a very fragile state.

I have personal experience with retrograde amnesia. When I was 21 (a brief period when I slightly approached being cool), I worked as a bartender. One night, while driving home after work, I stopped at a red light and was waiting to turn left onto my street, Belle Avenue. There was a car behind me, and behind that car was a police cruiser. When the light turned green, I started to make the left turn, when the cruiser broadsided my car, pushing the driver's side door into the middle of the car (it turned out they had just gotten a call and had sped off to answer it with no flashing lights or siren—remember the witness in the car behind me). I was taken by ambulance to the hospital half a block away. When I woke up in intensive care the next morning, I had no memory of the accident. And even though it was July, I thought it was April. Over the next few days, my memories gradually returned, but even today, I have no memory of the day of the accident, or the accident itself (thank goodness).

Case Studies of Retrograde Amnesia. Not all cases of retrograde amnesia follow the same pattern. What we have seen up to now is a typical pattern, but it can appear in other ways. Stracciari et al. (1994) describe two young men who had closed head injuries resulting in a temporally limited retrograde amnesia. They had trouble remembering what had happened to them during the past year. This amnesia was limited to autobiographical memories but not semantic and public memories (such as current events). So, not all information was lost for the amnesic period. However, even important personal information was lost. For example, one of them forgot that he had been seeing a particular woman for 6 months before the accident. This memory loss was profound enough that her name was unfamiliar to him—and he had her name tattooed on his forearm!

Although memories often return during recovery, in more severe cases they do not. One case without much improvement is that of P. S., who suffered profound anterograde amnesia as well (McCarthy & Hodges, 1995). As a result of a stroke when he was 67, P. S. sustained damage to his thalamus. The result was retrograde amnesia for all of his adult life, except for the period when he was in the British Navy during World War II. Because of his added problem with anterograde amnesia, he believed himself to be in this time. He interpreted and placed any knowledge within the framework of those war years. For example, while his autobiographical memory was severely compromised, he did have good memory for famous faces of the decades following World War II, and he could place them in the correct temporal sequence. However, when asked to date this information, he would place it in the early to mid-1940s. He does, however, have reasonably good memory for that time. When asked to describe his hometown, he can be very specific, but his description is of the town as it appeared in the 1940s. Here, the thalamus is not the storehouse of memories. Instead it is a connection between different sources of information that would place memories in time and in P. S.'s life. When this connection was severed, P. S. became trapped in time. (For another description of profound retrograde amnesia, see Hunkin, 1997, which describes a person who lost all memories before the age of 19.)

Electroconvulsive Therapy/Shock. Retrograde amnesia can also occur when a powerful electrical current is passed through the brain. In some cases this is done as part of a therapeutic treatment. This is **Electroconvulsive Therapy (ECT).** For ECT, electrodes are placed on the head. During ECT, the patient is strapped securely to a table, and series of electrical pulses are passed through the brain. Unless a person is administered anticonvulsant drugs, these shocks can make the whole body convulse violently and possibly be injured. Basically, the ECT treatment is inducing a grand mal seizure. This process is repeated 6 to 12 times over a 3- to 5-week period (Cahill & Frith, 1995). It is most often used with depressed patients after there has been little to no response to any other treatments and the patient is in a precarious state. ECT continues to be used and is effective at getting patients to a state where more conventional therapies can be used.

Electroconvulsive therapy has effects other than the alleviation of depressive symptoms, including amnesia. Initially, after ECT, there is a period of anterograde amnesia in which the person has trouble learning new things (Cahill & Frith, 1995). More prominent is the marked presence of retrograde amnesia (Cahill & Frith, 1995; Squire & Cohen, 1979), although some of the memories do eventually return. People undergoing this treatment lose memories from the recent past, including memories of the ECT session itself (which is probably a good thing). The amount of memory loss can vary, but it can be as long as 1 or 2 years prior to ECT (Squire, Slater, & Chace, 1975) (see Figure 16.1). This memory loss is found for both personal autobiographical memories (a more episodic memory loss) and for community-shared public memories (a more semantic memory loss); however, implicit memory seems unaffected (Vakil et al., 2000). For an interesting account of Benjamin Franklin's work on electricity, amnesia, and relief from depression, see Finger and Zaroub (2006).

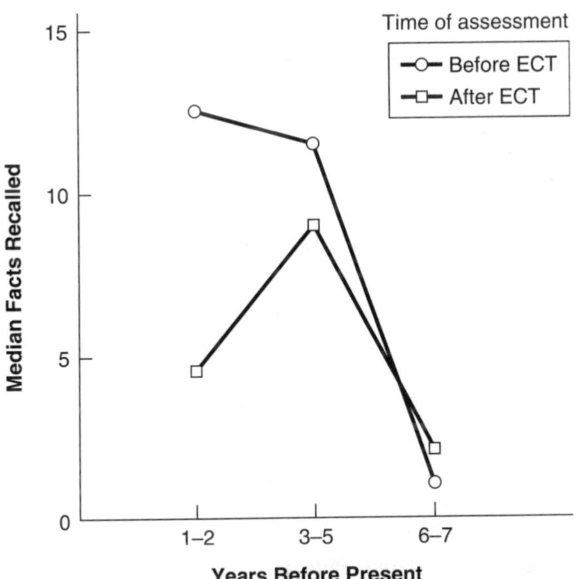

FIGURE 16.1 Graded Effects of Retrograde Amnesia

Source: Squire, L. R., & Cohen, N. (1979). Memory and amnesia: Resistance to disruption develops for years after learning. *Behavioral and Neural Biology, 25*, 115–125.

When used to study memory and not as a treatment, this procedure is called **Electroconvulsive Shock (ECS).** It is used on laboratory animals, such as rats. ECS provides a systematic assessment of retrograde amnesia. When ECS is given to rats shortly after a fear experience, such as receiving a painful shock, retrograde amnesia occurs, and there is no subsequent fear of that situation (Duncan, 1949; Madsen & McGaugh, 1961). In another ECS study by Chorover and Schiller (1965), rats were placed on a platform. If the rat stepped down from the platform, it received a shock, so it would no longer step down. Wires that delivered an ECS were attached to the rats' ears, and the amount of time between when the rat stepped off the platform and the delivery of the ECS was varied. As can be seen in Figure 16.2, in a study by Duncan (1949), the shorter the delay between the shock and the ECS, the less likely that rats learned to avoid stepping down, because the ECS had disrupted their memories. However, if there was a lengthy period between stepping down and the ECS, this information was stored in the rats' brains and thus was more permanent, stable, and resistant to the disruption by the ECS.

Synopsis

The loss of memories prior to an incident is retrospective amnesia. There is a graded loss of memories, with newer memories being more susceptible than older memories, suggesting a disruption of consolidation. Often, many of the memories initially lost are recovered, although those near the traumatic event may be lost forever. In addition to random accidents, retrograde amnesia can be deliberately induced through electrical shocks.

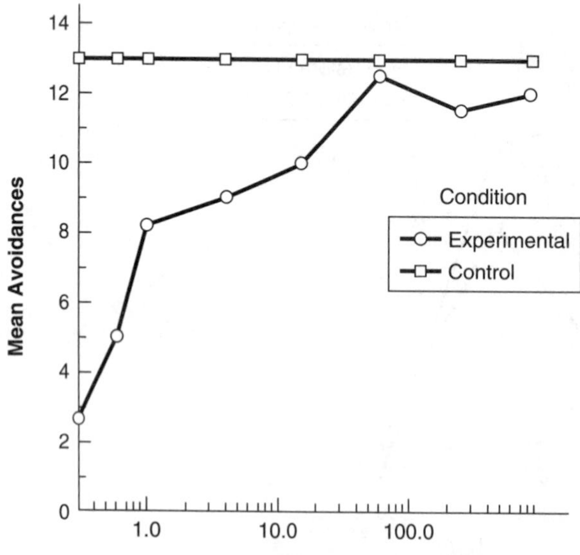

FIGURE 16.2 Retrograde Amnesia Following Electroconvulsive Shock

Source: Duncan, C. P. (1949). The retroactive effect of electroshock on learning. *Journal of Comparative Physiological Psychology, 42,* 32–44.

Anterograde Amnesia

Whereas retrograde amnesia is the loss of memories prior to an incident, **anterograde amnesia** is the inability to store new memories after an incident. This is a much more devastating condition. With anterograde amnesia, people lose the ability to fully benefit from their experiences, and they become, in some sense, frozen in time. Someone with severe anterograde amnesia needs to be given the same information repeatedly because they have great difficulty retaining it. Here, we first look at anterograde amnesia in terms of which part of the brain is damaged, to either the medial temporal lobes and the hippocampus or the diencephalon. After this, we consider issues of anterograde amnesia more generally (although, see Aggleton, 2008, and Aggleton & Brown, 1999, for a suggestion that the same basic memory processes are disrupted in both cases).

Medial Temporal Lobe and Hippocampus. The medial temporal lobes (B.A. 21) are adjacent to an important memory structure: the hippocampus. Damage to these areas of the brain as a result of surgical intervention, infection, stroke, or anoxia (lack of oxygen to the brain) can result in anterograde amnesia. Perhaps the most famous amnesic was Henry Molaison (February 26, 1926–December 2, 2008), better known as H. M. (Scoville & Milner, 1957). On August 23, 1953, at the age of 27, H. M. had brain surgery to relieve his severe epilepsy. H. M. was having several petit mal seizures each day (up to 12 in a 2-hour period) and weekly grand mal seizures, often resulting in injury. He was unable to work or lead a normal life. The surgeons removed much of his hippocampus and adjoining cortex on both sides. MRI scans (Corkin et al., 1997) showed that the brain damage included other structures, including portions of the amygdala and temporal cortex. The parts of the hippocampus that remained showed evidence of atrophy. In terms of his epilepsy, the operation was a success. The rate and severity of his seizures greatly diminished, although they were still present. Also, his intelligence stayed the same (if not improved), and his personality appeared unchanged. However, there was an unexpected side effect. H. M. had severe and dense anterograde amnesia. He was not able to learn new things.

Although H. M. had difficulty storing new memories, he had above normal intelligence. He had some retrograde amnesia for the time prior to the operation, but most of his memories remained intact (Scoville & Milner, 1957). However, he had difficulty in daily life because he could not remember much beyond the span of his short-term memory. He often commented that he felt as if he had just awakened from a dream. It was not unusual for him to do a jigsaw puzzle many times or to read the same magazine over and over and not have any memory of having read it before.

While H. M. had severe amnesia, not all of his memory was gone. He had a good short-term memory (Wickelgren, 1968), and his language abilities were largely intact (Skotko, Andrews, & Einstein, 2005). He could acquire new declarative memories if the information was salient enough and was repeatedly presented over a long period of time. For example, he was also able to remember his father's death after he had been absent from home for about a month (Milner, Corkin, & Teuber, 1968). He also showed some evidence of implicit memory, such as perceptual identification (Milner, Corkin, & Teuber, 1968), and procedural memory for motor tasks, such as mirror tracing or pursuit rotor tasks (Corkin, 1968). Note that H. M. was not the only person to get severe anterograde amnesia. Other ways of getting this condition include loss of oxygen to the brain, brain tumors, neurological disorders such as epilepsy, or viral attacks such as herpes simplex encephalitis.

Diencephalic Anterograde Amnesia. The diencephalon is a collection of brain structures, including the thalamus, hypothalamus, and mammillary bodies. Like damage to the medial temporal lobes and the hippocampus, damage to this area can cause anterograde amnesia. The most common way of getting this condition is as a symptom of Korsakoff's syndrome, which occurs in people who are chronic and severe alcoholics. They have damage in many brain areas, including the dorsomedial thalamic nuclei, the mammillary bodies, and the frontal lobe. This extensive brain damage is a function of a deficiency in thiamine (vitamin B1) as a result of alcoholism rather than an effect of the alcohol itself. It is also possible for the diencephalon to be damaged in other ways, such as through a stroke.

The diencephalon is closely associated with frontal lobe processing and the coordination and control of thought. People with anterograde amnesia may confabulate due to damage to these areas (see Chapter 17). Anterograde amnesia that results from damage to these structures may result in a decline in the ability to coordinate information in memory, making it difficult to recover memories in an effective way. These people also have more extensive retrograde amnesia than those with medial temporal lobe damage. This may also be due to a decreased ability to coordinate information in memory, which would make it difficult to retrieve old memories as well as store new ones.

Anterograde Amnesia More Generally. The part of memory most affected in anterograde amnesia is conscious, declarative memory, both episodic or autobiographical as well as semantic knowledge (but see Kitchner, Hodges, & McCarthy 1998). If you were to have a conversation with an anterograde amnesic, he or she might seem normal. However, if you were to get up, leave, and return 10 minutes later, he or she would not recognize you and may claim that he or she never met you before. There are other deficits that may arise. People do not show distinctiveness and novelty effects, such as the von Restorff effect (Kishiyama, Yonelinas, & Lazzara, 2004). Due to deficits in long-term memory encoding, they do not have the pool of memories needed to keep track of context. Because distinctiveness is defined by the context in which information is found (e.g., elephant is distinctive in a list of vehicles but not in a list of zoo animals), no von Restorff effect is seen.

While long-term memory is affected, short-term memory is intact (Baddeley & Warrington, 1970) but people forget things at a much faster rate (Warrington & Weiskrantz, 1968). So, they can consciously comprehend the experiences as they happen, but the experiences slip away quickly.

Note that, as with H. M., nondeclarative memories are relatively intact. Anterograde amnesics can learn new procedural tasks, although they may lack conscious awareness of learning the task. For example, amnesics might learn a motor task, such as mirror tracing, like normal people (Brooks & Baddeley, 1976). An example of an anterograde amnesic learning on a mirror tracing task is shown in Figure 16.3. Another well-known case of anterograde amnesia is that of Clive Wearing, a famed British classical musician who suffered from herpes simplex encephalitis in 1985. Despite his profound anterograde amnesia, his musical abilities remained largely intact, allowing him to play or conduct as he had done before, with degradations noticed only by expert musicians (Wilson & Wearing, 1995).

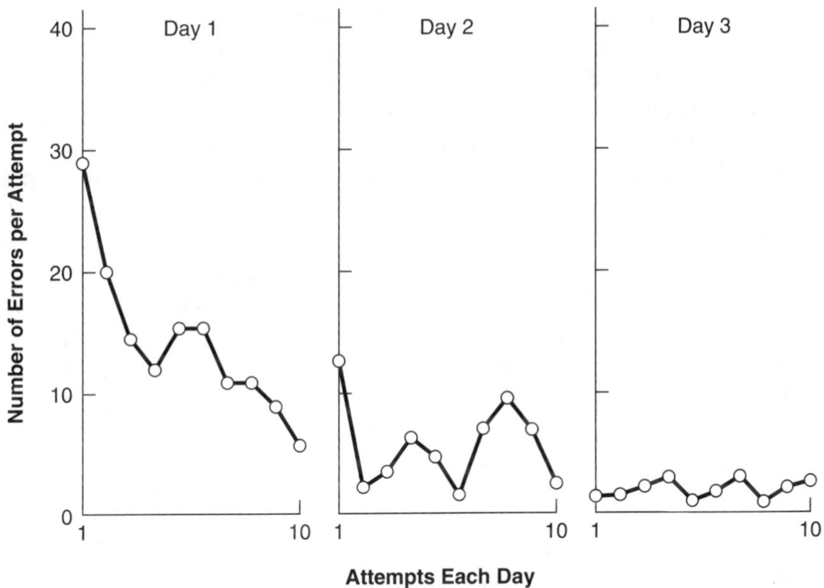

FIGURE 16.3 Performance of an Anterograde Amnesic on a Mirror Tracing Task. Illustrating preserved implicit memory

Source: Blakemore, C. (1977). Mechanics of the Mind. Cambridge, UK, Cambridge University Press. Reprinted with the permission of Cambridge University Press.

The preservation of nondeclarative memories also applies to implicit, linguistic tasks (Schacter, 1987), such as syntactic, semantic, and episodic priming of words (Ferreira, Bock, Wilson, & Cohen, 2008; Graf & Schacter, 1985; Graf, Shimamura, & Squire, 1985; Levy, Stark, & Squire, 2004), although priming is more likely to be preserved when it depends on perceptual than semantic characteristics (Rajaram & Coslett, 2000). Amnesics also perform similar to normal people on word fragment (Warrington & Weiskrantz, 1970), word stem (Graf, Squire, & Mandler, 1984), and perceptual identification tasks. For example, amnesics spend less time viewing pictures that are repeated. However, if something in a picture has been altered (e.g., the relationship among elements is changed), normal people spend more time looking in the region where the change occurred, whereas amnesics do not (Ryan, Althoff, Whitlow, & Cohen, 2000).

Again, it is important to keep in mind that no memory test process is pure. There is always an influence of multiple memory components. For example, the combined influence of explicit and implicit memory on a direct memory task in amnesics can be seen with recall and recognition. In Chapter 10, we saw how recall requires effort to generate information, whereas recognition requires only that a person, at a minimum, believes that the information is old. A feeling of familiarity does not require conscious recollection, but only unconscious, implicit influences. As such, anterograde amnesics have more difficulty with recall than with recognition. In some cases they may show no recognition deficit in conjunction with a clear recall deficit (Hirst et al., 1986; Hirst, Johnson, Phelps, & Volpe, 1988).

Other Case Studies of Anterograde Amnesia. It is possible for people to have anterograde amnesia for some types of information but not others. One case is that of A. B., who as a result of a hematoma had damage to his posterolateral frontal lobe (B.A. 4) and adjacent anterior parietal lobe (B.A. 1, 2, & 3) on the left side. A. B. cannot retain word or sentence lists in short-term memory. However, he can recall complex stories he reads or hears. Thus, A. B. has anterograde amnesia for words and unrelated sentences but has more normal memory for complex, interrelated, and meaningful prose (Romani & Martin, 1999). In other words, A. B. has poor memory at the surface form and textbase levels but good memory at the mental model level (see Chapter 7).

Another amnesic with selective problems is T. R. (Sirigu & Grafman, 1996). This man suffered cerebral anoxia after heart failure and then had amnesia consistent with damage to the hippocampus. Like many anterograde amnesics, T. R. has difficulty with new episodic memories. However, for him, it is only for certain types of information. He remembers events but only in terms of what happened and where it happened. However, he is amnesic for the identities of the people involved and for when it happened. This shows a selective loss of some episodic information, but not for others.

Living with Anterograde Amnesia. As you can imagine, anterograde amnesia has a profound effect on the ability to function normally. For example, people with anterograde amnesia may leave kitchen appliances on, leave fires burning, water running, and so on. They have a tendency to overeat because they consume multiple meals, not remembering that they had just eaten (Higgs, Williamson, Rothstein & Humphreys, 2008). Is there anything that can be done to help these people? An important thing to keep in mind is that it depends on how severe the amnesia is. Some people may have a relatively mild form of amnesia, which allows for some independence, whereas others are more profoundly affected. This section describes some amnesics on whom treatment has been attempted.

One of these is a special education teacher, Sheila Moakes (Kapur & Moakes, 1995). She became amnesic when a case of herpes simplex encephalitis at the age of 32 damaged parts of her temporal lobe and hippocampus, leaving her with some retrograde amnesia and profound anterograde amnesia. While she was initially nearly incapacitated, she eventually did recover some abilities. Although she can no longer work as a regular teacher, tracking students across the school year, she is able to tutor students on a lesson-by-lesson basis. She can also do many household tasks but only by keeping to a strict schedule (otherwise she does not do some things and does others repeatedly), and she can do light grocery shopping if she has a list and does not have to go to a new store. She can still drive well, with her only problem being that she may become lost if she ventures too far from home. She does watch television but avoids shows that have a plot that must be remembered. She also does not read much for the same reason. Some parts of her life have continued to deteriorate. She has become distant to her son and has lost many of her old friends and is not been able to make new ones. She has also lost the motivation to learn new tasks because she knows the enormous effort that is involved.

If a person's amnesia is milder, he or she may be aware of the problem and develop strategies to compensate for the loss, such as the case of J. C. (Wilson, J. C., & Hughes, 1997), a former law student, who became amnesic after an attack of herpes simplex encephalitis. Because of some spared memory and his high intelligence and motivation, he was able to overcome this disability to some degree. Although he had to quit law school, he was able to train to become a professional furniture refinisher. Still, it took him

20 trips to learn where to get off the bus for refinishing school. He also went on to start his own business. To keep his life in order, he developed a system using a watch with multiple alarms and a color-coded filofax for keeping notes about events in his life. If he goes to a new restaurant with friends, he needs to write down where he went and what he ate, or he won't remember. J. C. also started a new relationship, but he must record facts about his activities with the woman. He also needs to leave himself constant reminders, such as "clean contact lenses" or "check the oven." His life critically depends on sticky notes.

J. C. was able to show remarkable adaptation due in large part to the tremendous amount of support and monitoring he gets from his family and friends. However, not all anterograde amnesics are so fortunate. For example, Mr. S. became amnesic in his 70s as the result of a stroke (Squires, Hunkin, & Parkin, 1997). Although he used a notebook for reminders in the beginning, a lack of reinforcement from his wife and friends, as well as his own lack of motivation, made him soon stop. Thus, there was no improvement for Mr. S.

Mixture of Retrograde and Anterograde Amnesia

As noted earlier, it is rare to have only retrograde or anterograde amnesia. Here we consider a case of severe trauma in which both were present and how this changed over time (as reported in Barbizet, 1970). An overview of the situation is given in Figure 16.4.

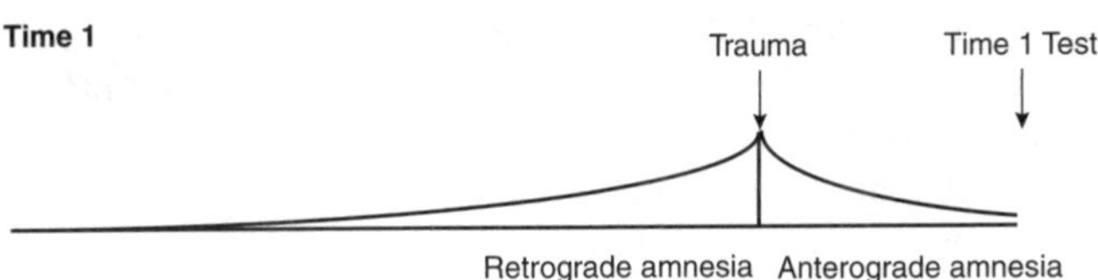

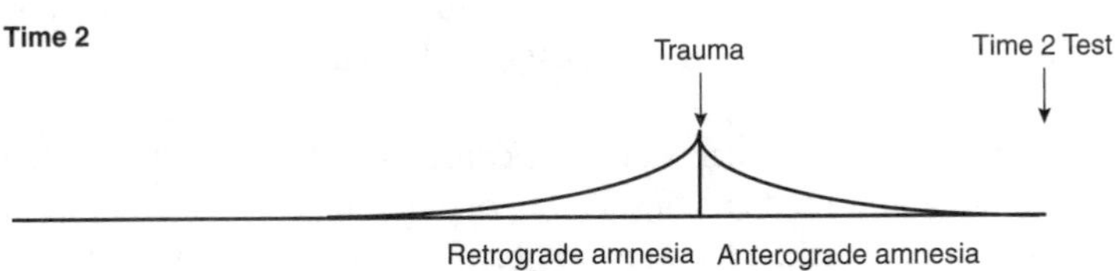

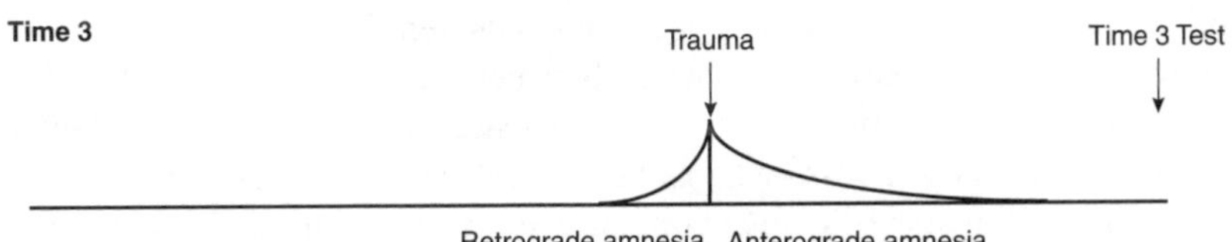

FIGURE 16.4 Illustration of Brain Damage Resulting in Both Retrograde and Anterograde Amnesias.

Initial testing occurred 5 months after the trauma in which there was both retrograde and anterograde amnesia. For the retrograde amnesia, the person was unable to remember events from the 2 years prior to the accident and had only partial memories for the time before that. For the anterograde amnesia, the person was not able to remember much of what happened after coming out of the coma, and was having trouble storing new memories.

As time progressed, things changed. The retrograde amnesia severity eases over time. By 8 months after the trauma, there was dense amnesia for only 1 year and partial amnesia for 4 years prior to that, and most other memories had returned to a normal. Ten months later, most of the retrograde amnesia had lifted, leaving only dense amnesia for the 2 weeks prior to the trauma, never to be recovered. As for the anterograde amnesia, there was some improvement as well. By 8 months after the trauma, some new information was being stored in long-term memory, and by 18 months memory had returned to a normal level. It is only for the 3.5-month period after the person emerged from the coma that there are no memories. Presumably, during this period the person was not able to store information effectively, so it will never be remembered.

Transient Global Amnesia. The types of amnesia that we have been talking about are the consequence of a clear traumatic injury, with no ambiguity about what brought it about, and the amnesia lasts for a substantial period of time. However, there is a rare form of amnesia that can occur where the cause is uncertain and the duration is brief, but that still affects a broad range of memories. This is **transient global amnesia (TGA).** During a TGA attack, a person has no memories of the recent past, anywhere from a few hours to several decades, although in most cases the memory loss is for a few months. This range of memory loss is shown in Figure 16.5. This amnesia can be very dense. For example, one person was surprised to see that some fingers on his left hand were missing, although they were lost in a farm machinery accident 4 months before.

Transient Global Amnesia episodes are short-lived, lasting only a few hours (typically 3–8 eight). A distribution of TGA durations is shown in Figure 16.6. This fleeting nature of TGA makes it hard to study, and although the concept of TGA has been around since the 1950s, it has been difficult to study until recently. Often, by the time a knowledgeable person is notified, the amnesia has begun to clear, and many incidents go unreported.

Often during a TGA episode, people are confused and repeatedly ask the same questions because of an anterograde amnesia component that prevents them from remembering that they had already asked the question or the answers. Although working memory appears to be fine, episodic knowledge is not retained or recovered. Semantic and procedural knowledge seem to be unaffected.

Part of what makes TGA so mysterious is that there is no clear indicator of its cause. The person seems fine but is experiencing a dense memory loss. As illustrated in Figure 16.7, TGAs often occur in people between the ages of 50 and 70, and typically only occur once in a lifetime. It has been suggested that TGAs are brought about by an emotional or physical stress or exertion, such as having an argument, playing an exciting card game, having sex (the most popular way to get it), driving, taking a hot shower, or having a coughing spell. There has been some suggestion that TGAs are a result of ischemias in the brain. These are temporary disruptions of blood flow. The parts of the

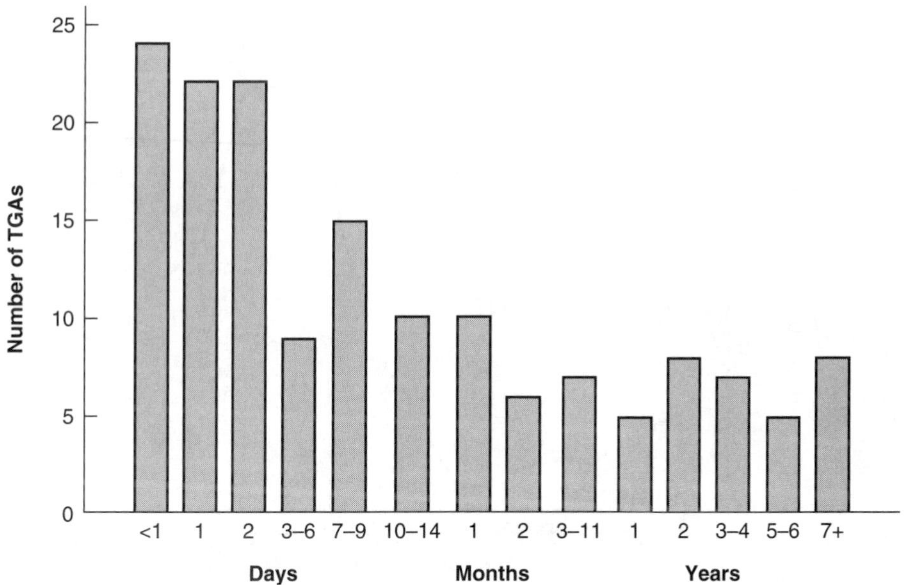

FIGURE 16.5 Degree of Retrograde Amnesia during a Transient Global Amnesia Episode

Source: Brown, A. S. (1998). Transient global amnesia. *Psychonomic Bulletin & Review, 5,* 401–427. Permission granted upon citation of source.

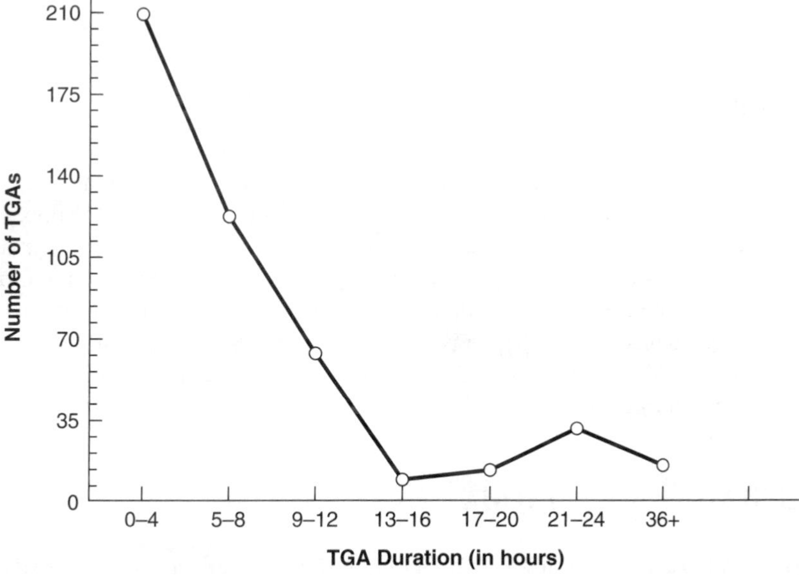

FIGURE 16.6 Duration of a Transient Global Amnesia

Source: Brown, A. S. (1998). Transient global amnesia. *Psychonomic Bulletin & Review, 5,* 401–427. Permission granted upon citation of source.

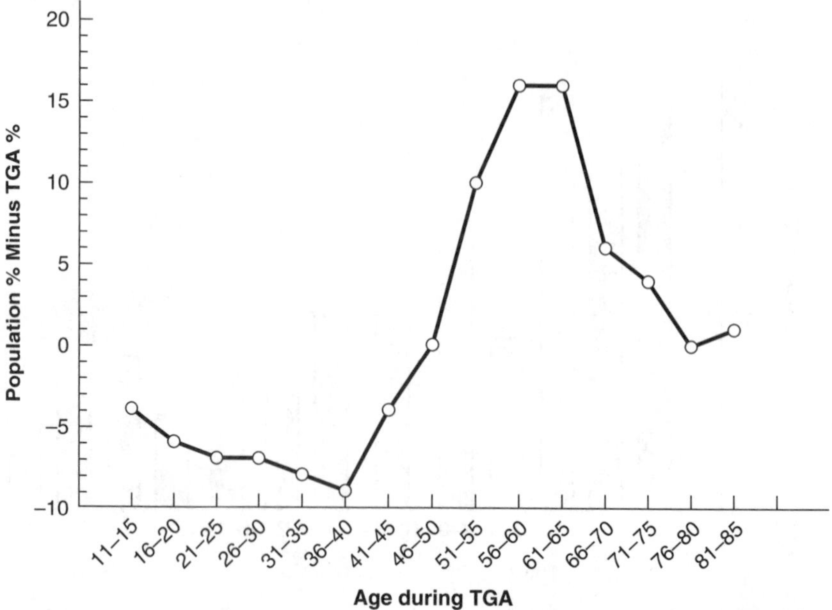

FIGURE 16.7 Age at Which a Transient Global Amnesia Episode Is Experienced

Source: Brown, A. S. (1998). Transient global amnesia. *Psychonomic Bulletin & Review, 5,* 401–427.

brain that are most often implicated are the temporal lobes, hippocampus, and thalamus. (For reviews of this phenomenon, see Brown, 1998, or Goldenberg, 1995.)

Synopsis

The loss of the ability to encode new memories is anterograde amnesia. Sometimes this deficit is quite severe, as with H. M. Anterograde amnesia can occur as a result of damage to either the hippocampus and medial temporal lobes or to the diencephalon. This amnesia results in profound loss of declarative memory abilities, whereas nondeclarative memory systems are less affected. People with anterograde amnesia need to be monitored for their own safety. However, people with less severe forms of this condition can have some limited independence. Finally, there is a form of amnesia known as transient global amnesia that is an odd loss of major periods of a person's life that can be triggered by mild to moderate stress during a person's early retirement years.

SHORT-TERM MEMORY AMNESIA

Most amnesias affect long-term memory, with preserved short-term memory. However, there are cases where short-term memory is damaged, but long-term memory is unaffected (e.g., Belleville, Caza, & Peretz, 2003). One example is the case of K. F. (Shallice & Warrington, 1970), who had a serial position curve recency effect of only one item (normal people have recency effects of five or six) and was not able to detect whether a probe letter was in a list if it was not the most recent one heard. However, long-term memory was relatively intact. Also there is the case of P. V. (Vallar & Baddeley, 1984; Vallar & Papagno, 1995), who had difficulty remembering spoken word lists over the short term but had normal memory for visually presented lists and good long-term retention. This led P. V. to have problems "understanding" short sequences that required verbal short-term memory, such as phone numbers or the prices of goods. She also had trouble doing mental calculations.

Many verbal short-term memory amnesias involved damage to the left parietal lobe (Vallar & Papagano, 1995)—in particular, the supramarginal gyrus (B.A. 40). In some cases, premotor areas of the frontal lobe are also implicated (e.g., Broca's area). This disrupts short-term memory rehearsal, and can have a spillover effect to influence more complex thinking, such as sentence comprehension. For example, a person with verbal short-term memory amnesia would have difficulty understanding sentences like "Touch the small green square and the large black circle," or "The cat that the dog chased was white." Comprehending these sentences requires keeping track of the words and the order in which they were heard. A person is less able to guess the intended message if there is some forgetting of some words or their order. People with short-term memory amnesia must rely on other sources of information. For example, patient I. R. could not use phonological information to help her remember but could use semantic information from long-term memory (Belleville, Caza, & Peretz, 2003).

Other short-term memory amnesias follow damage to the right parietal/occipital lobe resulting in visuo-spatial working memory problems (Vallar & Papagano, 1995), such as having difficulty counting the number of dots on a computer screen, identifying unfamiliar faces, doing mental rotation, or learning their way around an unfamiliar house.

Synopsis

Whereas most amnesias strike long-term memory, it is also possible to have short-term memory damaged, with long-term memory relatively intact. Rather than damaging short-term memory as a whole, different components of working memory appear to be compromised. This form of amnesia also deemphasizes the idea that long-term memory learning requires a fully functioning short-term memory.

PSYCHOGENIC AMNESIA

The amnesias we have seen so far are the result of physical brain damage, with a clear underlying cause. However, there are other types of amnesia that may arise based on psychological content, not the functioning of the nervous system. That is, a person may be so psychologically disturbed by something that it causes them to forget on a massive scale. These are **psychogenic amnesias** because they are brought about by psychological rather than neurological mechanisms. In most cases, the memory loss is associated with a traumatic event or circumstances in a person's life, and the knowledge lost is usually episodic or autobiographical in nature. Semantic and procedural memories remain intact.

The memory loss can be viewed as a way of coping with the trauma. If the oppressive knowledge is not consciously remembered, then it will no longer be stressful and anxiety provoking.

Repression

One of the best-known forms of psychogenic amnesia is **repression**, a concept associated with Freud and his followers. This view suggests that there are experiences people have that are traumatic or threatening to the point of potentially damaging the ability to function adequately in the world. These can be any number of traumas, including sexual abuse, violence, or even inappropriate sexual desires or feelings. To protect people from these damaging memories, a part of the mind actively represses them to keep them from entering consciousness. As such, repression is a defense mechanism.

The experimental support for repression is scarce. By its very nature, repression is difficult to study. First, one must recover repressed memories, but a problem is not knowing how accurate such memories are. As we saw in Chapter 12, it is easy for false memories to be generated, and there is no clear way, apart from independent evidence, to distinguish real recovered memories from false ones (Loftus, 1993). One of the more emotional debates in memory research has been whether or not recovered repressed memories are real. Some people have argued that there is no such thing as repression. All recovered repressed memories are either false memories or not really repressed in the first place. There are two lines of argument for this view. One is that many of the methods used to recover repressed memories are similar to those that would be used to generate false memories. Thus, many recovered memories are actually false memories. Another point is that the typical outcome for highly traumatic experiences is that people remember them very vividly and have difficulty forgetting them, even when they want to do so. This is the opposite of repression.

Dissociative Amnesia

Another psychogenic amnesia is **dissociative amnesia** in which a person is unable to remember segments of his or her life (Kihlstrom & Schacter, 1995). Typically, the forgotten knowledge is either traumatic itself or is associated with a traumatic event. For example, suppose you were the driver of a car in an accident that resulted in someone's death. If this pathologically troubled you, you might acquire dissociative amnesia in which you do not remember any of the events of that day. What makes this condition distinct from repression is that a person is aware of the memory loss and is troubled by it, whereas this may not be the case with repression.

There are three ways for dissociative amnesia to manifest itself (Nemiah, 1979). The first is as a **systematized amnesia,** where people are amnesic for information related to a traumatic event, regardless of when or where it occurred. Second, as a **localized amnesia,** in which a person has trouble remembering events within a block of time, such as a period of hours or weeks. Finally, as a **generalized amnesia,** in which nearly all of a person's life is forgotten. These different ways that dissociative amnesia manifests itself illustrate the psychological influence of its origins. This selectivity or breadth of coverage is almost never seen with organic amnesia.

Dissociative Fugue

A more profound psychogenic amnesia is a **dissociative fugue,** in which memory is disrupted to the point that a person forgets fundamental aspects of his or her identity, such as who he or she is, where he or she lives, and what he or she does for a living (Kihlstrom & Schacter, 1995). There are different fugue states, depending on the nature and extent of the loss (Fisher, 1945; Fisher & Joseph, 1949). First, there may be a change in both identity and location (where the person lives)—this is **fugue and flight.** Second, there may be a loss of memories, but the core identity is intact—this is **memory fugue.** Finally, there may be a reversion to an earlier state of life, with an inability to remember events after that period—this is **regression fugue.** Again, this sort of memory loss is psychological and is not seen with organic damage.

Although conscious awareness of previous memories is rendered inaccessible in the fugue state, if this is like other amnesias, one would expect implicit memory to be unaffected. This has been difficult to test, especially because the fugue state is so rare. However, there is some anecdotal evidence consistent with this idea. A dramatic illustration of preserved implicit memory of a fugal amnesic is a case of a woman who had been found wandering around but could provide no information about herself. She was asked on several occasions to dial a random number on a telephone. This number turned out to be her mother's (Lyon, 1985).

What is more fascinating is that when a person comes out of the fugue state, even if it had been going on for years, not only do memories from the original identity return, but memories from the fugue identity become forgotten. This return to the original identity can be slow or fast. Thus, even when there has been a recovery of the original identity, there is still an amnesic state associated with this condition.

Dissociative Identity Disorder

A final psychogenic amnesia is involved in **dissociative identity disorder**, in which a person acts as if he or she has many separate identities, each with its own autobiographical history. In some cases these alternative identities are aware of the others. Often one identity has no conscious memories of what another identity learned while he or she was dominant. In dissociative identity disorder, there may be asymmetrical amnesia across identities (Kihlstrom & Schacter, 1995). That is, one identity may be able to remember information that was learned when a second identity was dominant but not vice versa. This bears some resemblance to dissociative fugue, where the shift from one identity to another results in some amnesic forgetting of information learned while involved with a previous identity.

Still, this amnesia does not apply to all memories. Like organic amnesia, implicit memories may be intact with an otherwise amnesic loss across identities, as with procedural memory learning (Kihlstrom & Schacter, 1995) or priming (Huntjens et al., 2002).

Synopsis

It may be possible for people to be amnesic from psychological trauma. These psychogenic amnesias include repression, dissociative amnesia, dissociative fugue, and dissociative identity disorder.

SUMMARY

In this chapter we looked at a number of ways memory can be altered to create a state of pathological forgetting. Often this amnesia results from some sort of organic disturbance to the brain. In some cases, as with retrograde amnesia, a person is unable to remember a large number of events from his or her recent past. This can be the result of many events, such as a blow to the head or from electroconvulsive therapy treatments. With anterograde amnesia, a person is unable to acquire new memories. Sometimes this occurs as a result of damage to the hippocampus or the medial temporal lobe. In other cases it is a result of damage to diencephalic structures of the brain, such as the thalamus. In either case, a person with anterograde amnesia is effectively trapped in the present, with little to no abilities to adapt and change as a result of new information they are given. However, there may be a preservation of some unconscious memories, such as procedural memory. If a person were to acquire anterograde amnesia, life is changed dramatically, and only with a great deal of effort and support will the person be able to approach living a normal life. Finally, in the condition known as transient global amnesia, a person may become amnesic for a period of only a day.

Other types of amnesia have no clear organic source but seem to be due to more psychological stressors. For example, the Freudian concept of repression, if it exists, would be a broad-based defense mechanism that prevents threatening memories from entering conscious awareness. Well-documented cases of dissociative amnesia can occur if a person has certain memories that are highly traumatic. When pushed to an extreme, a person may become amnesic for his or her entire identity, as in a fugue state, and possibly wander off to form a new life as a new person. In one of the more intriguing psychopathologies that can arise, persons with dissociative identity disorder will behave as though they have different personalities with different identities. What is interesting is that some of these personalities may be amnesic for information that was learned when a different personality was dominant, at least for declarative memories.

STUDY QUESTIONS

1. How does retrograde amnesia occur? What are some of its defining characteristics? How does this relate to Ribot's Law?
2. What do electroconvulsive shocks do to memory? How extensive can the damage be?
3. What is transient global amnesia? How extensive is the loss? How long does it last? Who does this happen to?
4. What is anterograde amnesia? Damage to which brain structures produces this condition?
5. What types of memories are damaged in anterograde amnesia? What types of memories are preserved? What is the general prognosis for people with this condition?
6. What sorts of memory losses occur with short-term memory amnesias? How are these different losses associated with different parts of the brain?
7. What is psychogenic amnesia? What is repression? What is dissociative amnesia? What is a psychogenic fugue? What memory losses can occur in dissociative identity disorder?

KEY TERMS

amnesia, anterograde amnesia, consolidation, dissociative amnesia, dissociative fugue, dissociative identity disorder, Electroconvulsive Shock (ECS), Electroconvulsive Therapy (ECT), fugue and flight, generalized amnesia, localized amnesia, memory fugue, psychogenic amnesia, regression fugue, repression, retrograde amnesia, Ribot's Law, systematized amnesia, transient global amnesia (TGA)

CHAPTER SEVENTEEN

OTHER CONDITIONS THAT AFFECT MEMORY

In addition to the amnesia discussed in Chapter 16 there are other conditions that affect memory. These conditions are the focus of this chapter. Each of these is associated with some alteration of the typical pattern of neurological activity. Although most of these have a negative effect on memory, there are conditions that can lead to superior memory performance. The memory changes that are seen in these conditions are only part of a larger set of cognitive changes that are associated with each of them. This chapter first covers memory disorders that arise in various types of dementia that a person might be unfortunate enough to develop. These include conditions such as Alzheimer's, Parkinson's, and Huntington's diseases, as well as multiple sclerosis. Following this, there is an overview of how a serious psychotic condition, like schizophrenia, can have a profound and negative impact on memory. Other, milder psychological conditions, such as anxiety and depression, can also disrupt normal memory function. Also, a number of specific memory losses that occur with more localized and limited forms of brain damage are examined. Following this, perhaps closer to your own experience, the chapter discusses how the effects of drugs and alcohol can impair memory in some ways and help it in others. The chapter wraps up with a discussion of how the condition of synesthesia can sometimes improve memory.

DEMENTIA

Dementia is a condition in which there are serious impairments in many aspects of thinking, only one of which is memory, but without an impairment of consciousness. The memory problems that occur include a decline in the ability to learn new information and a loss of prior memories. Because of widespread degradation in the brain, this memory loss can even extend to well-ingrained memories. Generally, people often think of dementias as illnesses of only the elderly. Although it is true that many older adults will acquire some form of dementia (15 percent over the age of 65 and 25 to 47 percent over the age of 85), many younger people contract these diseases as well (Brandt & Rich, 1995). In this section we consider a number of the more prominent dementias in detail. These include Alzheimer's disease, Parkinson's disease, Huntington's disease, and the dementia associated with multiple sclerosis.

Alzheimer's Disease

Alzheimer's disease is a condition originally described by Alois Alzheimer in 1907. It is one of the most rapidly expanding health concerns, and as the population ages, more people will succumb to its effects. This disease occurs only in certain people as a result of specific neurological conditions. It is not a natural consequence of growing old. While far too many older adults contract Alzheimer's, most do not. Also, unfortunately, a person is often very aware of the progressive memory loss.

Characteristics. Alzheimer's disease is a cortical dementia that primarily affects the cerebral cortex. It is marked by a severe degradation in brain structure and function. In essence, with Alzheimer's disease, the mind and memory deteriorate. Three primary changes occur in this condition (Hodges, 2000). The first is a loss in the number of neurons and neural connections, primarily focused in the frontal and temporal lobes, which are critical for effective memory processing, with the primarily sensory and motor areas being better preserved. Second there is a presence of **neurofibrillary tangles** that occur within neurons and impede their ability to effectively transmit a signal. They grow over time, eventually pushing other neural structures, such as the nucleus, mitochondria, and ribosomes to one side, and disrupting their function and filling up the interior of the axons and dendrites. Finally, a third change is the presence of **amyloid plaques,** which are growths of old neural tissue with a core of amyloid proteins that occupy the regions around neurons and are surrounded by microglia. These plaques are about 70 microns in diameter, much larger than the neurons, which are often only 10 to 30 microns in diameter. Their presence makes it difficult for neurons to function because they degenerate the neurons' axons.

In addition, with Alzheimer's disease there are also changes in the cholinergic system (Bartus, Dean, Beer, & Lippa, 1982), particularly the manufacturing of the neurotransmitter acetylcholine (ACh), which is critical to learning and memory. The decrease can be mediated somewhat by people taking medications, such as Donepezil.

Causes of Alzheimer's Disease. No one knows for sure what causes Alzheimer's. However, a number of preconditions are known that indicate the likelihood of contracting the disease (Small, 1998). There is a strong genetic component. If a relative has Alzheimer's, there is a 25 to 50 percent probability that a person will develop it as well. If not, then the probability is only 10 percent. In identical twins, if one twin contracts the condition, there is a 40 to 50 percent chance that the other will contract it as well, and a 10 to 50 percent chance for fraternal twins. There is a higher rate of occurrence of the disease in people with Down syndrome, also suggesting a genetic component.

There are also external, environmental influences. For example, people who have suffered head traumas or long periods of depression are more likely to succumb. There are some protective factors. People who have been exposed to estrogen or antioxidants are less likely to get the disease. Similarly, people who experience body inflammations, such as arthritis, are less likely to contract Alzheimer's. There may also be some DNA combinations that are more resistant to this condition. Thus, many factors impact whether a person will one day suffer from Alzheimer's disease.

Memory Changes. People with Alzheimer's suffer from working memory problems. These tend not to be problems maintaining information but with controlling the flow of thought in the central executive. They have normal working memory spans for verbal and spatial information. However, they do not show normal recency effects for larger sets of information. In terms of central executive problems they have trouble managing memories under dual-task conditions where a person needs to keep track of two things at once. As such, they can become more easily confused and overwhelmed.

Alzheimer's has a profound effect on episodic memories, although there is a temporal gradient, with newer memories being more likely to be compromised than older memories (e.g., Sadek et al., 2004). This temporal gradient of memory loss can be extensive, reaching back several decades. As the disease progresses, there are losses of earlier memories that can result in changes and losses in a person's identity (Addis & Tippett, 2004). The temporal gradient of memory loss suggests that a problem in this condition is in encoding. It is even difficult for Alzheimer's patients to form new flashbulb memories (Budson & Gold, 2009). Neurological work using fMRI scanning has shown that the prefrontal lobes of Alzheimer's patients are not functioning as well as normal people's (Corkin, 1998). The rate with which Alzheimer's patients forget episodic information, once it has been encoded, is the same as that for people without the disease (White & Ruske, 2002). Thus, the episodic memory problems can be viewed as a form of anterograde amnesia. Retrieval, while difficult, is less of a problem, at least in the earlier stages of the disease. This deficit is more profound with recall than with recognition.

Although semantic memory is initially more resistant, it does eventually succumb. Alzheimer's patients may lose the ability to recall the names of objects and may substitute similar words—for example, using "tiger" or "animal" for "lion." Thus, there is a degree of noise and error in semantic memory. This can also be seen in how semantic memories are lost. Memory of how something is used to interact with other objects—that is, its functional relations—is lost sooner than knowledge about its parts and properties, with knowledge about categorical relations being the most resistant (Johnson & Hermann, 1995). Also, patients with Alzheimer's are more likely to have trouble remembering public information as compared to autobiographical information (Greene & Hodges, 1996). Here is a case where more stable, semantic information is more vulnerable than more episodic information.

Although many memory systems are affected by Alzheimer's, some systems are left relatively intact. For example, implicit memory processes are less affected. This also spills over into related metamemory processes. For example, using the remember-know distinction, Alzheimer's patients show declines in memory for information that is marked as "remember" but not when it is marked as "know" (Barba, 1997). Also, Alzheimer's patients have trouble making accurate source monitoring decisions (Mammarella & Fairfield, 2006). That said, some implicit memory processes are disrupted. For example, Alzheimer's patients often show impaired semantic priming.

Parkinson's Disease

The diseases we look at now—Parkinson's, Huntington's, and multiple sclerosis—are subcortical dementias. This is in contrast to Alzheimer's, which is a cortical dementia. It should be noted that not everyone who contracts these diseases become clearly demented.

These subcortical dementias are often associated with movement difficulties, as well as more minor problems with memory and thinking.

With **Parkinson's disease** there is damage to or loss of neurons in the basal ganglia and the substantia nigra. This condition is accompanied by a disruption in dopamine processing. This damage produces problems in coordinating movements, such as tremors, "pill rolling" (rubbing fingers together as if rolling a pill), problems in facial expression, and difficulty in walking. Parkinson's usually begins around the age of 50. In addition to the movement problems, there are cognitive and emotional deficits, including problems with memory (Brandt & Rich, 1995; Ivory, Knight, Longmore, & Caradoc-Davies, 1999; Prizzolo et al., 1982). There may be working memory problems, such as with updating spatial information in the visuo-spatial sketchpad. For example, when they travel through a new space with twists and turns, they may become more disoriented (Montgomery et al., 1993). In addition, they may experience problems identifying locations of previously seen pictures on a simple display grid (Pillon et al., 1997). They do not keep track of spatial contextual information like normal people would.

In addition, people with Parkinson's may have central executive and episodic buffer troubles (Altgassen, Phillips, Kopp, & Kliegel, 2007; Brown & Marsden, 1988). In fact, the visuo-spatial deficits may actually be a result of more central executive and episodic buffer problems (Altgassen et al., 2007). They have some difficulty controlling their stream of thought and how they use memories. For example, they have difficulty changing strategies and will continue doing things the way they've always done them before (Canavan et al., 1989). They also have difficulty evaluating the importance of events in a semantic schema or script, although they can order scripted information quite well (Zalla et al., 2000).

Like Alzheimer's, with Parkinson's the loss of episodic memories follows a temporal gradient, with older memories being more preserved than newer ones. However, the extent of the temporal gradient is far more subtle and is not as noticeable. Finally, while the forgetting of event content is less compromised in Parkinson's than in Alzheimer's, the opposite is true for event date memories. People with Parkinson's may have difficulty locating events in time (Sagar, Cohen et al., 1988; Sagar, Sullivan, et al., 1988), or putting information in a correct sequence, such as a telephone number. There is some suggestion that part of the problem is trouble in coordinating retrieval strategies and not so much in encoding or consolidation (Godbout & Doyon, 2000). Specifically, when recalling the components of a common script, such as going to the doctor, Parkinson's patients are more likely to leave out minor components, retrieve script components in the incorrect order, and have more irrelevant intrusions.

Huntington's Disease

Huntington's disease is characterized by uncontrolled muscle spasms, resulting in jerky movements. It is caused by damage to the basal ganglia and the caudate nucleus and often strikes around the age of 40, and the victim often dies by the age of 60. In addition, there are problems in memory (Brandt & Rich, 1995). Huntington's patients have problems with the central executive of working memory, resulting in a reduced memory span and difficulties in dual-task situations (Hodges, 2000). However, the rate of forgetting in episodic memory may be preserved along with recognition memory. Also, importantly, there is no temporal gradient to forgetting, but it is more uniform across time (e.g., Sadek et al., 2004). This suggests that the problem is with retrieval rather than the encoding and storage of memories.

With Huntington's disease, there may be problems with free recall, but not recognition, consistent with the idea that they are having trouble planning how to retrieve information. In general, the memory deficits are milder and similar to those observed with Parkinson's. However, Huntington's patients are more likely to have trouble with nonverbal information, such as memory for faces, spatial layouts, or visual images. Finally, people with Huntington's may have trouble with procedural memory, even though this memory system is often preserved in people with neurologically related memory losses.

Multiple Sclerosis

Multiple sclerosis involves a demyelinization of various neurons. Although this is generally associated with muscle control problems, it can also affect memory. There appears to be some atrophy of cells in area CA1 of the hippocampus, which is important for the creation of declarative memories (Sicotte et al., 2008). One of the larger areas of impact is short-term memory. There are problems in both creating and retrieving memories (Pelosi et al., 1997), but multiple sclerosis patients appear to have good awareness of their memory abilities (Randolph, Arnett, & Higginson, 2001). There is also a decline in the speed with which short-term memory is scanned, but not so much in working memory capacity (Janculjak, Mubrin, Brinar, & Spilich, 2002). Again, there is a greater disturbance of explicit over implicit memory.

Synopsis

Memory can be devastatingly altered by dementia. Alzheimer's, the most common disease that affects memory, results in memory being systematically destroyed as drastic changes are made to brain structure. Other conditions, such as Parkinson's, Huntington's, and multiple sclerosis, are subcortical diseases that can each have a memory loss component but are not as devastating to memory as Alzheimer's. How each condition affects memory depends on the brain structures that are damaged.

MEMORY PROBLEMS WITH OTHER PATHOLOGIES

In this section we consider the problems people can experience as a consequence of other conditions where memory loss is not necessarily the focus, nor are they dementias.

Confabulation

Some brain-damaged patients report things that are clearly not based on reality but are false memories generated by the patient. This is called **confabulation.** This is a symptom that may occur with damage to the frontal lobes. Thus, there is damage to the central executive of working memory. The false reports provided during confabulation are inconsistent with the patient's past and current situation, and are not lies as there is no intent to deceive. The patient is reporting what he or she believes to be the truth. Even when the confabulations are very bizarre, the person is unaware of any memory problems. Overall, a person is not able to effectively monitor memory and evaluate the results of retrieval. Thus, incorrect information is reported as if it were true. Confabulatory reports are often confined to episodic memory, with a strong metamemory sense of remembering. Semantic memory is largely unaffected (Barba, 1993). So, people are unconsciously inventing information about their lives, while their general understanding of how the world is structured and operates is relatively intact.

Schizophrenia

Schizophrenia is a class of serious mental disorders in which a person becomes detached from reality through a disruption in patterns of thinking and perception. Part of the cause of schizophrenia is an imbalance of neurotransmitters, such as dopamine. Schizophrenics may have amnesia for parts of episodic memory, with a temporal gradient present, with more severe memory impairment for newer memories. It is unclear to what degree this reflects actual problems with memory per se or of a general psychological disturbance. If people have disrupted and fragmented thought processes, it follows that they will have trouble structuring and organizing information. This low degree of structure will worsen memory. For semantic memory, the ability to retain information remains stable, although schizophrenics appear to be less organized in their use of semantic knowledge.

For schizophrenics, implicit memory is better preserved. For example, when asked to make remember-know distinctions, they are deficient for "remember" responses but not "know" responses (Huron, et al., 1995). Also, short-term memory appears to remain fairly intact (McKenna, Clare, & Baddeley, 1995). Looking at working memory in particular, the phonological loop and visuo-spatial sketchpad are less affected, but there are noticeable problems with the central executive. This is not surprising given that a role of the central executive is to help control the flow of thought, and schizophrenics' thinking patterns are very disturbed.

Depression

Memory problems can occur as a result of other psychological conditions as well, such as **depression.** Depression is a state that, if it persists for a long time, can create problems with memory (Watts, 1995). Depressed people find it difficult to encode new information, particularly positive information. Part of this may be due to a decline in motivation that not only affects the amount of information produced on a free recall test, although it can also worsen performance on forced recall and recognition tests. Part of this deficit may reflect a decreased likelihood that depressed people actively organize information.

People with depression may have selective memory problems. Consistent with mood-congruent memory, depressed people show a greater tendency to remember negative experiences. This may be due to decreased memory for positive information rather than increased memory for negative information (Blaney, 1986). In a study by Deldin, Keller, Gergen, and Miller (2001) people saw a series of faces. These faces expressed positive, neutral, or negative emotions. On a later memory test, during which ERPs were recorded, normal people showed a P300 when they saw positive faces they had seen before, indicating that they recognized them. However, depressed people did not show such a sign.

In addition to the mood-congruent effects, people in negative moods are limited in the amount of semantic memory information that is activated (Bolte, Goschke, & Kuhl, 2003). So, people in negative moods are less able to think creatively because less information is available in semantic memory.

With depression, short-term memory tends to be undisturbed. These people have normal memory spans, and they show normal recency effects, although the primacy effects might be compromised because depressed people are less likely to exert the effort needed to rehearse information and transfer it to long-term memory. In addition, there do not appear to be problems in implicit memory.

In very extreme and rare cases, depression can become so severe that a person suffers from the **Cotard delusion**, which is a belief that one is dead or that the world does not exist. This was first described by Jules Cotard, in 1882. This condition may occur with a profound depression and very little emotional response, accompanied by a decline in the ability to access episodic and semantic memories that would help identify the current surroundings and make them seem real (Leafhead & Kopelman, 1997). In essence, there is an almost a complete lack of a feeling of familiarity that would normally accompany memory retrieval.

Anxiety and Stress

With **anxiety** and **stress**, people exert a great deal of effort trying to resolve memory problems. These problems are more likely to occur with state anxiety (when an otherwise normal person is anxious) than with trait anxiety (people for whom anxiety is a part of their basic personality [Watts, 1995]). Unlike depression, there are noticeable problems with short-term memory. Because an anxious person is actively pursuing one or more lines of thought, there is less capacity available for other information (Beilock, 2008). As a result, short-term/working memory suffers. For example, people who are math-anxious tend to do worse on math problems they would otherwise be able to solve because their working memory capacity is consumed with irrelevant anxious thoughts (Ashcraft, 2002; Ashcraft & Krause, 2007). In long-term memory, if the task is easy, little disturbance is observed, but for more difficult tasks, an anxious person will show a deficit. Note that factors that can assist memory performance, such as accessing a wide range of semantic information, can actually lead anxious people to perform better.

One source of irrelevant information that can disrupt working memory is negative emotions (Kensinger & Corkin, 2003a). Negative and irrelevant information can clog up working memory. However, students who engage in expressive writing to disclose personal emotions can increase working memory span (Klein & Boals, 2001). This benefit is observed even weeks after the disclosure. Apparently, this expression decreases the implicit need or desire to think about it, so there are fewer intrusive anxious thoughts. People who write about negative experiences showed a larger increase in working memory span than people who wrote about neutral or positive experiences. So if you express thoughts that are troubling you, it might help you increase your working memory capacity later, and it could improve your memory overall.

Synopsis

Memory loss can be a symptom or side effect of many pathological conditions. Confabulation is a symptom in which a person has difficulty monitoring the contents and configurations of information retrieved from memory. Memories that would normally be rejected are accepted as genuine. People with severe mental disturbances, such as schizophrenia, have memory problems, such as metacognitive awareness of where memories come from. Depression and anxiety also have strong memory components. People with depression have difficulty remembering positive information. In contrast, people with severe anxiety have the same difficulty because they are remembering too much, with this extra information crowding out desired working memory processes.

LOSS OF MEMORY OF SPECIFIC KNOWLEDGE OR SKILLS

The distinction between autobiographical and semantic memories is observed with certain types of amnesia. For example, a person may have trouble with semantic memory but not autobiographical memory. Yasuda, Watanabe, and Ono (1997) describe a patient, M. N., who sustained (from a tumor) damage to her right hemisphere where the frontal and temporal lobes meet. She was able to give accurate accounts of her autobiographical memories, such as where she had gone to school, the places she had worked, and the various illnesses she had. However, she had difficulty identifying and remembering public events, recalling only 20 percent of those that most people could recall at a 100 percent level. She had problems with historical figures and famous monuments. This problem with semantic memory is also found in a condition called semantic amnesia.

Semantic Amnesia

Semantic amnesia is a deficit in the ability to retrieve semantic knowledge, often as a result of damage to the temporal lobes, particularly in the anterolateral portions (B.A. 38) and more likely with damage to the left hemisphere (Hodges, Patternson, Oxbuy, & Funnell, 1992; Patterson & Hodges, 1995; Snowden, Goulding, & Neary, 1989). This is a rare condition in the absence of other neurological syndromes, such as Alzheimer's disease, because many of the sources of damage tend to also affect other areas, and because this part of the brain is so well supported, such as this part of the temporal lobe being maintained by two major arteries, making it less likely to be damaged by a stroke.

People with semantic amnesia have difficulty retrieving word meanings, even for common words, despite otherwise normal language. For example, a person with semantic amnesia may not be able to remember what a cat or a robin is or whether a mouse has a beak or a long, skinny tail (Funnell, 1995). This loss is called **anomia** and can be very specific. For example, one patient, G. R., had difficulty with famous names but not with the names of friends or historical or literary figures (Lucchelli, Muggia, & Spinnler, 1997). G. R.'s memory for facts about a person was intact, such as knowing her line of work and any distinguishing achievements or physical features. The trouble was in remembering the names of these celebrities. For a first-hand account of the experience of anomia, see Ashcraft (1993).

With semantic amnesia and anomia, other parts of memory, including nondeclarative and episodic memories, are relatively intact. What distinguishes it from aphasia is that people also have difficulty with semantic judgments that do not require language, suggesting that semantic memory has been damaged (Bozeat et al., 2000). People have difficulty not only with the names of objects but also with how these objects are used. This is called **apraxia**. They may attempt to use objects incorrectly, such as trying to use a match as a pencil. Because of this, such people need to be constantly monitored to avoid harming themselves. It should be noted that they may be able to use some objects appropriately in cases where the use of the objects is clear and constrained (Hodges et al., 2000)—for example, using a pair of scissors with a piece of paper. There are only a limited number of ways that the scissors lend themselves to being used in that situation, and many people with apraxia perform normally.

Semantic amnesia can be restricted to particular types of information. This is illustrated by A. B. R., whose semantic amnesia occurred after a period of anoxia during open heart surgery. A. B. R. had trouble identifying pictures (but not names) of famous people (e.g., Queen Elizabeth and Napoleon) and landmarks (e.g., the White House and the Parthenon). The rest of his memories were relatively intact (Kartsounis & Shallice, 1996). Another distinction that may be affected is between abstract and concrete ideas. In normal people, concrete ideas (such as sock, pencil, dog) are easier to remember than abstract ones (such as truth, love, redemption). However, a patient, D. M., could identify abstract but not concrete words (Breedin, Saffran, & Coslett, 1994). A similar isolation in semantic amnesia can occur for knowledge of natural kinds versus artifacts (Patterson & Hodges, 1995).

Thus, there are a variety of ways memory can be affected in semantic amnesia. In an effort to bring some coherence to understanding semantic amnesia, Cree and McRae (2003) have broken down the trends seen in the various deficits into dimensions of processing. Essentially, these dimensions capture salient characteristics of knowledge, each of which is handled by a different part of the brain. Each dimension separates out different types of knowledge. These dimensions are listed below.

Dimension 1. Visual motion/complexity versus frequency/function

Dimension 2. Distinctive sounds versus distinctive features or names

Dimension 3. Touch/taste/color versus parts/textures

Dimension 4. Smell/correlated features/encyclopedic features versus parts/textures (p. 190)

This breakdown helps us understand the complexity of semantic information in normal people, and future theories of semantic memory need to take these sorts of findings into account. Moreover, it also helps us understand the problems that people face with semantic amnesia. Once we better understand their deficits, we can then more confidently link them with underlying neurological or psychological problems and be better prepared to treat them.

Before leaving semantic amnesia, let's think about what is going on in episodic memory a little more. As a reminder, despite problems in semantic memory, even complex forms of episodic memory, such as autobiographical memory, appear to be preserved (Simons, Graham, & Hodges, 2002). These autobiographical memories can be used to guide semantic dementia patients to derive semantic-like knowledge. Memories of previous experiences can help people derive some sort of semantic understanding, even though semantic memory itself may be compromised (Graham, Ralph, & Hodges, 1997). For example, a person could remember the names of other people he or she played golf with frequently by using autobiographical memories, but he or she would not be able to remember the names of people he or she had played with in the distant past or the names of famous golfers. Although there is some preservation of episodic memory, it is incomplete. There is an odd reversal of Ribot's Law with semantic amnesia, particularly for semantic aspects of those events, such as people's names (Piolino et al., 2003).

Aphasia, Amusia, and Prospagnosia

Some semantic amnesias are exclusive to certain types of knowledge and are identified as separate conditions. In some cases, people may lose the ability to remember how to use language, called **aphasia.** Because language is usually located in the left hemisphere of the brain, this is typically a result of damage to that area. There are two general kinds of aphasia. One is **Broca's aphasia,** which occurs when there is damage to caudal portions of the frontal lobe, and adjoining portions of the temporal lobe (B.A. 44 & 45). This is near the motor cortex of the frontal lobe. In this condition, a person has difficulty producing language, but language comprehension is better preserved. Another aphasia is **Wernicke's aphasia**, which occurs with damage to the posterior temporal lobe and the adjoining portions of the parietal lobe (B.A. 22). Here, a person has difficulty comprehending language, but language production is better preserved. This decline can get to the point where people cannot even monitor their own language. As a result, they produce a word salad that is grammatically correct but semantically anomalous. Unlike people with Broca's aphasia, people with Wernicke's aphasia are less aware of their deficit. A condition that is closely related to aphasia is called **amusia.** People with this deficit may have trouble either comprehending or producing music.

Another specific memory loss is **prosopagnosia,** or a failure to recognize faces, which can occur after damage to the fusiform gyrus (B. A. 37). Essentially, people with this condition retain memories of different people, but are unable to recognize a person's face, even when they know the person well. A patient may not even be able to recognize his or her own face in a mirror. Patients with this condition must use other cues to identify someone, such as the person's voice. Thus, different types of knowledge about people use different parts of the brain. Memory retrieval is not a discrete process of remembering. Instead, people may be able to partially remember some information but not all of it.

Synopsis

It is possible to have selective deficits that target memory for certain types of information but that leave other types of information relatively intact. In semantic amnesia, people have difficulty retrieving semantic information about the world, which makes it difficult for them to understand what is going on around them. However, their episodic and autobiographical memories are comparatively well preserved. Memory loss can also target specific abilities, such as loss of language skill memories with aphasia, loss of music skill memories with amusia, and loss of object name knowledge with anomia. Thus, different parts of the brain play specialized roles in remembering different types of knowledge.

DRUGS AND ALCOHOL

In this section we look at the influence of drugs that are known to produce dramatic changes in memory. In addition, we also look at the effects of alcohol on memory performance.

Drugs

One class of drugs that has a strong influence on memory is *benzodiazepines* (e.g., Valium and Halcion), which are depressants. These drugs have their influence by increasing GABA-related processes, which inhibit neural firing. Because of this suppressed neural activity, people taking these drugs have difficulty acquiring new episodic memories. In a sense, this is a drug-induced form of anterograde amnesia without retrograde amnesia, similar to what is seen in Korsakoff's syndrome patients (Curran, 1991; Mintzer & Griffiths, 2001). Thus, benzodiazepines primarily compromise declarative as compared to nondeclarative memory (Mintzer, 2003; Reder et al., 2006), with PET scans on one study showing suppressed processing in the right prefrontal cortex (B.A. 9), left parahippocampal gyrus (B.A. 35), and left anterior cingulated cortex (B.A. 32 [Mintzer et al., 2006]). A beneficial consequence of this drug-induced anterograde amnesia is that the retroactive interference effects are diminished, causing memory for information prior to taking the drug to be better than it would otherwise be (Fillmore, Kelly, Rush, & Hays, 2001). In addition, it should be noted that although memory is typically better for emotional information, people taking benzodiazepines do not show this benefit, suggesting that these drugs also disrupt processing in the amygdala (Buchanan, Karafin, & Adolphs, 2003).

Alcohol

Another substance that can have important influence on memory is *alcohol*. Alcohol can have a number of effects. Although we primarily focus on the consequences of individual episodes of drinking, there are other important memory topics that are not addressed here, including the consequences of chronic alcoholism and fetal alcohol syndrome. In general, memory is worse for information learned while under the influence of alcohol. This affects a broad range of memory processes (see Maylor & Rabbitt, 1993, for a review), including executive working memory function (Saults, Cowan, Sher, & Moreno, 2007), prospective memory (Leitz et al., 2009), and producing overconfidence in metamemory judgments (Nelson, McSpadden, Fromme, & Marlatt, 1986). Work using the process dissociation procedure has shown that this is more so for explicit, declarative knowledge than for implicit, nondeclarative knowledge (Kirchner & Sayette, 2003; Ray & Bates, 2006; Ray, Bates, & Bly, 2004). Part of the problem is that alcohol, as EEG recordings show, disrupts event-related synchronization and desynchronization (see Chapter 2) in the cortex in the theta and alpha band levels (Krause et al., 2002). At high enough blood alcohol levels, a person can experience blackouts during which there is no memory for any of the events of that time period. This is a sign of a serious drinking problem.

In addition to the negative effects of alcohol on memory, there are some positive effects as well. Specifically, information is remembered better if people consume alcohol immediately after some event, such as finding out about a big promotion at work, than if they do not (Moulton, et al., 2005; Parker et al., 1980). One idea is that because information is so poorly encoded when one is under the influence of alcohol, there are fewer new memory traces to produce retroactive interference, thereby making memory for the information present prior to alcohol consumption better than it would otherwise be. Another line of thinking is that alcohol may actually facilitate consolidation of the earlier memory traces, perhaps because of increased glucose levels (Hewitt, Holder, & Laird, 1996; Scholey & Fowles, 2002).

Alcohol can even influence memory when it is not present by just the suggestion that someone has consumed alcohol. For example, in a study by Assefi and Garry (2003) students at Victoria University of Wellington in New Zealand watched a slide show that involved a man shoplifting at a bookstore. Later, people were presented with misleading post-event information (see Chapter 13) Although all students drank tonic water, half of them were told that the water also contained vodka. The students who thought that they drank alcohol were more susceptible to the misleading information and were more confident in their responses. So, just the thought of drinking alcohol can influence how people use their memories.

SYNESTHESIA

A final condition that can influence memory is synesthesia. People with **synesthesia** have inappropriate and involuntary sensory experiences in addition to normal ones (see Grossenbacher & Lovelace, 2001; Hochel & Milán, 2008; Hubbard & Ramachandran, 2005; Rich & Mattingly, 2002 for reviews). For example, a person may experience colors when reading words. Two likely causes of synesthesia are a decreased ability to sufficiently suppress inappropriate feedback loops in perception (Grossenbacher &, 2001) or because of an incomplete pruning of cortical connections during development (Maurer, 1997). Accounts of the effects of synesthesia on memory began with Luria's (1968) subject S. (see Chapter 14). He had a phenomenal verbatim memory, in part because he used his synesthetic experience as a memory aid. In general, synesthetes not only report that they have better memories than most people (Yaro & Ward, 2007), but they also do better on memory tests, such as measures of working memory span or simple word lists (Mills et al., 2006; Radvansky, Gibson, & McNerney, 2009; Yaro & Ward, 2007).

Note that synesthesia does not uniformly improve memory. For example, if synesthetes and controls are given items to learn that are printed in black, colors congruent with the synesthetic experience, or colors incongruent with that experience, relative to words in black, synesthetes do better than the controls on memory for items presented in black or congruent colors but worse when the items were in incongruent colors (Smilek, Dixon, Cudahy, & Merikle, 2002; Radvansky et al., 2009). This suggests that synesthesia can impair memory when the synesthetic experience is inconsistent with the information in the world. Synesthetes also do not show a von Restorff effect if the unique word in a list is identified by color (e.g., a red word among a list of black words [Radvansky et al., 2009]).

SUMMARY

In this chapter we discussed a number of conditions a person may have that affect memory. The most common of these are the various dementias. Some of these, such as Alzheimer's disease, are primarily a result of damage to cortical structures that are important for memory. Others, such as Huntington's and Parkinson's diseases, are primarily a result of damage to subcortical structures. The fact that memory can be profoundly disrupted by damage to this wide variety of neurological structures shows that memory is a complex system made of many different interlocking components. There was some discussion of how memory can be compromised when people suffer from other disturbances, such as schizophrenia, or general frontal lobe damage (resulting in confabulation). We also discussed how memory can be disrupted by more common changes in psychological functioning, as with depression and anxiety. Finally, we discussed some problems that can occur with other forms of memory, such as semantic memory. Semantic memory deficits often leave a person with a decreased ability to store or retrieve certain types of information, such as words or music. Memory can also be altered in systematic ways by certain kinds of drugs or alcohol. In both of these cases, some form of anterograde amnesia is induced, although there may be some additional retroactive facilitation as well. Finally, this chapter discussed some of the possible consequences of synesthesia on memory in which it is enhanced for some kinds of information, as with enhanced working memory span scores, but compromised for others, such as the von Restorff effect.

STUDY QUESTIONS

1. What are the characteristics of Alzheimer's disease? What parts of the brain are affected? How is memory affected?
2. What are some of the subcortical dementias? What parts of the brain are affected? How is memory affected?
3. How does confabulation occur, and how does this inform us about the normal operation of memory?
4. What sorts of memory deficits occur in pathologies involving serious mental disturbances, such as schizophrenia?
5. What sorts of memory problems occur in affective disturbances? With depression? With anxiety?
6. What sort of memory disturbances occur with semantic amnesia? How does this relate to anomia? What types of memory systems are preserved in this condition?
7. What is interesting about episodic memory loss in semantic amnesia?
8. What are aphasia, amusia, and prosopagnosia? What sorts of memories are lost in each of these conditions?
9. How is memory affected by people taking benzodiazapines? By taking alcohol?
10. How does the condition of synesthesia make memory better? How does it make memory worse?

KEY TERMS

Alzheimer's disease, amusia, amyloid plaques, anomia, anxiety, aphasia, apraxia, Broca's aphasia, confabulation, Cotard delusion, depression, Huntington's disease, neurofibrillary tangles, Parkinson's disease, prosopagnosia, semantic amnesia, stress, synesthesia, Wernicke's aphasia

APPENDIX

MEMORY METHODS

This appendix provides you with methods that can be used to calculate various indices of memory. This is intended to be in addition to any statistical course you may have taken. The qualities of these methods are discussed in Chapter 3, as well as other places throughout the book.

The appendix is divided into three sections. The first describes a signal detection analysis method using easy-to-calculate measures of discrimination and bias. The second is a measure of clustering that can be applied to recall data. The third is a way to use the process dissociation procedure to provide estimates of implicit and explicit memory.

SIGNAL DETECTION ANALYSIS

As described in Chapter 3, signal detection analyses can correct for guessing and tease apart the influences of discrimination and bias in a person's responses. Signal detection analyses are typically applied to yes–no recognition data—that is, when people are presented with individual items and are asked to indicate whether each item is old or new. The following is a description of nonparametric measures of discrimination and bias that are relatively easy to calculate and interpret.

The measure of discrimination is A′, which is a lot like d′ but easier to calculate (following Donaldson, 1992, and Snodgrass & Corwin, 1988; see also Pollack, 1970). Note that the hits and false alarms need to be in proportions. Here is the equation for calculating A′ when the number of hits is greater than or equal to the number of false alarms:

$$A' = \frac{.5 + [(H - FA)(1 + H - FA)]}{[4H(1 - FA)]}$$

However, when the number of hits is less than the number of false alarms, the following formula should be used:

$$A' = \frac{.5 - [(FA - H)(1 + FA - H)]}{[4FA(1 - H)]}$$

B″ is a measure of bias, much like β, but, again, easier to calculate and based on the same principles as A′. Here is how to calculate B″ following Donaldson's (1992) correction:

$$B''_D = \frac{[(1 - H)(1 - FA) - HFA]}{[(1 - H)(1 - FA) + HFA]}$$

For these formulas, an A′ of .5 corresponds to chance discrimination (i.e., no discrimination). That is, when A′ values are around .5, it is unlikely that a person is reliably recognizing old information and rejecting new information. An A′ value of 1 corresponds to perfect discrimination. That is, the person is perfectly detecting old information in memory and rejecting new information. A′ values of less than .5 indicate below chance identification. This may mean that the person is using memory in a consistent and reliable way but not in the way you are hypothesizing. If A′ is negative, then you've calculated it wrong.

With regard to the bias measure, negative B″ values correspond to conservative responses. That is, people are being careful about what they are willing to identify as recognized. In contrast, positive B″ values correspond to liberal responses. That is, people are willing to say that any given item has been encountered before and is remembered. B″ values of zero correspond to no bias. B″ values greater than 1 or less than –1 indicate that you've done something wrong in your calculations.

CLUSTERING

Another thing you may want to know is how information is structured or organized in memory. One way to do this is by verifying if a person has structured information in memory in the way you think they will. For example, if you know that experts tend to organize information in a certain way, you can assess the degree to which a given person's own organization in memory matches that of the experts. This would tell you something about the level of this person's expertise.

One measure of organization is called an ARC score, for Adjusted Ratio of Clustering (Roenker, Thompson, & Brown, 1971). ARC scores are applied to data from recall tests. Essentially, people recall a set of information that was learned earlier. Then, using a preconceived idea about how the information could be organized in memory, you will assess the degree to which the organization approaches that ideal, taking chance into account. The basic formula for calculating an ARC score is as follows:

$$\text{ARC} = \frac{(R - E(R))}{(\text{max}R - E(R))}$$

In this formula, R stands for the number of observed categorical repetitions—that is, how many times during a person's recall were two items from the same predetermined category recalled together—for example, recalling two animal names one after the other. $E(R)$ is the number of categorical repetitions that would be expected by chance given the categories being tested for and how much the person actually recalled. In some sense, this is the amount of error that might be expected. This is the formula for calculating $E(R)$:

$$E(R) = \frac{\Sigma n_i^2}{N} - 1$$

Here, n refers to the number of items recalled from a given category i, and N is the number of items recalled by the person.

Finally, max$R$ refers to the maximum number of repetitions possible if clustering perfectly conformed to expectations, again given the categories being tested and the amount of information actually recalled. The formula for calculating max$R$ is as follows:

$$\text{max}R = N - k$$

Here, again, N is the number of items recalled by the person, and k is the number of categories present in a person's recall. This calculation will result in a number that is something like a ratio, although not quite. Perfect clustering will result in an ARC score of 1, whereas chance clustering will result in a score of 0. Variations in the degree of clustering will result in values between these two. It should also be noted that it is possible to get negative ARC scores. This indicates clustering below chance. If this value is a relatively large negative number, it might suggest that people have organized the information in memory in some way other than the categories that you defined.

A related measure is the ARC' score (Pellegrino, 1971) which looks at sequential order across multiple recall attempts, rather than categorical groupings. Here is a simplified version for pairs of repetitions (rather than triples or larger units) and assuming unidirectional recall. The basic structure of the formula is similar to the ARC score. The formula for ARC' is as follows:

$$\text{ARC}' = \frac{O(ITR) - E(ITR)}{\max(ITR) - E(ITR)}$$

Here ITR refers to intertrial repetitions. $O(ITR)$ are the number of observed repetitions, which is derived by counting up the number of times a particular item follows another. For example, if people were to recall the months of the year, this would count as 1 if July followed June on trial t and $t{+}1$. The formula for $E(ITR)$, the number of times a repetition would occur across trials by chance, is as follows:

$$\frac{E(ITR) = (N - 1)!(M - 3 + R)}{N!}$$

Here *M* is the number of items recalled on trial *t*, *N* is the number of items recalled on trial *t+1*, and *R* is number of items pairs that are recalled on trial *t*, but one or both of these items are not recalled on trial *t+1*. The explanation point is a mathematical symbol of a factorial function. Finally, the formula for max(*ITR*), the maximum number of intertrial repetitions that could occur, is as follows:

$$\max(ITR) = M - 3$$

PROCESS DISSOCIATION

The process dissociation procedure (Jacoby, 1991) is a simple way to separate out the influence of conscious and unconscious memory. Although this method is not completely precise and reliable in all cases, for the purposes of course work, it should be just fine. Essentially, this method works by comparing people's performance in two conditions. In one condition, both conscious and unconscious processes are working in the same way. This is the *inclusion condition*. In the second, these processes would be working in opposition to one another. This is the *exclusion condition*. By looking at the difference in performance in these two conditions, one can derive estimates of how each is being affected by the manipulation of interest.

In the inclusion condition, people do some task that theoretically would involve implicit and explicit memory working together—for example, asking a person to report words, such as animal names, that had been seen earlier on a list of animal names. A person can do this task using either conscious or unconscious influences. In the inclusion condition people can do the task using both explicit and implicit memory performance to produce words that were on the previous list. This is expressed in the following formula:

$$\mathrm{I} = \mathrm{R} + \mathrm{F} - \mathrm{RF}$$

Here, I stands for the inclusion condition, R stands for recollection, the explicit, conscious process—and F stands for familiarity—the implicit, unconscious process. So the rate of remembering old items on the inclusion condition reflects the rate of explicitly recollecting items, plus the rate of remembering items based solely on implicit familiarity, minus the portion where these two overlap (e.g., if you recall something consciously, the additional unconscious familiarity doesn't give you any additional benefit).

In contrast, in the exclusion condition, people are asked to do something that puts implicit and explicit memory processes in opposition. For example, people might see a list of animal names at the initial part of the study. Then a person would be asked to report a list of animals as long as he or she did not use any from the list heard earlier. Thus, words from the previous list that are reported are almost certainly due to unconscious memory because if the person consciously remembered them, he or she should not report it. This is expressed in this formula:

$$\mathrm{E} = \mathrm{F}(1 - \mathrm{R})$$

Here, E stands for the exclusion condition. So the rate of remembering old items is the rate at which the implicit memory processes retrieve this information, minus those that are rejected because they are also consciously remembered.

Thus, by separating out performance in the exclusion and inclusion conditions, one is left with the contribution of explicit memory. This can be expressed as:

$$\mathrm{R} = \mathrm{I} - \mathrm{E}$$

What is due to implicit memory can also be estimated. The estimate for familiarity is:

$$\frac{\mathrm{F} = \mathrm{E}}{(1 - \mathrm{I} + \mathrm{E})}$$

GLOSSARY

Acetylcholine (ACh) A neurotransmitter important for establishing new memories. For example, low levels of acetylcholine are implicated in Alzheimer's disease

action potential The electrical component of neural communication. The action potential occurs when a neuron "fires" by shifting the electrical charge of the neuron from –70 mv to +40 mv

additive factors logic A method of using response times, developed by Sternberg, to study human thought processes. This process is done by comparing various conditions of different levels of complexity

ad hoc categories Categories that are not stored previously in long-term memory but are generated on the fly in the service of some goal

"aha" effect This refers to better memory for problem solutions that are generated as compared to those that are simply provided

amnesia An inability to remember beyond what is observed with normal forgetting

amusia An inability to mentally process music

amygdala A portion of the brain that is critical for processing emotional aspects of memory

anomia A loss in the ability to retrieve word meanings

anorthoscopic perception An iconic memory phenomenon in which people are able to identify an object rapidly passed behind a narrow slit

anterograde amnesia Amnesia forward in time. An inability to acquire new memories

aphasia A loss in the ability to mentally process language

apraxia A loss in the ability to remember how to use objects

articulatory loop The portion of the phonological loop in working memory that actively rehearses verbal/auditory information

articulatory suppression Repeatedly saying a word out loud to prevent the rehearsal of verbal information in the phonological loop of working memory

artificial grammars A contrived system of generating string of letters or other items that illustrate that nondeclarative memory can acquire implicit rules for the structure of a serial order

associative interference Interference that occurs during memory retrieval as a result of increased numbers of associations with a concept (see also **fan effect**)

autobiographical memory Memory for one's life narrative

axons Parts of neurons used from transmitting neural signals

backward telescoping The finding that very recent memories will be reported as being older than they actually are

Baddeley's multicomponent model A popular model of working memory involving a central executive and three slave systems: the phonological loop, the visuo-spatial sketchpad, and the episodic buffer

basal ganglia A collection of subcortical structures that are involved in memory. These structures include the caudate nucleus, the putamen, the globus pallidus, and the subthalamic nucleus and are located above and around the thalamus. Important for memories involving habits and motor skills

behaviorism A school of psychological thought, dominant in the mid-twentieth century, that placed a heavy emphasis on studying observable behavior and actively avoided making assumptions about or studying thought

bias A tendency to be more liberal or conservative in reporting information from memory

boundary extension Remembering more of a scene than was actually viewed previously

Brodmann Areas (BA) A numerical mapping of different parts of the cortex

categorization The mental organization of information based on some form of similarity

category A group of individual members that are treated as is they were equivalent on one or more dimension

Category Adjustment Theory A fuzzy trace theory of memory that assumes that people use coarse-grained, categorical representations and fine-grained, detailed representations to make decisions about what is remembered from the past

central executive The control center in Baddeley's model of working memory

cerebellum A subcortical structure located at the back of the brain and involved in memory. This structure is involved in memory for fine motor skills

chunking The process of organizing multiple units of information into a single mental representation in memory

classical conditioning A form of nondeclarative memory that involves creating associations between environmental stimuli and ensuing responses

cognitive revolution The period in time during the 1950s and 1960s when there was a shift from behaviorism to an accepted study of mental processes (cognitive psychology)

collaborative facilitation Increased performance on a recognition test that occurs when people work in groups

collaborative inhibition Decreased performance on a recall test that occurs when people work in groups

complex span A working memory span test that requires both a processing and a retention component

computer-assisted tomography (CT) Also known as a CT or CAT scan. A neuroimaging technique that involves taking multiple x-ray "slices" of the brain

concreteness effect The finding that information that refers to concrete ideas (e.g., tree) is better remembered than information that refers to abstract ideas (e.g., truth)

confabulation The creation of false memories that a person presents as true, but without the intention to deceive, often as a result of damage to the frontal lobes

connectionist models See **parallel distributed processing models**

consolidation The process of solidifying memory traces in the neural structure over very long periods of time

Cotard delusion A severe state of depression in which one believes that one is dead

cryptomnesia Unconscious plagiarism brought about by lack of memory for source information

cued recall A recall method in which a person is given part of the information as a cue for the recall of the rest

decay Forgetting caused by the passage of time alone

declarative memory A portion of memory that is open to conscious inspection and verbalization

dendrites The part of an individual neuron that is primarily specialized for receiving signals from other neurons

diencephalon A portion of the brain including the thalamus and hypothalamus that primarily serves as a routing station. It is involved in memory for conscious, factual knowledge

direct memory task A memory test that explicitly asks a person to remember something, such as recall or recognition. Often strongly associated with explicit memory

directed forgetting The intentional forgetting of information. This usually occurs when people are instructed to forget or disregard some set of information

discrimination A component of signal detection theory of memory that refers to the ability to distinguish old from new information

dissociative amnesia A psychogenic amnesia in which people cannot remember traumatic events, but are aware of their inability to remember

dissociative fugue A psychogenic amnesia in which people flee from the source of a traumatic event, and may even take on a new identity

dissociative identity disorder A pathology in which a person behaves as if they can switch between multiple identities

distributed practice When the rehearsing of information in memory is spread out over several occasions rather than lumped into a single session (see **massed practice**). This leads to better memory

distributed storage models Models of memory that assume that information in memory traces are distributed across a large set of relatively simple individual units

dopamine This is a neurotransmitter that is important for memory. For example, people with Parkinson's disease have lower than normal dopamine levels

DRM paradigm A word list paradigm that reliably elicits false memories from a list of highly related semantic associates

Dual Code Theory A theory of memory that assumes that people are able to store information in either perceptual codes and/or verbal codes

dual process models Models of memory that assume there are two retrieval processes: one for an automatic activation and another for deliberative search

dynamic memory Memory for visuospatial information that is distorted by physical properties such as momentum, gravity, or friction

dysexecutive syndrome Loss in central executive control as a result of brain damage to the frontal lobes

Easterbrook hypothesis The theory that at heightened levels of emotion, attention becomes increasingly focused on a small subset of details, leaving poorer memory for peripheral details

echoic memory The sensory register dedicated to the brief retention of auditory information

eidetic imagery A term used to describe a type of photographic memory

elaborative rehearsal Rehearsing information in memory by building on and elaborating the information that is provided with other information which is already known. Thus, inferences make for more complex and elaborate memory trace

embodied cognition The theoretical idea that cognitive processes, including memory, are strongly influenced and guided by the fact that we inhabit bodies that interact with the world in certain ways. That is, our bodily interactions with the world are incorporated into how we think about things

emergent property A property of a system that does not exist in any of its parts but that emerges out of the combination of the parts into a new system

enactment effect The finding that memory is better for information that was actually performed

encoding specificity The finding that memory retrieval can sometimes be better when the retrieval context matches the encoding context

engram Another name for a memory trace

episodic buffer A part of working memory theory that helps integrate or bind information from different sources

episodic memory Memory for the individual events a person experiences

event-related desynchronization (ERD) A desynchronization of neural firing, often measured with EEG recordings, that may occur when mental work is being done

event-related potentials (ERP) A positive or negative wave of electrical charge, measured using EEG recordings, that regularly occurs following an event

executive controller A portion of working memory that manage attentional resources and the processing of the two slave systems

explicit memory Memory that involves conscious awareness—that is, a person is aware that he or she is using his or her memory to perform some task

false alarm Inappropriately identifying a new item as old on a recognition test

false fame effect Inappropriately labeling a nonfamous person as famous because his or her name elicits a feeling of familiarity

false memories Memories for events that never actually occurred

fan effect An increase in response times or error rates, with an increase in the number of associations with a concept

feeling of knowing A metacognitive judgment a person can make about the likelihood of later recognizing something that cannot be currently recalled

field memories The experience of remembering an event from one's own perspective

flashbulb memories Highly detailed memories for the events of learning highly surprising and significant news

forced choice recognition A type of recognition test in which a person must select one item from among a set of alternatives, such as a multiple-choice test

forced recall A type of recall test in which a person is forced to recall a certain amount of information

forgetting curve A change in memory performance over time as information is being lost over the retention period. Most forgetting curves are negatively accelerated functions, with the most forgetting occurring early on and less forgetting occurring later (per unit of time)

forward telescoping The finding that older memories will be reported as being more recent than they actually are

free recall A recall measure in which people are provided with very little information but are expected to generate and report as much as possible

frequency effect The influence of prior frequency of information on memory retrieval

frontal lobes The lobes of the cortex located at the front of the head. These lobes are involved in memory by controlling the flow and coordination of various memory processes, including both long-term memory and working memory

functional magnetic resonance imaging (fMRI) The neuroimaging technique of tracking oxygen level concentrations to measure cerebral blood flow under various conditions

functional stimulus what a research participant treats as the stimulus in an experiment

fuzzy trace theories These are theories of memory that assume that memory performance is a reflection of multiple types of mental representations working in combination

GABA (gamma-amino butyric acid) An inhibitory neurotransmitter

generation effect The finding that information that was generated by a person is remembered better than information that was only seen or heard

Gestalt psychology An early school of psychological thought, originating in Germany, that emphasized molar levels of analysis. Known for the concepts that the whole is different from the sum of its parts and representational isomorphism

global matching models Models of memory that assume that memory retrieval occurs through a massively parallel process in which all memory traces are compared with information in a memory probe but for which only some are activated

glutamate (Glu) An excitatory neurotransmitter critical for forming new memoires

HERA model The Hemispheric Encoding/Retrieval Asymmetry model. It suggests that the left frontal lobes are primarily involved in semantic retrieval and episodic encoding, whereas the right frontal lobes are primarily involved in episodic retrieval

hindsight bias The tendency to misremember the past in a way consistent with a person's current state of mind

hippocampus The brain structure that is often implicated in memory encoding

hypermnesia The phenomenon of greater memory retrieval after subsequent retrieval attempts

hypothalamus A subcortical structure that is part of the diencephalon

icon The form of the memory representation in iconic memory

iconic memory The sensory register dedicated to the brief retention of visual information

imagination inflation The greater likelihood of remembering something as having been experienced before when a person tries to imagine the event

implicit memory This refers to memory that is unconscious and out of awareness. That is, a person is not aware that they are using his or her memory to perform some task

incidental learning Situations in which a person memorizes information without explicitly trying to

indirect memory test Tasks that assess memory performance that minimize a person being consciously aware that his or her memory is being used and/or tested. Often associated with implicit memory

infantile amnesia Difficulty remembering life events from the period of infancy

inhibition A mental mechanism that actively suppresses related but irrelevant memory traces

instrumental conditioning A form of learning that involves either reinforcing or extinguishing associations between a response produced by an organism and the ensuing consequences of that response

intentional learning Situations in which a person explicitly memorizes information

interference A primary source of forgetting in memory in which different memory traces compete with one another for retrieval, making it difficult to access the desired information

inter-item delays The time between recalls that can be used to help identify chunks in memory

intrusions Information that is reported on a recall test that was not experienced previously

involuntary memories Memories that are retrieved spontaneously with conscious intention

irrelevant speech effect Decreased verbal working memory performance in the presence of irrelevant speech in the environment

Jost's law For memories of a similar strength, the older memories will decay more slowly relative to the newer memories

judgments of learning Metamemory ratings of how well a person feels that he has learned something

knew-it-all-along effect The tendency for people to misremember and think that they knew more in the past than they actually did

labor-in-vain effect The finding that people often try to initially learn the most difficult things first, causing them to end up exerting a lot of effort and learning very little

laterality The primary localization of a function in either the left or right hemisphere of the brain. Often laterality does not imply that one function is completely in one hemisphere but that one hemisphere is dominant for that function and does it much better than the other

learning Any change in the potential of a person to change his or her behavior as a consequence of some experience

learning curve A change in memory performance over time as information is being acquired. Most learning curves are negatively accelerated functions, with the most learning occurring early on and less learning occurring later (per unit of time)

levels of processing The idea that more elaboratively (or deeply) processed information is remembered better than more superficially (or shallowly) processed information

lexical decision task A commonly used indirect memory task that requires people to indicate whether a given string of letters is a word or not. Both response time and error rates are considered dependent variables

lexicality effect Superior short-term memory for words compared to nonwords

long-term depression (LTD) Relatively long-lasting suppression of neural connections as part of early memory formation

long-term memory This part of the modal model of memory is where information is held for longer periods of time (generally longer than 30 seconds) and that has a functionally unlimited capacity

long-term potentiation (LTP) Relatively long-lasting durability of neural connections that may serve as one of the initial encoding aspects to move information into long-term memory

long-term working memory A set of retrieval cues assembled in working memory to make accessing information in long-term memory more efficient. This develops in parallel with a cognitive skill

Latent Semantic Analysis (LSA). A formal memory model that takes a very large number of inputs to create a high dimensional (over 300) space to represent meaning

Magnetic Resonance Imaging (MRI) A neuroimaging technique that relies on the natural oscillations of atoms that make up various components of the brain and nervous system

Magnetoencephalography (MEG) A neuroimaging technique that relies on the electrical signals generated by clusters of neurons firing

massed practice When the rehearsing of information in memory is lumped into a single session rather than spread out over several occasions (see **distributed practice**). This leads to poorer memory

material appropriate processing Superior memory for information that is processed in a way the emphasizes characteristics that are not typically encoded, such as emphasizing relational information with expository texts

mediated priming Priming of concepts that are mediated by a related concept—for example, the priming of "stripes" by "lion" through the concept of "tiger"

memorists People with an exceptional memory ability of some sort

memory The retention of information over a period of time involving encoding, storage, and retrieval

mental rotation The ability to mentally turn visuospatial representations of objects

mere exposure effect The finding that people prefer things that they have been exposed to before relative to things they have not been exposed to, even if they are unaware of this exposure

metamemory Conscious knowledge of one's own memory contents, processes, and effectiveness

miss Inappropriately identifying a old item as new on a recognition test

mnemonic Any device (broadly speaking) used to help a person remember

modal model of memory This is the standard model of memory developed by Atkinson and Shiffrin (1968). This model is composed of the sensory registers, a short-term store, control processes, and a long-term store

mood-congruent memory The finding that people activate information in memory that is consistent with their current emotional state.

mood-dependent memory The finding that people remember information better when they are in the same mood at retrieval as they were in during encoding

Moses illusion The finding that people sometimes mistakenly accept incorrect information because it is semantically similar to the correct information, such as saying that Moses took two animals of each kind on the Ark, when it was Noah.

myelin sheath A fatty coating on a neural axon

naïve physics A person's intuitive understanding of the physical principles of the world

naming task An indirect memory task that requires a person to name words that are visually presented. Response time is the typical dependent measure

negative priming Slower responding to information that was recently a source of interference

negative transfer The decreased ability to learn new information because of prior known information that is related to it

network theories Theories of memory that assume that associative relations among concepts are stored directly in long-term memory

neural networks See **parallel distributed processing models**

neuron An individual cell that serves as the basic building block of the nervous system and, hence, memory

neurotransmitters Chemicals in the nervous system that are released from the terminal buttons of one neuron into a synapse. These neurotransmitters then affect the firing pattern of the postsynaptic neurons

nodes of Ranvier Gaps along a myelinated axon that facilitate the speed of neural transmission

nominal stimulus What the experimenter believes the stimulus to be in an experiment

nondeclarative memory A portion of memory that is not open to conscious inspection and verbalization

nonsense syllable A type of stimulus used to study memory performance in the absence of prior knowledge. These often come in the form of consonant-vowel-consonant (CVC) trigrams

norepinephrine A neurotransmitter that is thought to be important for memory consolidation

observer memories The experience of remembering an event in which one sees oneself from a third-person perspective

occipital lobes These are the lobes of the neocortex located at the back of the brain. These lobes are primarily responsible for visual processing

old-new recognition A form of recognition test in which a person is to indicate whether each item is either old (remembered) or new (not remembered)

organic amnesia Amnesia that is caused by brain damage or some other physiological cause

overlearning Continuing to study information even after perfect memory retrieval has been achieved. This often results in a greater resistance to forgetting

paired associate A pair of items presented during learning in a memory experiment. One word would serve as the context or cue for the retrieval of the other word during a memory test

parallel distributed processing models Theories of memory that assume that information is represented in a massively interconnected network in which information is encoded by the strength of the associations among the units

parallel processing When memory encoding or retrieval involves engaging multiple processes at the same time, possibly toward a common end

parietal lobes The lobes of the cerebral cortex located in front of the occipital lobes and behind the frontal lobes.

Often involved in working memory processes, such as those involving the visuo-spatial sketchpad

part-set cuing The finding that it is harder to retrieve any given item from a set after a person has been given a subset of that set as a retrieval cue

perceptual identification An indirect memory test in which people are asked to identify briefly presented items as old or new

permastore Memory traces that are in a long-term state in which very little is susceptible to forgetting

phantom limbs Memory traces that produce sensations of body parts that have been amputated

phonological loop One of the slave systems of working memory that is primarily responsible for processing auditory and verbal information

phonological similarity effect Inferior verbal working memory for items that are phonologically similar compared to phonologically dissimilar items

phonological store The portion of the phonological loop part of the working memory system that maintains auditory and verbal information over short periods of time

picture superiority effect The finding that memory is generally better for pictures than for words

Pollyanna Principle The idea that positive information tends to be remembered better than negative information

Positron Emission Tomography (PET) This is a neuroimaging technique that involves tracking blood flow under various conditions. This tracking is done by measuring concentrations of a radioactive isotope that has been injected into the bloodstream

primacy effect Better memory for information presented at the beginning of a series

priming A process of making some memories more available by previously retrieving memories that are similar to them in some way

proactive interference Interference forward in time. When previously known information makes it more difficult to retrieve information learned later that is related to it

process dissociation procedure By using inclusion and exclusion memory conditions, one can use this approach to derive estimates of explicit and implicit memory processes

prosopagnosia An inability to use memory for faces

prospective memory Memory to engage in actions in the future at a predetermined time or event

psychogenic amnesia Amnesia that is a result of psychological causes with no known underlying neurological abnormalities

psychological essentialism The categorization process in which people treat category members as if they share some common underlying essence, whether this is true or not

psychophysics relating physical properties to psychological experience

recall A type of memory test that requires a person to generate information

recency effect Better memory for information presented at the end of a series

recognition A type of memory test that requires a person to assess whether information that is presented has been encountered before

recognition failure Information that is recalled but not recognized

reminiscence The remembering of previously forgotten information

reminiscence bump A bump in a memory curve reflecting an increase in memory reports from the period between ages 15 and 25

repeated practice effect The finding that recall memory is worse for items that are the same category as other items that have received practice. This effects is often attributed to the operation of an active inhibition mechanism

repetition blindness Failing to consciously identify an entity (such as a word) in the environment when it follows soon after a person sees an initial entity of that type

repetition priming Faster processing of an item that was recently presented before

representational friction A dynamic memory finding in which memory for moving objects is decreased by the presumed effects of friction

representational gravity A dynamic memory finding in which memory for the trajectory of moving objects is influence by the presumed effects of gravity

representational momentum A dynamic memory finding in which memory for moving objects is biased to be further along a path of travel than what was last actually witnessed

repression A psychogenic amnesia in which people cannot remember traumatic events, and are unaware of their inability to remember

response time The time needed to respond to a stimulus, which can be used to make inferences about the complexity of memory processes

retrieval-induced inhibition Any finding in which the act of retrieval of some information makes it harder to remember other, related pieces of information

retrieval plan A system of retrieval cues subjectively devised by a person to aid in the recall of large sets of information

retroactive facilitation An increase in memory performance when subsequent information is prevented from being formed in long-term memory via LTP.

retroactive interference Interference backward in time. When newly learned information makes it more difficult to retrieve older, learned information that is related to it

retrograde amnesia Amnesia backward in time. An inability to retrieve memories of things that happened prior to an injury

retrospective memory The opposite of prospective memory. Memory for the past

revelation effect The increasing in reporting something as remembered (either accurately or not) when it is slowly revealed over time rather than revealed all at once

Ribot's Law The principle that, when retrograde amnesia occurs, more recent memories are more likely to be disrupted than older memories

rote rehearsal The practice of trying to memorize information simply by repeating it over and over, and ignoring the meaning of the information

savings A reduction in the amount of effort needed to learn a set of information on a subsequent attempt after some forgetting has already occurred

scale effect The finding that when people are asked to locate memories in time, they may be accurate at one scale (e.g., day of the week) but inaccurate at another (e.g., number of weeks in the past)

scripts Schemas that have a sequential ordering

semantic amnesia Severe loss of memory for general knowledge about the world

semantic memory Memory for general world, encyclopedic knowledge that is generally shared with one's community

sensory registers A part of the modal model of memory where sensory information is held in modality-specific stores. Sensory registers generally have a very large capacity but a very short duration

serial position curve Memory performance changes as a function of when items appeared in the series. Often there is a primacy effect and a recency effect

serial processing When memory encoding or retrieval involves engaging multiple processes in sequence

short-term memory A part of the modal model of memory is where information is held for a period of generally no longer than 30 seconds unless rehearsed. Control processes can operate on information in this memory store. Finally, short-term memory has a very limited capacity of 7 ± 2 chunks of information

signal detection theory A data analytical approach that allows researchers to separate out the influences of discrimination and bias on performance

single-cell recording The recording of the firing rate of a single neuron

sleeper effect The finding that people are more willing to accept previously rejected opinions over time when a low credible source is forgotten

SNARC effect Spatial-Numerical Association of Response Codes effect in which people respond faster to smaller numbers with the left hand and larger numbers with the right

soma The cell body of a neuron

source cuing Source information used to help a person retrieve a memory

source monitoring Remembering where information in memory came from

state-dependent memory The finding that it is easier to remember information when people are in a similar physiological state during retrieval as they were during the original encoding of the information

subtractive factors logic A method of using response times, developed by Donders, to study human thought processes. This is done by comparing various conditions in which the process of interest is present in one condition but absent in the other

suffix effect A decreased recency effect in a short-term memory serial position curve as a result of presenting an additional, nominally unrelated item at the end

synapse The gap between two neurons across which neurotransmitters are released

synesthesia A condition in which there are inappropriate and involuntary sensory experiences (e.g., experiencing colors when seeing letters) that can also influence memory

temporal lobes One of the lobes of the neocortex located below and behind the frontal lobes. Probably the portion of the cortex most strongly associated with memory storage

terminal buttons Part of a neuron at the end tips of an axon where the neurotransmitters are stored before being released into the synapse

thalamus A midbrain structure that is involved in memory by coordinating different types of information from different parts of the brain

threshold model A model of memory that assumes that retrieval occurs when the activation of a memory trace exceeds some preset level

tip-of-the-tongue state The feeling of imminent remembering in a case where a person has forgotten something, such as a word or name

Transcranial Magnetic Stimulation (TMS) The neuroscience measure of artificially stimulating a cortex to create a temporary "lesion"

transfer appropriate processing The finding that it is easier to remember information when the mental processes used at retrieval are more similar to the ones used at encoding

Transient Global Amnesia (TGA) A brief period of amnesia typically lasting 24 hours or less

Tulving's triarchic theory of memory A theory of memory by Endel Tulving that assumes that memory is divided into three primary components: (1) procedural memory, (2) semantic memory, and (3) episodic memory

Tulving-Wiseman Function A formal, mathematical function that describes recognition failure

tunnel memories Memories that focus on central details at the expense of peripheral information. These are often associated with more emotionally intense events.

verbal learning A research tradition in memory that existed in the context of a behaviorist psychology and stemmed from Ebbinghaus's work with nonsense syllables. People working in this tradition often used tasks such as the learning of paired-associate lists of words

verbal overshadowing Poorer memory for information that is later described as compared to information that is not described

verbal reports A method of studying memory by asking people to report the contents of their current state of consciousness—that is, what they are currently thinking about

visuo-spatial sketchpad The slave system of working memory primarily responsible for processing visual and spatial information

von Restorff effect The finding that information is remembered better if it is relatively distinct compared to other information a person was exposed to at the time

weapon focus effect The finding that attention, and hence memory, for an event is altered toward a weapon when one is present in an event, leading to poorer memory for non-weapon components of the event

wishful thinking bias a tendency for people to misremember desirable information as having come from reliable sources, and undesirable information as having come from unreliable sources

word length effect The finding that the number of words that can be held in working memory is decreased as the words become longer to articulate

working memory The portion of memory dedicated to processing information in the short term, including the active manipulation of that information. Baddeley's model is a common framework for understanding working memory

Yerkes-Dodson law The theory that memory performance overall declines at high levels of arousal.

BIBLIOGRAPHY

Abbot, V., Black, J. B., & Smith, E. E. (1985). The representation of scripts in memory. *Journal of Memory and Language, 24,* 179–199.

Abraham, W. C. (2006). Memory maintenance: The changing nature of neural mechanisms. *Psychological Science, 15,* 5–8.

Abrahamse, E. L., van der Lubbe, R. H. J., & Verway, W. B. (2008). Asymmetrical learning between a tactile and visual serial RT task. *Quarterly Journal of Experimental Psychology, 61,* 210–217.

Acheson, D. J., & McDonald, M. C. (2009). Twisting tongues and memories: Explorations of the relationship between language production and verbal working memory. *Journal of Memory and Language, 60,* 329–350.

Addis, D. R., & Tippett, L. J. (2004). Memory of myself: Autobiographical memory and identity in Alzheimer's disease. *Memory, 12,* 56–74.

Aggelton, J. P. (2008). Understanding anterograde amnesia: Disconnections and hidden lesions. *Quarterly Journal of Experimental Psychology, 61,* 1441–1471.

Aggleton, J. P., & Brown, M. W. (1999). Episodic memory, amnesia and the hippocampal-anterior thalamic axis. *Behavioral and Brain Sciences, 22,* 425–489.

Ahn, W., Kim, N. S., Lassaline, M. E., & Dennis, M. J. (2000). Causal status as a determinant of feature centrality. *Cognitive Psychology, 41,* 361–416.

Alba, J. W., & Hasher, L. (1983). Is memory schematic? *Psychological Bulletin, 93,* 203–231.

Albert, M. S., & Kaplan, E. (1980). Organic implications of neuropsychological deficits in the elderly. In L. W. Poon, J. L. Fozard, L. S. Cermak, D. Arenberg, & L. W. Thompson (Eds.), *New Directions in Memory and Aging,* pp. 403–432. Hillsdale, NJ: Erlbaum.

Alexander, K. W., Quas, J. A., Goodman, G. S. Ghetti, S., Edelstein, R. S., Redlich, A. D., Cordon, I. M., & Jones, D. P. H. (2005). Traumatic impact predicts long-term memory for documented child sexual abuse. *Psychological Science, 16,* 33–40.

Algom, D. (1992). Memory psychophysics: An examination of its perceptual and cognitive prospects. In D. Algom (Ed.), *Psychophysical Approaches to Cognition,* pp. 441–513. New York: North Holland.

Algom, D., & Lubel, S. (1994). Psychophysics in the field: Perception and memory for labor pain. *Perception & Psychophysics, 55,* 133–141.

Algom, D., Wolf, Y., & Bergman, B. (1985). Integration of stimulus dimensions in perception and memory: Composition rules and psychophysical relations. *Journal of Experimental Psychology: General, 114,* 451–471.

Alley, T. R., & Cunningham, M. R. (1991). Averaged faces are attractive, but very attractive faces are not average. *Psychological Science, 2,* 123–125.

Altgassen, M., Phillips, L., Kopp, U., & Kliegel, M. (2007). Role of working memory components in planning performance of individuals with Parkinson's disease. *Neuropsychologia, 45,* 2393–2397.

Amit, E., Algom, D., & Trope, Y. (2009). Distance-dependent processing of pictures and words. *Journal of Experimental Psychology: General, 138,* 400–415.

Anderson, J. R. (1974). Retrieval of propositional information from long-term memory. *Cognitive Psychology, 6,* 451–474.

Anderson, J. R. (1976). *Language, Memory, and Thought.* Hillsdale, NJ: Erlbaum.

Anderson, J. R. (1983). *The Architecture of Cognition.* Cambridge, MA: Harvard University Press.

Anderson, J. R. (2000). *Learning and Memory: An Integrated Approach.* New York: Wiley.

Anderson, J. R., & Schooler, L. J. (1991). Reflections of the environment in memory. *Psychological Science, 2,* 396–408.

Anderson, M. C. (2003). Rethinking interference theory: Executive control and the mechanisms of forgetting. *Journal of Memory and Language, 49,* 415–455.

Anderson, M. C., & Bell, T. (2001). Forgetting our facts: The role of inhibitory processes in the loss of prepositional knowledge. *Journal of Experimental Psychology: General, 130,* 544–570.

Anderson, M. C., Bjork, E. L., & Bjork, R. A. (2000). Retrieval-induced forgetting: Evidence for a recall-specific mechanism.*Psychonomic Bulletin & Review, 7,* 522–530.

Anderson, M. C., Bjork, R. A., & Bjork, E. L. (1994). Remembering can cause forgetting: Retrieval dynamics in long-term memory. *Journal of Experimental Psychology: Learning, Memory, and Cognition, 20,* 1063–1087.

Anderson, M. C., Green, C., & McCulloch, K. C. (2000). Similarity and inhibition in long-term memory: Evidence for a two-factor theory. *Journal of Experimental Psychology: Learning, Memory, and Cognition, 26,* 1141–1159.

Anderson, M. C., & McCulloch, K. C. (1999). Integration as a general boundary condition on retrieval-induced forgetting. *Journal of Experimental Psychology: Learning, Memory, and Cognition, 25,* 608–629.

Anderson, M. C., & Neely, J. H. (1996). Interference and inhibition in memory retrieval. In E. L. Bjork & R. A. Bjork (Eds.), *Memory: Handbook of Perception and Cognition,* pp. 237–313. San Diego, CA: Academic Press.

Anderson, M. C., & Spellman, B. A. (1995). On the status of inhibitory mechanisms in cognition: Memory retrieval as a model case. *Psychological Review, 102,* 68–100.

Anderson, R. B. (2001). The power law as an emergent property. *Memory & Cognition, 29,* 1061–1068.

Anderson, R. B., Garavan, H., Rivardo, M. G., & Chadwick, R. (1997). Inhibitory consequences of memory selection. *Acta Psychologica, 96,* 155–166.

Anderson, R. C., and Pichert, J. W. (1978). Recall of previously unrecallable information following a shift in perspective. *Journal of Verbal Learning and Verbal Behavior, 17,* 1–12.

Anderson, S. J., & Conway, M. A. (1993). Investigating the structure of autobiographical memories. *Journal of Experimental Psychology: Learning, Memory and Cognition, 19,* 1178–1196.

Anderson, S. J., & Conway, M. A. (1997). Representations of autobiographical memories. In M. A. Conway (Ed.), *Cognitive Models of Memory.* Cambridge, MA: MIT Press.

Andrade, J. (1995). Learning during anaesthesia: A review. *British Journal of Psychology, 86,* 479–506.

Andres, M., Olivier, E., & Badets, A. (2008). Actions, words, and numbers: A motor contribution to semantic processing? *Current Directions in Psychological Science, 17,* 313–317.

Andrés, P., Van der Linden, M., & Parmentier, F. B. R. (2004). Directed forgetting in working memory: Age-related differences. *Memory, 12,* 248–256.

Andrews, M., Vigliocco, G., & Vinson, D. (2009). Integrating experiential and distributional data to learn semantic representations. *Psychological Review, 116,* 463–498.

Anisfeld, M., & Lambert, W. E. (1966). When are pleasant words learned faster than unpleasant words. *Journal of Verbal Learning and Verbal Behavior, 5,* 132–141.

Arbuckle, T. Y., Cooney, R., Milne, J., & Melchior, A. (1994). Memory for spatial layouts in relation to age and schema typicality. *Psychology and Aging, 9,* 467–480.

Arbuckle, T. Y., & Cuddy, L. L. (1969). Discrimination of item strength at time of presentation. *Journal of Experimental Psychology, 81,* 126–131.

Arbuckle, T. Y., Vanderleck, V. F., Harsany, M., & Lapidus, S. (1990). Adult age differences in memory in relation to availability and accessibility of knowledge-based schemas. *Journal of Experimental Psychology: Learning, Memory, and Cognition, 16,* 305–315.

Ariel, R., Dunlosky, J., & Bailey, H. (2009). Agenda-based regulation of study-time allocation: When agendas override item-based monitoring. *Journal of Experimental Psychology: General, 138,* 432–447.

Arkes, H. R., Wortman, R. C., Saville, P. D., & Harkness, A. R. (1981). Hindsight bias among physicians weighing the likelihood of diagnosis. *Journal of Applied Psychology, 66,* 584–588.

Armstrong, S. L., Gleitman, L. R., & Gleitman, H. (1983). What some concepts might not be. *Cognition, 13,* 263–308.

Ash, I. K. (2009). Surprise, memory, and retrospective judgment making: Testing cognitive reconstruction theories of the hindsight bias effect. *Journal of Experimental Psychology: Learning, Memory and Cognition, 35,* 916–933.

Ashcraft, M. H. (1976). Priming and property dominance effects in semantic memory. *Memory & Cognition, 4,* 490–500.

Ashcraft, M. H. (1978a). Property dominance and typicality effects in property statement verification. *Journal of Verbal Learning and Verbal Behavior, 17,* 155–164.

Ashcraft, M. H. (1978b). Property norms for typical and atypical items from 17 categories: A description and discussion. *Memory & Cognition, 6,* 227–232.

Ashcraft, M. H. (1993). A personal case history of transient anomia. *Brain and Language, 44,* 47–57.

Ashcraft, M. H. (2002). Math anxiety: Personal, educational, and cognitive consequences. *Current Directions in Psychological Science, 11,* 181–185.

Ashcraft, M. H., & Krause, J. A. (2007). Working memory, math performance, and math anxiety. *Psychonomic Bulletin & Review, 14,* 243–248.

Aslan, A., Bäuml, K-H., & Grudbeiger, T. (2007). The role of inhibitory processes in part-list cuing. *Journal of Experimental Psychology: Learning, Memory, and Cognition, 33,* 335–341.

Aslan, A., Bäuml, K-H., & Pastötter, B. (2007). No inhibitory deficit in older adults' episodic memory. *Psychological Science, 18,* 72–78.

Assefi, S. L., & Garry, M. (2003). Absolute memory distortions: Alcohol placebos influence the misinformation effect. *Psychological Science, 14,* 77–80.

Atkins, A. S., & Reuter-Lorenz, P. A. (2008). False working memories? Semantic distortion in a mere 4 seconds. *Memory & Cognition, 36,* 74–81.

Atkinson, R. C., & Juola, J. F. (1973). Factors influencing speed and accuracy of word recognition. *Attention and Performance, 6,* 583–612.

Atkinson, R. C., & Juola, J. F. (1974). Search and decision processes in recognition memory. In D. H. Krantz, R. C. Atkinson, R. D. Luce, & P. Suppes (Eds.), *Contemporary Developments in Mathematical Psychology,* pp. 243–293. San Francisco, CA: Freeman.

Atkinson, R. C., & Shiffrin, R. M. (1968). Human memory: A proposed system and its control processes. *The Psychology of Learning and Motivation, 2,* 89–195.

Auble, P. M., Franks, J. J., Soraci, S. A. J. (1979). Effort toward comprehension: Elaboration or "aha!"? *Memory & Cognition, 7,* 426–434.

Averbach, E. (1963). The span of apprehension as a function of exposure duration. *Journal of Verbal Learning and Verbal Behavior, 2,* 60–64.

Ayers, T. J., Jonides, J., Reitman, J. S., Egan, J. C., & Howard, D. A. (1979). Differing suffix effects for the same physical suffix. *Journal of Experimental Psychology: Human Learning and Memory, 5,* 315–321.

Azimian-Faridani, N., & Wilding, E. L. (2004). An event-related potential study of the revelation effect. *Psychonomic Bulletin & Review, 11,* 926–931.

Bäckman, L., Small, B. J., & Fratiglioni, L. (2001). Stability of preclinical episodic memory deficit in Alzheimer's disease. *Brain, 124,* 96–102.

Baddeley, A. D. (1966). Short-term memory for word sequences as a function of acoustic, semantic, and formal similarity. *Quarterly Journal of Experimental Psychology, 18,* 302–309.

Baddeley, A. D. (1986). *Working Memory.* Oxford: Oxford University Press.

Baddeley, A. D. (2000). The episodic buffer: A new component of working memory? *Trends in Cognitive Science, 4,* 417–423.

Baddeley, A. D., & Andrade, J. (2000). Working memory and the vividness of imagery. *Journal of Experimental Psychology: General, 129,* 126–145.

Baddeley, A. D., & Hitch, G. (1974). Working memory. *Psychology of Learning and Motivation, 8,* 47–89.

Baddeley, A. D., Thomson, N., & Buchanan, M. (1975). Word length and the structure of short-term memory. *Journal of Verbal Learning and Verbal Behavior, 14,* 575–589.

Baddeley, A. D., & Warrington, E. K. (1970). Amnesia and the distinction between long- and short-term memory. *Journal of Verbal Learning and Verbal Behavior, 9,* 176–189.

Baddeley, A. D., & Wilson, B. (1985). Phonological coding and short-term memory in patients without speech. *Journal of Memory and Language, 24,* 490–502.

Bahrick, H. P. (1984). Semantic memory content in permastore: Fifty years of memory for Spanish vocabulary learned in school. *Journal of Experimental Psychology: General, 113,* 1–29.

Bahrick, H. P. (2000). Long-term maintenance of knowledge. In E. Tulving & F. I. M. Craik (Eds.), *The Oxford Handbook of Memory,* pp. 347–362. New York: Oxford University Press.

Bahrick, H. P., Bahrick, P. O., & Wittlinger, R. P. (1975). Fifty years of memory for names and faces: A cross-sectional approach. *Journal of Experimental Psychology: General, 104,* 54–75.

Bahrick, H. P., & Hall, L. K. (1991). Lifetime maintenance of high school mathematics content. *Journal of Experimental Psychology: General, 120,* 20–33.

Bailey, P. E., Henry, J. D., Rendell, P. G., Phillips, L. H., & Kliegel, M. (2010). Dismantling the age-prospective memory paradox: The classic laboratory paradigm simulated in a naturalistic setting. *Quarterly Journal of Experimental Psychology, 63,* 646–652.

Bajic, D., & Rickard, T. C. (2009). The temporal dynamics of strategy execution in cognitive skill learning. *Journal of Experimental Psychology, 35,*113–121.

Ball, C. T., & Little, J. C. (2006). A comparison of involuntary autobiographical memory retrievals. *Applied Cognitive Psychology, 20,* 1167–1179.

Ballard, P. B. (1913). Oblivescence and reminiscence. *British Journal of Psychology Monograph Supplements, 1,* 1–82.

Balota, D. A, & Duchek, J. M. (1988). Age-related differences in lexical access, spreading activation, and simple pronunciation. *Psychology and Aging, 3,* 84–93.

Balota, D. A., & Lorch, R. F. (1986). Depth of automatic spreading activation: Mediated priming effects in pronunciation but not in lexical decisions. *Journal of Experimental Psychology: Learning, Memory, and Cognition, 12,* 336–345.

Banks, W. P. (1970). Signal detection theory and human memory. *Psychological Bulletin, 74,* 81–99.

Banks, W. P. (1977). Encoding and processing of symbolic information in comparative judgments. *The Psychology of Learning and Motivation, 11,* 101–159.

Banks, W. P., Clark, H. H., & Lucy, P. (1975). The locus of the semantic congruity effect in comparative judgments. *Journal of Experimental Psychology: Human Perception and Performance, 104,* 35–47.

Barba, G. D. (1993). Confabulation: Knowledge and recollective experience. *Cognitive Neuropsychology, 10,* 1–20.

Barba, G. D. (1997). Recognition memory and recollective experience in Alzheimer's disease. *Memory, 5,* 657–672.

Barber, S. J., Gordon, R., & Franklin, N. (2009). Self-relevance and wishful thinking: Facilitation and distortion in source monitoring. *Memory & Cognition, 37,* 434–446.

Barbizet, J. (1970). *Human Memory and Its Pathology.* San Francisco: Freeman.

Barnier, A. J., Conway, M. A., Mayoh, L., Speyer, J., Avizmil, O., & Harris, C. B. (2007). Directed forgetting of recently recalled autobiographical memories. *Journal of Experimental Psychology: General, 136,* 301–322.

Barsalou, L. W. (1983). Ad hoc categories. *Memory & Cognition, 11,* 211–227.

Barsalou, L. W. (1988). The contents and organization of autobiographical memories. In U. Neisser & E. Winograd (Eds.) *Remembering Reconsidered: Ecological and Traditional Approaches to the Study of Memory.* New York: Cambridge University Press.

Barsalou, L. W. (2008). Grounded cognition. *Annual Review of Psychology, 59,* 617–645.

Barsalou, L. W., & Sewell, D. R. (1985). Contrasting the representation of scripts and categories. *Journal of Memory and Language, 24,* 646–665.

Bartlett, F. C. (1932). *Remembering: A Study in Experimental and Social Psychology.* Cambridge: Cambridge University Press.

Bartlett, J. C., & Snelus, P. (1980). Lifespan memory for popular songs. *American Journal of Psychology, 93,* 551–560.

Barton, S. B., & Sanford, A. J. (1993). A case study of anomaly detection: Shallow semantic processing and cohesion establishment. *Memory & Cognition, 21,* 477–487.

Bartus, R. T., Dean, R. L., Beer, B., & Lippa, A. S. (1982). The cholinergic hypothesis of geriatric memory dysfunction. *Science, 217,* 408–417.

Basden, B. H., Basden, D. R., Bryner, S., & Thomas, R. L. (1997). A comparison of group and individual remembering: Does collaboration disrupt retrieval strategies? *Journal of Experimental Psychology: Learning, Memory, and Cognition, 23,* 1176–1189.

Basden, B. H., Basden, D. R., & Morales, E. (2003). The role of retrieval practice in directed forgetting. *Journal of Experimental Psychology: Learning, Memory, and Cognition, 29,* 389–397.

Basden, B. H., Basden, D. R., & Stephens, J. P. (2002). Part-set cuing of order information in recall tests. *Journal of Memory and Language, 47,* 517–529.

Basden, D. R., Basden, B. H., & Galloway, B. C. (1977). Inhibition with part-list cuing: Some tests of the item strength hypothesis. *Journal of Experimental Psychology: Human Learning and Memory, 3,* 100–108.

Bassok, M., Pedigo, S. F., & Oskarsson, A. T. (2008). Priming addition facts with semantic relations. *Journal of Experimental Psychology: Learning, Memory, and Cognition, 34,* 343–352.

Bauer, P. J. (1996). What do infants recall of their lives? *American Psychologist, 51,* 29–41.

Bauer, P. J. (2002). Long-term recall memory: Behavioral and neuro-developmental changes in the first two years of life. *Current Directions in Psychological Science, 11,* 137–141.

Bauer, P. J. (2007). Recall in infancy. *Current Directions in Psychological Science, 16,* 142–146.

Bauer, P. J. (2009). The cognitive neuroscience of the development of memory. In M. L. Courage & N. Cowan (Eds.) *The Development of Memory in Infancy and Childhood*, pp. 115–144. New York: Psychology Press.

Bauer, P. J., Burch, M. M., Scholin, S. E., & Güler, O. E. (2007). Using cue words to investigate the distribution of autobiographical memories in childhood. *Psychological Science, 18,* 910–916.

Bauer, P. J., Wiebe, S. A., Carver, L. J., Waters, J. M., & Nelson, C. A. (2003). Developments in long-term memory late in the first year of life: Behavioral and electrophysiological indices. *Psychological Science, 14,* 629–635.

Bäuml, K-H. (2002). Semantic generation can cause episodic forgetting. *Psychological Science, 13,* 356–360.

Bäuml, K-H., & Aslan, A. (2006). Part-list cuing can be transient and lasting: The role of encoding. *Journal of Experimental Psychology: Learning, Memory, and Cognition, 32,* 33–43.

Bäuml, K-H., & Hartinger, A. (2002). On the role of item similarity in retrieval-induced forgetting. *Memory, 10,* 215–224.

Bäuml, K-H., & Kuhbandner, C. (2003). Retrieval-induced forgetting and part-list cuing in associatively structured lists. *Memory & Cognition, 31,* 1188–1197.

Bayen, U. J., Erdfelder, E., Bearden, J. N., & Lozito, J. P. (2006). Interplay of memory and judgment processes in effects of aging on hindsight bias. *Journal of Experimental Psychology: Learning, Memory, and Cognition, 32,* 1003–1018.

Bayen, U. J., Nakamura, G. V., Dupuis, S. E., & Yang, C. (2000). The use of schematic knowledge about sources in source monitoring. *Memory & Cognition, 28,* 480–500.

Begg, I. M., Robertson, R. K., Gruppuso, V., Anas, A., & Needham, D. R. (1996). The illusory-knowledge effect. *Journal of Memory and Language, 35,* 410–433.

Beilock, S. L. (2008). Math performance in stressful situations. *Current Directions in Psychological Science, 17,* 339–343.

Beilock, S. L., Bertenthal, B. I., McCoy, A. M., & Carr, T. H. (2004). Haste does not always make waste: Expertise, direction of attention, and speed versus accuracy in performing sensorimotor skills. *Psychonomic Bulletin & Review, 11,* 373–379.

Beilock, S. L., & Carr, T. H. (2001). On the fragility of skilled performance: What governs choking under pressure? *Journal of Experimental Psychology: General, 130,* 701–725.

Beilock, S. L., & Carr, T. H. (2005). When high-powered people fail: Working memory and "choking under pressure" in math. *Psychological Science, 16,* 101–105.

Beilock, S. L., & DeCaro, M. S. (2007). From poor performance to success under stress: Working memory, strategy selection, and mathematical problem solving under pressure. *Journal of Experimental Psychology: Learning, Memory, and Cognition, 33,* 983–998.

Beilock, S. L., Kulp, C. A., Holt, L. E., & Carr, T. H. (2004). More on the fragility of performance: Choking under pressure in mathematical problem solving. *Journal of Experimental Psychology: General, 133,* 584–600.

Belleville, S., Caza, N., & Peretz, I. (2003). A neuropsychology argument for a processing view of memory. *Journal of Memory and Language, 48,* 686–703.

Bellezza, F. S. (1992). Recall of congruent information in the self-reference task. *Bulletin of the Psychonomic Society, 30,* 275–278.

Belli, R. F., Lindsay, D. S., Gales, M. S., & McCarthy, T. T. (1994). Memory impairment and source misattribution in postevent misinformation experiments with short retention intervals. *Memory & Cognition, 22,* 40–54.

Benjamin, A. S. (2005). Response speeding mediates the contributions of cue familiarity and target retrievability to metamnemonic judgments. *Psychonomic Bulletin & Review, 12,* 874–879.

Benjamin, A. S., & Bird, R. D. (2006). Metacognitive control of the spacing of study repetitions. *Journal of Memory and Language, 55,* 126–137.

Bennett, D. J., & McEvoy, C. L. (1999). Mediated priming in younger and older adults. *Experimental Aging Research, 25,* 141–159.

Bentin, S. (1989). Electrophysiological studies of visual word perception, lexical organization, and semantic processing: A tutorial review. *Language and Speech, 32,* 205–220.

Bentin, S., McCarthy, G., & Wood, C. C. (1985). Event-related potentials, lexical decision and semantic memory. *Electroencephalography and Clinical Neurophysiology, 60,* 343–355.

Berkerian, D. A., & Bowers, J. M. (1983). Eyewitness testimony: Were we misled? *Journal of Experimental Psychology: Learning, Memory, and Cognition, 9,* 139–145.

Berman, G. L., & Cutler, B. L. (1996). Effects of inconsistencies in eyewitness testimony on mock-juror decision making. *Journal of Applied Psychology, 81,* 170–177.

Berman, M., Jonides, J., & Lewis, R. L. (2009). In search of decay in verbal short-term memory. *Journal of Experimental Psychology: Learning, Memory, and Cognition, 35,* 317–333.

Bernstein, D. M., Godfrey, R. D., Davidson, A., & Loftus, E. F. (2004). Conditions affecting the revelation effect for autobiographical memory. *Memory & Cognition, 32,* 455–462.

Bernstein, D. M., & Loftus, E. F. (2009). The consequences of false memories for food preferences and choices. *Perspectives on Psychological Science, 4,* 135–139

Bernstein, D. M., Whittlesea, B. W. A., & Loftus, E. F. (2002). Increasing confidence in remote autobiographical memory and general knowledge: Extensions of the revelation effect. *Memory & Cognition, 30,* 432–438.

Bernstein, D. W., Rudd, M. E., Erdfelder, E., Godfrey, R., & Loftus, E. F. (2009). The revelation effect for autobiographical memory: A mixture-model analysis. *Psychonomic Bulletin & Review, 16,* 463–468.

Berntsen, D. (1996). Involuntary autobiographical memories. *Applied Cognitive Psychology, 10,* 435–454.

Berntsen, D. (2001). Involuntary memories of emotional events: Do memories of traumas and extremely happy events differ? *Applied Cognitive Psychology, 15,* S135–S158.

Berntsen, D., & Hall, N. M. (2004). The episodic nature of in involuntary autobiographical memories. *Memory & Aging, 32,* 789–803.

Berntsen, D., & Rubin, D. C. (2002). Emotionally charged autobiographical memories across the life span: The recall of happy, sad, traumatic, and involuntary memories. *Psychology and Aging, 17,* 636–652.

Berntsen, D.. & Rubin, D. C. (2004). Cultural life scripts structure recall from autobiographical memory. *Memory & Cognition, 32,* 427–442.

Berntsen, D., & Rubin, D. C. (2006). Flashbulb memories and posttraumatic stress reactions across the life span: Age-related effects of the German occupation of Denmark during World War II. *Psychology and Aging, 21,* 127–139.

Berntsen, D., & Rubin, D.C. (2008). The reappearance hypothesis revisited: Recurrent involuntary memories after traumatic events and in everyday life. *Memory & Cognition, 36,* 449–460.

Bertsch, S., Pesta, B. J., Wiscott, R., & McDaniel, M. A. (2007). The generation effect: A meta-analytic review. *Memory & Cognition, 35,* 201–210.

Biederman, I., Cooper, E. E., Fox, P. W., & Mahadevan, R. S. (1992). Unexceptional spatial memory in an exceptional memorist. *Journal of Experimental Psychology: Learning, Memory, and Cognition, 18,* 654–657.

Bieman-Copland, M. C., & Charness, N. (1994). Memory knowledge and memory monitoring in adulthood. *Psychology and Aging, 9,* 287–302.

Bigand, E., Tillmann, B., Pulin-Charronnat, B., & Manderlier, D. (2005). Repetition priming: Is music special? *Quarterly Journal of Experimental Psychology, 58A,* 1347–1375.

Bireta, T. J., Neath, I., & Surprenant, A. M. (2006). The syllable-based word length effect and stimulus set specificity. *Psychonomic Bulletin & Review, 13,* 434–438.

Bireta, T. J., Surprenant, A. M., & Neath, I. (2008). Age-related differences in the von Restorff isolation effect. *Quarterly Journal of Experimental Psychology, 61,* 345–352.

Bishop, D. V. M., & Robson, J. (1989). Unimpaired short-term memory and rhyme judgment in congenitally speechless individuals: Implications for the notion of "articulatory coding." *Quarterly Journal of Experimental Psychology, 41A,* 123–140.

Bjork, E. L., & Bjork, R. A. (2003). Intentional forgetting can increase, not decrease, residual influences of to-be-forgotten information. *Journal of Experimental Psychology: Learning, Memory, and Cognition, 29,* 524–531.

Bjork, R. A. (1970). Positive forgetting: The noninterference of items intentionally forgotten. *Journal of Verbal Learning and Verbal Behavior, 9,* 255–268.

Bjork, R. A. (1989). Retrieval inhibition as an adaptive mechanism in human memory. In H. L. Roediger & F. I. M. Craik (Eds.),*Varieties of Memory and Consciousness*, pp. 309–330. Hillsdale, NJ: Erlbaum.

Bjorklund, D. F., Dukes, C., & Brown, R. D. (2009). The development of memory strategies. In M. L. Courage & N. Cowan (Eds.) *The Development of Memory in Infancy and Childhood*, pp. 145–175. New York: Psychology Press.

Bjorklund, D. F., & Zeman, B. R. (1982). Children's organization and metamemory awareness in their recall of familiar information. *Child Development, 53,* 799–810.

Björkman, M., Lundberg, I., & Tärnblom, S. (1960). On the relationship between percept and memory: A psychophysical approach *The Scandinavian Journal of Psychology, 1,* 136–144.

Blakemore, C. (1977). *Mechanics of the Mind.* Cambridge, England: Cambridge University Press.

Blakemore, C., & Cooper, G. F. (1970). Development of the brain depends on the visual environment. *Nature, 228,* 477–478.

Blanchet, S., Desganges, B., Denise, P., Lechevalier, B., Eustache, F., & Faure, S. (2001). New questions on the hemispheric encoding/retrieval asymmetry (HERA) model assessed by divided visual-field tachistoscopy in normal subjects. *Neuropsychologia, 39,* 502–509.

Blaney, P. H. (1986). Affect and Memory: A Review. *Psychological Bulletin, 99,* 229–246.

Blank, H., Fischer, V., & Erdfelder, E. (2003). Hindsight bias in political elections. *Memory, 11,* 491–504.

Blaxton, T. A., (1989). Investigating dissociations among memory measures: Support for a transfer-appropriate processing framework. *Journal of Experimental Psychology: Learning, Memory, and Cognition, 15,* 657–668.

Blaxton, T. A., & Neely, J. H. (1983). Inhibition from semantically related primes: Evidence of a category-specific inhibition. *Memory & Cognition, 11,* 500–510.

Bliss, J. C., Crane, H. D., Mansfield, P. K., & Townsend, J. T. (1966). Information available in brief tactile presentations. *Perception & Psychophysics, 1,* 273–283.

Bliss, T. V. P., & Collingridge, G. L. (1993). A synaptic model of memory: Long-term potentiation in the hippocampus. *Nature, 232,* 31–39.

Bliss, T. V. P., & Lomo, T. (1973). Long-lasting potentiation of synaptic transmission in the dentate area of the anaesthetized rabbit following stimulations of the preforant path. *Journal of Physiology, 232,* 331–356.

Block, R. A. (2009). Intent to remember briefly presented human faces and other pictorial stimuli enhances recognition memory. *Memory & Cognition, 37,* 667–678.

Bloom, L. C. (2006). Two-component theory of the suffix effect: Contrary evidence. *Memory & Cognition, 34,* 648–667.

Bohan, J., & Sanford, A. (2008). Semantic anomalies at the borderline of consciousness: An eye tracking investigation. *Quarterly Journal of Experimental Psychology, 61,* 232–239.

Bolte, A., Goschke, T., & Kuhl, J. (2003). Emotion and intuition: Effects of positive and negative mood on implicit judgments of semantic coherence. *Psychological Science, 14,* 416–421.

Bonn, A., & Berntsen, D. (2007). Pleasantness bias in flashbulb memories: Positive and negative flashbulb memories of the fall of the Berlin Wall among East and West Germans. *Memory & Cognition, 35,* 565–577.

Bornstein, R. F. (1989). Exposure and affect: A review and meta-analysis of research, 1968–1987. *Psychological Bulletin, 106,* 265–289.

Bornstein, B. H., & Neely, C. B. (2001). The revelation effect in frequency judgment. *Memory & Cognition, 29,* 209–213.

Bousfield, A. K., & Bousfield, W. A. (1966). Measurement of clustering and of sequential constancies in repeated free recall. *Psychological Reports, 19,* 935–942.

Bousfield, W. A., (1953). The occurrence of clustering in the recall of randomly arranged associates. *Journal of General Psychology, 49,* 229–240.

Bower, G. H. (1981). Mood and memory. *American Psychologist, 36,* 129–148.

Bower, G. H., Black, J. B., & Turner, T. J. (1979). Scripts in memory for text. *Cognitive Psychology, 11,* 117–220.

Bower, G. H., Clark, M. C., Lesgold, A. M., & Winzenz, D. (1969). Hierarchical retrieval schemes in recall of categorized word lists. *Journal of Verbal Learning and Verbal Behavior, 8,* 323–343.

Bower, G. H., Karlin, M. B., & Dueck, A. (1975). Comprehension and memory for pictures. *Memory & Cognition, 3,* 216–220.

Bower, G. H., & Rinck, M. (2001). Selecting one among many referents in spatial situation models. *Journal of Experimental Psychology: Learning, Memory, and Cognition, 27,* 81–98.

Bozeat, S., Lamdon Ralph, M. A., Patterson, K., Garrard, P., & Hodges, J. R. (2000). Non-verbal semantic impairment in semantic dementia. *Neuropsychologia, 38,* 1207–1215.

Bradburn, N. M., Rips, L. J., & Shevell, S. K. (1987). Answering autobiographical questions: The impact of memory and inference on surveys. *Science, 236,* 157–161.

Bradley, M. M., Greenwald, M. K., Petry, M. C., & Lang, P. J. (1992). Remembering pictures: Pleasure and arousal in memory. *Journal of Experimental Psychology: Learning, Memory, and Cognition, 18,* 379–390.

Brainerd, C. J., Payne, D. G., Wright, R., & Reyna, V. F. (2003). Phantom recall. *Journal of Memory and Language, 48,* 445–467.

Brainerd, C. J., Reyna, V. F., & Forrest, T. J. (2002). Are young children susceptible to the false-memory illusion? *Child Development, 73,* 1363–1377.

Brainerd, C. J., Reyna, V. F., & Howe, M. L. (2009). Trichotomous processes in early memory development, aging, and neurocognitive impairment: A unified theory. *Psychological Review, 116,* 783–832.

Brainerd, C. J., Reyna, V. F., & Mojardin, A. H. (1999). Conjoint recognition. *Psychological Review, 106,* 160–179.

Brainerd, C. J., Stein, L. M., Silveira, R. A., Rohenkohl, G., & Reyna, V. F. (2008). How does negative emotion cause false memories? *Psychological Science, 19,* 919–925.

Brainerd, C. J., Wright, R., Reyna, V. F., & Mojardin, A. H. (2001). Conjoint recognition and phantom recognition. *Journal of Experimental Psychology: Learning, Memory, and Cognition, 27,* 307–327.

Brandt, J., & Rich, J. B. (1995). Memory disorders in the dementias. In A. D. Baddeley, B. A. Wilson, & F. N. Watts (Eds.), *Handbook of Memory Disorders,* pp. 243–270. New York: Wiley.

Bransford, J. D., Barclay, J. R., & Franks, J. J. (1972). Sentence memory: A constructive versus interpretive approach. *Cognitive Psychology, 3,* 193–209.

Bransford, J. D., & Franks, J. J. (1971). The abstraction of linguistic ideas. *Cognitive Psychology, 2,* 331–350.

Bransford, J. D., & Johnson, M. K. (1972). Contextual prerequisites for understanding: Some investigations of comprehension and recall. *Journal of Verbal Learning and Verbal Behavior, 11,* 717–726.

Bransford, J. D., & Stein, B. S. (1984). *The Ideal Problem Solver.* New York: Freeman.

Braver, T. S., Barch, D. M., Keys, B. A., Carter, C. S., Cohen, J D., Kaye, J. A., Janowsky, J. S., Taylor, S. F., Yesavage, J. A., Mumenthaler, M. S., Jagust, W. J., & Reed, B. R. (2001). Context processing in older adults: Evidence for a theory relating cognitive control to neurobiology in healthy aging. *Journal of Experimental Psychology: General, 130,* 746–763.

Brédart, S., Lampinen, J. M., & Defeldre, A. C. (2003). Phenomenal characteristics of cryptomnesia. *Memory, 11,* 1–11.

Breedin, S. D., Saffran, E. M., & Coslett, H. B. (1994). Reversal of the concreteness effect in a patient with semantic dementia. *Cognitive Neuropsychology, 11,* 617–660.

Brewer, W. F., & Treyens, J. C. (1981). Role of schemata in memory for places. *Cognitive Psychology, 13,* 207–230.

Brigham, J. C., & Cairns, D. L. (1988). The effect of mugshot inspections on eyewitness identification accuracy. *Journal of Applied Social Psychology, 18,* 1394–1410.

Brooks, D. N., & Baddeley, A. D. (1976). What can amnesic patients learn? *Neuropsychologia, 14,* 111–122.

Brown, A. S. (1991). A review of the tip-of-the-tongue experience. *Psychological Bulletin, 109,* 204–223.

Brown, A. S. (1998). Transient global amnesia. *Psychonomic Bulletin & Review, 5,* 401–427.

Brown, A. S. (2002). Consolidation theory and retrograde amnesia in humans. *Psychonomic Bulletin & Review, 9,* 403–425.

Brown, A. S. (2003). A review of the déjà vu experience. *Psychological Bulletin, 129,* 394–413.

Brown, A. S., & Halliday, H. E. (1991). Cryptomnesia and source memory difficulties. *American Journal of Psychology, 104,* 475–490.

Brown, A. S., & Marsh, E. J. (2008). Evoking false beliefs about autobiographical experience. *Psychonomic Bulletin & Review, 15,* 186–190.

Brown, A. S. & Marsh, E. J. (2009). Creating illusions of past encounter through brief exposure. *Psychological Science, 20,* 534–538.

Brown, C., & Lloyd-Jones, T. J. (2005). Verbal facilitation of face recognition. *Memory & Cognition, 33,* 1442–1456.

Brown, C., & Lloyd-Jones, T. J. (2006). Beneficial effects of verbalization and visual distinctiveness on remembering and knowing faces. *Memory & Cognition, 34,* 277–286.

Brown, E., Deffenbacher, K., & Sturgill, W. (1977). Memory for faces and the circumstances of encounter. *Journal of Applied Psychology, 62,* 311–318.

Brown, G. D. A. (1997). Formal models of memory for serial order: A review. In M. A. Conway (Ed.), *Cognitive Models of Memory,* pp. 47–78. Cambridge, MA: MIT Press.

Brown, J. (1958). Some tests of the decay theory of immediate memory. *Quarterly Journal of Experimental Psychology, 10,* 12–21.

Brown, N. R. (1990). Organization of public events in long-term memory. *Journal of Experimental Psychology: General, 119,* 297–314.

Brown, N. R., Rips, L. J., & Shevell, S. K. (1985). The subjective dates of natural events in very-long-term memory. *Cognitive Psychology, 17,* 139–177.

Brown, N. S., & Schopflocher, D. (1998a). Event clusters: An organization of personal events in autobiographical memory. *Psychological Science, 9,* 470–475.

Brown, N. S., & Schopflocher, D. (1998b). Event cueing, event clusters, and the temporal distribution of autobiographical memories. *Applied Cognitive Psychology, 12,* 305–319.

Brown, R., & Kulik, J. (1977). Flashbulb memories. *Cognition, 5,* 73–99.

Brown, R., & McNeill, D. (1966). The "tip of the tongue" phenomenon. *Journal of Verbal Learning and Verbal Behavior, 5,* 325–337.

Brown, R. G., & Marsden, C. D. (1988). Internal versus external cues and the control of attention in Parkinson's disease.*Brain, 111,* 323–345.

Bruce, D., Wilcox-O'Hearn, L. A., Robinson, J. A., Phillips-Grant, K., Francis, L., & Smith, M. C. (2005). Fragmented memories mark the end of childhood amnesia. *Memory & Cognition, 33,* 567–576.

Bruck, M., & Cici, S. (2004). Forensic developmental psychology: Unveiling four misconceptions. *Current Directions in Psychological Science, 13,* 229–232.

Bruner, J. (1991). The narrative construction of reality. *Critical Inquiry, 18,* 1–21.

Bruner, J. S., Goodnow, J. J., & Austin, G. A. (1956). *A Study of Thinking.* Oxford, England: Wiley.

Buchanan, T. W., Karafin, M. S., & Adolphs, R. (2003). Selective effects of triazolam on memory for emotional, relative to neutral, stimuli: Differential effects on gist versus detail. *Behavioral Neuroscience, 117,* 517–525.

Buckner, R. L. (1996). Beyond HERA: Contributions of specific prefrontal brain areas to long-term memory retrieval. *Psychonomic Bulletin & Review, 3,* 149–158.

Budson, A. E., & Gold, C. A. (2009). Flashbulb, personal, and event memories in clinical populations. In O. Luminet & A. Curci (Eds.), *Flashbulb Memories: New Issues and New Perspectives*, pp. 141–162. New York: Psychology Press.

Bugmann, D., Coventry, K. R., & Newstead, S. E. (2007). Contextual cues and the retrieval of information from cognitive maps. *Memory & Cognition, 35,* 381–392.

Bunting, M. F., Conway, A. R. A., & Heitz, R. P. (2004). Individual differences in the fan effect and working memory capacity. *Journal of Memory and Language, 51,* 604–622.

Buratto, L. G., Matthews, W. J., & Lamberts, K. (2009). When are moving images remembered better? Study-test congruence and the dynamic superiority effect. *Quarterly Journal of Experimental Psychology, 62,* 1896–1903.

Burgess, A. P., & Ali, L. (2002). Functional connectivity of gamma EEG activity is modulated at low frequency during conscious recollection. *International Journal of Psychophysiology, 46,* 91–100.

Burgess, A. P., & Gruzelier, J. H. (2000). Short duration power changes in the EEG during recognition memory for words and faces. *Psychophysiology, 37,* 596–606.

Burgess, N. (2002). The hippocampus, space, and viewpoints in episodic memory. *Quarterly Journal of Experimental Psychology, 55A,* 1057–1080.

Burgess, N., & Hitch, G. J. (1992). Toward a network model of the articulatory loop. *Journal of Memory and Language, 31,* 429–460.

Burgess, P. W., & Shallice, T. (1997). The relationship between prospective and retrospective memory: Neurological evidence. In M. A. Conway (Ed.), *Cognitive Models of Memory,* pp. 247–272. Cambridge, MA: MIT Press.

Burke, D. M., White, H., & Diaz, D. L. (1987). Semantic priming in young and older adults: Evidence for age constancy in automatic and attentional processes. *Journal of Experimental Psychology: Human Perception and Performance, 13,* 79–88.

Burns, D. J. (1989). Proactive interference: An individual-item versus relational processing account. *Journal of Memory and Language, 28,* 345–359.

Burns, D. J. (1992). The consequences of generation. *Journal of Memory and Language, 31,* 615–633.

Burt, C. D. B. (1992). Retrieval characteristics of autobiographical memories: Event and date information. *Applied Cognitive Psychology, 6,* 389–404.

Burt, C. D. B., Kemp, S., & Conway, M. A. (2003). Themes, events, and episodes in autobiographical memory. *Memory & Cognition, 31,* 317–325.

Burt, C. D. B., Mitchell, D. A., Raggatt, P. T. F., Jones, C. A., & Cowan, T. M. (1995). A snapshot of autobiographical memory retrieval characteristics. *Applied Cognitive Psychology, 9,* 61–74.

Burt, C. D. B., Watt, S. C., Mitchell, D. A., & Conway, M. A. (1998). Retrieving the sequence of autobiographical event components. *Applied Cognitive Psychology, 12,* 321–338.

Butler, J., & Rovee-Collier, C. (1989). Contextual gating of memory retrieval. *Developmental Psychobiology, 22,* 533–552.

Butler, K. M., McDaniel, M. A., Dornberg, C. C., Price, A. L., & Roediger, H. L. (2004). Age differences in veridical and false recall are not inevitable: The role of frontal lobe function. *Psychonomic Bulletin & Review, 11,* 921–925.

Büttner, A. C. (2007). Questions versus statements: Challenging an assumption about semantic illusions. *Quarterly Journal of Experimental Psychology, 60,* 779–789.

Cabeza, R. (2002). Hemispheric asymmetry reduction in older adults: The HAROLD model. *Psychology and Aging, 17,* 85–100.

Cahill, C., & Frith, C. (1995). Memory following electroconvulsive therapy. In A. D. Baddeley, B. A. Wilson, & F. N. Watts (Eds.), *Handbook of Memory Disorders,* pp. 319–335. New York: Wiley.

Cameron, T. E., & Hockley, W. E. (2000). The revelation effect for item and associative recognition: Familiarity versus recollection. *Memory & Cognition, 28,* 176–183.

Camp, G., Pecher, D., & Schmidt, H. G. (2005). Retrieval-induced forgetting in implicit memory tests: The role of test awareness. *Psychonomic Bulletin & Review, 12,* 490–494.

Campbell, J. I. D., & Phenix, T. L.. (2009). Target strength and retrieval-induced forgetting in semantic recall. *Memory & Cognition, 37,* 65–72.

Campbell, R., & Dodd, B. (1982). Some suffix effects on lipread lists. *Canadian Journal of Psychology, 36,* 508–514.

Canas, J. J., & Nelson, D. L. (1986). Recognition and environmental context: The effect of testing by phone. *Bulletin of the Psychonomic Society, 24,* 407–409.

Canavan, A. G. M., Passingham, R. E., Marsden, C. D., Quinn, N., Wyke, M., & Polkey, C. E. (1989). The performance on learning tasks of patients in the early stages of Parkinson's disease. *Neuropsychologia, 27,* 141–156.

Candel, I., Merckelbach, H., & Zandbergen, M. (2003). Boundary distortions for neutral and emotional pictures. *Psychonomic Bulletin & Review, 10,* 691–695.

Cann, A., & Ross, D. A. (1989). Olfactory stimuli as context cues in human memory. *American Journal of Psychology, 102,* 91–102.

Cann, D., & Katz, A. M. (2005). Habitual acceptance of misinformation: Examination of individual differences and source attributions. *Memory & Cognition, 33,* 405–417.

Cantor, J., & Engle, R. W. (1993). Working-memory capacity as long-term memory activation: An individual differences approach. *Journal of Experimental Psychology: Learning, Memory, and Cognition, 19,* 1101–1114.

Cantor, J., Engle, R. W., & Hamilton, G. (1991). Short-term memory, working memory, and verbal abilities: How do they relate? *Intelligence, 15,* 229–246.

Carbon, C., & Leder, H. (2005). The wall inside the brain: Overestimation of distances crossing the former iron curtain. *Psychonomic Bulletin & Review, 12,* 746–750.

Carmichael, L., Hogan, H. P., & Walter, A. A. (1932). An experimental study of the effect of language on the reproductions of visually perceived forms. *Journal of Experimental Psychology, 15,* 73–86.

Carpenter, S. K. (2009). Cue strength as a moderator of the testing effect: The benefits of elaborative retrieval. *Journal of Experimental Psychology: Learning, Memory, and Cognition, 35,* 1563–1569.

Carpenter, S. K., Pashler, H., Wixted, J. T., & Vul, E. (2008). The effects of tests on learning and forgetting. *Memory & Cognition, 36,* 438–448.

Carrier, L. M., & Pashler, H. (1995). Attentional limits in memory retrieval. *Journal of Experimental Psychology: Learning, Memory, and Cognition, 21,* 1339–1348.

Carter, H. D. (1936). Emotional correlates of errors in learning. *Journal of Educational Psychology, 27,* 55–67.

Carter, H. D., Jones, H. E., & Shock, N. W. (1934). An experimental study of affective factors in learning. *Journal of Educational Psychology, 25,* 203–215.

Carver, L.J., & Bauer, P. J. (2001). The dawning of a past: The emergence of long-term explicit memory in infancy. *Journal of Experimental Psychology: General, 130,* 726–745.

Casasanto, D. (2009). Embodiment of abstract concepts: Good and bad in right- and left-handers. *Journal of Experimental Psychology: General, 138,* 351–367.

Case, R. (1972). Validation of a neo-Piagetian mental capacity construct. *Journal of Experimental Child Psychology, 14,* 287–302.

Castel, A. D., Farb, N. A. S., & Craik, F. I. M. (2007). Memory for general and specific value information in younger and older adults: Measuring the limits of strategic control. *Memory & Cognition, 35,* 689–700.

Castronovo, J., & Seron, X. (2007). Semantic numerical representation in blind subjects: The role of vision in the spatial format of the mental number line. *Quarterly Journal of Experimental Psychology, 60,* 101–119.

Čech, C. G., Shoben, E. J., & Love, M. (1990). Multiple congruity effects in judgments of magnitude. *Journal of Experimental Psychology: Learning, Memory, and Cognition, 16,* 1142–1152.

Ceci, S. J., & Bruck, M. (1993). Suggestibility of the child witness: A historical review and synthesis. *Psychological Bulletin, 113,* 403–439.

Cerella, J. (1994). Generalized slowing in Brinley plots. *Journal of Gerontology: Psychological Sciences, 49,* P65–P71.

Cermak, L. S., & O'Connor, M. (1983). The anterograde and retrograde retrieval ability of a patient with amnesia due to encephalitis.*Neuropsychologia, 21,* 213–234.

Chan, J. C. K. (2009). When does retrieval induce forgetting and when does it induce facilitation? Implications for retrieval inhibition, testing effect, and text processing. *Journal of Memory and Language, 61,* 153–170.

Chan, J. C. K., & McDermott, K. B. (2007). The effects of frontal lobe functioning and age on veridical and false recall.*Psychonomic Bulletin & Review, 14,* 606–611.

Chan, J. C. K., McDermott, K. B., & Roediger, H. L. (2006). Retrieval-induced facilitation: Initially nontested material can benefit from prior testing of related material. *Journal of Experimental Psychology: General, 135,* 553–571.

Chan, J. C. K., Thomas, A. K., & Bulevich, J. B. (2009). Recalling a witnessed event increases eyewitness suggestibility. *Psychological Science, 20,* 66–73.

Charles, S. T., Mather, M., & Carstensen, L. L. (2003). Aging and emotional memory: The forgettable nature of negative images for older adults. *Journal of Experimental Psychology: General, 132,* 310–324.

Chase, W. G., & Simon, H. A. (1973). Perception in chess. *Cognitive Psychology, 4,* 55–81.

Chasteen, A. L., Park, D. C., & Schwarz, N. (2001). Implementation intentions and facilitation of prospective memory. *Psychological Science, 12,* 457–461.

Chen, Y., & Blanchard-Fields, F. (2000). Unwanted thought: Age differences in the correction of social judgments. *Psychology and Aging, 15,* 475–482.

Cheng, P. W. (1997). From covariation to causation: A causal power theory. *Psychological Review, 104,* 367–405.

Chew, E. I., & Richardson, J. T. E. (1980). The relationship between perceptual and memorial psychophysics. *Memory & Cognition, 16,* 25–26.

Chi, M. T. H., & Koeske, R. D. (1983). Network representation of a child's dinosaur knowledge. *Developmental Psychology, 19,* 29–39.

Chiappe, P., Hasher, L., & Siegel, L. S. (2000). Working memory, inhibitory control, and reading disability. *Memory & Cognition, 28,* 8–17.

Chin-Parker, S., & Ross, B. H. (2002). The effect of category learning on sensitivity to within-category correlations. *Memory & Cognition, 30,* 353–362.

Chorover, S. L., & Schiller, P. H. (1965). Short-term retrograde amnesia in rats. *Journal of Comparative and Physiological Psychology, 59,* 73–78.

Christiaansen, R. E., & Ochalek, K. (1983). Editing misleading information from memory: Evidence for the co-existence of original and postevent information. *Memory & Cognition, 11,* 467–475.

Christianson, S. (1989). Flashbulb memories: Special, but not so special. *Memory & Cognition, 17,* 435–443.

Christianson, S. (1992). Emotional stress and eyewitness memory: A critical review. *Psychological Bulletin, 112,* 284–309.

Chrobak, Q. M., & Zaragoza, M. S. (2008). Inventing stories: Forcing witnesses to fabricate entire fictitious events leads to freely reported false memories. *Psychonomic Bulletin & Review, 15,* 1190–1195.

Chu, S., & Downes, J. J. (2002). Proust nose best: Odors are better cues of autobiographical memory. *Memory & Cognition, 30,* 511–518.

Chua, E. F., Schacter, D. L., & Sperling, R. A. (2009). Neural basis for recognition confidence in younger and older adults. *Psychology and Aging, 24,* 139–153.

Chugani, H. T., Phelps, M. E., & Mazziotta, J. C. (1986). Positron emission tomography study of human brain functional development. *Annals of Neurology, 22,* 487–497.

Chwilla, D. J., Kolk, H. J., & Mulder, G. (2000). Mediated priming in the lexical decision task: Evidence from event-related potentials and reaction time. *Journal of Memory and Language, 42,* 314–341.

Ciranni, M. A., & Shimamura, A. P. (1999). Retrieval-induced forgetting in episodic memory. *Journal of Experimental Psychology: Learning, Memory, and Cognition, 25,* 1403–1414.

Clare, J., & Lewandowsky, S. (2004). Verbalizing facial memory: Criterion effects in verbal overshadowing. *Journal of Experimental Psychology: Learning, Memory, and Cognition, 30,* 739–755.

Clark, S. E., Abbe, A., & Larson, R. P. (2006). Collaboration in associative recognition memory: Using recalled information to defend "new" judgments. *Journal of Experimental Psychology: Learning, Memory, and Cognition, 32,* 1266–1273.

Clark, S. E., & Godfrey, R. D. (2009). Eyewitness identification evidence and innocence risk. *Psychonomic Bulletin & Review, 16,* 22–42.

Clark, S. E., & Gronlund, S. D. (1996). Global matching models of recognition memory: How the models match the data. *Psychonomic Bulletin & Review, 3,* 37–60.

Clark, S. E., Hori, A., Putnam, A., & Martin, T. P. (2000). Group collaborations in recognition memory. *Journal of Experimental Psychology: Learning, Memory and Cognition, 26,* 1578–1588.

Clayton, K., & Habibi, A. (1991). Contributions of temporal contiguity to the spatial priming effect. *Journal of Experimental Psychology: Learning, Memory, & Cognition, 17,* 263–271.

Cleary, A. M. (2008). Recognition memory, familiarity, and déjà vu experiences. *Current Directions in Psychological Science, 17,* 353–357.

Cockburn, J. (1995). Task interruption in prospective memory: A frontal lobe function? *Cortex, 31* 87–97.

Cohen, A.-L., Jaudas, A., & Gollwitzer, P. M. (2008). Number of cues influences the cost of remembering to remember. *Memory & Cognition, 36,* 149–156.

Cohen, G. (1990). Recognition and retrieval of proper names: Age differences in the fan effect. *European Journal of Cognitive Psychology, 2,* 193–204.

Colcombe, S. J., Kramer, A. F., Erickson, K. I., & Scalf, P. (2005). The implications of cortical recruitment and brain morphology for individual differences in inhibitory function in aging humans. *Psychology and Aging, 20,* 363–375.

Colcombe, S. J., & Wyer, R. S. (2002). The role of prototypes in the mental representation of temporally related events. *Cognitive Psychology, 44,* 67–103.

Coles, M. G. H., Gratton, G., & Fabiani, M. (1990). Event-related brain potentials. In J. T. Cacioppo & L. G. Tassinary (Eds.), *Principles of Psychophysiology: Physical, Social, and Inferential Elements,* pp. 413–455. Cambridge, England: Cambridge University Press.

Colle, H. A., & Welsh, A. (1976). Acoustic masking in primary memory. *Journal of Verbal Learning and Verbal Behavior, 15,* 17–32.

Collins, A. M., & Loftus, E. F. (1975). A spreading activation theory of semantic processing. *Psychological Review, 82,* 407–428.

Collins, A. M., & Quillian, M. R. (1969). Retrieval time from semantic memory. *Journal of Verbal Learning and Verbal Behavior, 8,* 240–247.

Collins, A. M., & Quillian, M. R. (1972). How to make a language user. In E. Tulving & W. Donaldson (Eds.), *Organization and Memory,* pp. 309–351. New York: Academic Press.

Collins, K. A., Pillemer, D. B., Ivcevic, Z., & Gooze, R. A. (2007). Cultural scripts guide recall of intensely positive life events. *Memory & Cognition, 35,* 651–659.

Coman, A., Manier, D., & Hirst, W. (2009). Forgetting the unforgettable through conversation: Socially shared retrieval-induced forgetting of September 11 memories. *Psychological Science, 20,* 627–633.

Conrad, R. (1960). Very brief delay of immediate recall. *Quarterly Journal of Experimental Psychology, 12,* 45–47.

Conrad, R. (1965). Order error in immediate recall of sequences. *Journal of Verbal Learning and Verbal Behavior, 4,* 161–169.

Conrad, R. & Hull, A. (1964). Information, acoustic confusion, and memory span. *British Journal of Experimental Psychology, 55,* 75–84.

Conway, A. R. A., & Engle, R. W. (1994). Working memory and retrieval: A resource-dependent inhibition model. *Journal of Experimental Psychology: General, 123,* 354–373.

Conway, A. R. A., Kane, M. J., Bunting, M. F., Hambrick, D. Z., Wilhelm, O., & Engle, R. W. (2005). Working memory span tasks: A methodological review and users guide. *Psychonomic Bulletin & Review, 12,* 769–786.

Conway, M. A. (1990). Associations between autobiographical memories and concepts. *Journal of Experimental Psychology: Learning, Memory, and Cognition, 16,* 799–812.

Conway, M. A. (1996). Autobiographical memory. In E. L. Bjork & R. A. Bjork (Eds.), *Memory.* San Diego: Academic Press.

Conway, M. A., Anderson, S. J., Larsen, S. F., Donnelly C. M., McDaniel, M. A., McClelland, A. G. R., Rawles, R. E., & Logie, R. H. (1994). The formation of flashbulb memories. *Memory & Cognition, 22,* 326–343.

Conway, M. A., & Berkerian, D. A. (1987). Organization of autobiographical memory. *Memory & Cognition, 15,* 119–132.

Conway, M. A., Cohen, G., & Stanhope, N. (1991). On the very long-term retention of knowledge acquired through formal education: Twelve years of cognitive psychology. *Journal of Experimental Psychology: General, 120,* 395–409.

Conway, M. A., Harries, K., Noyes, J., Racma'ny, M., & Frankish, C. R. (2000). The disruption and dissolution of directed forgetting: Inhibitory control of memory. *Journal of Memory and Language, 43,* 409–430.

Conway, M. A. & Pleydell-Pearce, C. W. (2000). The construction of autobiographical memories in the self-memory system. *Psychological Review, 107,* 261–288.

Cook, G. I., Hicks, J. L., & Marsh, R. L. (2007). Source monitoring is not always enhanced for valenced material. *Memory & Cognition, 35,* 222–230.

Cook, G. I., Marsh, R. L., & Hicks, J. L. (2006a). Source memory in the absence of successful cued recall. *Memory & Cognition, 34,* 240–250.

Cook, G. I., Marsh, R. L., & Hicks, J. L. (2006b). The role of recollection and familiarity in the context variability mirror effect. *Journal of Experimental Psychology: Learning, Memory, and Cognition, 32,* 828–835.

Cooke, N. J., & Breedin, S. D. (1994). Constructing naive theories of motion on the fly. *Memory & Cognition, 22,* 474–493.

Copeland, D. E., & Radvansky, G. A. (2001). Phonological similarity in working memory. *Memory & Cognition, 29,* 774–776.

Copeland, D. E., Radvansky, G. A., & Goodwin, K. A. (2009). A novel study: Forgetting curves and the reminiscence bump. *Memory, 17,* 323–336.

Corkin, S. (1968). Acquisition of motor skill after bilateral medial temporal-lobe excision. *Neuropsychologia, 6,* 255–265.

Corkin, S. (1998). Functional MRI for studying episodic memory in aging and Alzheimer's disease. *Geriatrics, 53,* S13–S15.

Corkin, S., Amaral, D. G., González, R. G., Johnson, K. A., & Hyman, B. T. (1997). H. M.'s medial temporal lobe lesions: Findings from magnetic resonance imaging. *Journal of Neuroscience, 17,* 3964–3979.

Corson, Y., & Verrier, N. (2007). Emotions and false memories. *Psychological Science, 18,* 208–211.

Costermans, J., Lories, G., & Ansay, C. (1992). Confidence level and feeling of knowing in question answering: The weight of inferential processes. *Journal of Experimental Psychology: Learning, Memory, & Cognition, 18,* 142–150.

Courtney, J. R., & Hubbard, T. L. (2008). Spatial memory and explicit knowledge: An effect of instruction on representational momentum. *Quarterly Journal of Experimental Psychology, 61,* 1778–1784.

Cowan, N. (2000). The magical number 4 in short-term memory: A reconsideration of mental storage capacity. *Behavioral and Brain Sciences, 24,* 87–185.

Cowan, N., Baddeley, A. D., Elliott, E. M., & Norris, J. (2003). List composition and the word length effect in immediate recall: A comparison of localist and globalist assumptions. *Psychonomic Bulletin & Review, 10,* 74–79.

Cowan, N., Suomi, K., & Morae, P. A. (1982). Echoic storage in infant perception. *Child Development, 53,* 984–990.

Crabb, B. T., & Dark, V. J. (2003). Perceptual implicit memory relies on intentional load-sensitive processing at encoding. *Memory & Cognition, 31,* 997–1008.

Craik, F. I. M., & Byrd, M. (1982). Aging and cognitive deficits: The role of attentional resources. In F. I. M. Craik & S. Trehub (Eds.), *Aging and Cognitive Processes,* pp. 191–211. New York: Plenum Press.

Craik, F. I. M., & Lockhart, R. S. (1972). Levels of processing: A framework for memory research. *Journal of Verbal Learning and Verbal Behavior, 12,* 671–684.

Cree, G. S., & McRae, K. (2003). Analyzing the factors underlying the structure and computation of the meaning of chipmunk, cherry, chisel, cheese, and cello (and many other such concrete nouns). *Journal of Experimental Psychology: General, 132,* 163–201.

Crowder, R. G. (1972). Visual and auditory memory. In J. F. Kavanagh & I. G. Mattingly (Eds.), *Language by Ear and by Eye.* Cambridge, MA: MIT Press.

Crowder, R. G., & Morton, J. (1969). Precategorical acoustic storage (PAS). *Perception & Psychophysics, 5,* 365–373.

Crutch, S. J., Connell, S., & Warrington, E. K. (2009). The different representational frameworks underpinning abstract and concrete knowledge: Evidence form odd-one-out judgments. *Quarterly Journal of Experimental Psychology, 62,* 1377–1390.

Cue, A., Koppel, J., & Hirst, W. (2007). Silence is not golden: A case for socially shared retrieval-induced forgetting. *Psychological Science, 18,* 727–733.

Cuevas, K., Rovee-Collier, C., & Learmonth, A. E. (2006). Infants form associations between memory representations of stimuli that are absent. *Psychological Science, 17,* 543–549.

Curiel, J. M., & Radvansky, G. A. (1998). Mental organization in maps. *Journal of Experimental Psychology: Learning, Memory, & Cognition, 24,* 202–214.

Curran, T. (2000). Brain potentials of recollection and familiarity. *Memory & Cognition, 28,* 923–938.

Curran, H. V. (1991). Benzodiazapines, memory, and mood: A review. *Psychopharmacology, 105,* 1–8.

Cutting, J. E. (2003). Gustave Caillebotte, French Impressionism, and mere exposure. *Psychonomic Bulletin & Review, 10,* 319–343.

Dagenbach, D., Horst, S., and Carr, T. H. (1990). Adding new information to semantic memory: How much learning is enough to produce automatic priming? *Journal of Experimental Psychology: Learning, Memory, and Cognition, 16,* 581–591.

Dalgleish, T., Hauer, B., & Kuyken, W. (2008). The mental regulation of autobiographical recollection in the aftermath of trauma. *Current Directions in Psychological Science, 17,* 259–263.

Dalton, P., Lavie, N., & Spence, C. (2009). The role of working memory in tactile selective attention. *Quarterly Journal of Experimental Psychology, 62,* 635–644.

Daneman, M., & Carpenter, P. A. (1980). Individual differences in working memory and reading. *Journal of Verbal Learning and Verbal Behavior, 19,* 430–466.

Daneman, M., and Merikle, P. M. (1996). Working memory and language comprehension: A meta-analysis. *Psychonomic Bulletin and Review, 3,* 422–433.

Daniels, K. A., Toth, J. P., & Hertzog, C. (2009). Aging and recollection in the accuracy of judgments of learning. *Psychology and Aging, 24,* 494–500.

Danziger, K. (2008). *Marking the Mind.* Cambridge, England: Cambridge University Press.

Darling, S., Della Sala, S., & Logie, R. H. (2009). Dissociation between appearance and location within visuo-spatial working memory. *Quarterly Journal of Experimental Psychology, 62,* 417–425.

Darwin, C. J., Turvey, M. T., & Crowder, R. G. (1972). An auditory analogue of the Sperling partial report procedure: Evidence for brief auditory storage. *Cognitive Psychology, 3,* 255–267.

Davelaar, E. J., Goshen-Gottstein, Y., Ashkenazi, A., Haarmann, H. J., & Usher, M. (2005). The demise of short-term memory revisited: Empirical and computational investigations of recency effects. *Psychological Review, 112,* 3–42.

Davis, G., Shepherd, J., & Ellis, H. (1979). Effects of interpolated mugshot exposure on accuracy of eyewitness identification. *Journal of Applied Psychology, 64,* 232–237.

De Beni, R., Cornoldi, C., Larsson, M., Magnussen, S., & Ronnberg, J. (2007). Memory experts: Visual learning, wine tasting, orienterring, and speech-reading. In S. Magnussen & T. Helstrup (Eds.), *Everyday Memory,* pp. 201–228. Hove, England: Psychology Press.

Deese, J. (1959). On the prediction of occurrence of particular verbal intrusions in immediate recall. *Journal of Experimental Psychology, 58,* 17–22.

De Groot, A. M. B. (1983). The range of automatic spreading activation in word priming. *Journal of Verbal Learning and Verbal Behavior, 22,* 417–436.

Dehaene, S., Bossini, S., & Giraux, P. (1993). The mental representation of parity and number magnitude. *Journal of Experimental Psychology: General, 122,* 371–396.

Dehon, H., & Brédart, S. (2004). False memories: Young and older adults think of semantic associates at the same rate, but young adults are more successful at source monitoring. *Psychology and Aging, 19,* 191–197.

Delaney, P. F., Nghiem, K. N., & Waldum, E. R. (2009). The selective directed forgetting effect: Can people forget only part of a text? *Quarterly Journal of Experimental Psychology, 62,* 1542–1550.

Delaney, P. F., & Sahakyan, L. I. (2007). Unexpected costs of high working memory capacity following directed forgetting and contextual change manipulations. *Memory & Cognition, 35,* 1074–1082.

Deldin, P. J., Keller, J., Gergen, J. A., & Miller, G. A. (2001). Cognitive bias and emotion in neuropsychological models of depression. *Cognition and Emotion, 15,* 787–802.

DeLoache, J. S., Cassidy, D. J., & Brown, A. L. (1985). Precursors of mnemonic strategies in very young children's memory. *Child Development 56,* 125–137.

Dempster, F. N. (1992). The rise and fall of the inhibitory mechanism: Toward a unified theory of cognitive development and aging. *Developmental Review, 12,* 454–475.

Desjardnis, T., & Scoboria, A. (2007). "You and your best friend Suzy put Slime in Ms. Smollett's desk": Producing false memories with self-relevant details. *Psychonomic Bulletin & Review, 14,* 1090–1095.

Detmer, D. E., Fryback, D. G., & Gassner, K. (1978). Heuristics and biases in medical decision making. *Journal of Medical Education, 53,* 682–683.

Deutsch, D. (2002). The puzzle of absolute pitch. *Current Directions in Psychological Science, 11,* 200–204.

Dietrich, D., & Olson, M. (1993). A demonstration of hindsight bias using the Thomas confirmation vote. *Psychological Reports, 72,* 377–378.

Dijkstra, K., & Kaschak, M. P. (2006). Encoding in verbal, enacted and autobiographical tasks in young and older adults. *Quarterly Journal of Experimental Psychology, 59,* 1338–1345.

Dijkstra, K., & Kaup, B. (2005). Mechanisms of autobiographical memory retrieval in younger and older adults. *Memory & Cognition, 33,* 811–820.

Dinges, D. F., Whitehouse, W. G., Orne, E. C., Powell, J. W., Orne, M. T., & Erdelyi, M. H. (1992). Evaluating hypnotic memory enhancement (hypermnesia and reminiscence) using multitrial forced recall. *Journal of Experimental Psychology: Learning, Memory, and Cognition, 18,* 1139–1147.

Diwadkar, V. A., & McNamara, T. P. (1997). Viewpoint dependence in scene recognition. *Psychological Science, 8,* 302–307.

Dodd, D. H., & Bradshaw, J. M. (1980). Leading questions and memory: Pragmatic constraints. *Journal of Verbal Learning and Verbal Behavior, 19,* 695–704.

Dodd, M. D., Castel, A. D., & Roberts, K. E. (2006). A strategy disruption component to retrieval-induced forgetting. *Memory & Cognition, 34,* 102–111.

Dodd, M. D., & Shumborski, S. (2009). Examining the influence of action on spatial working memory: The importance of selection. *Quarterly Journal of Experimental Psychology, 62,* 1236–1247.

Dodson, C. S., Bawa, S., & Slotnik, S. D. (2007). Aging, source memory, and misrecollectiions. *Journal of Experimental Psychology: Learning, Memory, and Cognition, 33,* 169–181.

Dodson, C. S., Darragh, J., & Williams, A. (2008). Stereotypes and retrieval-provoked illusory source recollections. *Journal of Experimental Psychology: Learning, Memory, and Cognition, 34,* 460–477.

Dodson, C. S., Johnson, M. K., & Schooler, J. W. (1997). The verbal overshadowing effect: Why descriptions impair face recognition. *Memory & Cognition, 25,* 129–139.

Dodson, C. S., & Krueger, L. E. (2006). I misremember it well: Why older adults are unreliable eyewitnesses. *Psychonomic Bulletin & Review, 13,* 770–775.

Dodson, C. S., & Riesberg, D. (1991). Indirect testing of eyewitness memory: The (non)effect of misinformation. *Bulletin of the Psychonomic Society, 29,* 333–336.

Dodson, C. S., & Shimamura, A. P. (2000). Differential effects of cue dependency on item and source memory. *Journal of Experimental Psychology: Learning, Memory, and Cognition, 26,* 1023–1044.

Donaldson, W. (1992). Measuring recognition memory. *Journal of Experimental Psychology: General, 121,* 275–277.

Donaldson, W. (1996). The role of decision processes in remembering and knowing. *Memory & Cognition, 24,* 523–533.

Donders, F. C. (1868). Over de snelheid van psychische processen. Onderzoekingen gedaan in het Physiologisch Laboratorium der Utrechtsche Hoogeschool, 1868–1869, *Tweede Reeks, II,* 92–120.

Donley, R. D., & Ashcraft, M. H. (1992). The methodology of testing naïve beliefs in the physics classroom. *Memory & Cognition, 20,* 381–391.

Dopkins, S., & Ngo, C. T. (2002). Inhibition of verbal memory retrieval as a consequence of prior retrieval. *Journal of Memory and Language, 46,* 606–621.

Dopplemayr, M. M., Klimesch, W., Pachinger, T., & Ripper, B. (1998). The functional significance of absolute power with respect to event-related desynchronization. *Brain Topography, 11,* 133–140.

Dougal, S., & Schooler, J. W. (2007). Discovery misattribution: When solving is confused with remembering. *Journal of Experimental Psychology: General, 136,* 577–592.

Drosopoulos, S., Schulze, C., Fischer, S., & Born, J. (2007). Sleep's function in the spontaneous recovery and consolidating memories. *Journal of Experimental Psychology: General, 136,* 169–183.

Duchek, J. M. (1984). Encoding and retrieval differences between young and old: the impact of attentional capacity usage. *Developmental Psychology, 20,* 1173–1180.

Duchek, J. M., & Neely, J. H. (1989). A dissociative word-frequency X levels-of-processing interaction in episodic recognition and lexical decision tasks. *Memory & Cognition, 17,* 148–162.

Dudukovic, N. M., & Knowlton, B. J. (2006). Remember-know judgments and retrieval of contextual details. *Acta Psychologica, 122,* 160–173.

Duffy, S., Labrie, V., & Roder, J. C. (2008). D-serine augments NMDA-NR2B receptor-dependent hippocampal long-term depression and spatial reversal learning. *Neuropsychopharmacology, 33,* 1004–1018.

Duffy, S. A., & Keir, J. A. (2004). Violating stereotypes: Eye movements and comprehension processes when text conflicts with world knowledge. *Memory & Cognition, 32,* 551–559.

Dulany, D. E., Carlson, R. A., & Dewey, G. L. (1984). A case of syntactical learning and judgment: How conscious and how abstract? *Journal of Experimental Psychology: General, 113,* 541–555.

Dumay, N., & Gaskell, M. G. (2007). Sleep-associated changes in the mental representation of spoken words. *Psychological Science, 18,* 35–39.

Duncan, C. P. (1949). The retroactive effect of electroshock on learning. *Journal of Comparative Physiological Psychology, 42,* 32–44.

Dunlosky, J., Baker, J. M. C., Rawson, K. A., & Hertzog, C. (2006). Aging influence people's metacomprehension? Effects of processing ease on judgments of text learning. *Psychology and Aging, 21,* 390–400.

Dunlosky, J. & Hertzog, C. (2000). Updating knowledge about encoding strategies: A componential analysis of learning about strategy effectiveness from task experience. *Psychology and Aging, 15,* 462–474.

Dunlosky, J., & Nelson, T. O. (1994). Does the sensitivity of judgments of learning (JOLs) to the effects of various activities depend on when the JOLs occur? *Journal of Memory and Language, 33,* 545–565.

Dysart, J. E., Lindsay, R. C. L., Hammond, R., & Dupuis, P. (2001). Mugshot exposure prior to lineup identification: Interference, transference, and commitment effects. *Journal of Applied Psychology, 86,* 1280–1284.

Dywan, J., & Jacoby, L. L. (1990). Effects of aging on source monitoring: Differences in susceptibility to false fame. *Psychology and Aging, 5,* 379–387.

Dywan, J., Segalowitz, S. J., & Webster, L. (1998). Source monitoring: ERP evidence for greater reactivity to nontarget information in older adults. *Brain and Cognition, 36,* 390–430.

Eagle, M., & Leiter, E. (1964). Recall and recognition in intentional and incidental learning. *Journal of Experimental Psychology, 68,* 58–63.

Eakin, D. K., Schreiber, T. A., & Sergent-Marshall, S. (2003). Misinformation effects in eyewitness memory: The presence and absence of memory impairment as a function of warning and misinformation accessibility. *Journal of Experimental Psychology: Learning, Memory, and Cognition, 29,* 813–825.

Easterbrook, J. A. (1959). The effect of emotion on cue utilization and the organization of behavior. *Psychological Review, 66,* 183–201.

Ebbinghaus, H. (1885/1964). *Memory: A Contribution to Experimental Psychology.* Translated by H. A. Ruger & C. E. Bussenius. New York: Dover.

Echterhoff, G., Hirst, W., & Hussy, W. (2005). How eyewitnesses resist misinformation: Social postwarnings and the monitoring of memory characteristics. *Memory & Cognition, 33,* 770–782.

Eich, E. (1995). Mood as a mediator of place dependent memory. *Journal of Experimental Psychology: General, 124,* 293–308.

Eich, J. E., Weingartner, H., Stillman, R. C., & Gillin, J. C. (1975). State-dependent accessibility of retrieval cues in the retention of a categorized list. *Journal of Verbal Learning and Verbal Behavior, 14,* 408–417.

Eich, J. M. (1982). A composite holographic associative recall model. *Psychological Review, 89,* 627–661.

Eich, J. M. (1985). Levels of processing, encoding specificity, elaboration and CHARM. *Psychological Review, 92,* 1–38.

Eich, T. S., & Metcalfe, J. (2009). Effects of the stress of marathon running on implicit and explicit memory. *Psychonomic Bulletin & Review, 16,* 475–479.

Eichenbaum, H. (2002). *The Cognitive Neuroscience of Memory: An Introduction.* New York: Oxford.

Eimas, P. D., & Quinn, P. C. (1994). Studies on the formation of perceptually based basic-level categories in young infants. *Child Development, 65,* 903–917.

Einstein, G. O., & Hunt, R. R. (1980). Levels of processing and organization: Additive effects of individual-item and relational processing. *Journal of Experimental Psychology: Human Learning and Memory, 6,* 588–598.

Einstein, G. O., & McDaniel, M. A. (1990). Normal aging and prospective memory. *Journal of Experimental Psychology: Learning, Memory, and Cognition, 16,* 717–726.

Einstein, G. O., McDaniel, M. A., Owen, P. D., & Cote, N. C. (1990). Encoding and recall of texts: The importance of material appropriate processing. *Journal of Memory and Language, 29,* 566–581.

Einstein, G. O., McDaniel, M. A., Richardson, S. L., Guynn, M. L., & Cunfer, A. R. (1995). Aging and prospective memory: Examining influences of self-initiated retrieval processes. *Journal of Experimental Psychology: Learning, Memory, and Cognition, 21,* 996–1007.

Einstein, G. O., McDaniel, M. A., Smith, R., & Shaw, P. (1998). Habitual prospective memory and aging: Remembering instructions and forgetting actions. *Psychological Science, 9,* 284–288.

Eitam, B., Schul, Y., & Hassin, R. R. (2009). Goal relevance and artificial grammar learning. *Quarterly Journal of Experimental Psychology, 62,* 228–238.

Ekstrand, B. R. (1967). Effect of sleep on memory. *Journal of Experimental Psychology, 75,* 64–72.

Eldridge, M. A., Barnard, P. J., & Bekerian, D. A. (1994). Autobiographical memory and daily schemas at work. *Memory, 2,* 51–74.

Elliot, R., & Dolan, R. J. (1998). Neural response during preference and memory judgments for subliminally presented stimuli: A functional neuroimaging study. *The Journal of Neuroscience, 18,* 4697–4704.

Ellis, A. W., Young, A. W., & Critchley, E. M. R. (1989). Loss of memory for people following temporal lobe damage. *Brain, 112,* 1469–1483.

Elsley, J. V., & Parmentier, F. B. R. (2009). Is visual-spatial binding in working memory impaired by a concurrent memory load? *Quarterly Journal of Experimental Psychology, 62,* 1696–1705.

Emery, L., & Hess, T. M. (2008). Viewing instructions impact emotional memory differently in older and younger adults. *Psychology and Aging, 23,* 2–12.

Engelkamp, J., & Zimmer, H. D. (1989). Memory for action events: a new field of research. *Psychological Research, 51,* 153–157.

Engelkamp, J., & Zimmer, H. D. (1997). Sensory factors in subject-performed tasks. *Acta Psychologica, 96,* 43–60.

Engle, R. W., Fidler, D. S., & Reynolds, L. H. (1981). Does echoic memory develop? *Journal of Experimental Child Psychology, 32,* 459–473.

Engle, R. W., Tuholski, S. W., Laughlin, J. E., & Conway, A. R. A. (1999). Working memory, short-term memory, and general fluid intelligence: A latent variable approach. *Journal of Experimental Psychology: General, 128,* 309–331.

Enkvist, T., Newell, B., Juslin, P., & Olsson, H. (2006). On the role of causal intervention in multiple-cue judgment: Positive and negative effects on learning. *Journal of Experimental Psychology: Learning, Memory, and Cognition, 32,* 163–179.

Epstein, R., DeYoe, E. A., Press, D. Z., Rosen, A. C., & Kanwisher, N. (2001). Neuropsychological evidence of a topographical learning mechanism in parahippocampal cortex. *Cognitive Neuropsychology, 18,* 481–508.

Epstein, R., & Kanwisher, N. (1998). A cortical representation of the local visual environment. *Nature, 392,* 598–601.

Epstein, W., Wilder, L., & Robertson, L. (1975). The effect of directed forgetting on the time to remember. *Memory & Cognition, 3,* 401–404.

Erdelyi, M. H., & Becker, J. (1974). Hypermnesia for pictures: Incremental memory for pictures but not words in multiple recall trials. *Cognitive Psychology, 6,* 159–171.

Erdfelder, E., & Bechner, A. (1998). Decomposing the hindsight bias: A multinomial processing tree model for separating recollection and reconstruction in hindsight. *Journal of Experimental Psychology: Learning, Memory, and Cognition, 24,* 387–414.

Erickson, T. D., & Mattson, M. E. (1981). From words to meaning: A semantic illusion. *Journal of Verbal Learning and Verbal Behavior, 20,* 540–551.

Ericsson, K. A., Chase, W. G., & Faloon, S. (1980). Acquisition of a memory skill. *Science, 208,* 1181–1182.

Ericsson, K. A., & Kintsch, W. (1995). Long-term working memory. *Psychological Review, 102,* 211–245.

Ericsson, K. A., & Simon, H. A. (1980). Verbal reports as data. *Psychological Review, 87,* 215–251.

Estes, W. K. (1972). An associative basis for coding and organization in memory. In A. W. Melton & E. Martin (Eds.), *Coding Processes in Human Memory,* pp. 161–190. New York: Wiley.

Estes, Z. (2004). Confidence and gradedness in semantic categorization: Definitely somewhat artifactual, maybe absolutely natural. *Psychonomic Bulletin & Review, 11,* 1041–1047.

Evans, G. W., & Pezdek, K. (1980). Cognitive mapping: Knowledge of real-world distance and location information. *Journal of Experimental Psychology: Human Learning and Memory, 6,* 13–24.

Fein, S., McCloskey, A. L., & Tomlinson, T. M. (1997). Can the jury disregard the information? The use of suspicion to reduce the prejudicial effects of pretrial publicity and inadmissible testimony. *Personality and Social Psychology Bulletin, 23,* 1215–1226.

Feng, J., Spence, I., & Pratt, J. (2007). Playing an action video game reduces gender differences in spatial cognition. *Psychological Science, 18,* 850–855.

Fenker, D. B., Waldmann, M. E., & Holyoak, K. J. (2005). Accessing causal relations in semantic memory. *Memory & Cognition, 33,* 1036–1046.

Ferguson, R. P., & Hegarty, M. (1994). Properties of cognitive maps constructed from texts. *Memory & Cognition, 22,* 455–473.

Ferguson, R. P., & Martin, P. (1983). Long-term temporal estimation in humans. *Perception & Psychophysics, 33,* 585–592.

Ferguson, S. A., Hashtroudi, S., & Johnson, M. K. (1992). Age differences in using source-related cues. *Psychology and Aging, 7,* 443–452.

Fernandes, M., Ross, M., Wiegand, M., & Schryer, E. (2008). Are the memories of older adults positively biased? *Psychology and Aging, 23,* 297–306.

Ferreira, V. S., Bock, J. K., Wilson, M. P., & Cohen, N. J. (2008). Memory for syntax despite amnesia. *Psychological Science, 19,* 940–946.

Fields, A. W., & Shelton, A. L. (2006). Individual skill differences and large-scale environmental learning. *Journal of Experimental Psychology: Learning, Memory, and Cognition, 32,* 506–515.

Fillmore, M. T., Kelly, T. H., Rush, C. R., & Hays, L (2001). Retrograde facilitation of memory by triazolam: Effects on automatic processes. *Psychopharmacology, 158,* 314–321.

Finger, S., & Zaroub, F. (2006). Benjamin Franklin and shock-induced amnesia. *American Psychologist, 61,* 240–248.

Finlay, F., Hitch, G. J., & Meudell, P. R. (2000). Mutual inhibition in collaborative recall: Evidence for a retrieval-based account. *Journal of Experimental Psychology: Learning, Memory, and Cognition, 26,* 1556–1567.

Finkenhauer, C., Luminet, O., Gisle, L., El-ahmadi, A., van der Linden, M., & Philipott, P. (1998). Flashbulb memories and the underlying mechanisms of their formation: Toward an emotional-integrative model. *Memory & Cognition, 26,* 516–531.

Fischhoff, B. (1975). Hindsight does not equal foresight: The effect of outcome knowledge on judgment under uncertainty. *Journal of Experimental Psychology: Human Perception and Performance, 1,* 288–299.

Fisher, C. (1945). Amnesic states in war neuroses: The psychogenesis of fugues. *Psychoanalytic Quarterly, 14,* 437–468.

Fisher, C., & Joseph, E. D. (1945). Fugue with awareness of loss of personal identity. *Psychoanalytic Quarterly, 18,* 480–493.

Fisher, R. P., Geiselman, R. E., & Amador, M. (1989). Field test of the cognitive interview: Enhancing the recollection of actual victims and witnesses of crime. *Journal of Applied Psychology, 74,* 722–727.

Fisk, A. D., & Fisher, D. L. (1994). Brinley plots and theories of aging: The explicit, muddled, and implicit debates. *Journals of Gerontology: Psychological Sciences, 49,* P81–P88.

Fivush, R., & Nelson, K. (2004). Culture and language in the emergence of autobiographical memory. *Psychological Science, 15,* 573–577.

Flavell, J. H., Beach, D. H., & Chinsky, J. M. (1966). Spontaneous verbal rehearsal in a memory task as a function of age. *Child Development, 37,* 283–299.

Fleishman, D. A., Wilson, R. S., Gabrieli, J. D. E., Bienias, J. L., & Bennett, D. A. (2004). Longitudinal study of implicit and explicit memory in old persons. *Psychology and Aging, 19,* 617–625.

Flexser, A. J., & Tulving, E. (1975). Retrieval independence in recognition and recall. *Psychological Review, 85,* 153–171.

Freud, S. (1899/1938). Childhood and concealing memories. In A. A. Brill (Ed.), *The Basic Writings of Sigmund Freud.* New York: The Modern Library.

Freyd, J. J. (1987). Dynamic mental representations. *Psychological Review, 94,* 427–438.

Freyd, J. J., & Finke, R. A. (1984). Representational momentum. *Journal of Experimental Psychology: Learning, Memory, and Cognition, 10,* 126–132.

Freyd, J. J., & Finke, R. A. (1985). A velocity effect for representational momentum. *Bulletin of the Psychonomic Society, 23,* 443–446.

Freyd, J. J., Pantzer, T. M., & Cheng, J. L. (1988). Representing statics as forces in equilibrium. *Journal of Experimental Psychology: General, 117,* 395–407.

Friedman, A. (2009). The role of categories and spatial cuing in global-scale location estimates. *Journal of Experimental Psychology: Learning, Memory, and Cognition, 35,* 94–112.

Friedman, A., & Brown, N. R. (2000a). Reasoning about geography. *Journal of Experimental Psychology: General, 129,* 193–219.

Friedman, A., & Brown, N. R. (2000b). Updating geographical knowledge: Principles of coherence and inertia. *Journal of Experimental Psychology: Learning, Memory, and Cognition, 26,* 900–914.

Friedman, A., Brown, N. R., & McGaffey, A. P. (2002). A basis for bias in geographical judgments. *Psychonomic Bulletin & Review, 9,* 151–159.

Friedman, A., Kerkman, D. D., & Brown, N. R. (2002). Spatial location judgments: A cross-national comparison of estimation bias in subjective North American geography. *Psychonomic Bulletin & Review, 9,* 615–623.

Friedman, A., Kerkman, D. D., Brown, N. R., Stea, D., & Cappello, H. M. (2005). Cross-cultural similarities and differences in North Americans' geographic location judgments. *Psychonomic Bulletin & Review, 12,* 1054–1060.

Friedman, S. (1972). Newborn visual attention to repeated exposure of redundant vs. "novel" targets. *Perception & Psychophysics, 12,* 291–294.

Friedman, W. J. (1993). Memory for the time of past events. *Psychological Bulletin, 113,* 44–66.

Friedman, W. J. (2007). The role of reminding in long-term memory for temporal order. *Memory & Cognition, 35,* 66–72.

Frieske, D. A., & Park, D. C. (1999). Memory for news in young and old adults. *Psychology and Aging, 14,* 90–98.

Frigo, L. C., Reas, D. L., & LeCompte, D. C. (1999). Revelation without presentation: Counterfeit study list yields robust revelation effect. *Memory & Cognition, 27,* 339–343.

Fritz, C. O., Morris, P. E., Bjork, R. A., Gelman, R., & Wickens, T. D. (2000). When further learning fails: Stability and change following repeated presentation of text. *British Journal of Psychology, 91,* 493–511.

Frost, P. (2000). The quality of false memory over time: Is memory for misinformation "remembered" or "known"? *Psychonomic Bulletin & Review, 7,* 531–536.

Fu, Q., Fu, X., & Dienes, Z. (2008). Implicit sequence learning and conscious awareness. *Consciousness and Cognition, 17,* 185–202.

Funnell, E. (1995). A Case of Forgotten Knowledge. In R. Campbell & M. A. Conway (Eds.), *Broken Memories: Case*

Studies In Memory Impairment, pp. 225–236. Malden: Blackwell Publishing.

Furnham, A. (1986). The robustness of the recency effect: Studies using legal evidence. *The Journal of General Psychology, 113,* 351–357.

Gabbert, F., Memon, A., & Wright, D. B. (2006). Memory conformity: Disentangling the steps toward influence during a discussion. *Memory & Cognition, 13,* 480–485.

Gagne, C. L., & Shoben, E. J. (2002). Priming relations in ambiguous noun-noun combinations. *Memory & Cognition, 30,* 637–646.

Gailliot, M. T. (2008). Unlocking the energy dynamics of executive functioning: Linking executive functioning to brain glycogen. *Perspectives on Psychological Science, 3,* 245–263.

Galambos, J. A., & Rips, L. J. (1982). Memory for routines. *Journal of Verbal Learning and Verbal Behavior, 21,* 260–281.

Gallo, D. A., Cotel, S. C., Moore, C. D., & Schacter, D. L. (2007). Aging can spare recollection-based retrieval monitoring: The importance of event distinctiveness. *Psychology and Aging, 22,* 209–213.

Gallo, D. A., & Roediger, H. L. (2003). The effects of associations and aging on illusory recollection. *Memory & Cognition, 31,* 1036–1044.

Gardiner, J. M. (1988). Functional aspects of recollective experience. *Memory & Cognition, 16,* 309–313.

Gardiner, J. M., & Java, R. I. (1990). Recollective experience in word and nonword recognition. *Memory & Cognition, 18,* 23–30.

Gardiner, J. M., & Java, R. I. (1991). Forgetting in recognition memory with and without recollective experience. *Memory & Cognition, 19,* 617–623.

Gardiner, J. M., & Java, R. I. (1993). Recognizing and remembering. In A. F. Collins, S. E. Gathercole, M. A. Conway, & P. E. Morris (Eds.), *Theories of Memory,* pp. 163–188. Hillsdale, NJ: Erlbaum.

Gardiner, J. M., & Parkin, A. J. (1990). Attention and recollective experience in recognition memory. *Memory & Cognition, 18,* 579–583.

Gardiner, J. M., & Richardson-Klavehn, A. (2000). Remembering and knowing. In E. Tulving & F. I. M. Craik (Eds.), *The Oxford Handbook of Memory,* pp. 229–244. New York: Oxford University Press.

Garnham, A. (1981). Mental models as representations of text. *Memory & Cognition, 9,* 560–565.

Garry, M., & Gerrie, M. P. (2005). When photographs create false memories. *Current Directions in Psychological Science, 14,* 321–325.

Garry, M., & Polaschek, D. L. L. (2000). Imagination and memory. *Current Directions in Psychological Science, 9,* 6–10.

Garry, M., & Wade, K. A. (2005). Actually, a picture is worth less than 45 words: Narratives produce more false memories than photographs do. *Psychonomic Bulletin & Review, 12,* 359–366.

Garsoffky, B., Schwan, S., & Hesse, F. W. (2002). Viewpoint dependency in the recognition of dynamic scenes. *Journal of Experimental Psychology: Learning, Memory, and Cognition, 28,* 1035–1050.

Gathercole, S. E. (1997). Models of verbal short-term memory. In M. A. Conway (Ed.), *Cognitive Models of Memory*, pp. 13–45. Cambridge, MA: MIT Press.

Geghman, K. D., & Multhaup, K. S. (2004). How generation affects source memory. *Memory & Cognition, 32,* 819–823.

Geiselman, R. E. (1974). Positive forgetting of sentence material. *Memory & Cognition, 2,* 677–682.

Geiselman, R. E., Fisher, R. P., Firstenberg, L. Hutton, L. A., Sullivan, S., Avetissian, I., & Prosk, A. (1984). Enhancing eyewitness memory: An empirical evaluation of the cognitive interview. *Journal of Police Science and Administration, 12,* 74–80.

Geiselman, R. E., Fisher, R. P., MacKinnon, D. P., & Holland, H. L. (1985). Eyewitness memory enhancement in the police interview: Cognitive retrieval mnemonics versus hypnosis. *Journal of Applied Psychology, 70,* 401–412.

Gelman, S. A. (1988). The development of induction within natural kind and artifact categories. *Cognitive Psychology, 20,* 65–95.

Gelman, S. A., & O'Reilly, A. W. (1988). Children's inductive inferences within superordinate categories: The role of language and category structure. *Child Development, 59,* 876–887.

Geraci, L., McDaniel, M. A., Manzano, I., & Roediger, H. L. (2009). The influence of age on memory for distinctive events. *Memory & Cognition, 37,* 175–180.

Geraerts, E., Bernstein, D. M., Merekelbach, H., Linders, C., Raymaekers, L., & Loftus, E. F. (2008). Lasting false beliefs and their behavioral consequences. *Psychological Science, 19,* 749–753.

Gerard, L. D., Zacks, R. T., Hasher, L., & Radvansky, G. A. (1991). Age deficits in retrieval: The fan effect. *Journal of Gerontology, 46,* 131–136.

Gevins, A., Smith, M. E., McEvoy, L, & Yu, D. (1997). High-resolution EEG mapping of cortical activation related to working memory: Effects of task difficulty, type of processing, and practice. *Cerebral Cortex, 7,* 374–385.

Gevers, W., Reynvoet, B., & Fias, W. (2004). The mental representation of ordinal sequences is spatially organized: Evidence from days of the week. *Cortex, 40,* 171–172.

Ghetti, S. (2003). Memory for nonoccurrences: The role of metacognition. *Journal of Memory and Language, 48,* 722–739.

Gilbertson, L. J., Dietrich, D., Olson, M., & Guenther, R. K. (1994). A study of hindsight bias: The Rodney King case in retrospect. *Psychological Reports, 74,* 383–386.

Gillund, G., & Shiffrin, R. M. (1984). A retrieval model for both recognition and recall. *Psychological Review, 91,* 1–67.

Gilovich, T. (1981). Seeing the past in the present: The effect of associations to familiar events on judgments and decisions. *Journal of Personality and Social Psychology, 40,* 797–808.

Glanzer, M., & Cunitz, A. R. (1966). Two storage mechanisms in free recall. *Journal of Verbal Learning and Verbal Behavior, 5,* 351–360.

Glaze, J. A. (1928). The association value of nonsense syllables. *Journal of Genetic Psychology, 35,* 255–269.

Glenberg, A. M. (1976). Monotonic and nonmonotonic lag effects in paired-associate and recognition memory paradigms. *Journal of Verbal Learning and Verbal Behavior, 15,* 1–16.

Glenberg, A. M. (1979). Component-levels theory of the effects of spacing of repetitions on recall and recognition. *Memory & Cognition, 7,* 95–112.

Glenberg, A. M. (1997). What is memory for? *Behavioral and Brain Sciences, 20,* 1–55.

Glenberg, A. M., Bradley, M. M., Stevenson, J. A., Kraus, T. A., Tkachuk, M. J., Gretz, A. L., Fish, J. H., and Turpin, B. M. (1980). A two-process account of long-term serial position effects. *Journal of Experimental Psychology: Human Learning and Memory, 6,* 355–369.

Glenberg, A. M., & Lehmann, T. S. (1980). Spacing repetitions over 1 week. *Memory & Cognition, 8,* 528–538.

Glenberg, A. M., Meyer, M., & Lindem, K. (1987). Mental models contribute to foregrounding during text comprehension. *Journal of Memory and Language, 26,* 69–83.

Glenberg, A. M., Smith, S. M., & Green, C. (1977). Type I rehearsal: Maintenance and more. *Journal of Verbal Learning and Verbal Behavior, 16,* 339–352.

Glisky, E. L., Rubin, S. R., & Davidson, P. S. R. (2001). Source memory in older adults: An encoding or retrieval problem? *Journal of Experimental Psychology: Learning, Memory, and Cognition, 27,* 1131–1146.

Glück, J., & Bluck, S. (2007). Looking back across the life span: A life story account of the reminiscence bump. *Memory & Cognition, 35,* 1928–1939.

Glucksberg, S., & McCloskey, M. (1981). Decisions about ignorance: Knowing that you don't know. *Journal of Experimental Psychology: Human Learning and Memory, 7,* 311–325.

Godbout, L., & Doyon, J. (2000). Defective representation of knowledge in Parkinson's disease: Evidence from a script-production task. *Brain and Cognition, 44,* 490–510.

Godden, D. B., & Baddeley, A. D. (1975). Context-dependent memory in two natural environments: On land and underwater. *British Journal of Psychology, 66,* 325–331.

Goh, W. D. (2005). Talker variability and recognition memory: Instance-specific and voice-specific effects. *Journal of Experimental Psychology: Learning, Memory, and Cognition, 31,* 40–53.

Gold, J. M., Murray, R. F., Sekuler, A. B., Bennett, P.J., & Sekuler, R. (2005). Visual memory decay is deterministic. *Psychological Science, 16,* 769–774.

Goldenberg, G. (1995). Aphasic patients' knowledge about the visual appearance of objects. *Aphasiology, 9,* 50–56.

Golding, J. M., Fowler, S. B., Long, D. L., & Latta, H. (1990). Instructions to disregard potentially useful information: The effects of pragmatics on evaluative judgments and recall. *Journal of Memory and Language, 29,* 212–227.

Golding, J. M., & Hauselt, J. (1994). When instructions to forget become instructions to remember. *Personality and Social Psychology Bulletin, 20,* 178–183.

Golding, J. M., Long, D. L., & MacLeod, C. M. (1994). You can't always forget what you want: Directed forgetting of related words. *Journal of Memory and Language, 33,* 493–510.

Goldinger, S. D., Kleider, H. M., Azuma, T., & Beike, D. R. (2003). "Blaming the victim" under memory load. *Psychological Science, 14,* 81–85.

Goldsmith, M., Koriat, A., & Weinberg-Eliezer, A. (2002). Strategic regulation of grain size in memory reporting. *Journal of Experimental Psychology: General, 131,* 73–95.

Goldstein, A. G., & Chance, J. E. (1970). Visual recognition memory for complex configurations. *Perception & Psychophysics, 9,* 237–241.

Goldstone, R. L., Steyvers, M., & Rogosky, B. J. (2003). Conceptual interrelatedness and caricatures. *Memory & Cognition, 31,* 169–180.

Gómez-Ariza, C. J., & Bajo, M. T. (2003). Interference and integration: The fan effect in children and adults. *Memory, 11,* 505–523.

Gómez-Ariza, C. J., Lechuga, M. T., Pelegrina, S., & Bajo, M. T. (2005). Retrieval-induced forgetting in recall and recognition of thematically related and unrelated sentences. *Memory & Cognition, 33,* 1431–1441.

Gonsalves, B., Reber, P. J., Gitelman, D. R., Parrish, T. B., Mesulam, M-M., & Paller, K. A. (2004). Neural evidence that vivid imagining can lead to false remembering. *Psychological Science, 15,* 655–660.

Goodman, G. S., & Quas, J. A. (2008). Repeated interviews and children's memory: It's more than just how many. *Current Directions in Psychological Science, 17,* 386–390.

Goodwin, D. W., Powell, B., Bremer, D., Hoine, H., & Stern, J. (1969). Alcohol and recall: State-dependent effects in man. *Science, 163,* 2358–2360.

Gordon, R., Franklin, N., & Beck, J. (2005). Wishful thinking and source monitoring. *Memory & Cognition, 33,* 418–429.

Gorenstein, G. W., & Ellsworth, P. C. (1980). Effect of choosing an incorrect photograph on a later identification by an eyewitness. *Journal of Applied Psychology, 65,* 616–622.

Gottesman, C. V., & Intraub, H. (2002). Surface construal and the mental representation of scenes. *Journal of Experimental Psychology: Human Perception and Performance, 28,* 589–599.

Graesser, A. C., Gordon, S. E., & Sawyer, J. D. (1979). Recognition memory for typical and atypical actions in scripted activities: Tests of the script pointer + tag hypothesis. *Journal of Verbal Learning and Verbal Behavior, 18,* 319–332.

Graesser, A. C., & Nakamura, G. V. (1982). The impact of a schema on comprehension and memory. *The Psychology of Learning and Motivation, 16,* 59–109.

Graesser, A. C., Woll, S. B., Kowalski, D. J., & Smith, D. A. (1980). Memory for typical and atypical actions in scripted activities. *Journal of Experimental Psychology: Human Learning and Memory, 6,* 503–515.

Graf, P., Mandler, G., & Haden, P. E. (1982). Simulating amnesic symptoms in normal subjects. *Science, 218,* 1243–1244.

Graf. P., & Schacter, D. L. (1985). Implicit and explicit memory for new associations in normal and amnesic subjects. *Journal of Experimental Psychology: Learning, Memory, and Cognition, 11,* 501–518.

Graf. P., Shimamura, A. P, & Squire, L. R. (1985). Priming across modalities and priming across category levels: Extending the domain of preserved function in amnesia. *Journal of Experimental Psychology: Learning, Memory, and Cognition, 11,* 386–396.

Graf, P., Squire, L. R., & Mandler, G. (1984). The information that amnesic patients do not forget. *Journal of Experimental Psychology: Learning, Memory, and Cognition, 10,* 164–178.

Graham, K. S., Ralph, M. A. L., & Hodges, J. R. (1997). Determining the impact of autobiographical experience on "meaning": New insights from investigating sport-related vocabulary and knowledge in two cases with semantic dementia. *Cognitive Neuropsychology, 14,* 801–837.

Gray, C. R., & Gummerman, K. (1975). The enigmatic eidetic image: A critical examination of methods, data, and theories. *Psychological Bulletin, 82,* 383–407.

Greene, J. D. W., & Hodges, J. R. (1996). The fractionation of remote memory: Evidence from a longitudinal study of dementia of Alzheimer type. *Brain, 119,* 129–142.

Greene, R. L. (1989). Spacing effects in memory: Evidence for a two-process account. *Journal of Experimental Psychology: Learning, Memory, and Cognition, 15,* 371–377.

Grenier, J., Cappeliez, P., St-Onge, M., Vachon, J., Vinette, S., Roussy, F., Mercier, P., Lortie-Lussier, M., & de Koninck, J. (2005). Temporal references in dreams and autobiographical memory. *Memory & Cognition, 33,* 280–288.

Grossenbacher, P. G., & Lovelace, C. T. (2001). Mechanisms of synesthesia: Cognitive and physiological constraints. *Trends in Cognitive Science, 5,* 36–41.

Gruhn, D., Smith, J., & Baltes, P. B. (2005). No aging bias favoring memory for positive material: Evidence from a heterogeneity-homogeneity list paradigm using emotionally toned words. *Psychology and Aging, 20,* 579–588.

Gruppuso, V., Lindsay, D. S., & Masson, M. E. J. (2007). I'd know that face anywhere! *Psychonomic Bulletin, & Review, 14,* 1085–1089.

Guérard, K., & Tremblay, S. (2008). Revisiting evidence for modularity and functional equivalence across verbal and spatial domains in memory. *Journal of Experimental Psychology: Learning, Memory, and Cognition, 34,* 556–569.

Gunther, D. C., Ferraro, F. R., & Kirchner, T. (1996). Influence of emotional state on irrelevant thoughts. *Psychonomic Bulletin & Review, 3,* 491–494.

Gupta, P., Lipinski, J., & Aktunc, E. (2005). Reexamining the phonological similarity effect in immediate serial recall: The roles of type of similarity, category cuing, and item recall. *Memory & Cognition, 33,* 1001–1016.

Gustafsson, B., & Wigstrom, H. (1988). Physiological mechanisms underlying long-term potentiation. *Trends in Neuroscience, 11,* 156–163.

Haber, R. N. (1979). Twenty years of haunting eidetic imagery: Where's the ghost? *Behavioral and Brain Sciences, 2,* 583–629.

Haber, R. N., & Nathanson, L. S. (1968). Post-retinal storage? Some further observations on Parks' camel as seem through the eye of a needle. *Perception & Psychophysics, 3,* 349–355.

Haberlandt, K., & Bingham, G. (1984). The effect of input direction on the processing of script statements. *Journal of Verbal Learning and Verbal Behavior, 23,* 162–177.

Habib, R., Nyberg, L., & Tulving, E. (2003). Hemispheric asymmetries of memory: The HERA model revisited. *Trends in Cognitive Science, 7,* 241–245.

Halberstadt, J. & Rhodes, G. (2000). The attractiveness of non-face averages: Implications for an evolutionary explanation for the attractiveness of average faces. *Psychological Science, 11,* 285–289.

Halberstadt, J., & Rhodes, G. (2003). It's not just average faces that are attractive: Computer-manipulated averageness makes birds, fish, and automobiles attractive. *Psychonomic Bulletin & Review, 10,* 149–156.

Hannigan, S. L., & Reinitz, M. P. (2001). A demonstration and comparison of two types of inference-based memory errors. *Journal of Experimental Psychology: Learning, Memory, and Cognition, 27,* 931–940.

Harley, E. M., Carlsen, K. A., & Loftus, G. R. (2004). "Saw-it-all-along" effect: Demonstrations of visual hindsight bias. *Journal of Experimental Psychology: Learning, Memory, and Cognition, 30,* 960–968.

Harnishfeger, K. K., & Pope, R. S. (1996). Intending to forget: The development of cognitive inhibition in directed forgetting. *Journal of Experimental Child Psychology, 62,* 292–315.

Harrison, A. A., & Zajonc, R. B. (1970). The effects of frequency and duration of exposure on response competition and affective ratings. *The Journal of Psychology, 75,* 163–169.

Hart, J. T. (1965). Memory and the feeling-of-knowing experience. *Journal of Educational Psychology, 56,* 208–216.

Hartshorn, K., Rovee-Collier, C., Gerhardstein, P., Bhatt, R. S., Wondoloski, T. L., Klein, P., Gilch, J., Wurtzel, N., & Campos-de-Carvalho, M. (1998). The ontogeny of long-term memory over the first year-and-a-half of life. *Developmental Psychobiology, 32,* 69–9.

Hasher, L., Attig, M. S., & Alba, J. W. (1981). I knew it all along: Or did I? *Journal of Verbal Learning and Verbal Behavior, 20,* 86–96.

Hasher, L., & Griffin, M. (1978). Reconstructive and reproductive processes in memory. *Journal of Experimental Psychology: Human Learning and Memory, 4,* 318–330.

Hasher, L., & Zacks, R. T. (1979). Automatic and effortful processes in memory. *Journal of Experimental Psychology: General, 108,* 356–388.

Hasher, L., & Zacks, R. T. (1984). Automatic processing of fundamental information: The case of frequency of occurrance. *American Psychologist, 39,* 356–388.

Hasher, L., & Zacks, R. T. (1988). Working memory, comprehension, and aging: A review and a new view. *Psychology of Learning and Motivation, 22,* 1372–1388.

Hashtroudi, S., Ferguson, S. A., Rappold, V. A., & Chrosniak, L. D. (1988). Data-driven and conceptually driven processes in partial-word identification and recognition. *Journal of Experimental Psychology: Learning, Memory and Cognition, 14,* 749–757.

Hashtroudi, S., Johnson, M. K., & Chrosniak, L. D. (1990). Aging and qualitative characteristics of memories for perceived and imagined complex events. *Psychology and Aging, 5,* 119–126.

Hashtroudi, S., Johnson, M. K., Vnek, N., & Ferguson, S. A. (1994). Aging and the effects of affective and factual focus on source monitoring and recall. *Psychology and Aging, 9,* 160–170.

Hayne, H., & Simcock, G. (2009). Memory development in toddlers. In M. L. Courage & N. Cowan (Eds.) *The Development of Memory in Infancy and Childhood,* pp. 43–68. New York: Psychology Press.

Hayes-Roth, B., & Hayes-Roth, F. (1977). The prominence of lexical information in memory representations of meaning. *Journal of Verbal Learning and Verbal Behavior, 16,* 119–136.

Healy, A. F., Havas D. A., & Parker, J. T. (2000). Comparing serial position effects in semantic and episodic memory using reconstruction of order tasks. *Journal of Memory and Language, 42,* 147–167.

Heaps, C. M., & Nash, M. (2001). Comparing recollective experience in true and false autobiographical memories. *Journal of Experimental Psychology: Learning, Memory, and Cognition, 27,* 920–930.

Hebb, D. O. (1949). The *Organization of Behavior.* New York: Wiley.

Hege, A. C. G., & Dodson, C. S. (2004). Why distinctiveness information reduces false memories: Evidence for both impoverished relational-encoding and distinctiveness heuristics accounts. *Journal of Experimental Psychology: Learning, Memory, and Cognition, 30,* 787–795.

Heit, E., Brockdorff, N., & Lamberts, K. (2004). Strategic processes in false recognition memory. *Psychonomic Bulletin & Review, 11,* 380–386.

Hemmer, P., & Steyvers, M. (2009). Integrating episodic memories and prior knowledge at multiple levels of abstraction. *Psychonomic Bulletin & Review, 16,* 80–87.

Henderson, J. M., & Anes, M. D. (1994). Roles of object-file review and type priming in visual identification within and across eye fixations. *Journal of Experimental Psychology: Human Perception and Performance, 20,* 826–839.

Henkel, L. A. (2004). Erroneous memories arising from repeated attempts to remember. *Journal of Memory and Language, 50,* 26–46.

Henkel, L. A. (2007). The benefits and costs of repeated memory tests for young and older adults. *Psychology and Aging, 22,* 580–595.

Henkel, L. A., Franklin, N., & Johnson, M. K. (2000). Cross-modal source monitoring confusions between perceived and imagined events. *Journal of Experimental Psychology: Learning, Memory, and Cognition, 26,* 321–335.

Henkel, L. A., & Mather, M. (2007). Memory attributions for choices: How beliefs shape our memories. *Journal of Memory and Language,57,* 163–176.

Henry, J. D., MacLeod, M. S., Philips, L. H., & Crawford, J. R. (2004). A meta-analytic review of prospective memory and aging.*Psychology and Aging, 19,* 27–39.

Henson, R. N. A. (1998). Short-term memory for serial order: The start-end model. *Cognitive Psychology, 36,* 73–137.

Hertzog, C., Kramer, A. F., Wilson, R. S., & Lindenberger, U. (2008). Enrichment effects on adult cognitive development: Can the functional capacity of older adults be preserved and enhanced? *Psychological Science, in the Public Interest, 9,* 1–65.

Herz, R. S. (2004). A naturalistic analysis of autobiographical memories triggered by olfactory, visual, and auditory stimuli. *Chemical Senses, 29,* 217–224.

Herz, R. S., & Cupchik, G. C. (1995). The emotional distinctiveness of odor-evoked memories. *Chemical Senses, 20,* 517–528.

Herz, R. S., & Engen, T. (1996). Odor memory: Review and analysis. *Psychonomic Bulletin & Review, 3,* 300–313.

Herz, R. S., & Schooler, J. W. (2002). A naturalistic study of autobiographical memories evoked by olfactory and visual cues: Testing the Proustian hypothesis. *American Journal of Psychology, 115,* 21–32.

Hess, T. M. (2005). Memory and aging in context. *Psychological Bulletin, 131,* 383–406.

Hess, T. M. & Bolstad, C. A. (1998). Category-based versus attribute-based processing in different-aged adults. *Aging, Neuropsychology, and Cognition, 5,* 27–42.

Hess, T. M., & Flannagan, D. A. (1992). Schema-based retrieval processes in young and older adults. *Journal of Gerontology: Psychological Sciences, 47,* P52–P58.

Hess, T. M., & Follett, K. J. (1994). Adult age differences in the use of schematic and episodic information in making social judgments. *Aging and Cognition, 1,* 54–66.

Hess, T. M., Follett, K. J., & McGee, K. A. (1998). Aging and impression formation: The impact of processing skills and goals. *Journal of Gerontology: Psychological Sciences, 53B,* P175–P187.

Hess. T. M., & Hinson, J. T. (2006). Age-related variation in the influences of aging stereotypes on memory in adulthood. *Psychology and Aging, 21,* 621–625.

Hewitt, G. P., Holder, M., & Laird, J. (1996). Retrograde enhancement of human kinesthetic memory by alcohol: Consolidation or protection against interference. *Neurobiology of Learning and Memory, 65,* 269–277.

Hicks, J. L., & Cockman, D. W. (2003). The effect of general knowledge on source memory and decision processes. *Journal of Memory and Language, 48,* 489–501.

Hicks, J. L., & Marsh, R. L. (1998). A decrement-to-familiarity interpretation of the revelation effect from forced-choice tests of recognition memory. *Journal of Experimental Psychology: Learning, Memory, & Cognition, 24,* 1105–1120.

Hicks, J. L., & Marsh, R. L. (2002). On predicting the future states of awareness for recognition of unrecallable items. *Memory & Cognition, 30,* 60–66.

Hicks, J. L., Marsh, R. L., & Cook, G. I. (2005). Task interference in time-based, evnt-based, and dual intention prospective memory conditions. *Journal of Memory and Language, 53,* 430–444.

Hicks, J. L., Marsh, R. L., & Ritschel, L. (2002). The role of recollection and partial information in source monitoring.*Journal of Experimental Psychology: Learning, Memory, & Cognition, 28,* 503–508.

Hicks, J. L., Marsh, R. L., & Russell, E. J. (2000). The properties of retention intervals and their affect on retaining prospective memories. *Journal of Experimental Psychology: Learning, Memory, & Cognition, 26,* 1160–1169.

Hicks, J. L., & Starns, J. J. (2004). Retrieval-induced forgetting occurs in tests of item recognition. *Psychonomic Bulletin & Review, 11,* 125–130.

Higgs, S., Williamson, A. C., Rothstein, P., & Humphreys, G. W. (2008). Sensory-specific satiety is intact in amnesics who eat multiple meals. *Psychological Science, 19,* 623–628.

Hill, H., Strube, M., Roesch-Ely, D., & Weisbrod, M. (2002). Automatic vs. controlled processing in semantic memory: Differentiation by event-related potentials. *International Journal of Psychophysiology, 44,* 197–218.

Hill, J. W., & Bliss, J. C. (1968). Modeling a tactile sensory register. *Perception & Psychophysics, 4,* 91–101.

Hines, J. C., Touron, D. R., & Hertzog, C. (2009). Metacognitive influences on study time allocation in an associative recognition task: An analysis of adult age differences. *Psychology and Aging, 24,* 462–475.

Hinson, J. M., Jameson, T. L., & Whitney, P. (2003). Impulsive decision making and working memory. *Journal of Experimental Psychology: Learning, Memory, and Cognition, 29,* 298–306.

Hinsz, V. B. (1990). Cognitive and consensus processes in group recognition memory performance. *Journal of Personality and Social Psychology, 59,* 705–718.

Hintzman, D. L. (1986). "Schema abstraction" in a multiple-trace memory model. *Psychological Review, 93,* 411–428.

Hintzman, D. L. (1987). Recognition and recall in MINERVA 2: Analysis of the 'recognition-failure' paradigm. In P. Morris (Ed.) *Modelling Congition,* pp. 215–229. Oxford, England: Wiley.

Hintzman, D. L. (1988). Judgments of frequency and recognition memory in a multiple-trace memory model. *Psychological Review, 95,* 528–551.

Hintzman, D. L. (1990). Human learning and memory: Connections and Dissociations. *Annual Review of Psychology, 41,* 109–139.

Hintzman, D. L. (1992). Mathematical constraints on the Tulving-Wiseman Law. *Psychological Review, 99,* 536–542.

Hintzman, D. L., (2003). Robert Hooke's mode of memory. *Psychonomic Bulletin & Review, 10,* 3–14.

Hintzman, D. L., Summers, J. J., and Block, R. A. (1975). Spacing judgments as an index of study-phase retrieval. *Journal of Experimental Psychology: Human Learning and Memory, 1,* 31–40.

Hirst, W., Johnson, M. K., Kim, J. K., Phelps, E. A., Risse, G., & Volpe, B. T. (1986). Recognition and recall in amnesics. *Journal of Experimental Psychology: Learning, Memory, and Cognition, 12,* 445–451.

Hirst, W., Johnson, M. K., Phelps, E. A., & Volpe, B. T. (1988). More on recognition and recall in amnesics. *Journal of Experimental Psychology: Learning, Memory, and Cognition, 14,* 758–762.

Hirst, W., Phelps, E. A., Buckner, R. L., Budson, A. E., Cuc, A., Gabrieli, J. D. E., Johnson, M. K., Lustig, C., Lyle, K. B., Mather, M., Meksin, R., Mitchell, K. J., Ochsner, K. N., Schacter, D. L., Smions, J. S., & Vaisya, C. J. (2009). Long-term memory for the terrorist attack of September 11: Flashbulb memories, event memories, and the factors that influence their retention. *Journal of Experimental Psychology: General, 138,* 161–176.

Hitch, G. J., & Ferguson, J. (1991). Prospective memory for future intentions: Some comparisons with memory for past events. *European Journal of Cognitive Psychology, 3,* 285–295.

Hobson, J. A. (1988). *The Dreaming Brain.* New York, NY: Basic Books, Inc.

Hochberg, J., & Brooks, V. (1962). Pictorial recognition as an unlearned ability: A study of one child's performance. *American Journal of Psychology, 75,* 624–628.

Hochel, M., & Milán, E. G. (2008). Synaesthesia: The existing state of affairs. *Cognitive Neuropsychology, 25,* 93–117.

Hockley, W. E. (2008). The effects of environmental context on recognition memory and claims of remembering. *Journal of Experimental Psychology: Learning, Memory, and Cognition, 34,* 1412–1429.

Hodges, J. R. (2000). Memory in the Dementias. In E. Tulving & F. I. M. Craik (Eds.) *The Oxford handbook of Memory,* pp. 441–459. New York: Oxford University Press.

Hodges, J. R., Bozeat, S., Lambdon Ralph, M. A., Patterson, K., & Spatt, J. (2000). The role of conceptual knowledge in object use: Evidence from semantic dementia. *Brain, 123,* 1913–1925.

Hodges, J. R., & McCarthy, R. A. (1993). Autobiographical amnesia resulting from bilateral paramedian thalamic infarction. *Brain, 116,* 921–940.

Hodges, J. R., Patternson, K., Oxbuy, S., & Funnell, E. (1992). Semantic dementia: Progressive fluent aphasia with temporal lobe atrophy. *Brain, 115,* 1783–1806.

Hoffman, H. G., Granhag, P. A., See, S. T. K., & Loftus, E. F. (2001). Social influences on reality-monitoring decisions. *Memory & Cognition, 29,* 394–404.

Holcomb, P. J., Kounios, J., Anderson, J. E., & West, W. C. (1999). Dual-coding, context availability, and concreteness effects in sentence comprehension: An electrophysiological investigation. *Journal of Experimental Psychology: Learning, Memory, and Cognition, 25,* 721–742.

Holland, R. W., Hendriks, M., & Aarts, H. (2005). Smells like clean spirit: Nonconscious effects of scent on cognition and behavior. *Psychological Science, 16,* 689–693.

Hollingworth, A., & Henderson, J. M. (2003). Testing a conceptual locus for the inconsistent object change detection advantage in real-world scenes. *Memory & Cognition, 31,* 930–940.

Holloway, F. A. (1978). State dependent retrieval based on time of day. In B. Ho, D. Richards & D. Chute (Eds.), *Drug Discrimination and State Dependent Learning*, pp. 319–344. New York: Academic Press.

Holmes, D. S. (1970). Differential change in affective intensity and the forgetting of unpleasant personal experiences. *Journal of Personality and Social Psychology, 15,* 234–239.

Holtgraves, T. (2008). Conversation, speech acts, and memory. *Memory & Cognition, 36,* 361–374.

Holyoak, K. J., & Mah, W. A. (1982). Cognitive reference points in judgments of symbolic magnitude. *Cognitive Psychology, 14,* 328–352.

Hoosain, R., & Salili, F. (1988). Language differences, working memory, and mathematical ability. In M. M. Gruneberg, P. E. Morris, & R. N. Sykes (Eds.), *Practical Aspects of Memory: Current Research and Issues,* pp. 512–517. Chichester, England: Wiley.

Hornstein, S. L., Brown, A. S., & Mulligan, N. W. (2003). Long-term flashbulb memory for learning of Princess Diana's death. *Memory, 11,* 293–306.

Hovland, C. I., & Weiss, W. (1951). The influence of source credibility on communication effectiveness. *Public Opinion Quarterly, 15,* 635–650.

Howard, D. V., McAndrews, M. P., & Lasaga, M. I. (1981). Semantic priming of lexical decisions in young and old adults. *Journal of Gerontology, 36,* 707–714.

Howe, M. L. (2003). Memories from the cradle. *Current Directions in Psychological Science, 12,* 62–65.

Howe, M. L. (2007). Children's emotional false memories. *Psychological Science, 18,* 856–860.

Howe, M. L., & Courage, M. L. (1993). On resolving the enigma of infantile amnesia. *Psychological Bulletin, 113,* 305–326.

Hu, P., Stylos-Allan, M., & Walker, M. P. (2006). Sleep facilitates consolidation of emotional declarative memory. *Psychological Science, 17,* 891–898.

Hu, P., Ericsson, K. A., Yang, D., & Lu, C. (2009). Superior self-paced memorization of digits in spite of a normal digit span: The structure of a memorist's skill. *Journal of Experimental Psychology: Learning, memory, and Cognition, 35,* 1426–1442.

Hubel, D. H., & Wiesel, T. N. (1960). Receptive fields of optic nerve fibres in the spider monkey. *Journal of Physiology, 154,* 572–580.

Hubbard, E. M., & Ramachandran, V. S. (2005). Neurocognitive mechanisms of synesthesia. *Neuron, 48,* 509–520.

Hubbard, T. L. (1990). Cognitive representation of linear motion: Possible direction and gravity effects in judged displacement. *Memory & Cognition, 18,* 299–309.

Hubbard, T. L. (1995a). Cognitive representation of motion: Evidence for friction and gravity analogues. *Journal of Experimental Psychology: Learning, Memory, and Cognition, 21,* 241–254.

Hubbard, T. L. (1995b). Environmental invariants in the representation of motion: Implied dynamics and representational momentum, gravity, friction, and centripetal force. *Psychonomic Bulletin & Review, 2,* 322–338.

Hubbard, T. L. (1996). Representational momentum, centripetal force, and curvilinear impetus. *Journal of Experimental Psychology: Learning, Memory, and Cognition, 22,* 1049–1060.

Hubbard, T. L. (1997). Target size and displacement along the axis of implied gravitational attraction: Effects of implied weight and evidence of representational gravity. *Journal of Experimental Psychology: Learning, Memory, and Cognition, 23,* 1484–1493.

Hubbard, T. L. (2005). Representational momentum and related displacements in spatial memory: A review of the findings. *Psychonomic Bulletin & Review, 12,* 822–851.

Hubbard, T. L., & Bharucha, J. J. (1988). Judged displacement in apparent vertical and horizontal motion. *Perception & Psychophysics, 44,* 211–221.

Hulme, C. Maughan, S., & Brown, G. D. A. (1991). Memory for familiar and unfamiliar words: Evidence for a long-term memory contribution to short-term memory span. *Journal of Memory and Language, 30,* 685–701.

Hulme, C., Suprenant, A. M., Bireta, T. J., Stuart, G., & Neath, I. (2004). Abolishing the word-length effect. *Journal of*

Experimental Psychology: Learning, Memory, and Cognition, 30, 98–106.

Hulme, C., Thomson, N., Muir, C., & Lawrence, A. (1984). Speech rate and the development of short-term memory span. *Journal of Experimental Child Psychology, 38,* 241–253.

Hunkin, N. M. (1997). Focal retrograde amnesia: Implications for the organization of memory. In A. J. Parkin (Ed.), *Case Studies in the Neuropsychology of Memory,* pp. 63–82. Hove, England: Psychology Press.

Hunt, R. R. (1995). The subtlety of distinctiveness: What von Restorff really did. *Psychonomic Bulletin & Review, 2,* 105–112.

Hunt, R. R., Ausley, J. A., & Schultz, E. E. (1986). Shared and item-specific information in memory for event descriptions. *Memory & Cognition, 14,* 49–54.

Hunt, R. R., & Einstein, G. O. (1981). Relational and item-specific information in memory. *Journal of Verbal Learning and Verbal Behavior, 20,* 497–514.

Hunt, R. R., & McDaniel, M. A. (1993). The enigma of organization and distinctiveness. *Journal of Memory and Language, 32,* 421–445.

Hunt, R. R., & Seta, C. E. (1984). Category size effects in recall: The roles of relational and individual item information. *Journal of Experimental Psychology: Learning, Memory, and Cognition, 10,* 454–464.

Huntjens, R. J. C., Postma, A., Hamaker, E. L., Woertman, L., van der Hart, O., & Peters, M. (2002). Perceptual and conceptual priming in patients with dissociative identity disorder. *Memory & Cognition, 30,* 1033–1043.

Huron, C., Danion, J. M., Giacomoni, F., Grange, D., Robert, P., & Rizzo, L. (1995). Impairment of recognition memory with, but not without, conscious recollection in schizophrenia. *American Journal of Psychiatry, 152,* 1737–1742.

Hutenlocher, J., and Hedges, L. V., and Bradburn, N. M. (1990). Reports of elapsed time: Bounding and rounding processes in estimation. *Journal of Experimental Psychology: Learning, Memory, and Cognition, 16,* 196–213.

Huttenlocher, J., Hedges, L. V., & Duncan, S. (1991). Categories and particulars: Prototype effects in estimating spatial locations. *Psychological Review, 98,* 352–376.

Hyde, T. S., & Jenkins, J. J. (1973). Recall for words as a function of semantic, graphic, and syntactic orienting tasks. *Journal of Verbal Learning and Verbal Behavior, 12,* 471–480.

Intons-Peterson, M. J., & Roskos-Ewoldsen, B. B. (1989). Sensory-perceptual qualities of images. *Journal of Experimental Psychology: Learning, Memory, and Cognition, 15,* 188–199.

Intraub, H., Bender, R. S., & Mangels, J. A. (1992). Looking at pictures but remembering scenes. *Journal of Experimental Psychology: Learning, Memory, and Cognition, 18,* 180–191.

Intraub, H., & Berkowits, D. (1996). Beyond the edges of a picture. *American Journal of Psychology, 109,* 581–598.

Intraub, H., & Bodamer, J. L. (1993). Boundary extension: Fundamental aspect of pictorial representation or encoding artifact? *Journal of Experimental Psychology: Learning, Memory, and Cognition, 19,* 1387–1397.

Intraub, H., & Dickinson, C. A. (2008). False memory 1/20th of a second later: What the early onset of boundary extension reveals about perception. *Psychological Science, 19,* 1007–1014.

Intraub, H., Gottesman, C. V., & Bills, A. J. (1998). Effects of perceiving and imagining scenes on memory for pictures. *Journal of Experimental Psychology: Learning, Memory, and Cognition, 24,* 186–201.

Intraub, H., Gottesman, C. V., Willey, E. V., & Zuk, I. J. (1996). Boundary extension for briefly glimpsed photographs: Do common perceptual processes result in unexpected memory distortions? *Journal of Memory and Language, 35,* 118–134.

Intraub, H., & Hoffman, J. E. (1992). Reading and visual memory: Remembering scenes that were never seen. *American Journal of Psychology, 105,* 101–114.

Intraub, H., & Richardson, M. (1989). Wide-angle memories of close-up scenes. *Journal of Experimental Psychology: Learning, Memory, and Cognition, 15,* 179–187.

Irwin, D. E. (1996). Integrating information across saccadic eye movements. *Current Directions in Psychological Science, 5,* 94–100.

Irwin, D. E., & Brockmole, J. R. (2000). Mental rotation is suppressed during saccadic eye movements. *Psychonomic Bulletin & Review, 7,* 654–661.

Irwin, D. E., Brown, J. S., & Sun, J. S. (1988). Visual masking and visual integration across saccadic eye movements. *Journal of Experimental Psychology: General, 117,* 276–287.

Irwin, D. E., Yantis, S., & Jonides, J. (1983). Evidence against visual integration across saccadic eye movements. *Perception & Psychophysics, 34,* 49–57.

Ivory, S-J., Knight, R. G., Longmore, B. E., & Caradoc-Davies, T. (1999). Verbal memory in non-demented patients with idiopathic Parkinson's disease. *Neuropsychologia, 37,* 817–828.

Jacobs, L. F., & Schenk, F. (2003). Unpacking the cognitive map: The parallel map theory of hippocampal function. *Psychological Review, 110,* 285–315.

Jacoby, L. L. (1991). A process dissociation framework: Separating automatic from intentional uses of memory. *Journal of Memory and Language, 30,* 513–541.

Jacoby, L. L., & Dallas, M. (1981). On the relationship between autobiographical memory and perceptual learning. *Journal of Experimental Psychology: General, 110,* 306–340.

Jacoby, L. L., Kelley, C., Brown, J., & Jasechko, J. (1989). Becoming famous overnight: Limits on the ability to avoid unconscious influences of the past. *Journal of Personality and Social Psychology, 56,* 326–338.

Jacoby, L. L., & Rhodes, M. G. (2006). False remembering in the aged. *Current Directions in Psychological Science, 15,* 49–53.

Jacoby, L. L., Shimzu, Y., Daniels, K. A., & Rhodes, M. G. (2005). Modes of cognitive control in recognition and source memory: Depth of retrieval. *Psychonomic Bulletin & Review, 12,* 852–857.

Jacoby, L. L., & Whitehouse, K. (1989). An illusion of memory: False recognition influenced by unconscious perception. *Journal of Experimental Psychology: General, 118,* 126–135.

Jacoby, L. L., Woloshyn, V., & Kelley, C. (1989). Becoming famous without being recognized: Unconscious influences of memory produced by dividing attention. *Journal of Experimental Psychology: General, 118,* 115–125.

James, W. (1890 / 1950). *The Principles of Psychology.* New York: Dover.

Jahn, G. (2004). Three turtles in danger: Spontaneous construction of causally relevant spatial situation models. *Journal of Experimental Psychology: Learning, Memory, and Cognition, 30,* 969–987.

Janculjak, D., Mubrin, Z., Brinar, V., & Spilich, G. (2002). Changes of attention and memory in a group of patients with multiple sclerosis. *Clinical Neurology and Neurosurgery, 104,* 221–227.

Janowski, J. S., Shimamura, A. P., & Squire, L. R. (1989). Memory and metamemory: Comparisons between patients with frontal lobe lesions and amnesic patients. *Psychobiology, 17,* 3–11.

Janssen, S. M., Chessa, A. G., & Murre, J. M. J. (2006). Memory for time: How people date events. *Memory & Cognition, 34,* 138–147.

Jefferies, E., Lambon Ralph, M. A., & Baddeley, A. D. (2004). Automatic and controlled processing in sentence recall: The role of long-term and working memory. *Journal of Memory and Language, 51,* 623–643.

Jenkins, J. G., & Dallenbach, K. M. (1924). Oblivescence during sleep and waking. *American Journal of Psychology, 35,* 605–622.

Jessberger, S., & Gage, F. H. (2008). Stem-cell-associated structural and functional plasticity in the aging hippocampus. *Psychology and Aging, 23,* 684–691.

Jiménez, L., & Vázquez, G. A. (2008). Implicit sequence learning in a search task. *Quarterly Journal of Experimental Psychology, 61,* 1650–1657.

Johnson, M. K., De Leonardis, D. M., Hashtroudi, S., & Ferguson, S. A. (1995). Aging and single versus multiple cues in source monitoring. *Psychology and Aging, 10,* 507–517.

Johnson, M. K., Foley, M. A., & Leach, K. (1988). The consequences of memory of imagining in another person's voice. *Memory & Cognition, 16,* 337–342.

Johnson, M. K., Hashtroudi, S., & Lindsay, S. (1993). Source monitoring. *Psychological Bulletin, 114,* 3–28.

Johnson, M. K., & Hermann, A. M. (1995). Semantic relations and Alzheimer's disease: An early and disproportionate deficit in functional knowledge. *Journal of the International Neuropsychological Society, 1,* 568–574.

Johnson, M. K., Kounios, J., & Reeder, J. A. (1994). Time-course studies of reality monitoring and recognition. *Journal of Experimental Psychology: Learning, Memory, and Cognition, 20,* 1409–1419.

Johnson, M. K., & Raye, C. L. (1981). Reality monitoring. *Psychological Review, 88,* 67–85.

Johnson, S. J., & Anderson, M. C. (2004). The role of inhibitory control in forgetting semantic knowledge. *Psychological Science, 15,* 448–453.

Johnson-Laird, P. N. (1983). *Mental Models.* Cambridge, MA: Harvard University Press.

Johnson-Laird, P. N., Hermann, D. J., & Chaffin, R. (1984). Only connections: A critique of semantic networks. *Psychological Bulletin, 96,* 292–315.

Jonides, J. Lacy, S. C., & Nee, D. E. (2005). Processes of working memory in mind and brain. *Current Directions in Psychological Science, 14,* 2–5.

Joslyn, S., Loftus, E., McNoughton, A., & Powers, J. (2001). Memory for memory. *Memory & Cognition, 29,* 789–797.

Joslyn, S. L., & Oakes, M. A. (2005). Directed forgetting of autobiographical events. *Memory & Cognition, 33,* 577–587.

Jost, A. (1897). Die Assoziationsfestigkeit in ihrer Abha¨ngigkeit von der Verteilung der Wiederholungen [The strength of associations in their dependence on the distribution of repetitions]. *Zeitschrift fur Psychologie und Physiologie der Sinnesorgane, 16,* 436–472.

Just, M. A., Carpenter, P. A., Maguire, M., Diwadkar, V., & McManis, S. (2001). Mental rotation of objects retrieved from memory: A functional MRI study of spatial processing. *Journal of Experimental Psychology: General, 130,* 493–504.

Kahana, M. J., & Wingfield, A. (2000). A functional relation between learning and organization in free recall. *Psychonomic Bulletin & Review, 7,* 516–521.

Kahneman, D., Treisman, A., and Gibbs, B. J. (1992). The reviewing of objects files: Object-specific integration of information. Cognitive *Psychology, 24,* 175–219.

Kail, R. (1991). Processing time declines exponentially during childhood and adolescence. *Developmental Psychology, 27,* 259–266.

Kail, R. (1997). Processing time, imagery, and spatial memory. *Journal of Experimental Child Psychology, 64,* 67–78.

Kaiser, M. K., Proffitt, D. R., & Anderson, K. (1985). Judgments of natural and anomalous trajectories in the presence and absence of motion. *Journal of Experimental Psychology: Learning, Memory, and Cognition, 11,* 795–803.

Kalakoski, V., & Saarilouma, P. (2001). Taxi drivers' exceptional memory of street names. *Memory & Cognition, 29,* 634–638.

Kalénine, S., & Bonthoux, F. (2008). Object manipulability affects children's and adults' conceptual processing. *Psychonomic Bulletin & Review, 15,* 667–672.

Kalish, C. W. (2002). Essentialist to some degree: Beliefs about the structure of natural kinds categories. *Memory & Cognition, 30,* 340–352.

Kane, M. J. Bleckley, M. K., Conway, A. R. A., & Engle, R. W. (2001). A controlled-attention view of working memory capacity. *Journal of Experimental Psychology: General, 130,* 169–183.

Kane, M. J., & Engle, R. W. (2000). Working-memory capacity: Proactive interference, and divided attention: Limits on long-term memory retrieval. *Journal of Experimental Psychology: Learning, Memory, and Cognition, 26,* 336–358.

Kane, M. J., & Engle, R. W. (2002). The role of prefrontal cortex in working-memory capacity, executive attention, and general fluid intelligence: An individual-differences perspective. *Psychonomic Bulletin & Review, 9,* 637–671.

Kang, S. H. K., McDermott, K. B., & Cohen, S. M. (2008). The mnemonic advantage of processing fitness-relevant information. *Memory & Cognition, 36,* 1151–1156.

Kanwisher, N. (1987). Repetition blindness: Type recognition without token individuation. *Cognition, 27,* 117–143.

Kapur, N. (1999). Syndromes of retrograde amnesia: A conceptual and empirical synthesis. *Psychological Bulletin, 125,* 800–825.

Kapur, N., & Moakes, D. (1995). Living with amnesia. In R. Campbell & M. A. Conway (Eds.), *Broken Memories: Case Studies in Memory Impairment,* pp. 1–7. Malden, MA: Blackwell.

Karney, B. R., & Coombs, R. H. (2000). Memory bias in long-term close relationships: Consistency or improvement? *Personality and Social Psychology Bulletin, 26,* 959–970.

Kassam, K. S., Gilbert, D. T., Swencionis, J. K., & Wilson, T. D. (2009). Misconceptions of memory: The Scooter Libby effect. *Psychological Science, 20,* 551–552.

Kartsounis, L. D., & Shallice, T. (1996). Modality specific semantic knowledge loss for unique items. *Cortex, 32,* 109–119.

Kay, H. (1955). Learning and retaining verbal material. *British Journal of Psychology, 46,* 81–100.

Kelly, J. W., & McNamara, T. P. (2008). Response mode differences in perspective taking: Differences in representation or differences in retrieval? *Memory & Cognition, 36,* 863–872.

Kelly, M. H., & Freyd, J. J. (1987). Explorations of representational momentum. *Cognitive Psychology, 19,* 369–401.

Kemp, S. (1988). Memorial psychophysics for visual area: The effect of retention interval. *Memory & Cognition, 16,* 431–436.

Kennedy, Q., Mather, M., & Carstensen, L. L. (2004). The role of motivation in the age-related positivity effect in autobiographical memory. *Psychological Science, 15,* 208–214.

Kenny, L. M., Bryant, R. A., Silove, D., Creamer, M., O'Donnell, M., & McFarlane, A. C. (2009). Distant memories: A prospective study of vantage point of trauma memories. *Psychological Science, 20,* 1049–1052.

Kensinger, E. A. (2007). Negative emotion enhances memory accuracy: Behavioral and neuroimaging evidence. *Current Directions in Psychological Science, 16,* 213–218.

Kensinger, E. A. (2009). *Emotional Memory Across the Adult Lifespan*. Psychology Press: New York.

Kensinger, E. A., & Choi, E. S. (2009). When side matters: Hemispheric processing and the visual specificity of emotional memories. *Journal of Experimental Psychology: Learning, Memory, and Cognition, 35,* 247–253.

Kensinger, E. A., & Corkin, S. (2003a). Memory enhancement for emotional words: Are emotional words more vividly remembered than neutral words? *Memory & Cognition, 31,* 1169–1180.

Kensinger, E. A., & Corkin, S. (2003b). Effect of negative emotional content on working memory and long-term memory. *Emotion, 3,* 378–393.

Kensinger, E. A., Garoff-Easton, R. J., & Schacter, D. L. (2007). Effects of emotion on memory specificity: Memory tradeoffs elicited by negative visually arousing stimuli. *Journal of Memory and Language, 56,* 575–591.

Kensinger, E. A., O'Brien, J. L., Swanberg, K., Garoff-Eaton, R. J., & Schacter, D. L. (2007). The effects of emotional content on reality-monitoring performance in young and older adults. *Psychology and Aging, 22,* 752–764.

Kensinger, E. A., & Schacter, D. L. (2006). Reality monitoring and memory distortion: Effects of negative, arousing content. *Memory & Cognition, 34,* 251–260.

Kensinger, E. A., & Schacter, D. L. (2006). When the Red Sox shocked the Yankees: Comparing negative and positive memories. *Psychonomic Bulletin & Review, 13,* 757–763.

Keppel, G., & Underwood, B. J. (1962). Proactive inhibition in short-term retention of single items. *Journal of Verbal Learning and Verbal Behavior, 1,* 153–161.

Kerst, S. M., & Howard, J. H. (1983). Mental processes in magnitude estimation of length and loudness. *Bulletin of the Psychonomic Society, 21,* 141–144.

Kerstholt, J. H., & Jackson, J. L. (1998). Judicial decision making: Order of evidence presentation and availability of background information. *Applied Cognitive Psychology, 15,* 445–454.

Khaneman, D., Triesman, A., & Gibbs, B. J. (1992). The reviewing of object files: Object-specific integration of information. *Cognitive Psychology, 24,* 175–219.

Kihlstrom, J. F., & Schacter, D. L. (1995). Functional disorders of autobiographical memory. In A. D. Baddeley, B. A. Wilson, & F. N. Watts (Eds.), *Handbook of Memory Disorders,* pp. 337–364. New York: Wiley.

Kim, M-S., Kim, J. C., & Chung, C. K. (2008). Neural correlates of immediate and delayed word recognition memory: An MEG study. *Brain Research,* 1240, 132–142.

Kimball, D. R., & Bjork, R. A. (2002). Influences of intentional and unintentional forgetting on false memories. *Journal of Experimental Psychology: General, 131,* 116–130.

Kimball, D. R., Bjork, E. L., Bjork, R. A., & Smith, T. A. (2008). Part-list cuing and the dynamics of false recall. *Psychonomic Bulletin & Review, 15,* 296–301.

Kimball, D. R., & Metcalfe, J. (2003). Delaying judgments of learning affects memory, not metamemory. *Memory & Cognition, 31,* 918–929.

Kintsch, W. (1968). Recognition and free recall of organized lists. *Journal of Experimental Psychology, 78,* 481–487.

Kintsch, W. (1970). Models for free recall and recognition. In D. A. Norman (Ed.), *Models of Human Memory,* pp. 331–373. New York: Academic Press.

Kintsch, W., & Bates, E. (1977). Recognition memory for statements from a classroom lecture. *Journal of Experimental Psychology: Human Learning and Memory, 3,* 150–159.

Kintsch, W., & Bowles, A. (2002). Metaphor comprehension: What makes a metaphor difficult to understand? *Metaphor and Symbol, 17,* 249–262.

Kintsch, W., Mandel, T. S., & Kozminsky, E. (1977). Summarizing scrambled stories. *Memory & Cognition, 5,* 547–552.

Kintsch, W., Welsch, D., Schmalhofer, F., & Zimny, S. (1990). Sentence memory: A theoretical analysis. *Journal of Memory and Language, 29,* 133–159.

Kirchner, T. R., & Sayette, M. A. (2003). Effects of alcohol on controlled and automatic memory processes. *Experimental and Clinical Psychopharmacology, 11,* 167–175.

Kirschen, M. P., Davis-Ratner, M. S., Jerde, T. E., Schraedley-Desmond, P., & Desmond, J. E. (2006). Enhancement of phonological memory following Transcranial Magnetic Stimulation (TMS). *Behavioural Neurology, 17,* 187–194.

Kishiyama, M. M., & Yonelinas, A. P. (2003). Novelty effects on recollection and familiarity in recognition memory. *Memory & Cognition, 31,* 1045–1051.

Kishiyama, M. M., Yonelinas, A. P., & Lazzara, M. M. (2004). The Von Restorff effect in amnesia: The contribution of the hippocampal system to novelty-related memory enhancements. *Journal of Cognitive Neuroscience, 16,* 15–23.

Kitchner, E. G., Hodges, J. R., & McCarthy, R. (1998). Acquisition of post-morbid vocabulary and semantic facts in the absence of episodic memory. *Brain, 121,* 1313–1327.

Klauer, K.C., & Zhao, Z. (2004). Double dissociations in visual and spatial short-term memory. *Journal of Experimental Psychology: General, 133,* 355–381.

Klein, K., & Boals, A. (2001). Expressive writing can increase working memory capacity. *Journal of Experimental Psychology: General, 130,* 520–533.

Klein, S. B., Cosmides, L., Tooby, J., & Chance, S. (2002). Decisions and the evolution of memory: Multiple systems, multiple functions. *Psychological Review, 109,* 306–329.

Kleinsmith, L. J., & Kaplan, S. (1963). Paired-associate learning as a function of arousal and interpolated interval. *Journal of Experimental Psychology, 65,* 190–193.

Kliegel, M., McDaniel, M. A., & Einstein, G. O. (2000). Plan formation, retention, and execution in prospective memory: A new approach and age-related effects. *Memory & Cognition, 28,* 1041–1049.

Klimesch, W. (1999). EEG alpha and theta oscillations reflect cognitive and memory performance: A review and analysis. *Brain Research Reviews, 29,* 169–195.

Klimesch, W., Doppelmayr, M., Russegger, H., & Pachinger, T. (1996). Theta band power in the human scalp EEG and the encoding of new information. *Neuroreport, 7,* 1235–1240.

Klimesch, W., Schimke, H., Dopplemayr, M., Ripper, B., Schwaiger, J., & Pfurtscheller, G. (1996). Event-related deschronization (ERD) and the Dm effect: Does alpha desychronization during encoding predict later recall performance? *International Journal of Psychophysiology, 24,* 47–60.

Knight, B. G., Maines, M. L., & Robinson, G. S. (2002). The effects of sad mood on memory in older adults: A test of the mood congruence effect. *Psychology and Aging, 17,* 653–661.

Kole, J. A., & Healy, A. F. (2007). The effects of memory set size and information structure on learning and retention. *Psychonomic Bulletin & Review, 14,* 693–698.

Kolers, P. A. (1976). Reading a year later. *Journal of Experimental Psychology: Human Learning and Memory, 2,* 554–565.

Kolers, P. A., & Palef, S. R. (1976). Knowing not. *Memory & Cognition, 4,* 553–558.

Kolers, P. A., & Roediger, H. L. (1984). Procedures of mind. *Journal of Verbal Learning and Verbal Behavior, 23,* 425–449.

Koriat, A. (1993). How do we know that we know? The accessibility model of the feeling of knowing. *Psychological Review, 100,* 609–639.

Koriat, A. (1995). Dissociating knowing and the feeling of knowing: Further evidence for the accessibility model. *Journal of Experimental Psychology: General, 124,* 311–333.

Koriat, A. (1997). Monitoring one's own knowledge during study: A cue utilization approach to judgments of learning. *Journal of Experimental Psychology: General, 126,* 349–370.

Koriat, A. (2002). Comparing objective and subjective learning curves: Judgments of learning exhibit increased underconfidence with practice. *Journal of Experimental Psychology: General, 131,* 147–162.

Koriat, A., & Bjork, R. A. (2006). Illusions of competence during study can be remedied by manipulations that enhance learners' sensitivity to retrieval conditions at test. *Memory & Cognition, 34,* 959–972.

Koriat, A., & Levy-Sadot, R. (2001). The combined contributions of the cue-familiarity and accessibility heuristics to feelings of knowing. *Journal of Experimental Psychology: Learning, Memory, and Cognition, 27,* 34–53.

Koriat, A., Levy-Sadot, R., Edry, E., & de Marcas, S. (2003). What do we know about what we cannot remember? Accessing the semantic attributes of words that cannot be recalled. *Journal of Experimental Psychology: Learning, Memory, and Cognition, 29,* 1095–1105.

Koriat, A., & Pearlman-Avnion, S. (2003). Memory organization of action events and its relationship to memory performance. *Journal of Experimental Psychology: General, 132,* 435–454.

Kornell, N., Hays, M. J., & Bjork, R. A. (2009). Unsuccessful retrieval attempts enhance subsequent learning. *Journal of Experimental Psychology: Learning, Memory, and Cognition, 35,* 989–998.

Kosslyn, S. M. (1975). Information representation in visual images. *Cognitive Psychology, 7,* 341–370.

Kosslyn, S. M. (1980). *Image and Mind.* Cambridge, MA: Harvard University Press.

Kosslyn, S. M., Ball, T. M., and Reiser, B. J. (1978). Visual images preserve metric spatial information: Evidence from studies of image scanning. *Journal of Experimental Psychology: Human Perception and Performance, 4,* 47–60.

Kosslyn, S. M., & Pomerantz, J. R. (1977). Imagery, propositions, and the form of internal representations. *Cognitive Psychology, 9,* 52–76.

Kounios, J., & Holcombe, P. J. (1994). Concreteness effects in semantic processing: ERP evidence supporting dual-coding theory. *Journal of Experimental Psychology: Learning, Memory, and Cognition, 20,* 804–823.

Kounios, J., Montgomery, E. C., & Smith, R. W. (1994). Semantic memory and the granularity of semantic relations: Evidence from speed-accuracy decomposition. *Memory & Cognition, 22,* 729–741.

Koutstaal, W. (2006). Flexible remembering. *Psychonomic Bulletin & Review, 13,* 84–91.

Koutstaal, W., Reddy, C., Jackson, E. M., Prince, S., Cendan, D. L., & Schacter, D. L. (2003). False recognition of abstract versus common objects in older and younger adults: Testing the semantic categorization account. *Journal of Experimental Psychology: Learning, Memory and Cognition, 29,* 499–510.

Koutstaal, W., & Schacter, D. L. (1997). Gist-based false recognition of pictures in older and younger adults. *Journal of Memory and Language, 37,* 555–583.

Kozhevnikov, M., & Hegarty, M. (2001). Impetus beliefs as default heuristics: Dissociation between explicit and implicit knowledge about motion. *Psychonomic Bulletin & Review, 8,* 439–453.

Kozhevnikov, M., Louchakova, O., Josipovic, Z., & Motes, M. A. (2009). The enhancement of visuospatial processing efficiency through Buddhist deity meditation. *Psychological Science, 20,* 645–653.

Kramer, T. H., Buckout, R., & Eugenio, P. (1990). Weapon focus, arousal, and eyewitness memory. *Law and Human Behavior, 14,* 167–184.

Krause, C. M., Aromäki, A., Sillanmäki, L., Åström, T., Alanko, K., Salonen, E., & Peltola, O. (2002). Alcohol-induced alterations in ERD/ERS during an auditory memory task. *Alcohol, 26,* 145–153.

Krause, W., Gibbons, H., & Schack, B. (1998). Concept activation and coordination of activation procedures require two different networks. *Neuroreport, 9,* 1649–1653.

Kroll, N. E. A., & Klimesch, W. (1992). Semantic memory: Complexity or connectivity. *Memory & Cognition, 20,* 192–210.

Kumkale, G. T., & Albarracin, D. (2003). The sleeper effect in persuasion: A meta-analytic review. *Psychological Bulletin, 130,* 143–172.

Kunst-Wilson, W. R., & Zajonc, R. B. (1980). Affective discrimination of stimuli that cannot be recognized. *Science, 207,* 557–558.

Kutas, M., & Hillyard, S. A. (1980). Reading senseless sentences: Brain potentials reflect semantic incongruity. *Science, 207,* 203–205.

Kvavilashvili, L., & Mandler, G. (2004). Out of one's mind: A study of involuntary semantic memories. *Cognitive Psychology, 48,* 47–94.

LaBar, K. S., & Cabeza, R. (2006). Cognitive neuroscience of emotional memory. *Nature Reviews: Neuroscience, 7,* 54–64.

Lampinen, J. M., Copeland, S. M., & Neuscatz, J. S. (2001). Recollections of things schematic: Room schemas revisited. *Journal of Experimental Psychology: Learning, Memory, and Cognition, 27,* 1211–1222.

Lancaster, J. S., & Barsalou, L. W. (1997). Multiple organizations of events in memory. *Memory, 5,* 569–599.

Landau, J. D. (2001). Altering the balance of recollection and familiarity influences the revelation effect. *American Journal of Psychology, 114,* 425–437.

Landauer, T. K. (1969). Reinforcement as consolidation. *Psychological Review, 76,* 82–96.

Landauer, T. K. & Dumais, S. T. (1997). A solution to Plato's problem: The latent semantic analysis theory of acquisition, induction, and representation of knowledge. *Psychological Review, 104,* 211–240.

Lane, S. M., & Zaragoza, M. S. (2007). A little elaboration foes a long way: The role of generation in eyewitness suggestibility. *Memory & Cognition, 35,* 1255–1266.

Laney, C., Campbell, H. V., Heuer, F., & Reisberg, D. (2005). Memory for thematically arousing events. *Memory & Cognition, 32,* 1149–1159.

Langlois, J. H., & Roggman, L. A. (1990). Attractive faces are only average. *Psychological Science, 1,* 115–121.

Langlois, J. H., Roggman, L. A., & Musselman, L. (1994). What is average and what is not average about attractive faces. *Psychological Science, 5,* 214–220.

La Rooy, D., Pipe, M-E., & Murray, J. E. (2005). Reminiscence and hypermnesia in children's eyewitness memory. *Journal of Experimental Child Psychology, 90,* 235–254.

Lashley, K. S. (1950). In search of the engram. *Symposia of the Society for Experimental Biology: Physiological Mechanisms of Animal Behavior,* Vol. 4. New York: Academic Press.

Lavaer, G. D, & Burke, D. M. (1993). Why do semantic priming effects increase in old age? A meta-analysis. *Psychology and Aging, 8,* 34–43.

LaVoie, D. J., & Malmstrom, T. (1998). False recognition effects in younger and older adults' memory for text passages. *Journals of Gerontology: Psychological Sciences, 53B,* P255–P262.

Leafhead, K. M., & Kopelman, M. D. (1997). Face memory impairment in the Cotard delusion. In A. J. Parkin (Ed.), *Case Studies in the Neuropsychology of Memory,* pp. 165–177. Hove, England:Psychology Press.

Leary, M. R. (1981). The distorted nature of hindsight. *Journal of Social Psychology, 115,* 25–29.

Leary, M. R. (1982). Hindsight distortion and the 1980 Presidential election. *Personality and Social Psychology Bulletin, 8,* 257–263.

LeBoe, J. P., & Whittlesea, B. W. A. (2002). The inferential basis of familiarity and recall: Evidence for a common underlying process. *Journal of Memory and Language, 46,* 804–829.

LeCompte, D. C. (1995). Recollective experience in the revelation effect: Separating the contributions of recollection and familiarity. *Memory & Cognition, 23,* 324–334.

Lee, J. L., & Brown, N R. (2003). Delay related changes in personal memory for September 11 2001. *Applied Cognitive Psychology, 17,* 1007–1015.

Leitz, J. R., Morgan, C., J. A., Bisby, J. A., Rendell, P. G., & Curran, H. V. (2009). Global impairment of prospective memory following acute alcohol. *Psychopharmacology, 205,* 379–387.

Levin, D. T., & Simons, D. J. (1997). Failure to detect changes to attended objects in motion pictures. *Psychonomic Bulletin & Review, 4,* 501–506.

Levine, B., Svaboda, E., Hay, J. F., Winocur, G, & Moscovitch, M. (2002). Aging and autobiographical memory: Dissociating episodic from semantic retrieval. *Psychology and Aging, 17,* 677–689.

Levine, L. J., Prohaska, V., Burgess, S. L., Rice, J. A., & Laulhere, T. M. (2001). Remembering past emotions: The role of current appraisals. *Cognition and Emotion, 15,* 393–417.

Levine, M., Jankovic, I. N., & Palij, M. (1982). Principles of spatial problem solving. *Journal of Experimental Psychology: General, 111,* 157–175.

Levy, B. (1996). Improving memory in old age through implicit self-stereotyping. *Journal of Personality and Social Psychology, 71,* 1092–1107.

Levy, B. A., & Kirsner, K. (1989). Reprocessing text: Indirect measures of word and message level processes. *Journal of Experimental Psychology: Learning, Memory, and Cognition, 15,* 407–417.

Levy, D. A., Stark, C. E. L., & Squire, L. R. (2004). Intact conceptual priming in the absence of declarative memory. *Psychological Science, 15,* 680–686.

Lewandowsky, S., & Murdock, B. B. (1989). Memory for serial order. *Psychological Review, 96,* 25–57.

Lewandowsky, S., & Oberauer, K. (2009). No evidence for temporal decay in working memory. *Journal of Experimental Psychology: Learning, Memory, and Cognition, 35,* 1545–1551.

Lewandowsky, S., Stritzke, W. G. K., Oberauer, K., & Morales, M. (2005). Memory for fact, fiction, and misinformation: The Iraq war 2003. *Psychological Science, 16,* 190–195.

Leynes, P. A., & Phillips, M. C. (2008). Event-related potential (ERP) evidence for varied recollection during source monitoring. *Journal of Experimental Psychology: Learning, Memory, and Cognition, 34,* 741–751.

Li, X., Schweickert, R., & Gandour, J. (2000). The phonological similarity effect in immediate recall: Positions of shared phonemes. *Memory & Cognition, 28,* 1116–1125.

Libby, L. K. (2003). Imagery perspective and source monitoring in imagination inflation. *Memory & Cognition, 31,* 1072–1081.

Lidji, P., Kolinsky, R., Lochy, A., & Morais, J. (2007). Spatial associations for musical stimuli: A piano in the head? *Journal of Experimental Psychology: Human Perception and Performance, 33,* 1189–1207.

Light, L. L., & Anderson, P. A. (1983). Memory for scripts in young and older adults. *Memory & Cognition, 11,* 435–444.

Light, L. L., & Capps, J. L. (1986). Comprehension of pronouns in young and older adults. *Developmental Psychology, 22,* 580–585.

Light, L. L., Hollander, S., & Kayra-Stuart, F. (1981). Why attractive people are harder to remember. *Personality and Social Psychology Bulletin, 7,* 269–276.

Lindberg, M. A. (1980). Is knowledge base development a necessary and sufficient condition for memory development? *Journal of Experimental Child Psychology, 30,* 401–410.

Lindsay, D. S., Allen, B. P., Chan, J. C. K., & Dahl, L. C. (2004). Eyewitness suggestibility and source similarity: Intrusions of details from one event into memory reports of another event. *Journal of Memory and Language, 50,* 96–111.

Lindsay, D. S., Hagen, L., Read, J. D., Wade, K. A., & Garry, M. (2004). True photographs and false memories. *Psychological Science, 15,* 149–154.

Lindsay, D. S., & Johnson, M. K. (1991). Developmental changes in memory source monitoring. *Journal of Experimental Child Psychology, 52,* 297–318.

Lindsay, D. S., Johnson, M. K., & Kwon, P. (1991). Recognition memory and source monitoring. *Bulletin of the Psychonomic Society, 29,* 203–205.

Lindsay, R. C. L., & Wells, G. L. (1980). What price justice? *Law and Human Behavior, 4,* 303–313.

Lindsay, R. C. L., & Wells, G. L. (1985). Improving eyewitness identifications from lineups: Simultaneous versus sequential lineup presentations. *Journal of Applied Psychology, 70,* 556–564.

Liu, L. L., & Park, D. C. (2004). Aging and medical adherence: The use of automatic processes to achieve effortful things. *Psychology and Aging, 19,* 318–325.

Liu, T., & Cooper, L. A. (2001). The influence of task requirements on priming in object decision and matching. *Memory & Cognition, 29,* 874–882.

Liu, T. & Cooper, L. A. (2003). Explicit and implicit memory for rotating objects. *Journal of Experimental Psychology: Learning, Memory and Cognition, 29,* 554–562.

Liu, Y., Su, Y., Xu, G., & Chan, R. C. K. (2007). Two dissociable aspects of feeling-of-knowing: Knowing that you know and knowing that you do not know. *Quarterly Journal of Experimental Psychology, 60,* 672–680.

Lloyd-Jones, T., & Vernon, D. (2003). Semantic interference from visual object recognition on visual imagery. *Journal of Experimental Psychology: Learning, Memory and Cognition, 29,* 563–580.

Lockhart, R. S., & Murdock, B. B. (1970). Memory and the theory of signal detection. *Psychological Bulletin, 74,* 100–109.

Loftus, E. F. (1971). Memory for intentions: The effect of presence of a cue and interpolated activity. *Psychonomic Science, 23,* 315–316.

Loftus, E. F. (1979). The malleability of human memory. *American Scientist, 67,* 312–320.

Loftus, E. F. (1993). The reality of repressed memories. *American Psychologist, 48,* 518–537.

Loftus, E. F. (2004). Memories of things unseen. *Current Directions in Psychological Science, 13,* 145–147.

Loftus, E. F., & Loftus, G. R. (1980). On the permanence of stored information in the human brain. *American Psychologist, 35,* 409–420.

Loftus, E. F., Loftus, G. R., & Messo, J. (1987) Some facts about "weapon focus." *Law and Human Behavior, 11,* 55–62.

Loftus, E. F., Miller, D. G., & Burns, H. J. (1978). Semantic integration of verbal information into a visual memory. *Journal of Experimental Psychology: Human Learning and Memory, 4,* 19–31.

Loftus, E. F., & Palmer, J. C. (1974). Reconstruction of automobile destruction: An example of the interaction between language and memory. *Journal of Verbal Learning and Verbal Behavior, 13,* 585–589.

Loftus, E. F., & Zanni, G. (1975). Eyewitness testimony: The influence of the wording of a question. *Bulletin of the Psychonomic Society, 5,* 86–88.

Logie. R. H., & Maylor, E. A. (2009). An internet study of prospective memory across adulthood. *Psychology and Aging, 24,* 767–774.

London, K., & Nunez, N. (2000). The effect of jury deliberations on jurors' propensity to disregard inadmissible evidence. *Journal of Applied Psychology, 85,* 932–939.

Long, D. L., & Prat, C. S. (2002). Memory for Star Trek: The role of prior knowledge in recognition revisited. *Journal of Experimental Psychology: Learning, Memory, and Cognition, 28,* 1073–1082.

Lövdén, M. (2003). The episodic memory and inhibitory accounts of age-related increases in false memories: A consistency check. *Journal of Memory and Language, 49,* 268–283.

Love, B. C. (2005). Environment and goals jointly direct category acquisition. *Current Directions in Psychological Science, 14,* 195–199.

Lucchelli, F., Muggia, S., & Spinnler, H. (1997). Selective proper name anomia: A case involving only contemporary celebrities. *Cognitive Neuropsychology, 14,* 881–900.

Luminet, O. (2009). Models for the formation of flashbulb memories. In O. Luminet & A. Curci (Eds.), *Flashbulb Memories: New Issues and New Perspectives,* pp. 51–76. New York: Psychology Press.

Luo, C. R. (1993). Enhanced feeling of recognition: Effects of identifying and manipulating test items on recognition memory. *Journal of Experimental Psychology: Learning, Memory, and Cognition, 19,* 405–413.

Luo, L., & Craik, F. I. M. (2009). Age differences in recollection: Specificity effects at retrieval. *Journal of Memory and Language, 60,* 421–436.

Lupyan, G. (2008). From chair to "chair": A representational shift account of object labeling effects on memory. *Journal of Experimental Psychology: General, 137,* 348–369.

Luria, A. R. (1968). *The Mind of a Mnemonist: A Little Book About a Vast Memory.* New York: Basic Books.

Luus, C. A. E., & Wells, G. L. (1994). The malleability of eyewitness confidence: co-witness and perseverance effects. *Journal of Applied Psychology, 79,* 714–723.

Lyle, K. B., Bloise, S. M., & Johnson, M. K. (2006). Age-related binding deficits and the content of false memories. *Psychology and Aging, 21,* 86-95.

Lyle, K. B., & Johnson, M. K. (2004). Effects of verbalization on lineup face recognition in an interpolated inspection paradigm. *Applied Cognitive Psychology, 18,* 393–403.

Lynch, S., & Yarnell, P. R. (1973). Retrograde amnesia: Delayed forgetting after concussion. *American Journal of Psychology, 86,* 643–645.

Lyon, L. S. (1985). Facilitating telephone number recall in a case of psychogenic amnesia. *Journal of Behavior Therapy and Experimental Psychiatry, 16,* 147–149.

Maass, A., & Köhnken, G. (1989). Simulating the "weapon effect." *Law and Human Behavior, 13,* 397–408.

Macken, W. J. (2002). Environmental context and recognition: The role of recollection and familiarity. *Journal of Experimental Psychology: Learning, Memory, and Cognition, 28,* 153–161.

MacLeod, C., Dodd, M. D., Sheard, E. D., Wilson, D. E., & Bibi, U. (2003). In opposition to inhibition. *The Psychology of Learning and Motivation, 43,* 163–214.

MacLeod, C. M. (1989). Directed forgetting affects both direct and indirect tests of memory. *Journal of Experimental Psychology: Learning, Memory, and Cognition, 15,* 13–21.

MacLeod, M. D., & Saunders, J. (2005). The role of inhibitory control in the production of misinformation effects. *Journal of Experimental Psychology: Learning, Memory, and Cognition, 31,* 964–979.

MacLeod, M. D., & Saunders, J. (2008). Retrieval inhibition and memory distortion. *Current Directions in Psychological Science, 17,* 26–30.

MacPherson, S. E., Phillips, L. H., & Sala, S. D. (2002). Age, executive functioning, and social decision making: A dorsolateral prefrontal theory of cognitive aging. *Psychology and Aging, 17,* 598–609.

Macrae, C. N., & Roseveare, T. A. (2002). I was always on my mind: The self and temporary forgetting. *Psychonomic Bulletin & Review, 9,* 611–614.

Maddox, K. B., Rapp, D. N., Brion, S., & Taylor, H. A. (2008). Social influences on spatial memory. *Memory & Cognition, 36, 479–494.*

Madigan, S., & O'Hara, R. (1992). Short-term memory at the turn of the century: Mary Whiton Calkins's memory research. *American Psychologist, 47,* 170–174.

Madsen, M. C., & McGaugh, J. L. (1961). The effect of ECS on one-trial avoidance learning. *Journal of Comparative and Physiological Psychology, 54,* 522–523.

Magliano, J. P., Miller, J., & Zwaan, R. A. (2001). Indexing space and time in film understanding. *Applied Cognitive Psychology, 15,* 533–545.

Magno, E., & Allen, K. (2007). Self-reference during explicit memory retrieval: An event-related potential analysis. *Psychological Science, 18,* 672–677.

Mahmood, D., Manier, D., & Hirst, W. (2004). Memory for how one learned of multiple deaths from AIDS: Repeated exposure and distinctiveness. *Memory & Cognition, 32,* 125–134.

Mahrer, P., & Miles, C. (1999). Memorial and strategic determinants of tactile memory. *Journal of Experimental Psychology: Learning, Memory and Cognition, 25,* 630–643.

Mahut, H., Zola-Morgan, S., & Moss, M. (1982). Hippocampal resections impair associative learning and recognition memory in the monkey. *The Journal of Neuroscience, 2,* 1214–1229.

Maki, R. H., Weigold, A., & Arellano, A. (2008). False memory for associated word lists in individuals and collaborating groups. *Memory & Cognition, 36,* 598–603.

Malmberg, K. J., Steyvers, M., Stephens, J. D., & Shiffrin, R. M. (2002). Feature frequency effects in recognition memory. *Memory & Cognition, 30,* 607–613.

Malpass, R. S., & Devine, P. G. (1981). Eyewitness identification: Lineup instructions and the absence of the offender. *Journal of Applied Psychology, 66,* 482–489.

Mammarella, N., & Fairfield, B. (2006). The role of encoding in reality monitoring: A running memory test with Alzheimer's type dementia. *Quarterly Journal of Experimental Psychology, 59,* 1701–1708.

Mandler, G. (1967). Organization and memory. In K. W. Spence and J. T. Spence (Eds.), *The Psychology of Learning and Motivation.* New York: Academic Press.

Mandler, G. (1980). Recognizing: The judgment of previous occurrence. *Psychological Review, 87,* 252–271.

Mandler, G. (2008). Familiarity breeds attempts: A critical review of dual-process theories of recognition. *Perspectives on Psychological Science, 3,* 390–399.

Mandler, J. M. (1988). How to build a baby: On the development of an accessible representational system. *Cognitive Development, 3,* 113–136.

Mandler, J. M. (1992). How to build a baby: II. conceptual primitives. *Psychological Review, 99,* 587–604.

Mandler, J. M., Bauer, P. J., & McDonough, L. (1991). Separating the sheep from the goats: Differentiating global categories. *Cognitive Psychology, 23,* 263–298.

Mandler, J. M., Fivush, R., & Reznick, J. S. (1987). The development of contextual categories. *Cognitive Development, 2,* 339–354.

Mandler, J. M., & McDonough, L. (1996). Drinking and driving don't mix: Inductive generalization in infancy. *Cognition, 59,* 307–335.

Mandler, J. M., & Ritchey, G. H. (1977). Long-term memory for pictures. *Journal of Experimental Psychology: Human Learning and Memory, 3,* 386–396.

Mäntylä, T. (2003). Assessing absentmindedness: Prospective memory complaint and impairment in middle-aged adults. *Memory & Cognition, 31,* 15–25.

Maratos, E. J., Dolan, R. J., Morris, J. S., Henson R. M. A., & Rugg, M. D. (2001). Neural activity associated with episodic memory for emotional context. *Neuropsychologia, 39,* 910–920.

Mark, M. M., & Mellor, S. (1991). Effect of self-relevence of an event on hindsight bias: The foreseeability of a layoff. *Journal of Applied Psychology, 76,* 569–577.

Markman, A. B., & Ross, B. H. (2003). Category use and category learning. *Psychological Bulletin, 129,* 592–613.

Marsh, E. J., Dolan, P. O., Balota, D. A., & Roediger, H. L. (2004). Part-set cuing effects in younger and older adults. *Psychology and Aging, 19,* 134–144.

Marsh, E. J., Edelman, G., & Bower, G. H. (2001). Demonstrations of a generation effect in context memory. *Memory & Cognition, 29,* 798–805.

Marsh, E. J., & Fazio, L. K. (2006). Learning errors from fiction: Difficulties in reducing reliance on fictional stories. *Memory & Cognition, 34,* 1140–1149.

Marsh, E. J., Meade, M. L., & Roediger, H. L. (2003). Learning facts from fiction. *Journal of Memory and Language, 49,* 519–536.

Marsh, R. L., Hicks, J. L., Cook, G. I., Hansen, J. S., & Pallos, A. L. (2003). Interference to ongoing activities covaries with the characteristics of an event-based intention. *Journal of Experimental Psychology: Learning, Memory, and Cognition, 29,* 861–870.

Marsh, R. L., Hicks, J. L., Hancock, T. W., & Munsayac, K. (2002). Investigating the output monitoring component of event-based prospective memory performance. *Memory & Cognition, 30,* 302–311.

Marshall, P. J. (2009). Relating psychology and neuroscience. *Perspectives on Psychological Science, 4,* 113–125.

Marshuetz, C. (1998). Order information in working memory: An integrative review of evidence from brain and behavior. *Psychological Bulletin, 131,* 323–339.

Martin, A., & Chao, L. L. (2001). Semantic memory and the brain: Structure and processes. *Current Opinion in Neurobiology, 11,* 194–201.

Martin, T., McDaniel, M. A., Guynn, M. J., Houck, J. M., Woodruff, C. C., Pearson Bish, J., Moses, S. N., Kičeć, D., & Tesche, C. D. (2007). Brain regions and their dynamics in prospective memory retrieval: A MEG study. *International Journal of Psychophysiology, 64,* 247–258.

Martin-Loeches, M., Hinojosa, J. A., Fernandez-Frias, C., & Rubia, F. J. (2001). Functional differences in the semantic processing of concrete and abstract words. *Neuropsychologia, 39,* 1086–1096.

Mason, M. F., Hood, B. M., & Macrae, C. N. (2004). Look into my eyes: Gaze direction and person memory. *Memory, 12,* 637–643.

Mather, M. (2007). Emotional arousal and memory binding: An object-based framework. *Perspectives on Psychological Science, 2,* 33–52.

Mather, M., & Johnson, M. K. (2000). Choice-supportive source monitoring: Do our decisions seem better to us as we age? *Psychology and Aging, 15,* 596–606.

Mather, M., Johnson, M. K., & De Leonardis, D. M. (1999). Stereotype reliance in source monitoring: Age differences and neuropsychological test correlates. *Cognitive Neuropsychology, 16,* 437–458.

Mather, M., & Knight, M. (2005). Goal-directed memory: The role of cognitive control in older adults' emotional memory. *Psychology and Aging, 20,* 554–570.

Mather. M., & Nesmith, K. (2008). Arousal-enhanced location memory for pictures. *Journal of Memory and Language, 58,*449–464.

Mather, M., Shafir, E., & Johnson, M. K. (2000). Misremembrance of options past: Source monitoring and choice. *Psychological Science, 11,* 132–138.

Mather, M., Shafir, E., & Johnson, M. K. (2003). Remembering chosen and assigned options. *Memory & Cognition, 31,* 422–433.

Matthews, W. J., Benjamin, C., & Osborne, C. (2007). Memory for moving and static images. *Psychonomic Bulletin & Review, 14,* 989–993.

Matvey, G., Dunlosky, J., Shaw, R. J., Parks, C., & Hertzog, C. (2002). Age-related equivalence and deficit in knowledge updating of cue effectiveness. *Psychology and Aging, 17,* 589–597.

Maurer, D. (1997). Neonatal synaesthesia: implications for the processing of speech and faces. In S. Baron-Cohen & J.E. Harrison (Eds.), *Synaesthesia: Classic and Contemporary Readings*, pp. 224–242. Malden, MA.: Blackwell.

May, C. P., Rahhal, T., Berry, E. M., & Leighton, E. A. (2005). Aging, source memory, and emotion. *Psychology and Aging, 20,* 571–578.

Mayes, A. R., & Montaldi, D. (1999). The neuroimaging of long-term memory encoding processes. *Memory, 7,* 613–659.

Maylor, E. A. (1993). Aging and forgetting in prospective and retrospective memory tasks. *Psychology and Aging, 8,* 420–428.

Maylor, E. A. (2002). Serial position effects in semantic memory: Reconstructing the order of versus of hymns. *Psychonomic Bulletin & Review, 9,* 816–820.

Maylor. E. A., & Rabbitt, P. M. A. (1993). Alcohol, reaction time and memory: A meta-analysis. *British Journal of Psychology, 84,* 301–317.

Mazzoni, G. A. L., Loftus, E. F., & Kirsch, I. (2001). Changing beliefs about implausible autobiographical events: A little plausibility goes a long way. *Journal of Experimental Psychology: Applied, 7,* 51–59.

Mazzoni. G. A. L., & Memon, A. (2003). Imagination can create false autobiographical memories. *Psychological Science, 14,* 186–188.

McAdams, D. P. (2001). The psychology of life stories. *Journal of General Psychology, 5,* 100–122.

McCabe, D. P., Smith, A. D., & Parks, C. M. (2007). Inadvertent plagiarism in young and older adults: the role of working memory capacity in reducing memory errors. *Memory & Cognition, 35,* 231–241.

McCarthy, R. A., & Hodges, J. R. (1995). Trapped in time: Profound autobiographical memory loss following thalamic stroke. In R. Campbell & M. A. Conway (Eds.), *Broken Memories: Case Studies in Memory Impairment.* Cambridge, MA: Blackwell.

McCarthy, R. A., & Warrington, E. K. (1992). Actors but not scripts: The dissociation of people and events in retrograde amnesia. *Neuropsychologia, 30,* 633–644.

McClelland, J. L. (2000). Connectionist models of memory. In E. Tulving & F. I. M. Craik (Eds.), *The Oxford Handbook of Memory,* pp. 583–596. New York: Oxford University Press.

McCloskey, M. (1983). Naive theories of motion. In D. Gentner & A. L. Stevens (Eds.), *Mental models*, pp. 299–324. Hillsdale, NJ: Erlbaum.

McCloskey, M., Caramazza, A., & Green, B. (1980). Curvilinear motion in the absence of external forces: Naive beliefs about the motion of objects. *Science, 210,* 1139–1141.

McCloskey, M., & Kohl, D. (1983). Naive physics: The curvilinear impetus principle and its role in interactions with moving objects. *Journal of Experimental Psychology: Learning, Memory, and Cognition, 9,* 146–156.

McCloskey, M., & Watkins, M. J. (1978). The seeing-more-than-is-there phenomenon: Implications for the locus of iconic storage. *Journal of Experimental Psychology: Human Perception and Performance, 4,* 553–564.

McCloskey, M. Wible, C. G., & Cohen, N. J. (1988). Is there a special flashbulb-memory mechanism? *Journal of Experimental Psychology: General, 117,* 171–181.

McCloskey, M. & Zaragoza, M. (1985). Misleading postevent information and memory for events: Arguments and evidence against memory impairment hypotheses. *Journal of Experimental Psychology: General, 114,* 1–16.

McDaniel, M. A., & Bugg, J. M. (2008). Instability in memory phenomena: A common puzzle and a unifying explanation. *Psychonomic Bulletin & Review, 15,* 237–255.

McDaniel, M. A., & Einstein, G. O. (1986). Bizarre imagery as an effective memory aid: The importance of distinctiveness.*Journal of Experimental Psychology: Learning, Memory, and Cognition, 12,* 54–65.

McDaniel, M. A., Einstein, G. O., Dunay, P. K., & Cobb, R. E. (1986). Encoding difficulty and memory: Toward a unifying theory. *Journal of Memory and Language, 25,* 645–656.

McDaniel, M. A., Einstein, G. O., & Lollis, T. (1988). Qualitative and quantitative considerations in encoding difficulty effects. *Memory & Cognition, 16,* 8–14.

McDaniel, M. A., Guynn, M. J., Einstein, G. O., & Breneiser, J. (2004). Cue-focused and reflexive-associative processes in prospective memory retrieval. *Journal of Experimental Psychology: Learning, Memory, and Cognition, 30,* 605–614.

McDaniel, M. A., Howard, D. C., & Butler, K. M. (2008). Implementation intentions facilitate prospective memory under high attention demands. *Memory & Cognition, 36,* 716–724.

McDaniel, M. A., & Waddill, P. J. (1990). Generation effects for context words: Implications for item-specific and multifactor theories. *Journal of Memory and Language, 29,* 201–211.

McDermott, K. B., & Chan, J. C. K. (2006). Effects of repetition on memory for pragmatic inferences. *Memory & Cognition, 34,* 1273–1284.

McFarland, C., & Ross, M. (1987). The relation between current impressions and memories of self and dating partners. *Personality and Social Psychology Bulletin, 13,* 228–238.

McGaugh, J. L. (1966). Time-dependent processes in memory storage. *Science, 153,* 1351–1358.

McGeoch, J. A. (1932). Forgetting and the law of disuse. *Psychological Review, 39,* 352–370.

McGovern, J. B. (1964). Extinction of associations in four transfer paradigms. *Psychological Monographs, 78(*16). 1–21

McGuire, M. J., & Maki, R. H. (2001). When knowing more means less: The effect of fan on metamemory judgments. *Journal of Experimental Psychology: Learning, Memory, and Cognition, 27,* 1172–1179.

McIsaac, H. K., & Eich, E. (2004). Vantage point in traumatic memory. *Psychological Science, 15,* 248–253.

McKay, D. G., & Ahmetzanov, M. V. (2005). Emotion, memory, and attention in the taboo Stroop paradigm: An experimental analogue of flashbulb memories. *Psychological Science, 16,* 25–32.

McKenna, P., Clare, L., & Baddeley, A. D. (1995). Schizophrenia. In A. D. Baddeley, B. A. Wilson, & F. N. Watts (Eds.), *Handbook of Memory Disorders,* pp. 271–292. Oxford, England: Wiley.

McNamara, T. P. (1986). Mental representations of spatial relations. *Cognitive Psychology, 18,* 87–121.

McNamara, T. P., & Altarriba, J. (1988). Depth of spreading activation revisited: Semantic mediated priming occurs in lexical decisions. *Journal of Memory and Language, 27,* 545–559.

McNamara, T. P., Altarriba, J., Bendele, M., Johnson, S. C., & Clayton, K. N. (1989). Constraints on priming in spatial memory: Naturally learned and experimentally learned environments. *Memory & Cognition, 17,* 444–453.

McNamara, T. P., Halpin, J. A., & Hardy, J. K. (1992a). Spatial and temporal contributions to the structure of spatial memory. *Journal of Experimental Psychology: Learning, Memory, and Cognition, 18,* 555–564.

McNamara, T. P., Halpin, J. A., & Hardy, J. K. (1992b). The representation and integration in memory of spatial and nonspatial information. *Memory & Cognition, 20,* 519–532.

McNamara, T. P., Hardy, J. K., & Hirtle, S. C. (1989). Subjective hierarchies in spatial memory. *Journal of Experimental Psychology: Learning, Memory, and Cognition, 15,* 211–227.

McNamara, T. P., & LeSueur, L. L. (1989). Mental representations of spatial and nonspatial relations. *The Quarterly Journal of Experimental Psychology, 41A,* 215–233.

McNamara, T. P., Ratcliff, R. & McKoon, G. (1984). The mental representation of knowledge acquired from maps. *Journal of Experimental Psychology: Learning, Memory and Cognition, 10,* 723–732.

McNamara, T. P., Rump, B., & Werner, S. (2003). Egocentric and geocentric frames of reference in memory for large-scale space. *Psychonomic Bulletin & Review, 10,* 589–595.

Meade, M. L., & Roediger, H. L. (2002). Explorations in the social contagion of memory. *Memory & Cognition, 30,* 995–1009.

Medin, D. L. (1989). Concepts and conceptual structure. *American Psychologist, 44,* 1469–1481.

Medin, D. L., & Shaffer, M. M. (1978). Context theory of classification learning. *Psychological Review, 85,* 207–238.

Medin, D. L., & Shoben, E. J. (1988). Context and structure in conceptual combination. *Cognitive Psychology, 20,* 158–190.

Medin, D. L., & Smith, E. E. (1984). Concepts and concept formation. *Annual Review of Psychology, 35,* 113–138.

Meeter, M., Murre, J. M. J., & Janssen, S. M. J. (2005). Remembering the news: Modeling retention data from a study with 1,400 participants. *Memory & Cognition, 33,* 793–810.

Meeter, M., Myers, C. E., & Gluck, M. A. (2005). Integrating incremental learning and episodic memory models of the hippocampal region. *Psychological Review, 112,* 560–585.

Meissner, C. A., Brigham, J. C., & Kelley, C. M. (2002). The influence of retrieval processes in verbal overshadowing. *Memory & Cognition, 29,* 176–186.

Melton, A. W., & Irwin, J. M., (1940). The influence of degree of interpolated learning on retroactive inhibition and the overt transfer of specific responses. *American Journal of Psychology, 53,* 173–203.

Meltzer, H. (1930). Individual differences in forgetting pleasant and unpleasant experiences. *Journal of Educational Psychology, 21,* 399–409.

Memon, A., Hope, L., Bartlett, J., & Bull, R. (2002). Eyewitness recognition errors: The effects of mugshot viewing and choosing in young and old adults. *Memory & Cognition, 30,* 1219–1227.

Merrill, A. A., & Baird, J. C. (1987). Semantic and spatial factors in environmental memory. *Memory & Cognition, 15,* 101–108.

Metcalfe, J. (2000). Metamemory: Theory and data. In E. Tulving & F. I. M. Craik (Eds.), *The Oxford Handbook of Memory,* pp. 197–211. New York: Oxford University Press.

Metcalfe, J. (2002). Is study time allocated selectively to a region of proximal learning? *Journal of Experimental Psychology: General, 131,* 349–363.

Metcalfe, J. (2009). Metacognitive judgments and control of study? *Current Directions in Psychological Science, 18,* 159–163.

Metcalfe, J., & Finn, B. (2008a). Evidence that judgments of learning are causally related to study choice. *Psychonomic Bulletin & Review, 15,* 174–179.

Metcalfe, J., & Finn, B. (2008b). Familiarity and retrieval processes in delayed judgments of learning. *Journal of Experimental Psychology: Learning, Memory, and Cognition, 34,* 1084–1097.

Metcalfe, J., & Kornell, N. (2003). The dynamics of learning and allocation of study time to a region of proximal learning. *Journal of Experimental Psychology: General, 132,* 530–542.

Meyer, D. E., Irwin, D. E., Osman, A. M., & Kounios, J. (1988). The dynamics of cognition and action: Mental processes inferred from speed-accuracy decomposition. *Psychological Review, 95,* 183–237.

Meyer, D. E. & Schvanevelt, R. W. (1971). Facilitation in recognizing pairs of words: Evidence of a dependence between retrieval operations. *Journal of Experimental Psychology, 90,* 227–234.

Mikels, J. A., Larkin, G. R., Reuter-Lorenz, P. A., & Carstensen, L. L. (2005). Divergent trajectories in the aging mind: Changes in working memory for affective versus visual information with age. *Psychology and Aging, 20,* 542–553.

Miles, C., & Hodder, K. (2005). Serial position effects in recognition memory for odors: A reexamination. *Memory & Cognition, 33,* 1303–1314.

Miles, C., & Jenkins, R. (2000). Recency and suffix effects with immediate recall of olfactory stimuli. *Memory, 8,* 195–206.

Miles, J. R., & Stine-Morrow, E. A. L. (2004). Differences in self-regulated learning from reading sentences. *Psychology and Aging, 19,* 626–636.

Miller, A. R., Baratta, C., Wynveen, C., & Rosenfeld, J. P. (2001). P300 latency, but not amplitude or topography, distinguishes between true and false recognition. *Journal of Experimental Psychology: Learning, Memory, and Cognition, 27,* 354–361.

Miller, G. A. (1956). The magical number seven, plus or minus two: Some limits on our capacity for processing information. *Psychological Review, 63,* 81–97.

Mills, C. B., Innis, J., Westendorf, T., Owsianiecki, L., & McDonald, A. (2006). Effect of a synesthete's photisms on name recall. *Cortex, 42,* 155–163.

Milner, B., Corkin, S., & Teuber, H. L. (1968). Further analysis of the hippocampal amnesic syndrome: 14-year follow-up study of H. M. *Neuropsychologia, 6,* 215–234.

Minsky, M. L. (1986). *The Society of Mind.* New York: Simon & Schuster.

Mintzer, M. Z. (2003). Triazolam-induced amnesia and the word-frequency effect in recognition memory: Support for a dual process account. *Journal of Memory and Language, 48,* 596–602.

Mintzer, M. Z., & Griffiths, R. R. (2001). False recognition in triazolam-induced amnesia. *Journal of Memory and Language, 44,* 475–492.

Mintzer, M. Z., Kuwabara, H., Alexander, M., Brasic, J. R., Ye, W., Ernst, M., Griffiths, R. R., & Wong, D. F. (2006). Dose effects of triazolam on brain activity curing episodic memory encoding: A PET study. *Psychopharmacology, 188,* 445–461.

Mirman, D., & Magnuson, J. S. (2009). The effect of frequency of shared features on judgments of semantic similarity. *Psychonomic Bulletin & Review, 16,* 671–677.

Mishkin, M., & Appenzeller, T. (1987). The anatomy of memory. *Scientific American, 256,* 80–89.

Mitchell, C. J., Lovibond, P. F., & Gan, C. Y. (2005). A dissociation between causal judgment and outcome recall. *Psychonomic Bulletin & Review, 12,* 950–954.

Mitchell, C. J., Lovibond, P. F., Minard, E., & Lavis, Y. (2006). Forward blocking in human learning sometimes reflects the failure to encode a cue-outcome relationship. *Quarterly Journal of Experimental Psychology, 59,* 830–844.

Mitchell, D. B. (2006). Nonconscious priming after 17 years. *Psychological Science, 17,* 925–929.

Mogle, J. A., Lovett, B. J., Stawski, R. A., & Sliwinski, M. J. (2008). What's so special about working memory? An examination of the relationships among working memory, secondary memory, and fluid intelligence. *Psychological Science, 19,* 1071–1077.

Montgomery, P., Siverstein, P., Wichmann, R., Fleischaker, K., & Andberg, M. (1993). Spatial updating in Parkinson's disease. *Brain and Cognition, 23,* 113–126.

Morey, C. C., & Cowan, N. (2005). When do visual and verbal memories conflict? The importance of working memory load and retrieval. *Journal of Experimental Psychology: Learning, Memory, and Cognition, 31,* 703–713.

Morris, C. D., Bransford, J. D., & Franks, J. J. (1977). Levels of processing versus transfer appropriate processing. *Journal of Verbal Learning and Verbal Behavior, 16,* 519–533.

Morrow, D. G., Greenspan, S. L., & Bower, G. H. (1987). Accessibility and situation models in narrative comprehension. *Journal of Memory and Language, 26,* 165–187.

Morton, J., Crowder, R. G., & Prussin, H. A. (1971). Experiments with the stimulus suffix effect. *Journal of Experimental Psychology: Monograph, 91,* 169–190.

Motes, M. A., Hubbard, T. L., Courtney, J. R., & Rypma, B. (2008). A principal components analysis of dynamic spatial memory biases. *Journal of Experimental Psychology: Learning, Memory, and Cognition, 34,* 1076–1083.

Moulton, P. L., Ptros, T. V., Apostal, K. J., Park, R. V., Ronning, E. A., King, B. M., & Penland, J. G. (2005). Alcohol-induced impairment and enhancement of memory: A test of the interference theory. *Physiology & Behavior, 85,* 240–245.

Moyer, R. S., Bradley, D. R., Sorensen, M. H., Whiting, J. C., & Mansfield, D. P. (1977). Psychophysical functions for perceived and remembered size. *Science, 200,* 330–332.

Moyer, R. S., Sklarew, P., & Whiting, J. (1982). Memory psychophysics. In H. Geissler & P. Patzold (Eds.), *Psychophysical Judgment and the Process of Perception,* pp. 35–46. New York: North-Holland.

Muller, R. U., Kuble, J. L., & Ranck, J. B. (1987). Spatial firing patterns of hippocampal complex-spike cells in a fixed environment. *The Journal of Neuroscience, 7,* 1935–1950.

Mulligan, N. W. (2001). Generation and hypermnesia. *Journal of Experimental Psychology: Learning, Memory, and Cognition, 27,* 436–450.

Mulligan, N. W., & Lozito, J. P. (2006). An asymmetry between memory encoding and retrieval. *Psychological Science, 17,* 7–11.

Munger, M. P., Solberg, J. L., & Horrocks, K. K. (1999). The relationship between mental rotation and representational momentum. *Journal of Experimental Psychology: Learning, Memory, and Cognition, 25,* 1557–1568.

Murdock, B. B. A distributed memory model for serial order information, *Psychological Review, 90,* 316–338.

Murdock, B. B. (1962). The serial position effect of free recall. *Journal of Experimental Psychology, 64,* 482–488.

Murdock, B. B. (1974). *Human Memory: Theory and Data.* Potomac, MD: Erlbaum.

Murdock, B. B. (1982a). A theory for the storage and retrieval of item and associative information. *Psychological Review, 89,* 609–626.

Murdock, B. B. (1982b). A distributed memory model for serial-order information. *Psychological Review, 90,* 316–338.

Murdock, B. B. (1993). TODAM2: A model for the storage and retrieval of item, associative, and serial-order information. *Psychological Review, 100,* 183–203.

Murdock, B. B. (1995). Developing TODAM: Three models for serial-order information. *Memory & Cognition, 23,* 631–645.

Murphy, N. A., & Isaacowitz, D. M. (2008). Preferences for emotional information in older and younger adults: A meta-analysis of memory and attention tasks. *Psychology and Aging, 23,* 263–286.

Murray, D. J. (1967). The role of speech responses in short-term memory. *Canadian Journal of Psychology, 21,* 263–276.

Muzzio, I. A., Kentros, C., & Kandel, E. (2009). What is remembered? Role of attention on the encoding and retrieval of hippocampal representations. *Journal of Physiology, 587,* 2837–2854.

Myers, J. L., O'Brien, E. J., Balota, D. A., & Toyofuku, M. L. (1984). Memory search without interference: The role of integration. *Cognitive Psychology, 16,* 217–242.

Myerson, J., Ferraro, F. R., Hale, S., & Lima, S. D. (1992). General slowing in semantic priming and word recognition. *Psychology and Aging, 7,* 257–270.

Myerson, J., Hale, S., Wagstaff, D., Poon, L. W., & Smith, G. A. (1990). The information-loss model: A mathematical theory of age-related cognitive slowing. *Psychological Review, 97,* 475–487.

Myerson, J., Wagstaff, D., & Hale, S. (1994). Brinley plots, explained variance, and the analysis of age differences in response latencies. *Journal of Gerontology: Psychological Sciences, 49,* P72–P80.

Nadel, L., & Zola-Morgan, S. (1984). Infantile amnesia: A neurobiological perspective. In M. Moscovitch (Ed.), *Infant Memory.* New York: Plenum Press.

Nairne, J. S., & Pandeirada, J. N. S. (2008a). Adaptive memory: Is survival processing special? *Journal of Memory and Language, 59,* 377–385.

Nairne, J. S., & Pandeirada, J. N. S. (2008b). Adaptive memory: Remembering with a stone-age brain. *Current Directions in Psychological Science, 17,* 239–243.

Nairne, J. S., Pandeirada, J. N. S., & Thompson, S. R., & (2008). Adaptive memory: The comparative value of survival processing. *Psychological Science, 19,* 176–180.

Nairne, J. S., Thompson, S. R., & Pandeirada, J. N. S. (2007). Adaptive memory: Survival processing enhances retention. *Journal of Experimental Psychology: Learning, Memory, and Cognition, 33,* 263–273.

Nakamura, G. V., & Graesser, A. C. (1985). Memory for script typical and atypical actions: A reaction time study. *Bulletin of the Psychonomic Society, 23,* 384–386.

Nakamura, G. V., Graesser, A. C., Zimmerman, J. A., & Riha, J. (1985). Script processing in a natural situation. *Memory & Cognition, 13,* 140–144.

Nathan, M. B., Shaki, S., Salti, M., & Algom, D. (2009). Numbers and space: Associations and dissociations. *Psychonomic Bulletin & Review, 16,* 578–582.

Neath, I. (1998). *Human Memory: An Introduction to Research Data, and Theory.* Pacific Grove: Brooks/Cole.

Neath, I., Surprenant, A. M., & Crowder, R. G. (1993). The context-dependent stimulus suffix effect. *Journal of Experimental Psychology: Learning, Memory and Cognition, 19,* 698–703.

Nee, D. E., & Jonides, J. (2008). Dissociable interference-control processes in perception and memory. *Psychological Science, 19,* 490–500.

Neely, J. H. (1977). Semantic priming and retrieval from lexical memory: Roles of inhibitionless spreading activation and limited-capacity attention. *Journal of Experimental Psychology: General, 106,* 226–254.

Neisser, U. (1981). John Dean's memory: A case study. *Cognition, 9,* 1–22.

Neisser, U. (1982). Snapshots or benchmarks? In U. Neisser (Ed.), *Memory Observed: Remembering in Natural Contexts,* pp. 43–48. San Francisco: Freeman.

Nelson, K. (1993). The psychological and social origins of autobiographical memory. *Psychological Science, 4,* 7–14.

Nelson, K., & Fivush, R. (2004). The emergence of autobiographical memory: A social cultural developmental theory. *Psychological Review, 111,* 486–511.

Nelson, K., & Gruendel, J. M. (1988). At moring it's lunchtime: A scriptal view of children's dialogue. In M. B. Franklin & S. S. Barten (Eds.), *Child language: A Reader,* pp. 263–277. New York: Oxford University press.

Nelson, T. O. (1978). Detecting small amounts of information in memory: Savings for nonrecognized items. *Journal of Experimental Psychology: Human Learning and Memory, 4,* 453–468.

Nelson, T. O., & Dunlosky, J. (1991). When people's judgments of learning (JOLs) are extremely accurate at predicting subsequent recall: The "Delayed-JOL effect." *Psychological Science, 2,* 267–270.

Nelson, T. O., & Leonesio, R. J. (1988). Allocation of self-paced study time and the "labor-in vain effect." *Journal of Experimental Psychology: Learning, Memory, and Cognition, 14,* 676–686.

Nelson, T. O., McSpadden, M., Fromme, K., & Marlatt, G. A. (1986). Effects of alcohol intoxication on metamemory and on retrieval from long-term memory. *Journal of Experimental Psychology: General, 115,* 247–254.

Nemiah, J. C. (1979). Dissociative amnesia: A clinical and theoretical reconsideration. In J. F. Kihlstrom and F. J. Evans (Eds.), *Functional Disorders of Memory.* Hillsdale, NJ: Erlbaum.

Newcombe, N., Huttenlocher, J., Sandberg, E., Lie, E., & Johnson, S. (1999). What do misestimations and asymmetries in spatial judgment indicate about spatial representation? *Journal of Experimental Psychology: Learning, Memory and Cognition, 25,* 986–996.

Newcombe, N. S., & Chiang, N. C. (2007). Learning geographical information from hypothetical maps. *Memory & Cognition, 35,* 895–909.

Newcombe, N. S., Drummy, A. B., Fox, N. A., Lie, E., & Ottinger-Alberts, W. (2000). Remembering early childhood: How much, how, and (why (or why not). *Current Directions in Psychological Science, 9,* 55–58.

Newtson, D. (1976). Foundations of attribution: The perception of ongoing behavior. In J. H. Harvey, W. J. Ickes, & R. F. Kidd (Eds.), *New Directions in Attribution Research.* New York: Erlbaum.

Ngo, C. T., Sargent, J., & Dopkins, S. (2007). Level of discrimination for recognition judgments reduced following the recognition of semantically related words. *Journal of Memory and Language, 57,* 415–436.

Nickerson, R. S. (1984). Retrieval inhibition from part-set cuing: A persistent enigma in memory research. *Memory & Cognition, 12,* 531–552.

Nickerson, R. S., & Adams, M. J. (1979). Long-term memory for a common object. *Cognitive Psychology, 11,* 287–307.

Nicolas, S., & Worthen, J. B. (2009). Adult age differences in memory for distinctive information: Evidence from the bizarreness effect. *Quarterly Journal of Experimental Psychology, 62,* 1983–1990.

Niedwieska, A. (2003) Misleading postevent information and flashbulb memories. *Memory, 11,* 594–558.

Niewiadomski, M. W., & Hockley, W. E. (2001). Interrupting recognition memory: Tests of familiarity-based accounts of the revelation effect. *Memory & Cognition, 29,* 1130–1138.

Nigro, G., & Neisser, U. (1983). Point of view in personal memories. *Cognitive Psychology, 15,* 467–482.

Nisbett, R. E., & Wilson, T. D. (1977). Telling more than we can know: Verbal reports on mental processes. *Psychological Review, 84,* 231–259.

Nissen, M. J., & Bullemer, P. (1987). Attentional requirements of learning: Evidence from performance measures. *Cognitive Psychology, 19,* 1–32.

Nittono, H., Suehiro, M., & Hori, T. (2002). Word imagability and N400 in an incidental memory paradigm. *International Journal of Pychophysiology, 44,* 219–229.

Noice, T., & Noice, H. (2002). Very long-term recall and recognition of well-learned material. *Applied Cognitive Psychology, 16,* 259–272.

Noice, H., & Noice, T. (2006). What studies of actors and acting can tell us about memory and cognitive functioning. *Current Directions in Psychological Science, 15,* 14–18.

Norman, K. A., Newman, E. L., & Detre, G. (2007). A neural network model of retrieval induced forgetting. *Psychological Review, 114,* 887–953.

Norman, K. A., & Schacter, D. L. (1997). False recognition in younger and older adults: Exploring the characteristics of illusory memories. *Memory & Cognition, 25,* 838–848.

Nosofsky, R. M. (1988). Exemplar-based accounts of relations between classification, recognition, and typicality. *Journal of Experimental Psychology: Learning, Memory, and Cognition, 14,* 700–708.

Novak, D. L., & Mather, M. (2009). The tenacious nature of memory binding for arousing items. *Memory & Cognition, 37,* 945–952.

Nyberg, L., Cabeza, R., & Tulving, E. (1996). PET studies of encoding and retrieval: The HERA model. *Psychonomic Bulletin & Review, 3,* 135–148.

Nyberg, L., Maitland, S. B., Rönnlund, M., Bäckman, L., Dixon, R. A., Wahlin, A., & Nilsson, L. (2003). Selective adult age differences in an age-invariant multifactor model of declarative memory. *Psychology and Aging, 18,* 149–160.

Oakhill, J., Garnham, A., & Reynolds, D. (2005). Immediate activation of stereotypical gender information. *Memory & Cognition, 33,* 972–983.

Oberle, C. D., McBeath, M. K., Madigan, S. C., & Sugar, T. G. (2005). The Galileo bias: A naïve conceptual belief that influences people's perceptions and performance in a ball-dropping task. *Journal of Experimental Psychology: Learning, Memory and Cognition, 31,* 643–653.

O'Connor, M., Verfaellie, M., & Cermak, L. S. (1995). Clinical differentiation of amnesic subtypes. In A. D. Baddeley, B. A. Wilson, & F. N. Watts (Eds.), *Handbook of Memory Disorders,* pp. 53–80. New York: Wiley.

Odegard, T. N., Lampinen, J. M., & Wirth-Beaumont, E. T. (2004). Organisation and retrieval: the generation of event clusters. *Memory, 12,* 685–695.

O'Keefe, J., & Dostrovsky, J. (1971). The hippocampus as a spatial map. *Brain Research, 34,* 171–175.

Olafson, K. M., & Ferraro, F. R. (2001). Effects of emotional state on lexical decision performance. *Brain and Cognition, 45,* 15–20.

Oliphant, G. W. (1982). Repetition and recency effects in word recognition. *Australian Journal of Psychology, 35,* 393–403.

Opacic, T., Stevens, C., & Tillmann, B. (2009). Unspoken knowledge: Implicit learning of structured human dance movement. *Journal of Experimental Psychology: Learning, Memory, and Cognition, 35,* 1570–1577.

O'Reilly, R. C., & Rudy, J. W. (2001). Conjunctive representations in learning and memory: Principles of cortical and hippocampal function. *Psychological Review, 108,* 311–345.

Ornstein, P. A., Naus, M. J., & Liberty, C. (1975). Rehearsal and organization processes in children's memory. *Child Development 46,* 818–830.

Ortony, A., Turner, T. J., & Antos, S. J. (1983). A puzzle about affect and recognition memory. *Journal of Experimental Psychology: Learning, Memory, and Cognition, 9,* 725–729.

Oswald, K. M., Serra, M., & Krishna, A. (2006). Part-list cuing in speeded recognition and free recall. *Memory & Cognition, 34,* 518–526.

Otani, H., & Hodge, M. H. (1991). Does hypermnesia occur in recognition and cued recall? *American Journal of Psychology, 104,* 101–116.

Pansky, A., & Koriat, A. (2004). The basic-level convergence effect in memory distortions. *Psychological Science, 15,* 52–59.

Papanicolaou, A. C., Simos, P. G., Castillo, E. M., Breier, J. I., Katz, J. S., & Wright, A. A. (2002). The hippocampus and memory of verbal and pictoral material. *Learning and Memory, 9,* 99–104.

Paris, S. C., & Lindaur, B. K. (1976). The role of inference in children's comprehension and memory for sentences. *Cognitive Psychology, 8,* 217–227.

Park, D. C., Hertzog, C., Kidder, D. P., Morrell, R. W., & Mayhorn, C. B. (1997). Effect of age on event-based and time-based prospective memory. *Psychology and Aging, 12,* 314–327.

Park, D. C., Nisbett, R., & Heeden, T. (1999). Aging, culture, and cognition. *Journals of Gerontology: Psychological Sciences, 54B,* P75–P84.

Parker, E. S., Birnbaum, I. M., Weingartner, H., Hartley, J. T., Stillman, R. C., & Lyatt, R. J. (1980). Retrograde enhancement of human memory. *Psychopharmacology, 69,* 219–222.

Parker, J. F. (1995). Age differences in source monitoring of performed and imagined actions on immediate and delayed tests. *Journal of Experimental Child Psychology, 60,* 84–101.

Parks, T. E. (1965). Post-retinal visual storage. *American Journal of Psychology, 78,* 145–147.

Parmentier, F. B. R., Tremblay, S., & Jones, D. M. (2004). Exploring the suffix effect in serial visuospatial short-term memory. *Psychonomic Bulletin & Review, 11,* 289–295.

Pashler, H., Rohrer, D., Cepeda, N. J., & Carpenter, S. K. (2007). Enhancing learning and retarding forgetting: Choices and consequences. *Psychonomic Bulletin & Review, 14,* 187–193.

Patterson, K., & Hodges, J. R. (1995). Disorders of semantic memory. In A. D. Baddeley, B. A. Wilson, & F. N. Watts (Eds.), *Handbook of Memory Disorders,* pp. 167–186. New York: Wiley.

Patternson, K. E., Meltzer, R. H., & Mandler, G. (1971). Inter-response times in categorized free recall. *Journal of Verbal Learning and Verbal Behavior, 10,* 417–426.

Paivio, A. (1969). Mental imagery in associative learning and memory. *Psychological Review, 76,* 241–263.

Pavlov, I. P., (1923). New researchers on conditioned reflexes. *Science, 58,* 359–361.

Payne, D. G. (1987). Hypermnesia and reminiscence in recall: A historical and empirical review. *Psychological Bulletin, 101,* 5–27.

Payne, J. D., Stickgold, R., Swanberg, K., & Kensinger, E. A. (2008). Sleep preferentially enhances memory for emotional components of scenes. *Psychological Science, 19,* 781–788.

Pearse, S. A., Isherwood, S., Hrouda, D., Richardson, P. H., Erskine, A., & Skinner, J. (1990). Memory and pain: Tests of mood congruity and state dependent learning in experimentally induced and clinical pain. *Pain, 43,* 187–193.

Pecher, D., Zeelenberg, R., & Barsalou, L. W. (2003). Verifying different-modality properties for concepts produces switching costs. *Psychological Science, 14,* 119–124.

Pellegrino, J. W. (1971). A general measure of organization in free recall for variable unit size and internal sequential consistency. *Behavior Research Methods & Instruments, 3,* 241–246.

Pelosi, L., Geesken, J. M., Holly, M., Hayward, M., & Blumhardt, L. D. (1997). Working memory impairment in early multiple sclerosis: Evidence from an event-related potential study of patients with clinically isolated myelopathy. *Brain, 120,* 2039–2058.

Penfield, W. (1955). The permanent record of the stream of consciousness. *Acta Psychologica, 11,* 47–69.

Pennington, N., & Hastie, R. (1986). Evidence evaluation in complex decision making. *Journal of Personality and Social Psychology, 51,* 242–258.

Pennington, N., & Hastie, R. (1988). Explanation-based decision making: Effects of memory structure on judgment. *Journal of Experimental Psychology: Learning, Memory and Cognition, 14,* 521–533.

Pennington, N., & Hastie, R. (1992). Explaining the evidence: Tests of the story model for juror decision making. *Journal of Personality and Social Psychology, 62,* 189–206.

Perales J. C., & Shanks, D. R. (2007). Models of covariation-based causal judgment: A review and synthesis. *Psychonomic Bulletin & Review, 14,* 577–596.

Perfect, T. J. (1994). What can Brinley plots tell us about cognitive aging? *Journal of Gerontology: Psychological Sciences, 49,* P60–P64.

Perfect, T. J., Moulin, C. J. A., Conway, M. A., & Perry, E. (2002). Assessing the inhibitory account of retrieval-induced forgetting with implicit-memory tests. *Journal of Experimental Psychology: Learning, Memory and Cognition, 28,* 1111–1119.

Perfect, T. J., Stark, L., Tree, J. J., Moulin, C. J. A., Ahmed, L., & Hutter, R. (2004). Transfer appropriate forgetting: The cue-dependent nature of retrieval-induced forgetting. *Journal of Memory and Language, 51,* 399–417.

Perham, N., Marsh, J. E., & Jones, D. M. (2009). Syntax and serial recall: How language supports short-term memory for order. *Quarterly Journal of Experimental Psychology, 62,* 1285–1293.

Peters, R., & McGee, R. (1982). Cigarette smoking and state-dependent memory. *Psychopharmacology, 76,* 232–235.

Peterson, L. R., & Johnson, S. F. (1971). Some effects of minimizing articulation of short-term retention. *Journal of Verbal Learning and Verbal Behavior, 10,* 346–354.

Peterson, L. R., & Peterson, M. J. (1959). Short-term retention of individual verbal items. *Journal of Experimental Psychology, 58,* 193–198.

Petrician, R., Moscovitch, M., & Schimmack, U. (2008). Cognitive resources, valence, and memory retrieval of emotional events in older adults. *Psychology and Aging, 23,* 585–594.

Pexman, P. M., Hargreaves, I. S., Edwards, J. D., Henry, L. C., & Goodyear, B. G. (2007). The neural consequences of semantic richness: When more comes to mind, less activation is observed. *Psychological Science, 18,* 401–406.

Peynircioğlu, Z. F., & Tekcan, A. I. (1993). Revelation effect: Effort or priming does not create the sense of familiarity. *Journal of Experimental Psychology: Learning, Memory and Cognition, 19,* 382–388.

Pezdek, K., Blandon-Gitlin, I., & Gabbay, P. (2006). Imagination and memory: Does imagining implausible events lead to false autobiographical memories? *Psychonomic Bulletin & Review, 13,* 764–769.

Pezdek, K., Blandon-Gitlin, I., Lam, S., Hart, R. E., & Schooler, J. W. (2006). Is knowing believing? The role of event plausibility and background knowledge in planting false beliefs about the personal past. *Memory & Cognition, 34,* 1628–1635.

Pezdek, K., Finger, K., & Hodge, D. (1997). Planting false childhood memories: The role of event plausibility. *Psychological Science, 8,* 437–441.

Phelps, E. A. (2006). Emotion and cognition: Insights from studies of the human amygdala. *Annual Review of Psychology, 57,* 27–53.

Pickel, K. L. (1998). Unusualness and threat as possible causes of "weapon focus." *Memory, 6,* 277–295.

Pickel, K. L. (2004). When a lie becomes the truth: The effects of self-generated misinformation on eyewitness memory. *Memory, 12,* 14–26.

Pillemer, D. B. (2001). Momentous events and the life story. *Journal of General Psychology, 5,* 123–134.

Pillemer, D. B. (2009). "Hearing the news" versus "being there": Comparing flashbulb memories and recall of first hand experiences. In O. Luminet & A. Curci (Eds.), *Flashbulb Memories: New Issues and New Perspectives*, pp. 125–140. New York: Psychology Press.

Pillon, B., Ertle, S., Deweer, B., Bonnet, A. Vidailhet, M., & Dubois, B. (1997). Memory for spatial location in "de novo" Parkinsonian patients. *Neuropschologia, 35,* 221–228.

Piolino, P., Belliard, S., Desgranges, B., Perron, M., & Eustache, F. (2003). Autobiographical memory and autonoetic consciousness in a case of semantic dementia. *Cognitive Neuropsychology, 20,* 619–639.

Piolino, P., Desgranges, B., Clarys, D., Guillery-Girard, B., Taconnat, L., Isigrini, M., & Eustache, F. (2006). Autobiographical memory, autonoetic consciousness, and self-perspective in aging. *Psychology and Aging, 21,* 510–525.

Pirolli, P. L., & Anderson, J. R. (1985). The role of practice in fact retrieval. *Journal of Experimental Psychology: Learning, Memory, and Cognition, 11,* 136–153.

Plumert, J. M. (1994). Flexibility in children's use of spatial and categorical organizational strategies in recall. *Developmental Psychology, 30,* 738–747.

Poletiek, F. H., & Wolters, G. (2009). What is learned about fragments in artificial grammar learning? A transitional probabilities approach. *Quarterly Journal of Experimental Psychology, 62,* 868–876.

Pollack, I. (1970). A nonparametric procedure for evaluation of true and false positives. *Behavioral Research Methods & Instruments, 2,* 155–156.

Pollio, H. R., Richards, S., & Lucas, R. (1969). Temporal properties of category recall. *Journal of Verbal Learning and Verbal Behavior, 8,* 529–536.

Poole, D. A., & Lindsay, D. S. (2001). Children's eyewitness reports after exposure to misinformation from parents. *Journal of Experimental Psychology: Applied, 7,* 27–50.

Porter, S., Birt, A. R., Yuille, J. C., & Lehman, D. R. (2000). Negotiating false memories: Interviewer and rememberer characteristics relate to memory distortion. *Psychological Science, 11,* 507–510.

Portrat, S., Barrouillet, P., & Camos, V. (2008). Time-related decay or interference-based forgetting in working memory? *Journal of Experimental Psychology: Learning, Memory, and Cognition, 34,* 1561–1564.

Porter, S., & Peace, K. A. (2007). The scars of memory: A prospective, longitudinal investigation of the consistency of traumatic and positive emotional memories in adulthood. *Psychological Science, 18,* 435–441.

Posner, M. I., & Keele, S. W. (1968). On the genesis of abstract ideas. *Journal of Experimental Psychology, 77,* 353–363.

Posner, M. I., & Keele, S. W. (1970). Retention of abstract ideas. *Journal of Experimental Psychology, 83,* 304–308.

Posner, M. I., & Raichle, M. E. (1994). *Images of Mind.* New York: Scientific American Library.

Postman, L., & Adams, P. A. (1956). Studies in incidental learning: IV. The interaction of orienting tasks and stimulus materials. *Journal of Experimental Psychology, 51,* 329–333.

Postman, L., Adams, P. A., & Philips, L. W. (1955). Studies in incidental learning: II. The effects of association value and of the method of testing. *Journal of Experimental Psychology, 49,* 1–10.

Postman, L., & Keppel, G. (1977). Conditions of cumulative proactive inhibition. *Journal of Experimental Psychology: General, 106,* 376–403.

Postman, L., & Stark, K. (1969). Role of response availability in transfer and interference. *Journal of Experimental Psychology, 79,* 168–177.

Pothos, E. M. (2005). Expectations about stimulus structure in implicit learning. *Memory & Cognition, 33,* 171–181.

Pothos, E. M. (2007). Theories of artificial grammar learning. *Psychological Bulletin, 133,* 227–244.

Potts, G. R. (1972). Information processing strategies used in the encoding of linear orderings. *Journal of Verbal Learning and Verbal Behavior, 11,* 727–740.

Powell, J. L. (1988). A test of the knew-it-all-along effect in the 1984 presidential statewide elections. *Journal of Applied Social Psychology, 18,* 760–773.

Prado, J., van der Henst, J-B., & Noveck, I. A. (2008). Spatial associations in relational reasoning: Evidence for a SNARC-like effect. *Quarterly Journal of Experimental Psychology, 61,* 1143–1150.

Presson, C. C., DeLange, N., & Hazelrigg, M. D. (1989). Orientation specificity in spatial memory: What makes a path different from a map of a path? *Journal of Experimental Psychology: Learning, Memory and Cognition, 15,* 887–897.

Pretkanis, A. R., Greenwald, A. G., Leippe, M. R., & Baumgarder, M. H. (1988). In search of reliable persuasion effects: III. The sleeper effect is dead: Long live the sleeper effect. *Journal of Personality and Social Psychology, 54,* 203–218.

Prizzolo, F. J., Hansch, E. C., Mortimer, J. A., Webster, D. D., & Kuskowski, M. A. (1982). Dementia in Parkinson's disease: A neuropsychological analysis. *Brain and Cognition, 1,* 71–83.

Prull, M. W., Crandall Dawes, L. L., McLeish Martin, A., Rosenberg, H. F., & Light, L. L. (2006). Recollection and familiarity in recognition memory: Adult age differences and neuropsychological test correlates. *Psychology and Aging, 21,* 107–118.

Prull, M. W., Light, L. L., Collett, M. E., & Kennison, R. F. (1998). Age-related differences in memory illusions: Revelation effect. *Aging, Neuropsychology and Cognition, 5,* 147–165

Pulvermüller, F., Lutzenberger, W., & Preissl, H. (1999). Nouns and verbs in the intact brain: Evidence from event-related potentials and high-frequency cortical responses. *Cerrebral Cortex, 9,* 497–506.

Quesada, J.F, Kintsch, W. and Gomez, E. (2001) Complex problem-solving: A field in search of a definition? *Theoretical Issues in Ergonomics Science, 6,* 117–131.

Quinn, P. C., Eimas, P. D., & Rosenkrantz, S. L. (1993). Evidence for representations of perceptually similar natural categories by 3-month-old and 4-month-old infants. *Perception, 22,* 463–475.

Quinn, P.C., & Tanaka, J. W. (2007). Early development of perceptual expertise: Within-basic-level categorization experience facilitates the formation of subordinate-level category representation in 6- to 7-month-old infants. *Memory & Cognition, 35,* 1422–1431.

Raaijmakers, J. G. W., & Shiffrin, R. M. (1980). SAM: A theory of probabilistic search of associative memory. *The Psychology of Learning and Motivation, 14,* 207–262.

Raaijmakers, J. G. W., & Shiffrin, R. M. (1981). Search of associative memory. *Psychological Review, 88,* 93–134.

Raaijmakers, J. G. W., & Shiffrin, R. M. (1992). Models for recall and recognition. *Annual Review of Psychology, 43,* 205–234.

Racsmány, M., & Conway, M. A. (2006). Episodic inhibition. *Journal of Experimental Psychology: Learning, Memory and Cognition, 32,* 44–57.

Racsmány, M., Conway, M. A., Garab, E. A., & Nagmáté, G. (2008). Memory awareness following episodic inhibition. *Quarterly Journal of Experimental Psychology, 61,* 525–534.

Radvansky, G. A. (1999). Memory retrieval and suppression: The inhibition of situation models. *Journal of Experimental Psychology: General, 128,* 563–579.

Radvansky, G. A., Carlson-Radvansky, J., & Irwin, D. E. (1995). Uncertainty in estimating distances from memory. *Memory & Cognition, 23,* 596–606.

Radvansky, G. A., & Copeland, D. E. (2006) Memory retrieval and interference: Working memory issues. *Journal of Memory and Language, 55,* 33–46.

Radvansky, G. A., Copeland, D. E., & von Hippel, W. (2010). Stereotype activation, inhibition, and aging. *Journal of Experimental Social Psychology, 46,* 51–60.

Radvansky, G. A. & Dijkstra, K. (2007) Aging and situation model processing. *Psychonomic Bulletin & Review, 14,* 1027–1042.

Radvansky, G. A., Fleming, K. J., & Simmons, J. A. (1995). Timbre reliance in nonmusicians' and musicians' memory for melodies. *Music Perception, 13,* 127–140.

Radvansky, G. A., Gerard, L. D., Zacks, R. T., & Hasher, L. (1990). Younger and older adults' use of mental models as representations of text materials. *Psychology and Aging, 5,* 209–214.

Radvansky, G. A., Gibson, B. S., & McNerney, M. W. (2009). Synesthesia, memory, and comprehension. Unpublished manuscript

Radvansky, G. A., Lynchard, N. N. A., & von Hippel, W. (2009). Aging and stereotype deactivation. *Aging, Neuropsychology and Cognition, 16,* 22–32.

Radvansky, G. A., and Potter, J. K. (2000). Source cuing: Memory for melodies. *Memory and Cognition, 28,* 693–699.

Radvansky, G. A., Spieler, D. H., & Zacks, R. T. (1993). Mental model organization. *Journal of Experimental Psychology: Learning, Memory, and Cognition, 19,* 95–114.

Radvansky, G. A., Wyer, R. S., Curiel, J. M., & Lutz, M. F. (1997). Situation models and abstract ownership relations. *Journal of Experimental Psychology: Learning, Memory, and Cognition, 23,* 1233–1246.

Radvansky, G. A., & Zacks, R. T. (1991). Mental models and the fan effect. *Journal of Experimental Psychology: Learning, Memory, and Cognition, 17,* 940–953.

Radvansky, G. A., Zwaan, R. A., Curiel, J. M., & Copeland, D. E. (2001). Situation models and aging. *Psychology and Aging, 16,* 145–160.

Radvansky, G. A., Zwaan, R. A., Federico, T., & Franklin, N. (1998). Retrieval from temporally organized situation models. *Journal of Experimental Psychology: Learning, Memory, and Cognition, 24,* 1224–1237.

Ranganath, C., & Pallar, K. A. (1999). Frontal brain activity during episodic and semantic retrieval: Insights from event-related potentials. *Journal of Cognitive Neuroscience, 11,* 598–609.

Rahhal, T. A., May, C. P., & Hasher, L. (2002). Truth and character: Sources that older adults can remember. *Psychological Science, 13,* 101–105

Rajaram, S. (1993). Remembering and knowing: Two means of access to the personal past. *Memory & Cognition, 21,* 89–102.

Rajaram, S., & Coslett, H. B. (2000). Conceptual associative learning in amnesia: A case study. *Journal of Memory and Language, 43,* 291–315.

Rajaram, S., & Pereira-Pararin, L. P. (2007). Collab-oration can improve individual recognition memory: Evidence from immediate and delayed tests. *Psychonomic Bulletin & Review, 14,* 95–100.

Rand, G., & Wapner, S. (1967). Postural states as a factor in memory. *Journal of Verbal Learning and Verbal Behavior, 6,* 268–271.

Randolph, J. J., Arnett, P. A., & Higginson, C. I. (2001). Metamemory and tested cognitive functioning in multiple sclerosis. *Clinical Neuropsychologist, 15,* 357–368.

Raney, G. E. (2003). A context-dependent representation model for explaining text repetition effects. *Psychonomic Bulletin & Review, 10,* 15–28.

Rasch, B., & Born, J. (2008). Reactivation and consolidation of memory during sleep. *Current Directions in Psychological Science, 17,* 188–192.

Rathbone, C. J., Moulin, C. J. A., & Conway, M. A. (2008). Self-centered memories: The reminiscence bump and the self. *Memory & Cognition, 36,* 1403–1414.

Rawson, K. A., & Van Overschelde, J. P. (2008). How does knowledge promote memory? The distinctiveness theory of skilled memory. *Journal of Memory and Language, 58,* 646–668.

Ray, S., & Bates, M. E. (2006). Acute alcohol effects on repetition priming and word recognition memory with equivalent memory cues. *Brain and Cognition, 60,* 118–127.

Ray, S., Bates, M. E., & Bly, B. M. (2004). Alcohol's dissociation of implicit and explicit memory processes: Implications of a parallel distributed processing model of semantic priming. *Experimental and Clinical Psychopharmacology, 12,* 118–125.

Read, J. D. (1994). Understanding bystander misidentifications: The role of familiarity and contextual knowledge. In D. F. Ross, J. D. Read, and M. P. Toglia (Eds.), *Adult Eyewitness Testimony: Current Trends and Developments,* pp. 56–79. Cambridge: Cambridge University Press.

Read, J. D. (1996). From a passing thought to a false memory is two minutes: Confusing real and illusory events. *Psychonomic Bulletin & Review, 31,* 105–111.

Reber, A. S. (1967). Implicit learning of artificial grammars. *Journal of Verbal Learning and Verbal Behavior, 6,* 855–863.

Reber, A. S. (1969). Transfer of syntactic structure in synthetic languages. *Journal of Experimental Psychology, 81,* 115–119.

Reder, L. M. (1987). Strategy selection in question answering. *Cognitive Psychology, 19,* 90–138.

Reder, L. M., & Cleermans, A. (1990). The role of partial matches in comprehension: The Moses illusion revisited. *Psychology of Learning and Motivation, 25,* 233–258.

Reder, L. M., & Kusbit, G. W. (1991). Locus of the Moses Illusion: Imperfect encoding, retrieval or match? *Journal of Memory and Language, 30,* 385–406.

Reder, L. M., Oates, J. M., Thornton. E. R., Quinlan, J. J., Kaufer, A., & Sauer, J. (2006). Drug-induced amnesia hurts recognition, but once for memories that can be unitized. *Psychological Science, 17,* 562–567.

Reder, L. M., Wible, C., & Martin, J. (1986). Differential memory changes with age: Exact retrieval versus plausible inference. *Journal of Experimental Psychology: Learning, Memory, and Cognition, 12,* 72–81.

Reed, C. L., & Vinson, N. G. (1996). Conceptual effects on representational momentum. *Journal of Experimental Psychology: Human Perception and Performance, 22,* 839–850.

Rehder, B., & Hastie, R. (2001). Causal knowledge and categories: The effects of causal beliefs on categorization, induction, and similarity. *Journal of Experimental Psychology: General, 130,* 323–360.

Rehder, B., & Ross, B. H. (2001). Abstract coherent categories. *Journal of Experimental Psychology: Learning, Memory, and Cognition, 27,* 1261–1275.

Reitman, J. S., & Rueter, H. H. (1980). Organization revealed by recall orders and confirmed by pauses. *Cognitive Psychology, 12,* 554–581.

Rescorla, R. A., & Wagner, A. R. (1972). A theory of Pavlovian conditioning: Variations of the effectiveness of reinforcement and nonreinforcement. In A. H. Black & W. F. Prokasy (Eds.), *Classical Conditioning II: Current Research and Theory* (pp. 64–99). New York: Appleton-Century-Crofts.

Reuter-Lorenz, P. A., & Cappell, K. A. (2008). Neurocognitive aging and the compensation hypothesis. *Current Directions in Psychological Science, 17,* 177–182.

Reysen, M. B. (2003). The effects of social pressure on group recall. *Memory & Cognition, 31,* 1163–1168.

Reysen, M. B. (2007). The effects of social pressure on false memories. *Memory & Cognition, 35,* 59–65.

Reysen, M. B., & Adair, S. A. (2008). Social processing improves recall performance. *Psychonomic Bulletin & Review, 15,* 197–201.

Rhodes, G., Jeffery, L., Watson, T. L., Clifford, C. W. G., & Nakayama, K. (2003). Fitting the mind to the world: Face adaptation and attractiveness after effects. *Psychological Science, 14,* 558–566.

Rhodes, G., & Tremewan, T. (1996). Averageness, exaggeration, and facial attractiveness. *Psychological Science, 7,* 105–110.

Rich, A. N., & Mattingly, J. B. (2002). Anomalous perception in synaesthesia: A cognitive neuroscience perspective. *Nature Reviews: Neuroscience, 3,* 43–51.

Richardson, R., Guanowsky, V., Ahlers, S. T., & Riccio, D. D. (1984). Role of body temperature in the onset of, and recovery from, hypothermia-induced anterograde amnesia. *Physiological Psychology, 12,* 125–132.

Richardson, R., & Hayne, H. (2007). You can't take it with you: The translation of memory across development. *Current Directions in Psychological Science,16,* 223–227.

Riccio, D. C., Millin, P. M., & Gisquet-Verrier, P. (2003). Retrograde amnesia: Forgetting back. *Current Directions in Psychological Science, 12,* 41–44.

Riefer, D. M., & Rouder, J. N. (1992). A multinomial modeling analysis of the mnemonic benefits of bizarre imagery. *Memory & Cognition, 20,* 601–611.

Rinck, M., and Bower, G. H. (1995). Anaphora resolution and the focus of attention in situation models. *Journal of Memory and Language, 34,* 110–131.

Rinck, M., Haehnel, A., Bower, G. H., & Glowalla, U. (1997). The metrics of spatial situation models. *Journal of Experimental Psychology: Learning, Memory, and Cognition, 23,* 622–637.

Rinck, M., Hähnel, A., & Becker, G. (2001). Using temporal information to construct, update, and retrieve situation models of narratives. *Journal of Experimental Psychology: Learning, Memory, and Cognition, 27,* 67–80.

Rips, L. J., Shoben, E. J., & Smith, E. E. (1973). Semantic distance and the verification of semantic relations. *Journal of Verbal Learning and Verbal Behavior, 12,* 1–20.

Roberts, K. P., & Blades, M. (2000). Children's memory and source monitoring of real-life and televised events. *Journal of Applied Developmental Psychology, 20,* 575–596.

Roberts, W. T., & Higham, P. A. (2002). Selecting accurate statements from the cognitive interview using confidence ratings. *Journal of Experimental Psychology: Applied, 8,* 33–43.

Robinson, M. D., & Johnson, J. T. (1998). How not to enhance the confidence-accuracy relation: The detrimental effects of attention to the identification process. *Law and Human Behavior, 22,* 409–428.

Roediger, H. L. (1980). Memory metaphors in cognitive psychology. *Memory & Cognition, 8,* 231–246.

Roediger, H. L., & Blaxton, T. A. (1987). Effects of varying modality, surface features, and retention interval on priming in word-fragment completion. *Memory & Cognition, 15,* 379–388.

Roediger, H. L., and Crowder, R. G. (1976). A serial position effect in recall of United States presidents. *Bulletin of Psychonomic Society, 8,* 275–278.

Roediger, H. L., & Geraci, L. (2007). Aging and the misinformation effect: A neurological analysis. *Journal of Experimental Psychology: Learning, Memory, and Cognition, 33,* 321–334.

Roediger, H. L., & Karpicke, J. D. (2006). Test-enhanced learning: Taking memory tests improves long-term retention. *Psychological Science, 17,* 249–255.

Roediger, H. L., & McDermott, K. B. (1995). Creating false memories: Remembering words not presented in lists. *Journal of Experimental Psychology: Learning, Memory, and Cognition, 21,* 803–814.

Roediger, H. L., Meade, M. L., & Bergman, E. T. (2001). Social contagion of memory. *Psychonomic Bulletin & Review, 8,* 365–371.

Roediger, H. L., Neely, J. H., & Blaxton, T. A. (1983). Inhibition from related primes in semantic memory retrieval: A reappraisal of Brown's (1979) paradigm. *Journal of Experimental Psychology: Learning, Memory, and Cognition, 9,* 478–485.

Roediger, H. L., Stellon, C. C., & Tulving, E. (1977). Inhibition from part-list cues and rate of recall. *Journal of Experimental Psychology: Human Learning and Memory, 3,* 174–188.

Roediger, H. L., Watson, J. M., McDermott, K. B., & Gallo, D. A. (2001). Factors that determine false recall: A multiple regression analysis. *Psychonomic Bulletin & Review, 8,* 385–407.

Roenker, D. L., Thompson, C. P, & Brown, S. C. (1971).Comparison of measures for the estimation of clustering in free recall. *Psychological Bulletin, 76,* 45–48.

Rohrer, D. (2003). The natural appearance of unnatural incline speed. *Memory & Cognition, 31,* 816–826.

Rohrer, D. & Pashler, H. E. (2003). Concurrent task effects on memory retrieval. *Psychonomic Bulletin & Review, 10,* 96–103.

Romani, C., & Martin, R. (1999). A deficit in the short-term retention of lexical-semantic information: Forgetting words but remembering a story. *Journal of Experimental Psychology: General, 128,* 56–77.

Rönnlund, M., Nyberg, L., Bäckman, L., & Nilsson, L-G., (2005). Stability, growth, and decline in adult life span development of declarative memory: Cross-sectional and longitudinal data from a population-based study. *Psychology and Aging, 20,* 3–18.

Rosch, E. (1975). Cognitive representations of semantic categories. *Journal of Experimental Psychology: General, 104,* 192–233.

Rosch, E., & Mervis, C. B. (1975). Family resemblances: Studies in the internal structure of categories. *Cognitive Psychology, 7,* 573–605.

Rosch, E., Mervis, C. B., Gray, W. D., Johnson, D. M., & Boyes-Braem, P. (1976). Basic objects in natural categories. *Cognitive Psychology, 8,* 382–439.

Ross, D. F., Ceci, S. J., Dunning, D., & Toglia, M. P. (1994). Unconscious transference and mistaken identity: When a witness misidentifies a familiar but innocent person. *Journal of Applied Psychology, 79,* 918–930.

Ross, L., Greene, D., & House, P. (1977). The "false consensus effect": An egocentric bias in social perception and attribution processes. *Journal of Experimental Social Psychology, 13,* 279–301.

Rossano, M. J., Warren, D. H, & Kenan, A. (1995). Orientation specificity: How general is it? *American Journal of Psychology, 108,* 359–380.

Rotello, C. M., & McMillan, N. A. (2006). Remember-know models as decision strategies in two experimental paradigms. *Journal of Memory and Language, 55,* 479–494.

Rouder, J. N., & Ratcliff, R. (2006). Comparing exemplar- and rule-based theories of categorization. *Current Directions in Psychological Science, 15,* 9–13.

Rovee-Collier, C. (1997). Dissociations in infant memory: Rethinking the development of implicit and explicit memory. *Psychological Review, 104,* 467–498.

Rovee-Collier, C., & Cuevas, K. (2009). The development of infant memory. In M. L. Courage & N. Cowan (Eds.) *The Development of Memory in Infancy and Childhood*, pp. 11–41. New York: Psychology Press.

Rovee-Collier, C., & Fagan, J. W. (1981). The retrieval of memory in early infancy. *Advances in Infancy Research, 1,* 225–254.

Rubin, D. C. (1982). On the retention function for autobiographical memory. *Journal of Verbal Learning & Verbal Behavior, 21,* 21–38.

Rubin, D. C. (1998). Knowledge and judgments about events that occurred prior to birth: The measurement of the persistence of information. *Psychonomic Bulletin & Review, 5,* 397–400.

Rubin, D.C. (2006). The basic-systems model of episodic memory. *Perspectives on Psychological Science, 1,* 277–311.

Rubin, D. C., and Baddeley, A. D. (1989). Telescoping is not time compression: A model of the dating of autobiographical events. *Memory and Cognition, 17,* 653–661.

Rubin, D. C., & Berntsen, D. (2003). Life scripts help to maintain autobiographical memories of highly positive, but not highly negative, events. *Memory & Cognition, 31,* 1–14.

Rubin, D. C., Berntsen, D., & Bohni, M. K. (2008). A memory-based model of posttraumatic stress disorder: Evaluating basic assumptions underlying the PTSD diagnosis. *Psychological Review, 115,* 985–1011.

Rubin, D. C., Boals, A., & Berntsen, D. (2008). Memory in posttraumatic stress disorder: Properties of voluntary and involuntary, traumatic and nontraumatic autobiographical memories in people with and without posttraumatic stress disorder symptoms. *Journal of Experimental Psychology: General, 137,* 591–614.

Rubin, D. C., Groth, E., & Goldsmith, D. J. (1984). Olfactory cuing of autobiographical memory. *American Journal of Psychology, 97,* 493–507.

Rubin, D. C., Rahhal, T. A., & Poon, L. W. (1998). Things learned in early adulthood are remembered best. *Memory & Cognition, 26,* 3–19.

Rubin, D. C., Schrauf, R. W., & Greenberg, D. L. (2003). Belief and recollection of autobiographical memories. *Memory & Cognition, 31,* 887–901.

Rundus, D. (1971). Analysis of rehearsal processes in free recall. *Journal of Experimental Psychology, 89,* 63–77.

Russo, R., Parkin, A. J., Taylor, S. R., & Wilks, J. (1998). Revising current two-process accounts of spacing effects in memory. *Journal of Experimental Psychology: Learning, Memory, and Cognition, 24,* 161–172.

Ryan, J. D., Althoff, R. R., Whitlow, S., & Cohen, N. J. (2000). Amnesia is a deficit in relational memory. *Psychological Science, 11,* 454–460.

Rypma, B., Prabhakaran, V., Desmond, J. E., & Gabriei, D. E. (2001). Age differences in prefrontal cortical activity in working memory. *Psychology and Aging, 16,* 371–384.

Sachs, J. S. (1967). Recognition memory for syntactic and semantic aspects of connected discourse. *Perception & Psychophysics, 2,* 437–442.

Sachs, J. S. (1974). Memory in reading and listening to discourse. *Memory & Cognition, 2,* 95–100.

Sadalla, E. K., Burroughs, J., & Staplin, L. J. (1980). Reference points in spatial cognition. *Journal of Experimental Psychology: Human Learning and Memory, 5,* 516–528.

Sadek, J. R., Johnson, S. A., White, D. A., Salmon, D. P., Taylor, K. I., DeLaPena, J. H., Paulsen, J. S., Heaton, R. K., & Grant, I. (2004). Retrograde amnesia in dementia: Comparison of HIV-associated dementia, Alzheimer's disease, and Huntington's disease. *Neuropsychology, 18,* 692–699.

Safer, M. A., Bonanno, G. A., & Field, N. P. (2001). "It was never that bad": Biased recall of grief and long-term adjustment to the death of a spouse. *Memory, 9,* 195–204.

Safer, M. A., Christianson, S., Autry, M. W., & Österlund, K. (1998). Tunnel memory for traumatic events. *Applied Cognitive Psychology, 12,* 99–117.

Sagar, H. J., Cohen, N. J., Sullivan, E. V., Corkin, S., & Growden, J. H. (1988). Remote memory function in Alzheimer's disease and Parkinson's disease. *Brain, 111,* 185–206.

Sagar, H. J., Sullivan, E. V., Gabrieli, J. D. E., Corkin, S., & Growdon, J. H. (1988). Temporal ordering and short-term memory deficits in Parkinson's disease. *Journal of Clinical and Experimental Neuropsychology,* 11, 525–539.

Sahakyan, L. (2004). Destructive effects of "forget" instructions. *Psychonomic Bulletin & Review, 11,* 555–559.

Sahakyan, L., Delaney, P. F., & Goodmon, L. B. (2008). Honey, I already forgot that: Strategic control of directed forgetting in older and younger adults. *Psychology and Aging, 23,* 621–633.

Sahakyan, L., & Foster, N. L. (2009). Intentional forgetting of actions: Comparison of list-method and item-method directed forgetting. *Journal of Memory and Language, 61,* 134–152.

Salame, P., & Baddeley, A. (1989). Effects of background music on phonological short-term memory. *Quarterly Journal of Experimental Psychology, 41A,* 107–122.

Sallas, B., Mathews, R. C., Lane, S. M., & Sun, R. (2007). Developing rich and quickly accessed knowledge of an artificial grammar. *Memory & Cognition, 35,* 2118–2133.

Salthouse, T. A. (1996). The processing-speed theory of adult age differences in cognition. *Psychological Review, 103,* 403–428.

Salthouse, T. A., Berish, D. E., & Siedlecki, K. L. (2004). Construct validity and age sensitivity of prospective memory. *Memory & Cognition, 32,* 1133–1148.

Salthouse, T. A., & Pink, J. E. (2008). Why is working memory related to fluid intelligence? *Psychonomic Bulletin & Review, 15,* 364–371.

Salzman, I. J. (1953). The orienting task in incidental and intentional learning. *American Journal of Psychology, 64,* 593–598.

Salzman, I. J. (1956). Comparisons of incidental and intentional learning with different orienting tasks. *American Journal of Psychology, 69,* 274–277.

Sampaio, C., & Wang, R. F. (2008). Category-based errors and the accessibility of unbiased spatial memories: A retrieval model. *Journal of Experimental Psychology: Learning, Memory, and Cognition, 35,* 1331–1337.

Samuel, A. G. (1978). Organizational vs. retrieval factors in the development of digit span. *Journal of Experimental Child Psychology, 26,* 308–319.

Sanna, L. J., & Schwartz, N. (2004). Integrating temporal biases: The interplay of focal thoughts and accessibility experiences. *Psychological Science, 15,* 474–481.

Sanna, L. J., Schwartz, N., & Small, E. M. (2002). Accessibility experiences and the hindsight bias: I knew it all along versus it could never have happened. *Memory & Cognition, 30,* 1288–1296.

Santens, S., & Gevers, W. (2008). The SNARC effect does not imply a mental number line. *Cognition, 108,* 263–270.

Saunders, J., Fernandes, M., & Kosnes, L. (2009). Retrieval-induced forgetting and mental imagery. *Memory & Cognition, 37,* 819–828.

Saunders, J., & MacLeod, M. D. (2006). Can inhibition resolve retrieval competition through the control of spreading activation? *Memory & Cognition, 34,* 307–322.

Saults, J. S., Cowan, N., Sher, K. J., & Moreno, M. V. (2007). Differential effects of alcohol on working memory: Distinguishing multiple processes. *Experimental and Clinical psychopharmacology, 15,* 576–587.

Schacter, D. L. (1987). Implicit memory: History and current status. *Journal of Experimental Psychology: Learning, Memory, and Cognition, 13,* 501–518.

Schacter, D. L., & Badgaiyan, R. D. (2001). Neuroimaging of priming: New perspectives on implicit and explicit memory. *Current Directions in Psychological Science, 10,* 1–4.

Schacter, D. L., Cooper, L. A., & Delaney, S. M. (1990). Implicit memory for unfamiliar objects depends on access to structural descriptions. *Journal of Experimental Psychology: General, 119,* 5–24.

Schacter, D. L., Eich, J. E., & Tulving, E. (1978). Richard Semon's theory of memory. *Journal of Verbal Learning and Verbal Behavior, 17,* 721–743.

Scheck, P., Meeter, M., & Nelson, T. O. (2004). Anchoring effects in the absolute accuracy of immediate versus delayed judgments of learning. *Journal of Memory and Language, 51,* 71–79.

Schendan, H. E., & Kutas, M. (2007). Neurophysiological evidence for transfer appropriate processing of memory: Processing versus feature similarity. *Psychonomic Bulletin & Review, 14,* 612–619.

Schlagman, S., Kliegel, M., Schulz, J., & Kvavilashvili, L. (2009). Differential effects of age on involuntary and voluntary autobiographical memory. *Psychology and Aging, 24,* 397–411.

Schmidt, S. R. (2004). Autobiographical memories for the September 11th attacks: Reconstructive errors and emotional impairment of memory. *Memory & Cognition, 32,* 443–454.

Schmidt, S. R., & Saari, B. (2007). The emotional memory effect: Differential processing or item distinctiveness? *Memory & Cognition, 35,* 1905–1916.

Schmolck, H., Buffalo, E. A., & Squire, L. R. (2000). Memory distortions over time: Recollections of the O. J. Simpson trial verdict after 15 and 32 months. *Psychological Science, 11,* 39–45.

Schnorr, J. A., & Atkinson, R. C. (1969). Repetition versus imagery instructions in the short- and long-term retention of paired-associates. *Psychonomic Science, 15,* 183–184.

Schooler, J. W., & Engstler-Schooler, T. Y. (1990). Verbal overshadowing of visual memories: Some things are better left unsaid. *Cognitive Psychology, 22,* 36–71.

Scholey, A. B., & Fowles, K. A. (2002). Retrograde enhancement of kinesthetic memory by alcohol and by glucose. *Neurobiology of Learning and Memory, 78,* 477–483.

Schrauf, R. W., & Rubin, D. C. (1998). Bilinguial autobiographical memory in older adult immigrants: A test of cognitive explanations of the reminiscence bump and the linguistic encoding of memories. *Journal of Memory and Language, 39,* 437–457.

Schreiber, T. A. (1998). Effects of target set size on feelings of knowing and cued recall: Implications for the cue effectiveness and partial-retrieval hypotheses. *Memory & Cognition, 26,* 553–571.

Schreiber, T. A. & Nelson, D. L. (1998). The relation between feelings of knowing and the number of neighboring concepts linked to the test cue. *Memory & Cognition, 26,* 869–883.

Schwartz, B. L. (1994). Sources of information in metamemory: Judgments of learning and feelings of knowing. *Psychonomic Bulletin & Review, 1,* 357–375.

Schwartz, B. L. (2001). The relation of tip-of-the-tongue states to retrieval time. *Memory & Cognition, 29,* 117–126.

Schwartz, B. L. (2008). Working memory load differentially affects tip-of-the-tongue states and feeling-of-knowing judgments. *Memory & Cognition, 36,* 9–19.

Schwender, D., Kaiser, A., Klasing, S., Peter, K., and Poeppel, E. (1993). Explicit and implicit memory and mid-latency auditory evoked potentials during cardiac surgery. In B. Bonke (Ed.), *Memory and Awareness in Anesthesia,.* pp. 85–98. Upper Saddle River, NJ: Prentice-Hall.

Scoboria, A., Mazzoni, G., Kirsch, I., Milling, L. S. (2002). Immediate and persisting effects of misleading questions and hypnosis on memory reports. *Journal of Experimental Psychology: Applied, 8,* 26–32.

Scott, R. B., & Dienes, Z. (2008). The conscious, the unconscious, and familiarity. *Journal of Experimental Psychology: Learning, Memory, and Cognition, 34,* 1264–1288.

Scoville, W. B., & Milner, B. (1957). Loss of recent memory after bilateral hippocampal lesions. *Journal of Neurology, Neurosurgery, and Psychiatry, 20,* 11–21.

Seamon, J. G., Luo, C. R., Kopecky, J. J., Price, C. A., Rothschild, L., Fung, N. S., & Schwartz, M. A. (2002). Are false memories more difficult to forget than accurate memories? The effect of retention interval on recall and recognition. *Memory & Cognition, 30,* 1054–1064.

Sederberg, P. B., Schulze-Bonhage, A., Madsen, J. R., Bromfield, E. B., Litt, B., Brandt, A., & Kahana, M. J. (2007). Gamma oscillations distinguish true from false memories. *Psychological Science, 18,* 927–932.

Segal, S. J., & Fusella, V. (1970). Influence of imaged pictures and sounds on detection of visual and auditory signals. *Journal of Experimental Psychology, 83,* 458–464.

Segal, S. J., & Fusella, V. (1971). Effect of images in six sense modalities on detection of visual signal from noise. *Psychonomic Science, 24,* 55–56.

Sehulster, J. R. (1989). Content and temporal structure of autobiographical knowledge: Remembering twenty-five seasons at the Metropolitan Opera. *Memory & Cognition, 17,* 590–606.

Seiler, K. H., & Engelkamp, J. (2003). The role of item-specific information for the serial position curve in free recall. *Journal of Experimental Psychology: Learning, Memory, and Cognition, 29,* 954–964.

Senkfor, A. J., & Van Petten, C. (1998). Who said what? An event-related potential investigation of source and item memory. *Journal of Experimental Psychology: Learning, Memory, and Cognition, 24,* 1005–1025.

Senkfor, A. J., Van Petten, C., & Kutas, M. (2008). Enactment versus conceptual encoding: Equivalent item memory but different source memory. *Cortex, 44,* 649–664.

Sereno, S. C., O'Donnell, P. J., & Sereno, M. E. (2009). Size matters: Bigger is faster. *Quarterly Journal of Experimental Psychology, 62,* 1115–1122.

Shafto, M., & MacKay, D. G. (2000). The Moses, mega-Moses, and Armstrong illusions: Integrating language comprehension and semantic memory. *Psychological Science, 11,* 372–378.

Shah, P., & Miyake, A. (1996). The separability of working memory resources for spatial thinking and language processing: An individual differences approach. *Journal of Experimental Psychology: General, 125,* 4–27.

Shaki, S., & Fischer, M. H. (2008). Reading space into numbers—A cross-linguistic comparison of the SNARC effect. *Cognition, 108,* 590–599.

Shallice, T., Fletcher, P., & Dolan, R. (1998). The functional imaging of recall. In M. A. Conway, S. E. Gathercole, and C. Cornoldi (Eds.), *Theories of Memory: Volume II,* pp. 247–258. Hove, England: Psychology Press.

Shallice, T., & Warrington, E. K. (1970). Independent functioning of verbal memory stores: A neuropsychological study. *Quarterly Journal of Experimental Psychology, 22,* 261–273.

Shanks, D. R., & Dickinson, A. (1987). Associative accounts of causality judgment. *The Psychology of Learning and Motivation, 21,* 229–261.San Diego: Academic Press.

Shapiro, M. L., Tanila, H., & Eichenbaum, H. (1997). Cues that hippocampal place cells encode: Dynamic and hierarchical representation of local and distal stimuli. *Hippocampus, 7,* 624–642.

Shaw, J. S. (1996). Increases in eyewitness confidence resulting from postevent questioning. *Journal of Experimental Psychology: Applied, 2,* 126–146.

Shaw, J. S. & Kerr, T. K. (2003). Extra effort during memory retrieval may be associated with increases in eyewitness confidence. *Law and Human Behavior, 27,* 315–329.

Shaw, J. S., & McClure, K. A. (1996). Repeated postevent questioning can lead to elevated levels of eyewitness confidence. *Law and Human Behavior, 20,* 629–653.

Shelton, A. L., & McNamara, T. P. (1997). Multiple views of spatial memory. *Psychonomic Bulletin & Review, 4,* 102–106.

Shelton, A. L., & McNamara, T. P. (2004). Orientation and perspective dominance in route and survey learning. *Journal of Experimental Psychology: Learning, Memory, and Cognition, 30,* 158–170.

Shepard, R. N. (1967). Recognition memory for words, sentences, and pictures. *Journal of Verbal Learning and verbal Behavior, 6,* 156–163.

Shepard, R. N. (1984). Ecological constraints on internal representation: Resonant kinematics of perceiving, imagining, thinking, and dreaming. *Psychological Review, 9,* 417–447.

Shepard, R. N., & Chipman, S. (1970). Second-order isomorphs of internal representations: Shapes of states. *Cognitive Psychology, 1,* 1–17.

Shepard, R. N., & Metzler, J. (1971). Mental rotation of three-dimensional objects. *Science, 171,* 701–703.

Sherman. R. C., & Lim, K. M. (1991). Determinants of spatial priming in environmental memory. *Memory & Cognition, 19,* 283–292.

Sherry, D. F., & Schacter, D. L. (1987). The evolution of multiple memory systems. *Psychological Review, 94,* 439–454.

Shiffrin, R. M. & Steyvers, M. (1997). A model for recognition memory: REM—retrieving effectively from memory. *Psychonomic Bulletin & Review, 4,* 145–166.

Shoben, E. J.,Čech, C. G., Schwanenflugel, P. J., & Sailor, K. M. (1989). Serial position effects in comparative judgments. *Journal of Experimental Psychology: Human Perception and Performance, 15,* 273–286.

Sholl, J. M. (1987). Cognitive maps as orienting schemata. *Journal of Experimental Psychology: Learning, Memory, and Cognition, 13,* 615–628.

Sicotte, N. L., Kern, K. C., Giesser, B. S., Arshanapalli, A., Schultz, A., Montag, M., Wang, H., & Bookheimer, S. Y. (2008). Regional hippocampal atrophy in multiple sclerosis. *Brain, 131,* 1134–1141.

Simcock, G., & Hayne, H. (2002). Breaking the barrier? Children fail to translate their preverbal memories into language. *Psychological Science, 13,* 225–231.

Simons, D. J., & Levin, D. T. (1998). Failure to detect changes to people during real-world interaction. *Psychological Bulletin & Review, 5,* 644–649.

Simons, J. S., Dodson, C. S., Bell, D., & Schacter, D. L. (2004). Specific- and partial-source memory: Effects of aging. *Psychology and Aging, 19,* 689–694.

Simons, J. S., Graham, K. S, & Hodges, J. R. (2002). Perceptual and semantic contributions to episodic memory: Evidence from semantic dementia and Alzheimer's disease. *Journal of Memory and Language, 47,* 197–213.

Sirigu, A., & Grafman, J. (1996). Selective impairments within episodic memories. *Cortex, 32,* 83–95.

Skotko, B. G., Andrews, E., & Einstein, G. (2005). Language and the medial temporal lobe: Evidence from H.M.'s spontaneous discourse. *Journal of Memory and Language, 53,* 397–415.

Slamecka, N. J. (1968). An examination of trace storage in free recall. *Journal of Experimental Psychology, 4,* 504–513.

Slamecka, N. J., & Graf, P. (1978). The generation effect: Delineation of a phenomenon. *Journal of Experimental Psychology: Human Learning and Memory, 4,* 592–604.

Sloman, S. A., Bower, G. H., & Rohrer, D. (1991). Congruency effects in part-list cuing inhibition. *Journal of Experimental Psychology: Learning, Memory, and Cognition, 17,* 974–982.

Small, B. J., Dixon, R. A., Hultsch, D. F., & Hertzog, C. (1999). Longitudinal changes in quantitative and qualitative indicators of word and story recall in young-old and old-old adults. *Journal of Gerontology: Psychological Sciences 54B,* P107–P115.

Small, G. W. (1998). The pathogenesis of Alzheimer's disease. *Journal of Clinical Psychiatry, 59,* 7–14.

Smilek, D., Dixon, M. J., Cudahy, C., & Merikle, P.M. (2002). Synesthetic color experiences influence memory. *Psychological Science, 13,* 548–552.

Smith, E. E. (2000). Neural bases of human working memory. *Current Directions in Psychological Science, 9,* 45–49.

Smith. E. E., Adams, N., & Schorr, D. (1978). Fact retrieval and the paradox of interference. *Cognitive Psychology, 10,* 438–464.

Smith, M. C. (1983). Hypnotic memory enhancement of witnesses: Does it work? *Psychological Bulletin, 94,* 387–407.

Smith, R. E., & Hunt, R. R. (2000). The influence of distinctive processing on retrieval-induced forgetting. *Memory & Cognition, 28,* 503–508.

Smith, R. E., & Bayen, U. J. (2006). The source of adult age differences in event-based prospective memory: A multinomial approach. *Journal of Experimental Psychology: Learning, Memory, and Cognition, 32,* 623–635.

Smith, R. E., Lozito, J. P., & Bayen, U. J. (2005). Adult age differences in distinctive processing: the modality effect on false recall. *Psychology and Aging, 20,* 486–492.

Smith, S. M., (1979). Remembering in and out of context. *Journal of Experimental Psychology: Human Learning and Memory, 5,* 460–471.

Smith, S. M. (1984). A comparison of two techniques for reducing context-dependent forgetting. *Memory & Cognition, 12,* 477–482.

Smith, S. M. (1985). Background music and context-dependent memory. *American Journal of Psychology, 98,* 591–603.

Smith, S. M., (1988). Environmental context–dependent memory. In G. M. Davies & D. M. Thomas (Eds.), *Memory in Context: Context in Memory,* pp. 13–34. New York: Wiley.

Smith, S. M., Glenberg, A., & Bjork, R. A. (1978). Environmental context and human memory. *Memory & Cognition, 6,* 342–353.

Smith, S. M., & Vela, E. (2001). Environmental context-dependent memory: A review and meta-analysis. *Psychonomic Bulletin & Review, 8,* 203–220.

Snodgrass, J. G., & Corwin, J. (1988). Pragmatics of measuring recognition memory: Applications to dementia and amnesia. *Journal of Experimental Psychology: General, 117,* 34–50.

Snodgrass, J. G., Volvovitz, R., & Walfish, E. R. (1972). Recognition memory for words, pictures, and words + pictures. *Psychonomic Science, 27,* 345–347.

Snowden, J., Goulding, J., & Neary, D. (1989). Semantic dementia: A form of circumscribed cerebral atrophy. *Behavioral Neurology, 2,* 167–182.

Snyder, K. A., Blank, M. P., & Marsolek, C. J. (2008). What form of memory underlies novelty preferences? *Psychonomic Bulletin & Review, 15,* 315–321.

Solomon, K. O., & Barsalou, L. W. (2001). Representing properties locally. *Cognitive Psychology, 43,* 129–169.

Solomon, K. O., & Barsalou, L. W. (2004). Perceptual simulation in property verification. *Memory & Cognition, 32,* 244–259.

Son, L. K. (2004). Spacing one's study: Evidence for a metacognitive control strategy. *Journal of Experimental Psychology: Learning, Memory, and Cognition, 30,* 601–604.

Souchey, C., Isingrini, M., & Espagnet, L. (2000). Aging, episodic memory feeling-of-knowing, and frontal functioning. *Neuropsychology, 14,* 299–309.

Spaniol, J., Madden, D. J., & Voss, A. (2006). A diffusion model analysis of adult age differences in episodic and semantic long-term memory retrieval. *Journal of Experimental Psychology: Learning, Memory, and Cognition, 32,* 101–117.

Spear, N. E., & Riccio, D. C. (1994). *Memory: Phenomena and Principles.* New York: Allyn and Bacon.

Sperling, G. (1960). The information available in brief visual presentations. *Psychological Monographs: General and Applied, 74 (11),* 1–29.

Sporer, S. L., Penrod, S., Read, D., & Cutler, B. (1995). Choosing, confidence, and accuracy: A meta-analysis of the confidence-accuracy relation in eyewitness identification studies. *Psychological Bulletin, 118,* 315–327.

Sprecher, S. (1999). "I love you more today than yesterday": Romantic partners' perceptions of change in love and related affect over time. *Journal of Personality and Social Psychology, 76,* 46–53.

Squire, L. R., & Cohen, N. (1979). Memory and amnesia: Resistance to disruption develops for years after learning. *Behavioral and Neural Biology, 25,* 115–125.

Squire, L. R., Slater, P. C., & Chace, P. M. (1975). Retrograde amnesia: Temporal gradient in very long term memory following electroconvulsive therapy. *Science, 187,* 77–79.

Squires, E. J., Hunkin, N. M., & Parkin, A. J. (1997). Take note: Using errorless learning to promote memory notebook training. In A. J. Parkin (Ed.), *Case Studies in the Neuropsychology of Memory,* pp. 191–203. Hove, England: Psychology Press.

Srivinas, K., & Roediger, H. L. (1990). Classifying implicit memory tests: Category association and anagram solution. *Journal of Memory and Language, 29,* 389–412.

Stagner, R. (1933). Factors influencing the memory value of words in a series. *Journal of Experimental Psychology, 16,* 129–137.

Standing, L. (1973). Learning 10,000 pictures. *Quarterly Journal of Experimental Psychology, 25,* 207–222.

Stark. L.-J. & Perfect, T. J. (2006). Elaboration inflation: How your ideas become mine. *Applied Cognitive Psychology, 20,* 641–648.

Stark. L.-J. & Perfect, T. J. (2007). Whose idea was that? Source monitoring for idea ownership following elaboration. *Memory, 15,* 776–783.

Stark. L.-J. & Perfect, T. J. (2008). The effects of repeated idea elaboration on unconscious plagiarism. *Memory & Cognition, 36,* 65–73.

Starns, J. J., Hicks, J. L., Brown, N. L., & Martin, B. A. (2008). Source memory for unrecognized items: Predictions from multivariate signal detection theory. *Memory & Cognition, 36,* 1–8.

Stebbins, G. T., Carrillo, M. C., Dorfman, J., Dirksen, C., Desmond, J. E., Turner, D. A., Bennett, D. A., Wilson, R. S., Glover, G., & Gabrieli, J. D. E. (2002). Aging effects on memory encoding in the frontal lobes. *Psychology and Aging, 17,* 44–55.

Steblay, N. M. (1992). A meta-analytic review of the weapon focus effect. *Law and Human Behavior, 16,* 413–424.

Steblay, N. M. (1997). Social influence in eyewitness recall: A meta-analytic review of lineup instruction effects. *Law and Human Behavior, 21,* 283–297.

Steffens, M. C. (2007). Memory for goal-directed sequences of actions: Is doing better than seeing? *Psychonomic Bulletin & Review, 14,* 1194–1198.

Steffens, M. C., Buchner, A., Martensen, H., & Erdfelder, E. (2000). Further evidence on the similarity of memory processes in the process dissociation procedure and in source monitoring. *Memory & Cognition, 28,* 1152–1164.

Steffens, M. C., Buchner, A., & Wender, K. F. (2003). Quite ordinary retrieval cues may determine free recall of actions. *Journal of Memory and Language, 48,* 399–415.

Steinhart, D. (2001). Summary Street: An intelligent tutoring system for improving student writing through the use of latent semantic analysis. *Unpublished doctoral dissertation, Institute of Cognitive Science, University of Colorado, Boulder.*

Sternberg, S. (1966). High-speed scanning in human memory. *Science, 153,* 652–654.

Sternberg, S. (1969). The discovery of processing stages: Extensions of Donders' method. *Acta Pscyhologica, 30,* 276–315.

Sternberg, S. (1975). Memory scanning: New findings and current controversies. *Quarterly Journal of Experimental Psychology, 27,* 1–32.

Stevens, A. & Coupe, P. (1978). Distortions in judged spatial relations. *Cognitive Psychology, 10,* 422–437.

Stevens, S. S., & Galantner, E. H. (1957). Ratio scales and category scales for a dozen perceptual continua. *Journal of Experimental Psychology, 54,* 377–411.

Stewart, B. D., von Hippel, W., & Radvansky, G. A. (2009). Age, race, and implicit prejudice. Using process dissociation to separate the underlying components. *Psychological Science, 20,* 164–168.

St. Jacques, P. L., Dolcos, F., & Cabeza, R. (2009). Effects of aging on functional connectivity of the amygdala for subsequent memory of negative pictures. *Psychological Science, 20,* 74–84.

Storbeck, J., & Clore, G. L. (2005). With sadness comes accuracy; with happiness, false memory: Mood and the false memory effect. *Psychological Science,16,* 785–791.

Stracciari, A., Ghidoni, E., Guarino, M., Poletti, M., & Pazzaglia, P. (1994). Post-traumatic retrograde amnesia with selective impairment of autobiographical memory. *Cortex, 30,* 459–468.

Stromeyer, C. F., & Psotka, J. (1970). The detailed texture opf eidetic images. *Nature, 255,* 346–349.

Summers, W. V., Horton, D. L., & Diehl, V. A. (1985). Contextual knowledge during encoding influences sentence recognition. *Journal of Experimental Psychology: Learning, Memory, and Cognition, 11,* 771–779.

Sun, H. J., Chan, G. S. W., & Campos, J. L. (2004). Active navigation and orientation-free spatial representations. *Memory & Cognition, 32,* 51–71.

Swaab, T. Y., Baynes, K., & Knight, R. T. (2002). Separable effects of priming and imageability on word processing: An ERP study. *Cognitive Brain Research, 15,* 99–103.

Swanson, J. M., & Kinsbourne, M. (1976). Stimulant-related state-dependent learning in hyperactive children. *Science, 192,* 1354–1356.

Symons, C. S., & Johnson, B. T. (1997). The self-reference effect in memory: A meta-analysis. *Psychological Bulletin, 121,* 371–394.

Szupnar, K. K., McDermott, K. B., & Roediger, H. L. (2008). Testing during study insulates against the buildup of proactive interference. *Journal of Experimental Psychology: Learning, Memory, and Cognition, 34,* 1392–1399.

Taft, M. (1979). Recognition of affixed words and the word frequency effect. *Memory & Cognition, 7,* 263–272.

Takahashi, M., Shimizu, H., Saito, S., & Tomoyori, H. (2006). One percent ability and ninety-nine percent perspiration: A study of a Japanese memorist. *Journal of Experimental Psychology: Learning, Memory, and Cognition, 32,* 1195–1200.

Talarico, J. M., & Rubin, D. C. (2003). Confidence, not consistency, characterizes flashbulb memories. *Psychological Science, 14,* 455–461.

Talarico, J. M., & Rubin, D. C. (2009). Flashbulb memories results from ordinary memory processes and extraordinary event characteristics. In O. Luminet & A. Curci (Eds.), *Flashbulb Memories: New Issues and New Perspectives,* pp. 79–98. New York: Psychology Press.

Talarico, J. M., LaBar, K. S., & Rubin, D. C. (2004). Emotional intensity predicts autobiographical memory experience. *Memory & Cognition, 32,* 1118–1132.

Talmi, D., Grady, C. L., Goshen-Gottstein, Y., & Moscovitch, M. (2005). Neuroimaging the serial position curve: A test of single-store versus dual-store models. *Psychological Science, 16,* 716–723.

Talmi, D., Luk, B. T. C., McGarry, L. M., & Moscovitch, M. (2007). The contribution of relatedness and distinctiveness to emotionally-enhanced memory. *Journal of Memory and Language, 56,* 555–574.

Taylor, H. A., & Tversky, B. (1992). Spatial mental models derived from survey and route descriptions. *Journal of Memory and Language, 31,* 261–292.

Tekcan, A. I., Ece, B., Gülgöz, S., & Er, N. (2003). Autobiographical and event memory for 9/11: Changes across one year. *Applied Cognitive Psychology, 17,* 1057–1066.

Terry, W. S. (2000). *Learning and Memory: Basic Principles, Processes, and Procedures.* Boston: Allyn & Bacon.

Thapar, A., & Sniezek, S. M. (2008). Aging and the revelation effect. *Psychology and Aging, 23,* 473–477.

Thapar, A., & Westerman, D. L. (2009). Aging and fluency-based illusions in recognition memory. *Psychology and Aging, 24,* 595–603.

Thomas, A. K., & Bulevich, J. B. (2006). Effective cue utilization reduces memory errors in older adults. *Psychology and Aging, 21,* 379–389.

Thomas, A. K., Bulevich, J. B., & Loftus, E. F. (2003). Exploring the role of repetition and sensory elaboration in the imagination inflation effect. *Memory & Cognition, 31,* 630–640.

Thomas, A. K., & Loftus, E. F. (2002). Creating bizarre false memories through imagination. *Memory & Cognition, 30,* 423–431.

Thomas, R. C., & Hasher, L. (2006). The influence of emotional valence on age differences in early processing and memory. *Psychology and Aging, 21,* 821–825.

Thompson, C. P., Cowan, T. M. & Frieman, J. (1993). *Memory Search by a Memorist.* Hillsdale, NJ: Erlbaum.

Thompson, C. P., Cowan, T. M., Frieman, J., Mahadevan, R. S., & Vogl, R. J. (1991). Rajan: A study of a memorist. *Journal of Memory and Language, 30,* 702–724.

Thompson, C. P., Skowronski, J. J., & Lee, D. J. (1988). Telescoping in dating naturally occurring events. *Memory & Cognition, 16,* 461–468.

Thompson, C. P., Skowronski, J. J., Larsen, S. F., & Betz, A. L. (1996). *Autobiographical Memory: Remembering What and Remembering When.* Mahwah, New Jersey: Erlbaum.

Thompson, D. M., & Tulving, E. (1970). Associative encoding and retrieval: Weak and strong cues. *Journal of Experimental Psychology, 86,* 255–262.

Thompson, R., Emmorey, K., & Gollan, T. H. (2005). "Tip of the fingers" experiences in deaf signers: Insights into the organization of a sign-based lexicon. *Psychological Science, 16,* 856–860.

Thompson, W. C., Fong, G. T., & Rosenhan, D. L. (1981). Inadmissible evidence and juror verdicts. *Journal of Personality and Social Psychology, 40,* 453–463.

Thompson-Schill, S. L., Kurtz, K. J., & Gabrieli, J. D. E. (1998). Effects of semantic and associative relatedness on automatic priming. *Journal of Memory and Language, 38,* 440–458.

Thorndyke, P. W. (1981). Distance estimation from cognitive maps. *Cognitive Psychology, 13,* 526–550.

Titchener, E. B. (1928). *A Textbook of Psychology.* New York: Macmillan.

Toglia, M. P., & Kimble, G. A. (1976). Recall and use of serial position information. *Journal of Experimental Psychology: Human Learning and Memory, 2,* 431–445.

Tolman, E. C. (1948). Cognitive maps in rats and men. *Psychological Review, 55,* 189–208.

Topolinski, S., & Strack, F. (2009a). The architecture of intuition: Fluency and affect determine intuitive judgments of semantic and visual coherence and judgments of grammaticality in artificial grammar learning. *Journal of Experimental Psychology: General, 138,* 39–63.

Topolinski, S., & Strack, F. (2009b). Motormouth: Mere exposure depends on stimulus-specific motor simulations. *Journal of Experimental Psychology: Learning, Memory, and Cognition, 35,* 423–433.

Toppino, T. C., & Bloom, L. C. (2002). The spacing effect, free recall, and two-process theory: A closer look. *Memory & Cognition, 28,* 437–444.

Toth, J. P., Reingold, E. M., & Jacoby, L. L. (1994). Toward a redefinition of implicit memory: Process dissociations following elaborative processing and self-generation. *Journal of Experimental Psychology: Learning, Memory, and Cognition, 20,* 290–303.

Townsend, J. T. (1990). Serial vs. parallel processing: Sometimes they look like Tweedledum and Tweedledee but they can (and should) be distinguished. *Psychological Science, 1,* 46–54.

Trabasso, T., & van den Broek, P. W. (1985). Causal thinking and the representation of narrative events. *Journal of Memory and Language, 24,* 612–630.

Trafimow, D., & Wyer, R. S. (1993). Cognitive representations of mundane social events. *Journal of Personality and Social Psychology, 64,* 365–376.

Tremblay, S., & Saint-Aubin, J. (2009). Evidence of anticipatory eye movements in the spatial Hebb repetition effect: Insights for modeling sequential learning. *Journal of Experimental Psychology, Learning, Memory, and Cognition, 35,* 1256–1265.

Tulving, E. (1962). Subjective organization in free recall of "unrelated" words. *Psychological Review, 69,* 344–354.

Tulving, E. (1972). Episodic and semantic memory. In E. Tulving & W. Donaldson (Eds.), *Organization of Memory,* pp. 381–403. New York: Academic Press.

Tulving, E. (1985a). How many memory systems are there? *American Psychologist, 40,* 385–398.

Tulving, E. (1985b). Memory and consciousness. *Canadian Psychology, 26,* 1–12.

Tulving. E., & Hastie, R. (1972). Inhibition effects of intralist repetition in free recall. *Journal of Experimental Psychology, 92,* 297–304.

Tulving, E., & Madigan, S. A. (1970). Memory and verbal learning. *Annual Review of Psychology, 21,* 437–484.

Tulving. E., & Pearlstone, Z. (1966). Availability versus accessibility of information in memory for words. *Journal of Verbal Learning and Verbal Behavior, 5,* 381–391.

Tulving, E., & Psotka, J. (1971). Retroactive inhibition in free recall: Inaccessibility of information available in the memory store. *Journal of Experimental Psychology, 87,* 1–8.

Tulving, E., & Schacter, D. L. (1990). Priming in human memory systems. *Science, 247,* 301–306.

Tulving, E., Schacter, D. L., McLachlan, D. R., & Moscovitch, M. (1988). Priming of semantic autobiographical knowledge: A case study of retrograde amnesia. *Brain and Cognition, 8,* 3–20.

Tulving, E., Schacter, D. L., & Stark, H. A. (1982). Priming effects in word-fragment completion are independent of recognition memory. *Journal of Experimental Psychology: Learning, Memory and Cognition, 8,* 336–342.

Tulving, E., & Watkins, O. C. (1977). Recognition failure of words with a single meaning. *Memory & Cognition, 5,* 513–522.

Tulving, E., & Wiseman, S. (1975). Relation between recognition and recognition failure of recallable words. *Bulletin of the Psychonomic Society, 6,* 79–82.

Turkheimer, E. (1998). Heretibility and biological explanation. *Psychological Review, 105,* 782–791.

Turner, M. L., & Engle, R. W. (1989). Is working memory capacity task dependent? *Journal of Memory and Language, 28,* 127–154.

Tversky, B. (1981). Distortions in memory for maps. *Cognitive Psychology, 13,* 417–433.

Tversky, B., & Hemenway, K. (1984). Objects, parts, and categories. *Journal of Experimental Psychology: General, 113,* 169–193.

Tversky, B., & Marsh, E. J. (2000). Biased retellings of events yield biased memories. *Cognitive Psychology, 40,* 1–38.

Tzeng, O. J. L. (1976). A precedence effect in the processing of verbal information. *American Journal of Psychology, 89,* 577–599.

Underwood, B. J. (1957). Interference and forgetting. *Psychological Review, 64,* 49–60.

Underwood, J., & Pezdek, K. (1998). Memory suggestibility as an example of the sleeper effect. *Psychonomic Bulletin & Review, 5,* 449–453.

Unsworth, N. (2007). Individual differences in working memory capacity and episodic retrieval: Examining the dynamics of delayed and continuous distractor free recall. *Journal of Experimental Psychology: Learning, Memory, and Cognition, 33,* 1020–1034.

Unsworth, N., & Engle, R. W. (2006). Simple and complex memory spans and their relation to fluid abilities: Evidence from list-length effects. *Journal of Memory and Language, 54,* 68–80.

Unsworth, N., & Engle, R. W. (2007). The nature of individual differences in working memory capacity: Active maintenance in primary memory and controlled search from secondary memory. *Psychological Review, 114,* 104–132.

Urbach, T. P., Windmann, S. S., Payne, D. G., & Kutas, M. (2005). Mismaking memories: Neural precursors of memory illusions in electrical brain activity. *Psychological Science, 16,* 19–24.

Vaidya, C. J., Zhao, M., Desmond, J. E., & Gabrieli, J. D. E. (2002). Evidence for cortical encoding specificity in episodic memory: Memory-induced re-activation of picture processing areas. *Neuropsychologia, 40,* 2136–2143.

Valiquette, C. M., McNamara, T. P., & Smith, K. (2003). Locomotion, incidental learning, and the selection of spatial reference systems. *Memory & Cognition, 31,* 479–489.

Vallar, G., & Baddeley, A. D. (1985). Fractionation of working memory: Neuropsychological evidence for a phonological short-term store. *Journal of Verbal Learning and Verbal Behavior, 23,* 151–161.

Vallar, G., & Papagano, C. (1995). Neuropsychological impairments of short-term memory. In A. D. Baddeley, B. A. Wilson, & F. N. Watts (Eds.), *Handbook of Memory Disorders,* pp. 135–165. New York: Wiley.

Vakil, E., Grunhaus, L., Nagar, I., Ben-Chaim, E., Dolberg, O. T., Dannon, P. N., Schrieber, S. (2000). The effect of electroconvulsive therapy (ECT) on implicit memory: Skill learning and perceptual priming in patients with major depression. *Neuropsychologia, 38,* 1405–1414.

van der Meulen, M., Logie, R. H., & Della Sala, S. (2009). Selective interference with image retention and generation: Evidence for the workspace model. *Quarterly Journal of Experimental Psychology, 62,* 1568–1580.

van Dijk, T. A., & Kintsch, W. (1983). *Strategies in Discourse Comprehension.* New York: Academic Press.

Vandorpe, S., & De Houwer, J. (2005). A comparison of forward blocking and reduced overshadowing in human causal learning. *Psychonomic Bulletin & Review, 12,* 945–949.

Veling, H., & van Knippenberg, A. (2004). Remembering can cause inhibition: Retrieval induced inhibition as cue independent process. *Journal of Experimental Psychology: Learning, Memory, and Cognition, 30,* 315–318.

Verde, M. F. (2004). The retrieval practice effect in associative recognition. *Memory & Cognition, 32,* 1265–1272.

Verfaillie, K., & Y'dewalle, G. (1991). Representational momentum and event course anticipation in the perception of implied periodic motions. *Journal of Experimental Psychology: Learning, Memory, and Cognition, 17,* 302–313.

Verkoeijen, P. P. J. L., Rikers, R. M. J. P., & Schmidt, H. G. (2004). Detrimental influence of contextual change on spacing effects. *Journal of Experimental Psychology: Learning, Memory, and Cognition, 30,* 796–800.

Viney, W., & King, D. B. (1998). *A History of Psychology: Ideas and Context.* Boston: Allyn and Bacon.

Vokey, J. R., & Highham, P. A. (2005). Abstract analogies and positive transfer in artificial grammar learning. *Canadian Journal of Experimental Psychology, 59,* 54–61.

Vollrath, D. A., Sheppard, B. H., Hinsz, V. B., & Davis, J. H. (1989). Memory performance by decision-making groups and individuals. *Organizational Behavior and Human Decision Processes, 43,* 289–300.

von Essen, J. D., & Nilsson, L. (2003). Memory effects of motor activation in subject-performed tasks and sign language. *Psychonomic Bulletin & Review, 10,* 445–449.

von Hippel, W., Silver, L. A., & Lynch, M. E. (2000). Stereotyping against your will: The role of inhibitory ability in stereotyping and prejudice among the elderly. *Personality and Social Psychology Bulletin, 26,* 523–532.

Wagenaar, W. A. (1986). My memory: A study of autobiographical memory over six years. *Cognitive Psychology, 18,* 225–252.

Wagner, S. M., Nusbaum, H., & Goldin-Meadow, S. (2004). Probing the mental representation of gesture: Is handwaving spatial? *Journal of Memory and Language, 50,* 395–407.

Walker, W. R., Skowronski, J. J., & Thompson, C. P. (2003). Life is pleasant—and memory helps keep it that way! *Review of General Psychology, 7,* 203–210.

Walker, W. R., Vogl, R. J., & Thompson, C. P. (1997). Autobiographical memory: Unpleasantness fades faster than pleasantness over time. *Applied Cognitive Psychology, 11,* 399–413.

Waller, D., Loomis, J. M., & Haun, D. B. M. (2004). Body-based senses enhance knowledge of directions in large-scale environments. *Psychonomic Bulletin & Review, 11,* 157–163.

Waller, D., Montello, D. R., Richardson, A. E., & Hegarty, M. (2002). Orientation specificity and spatial layout updating of memories for layouts. *Journal of Experimental Psychology: Learning, Memory and Cognition, 28,* 1051–1063.

Wang, Q. (2004). Infantile amnesia reconsidered: A cross-cultural analysis. *Memory, 11,* 65–80.

Waring, J. D., & Kensinger, E. A. (2009). Effects of emotional valence and arousal upon memory trade-offs with aging. *Psychology and Aging, 24,* 412–422.

Warrington, E. K., & Weiskrantz, L. (1968). A study of learning and retention in amnesic patients. *Neuropsychologia, 6,* 283–291.

Warrington, E. K., & Weiskrantz, L. (1970). Amnestic syndrome: Consolidation or retrieval? *Nature, 228,* 628–630.

Was, C. A., & Woltz, D. J. (2007). Reexamining the relationship between working memory and comprehension: The role of available long-term memory. *Journal of Memory and Language, 56,* 86–102.

Waters, G. S., & Caplan, D. (1996). The measurement of verbal working memory capacity and its relation to reading comprehension. *Quarterly Journal of Experimental Psychology, 49A,* 51–79.

Watkins, M. J., & Peynircioğlu, Z. F. (1990). The revelation effect: When disguising test items induces recognition. *Journal of Experimental Psychology: Learning, Memory and Cognition, 16,* 1012–1020.

Watts, F. N. (1995). Depression and anxiety. In A. D. Baddeley, B. A. Wilson, & F. N. Watts (Eds.), *Handbook of Memory Disorders,* pp. 293–318. New York: Wiley.

Waugh, N. C., & Norman, D. A. (1965). Primary memory. *Psychological Review, 72,* 89–104.

Weaver, C. A., & Krug, K. S. (2004). Consolidation-like effects in flashbulb memories: Evidence from September 11, 2001. *American Journal of Psychology, 117,* 517–530.

Wegner, D. M. (1989). *White Bears and Other Unwanted Thoughts: Suppression, Obsession, and the Psychology of Mental Control.* New York: Viking.

Weinstein, Y., Bugg, J. M., & Roediger, H. L. (2008). Can the survival recall advantage be explained by basic memory processes? *Memory & Cognition, 36,* 913–919.

Weiss, W. (1953). A "sleeper" effect in opinion change. *Journal of Abnormal and Social Psychology, 48,* 173–180.

Weldon, M. S., & Bellinger, K. D. (1997). Collective memory: Collaborative and individual processes in remembering. *Journal of Experimental Psychology: Learning, Memory, and Cognition, 23,* 1160–1175.

Weldon, M. S., Blair, C., & Huebsch, P. D. (2000). Group remembering: Does social loafing underlie collaborative inhibition? *Journal of Experimental Psychology: Learning, Memory and Cognition, 26,* 1568–1577.

Wells, G. L. (1984). The psychology of lineup identification. *Journal of Applied Social Psychology, 14,* 89–103.

Wells, G. L., & Bradfield, A. L. (1998). "Good, you identified the suspect": Feedback to eyewitnesses distorts their reports of the witnessing experience. *Journal of Applied Psychology, 83,* 360–376.

Wells, G. L., & Bradfield, A. L. (1999). Distortion in eyewitnesses' recollections: Can the postidentification-feedback effect be moderated? *Psychological Science, 10,* 138–144.

Wells, G. L., & Hasel, L. E. (2007). Facial composite production by eyewitnesses. *Current Directions in Psychological Science, 16,* 6–10.

Wells, G. L., Malpass, R. S., Lindsay, R. C. L., Fisher, R. P., Turtle, J. W., & Fulero, S. M. (2000). From the lab to the police station: A successful application of eyewitness research. *American Psychologist, 55,* 581–598.

Wells, G. L., Memon, A., & Penrod, S. D. (2006). Eyewitness evidence: Improving its probative value. *Psychological Science in the Public Interest, 7,* 45–75.

Wells, G. L., Rydell, S. M., & Seelau, E. P. (1993). The selection of distractors for eyewitness lineups. *Journal of Applied Psychology, 78,* 835–844.

West, R. L. (1988). Prospective memory and aging. In M. M. Gruneberg, P. E. Morris, & R. N. Sykes (Eds.), *Practical Aspects of Memory,* pp. 119–125. Chichester, England: Wiley.

West, R. L., Thorn, R. M., & Bagwell, D. K. (2003). Memory performance and beliefs as a function of goal setting and aging. *Psychology and Aging, 18,* 111–125.

Westerman, D. L. (2000). Recollection-based recognition eliminates the revelation effect in memory. *Memory & Cognition, 28,* 167–175.

Westerman, D. L., & Greene, R. L. (1996). On the generality of the revelation effect. *Journal of Experimental Psychology Learning, Memory, and Cognition, 22,* 1147–1153.

Westerman, D. L., & Greene, R. L. (1998). The revelation that the revelation effect is not due to revelation. *Journal of Experimental Psychology Learning, Memory, and Cognition, 24,* 377–386.

Westerman, D. L., & Larsen, J. D. (1997). Verbal-overshadowing effect: Evidence for a general shift in processing. *American Journal of Psychology, 110,* 417–428.

Westmacott, R., & Moscovitch, M. (2003). The contribution of autobiographical significance to semantic memory. *Memory & Cognition, 31,* 761–774.

Wheeler, M. A., & Roediger, H. L. (1992). Disparate effects of repeated testing: Reconciling Ballard's (1913) and Barlett's (1932) results. *Psychological Science, 3,* 240–245.

White, K. G., & Ruske, A. C. (2002). Memory deficits in Alzheimer's disease: The encoding hypothesis and cholinergic function. *Psychonomic Bulletin & Review, 9,* 426–437.

White, K. K., & Abrams, L. (2002). Does priming specific syllables during tip-of-the-tongue states facilitate word retrieval in older adults? *Psychology and Aging, 17,* 226–235.

Whitten, W. B., & Leonard, J. M. (1981). Directed search through autobiographical memory. *Memory & Cognition, 9,* 566–579.

Wickelgren, W. A. (1968). Sparing of short-term memory in an amnesic patient: Implications for strength theory of short-term memory. *Neuropsychologia, 6,* 235–244.

Wickens, D. D. (1972). Characteristics of word encoding. In A. W. Melton & E. Martin (Eds.), *Coding Processes in Human Memory,* pp. 191–215. New York: Wiley.

Widner, R. L., Otani, H., & Smith, A. D. (2000). Hypermnesia: Age-related differences between young and older adults. *Memory & Cognition, 28,* 556–564.

Wiest, W. M., & Bell, B. (1985). Stevens's exponent for psychophysical scaling of perceived, remembered and inferred distance. *Psychological Bulletin, 98,* 457–470.

Wiggs, C. L., Weisberg, J., & Martin, A. (1999). Neural correlates of semantic and episodic memory retrieval. *Neuropsychologia, 37,* 103–118.

Wildber, D. J., & Wilson, P. N. (2008). Influences on the first-perspective alignment effect from text route descriptions. *Quarterly Journal of Experimental Psychology, 61,* 763–783.

Wilding, E. L. (2000). In what way does the parietal ERP old/new effect index recollection? *International Journal of Psychophysiology, 35,* 81–87.

Wilkinson, L., Scholey, A., & Wesnes, K. (2002). Chewing gum selectively improves aspects of memory in healthy volunteers. *Appetite, 38,* 235–236.

Wilkinson, L., & Shanks, D. R. (2004). Intentional control and implicit sequence learning. *Journal of Experimental Psychology: Learning, Memory, and Cognition, 30,* 354–369.

Willander, J. & Larsson, M. (2006). Smell your way back to childhood: Autobiographical odor memory. *Psychonomic Bulletin & Review, 13,* 240–244.

Willander, J. & Larsson, M. (2007). Olfaction and emotion: The case of autobiographical memory. *Memory & Cognition, 35,* 1659–1663.

Williams, C. C., & Zacks, R. T. (2001). Is retrieval-induced forgetting an inhibitory process? *American Journal of Psychology, 114,* 329–354.

Wills, T. W., Soraci, S. A., Chechile, R. A., & Taylor, H. A. (2000). "Aha" effects in the generation of pictures. *Memory & Cognition, 28,* 939–948.

Wilson, B. A., J. C., & Hughes, E. (1997). Coping with amnesia: The natural history of a compensatory memory system. In A. J. Parkin (Ed.), *Case Studies in the Neuropsychology of Memory,* pp. 179–190. East Sussex, England: Psychology Press.

Wilson, B. A., & Wearing, D. (1995). Prisoner of consciousness: A state of just awakening following herpes simplex encephalitis. In R. Campbell & M. A. Conway (Eds.), *Broken Memories: Case Studies in Memory Impairment.* Cambridge, MA: Blackwell.

Wilson, M. (2002). Six views of embodied cognition. *Psychonomic Bulletin & Review, 9,* 625–636.

Wilson, M. & Emmorey, K. (2006). Comparing sign language and speech reveals a universal limit on short-term memory capacity. *Psychological Science, 17,* 682–683.

Wilson, M., & Fox, G. (2007). Working memory for language is not special: Evidence for an articulatory loop for novel stimuli. *Psychonomic Bulletin & Review, 14,* 470–473.

Winer, G. A., Cottrell, J E., Gregg, V., Fournier, J. S., & Bica, L. A. (2002). Fundamentally misunderstanding visual perception. *American Psychologist, 57,* 417–424.

Winkielman, P., Halberstadt, J., Fazendeiro, T., & Catty, S. (2006). Prototypes are attractive because they are easy on the mind. *Psychological Science, 17,* 799–806.

Winkielman, P., & Schwartz, N. (2001). How pleasant was your childhood? Beliefs about memory shape inferences from experienced difficulty of recall. *Psychological Science, 12,* 176–179.

Wixted, J. T. (2004a). On common ground: Jost's (1897) law of forgetting and Ribot's (1881) law of anterograde amnesia. *Psychological Review, 111,* 864–879.

Wixted, J. T. (2004b). The psychology and neuroscience of forgetting. *Annual Review of Psychology, 55,* 235–269.

Wixted, J. T. (2005). A theory about why we forget what we once knew. *Current Directions in Psychological Science, 14,* 6–9.

Wolpe, J. (1958). *Psychotherapy by Reciprocal Inhibition.* Stanford, CA.: Stanford University Press.

Wood, G. (1978). The knew-it-all-along effect. *Journal of Experimental Psychology: Human Perception and Performance, 4,* 345–353.

Wraga, M., Creem, S. H., & Proffitt, D. R. (2000). Updating displays after imagined object and viewer rotations. *Journal of Experimental Psychology: Learning, Memory, and Cognition, 26,* 151–168.

Wraga, M., Swaby, M., & Flynn, C. M. (2008). Passive tactile feedback facilitates mental rotation of handheld objects. *Memory & Cognition, 36,* 271–281.

Wright, D. B., Memon, A., Skagerberg, E. M., & Gabbert, F. (2009). When eyewitnesses talk. *Current Directions in Psychological Science, 18,* 174–178.

Wurm, L. H. (2006). Danger and Usefulness: An alternative framework for understanding rapid evaluation effects n perception. *Psychonomic Bulletin & Review, 14,* 1218–1225.

Wurm, L. H., & Seaman, S. R. (2008). Semantic effects in naming and perceptual identification but not in delayed naming: Implications for models and tasks. *Journal of Experimental Psychology: Learning, Memory, and Cognition, 34,* 381–398.

Wyer, R. S., & Unverzagt, W. H. (1985). Effects of instructions to disregard information on its subsequent recall and use in making judgments. *Journal of Personality and Social Psychology, 48,* 533–549.

Yaro, C., & Ward, J. (2007). Searching for Shereshevskii: What is superior about the memory of synaesthetes? *Quarterly Journal of Experimental Psychology, 60,* 681–695.

Yasuda, K., Watanabe, O., & Ono, Y. (1997). Dissociation between semantic and autobiographical memory: A case report. *Cortex, 33,* 623–638.

Yerkes, R. M., & Dodson, J. D. (1908). The relation of strength of stimulus to rapidity of habit-formation. *Journal of Comparative Neurology and Psychology, 18,* 459–482.

Yonelinas, A. P. (2002). The nature of recollection and familiarity: A review of 30 years of research. *Journal of Memory and Language, 46,* 441–517.

Young, K. D., Peynircioğlu, Z. F., & Hohman, T. J. (2009). Revelation effect in metamemory. *Psychonomic Bulletin & Review, 16,* 952–956.

Zacks, J. M., Speer, N. K., & Reynolds, J. R. (2009). Segmentation in reading and film comprehension. *Journal of Experimental Psychology: General, 138,* 307–327.

Zacks, R. T., Hasher, L., & Li, K. Z. H. (2000). Human memory. In F. I. M. Craik and T. A. Salthouse (Eds.), *Handbook of Aging and Cognition* (2nd ed.). Mahwah, NJ: Erlbaum.

Zacks, R. T., Radvansky, G. A., & Hasher, L. (1996). Studies of directed forgetting in older adults. *Journal of Experimental Psychology: Learning, Memory, and Cognition, 22,* 143–156.

Zalla, T., Sirigu, A., Pillon, B., Dubois, B., Agid, Y., & Grafman, J. (2000). How patients with Parkinson's disease retrieve and manage cognitive event knowledge. *Cortex, 36,* 163–179.

Zajonc, R. B. (1968). Attitudinal effects of mere exposure. *Journal of Personality and Social Psychology Monograph Supplement, 9,* 1–27.

Zajonc, R. B. (2001). Mere exposure: A gateway to the subliminal. *Current Directions in Psychological Science, 10,* 224–228.

Zaragoza, M. S., & Koshmider, J. W. (1989). Misled subjects may know more than their performance implies. *Journal of Experimental Psychology: Learning, Memory, and Cognition, 15,* 246–255.

Zaragoza, M. S., & Lane, S. M. (1994). Source misattributions and the suggestibility of eyewitness memory. *Journal of Experimental Psychology: Learning, Memory, and Cognition, 20,* 934–945.

Zaragoza, M. S., Payment, K. E., Ackil, J. K., Drivdahl, S. B., & Beck, M. (2001). Interviewing witnesses: Forced confabulation and confirmatory feedback increase false memories. *Psychological Science, 12,* 473–477.

Zechmeister, E. B., & Nyberg, S. E. (1982). *Human Memory: An Introduction to Research and Theory.* Pacific Grove: Brook/Cole Publishing.

Zechmeister, E. B., & Shaughnessy, J. J. (1980). When you think that you know and when you think that you know but you don't. *Bulletin of the Psychonomic Society, 15,* 41–44.

Zelinski, E. M., & Miura, S. A. (1988). Effects of thematic information on script memory in young and older adults. *Psychology and Aging, 3,* 292–299.

Zelinski, E. M., & Stewart, S. T. (1998). Individual differences in 16 year memory changes. *Psychology and Aging, 13,* 622–630.

Zellner, M.., & Bäuml, K-H. (2005). Intact retrieval inhibition in children's episodic recall. *Memory & Cognition, 33,* 396–404.

Zellner, M., & Bäuml, K-H. (2006). Inhibitory deficits in older adults: List-method directed forgetting revisited. *Journal of Experimental Psychology: Learning, Memory, and Cognition, 32,* 290–300.

Zimmer, H. D., & Engelkamp, J. (2003). Signing enhances memory like performing actions. *Psychonomic Bulletin & Review, 10,* 450–454.

Zimmerman, J., and Underwood, B. J. (1968). Ordinal position knowledge within and across lists as a function of instructions in free-recall learning. *Journal of General Psychology, 79,* 301–307.

Zimmermann, T. D., & Meier, B. (2006). The rise and decline of prospective memory performance across the lifespan. *Quarterly Journal of Experimental Psychology, 12,* 2040–2046.

Zwaan, R. A., & Radvansky, G. A. (1998). Situation models in comprehension and memory. *Psychological Bulletin, 123,* 162–185.

NAME INDEX

SUBJECT INDEX